VIZ GRAPHIC NOVEL

MAISON IKKOKU™

DOMESTIC
DISPUTE

This volume contains MAISON IKKOKU PART SIX #1 through #6 (first half)
in their entirety.

STORY AND ART BY
RUMIKO TAKAHASHI

ENGLISH ADAPTATION BY
GERARD JONES

Translation/Mari Morimoto
Touch-Up Art & Lettering/Bill Spicer
Cover Design/Viz Graphics
Editor/Trish Ledoux
Assistant Editor/Annette Roman

Managing Editor/Hyoe Narita
Editor-in-Chief/Satoru Fujii
Publisher/Seiji Horibuchi

Printed in Canada

Published by Viz Communications, Inc.
P.O. Box 77010 • San Francisco, CA 94107

10 9 8 7 6 5 4 3 2
First printing, November 1997

Vizit us at our World Wide Web site at www.viz.com and
our Internet magazine, j-pop.com, at www.j-pop.com!

From the company that has its finger on the pulse of Japanese popular culture and art
comes j-pop.com, Viz Communications' Internet magazine, featuring the latest news
about Japanese anime, manga, video games, music, and pop culture!

MAISON IKKOKU GRAPHIC NOVELS TO DATE

MAISON IKKOKU
FAMILY AFFAIRS
HOME SWEET HOME
GOOD HOUSEKEEPING
EMPTY NEST
BEDSIDE MANNERS
INTENSIVE CARE
DOMESTIC DISPUTE

VIZ GRAPHIC NOVEL

MAISON IKKOKU™ VOLUME EIGHT

DOMESTIC DISPUTE

STORY AND ART BY
RUMIKO TAKAHASHI

CONTENTS

PART 1
ONE BIG HAPPY FAMILY

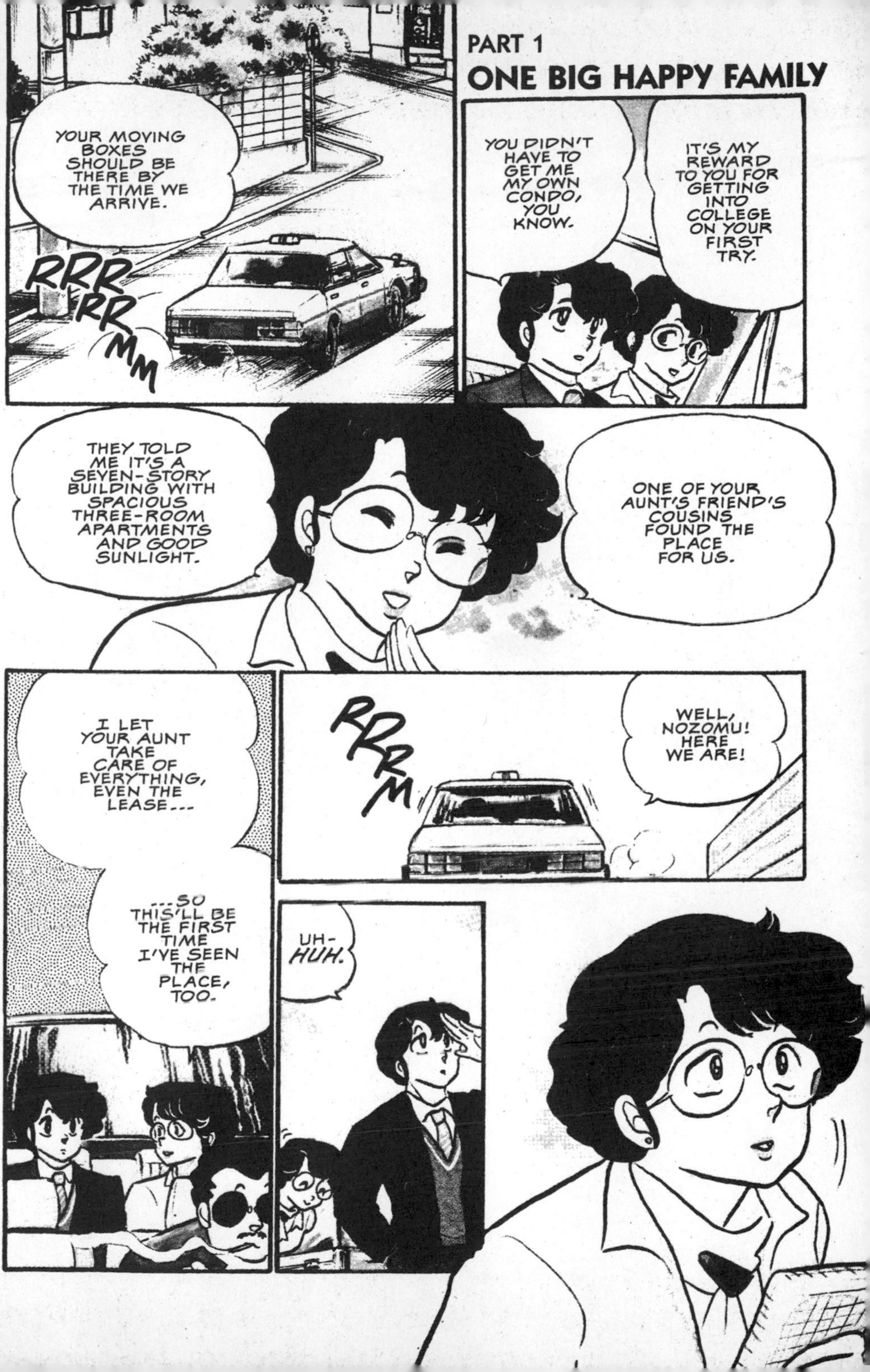
YOUR MOVING BOXES SHOULD BE THERE BY THE TIME WE ARRIVE.
RRRRRMM
YOU DIDN'T HAVE TO GET ME MY OWN CONDO, YOU KNOW.
IT'S MY REWARD TO YOU FOR GETTING INTO COLLEGE ON YOUR FIRST TRY.
THEY TOLD ME IT'S A SEVEN-STORY BUILDING WITH SPACIOUS THREE-ROOM APARTMENTS AND GOOD SUNLIGHT.
ONE OF YOUR AUNT'S FRIEND'S COUSINS FOUND THE PLACE FOR US.
I LET YOUR AUNT TAKE CARE OF EVERYTHING, EVEN THE LEASE...
...SO THIS'LL BE THE FIRST TIME I'VE SEEN THE PLACE, TOO.
RRRM
WELL, NOZOMU! HERE WE ARE!
UH-HUH.

PART 1
ONE BIG HAPPY FAMILY

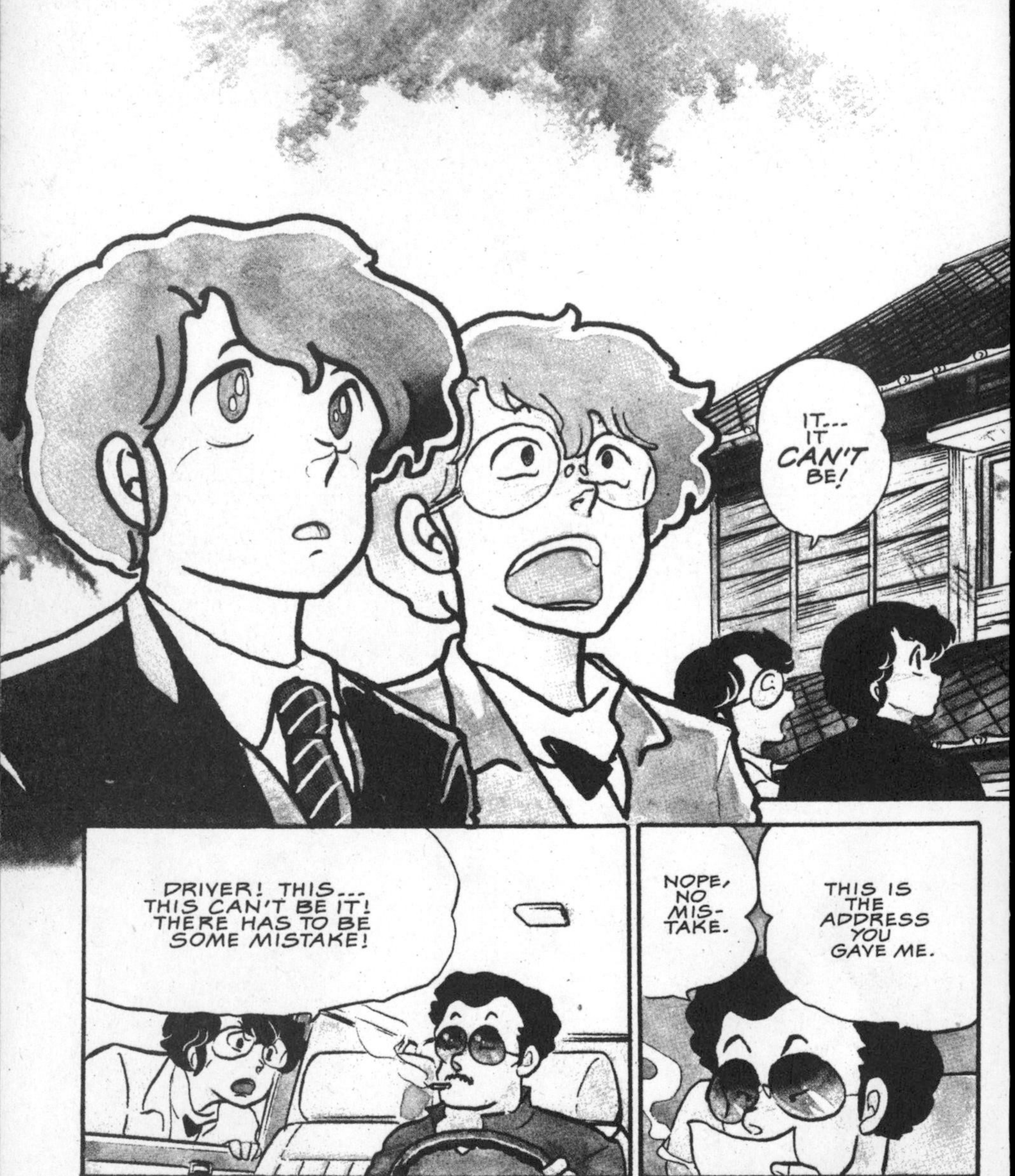
IT... IT CAN'T BE!
DRIVER! THIS... THIS CAN'T BE IT! THERE HAS TO BE SOME MISTAKE!
NOPE, NO MIS-TAKE.
THIS IS THE ADDRESS YOU GAVE ME.

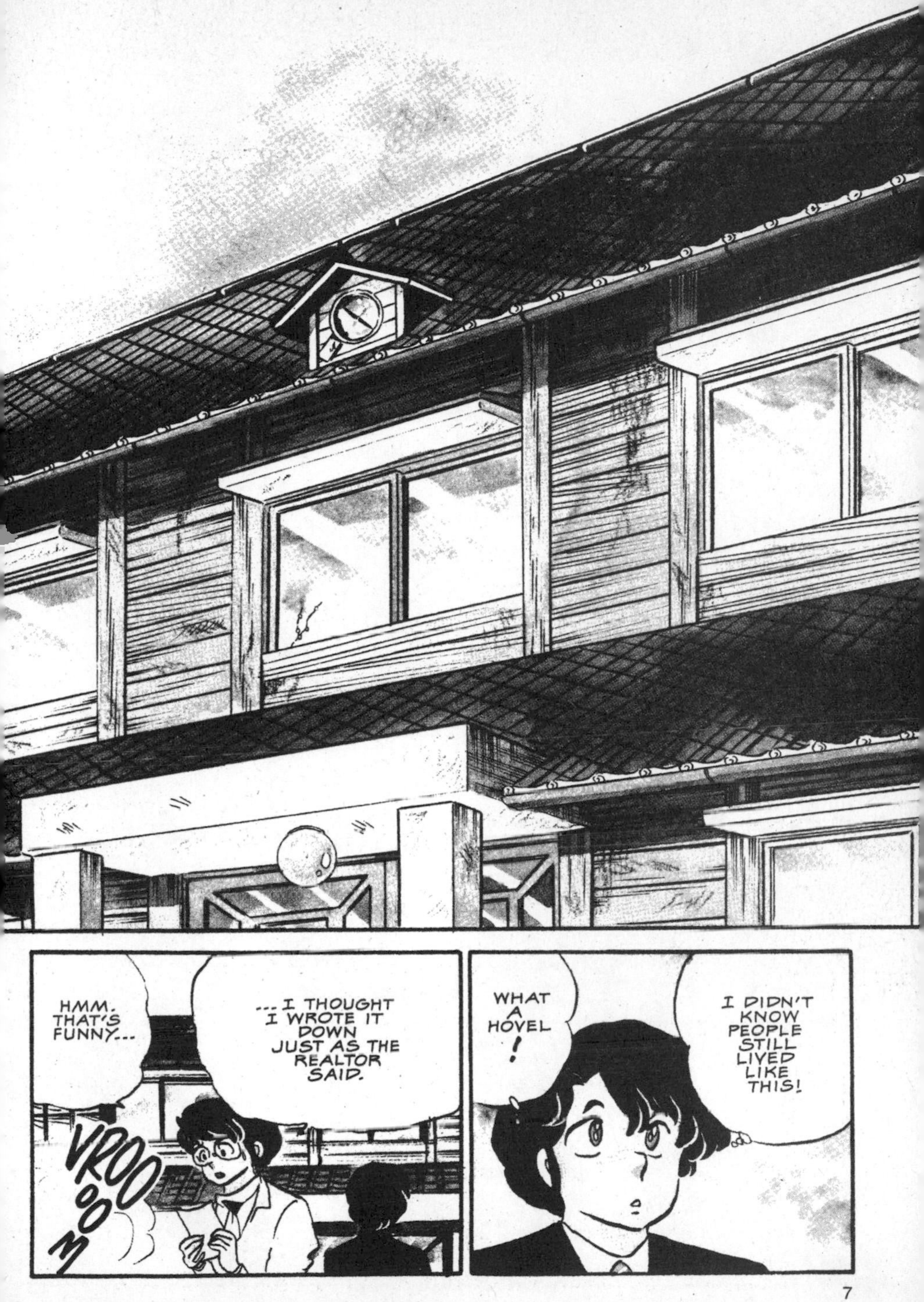
HMM. THAT'S FUNNY...
...I THOUGHT I WROTE IT DOWN JUST AS THE REALTOR SAID.
VROOOOM
WHAT A HOVEL!
I DIDN'T KNOW PEOPLE STILL LIVED LIKE THIS!

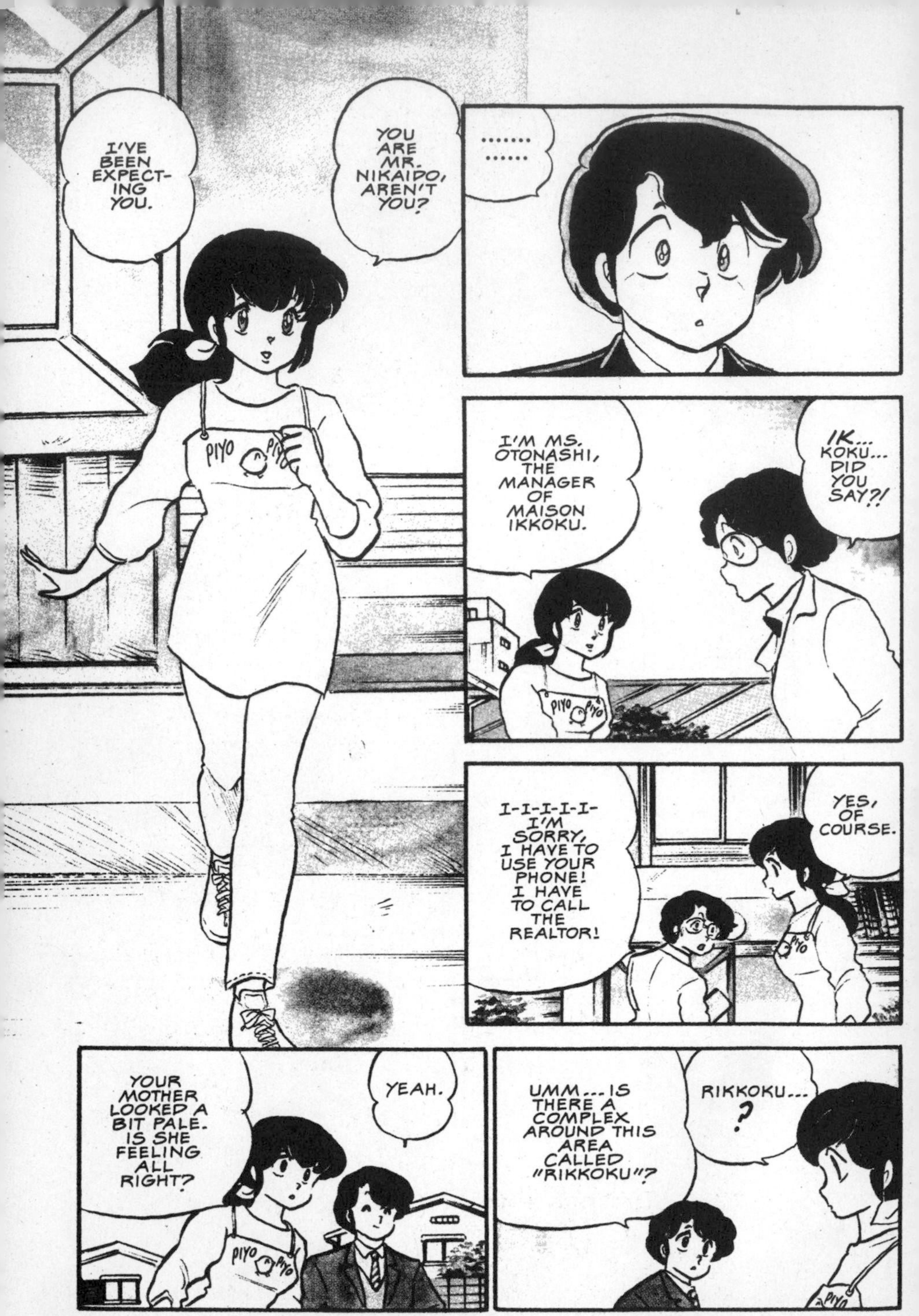
I'VE BEEN EXPECTING YOU.
YOU ARE MR. NIKAIDO, AREN'T YOU?
....
......
I'M MS. OTONASHI, THE MANAGER OF MAISON IKKOKU.
IK... KOKU... DID YOU SAY?!
I-I-I-I-I-I'M SORRY, I HAVE TO USE YOUR PHONE! I HAVE TO CALL THE REALTOR!
YES, OF COURSE.
YOUR MOTHER LOOKED A BIT PALE. IS SHE FEELING ALL RIGHT?
YEAH.
UMM... IS THERE A COMPLEX AROUND THIS AREA CALLED "RIKKOKU"?
RIKKOKU... ?

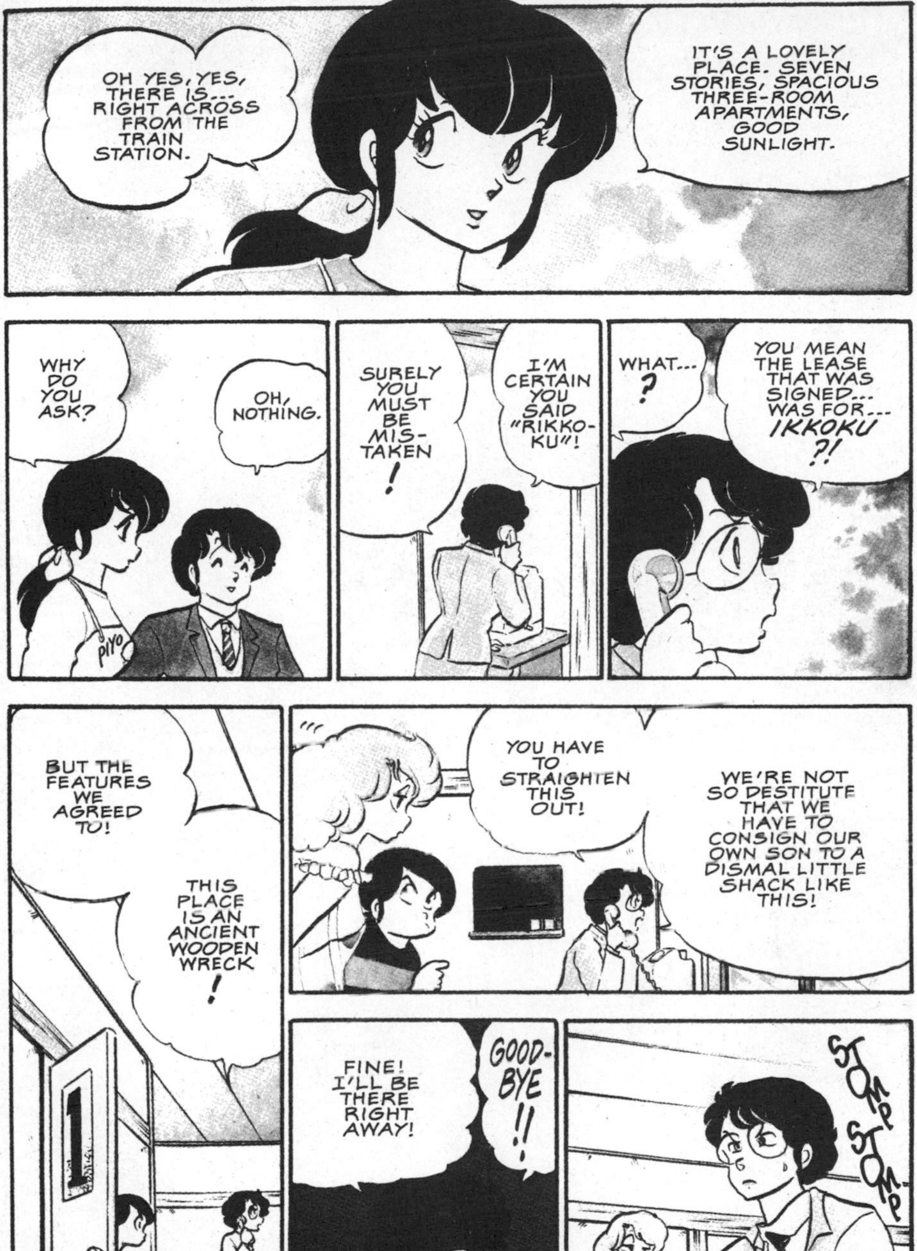
OH YES, YES, THERE IS... RIGHT ACROSS FROM THE TRAIN STATION.
IT'S A LOVELY PLACE. SEVEN STORIES, SPACIOUS THREE-ROOM APARTMENTS, GOOD SUNLIGHT.
WHY DO YOU ASK?
OH, NOTHING.
PIYO
SURELY YOU MUST BE MIS-TAKEN!
I'M CERTAIN YOU SAID "RIKKOKU"!
WHAT...?
YOU MEAN THE LEASE THAT WAS SIGNED... WAS FOR... IKKOKU?!
BUT THE FEATURES WE AGREED TO!
THIS PLACE IS AN ANCIENT WOODEN WRECK!
YOU HAVE TO STRAIGHTEN THIS OUT!
WE'RE NOT SO DESTITUTE THAT WE HAVE TO CONSIGN OUR OWN SON TO A DISMAL LITTLE SHACK LIKE THIS!
FINE! I'LL BE THERE RIGHT AWAY!
GOOD-BYE!!
STOMP STOMP

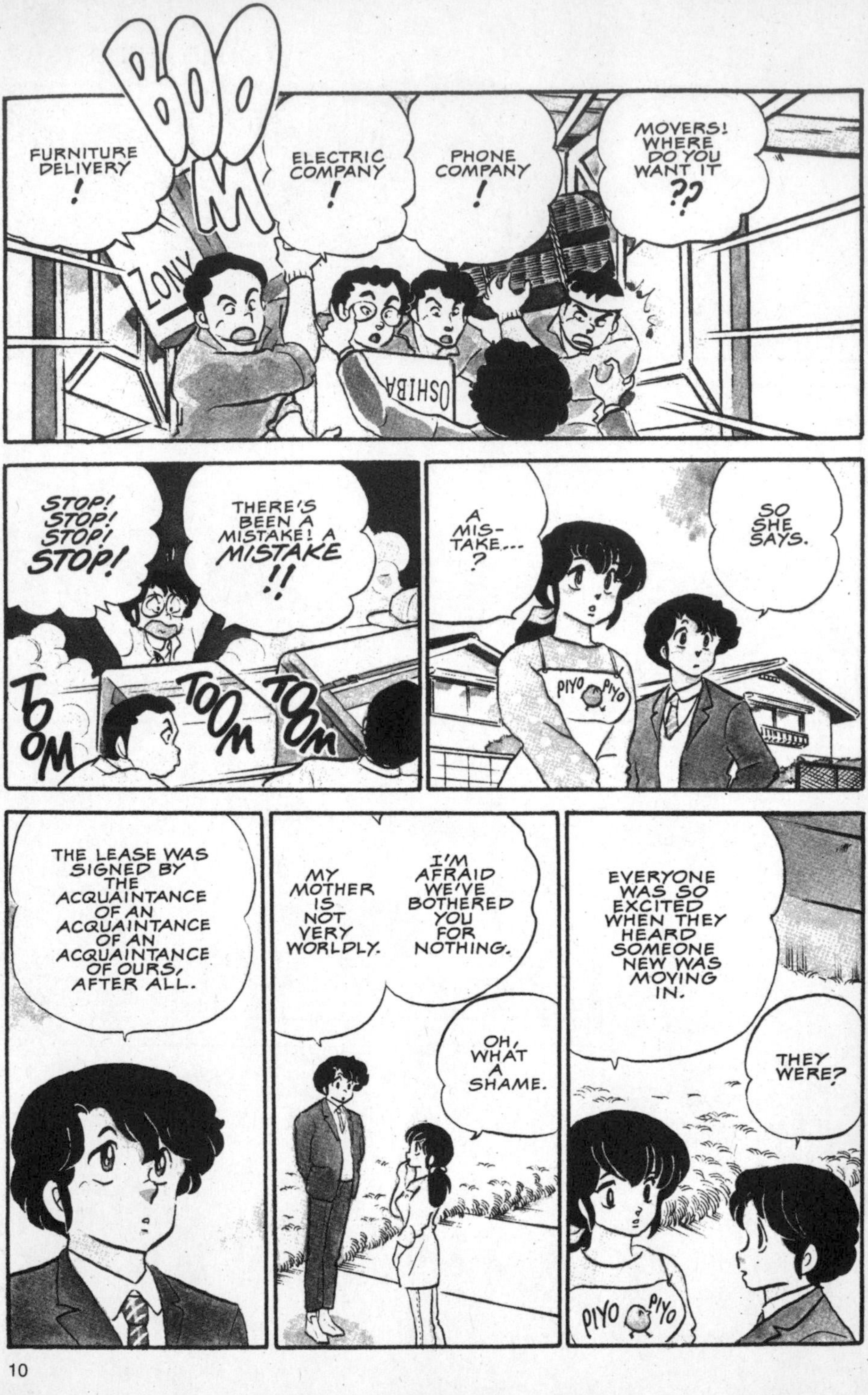

FURNITURE DELIVERY !
BOOM
ELECTRIC COMPANY !
PHONE COMPANY !
MOVERS! WHERE DO YOU WANT IT ??
ZONY
OSHIBA
STOP! STOP! STOP! STOP!
THERE'S BEEN A MISTAKE! A MISTAKE !!
TOOM TOOM TOOM
A MISTAKE... ?
SO SHE SAYS.
PIYO PIYO
THE LEASE WAS SIGNED BY THE ACQUAINTANCE OF AN ACQUAINTANCE OF AN ACQUAINTANCE OF OURS, AFTER ALL.
MY MOTHER IS NOT VERY WORLDLY.
I'M AFRAID WE'VE BOTHERED YOU FOR NOTHING.
OH, WHAT A SHAME.
EVERYONE WAS SO EXCITED WHEN THEY HEARD SOMEONE NEW WAS MOVING IN.
THEY WERE?
PIYO PIYO

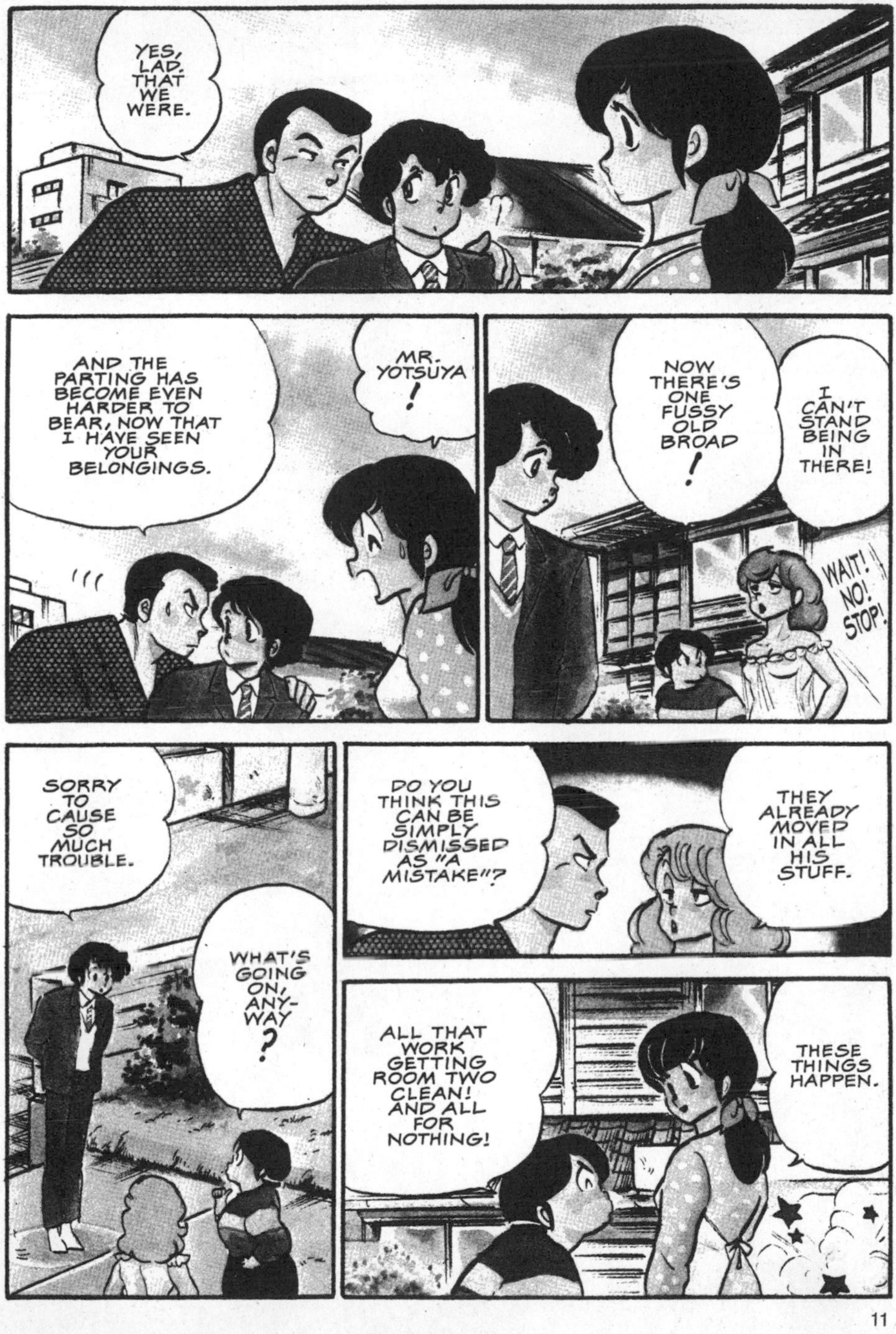
YES, LAD. THAT WE WERE.
AND THE PARTING HAS BECOME EVEN HARDER TO BEAR, NOW THAT I HAVE SEEN YOUR BELONGINGS.
MR. YOTSUYA!
NOW THERE'S ONE FUSSY OLD BROAD!
I CAN'T STAND BEING IN THERE!
WAIT! NO! STOP!
SORRY TO CAUSE SO MUCH TROUBLE.
WHAT'S GOING ON, ANYWAY?
DO YOU THINK THIS CAN BE SIMPLY DISMISSED AS "A MISTAKE"?
THEY ALREADY MOVED IN ALL HIS STUFF.
ALL THAT WORK GETTING ROOM TWO CLEAN! AND ALL FOR NOTHING!
THESE THINGS HAPPEN.

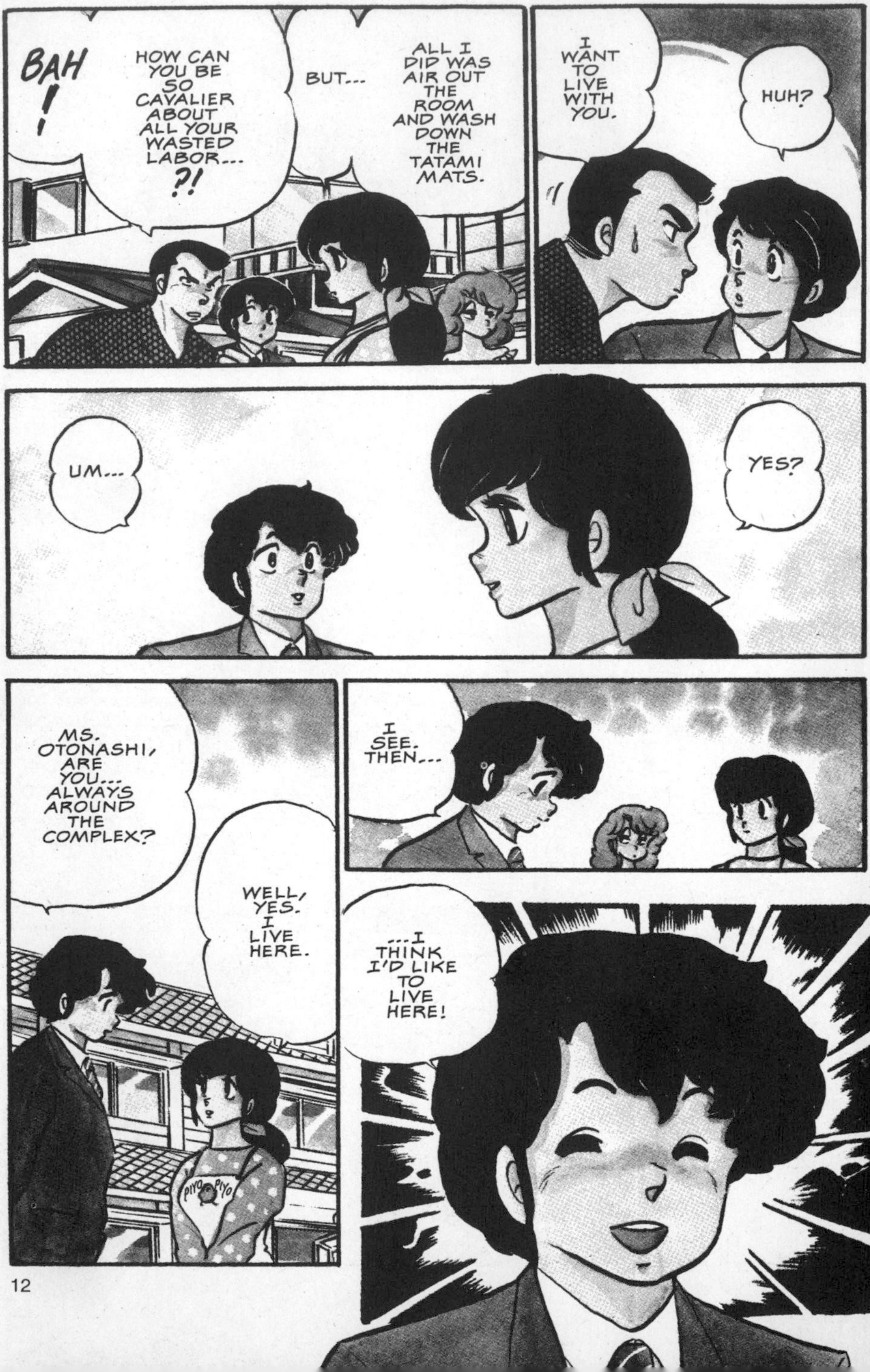
BAH!
HOW CAN YOU BE SO CAVALIER ABOUT ALL YOUR WASTED LABOR...?!
BUT...
ALL I DID WAS AIR OUT THE ROOM AND WASH DOWN THE TATAMI MATS.
I WANT TO LIVE WITH YOU.
HUH?
UM...
YES?
MS. OTONASHI, ARE YOU... ALWAYS AROUND THE COMPLEX?
WELL, YES. I LIVE HERE.
PIYO PIYO
I SEE. THEN...
...I THINK I'D LIKE TO LIVE HERE!

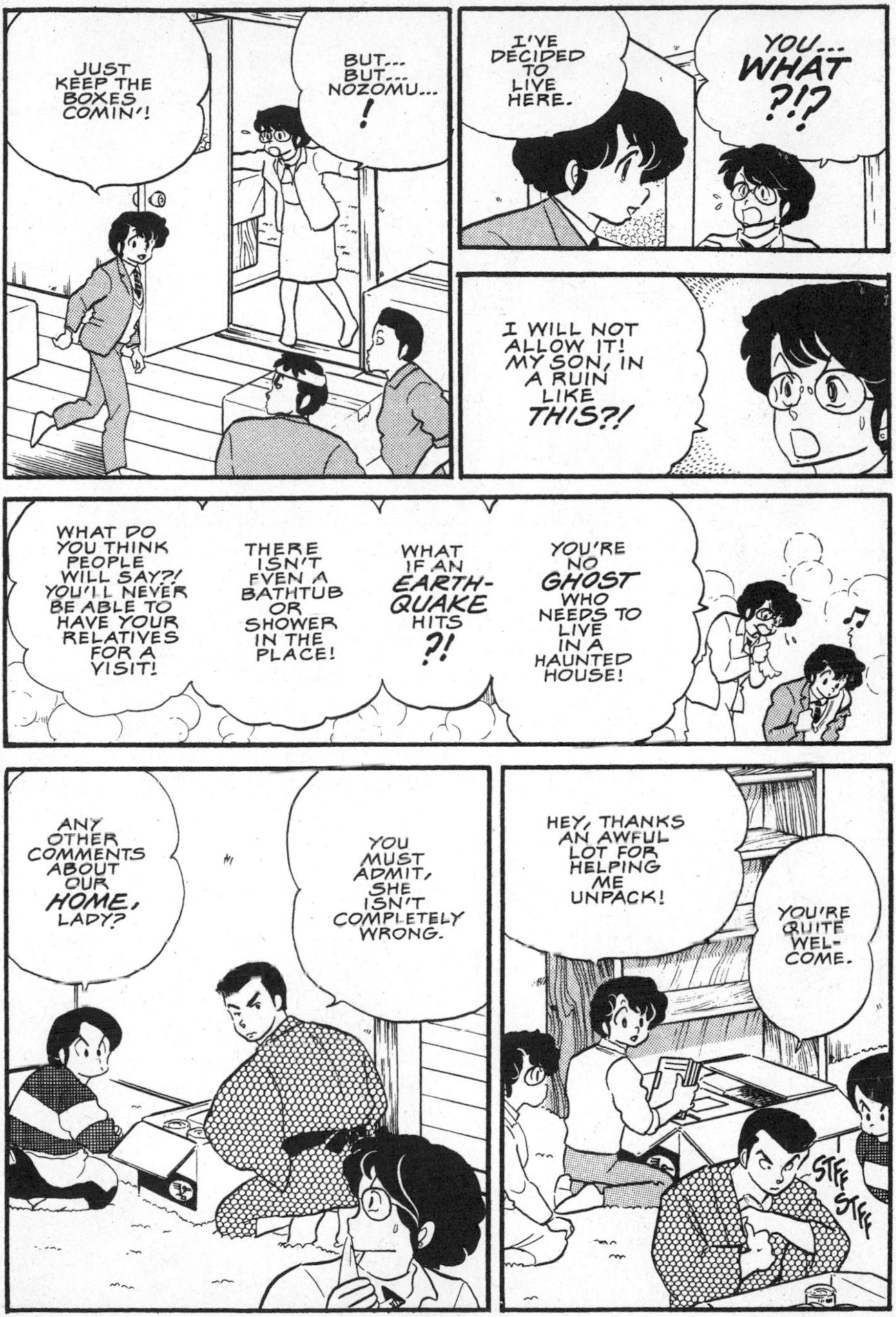
JUST KEEP THE BOXES COMIN'!
BUT... BUT... NOZOMU... !
I'VE DECIDED TO LIVE HERE.
YOU... WHAT ?!?
I WILL NOT ALLOW IT! MY SON, IN A RUIN LIKE THIS?!
WHAT DO YOU THINK PEOPLE WILL SAY?! YOU'LL NEVER BE ABLE TO HAVE YOUR RELATIVES FOR A VISIT!
THERE ISN'T EVEN A BATHTUB OR SHOWER IN THE PLACE!
WHAT IF AN EARTHQUAKE HITS ?!
YOU'RE NO GHOST WHO NEEDS TO LIVE IN A HAUNTED HOUSE!
ANY OTHER COMMENTS ABOUT OUR HOME, LADY?
YOU MUST ADMIT, SHE ISN'T COMPLETELY WRONG.
HEY, THANKS AN AWFUL LOT FOR HELPING ME UNPACK!
YOU'RE QUITE WEL- COME.
STFF STFF

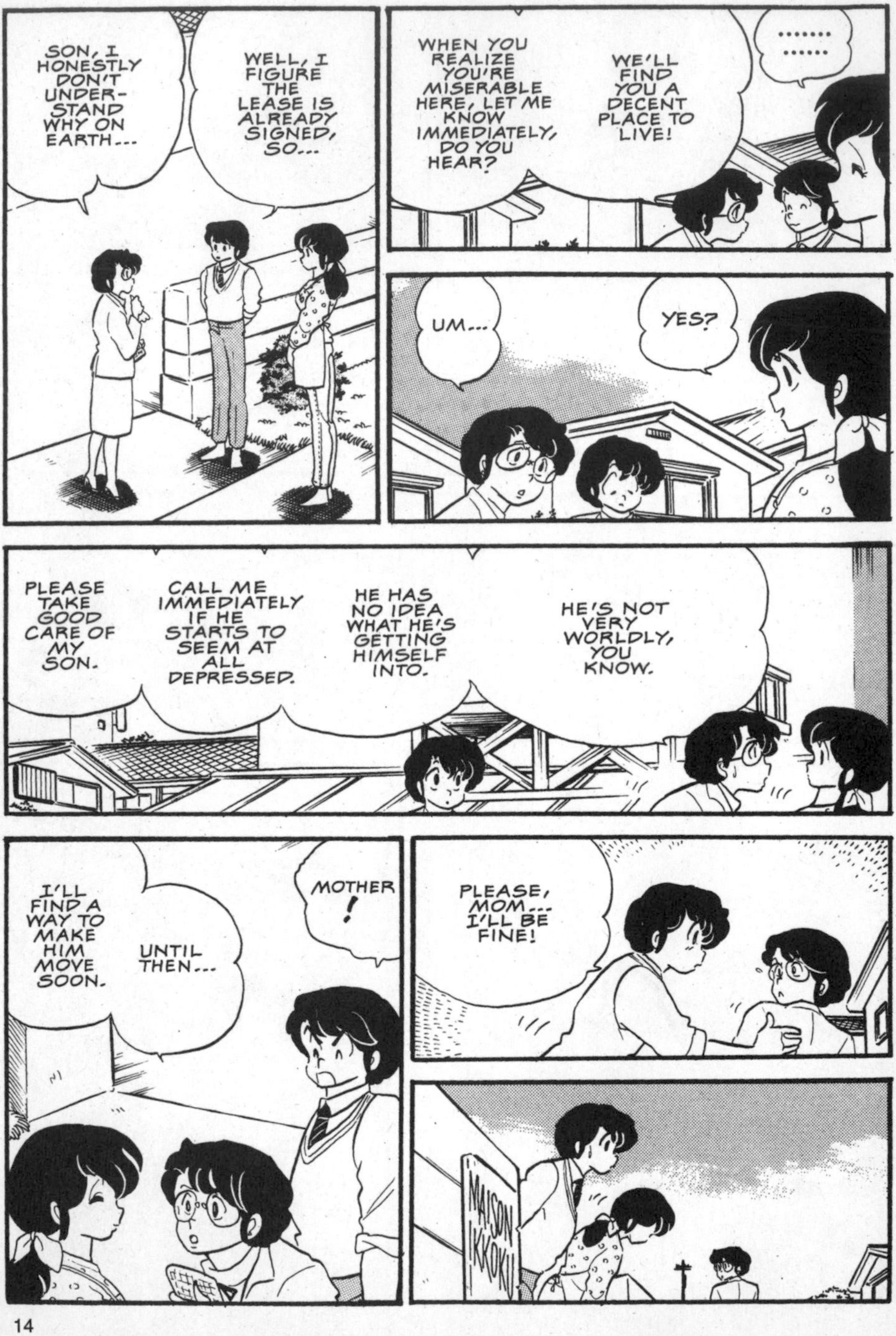
SON, I HONESTLY DON'T UNDER-STAND WHY ON EARTH...
WELL, I FIGURE THE LEASE IS ALREADY SIGNED, SO...
WHEN YOU REALIZE YOU'RE MISERABLE HERE, LET ME KNOW IMMEDIATELY, DO YOU HEAR?
WE'LL FIND YOU A DECENT PLACE TO LIVE!
....
......
UM...
YES?
PLEASE TAKE GOOD CARE OF MY SON.
CALL ME IMMEDIATELY IF HE STARTS TO SEEM AT ALL DEPRESSED.
HE HAS NO IDEA WHAT HE'S GETTING HIMSELF INTO.
HE'S NOT VERY WORLDLY, YOU KNOW.
I'LL FIND A WAY TO MAKE HIM MOVE SOON.
UNTIL THEN...
MOTHER!
PLEASE, MOM... I'LL BE FINE!
MAISON IKKOKU

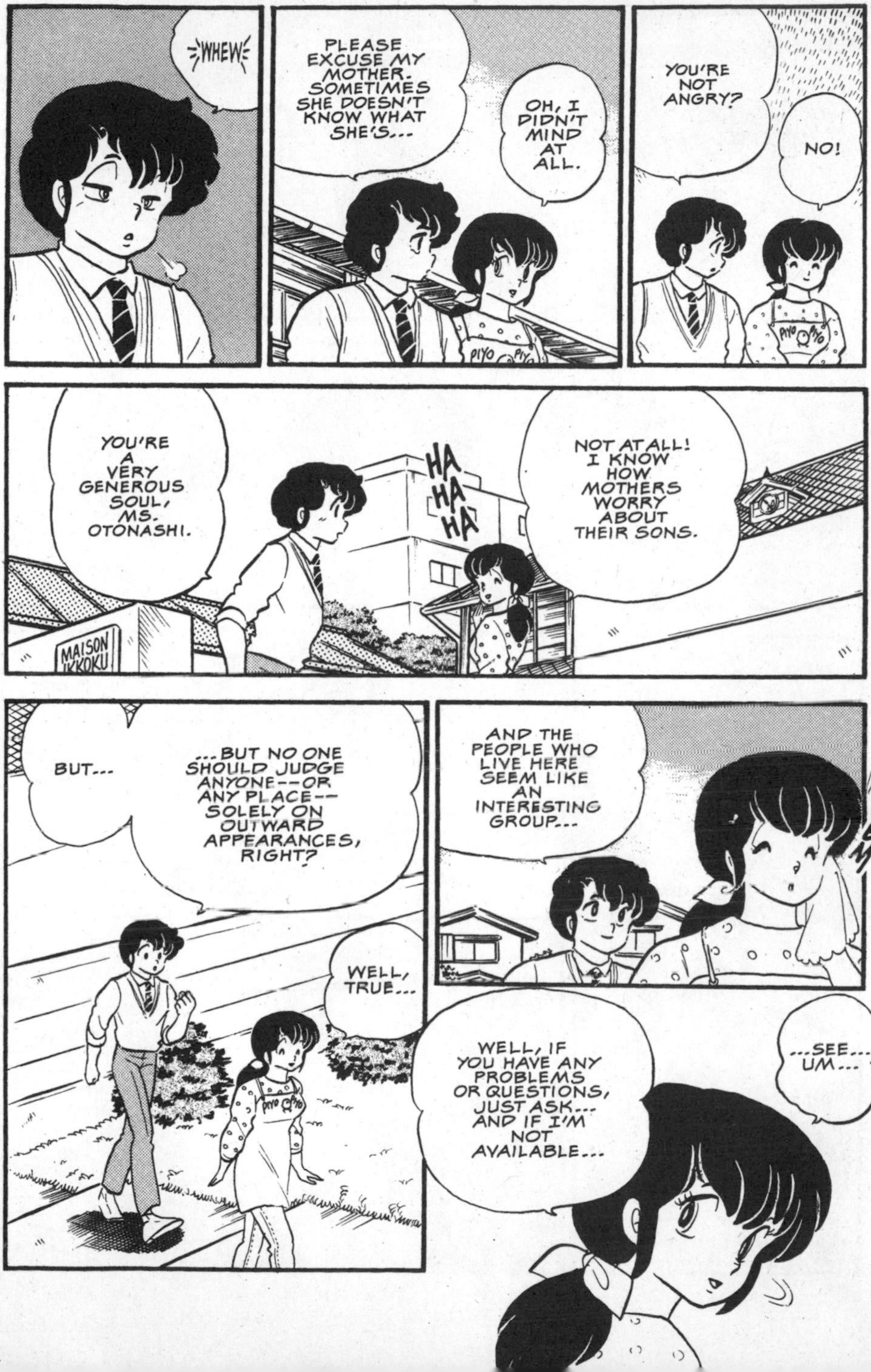
WHEW
PLEASE EXCUSE MY MOTHER. SOMETIMES SHE DOESN'T KNOW WHAT SHE'S...
OH, I DIDN'T MIND AT ALL.
YOU'RE NOT ANGRY?
NO!
PIYO PIYO
YOU'RE A VERY GENEROUS SOUL, MS. OTONASHI.
HA HA HA
NOT AT ALL! I KNOW HOW MOTHERS WORRY ABOUT THEIR SONS.
MAISON IKKOKU
BUT...
...BUT NO ONE SHOULD JUDGE ANYONE--OR ANY PLACE--SOLELY ON OUTWARD APPEARANCES, RIGHT?
WELL, TRUE...
AND THE PEOPLE WHO LIVE HERE SEEM LIKE AN INTERESTING GROUP...
AHEM
WELL, IF YOU HAVE ANY PROBLEMS OR QUESTIONS, JUST ASK... AND IF I'M NOT AVAILABLE...
...SEE... UM...

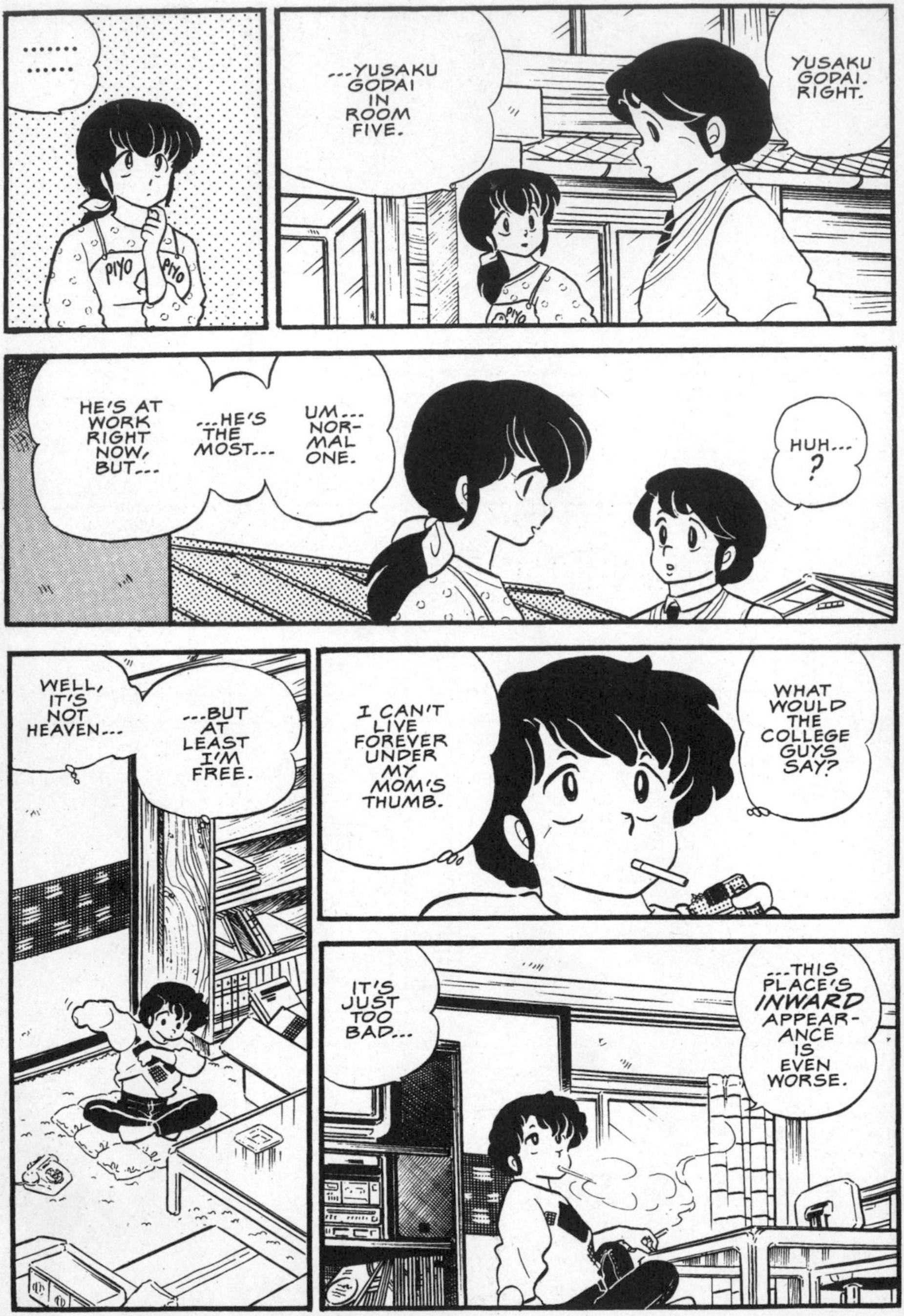

....
....
PIYO
PIYO
...YUSAKU GODAI IN ROOM FIVE.
YUSAKU GODAI. RIGHT.
PIYO
HE'S AT WORK RIGHT NOW, BUT...
...HE'S THE MOST...
UM... NOR-MAL ONE.
HUH...?
WELL, IT'S NOT HEAVEN...
...BUT AT LEAST I'M FREE.
I CAN'T LIVE FOREVER UNDER MY MOM'S THUMB.
WHAT WOULD THE COLLEGE GUYS SAY?
IT'S JUST TOO BAD...
...THIS PLACE'S *INWARD* APPEARANCE IS EVEN WORSE.

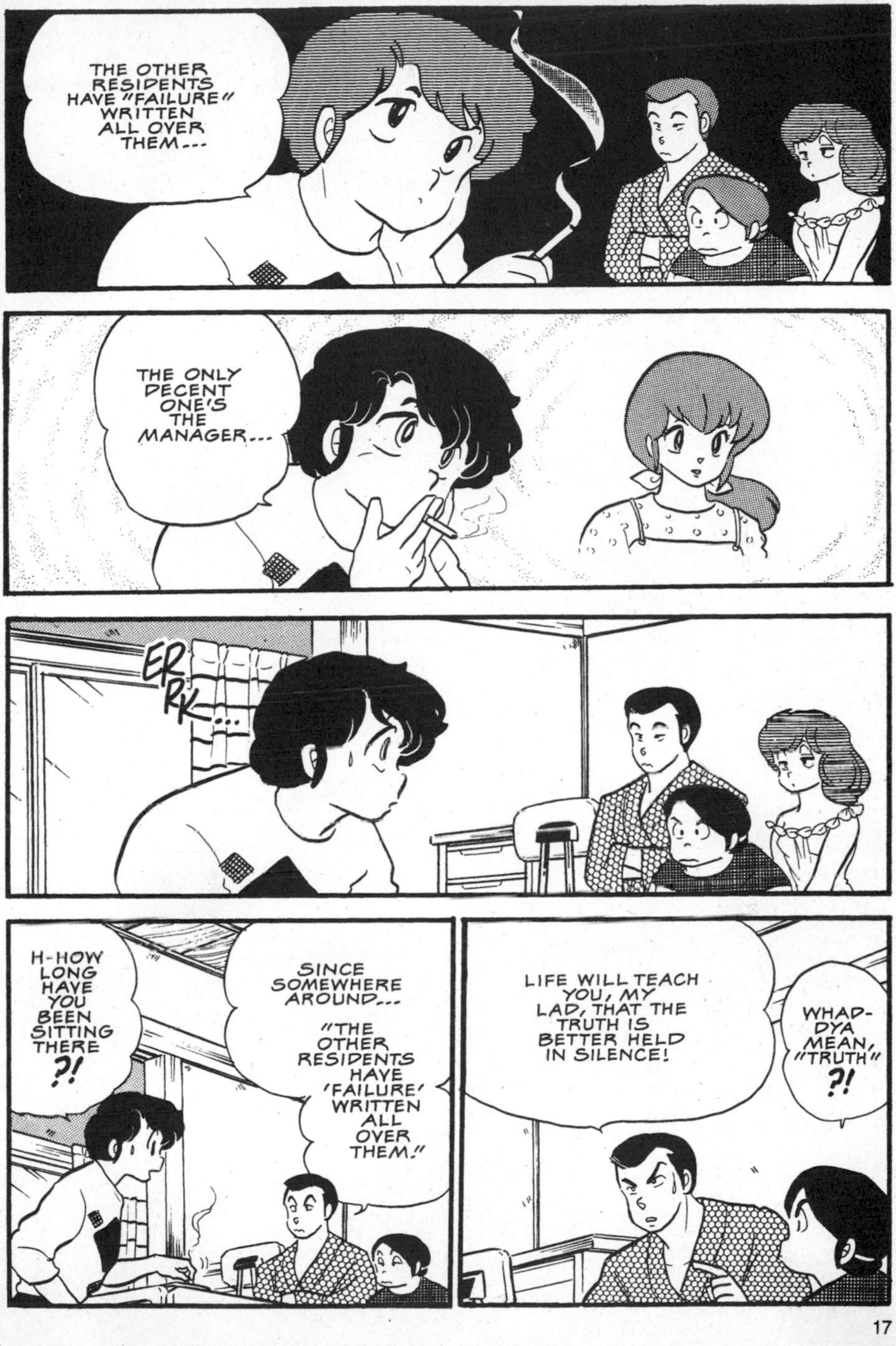
THE OTHER RESIDENTS HAVE "FAILURE" WRITTEN ALL OVER THEM...
THE ONLY DECENT ONE'S THE MANAGER...
ERRK...
H-HOW LONG HAVE YOU BEEN SITTING THERE ?!
SINCE SOMEWHERE AROUND... "THE OTHER RESIDENTS HAVE 'FAILURE' WRITTEN ALL OVER THEM."
LIFE WILL TEACH YOU, MY LAD, THAT THE TRUTH IS BETTER HELD IN SILENCE!
WHAD-DYA MEAN, "TRUTH" ?!

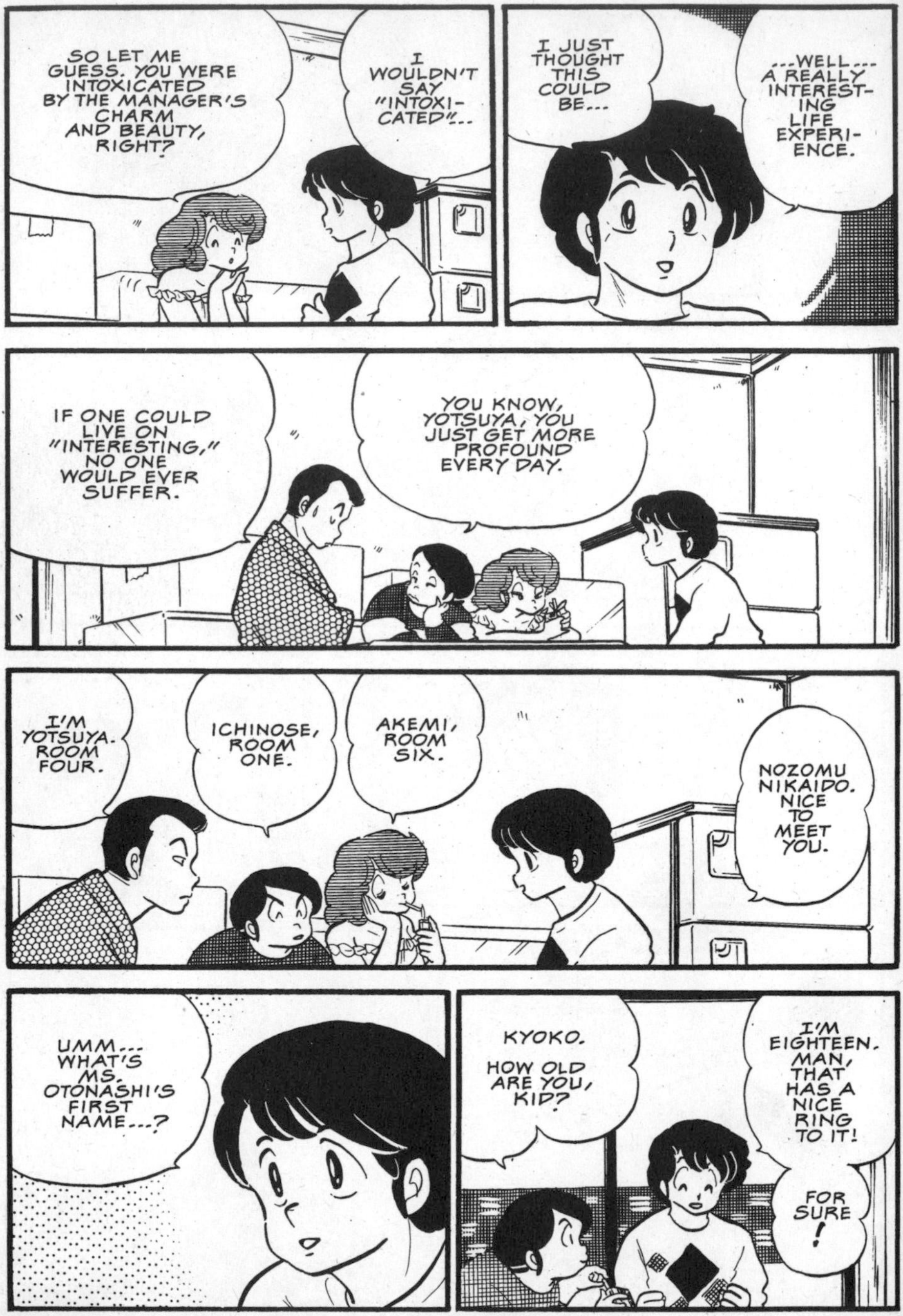
SO LET ME GUESS. YOU WERE INTOXICATED BY THE MANAGER'S CHARM AND BEAUTY, RIGHT?
I WOULDN'T SAY "INTOXICATED"...
I JUST THOUGHT THIS COULD BE...
...WELL... A REALLY INTERESTING LIFE EXPERIENCE.
IF ONE COULD LIVE ON "INTERESTING," NO ONE WOULD EVER SUFFER.
YOU KNOW, YOTSUYA, YOU JUST GET MORE PROFOUND EVERY DAY.
I'M YOTSUYA. ROOM FOUR.
ICHINOSE, ROOM ONE.
AKEMI, ROOM SIX.
NOZOMU NIKAIDO. NICE TO MEET YOU.
UMM... WHAT'S MS. OTONASHI'S FIRST NAME...?
KYOKO.
HOW OLD ARE YOU, KID?
I'M EIGHTEEN. MAN, THAT HAS A NICE RING TO IT!
FOR SURE!

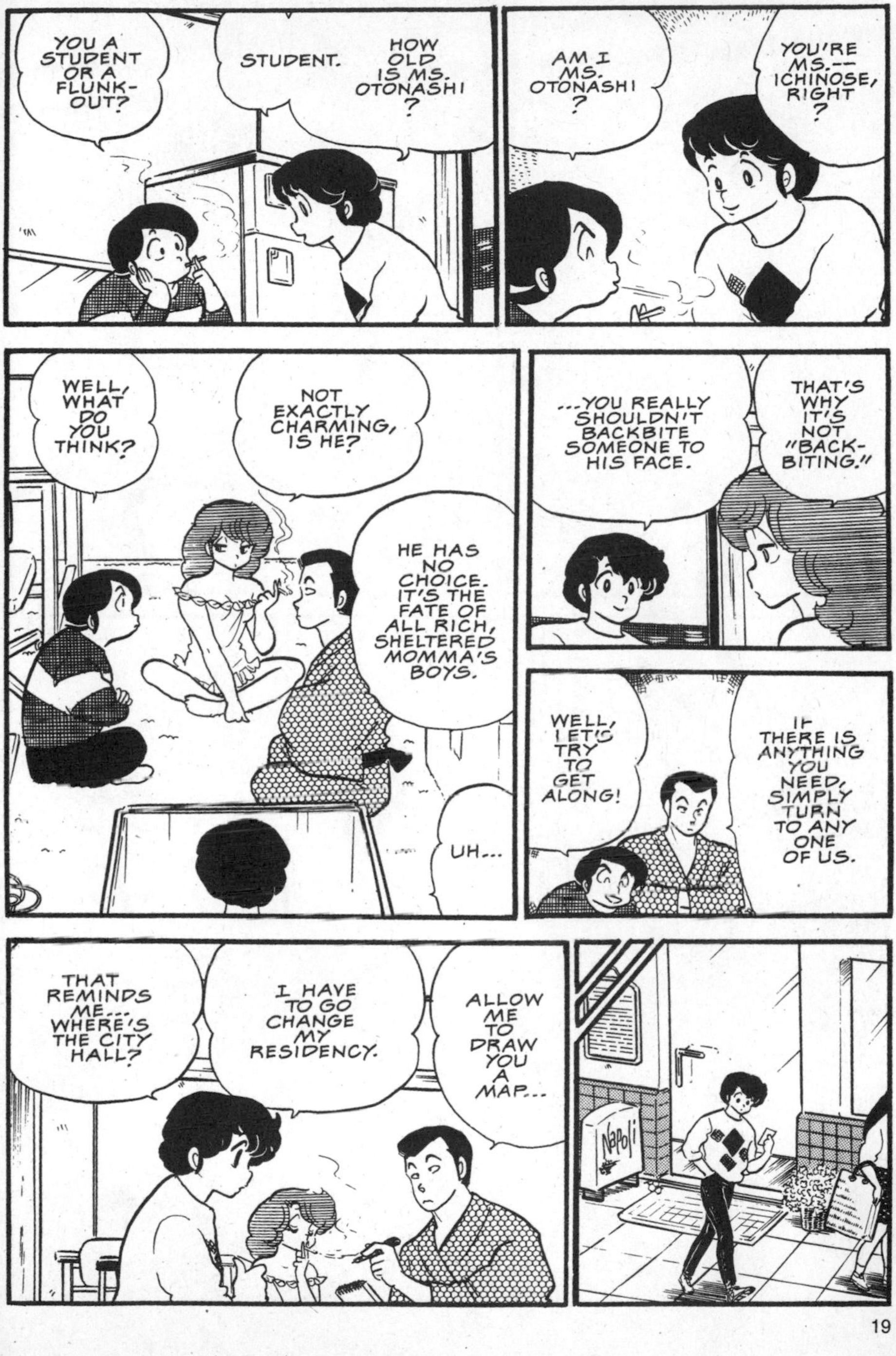
YOU A STUDENT OR A FLUNK-OUT?
STUDENT.
HOW OLD IS MS. OTONASHI?
AM I MS. OTONASHI?
YOU'RE MS.-- ICHINOSE, RIGHT?
WELL, WHAT DO YOU THINK?
NOT EXACTLY CHARMING, IS HE?
HE HAS NO CHOICE. IT'S THE FATE OF ALL RICH, SHELTERED MOMMA'S BOYS.
UH...
...YOU REALLY SHOULDN'T BACKBITE SOMEONE TO HIS FACE.
THAT'S WHY IT'S NOT "BACK-BITING."
WELL, LET'S TRY TO GET ALONG!
IF THERE IS ANYTHING YOU NEED, SIMPLY TURN TO ANY ONE OF US.
THAT REMINDS ME... WHERE'S THE CITY HALL?
I HAVE TO GO CHANGE MY RESIDENCY.
ALLOW ME TO DRAW YOU A MAP...
Napoli

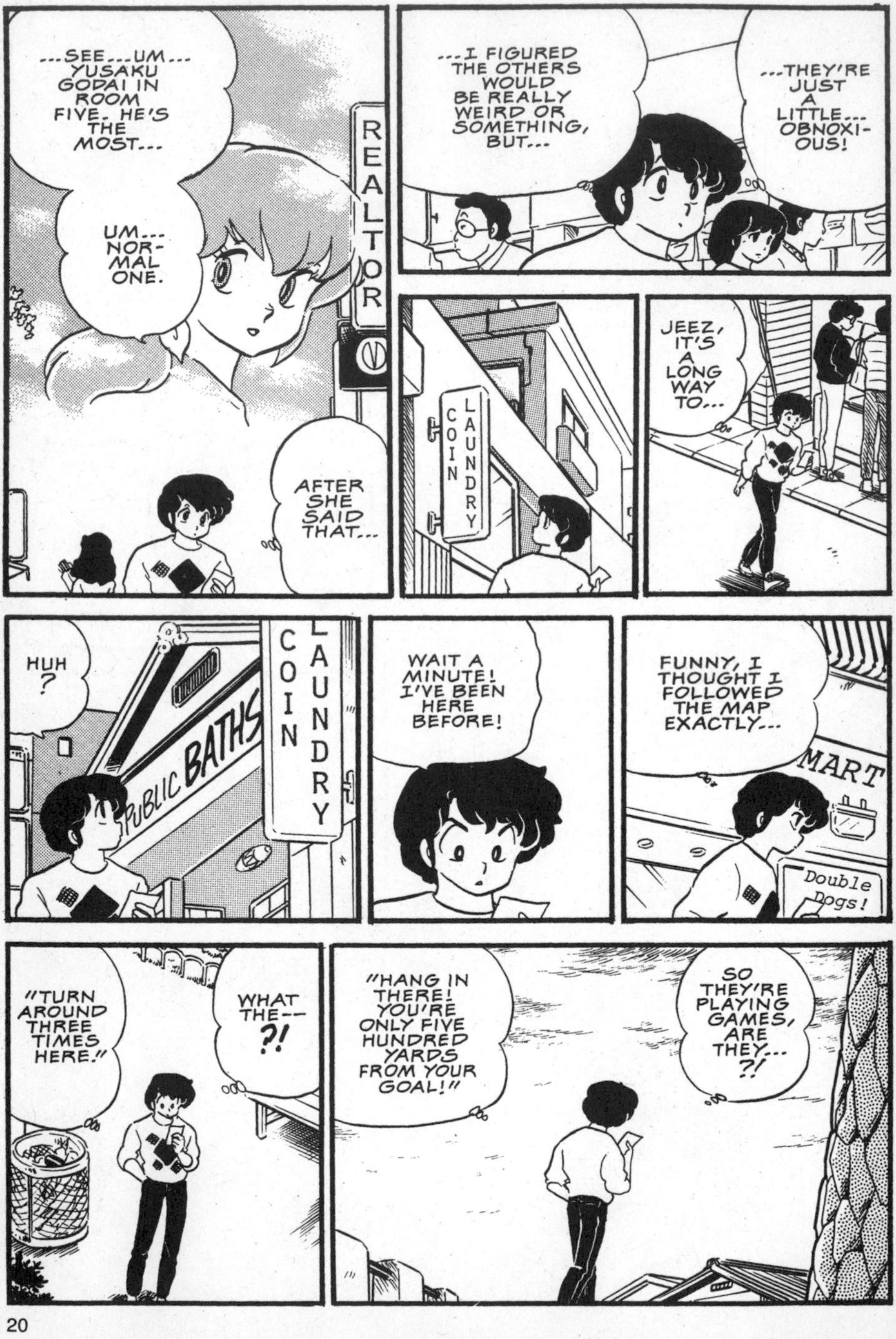
...SEE...UM... YUSAKU GODAI IN ROOM FIVE. HE'S THE MOST...
REALTOR
UM... NOR-MAL ONE.
AFTER SHE SAID THAT...
...I FIGURED THE OTHERS WOULD BE REALLY WEIRD OR SOMETHING, BUT...
...THEY'RE JUST A LITTLE... OBNOXI-OUS!
COIN LAUNDRY
JEEZ, IT'S A LONG WAY TO...
HUH?
PUBLIC BATHS
COIN LAUNDRY
WAIT A MINUTE! I'VE BEEN HERE BEFORE!
FUNNY, I THOUGHT I FOLLOWED THE MAP EXACTLY...
MART
Double Dogs!
"TURN AROUND THREE TIMES HERE."
WHAT THE--?!
"HANG IN THERE! YOU'RE ONLY FIVE HUNDRED YARDS FROM YOUR GOAL!"
SO THEY'RE PLAYING GAMES, ARE THEY...?!

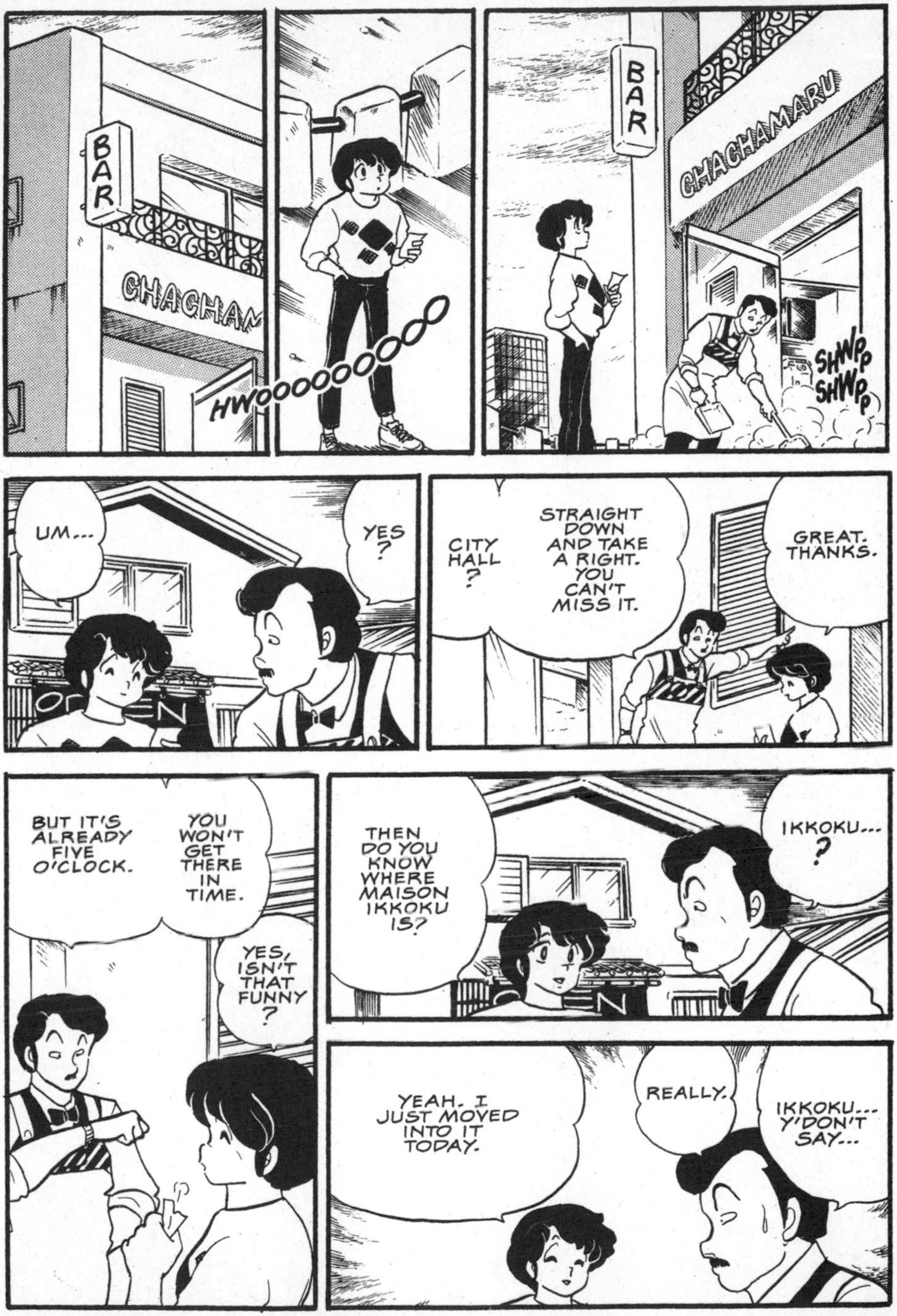
BAR
CHACHAM
HWOOOOOOOOOO
BAR
CHACHAMARU
SHWPP SHWPP
UM...
YES?
CITY HALL?
STRAIGHT DOWN AND TAKE A RIGHT. YOU CAN'T MISS IT.
GREAT. THANKS.
BUT IT'S ALREADY FIVE O'CLOCK.
YOU WON'T GET THERE IN TIME.
YES, ISN'T THAT FUNNY?
THEN DO YOU KNOW WHERE MAISON IKKOKU IS?
IKKOKU...?
YEAH. I JUST MOVED INTO IT TODAY.
REALLY.
IKKOKU... Y'DON'T SAY...

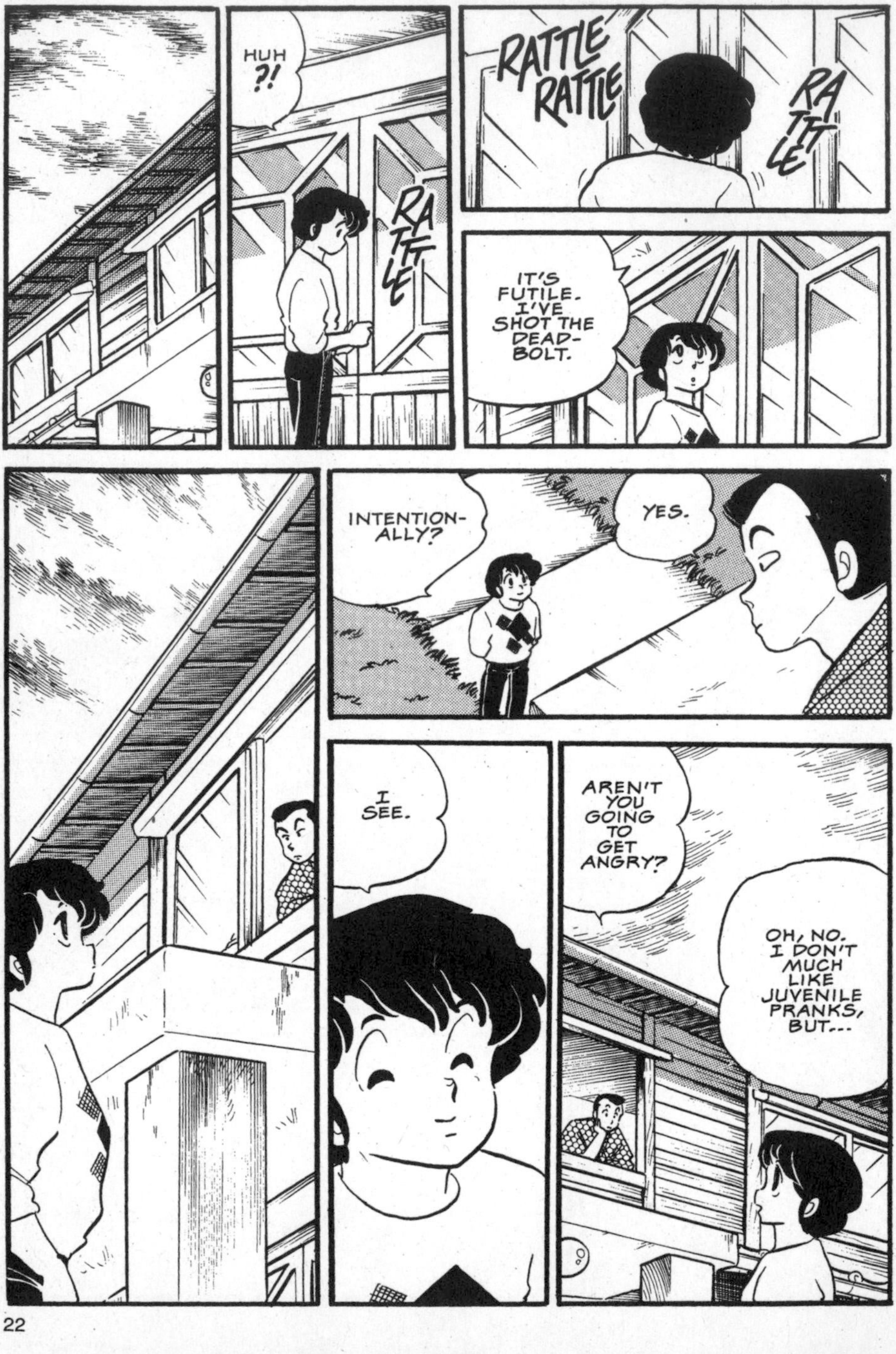
HUH ?!
RATTLE
RATTLE RATTLE
RATTLE
IT'S FUTILE. I'VE SHOT THE DEAD-BOLT.
INTENTION-ALLY?
YES.
I SEE.
AREN'T YOU GOING TO GET ANGRY?
OH, NO. I DON'T MUCH LIKE JUVENILE PRANKS, BUT...

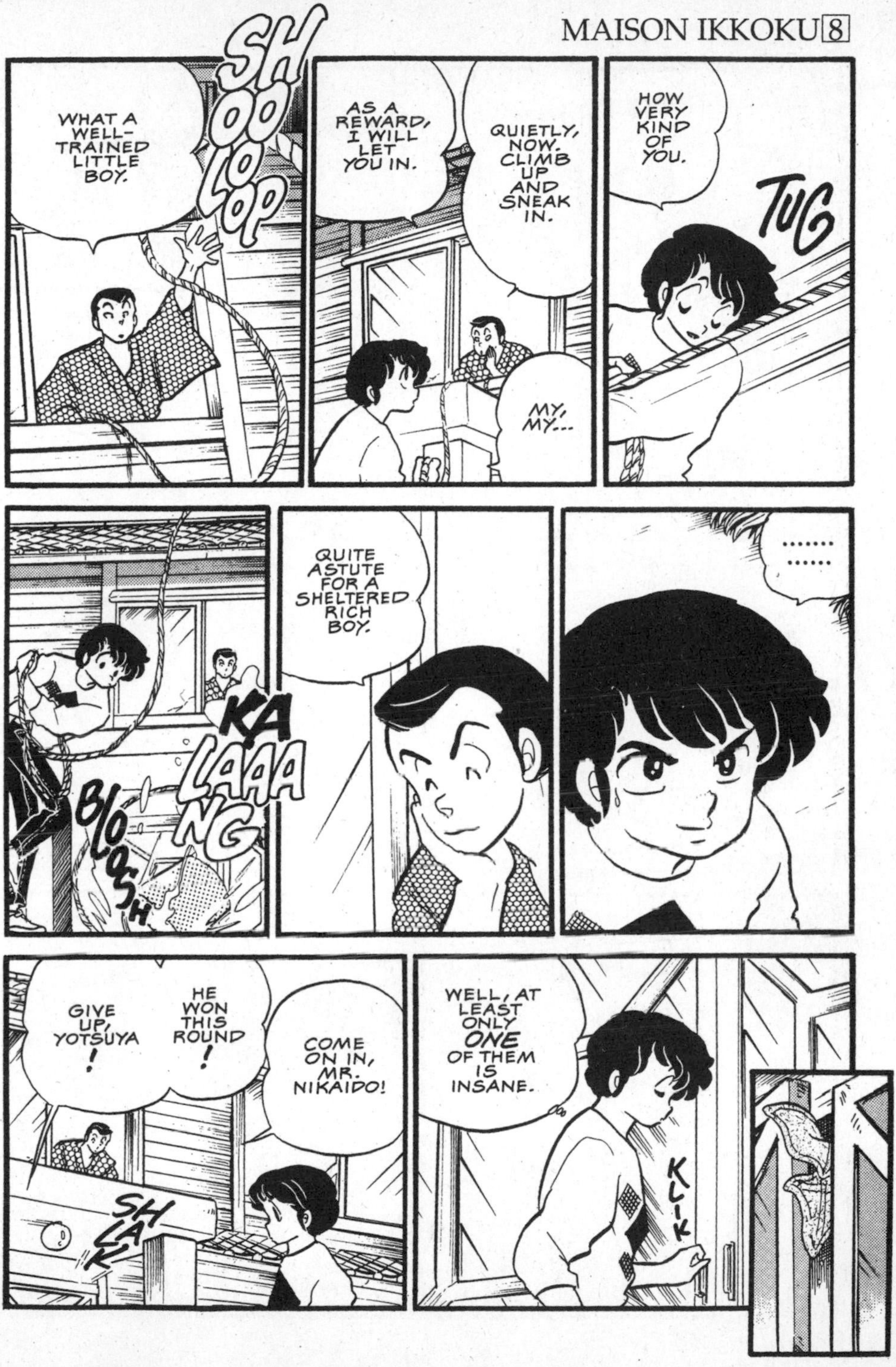
WHAT A WELL-TRAINED LITTLE BOY.
SHOOLOLOP
AS A REWARD, I WILL LET YOU IN.
QUIETLY, NOW. CLIMB UP AND SNEAK IN.
MY, MY...
HOW VERY KIND OF YOU.
TUG
KA LAAAA NG
BLOOOSH
QUITE ASTUTE FOR A SHELTERED RICH BOY.
....
......
GIVE UP, YOTSUYA!
HE WON THIS ROUND!
COME ON IN, MR. NIKAIDO!
SHLAK
WELL, AT LEAST ONLY *ONE* OF THEM IS INSANE.
KLIK

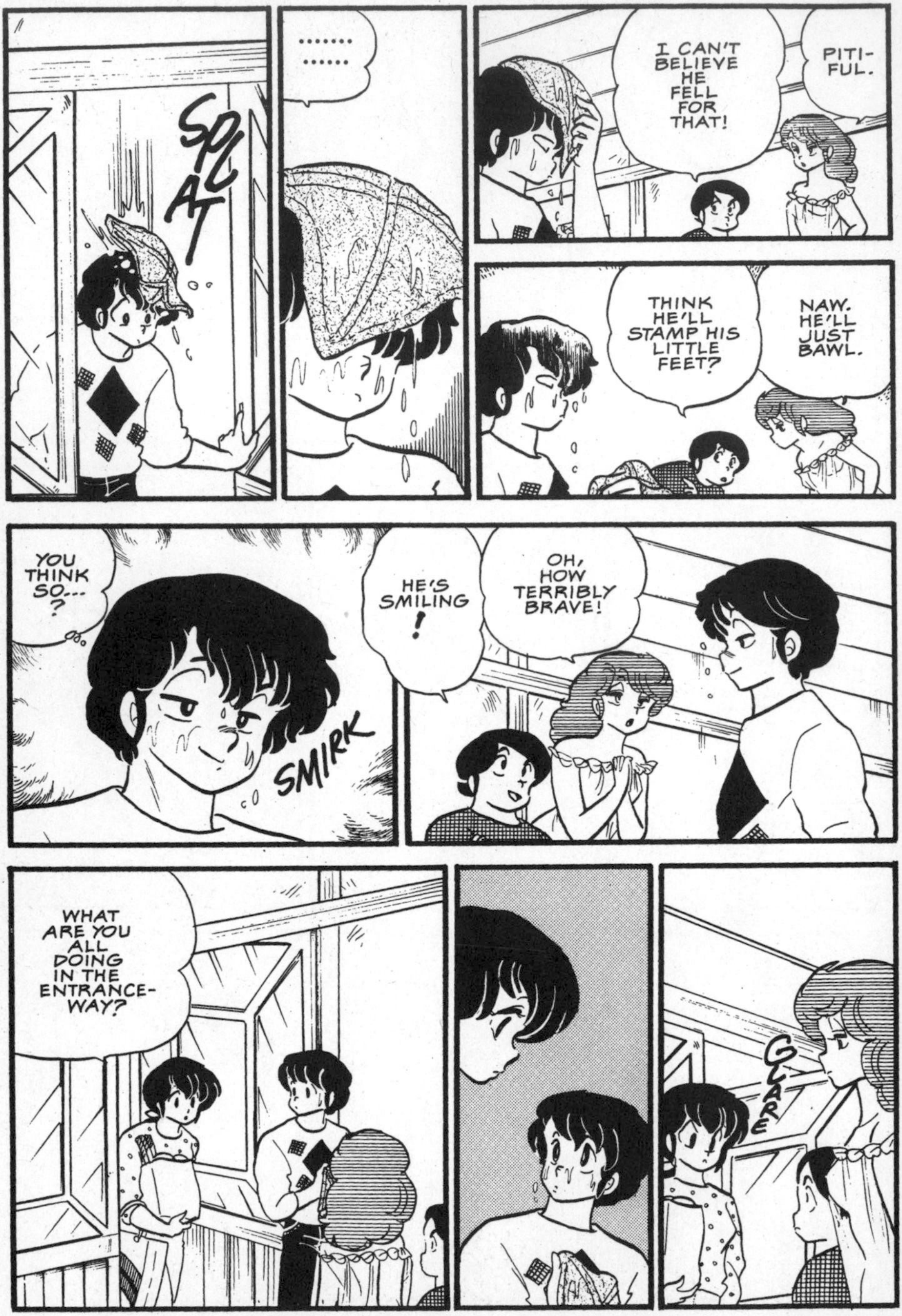
SPLAT
....
....
I CAN'T BELIEVE HE FELL FOR THAT!
PITI-FUL.
THINK HE'LL STAMP HIS LITTLE FEET?
NAW. HE'LL JUST BAWL.
YOU THINK SO...?
SMIRK
HE'S SMILING!
OH, HOW TERRIBLY BRAVE!
WHAT ARE YOU ALL DOING IN THE ENTRANCE-WAY?
GLARE

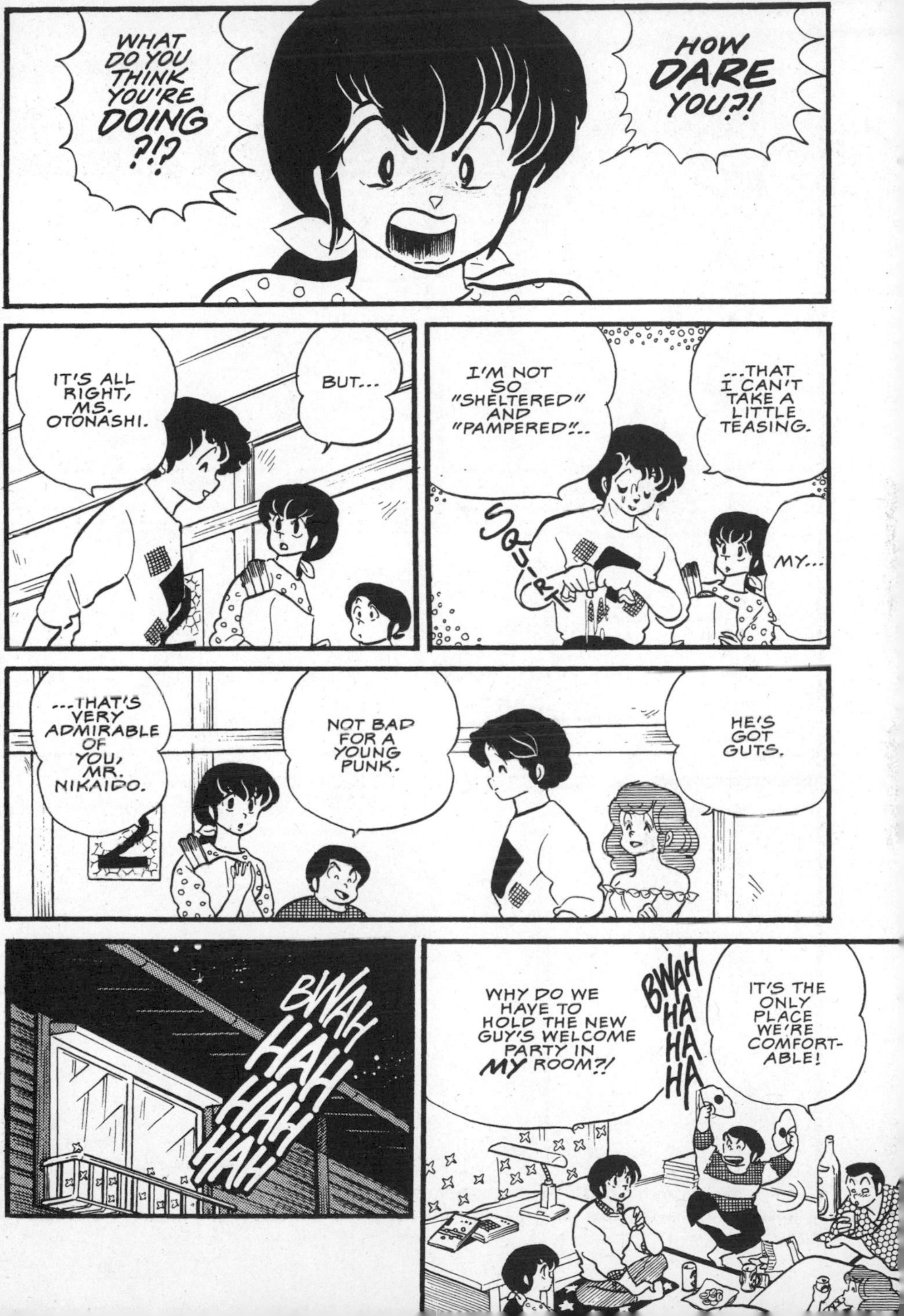
WHAT DO YOU THINK YOU'RE DOING ?!?
HOW DARE YOU?!
IT'S ALL RIGHT, MS. OTONASHI.
BUT...
I'M NOT SO "SHELTERED" AND "PAMPERED"...
...THAT I CAN'T TAKE A LITTLE TEASING.
SQUIRT
MY...
...THAT'S VERY ADMIRABLE OF YOU, MR. NIKAIDO.
NOT BAD FOR A YOUNG PUNK.
HE'S GOT GUTS.
BWAH HAH HAH HAH HAH
WHY DO WE HAVE TO HOLD THE NEW GUY'S WELCOME PARTY IN MY ROOM?!
BWAH HA HA HA HA
IT'S THE ONLY PLACE WE'RE COMFORT-ABLE!

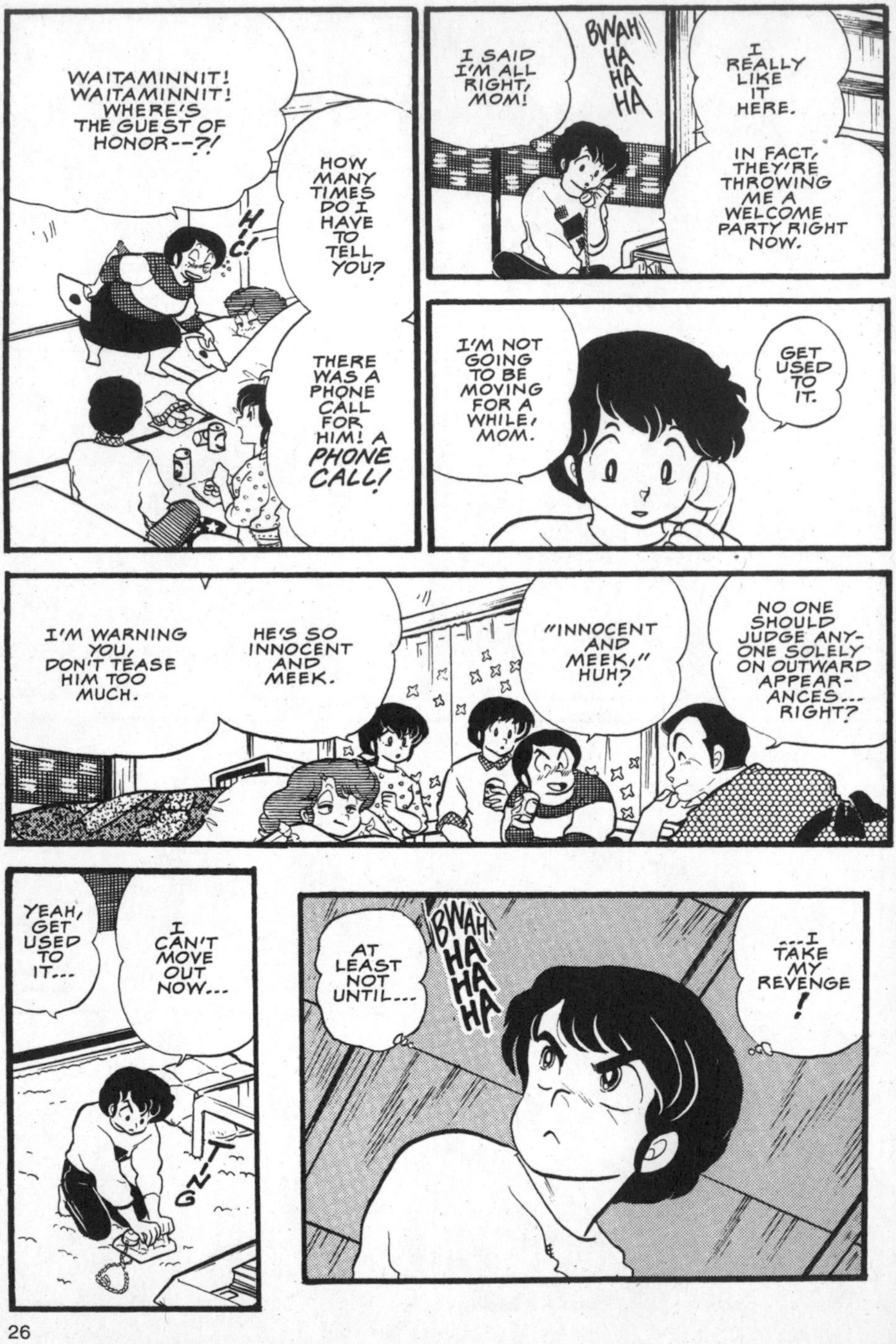
WAITAMINNIT! WAITAMINNIT! WHERE'S THE GUEST OF HONOR--?!
HIC!
HOW MANY TIMES DO I HAVE TO TELL YOU?
THERE WAS A PHONE CALL FOR HIM! A PHONE CALL!
I SAID I'M ALL RIGHT, MOM!
BWAH HA HA HA
I REALLY LIKE IT HERE.
IN FACT, THEY'RE THROWING ME A WELCOME PARTY RIGHT NOW.
I'M NOT GOING TO BE MOVING FOR A WHILE, MOM.
GET USED TO IT.
I'M WARNING YOU, DON'T TEASE HIM TOO MUCH.
HE'S SO INNOCENT AND MEEK.
"INNOCENT AND MEEK," HUH?
NO ONE SHOULD JUDGE ANY-ONE SOLELY ON OUTWARD APPEAR-ANCES... RIGHT?
YEAH, GET USED TO IT...
I CAN'T MOVE OUT NOW...
TING
AT LEAST NOT UNTIL...
BWAH HA HA HA HA
...I TAKE MY REVENGE!

PART 2
ATTACK AND COUNTERATTACK

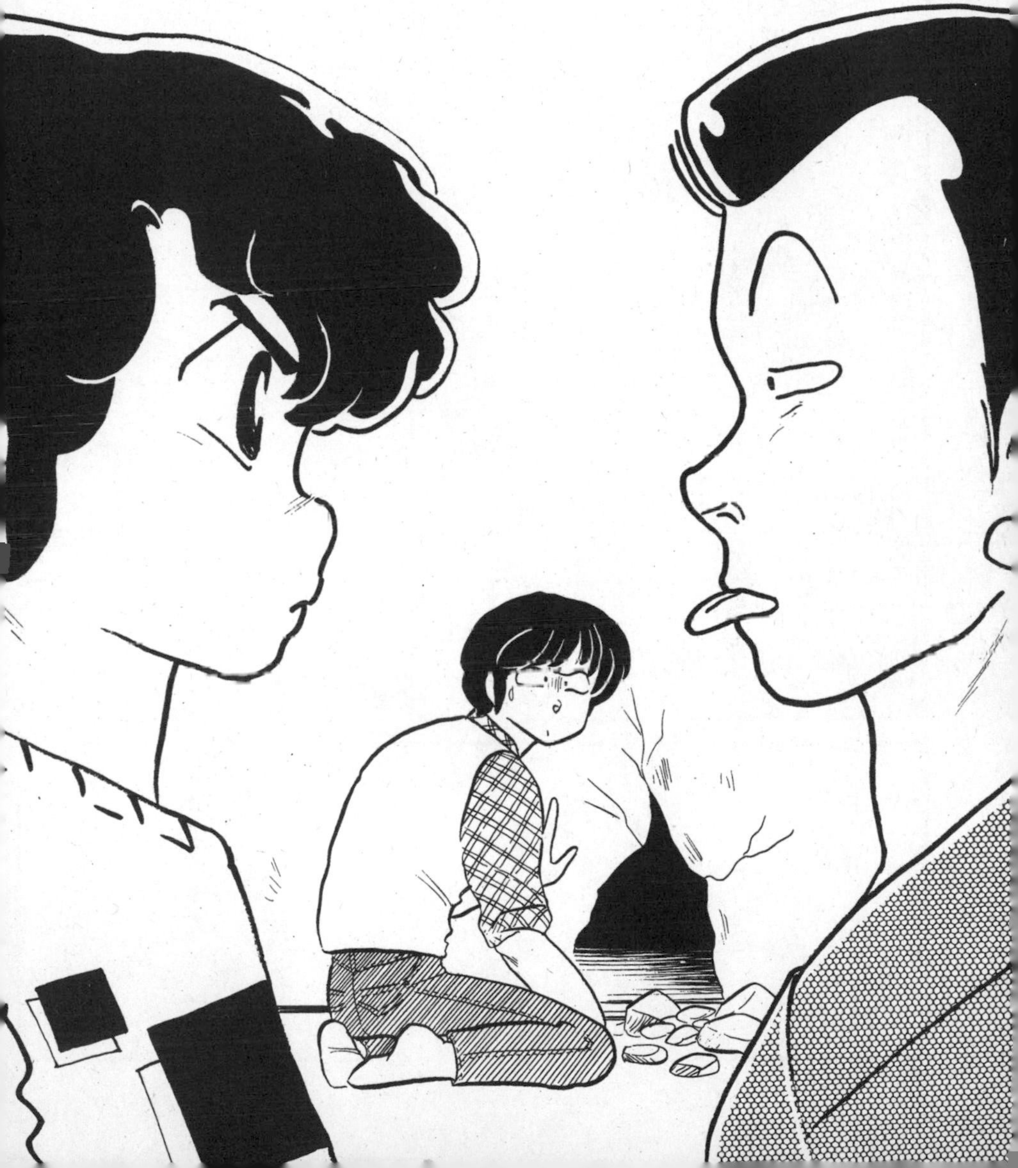

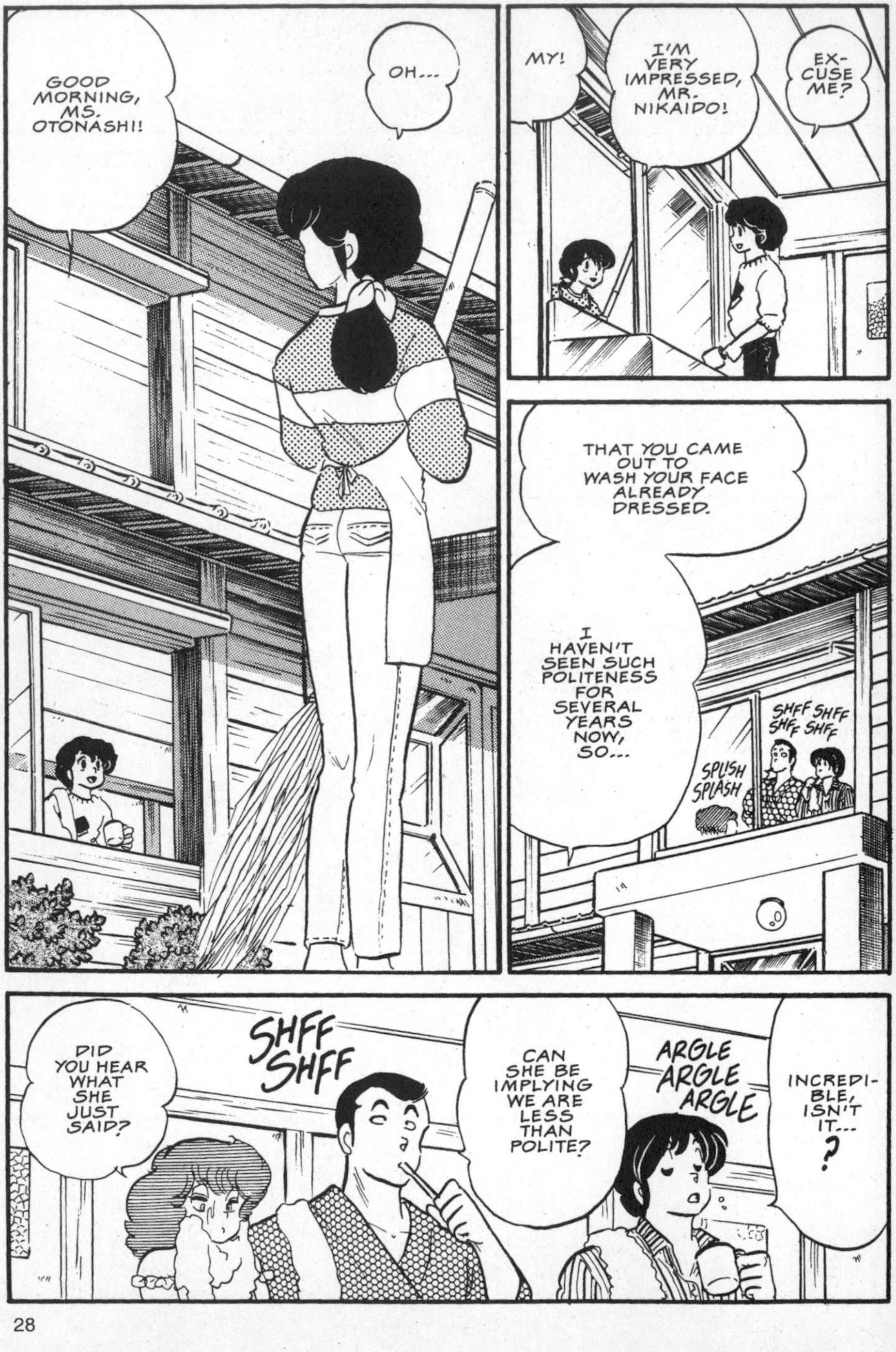

GOOD MORNING, MS. OTONASHI!
OH...
MY!
I'M VERY IMPRESSED, MR. NIKAIDO!
EX-CUSE ME?
THAT YOU CAME OUT TO WASH YOUR FACE ALREADY DRESSED.
I HAVEN'T SEEN SUCH POLITENESS FOR SEVERAL YEARS NOW, SO...
SPLISH SPLASH
SHFF SHFF SHFF SHFF
DID YOU HEAR WHAT SHE JUST SAID?
SHFF SHFF
CAN SHE BE IMPLYING WE ARE LESS THAN POLITE?
ARGLE ARGLE ARGLE
INCREDI-BLE, ISN'T IT...
?

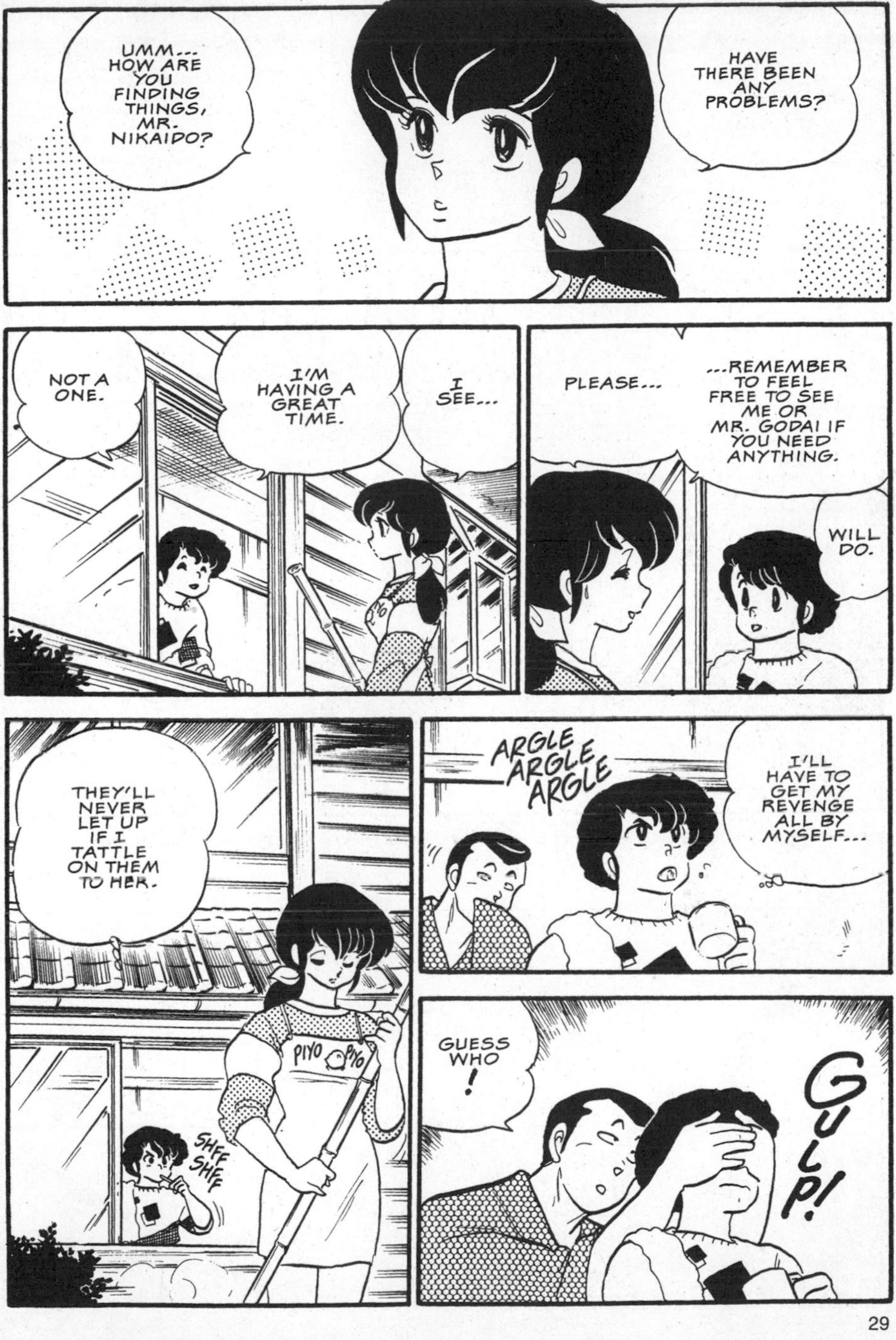
UMM... HOW ARE YOU FINDING THINGS, MR. NIKAIDO?
HAVE THERE BEEN ANY PROBLEMS?
NOT A ONE.
I'M HAVING A GREAT TIME.
I SEE...
PLEASE...
...REMEMBER TO FEEL FREE TO SEE ME OR MR. GODAI IF YOU NEED ANYTHING.
WILL DO.
THEY'LL NEVER LET UP IF I TATTLE ON THEM TO HER.
PIYO PIYO
SHFF SHFF
ARGLE ARGLE ARGLE
I'LL HAVE TO GET MY REVENGE ALL BY MYSELF...
GUESS WHO!
GULP!

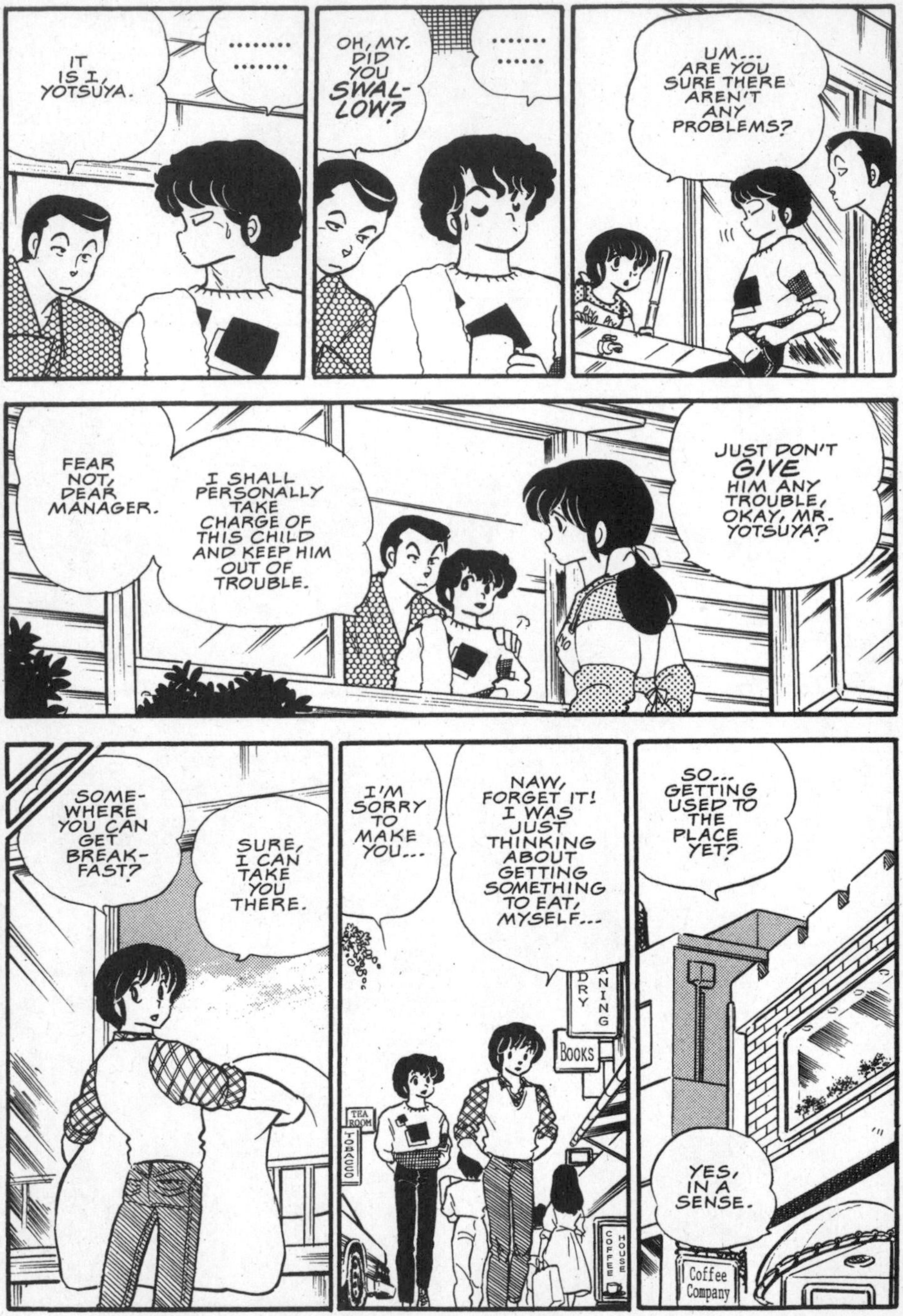

IT IS I, YOTSUYA.
....
OH, MY. DID YOU SWAL-LOW?
....
UM... ARE YOU SURE THERE AREN'T ANY PROBLEMS?
FEAR NOT, DEAR MANAGER.
I SHALL PERSONALLY TAKE CHARGE OF THIS CHILD AND KEEP HIM OUT OF TROUBLE.
JUST DON'T GIVE HIM ANY TROUBLE, OKAY, MR. YOTSUYA?
SOME-WHERE YOU CAN GET BREAK-FAST?
SURE, I CAN TAKE YOU THERE.
I'M SORRY TO MAKE YOU...
NAW, FORGET IT! I WAS JUST THINKING ABOUT GETTING SOMETHING TO EAT, MYSELF...
TEA ROOM
TOBACCO
BOOKS
COFFEE HOUSE
SO... GETTING USED TO THE PLACE YET?
YES, IN A SENSE.
Coffee Company

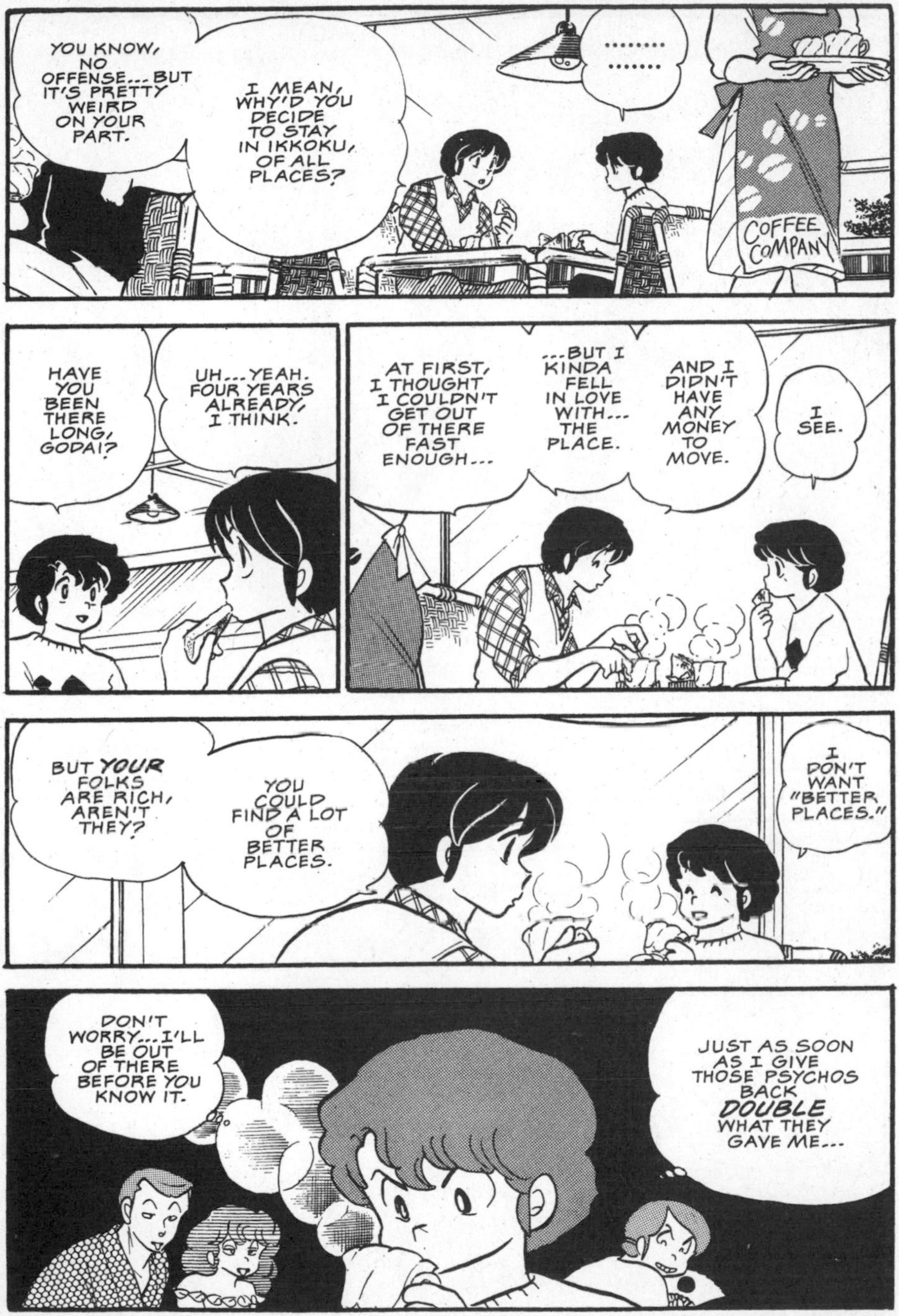

YOU KNOW, NO OFFENSE... BUT IT'S PRETTY WEIRD ON YOUR PART.
I MEAN, WHY'D YOU DECIDE TO STAY IN IKKOKU, OF ALL PLACES?
....
COFFEE COMPANY
HAVE YOU BEEN THERE LONG, GODAI?
UH... YEAH. FOUR YEARS ALREADY, I THINK.
AT FIRST, I THOUGHT I COULDN'T GET OUT OF THERE FAST ENOUGH...
...BUT I KINDA FELL IN LOVE WITH... THE PLACE.
AND I DIDN'T HAVE ANY MONEY TO MOVE.
I SEE.
BUT YOUR FOLKS ARE RICH, AREN'T THEY?
YOU COULD FIND A LOT OF BETTER PLACES.
I DON'T WANT "BETTER PLACES."
DON'T WORRY... I'LL BE OUT OF THERE BEFORE YOU KNOW IT.
JUST AS SOON AS I GIVE THOSE PSYCHOS BACK DOUBLE WHAT THEY GAVE ME...

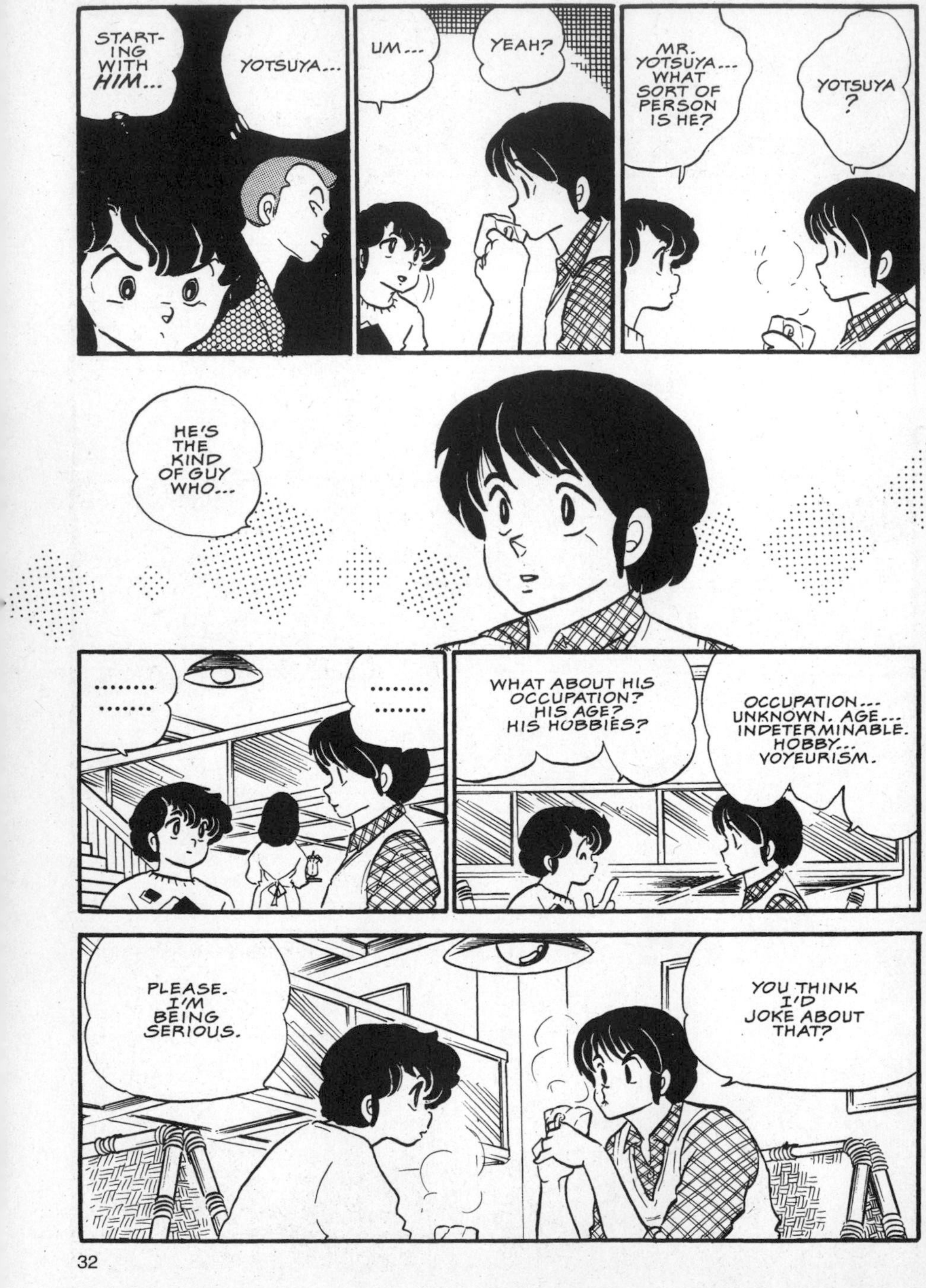

START-ING WITH HIM...
YOTSUYA...
UM...
YEAH?
MR. YOTSUYA... WHAT SORT OF PERSON IS HE?
YOTSUYA?
HE'S THE KIND OF GUY WHO...
....
....
WHAT ABOUT HIS OCCUPATION? HIS AGE? HIS HOBBIES?
OCCUPATION... UNKNOWN. AGE... INDETERMINABLE. HOBBY... VOYEURISM.
PLEASE. I'M BEING SERIOUS.
YOU THINK I'D JOKE ABOUT THAT?

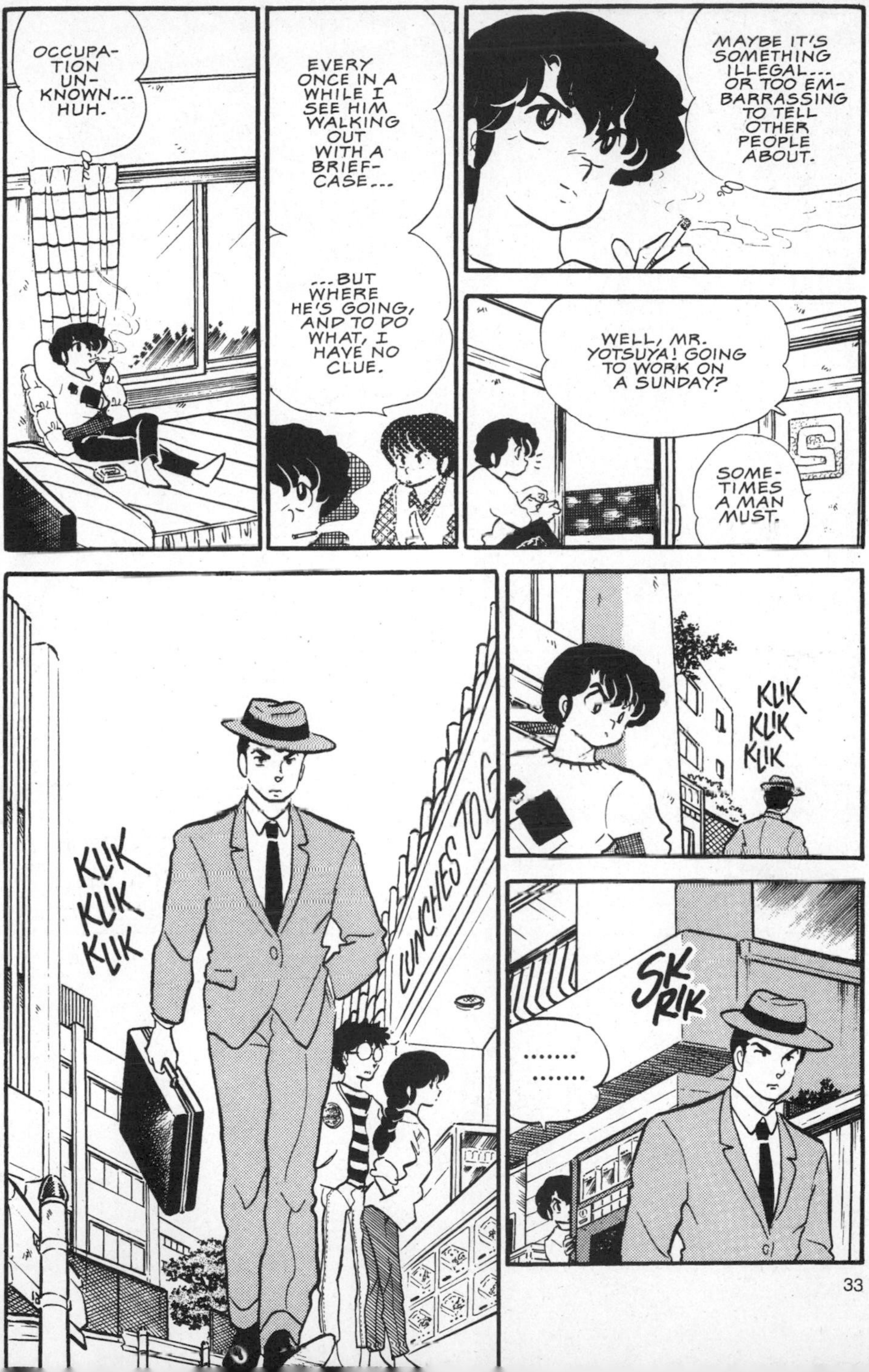
OCCUPATION UNKNOWN... HUH.
EVERY ONCE IN A WHILE I SEE HIM WALKING OUT WITH A BRIEFCASE...
...BUT WHERE HE'S GOING, AND TO DO WHAT, I HAVE NO CLUE.
MAYBE IT'S SOMETHING ILLEGAL... OR TOO EMBARRASSING TO TELL OTHER PEOPLE ABOUT.
WELL, MR. YOTSUYA! GOING TO WORK ON A SUNDAY?
SOMETIMES A MAN MUST.
KLIK KLIK KLIK
LUNCHES TO G
KLIK KLIK KLIK
SK RIK
....
....

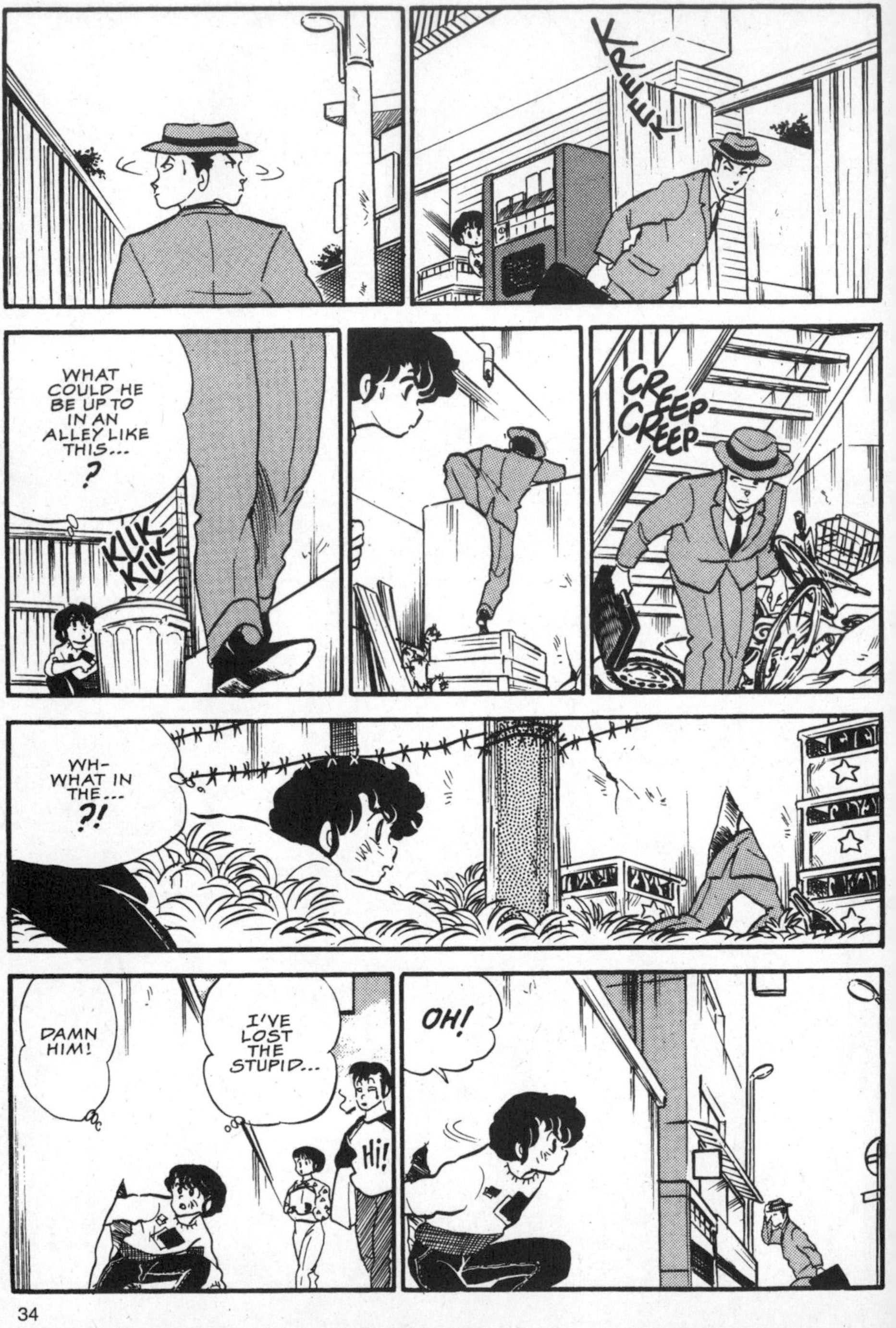
KREEEK
WHAT COULD HE BE UP TO IN AN ALLEY LIKE THIS...?
KLIK KLIK
CREEP CREEP
WH-WHAT IN THE...?!
DAMN HIM!
I'VE LOST THE STUPID...
Hi!
OH!

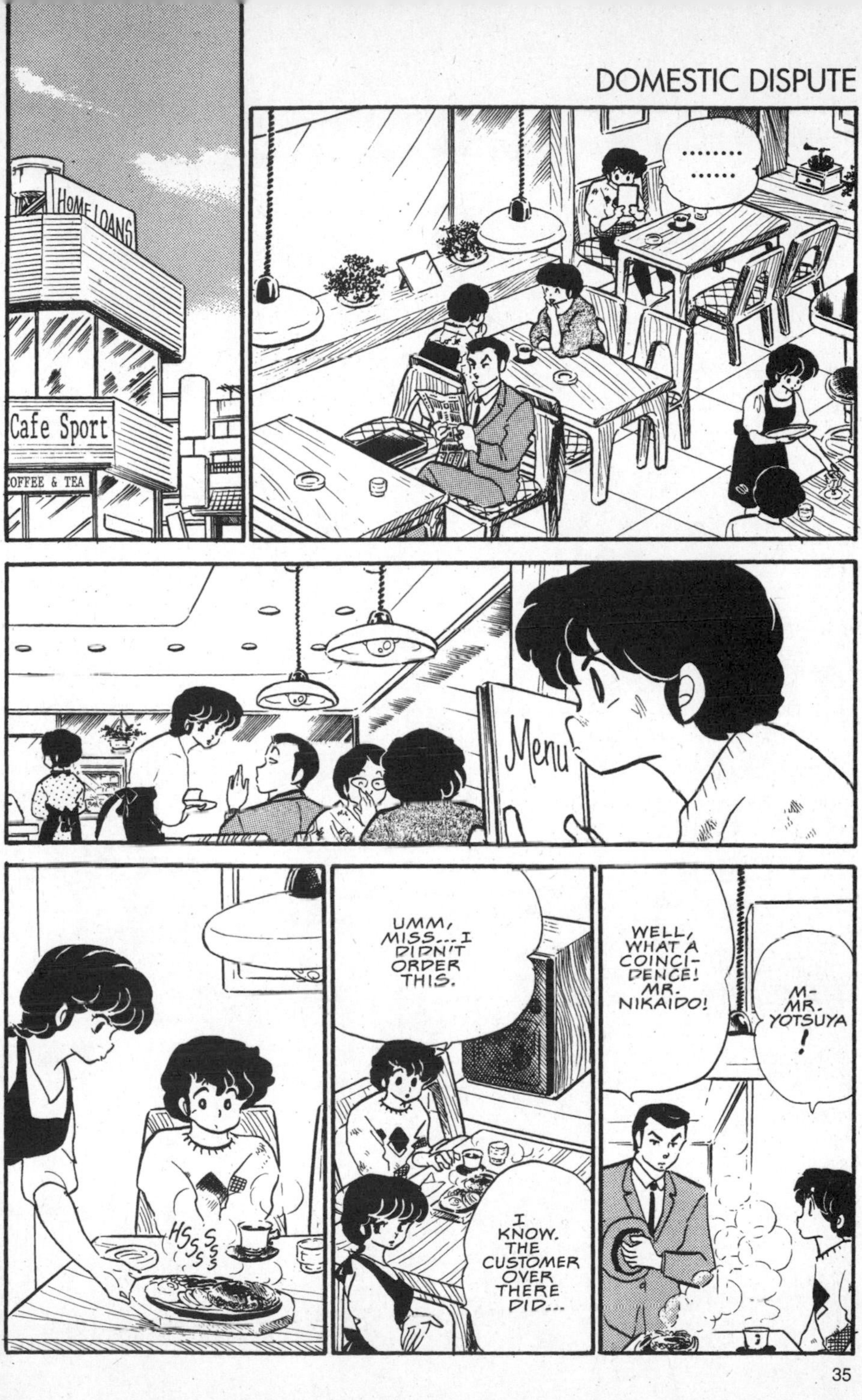
HOME LOANS
Cafe Sport
COFFEE & TEA
....
......
Menu
HSSSSSS
UMM, MISS... I DIDN'T ORDER THIS.
I KNOW. THE CUSTOMER OVER THERE DID...
WELL, WHAT A COINCIDENCE! MR. NIKAIDO!
M-MR. YOTSUYA!

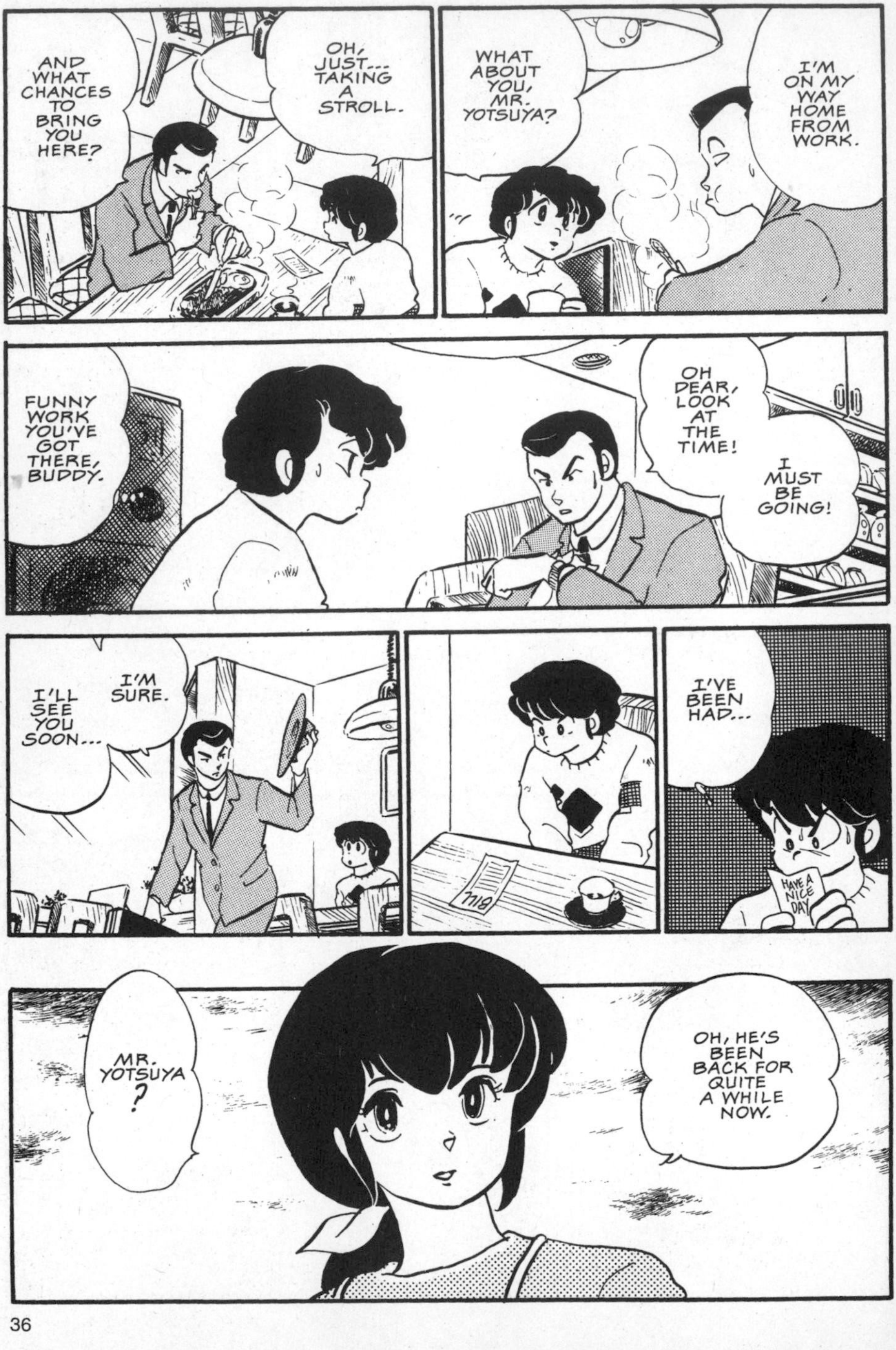
AND WHAT CHANCES TO BRING YOU HERE?
OH, JUST... TAKING A STROLL.
WHAT ABOUT YOU, MR. YOTSUYA?
I'M ON MY WAY HOME FROM WORK.
FUNNY WORK YOU'VE GOT THERE, BUDDY.
OH DEAR, LOOK AT THE TIME!
I MUST BE GOING!
I'M SURE.
I'LL SEE YOU SOON...
BILL
I'VE BEEN HAD...
HAVE A NICE DAY
MR. YOTSUYA?
OH, HE'S BEEN BACK FOR QUITE A WHILE NOW.

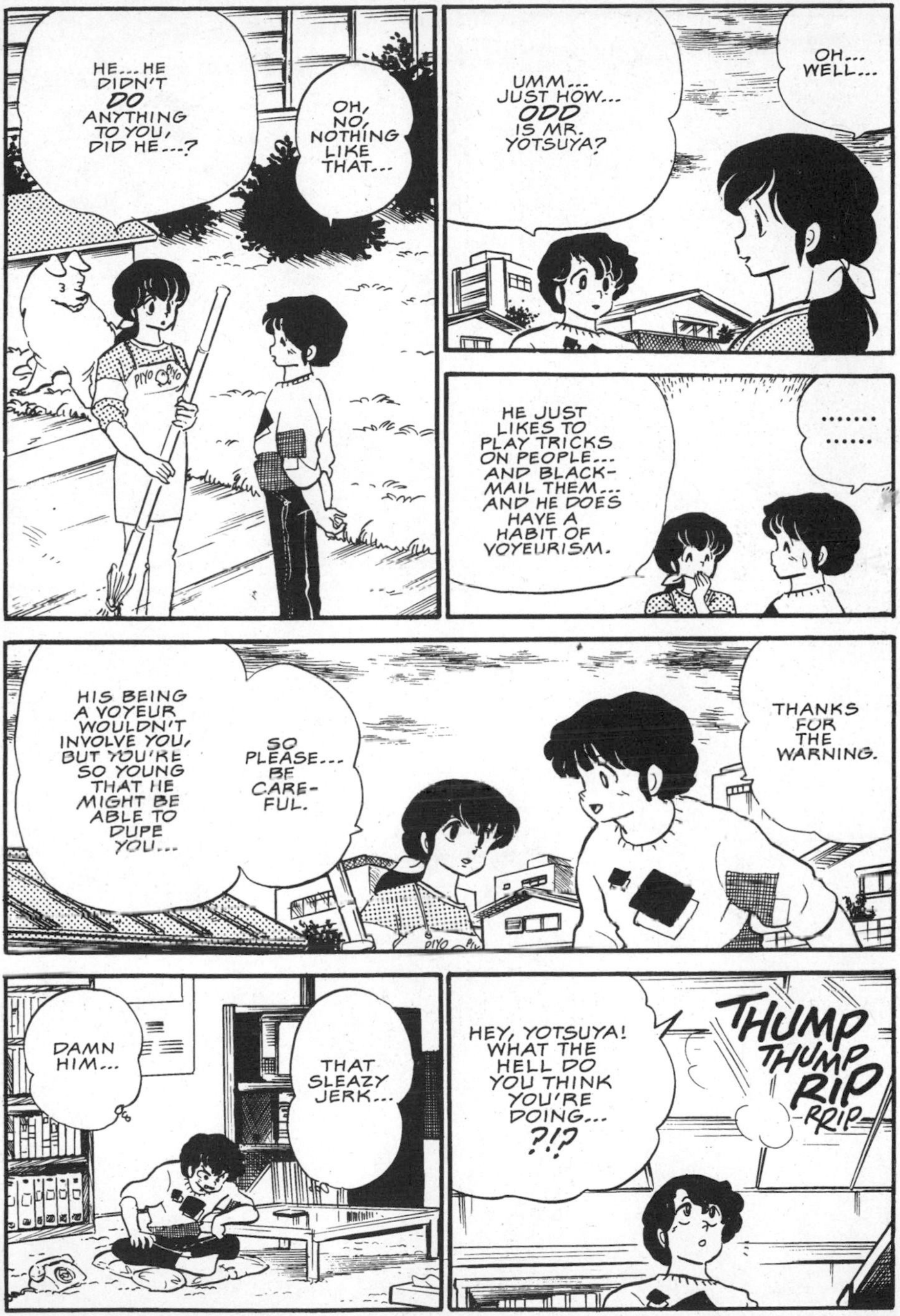
HE... HE DIDN'T DO ANYTHING TO YOU, DID HE...?
OH, NO, NOTHING LIKE THAT...
UMM... JUST HOW... ODD IS MR. YOTSUYA?
OH... WELL...
HE JUST LIKES TO PLAY TRICKS ON PEOPLE... AND BLACK-MAIL THEM... AND HE DOES HAVE A HABIT OF VOYEURISM.
....
....
HIS BEING A VOYEUR WOULDN'T INVOLVE YOU, BUT YOU'RE SO YOUNG THAT HE MIGHT BE ABLE TO DUPE YOU...
SO PLEASE... BE CARE-FUL.
THANKS FOR THE WARNING.
DAMN HIM...
THAT SLEAZY JERK...
HEY, YOTSUYA! WHAT THE HELL DO YOU THINK YOU'RE DOING...?!?
THUMP THUMP RIP RRIP

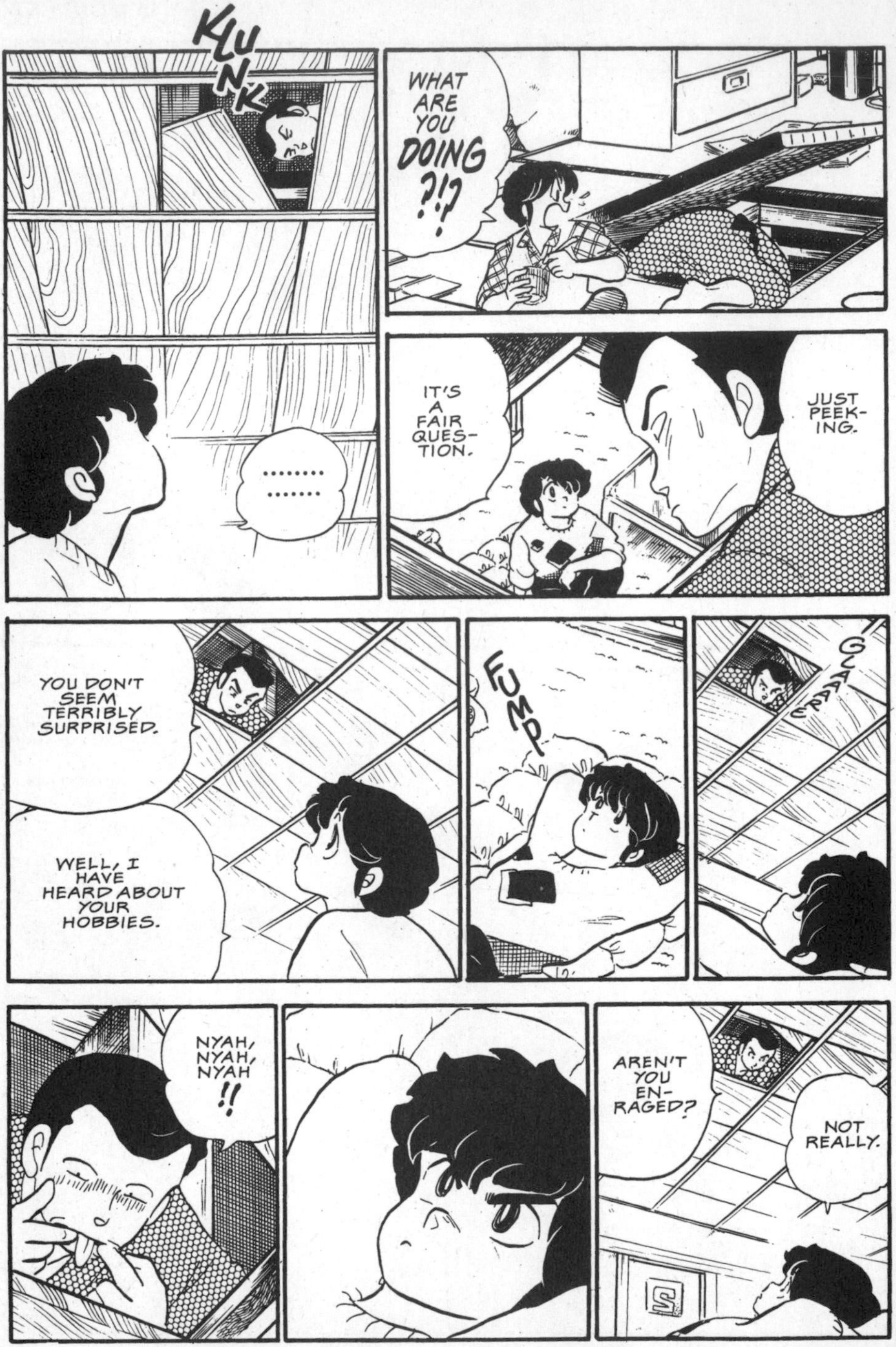
KLUNK
....
....
WHAT ARE YOU DOING ?!?
IT'S A FAIR QUESTION.
JUST PEEKING.
YOU DON'T SEEM TERRIBLY SURPRISED.
WELL, I HAVE HEARD ABOUT YOUR HOBBIES.
FUMP
GLAARE
NYAH, NYAH, NYAH !!
AREN'T YOU ENRAGED?
NOT REALLY.

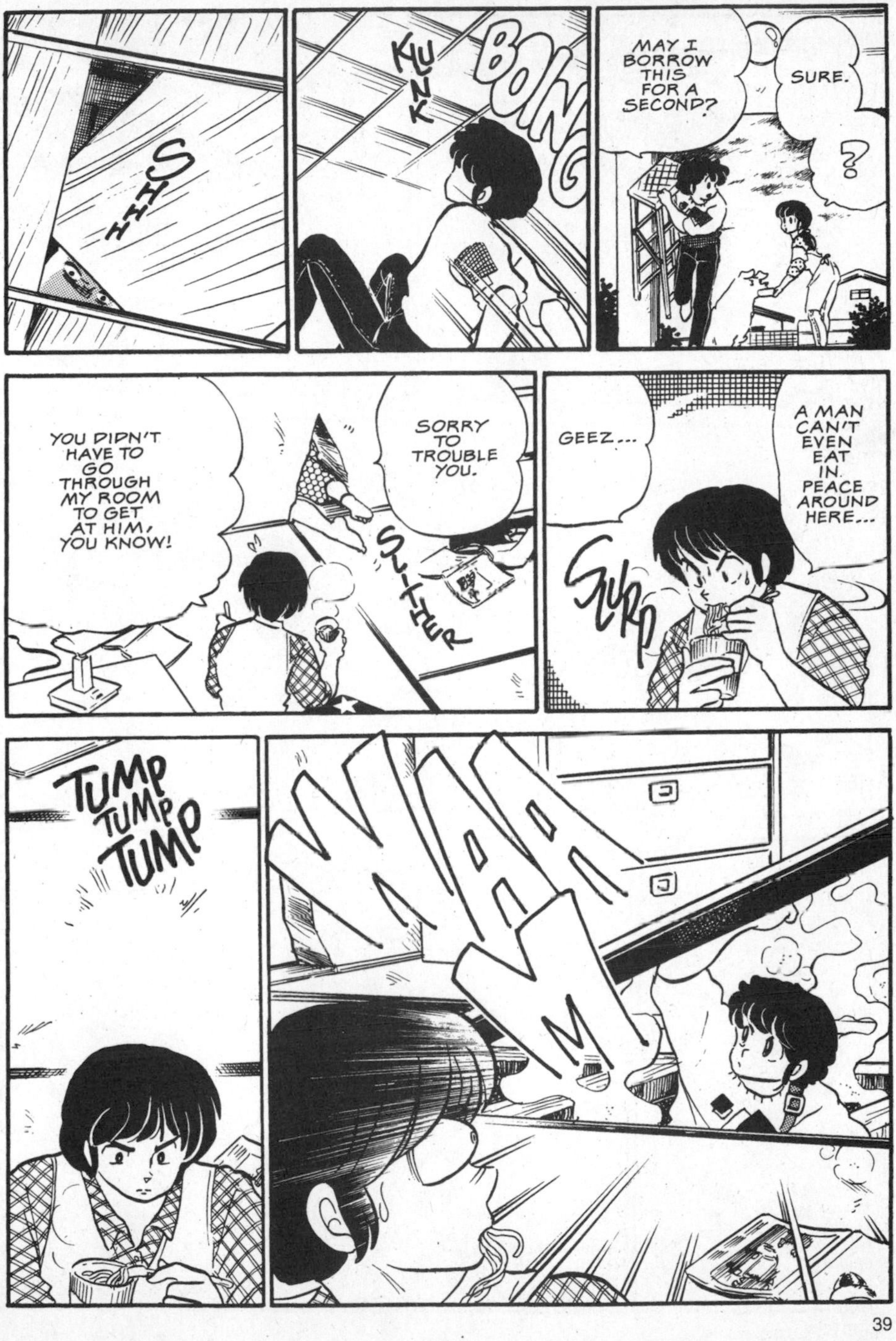
SHHH
KLUNK
BOING
MAY I BORROW THIS FOR A SECOND?
SURE.
?
YOU DIDN'T HAVE TO GO THROUGH MY ROOM TO GET AT HIM, YOU KNOW!
SORRY TO TROUBLE YOU.
SLITHER
GEEZ...
A MAN CAN'T EVEN EAT IN PEACE AROUND HERE...
SLURP
TUMP TUMP TUMP
WHAAM

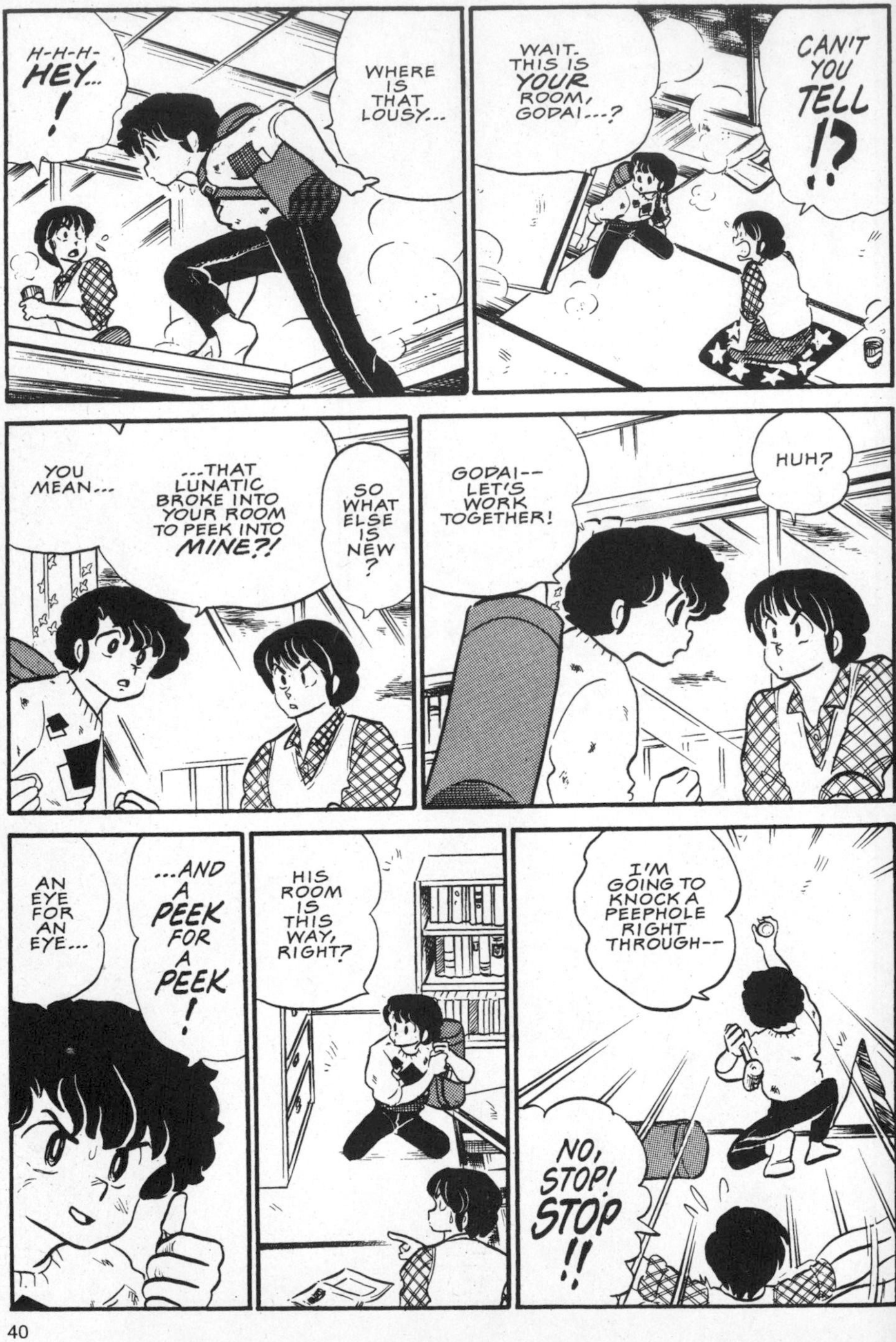
H-H-H-HEY...!
WHERE IS THAT LOUSY...
WAIT- THIS IS YOUR ROOM, GODAI...?
CAN'T YOU TELL!?
YOU MEAN...
...THAT LUNATIC BROKE INTO YOUR ROOM TO PEEK INTO MINE?!
SO WHAT ELSE IS NEW?
GODAI-- LET'S WORK TOGETHER!
HUH?
AN EYE FOR AN EYE...
...AND A PEEK FOR A PEEK!
HIS ROOM IS THIS WAY, RIGHT?
I'M GOING TO KNOCK A PEEPHOLE RIGHT THROUGH--
NO, STOP! STOP!!

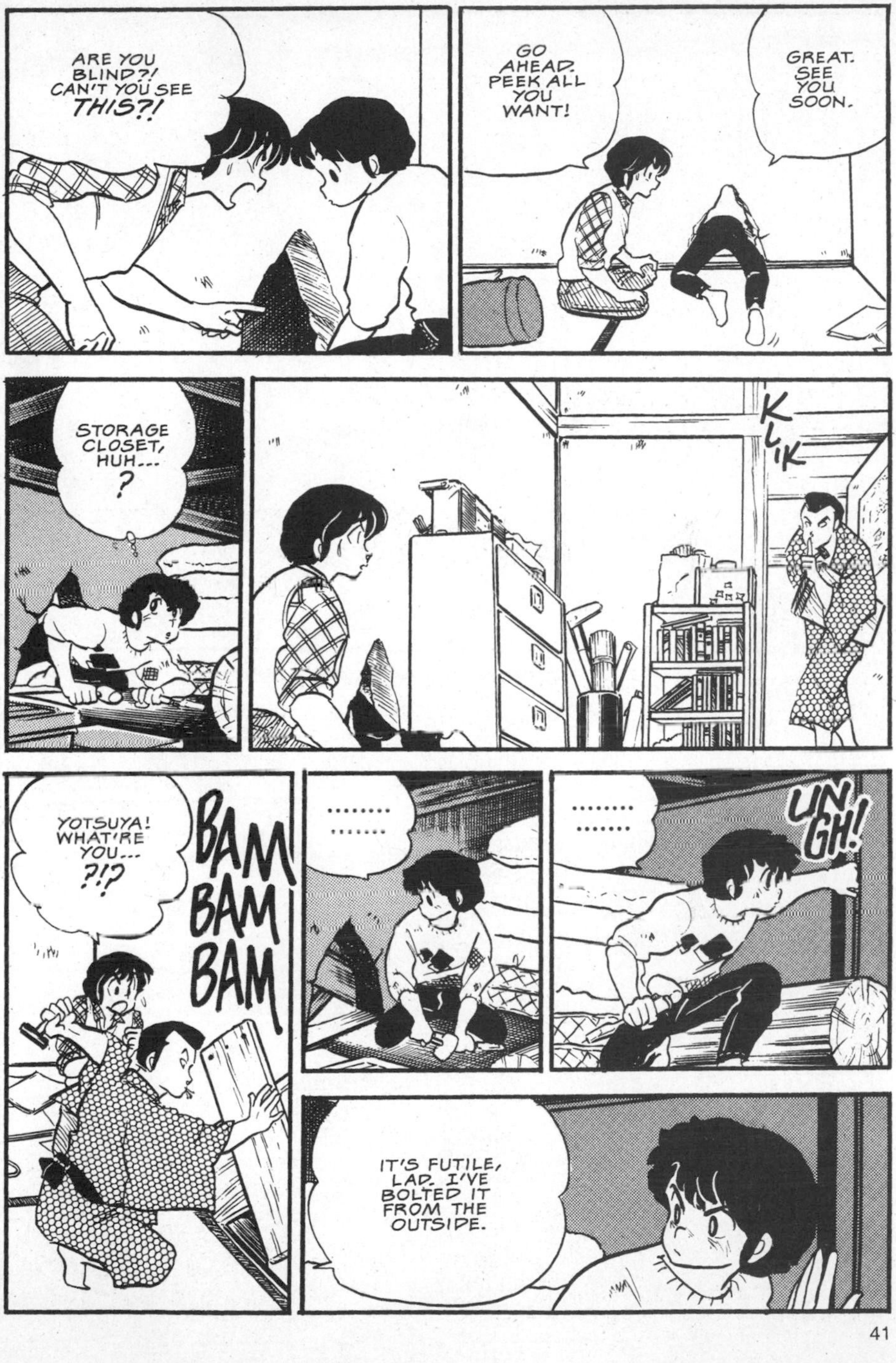
ARE YOU BLIND?! CAN'T YOU SEE THIS?!
GO AHEAD. PEEK ALL YOU WANT!
GREAT. SEE YOU SOON.
STORAGE CLOSET, HUH... ?
KLIK
YOTSUYA! WHAT'RE YOU... ?!?
BAM BAM BAM
....
....
UNGH!
IT'S FUTILE, LAD. I'VE BOLTED IT FROM THE OUTSIDE.

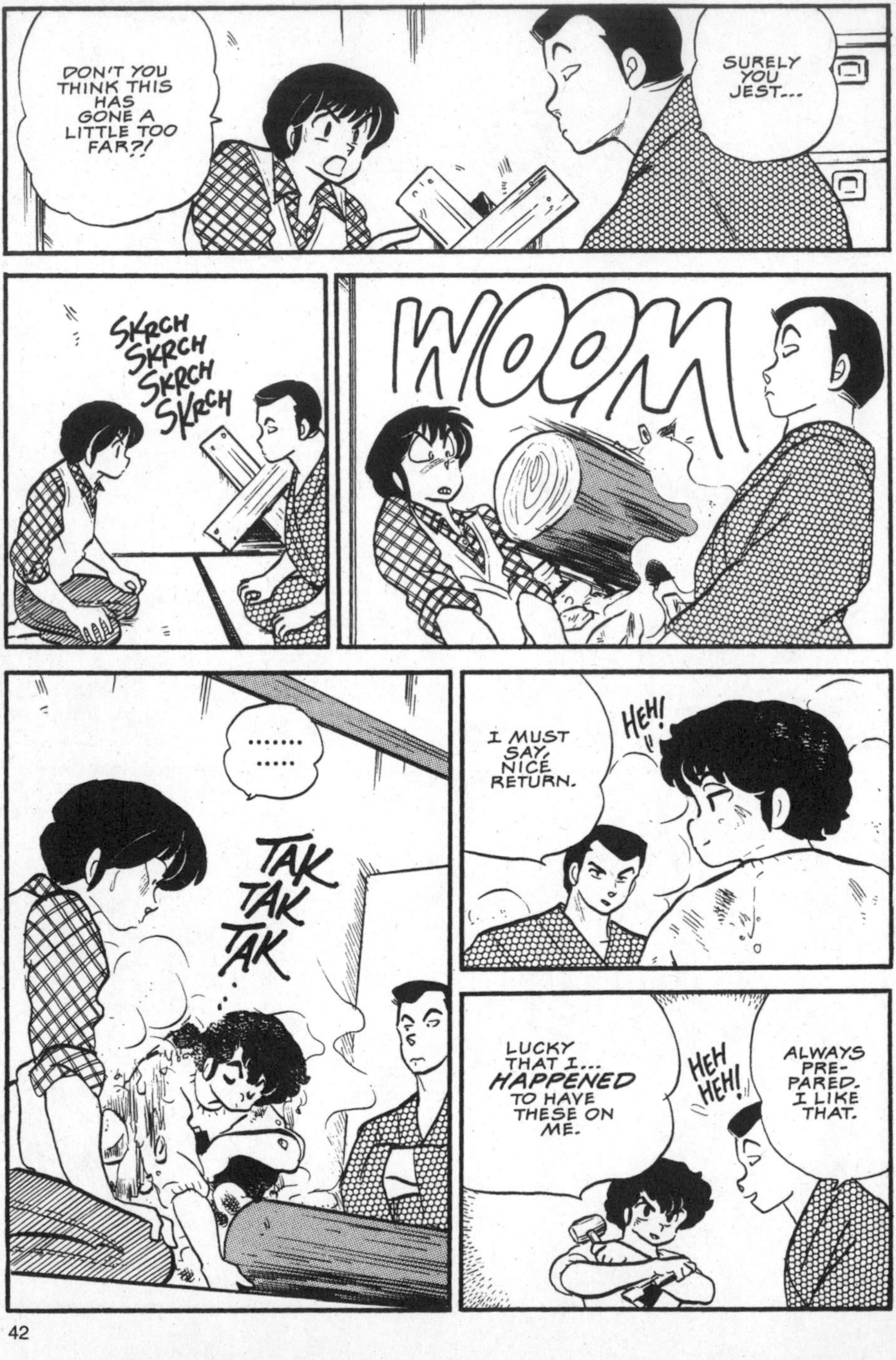
DON'T YOU THINK THIS HAS GONE A LITTLE TOO FAR?!
SURELY YOU JEST...
SKRCH SKRCH SKRCH SKRCH
WOOM
....
......
TAK TAK TAK
I MUST SAY, NICE RETURN.
HEH!
LUCKY THAT I... HAPPENED TO HAVE THESE ON ME.
HEH HEH!
ALWAYS PREPARED. I LIKE THAT.

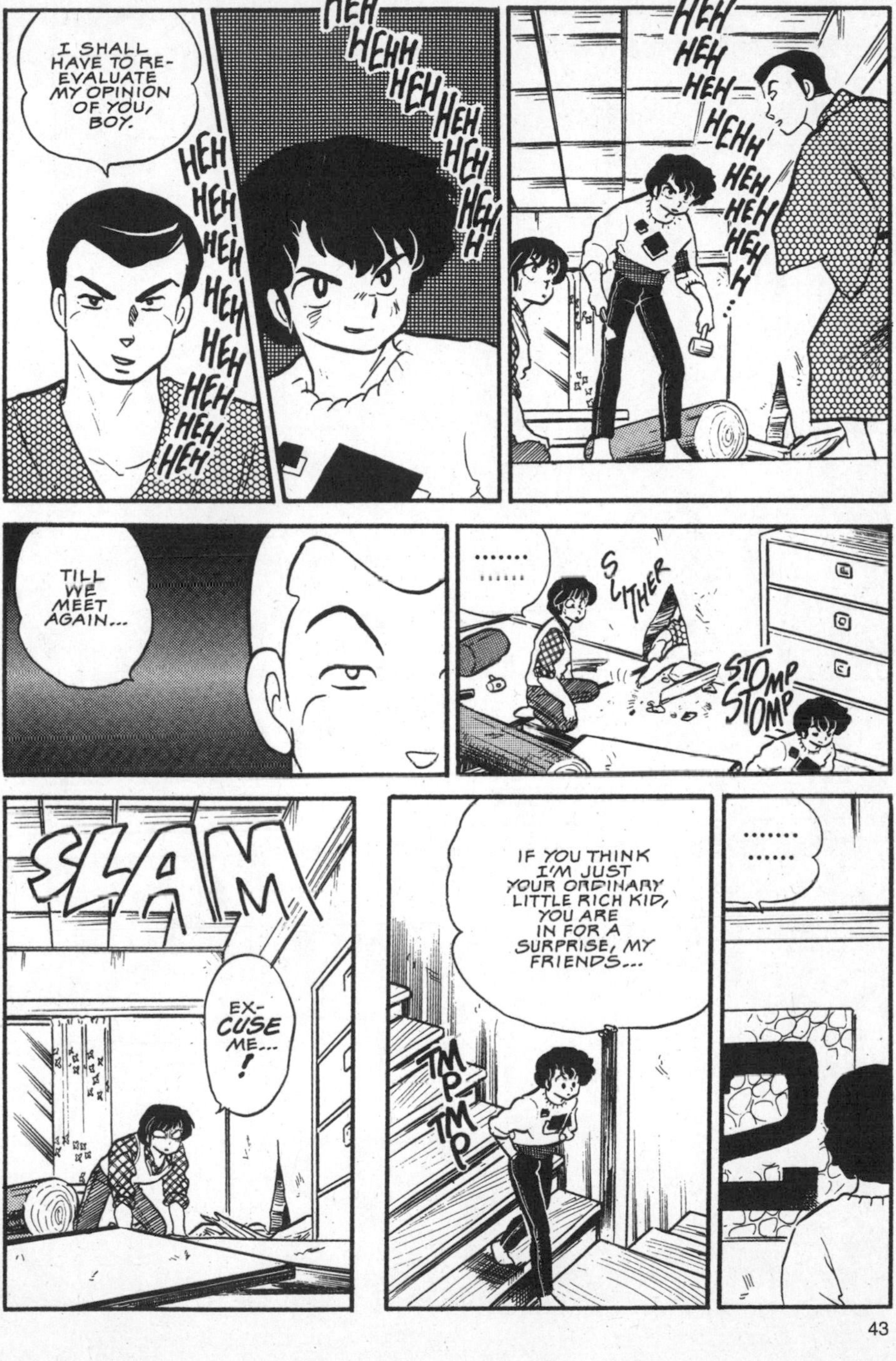
I SHALL HAVE TO RE-EVALUATE MY OPINION OF YOU, BOY.
HEH HEH HEH HEH HEH HEH HEH HEH
HEH HEHH HEH HEH HEH HEH HEH H
HEH HEH HEH HEHH HEH HEH HEH H...
TILL WE MEET AGAIN...
......
......
SLITHER
STOMP STOMP
SLAM
EX-CUSE ME...!
TMP TMP
IF YOU THINK I'M JUST YOUR ORDINARY LITTLE RICH KID, YOU ARE IN FOR A SURPRISE, MY FRIENDS...
......
......

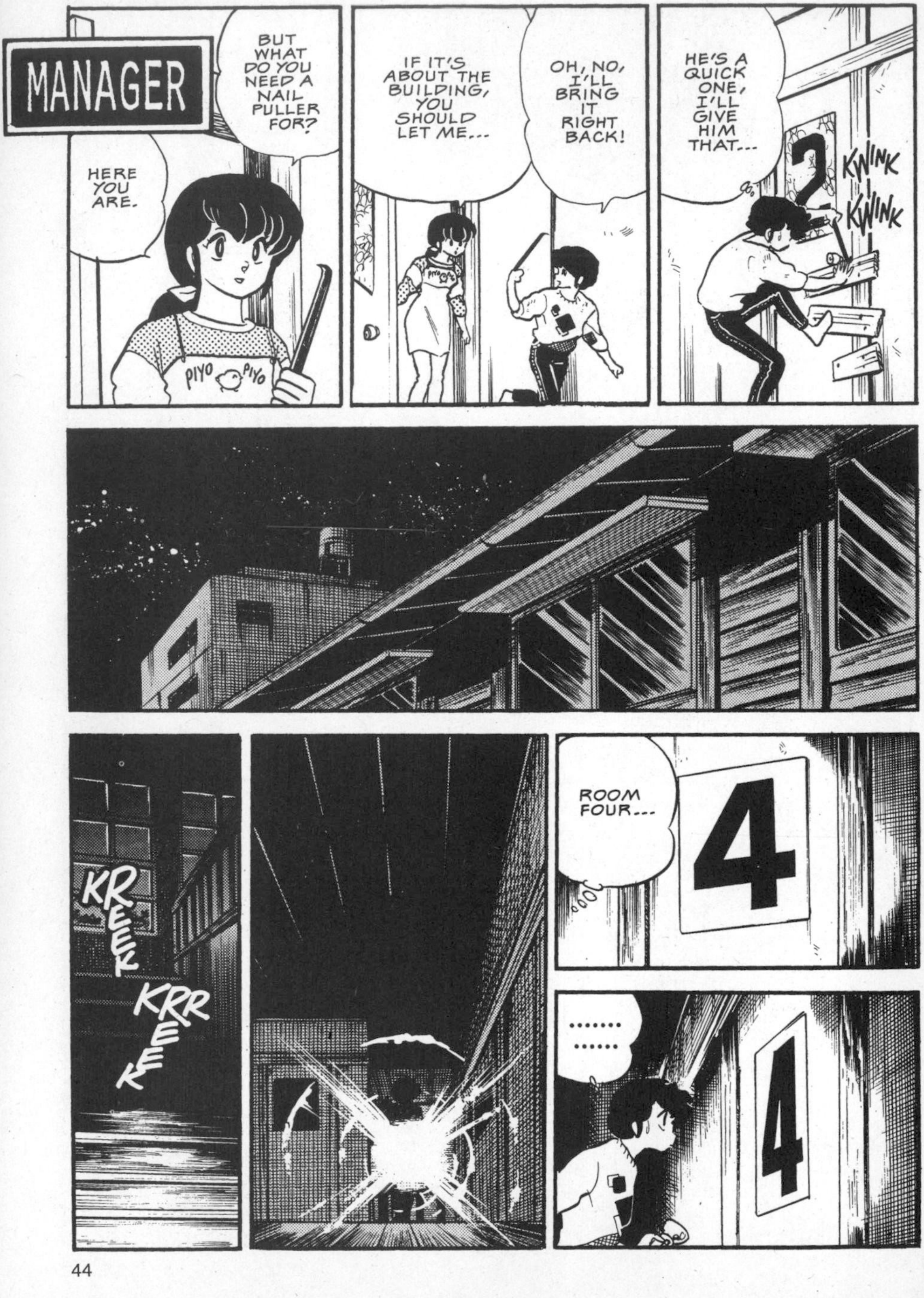
MANAGER
BUT WHAT DO YOU NEED A NAIL PULLER FOR?
HERE YOU ARE.
PIYO PIYO
IF IT'S ABOUT THE BUILDING, YOU SHOULD LET ME...
OH, NO, I'LL BRING IT RIGHT BACK!
HE'S A QUICK ONE, I'LL GIVE HIM THAT...
KWINK
KWINK
KREEK
KRREEK
ROOM FOUR...
4
....
....
4

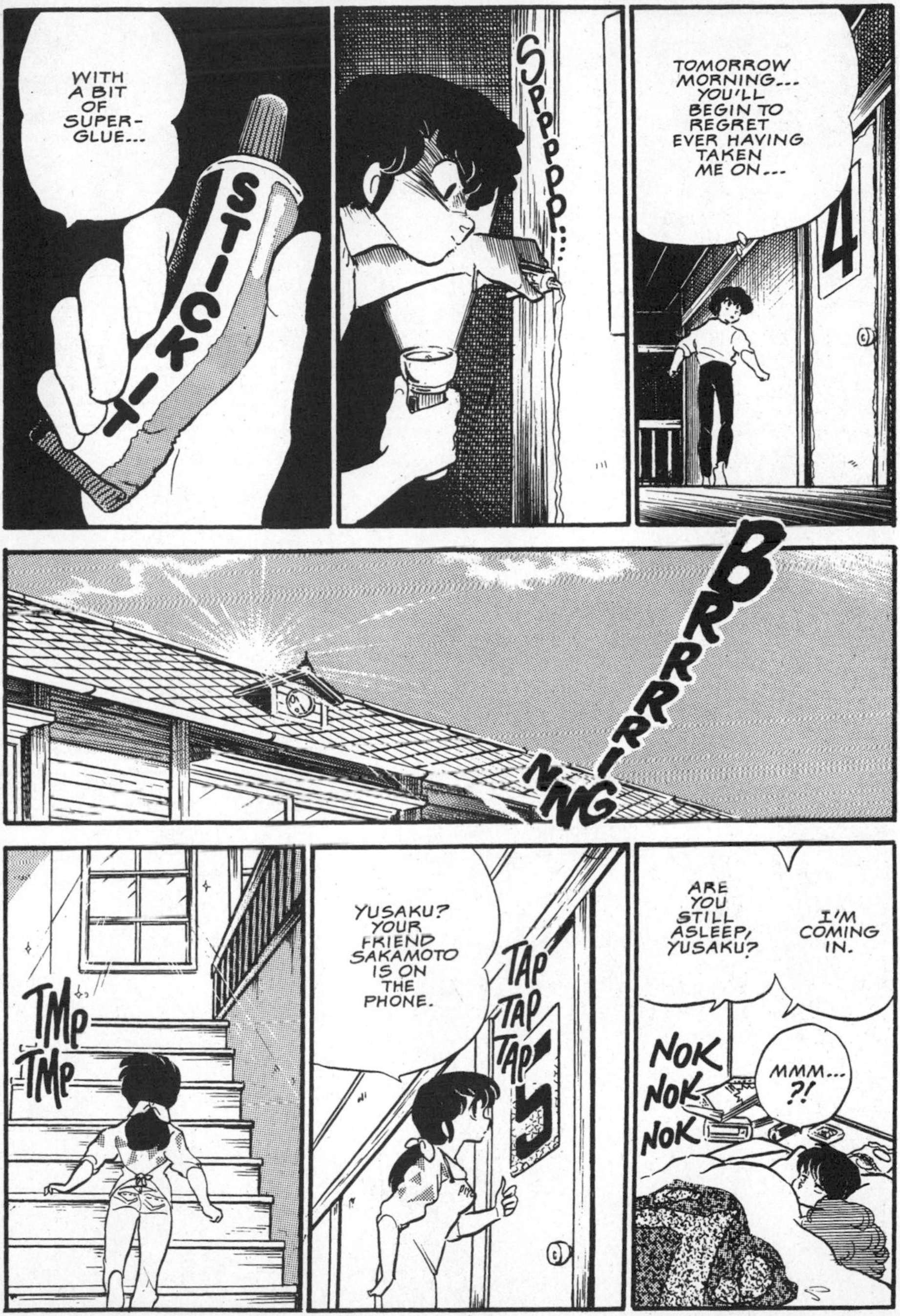
WITH A BIT OF SUPER-GLUE...
STICK-IT
SPPPPPP...
TOMORROW MORNING... YOU'LL BEGIN TO REGRET EVER HAVING TAKEN ME ON...
4
BRRRRRIING
TMP TMP
YUSAKU? YOUR FRIEND SAKAMOTO IS ON THE PHONE.
TAP TAP TAP
5
ARE YOU STILL ASLEEP, YUSAKU?
I'M COMING IN.
NOK NOK NOK
MMM... ?!

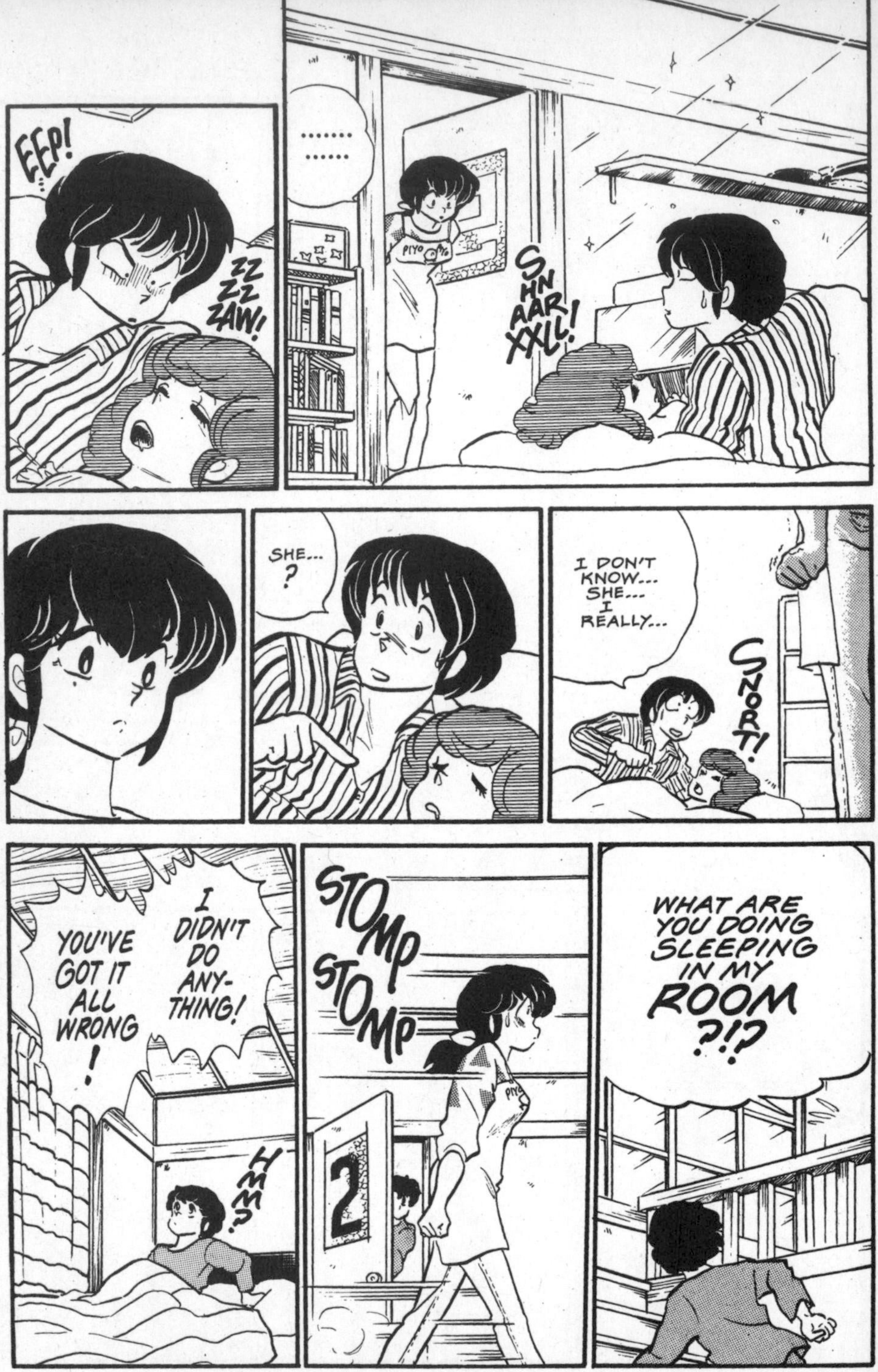
EEP!
ZZ ZZ ZAW!
....
......
SHN AAR XXLL!
SHE... ?
I DON'T KNOW... SHE... I REALLY...
SNORT!
YOU'VE GOT IT ALL WRONG!
I DIDN'T DO ANYTHING!
HMM?
STOMP STOMP
PIYO
2
WHAT ARE YOU DOING SLEEPING IN MY ROOM ?!?

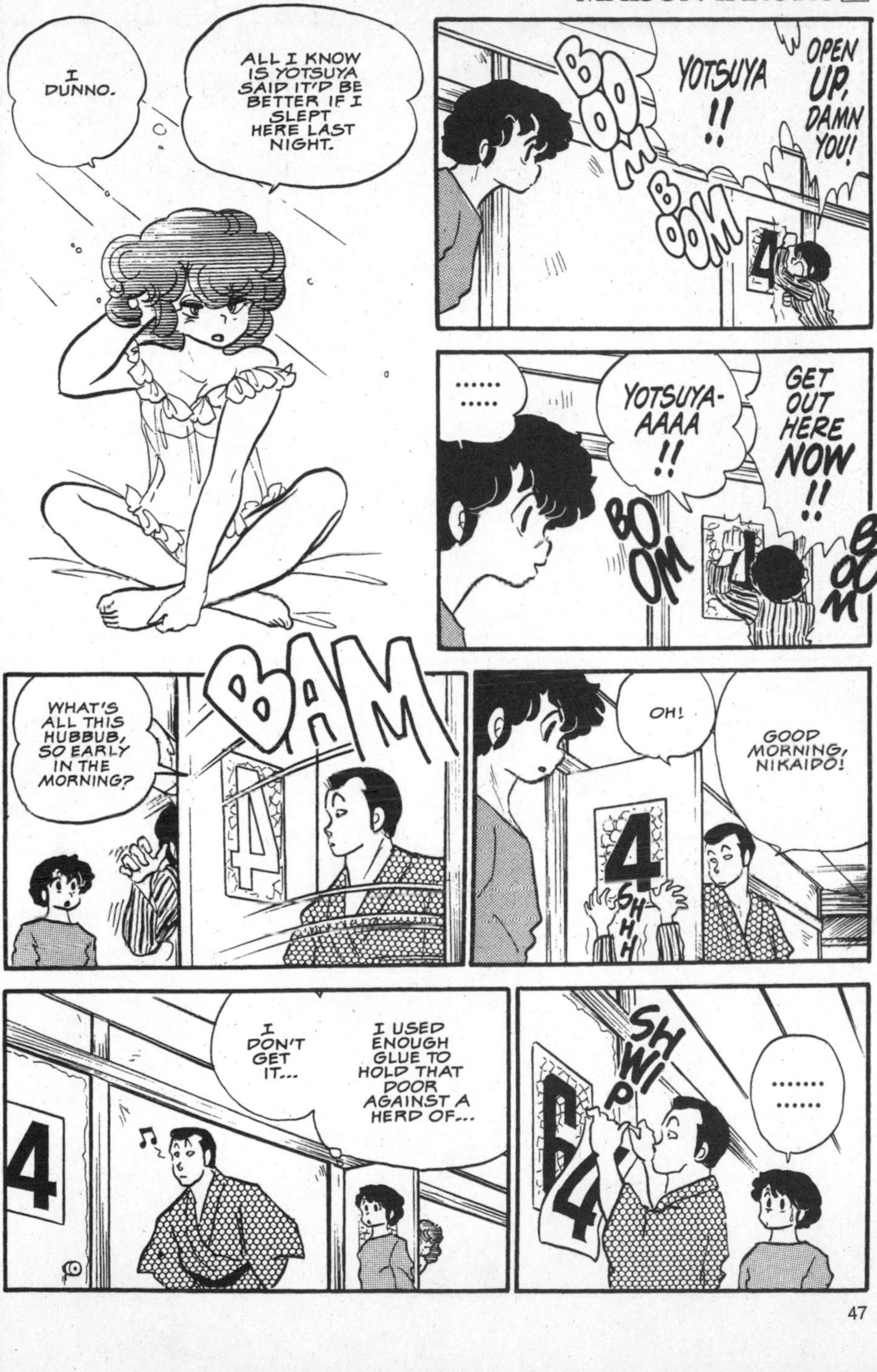
I DUNNO.
ALL I KNOW IS YOTSUYA SAID IT'D BE BETTER IF I SLEPT HERE LAST NIGHT.
BOOM
YOTSUYA!!
OPEN UP, DAMN YOU!
BOOM
......
......
YOTSUYA-AAAA!!
GET OUT HERE NOW!!
BOOM
BOOM
WHAT'S ALL THIS HUBBUB, SO EARLY IN THE MORNING?
BAM
OH!
GOOD MORNING, NIKAIDO!
SHHH
I DON'T GET IT...
I USED ENOUGH GLUE TO HOLD THAT DOOR AGAINST A HERD OF...
SHWIP
......
......

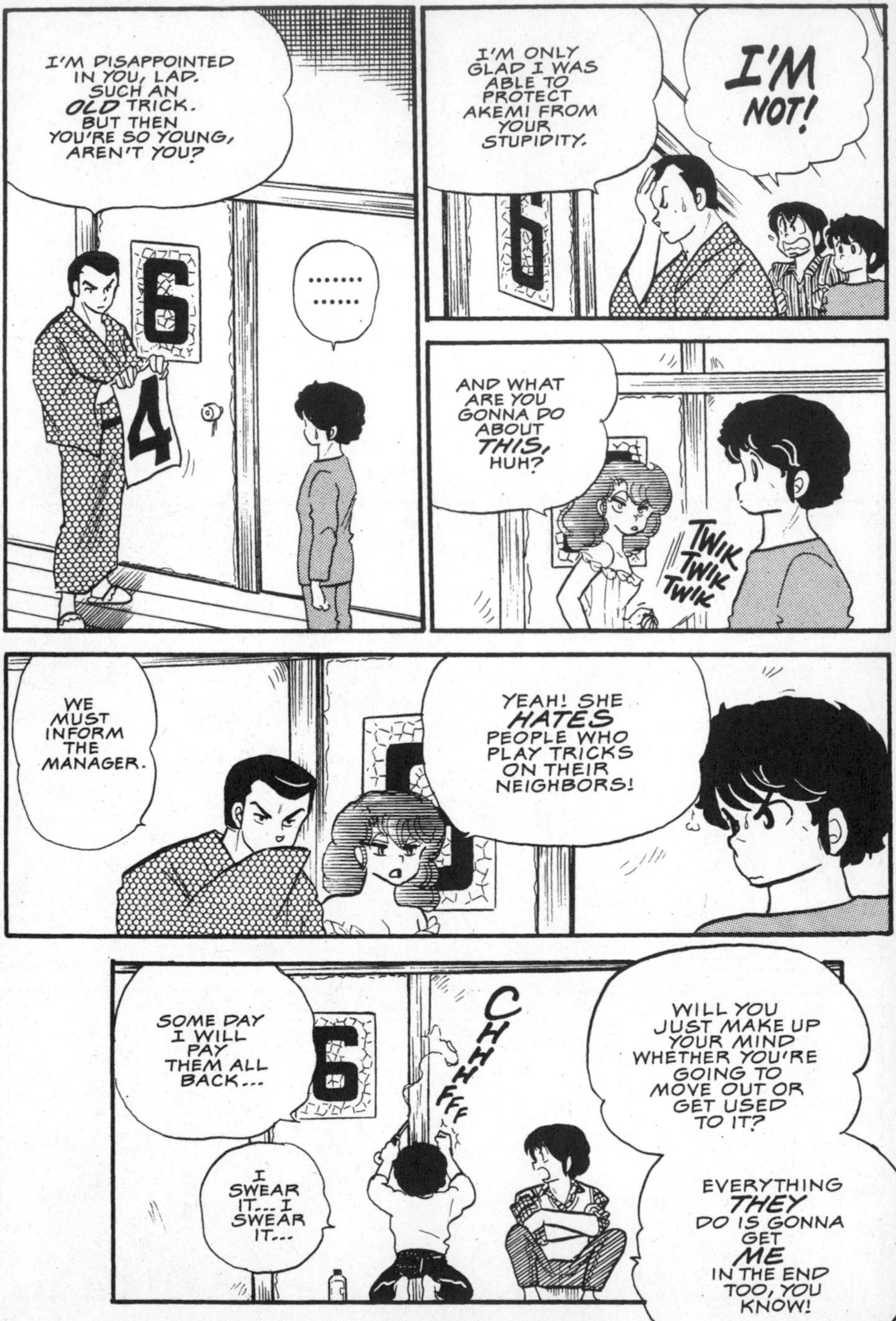

I'M DISAPPOINTED IN YOU, LAD. SUCH AN OLD TRICK. BUT THEN YOU'RE SO YOUNG, AREN'T YOU?
....
....
I'M ONLY GLAD I WAS ABLE TO PROTECT AKEMI FROM YOUR STUPIDITY.
I'M NOT!
AND WHAT ARE YOU GONNA DO ABOUT THIS, HUH?
TWIK TWIK TWIK
WE MUST INFORM THE MANAGER.
YEAH! SHE HATES PEOPLE WHO PLAY TRICKS ON THEIR NEIGHBORS!
SOME DAY I WILL PAY THEM ALL BACK...
I SWEAR IT... I SWEAR IT...
CHHHFFF
WILL YOU JUST MAKE UP YOUR MIND WHETHER YOU'RE GOING TO MOVE OUT OR GET USED TO IT?
EVERYTHING THEY DO IS GONNA GET ME IN THE END TOO, YOU KNOW!

PART 3

CAN'T WE BE FRIENDS?

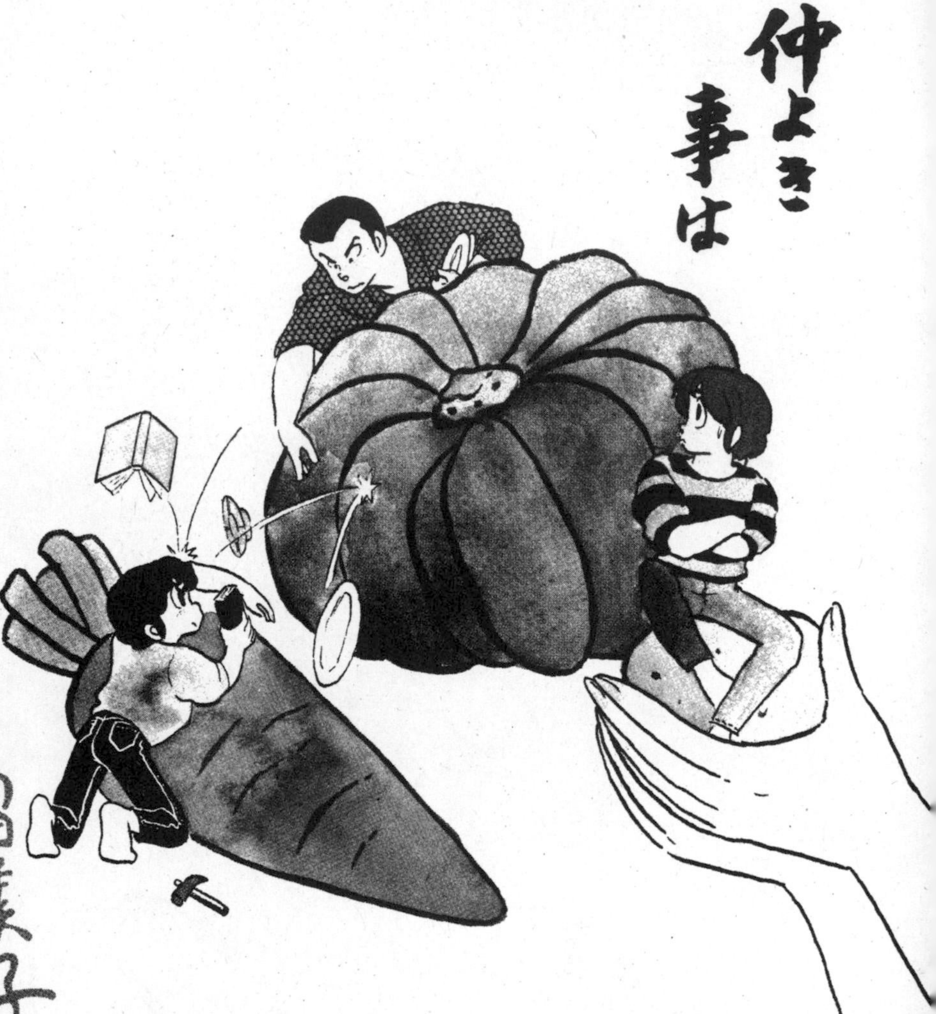
仲よき事は
留美子

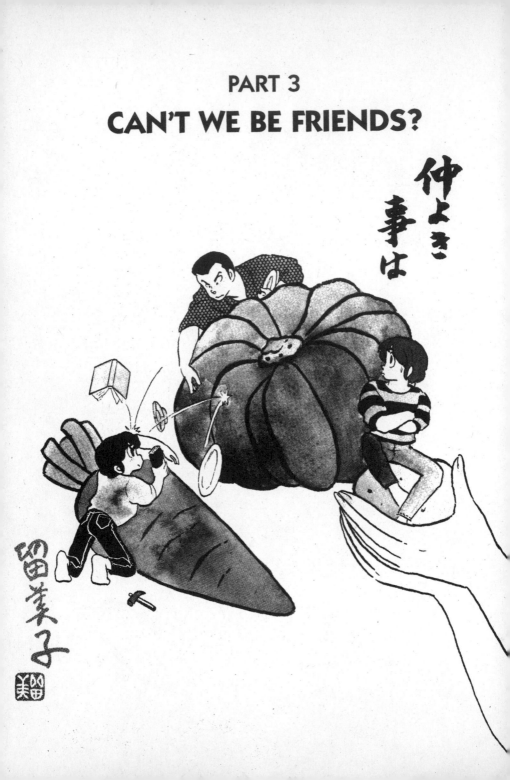

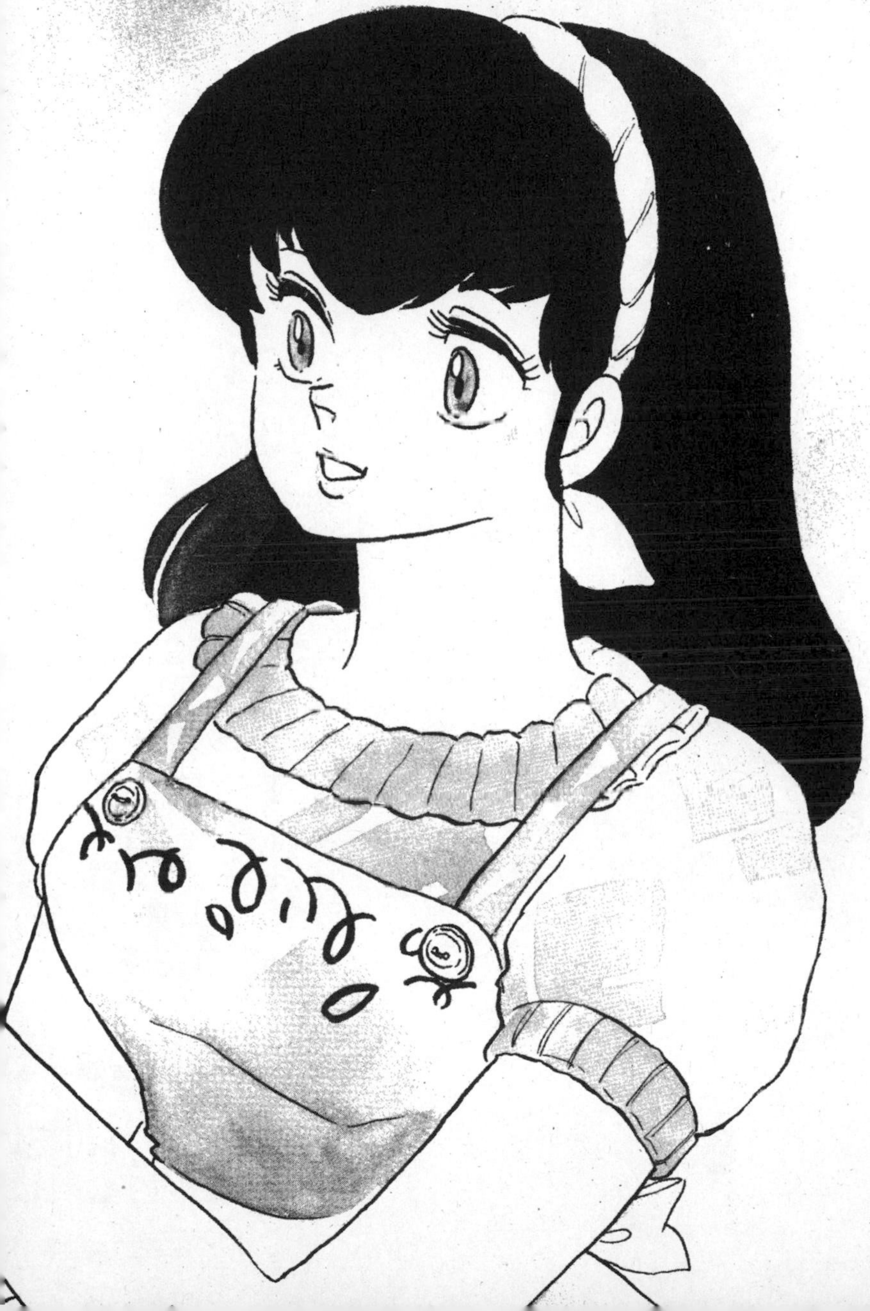

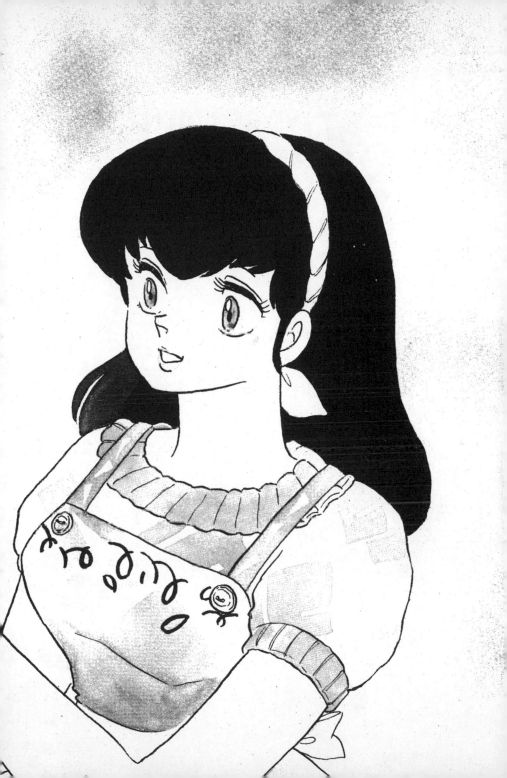

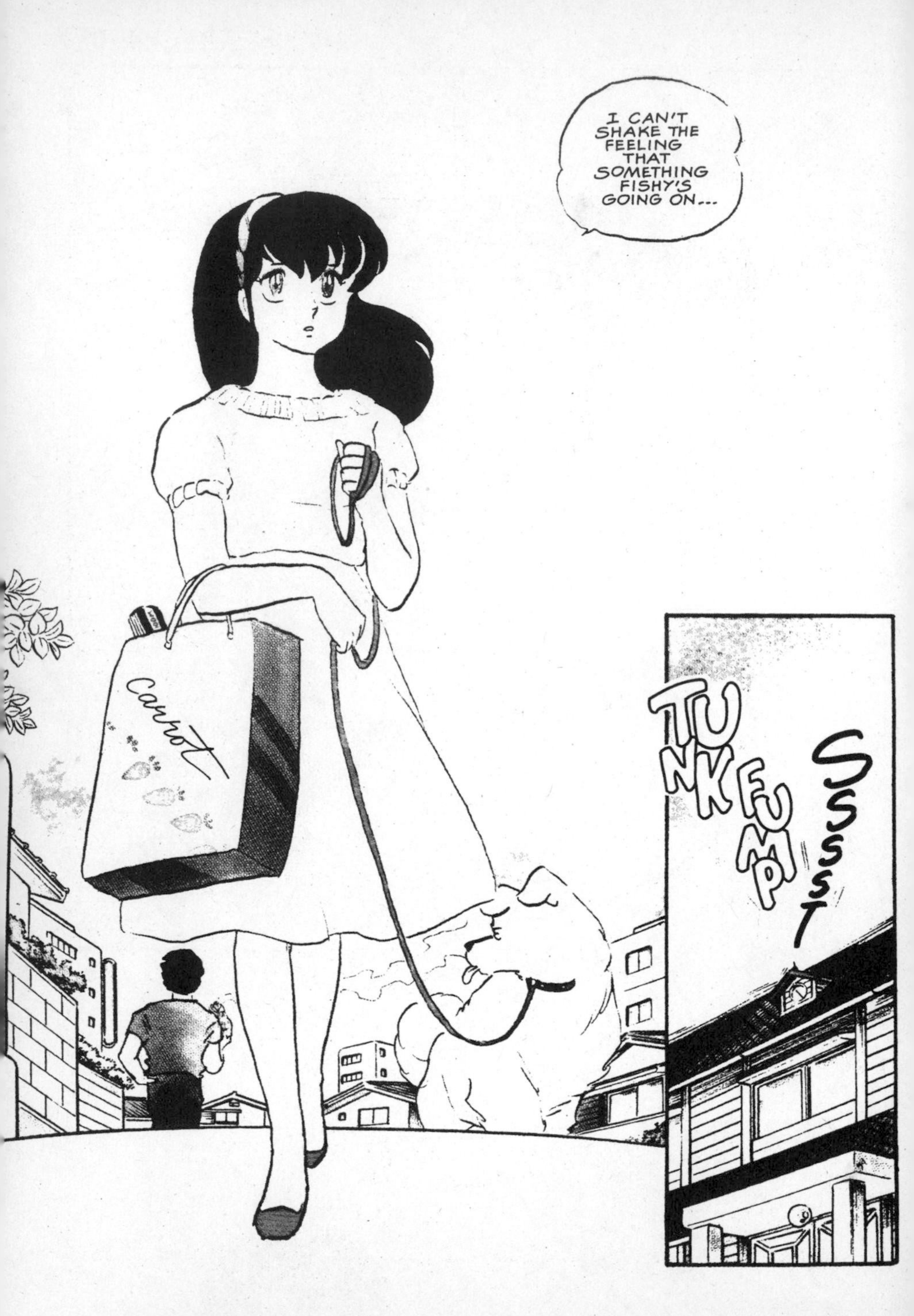
I CAN'T SHAKE THE FEELING THAT SOMETHING FISHY'S GOING ON...
Carrot
TUNK
FUMP
SSSST

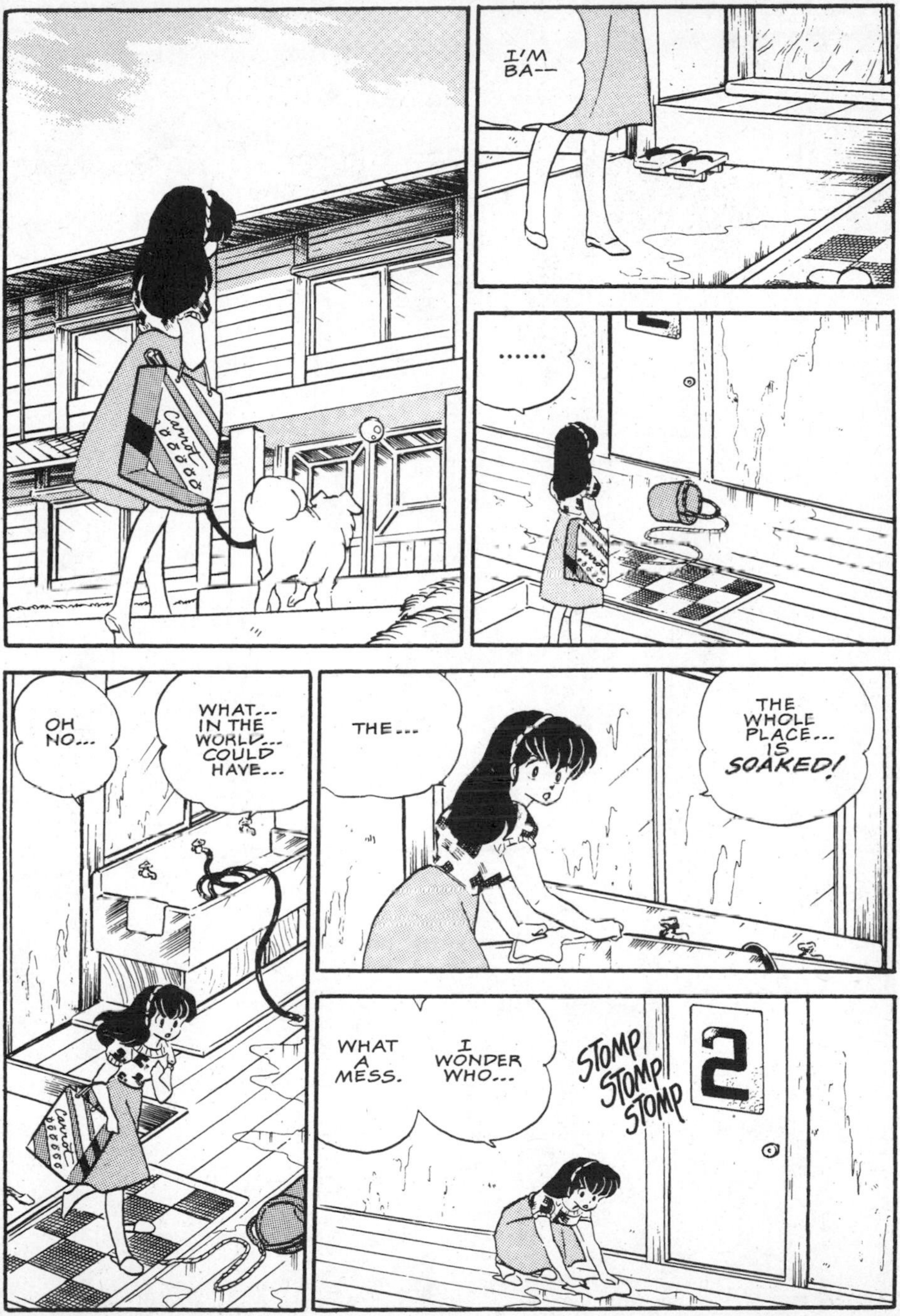
I'M BA--
......
OH NO...
WHAT... IN THE WORLD... COULD HAVE...
THE...
THE WHOLE PLACE... IS SOAKED!
WHAT A MESS.
I WONDER WHO...
STOMP STOMP STOMP
2

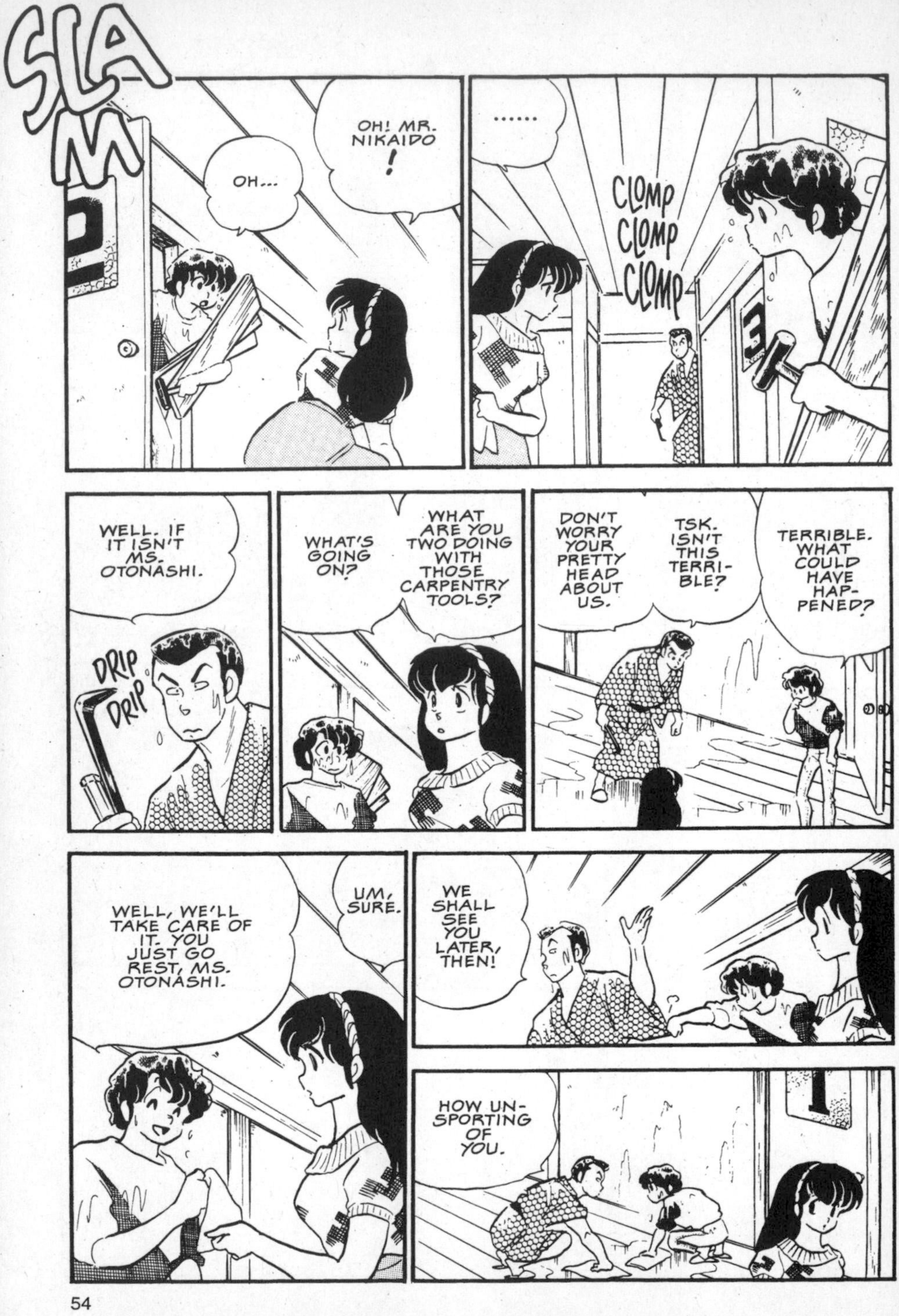
SLAM
OH...
OH! MR. NIKAIDO!
......
CLOMP CLOMP CLOMP
WELL. IF IT ISN'T MS. OTONASHI.
DRIP DRIP
WHAT'S GOING ON?
WHAT ARE YOU TWO DOING WITH THOSE CARPENTRY TOOLS?
DON'T WORRY YOUR PRETTY HEAD ABOUT US.
TSK. ISN'T THIS TERRI-BLE?
TERRIBLE. WHAT COULD HAVE HAP-PENED?
WELL, WE'LL TAKE CARE OF IT. YOU JUST GO REST, MS. OTONASHI.
UM, SURE.
WE SHALL SEE YOU LATER, THEN!
HOW UN-SPORTING OF YOU.

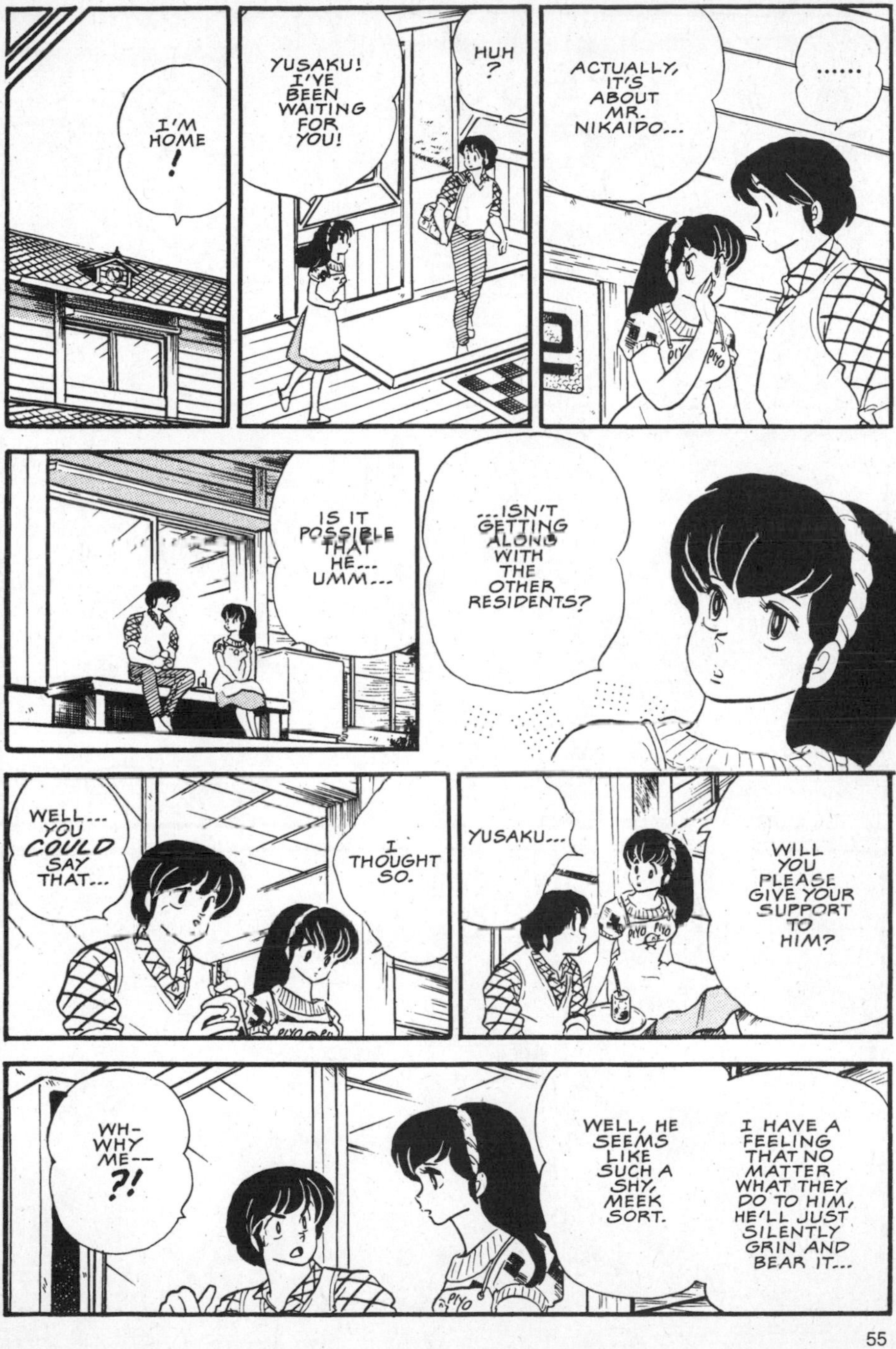
I'M HOME !
YUSAKU! I'VE BEEN WAITING FOR YOU!
HUH ?
ACTUALLY, IT'S ABOUT MR. NIKAIDO...
......
IS IT POSSIBLE THAT HE... UMM...
...ISN'T GETTING ALONG WITH THE OTHER RESIDENTS?
WELL... YOU COULD SAY THAT...
I THOUGHT SO.
YUSAKU...
WILL YOU PLEASE GIVE YOUR SUPPORT TO HIM?
WH-WHY ME-- ?!
WELL, HE SEEMS LIKE SUCH A SHY, MEEK SORT.
I HAVE A FEELING THAT NO MATTER WHAT THEY DO TO HIM, HE'LL JUST SILENTLY GRIN AND BEAR IT...

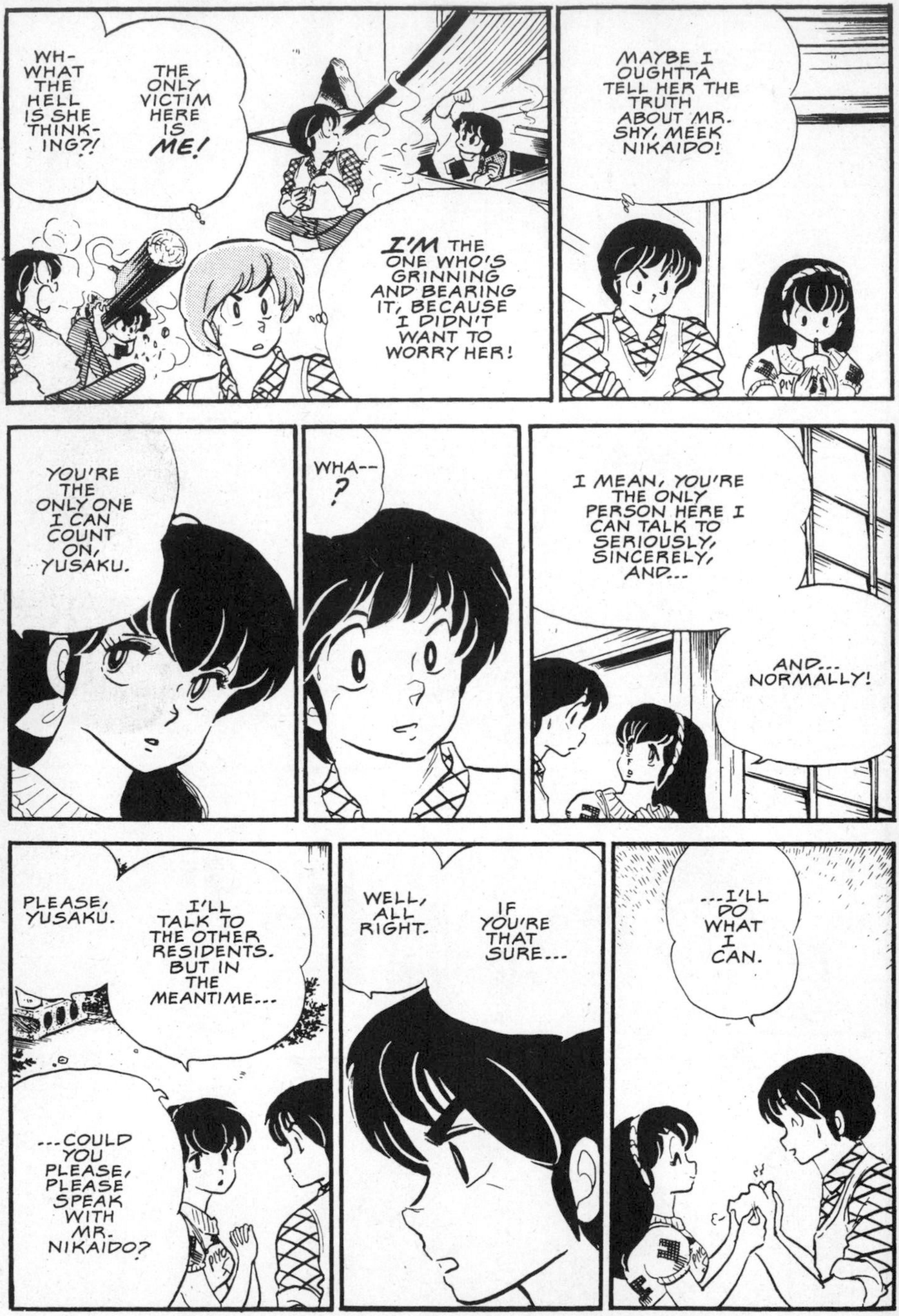
WH- WHAT THE HELL IS SHE THINKING?!
THE ONLY VICTIM HERE IS ME!
I'M THE ONE WHO'S GRINNING AND BEARING IT, BECAUSE I DIDN'T WANT TO WORRY HER!
MAYBE I OUGHTTA TELL HER THE TRUTH ABOUT MR. SHY, MEEK NIKAIDO!
YOU'RE THE ONLY ONE I CAN COUNT ON, YUSAKU.
WHA-- ?
I MEAN, YOU'RE THE ONLY PERSON HERE I CAN TALK TO SERIOUSLY, SINCERELY, AND...
AND... NORMALLY!
PLEASE, YUSAKU.
I'LL TALK TO THE OTHER RESIDENTS. BUT IN THE MEANTIME...
...COULD YOU PLEASE, PLEASE SPEAK WITH MR. NIKAIDO?
WELL, ALL RIGHT.
IF YOU'RE THAT SURE...
...I'LL DO WHAT I CAN.

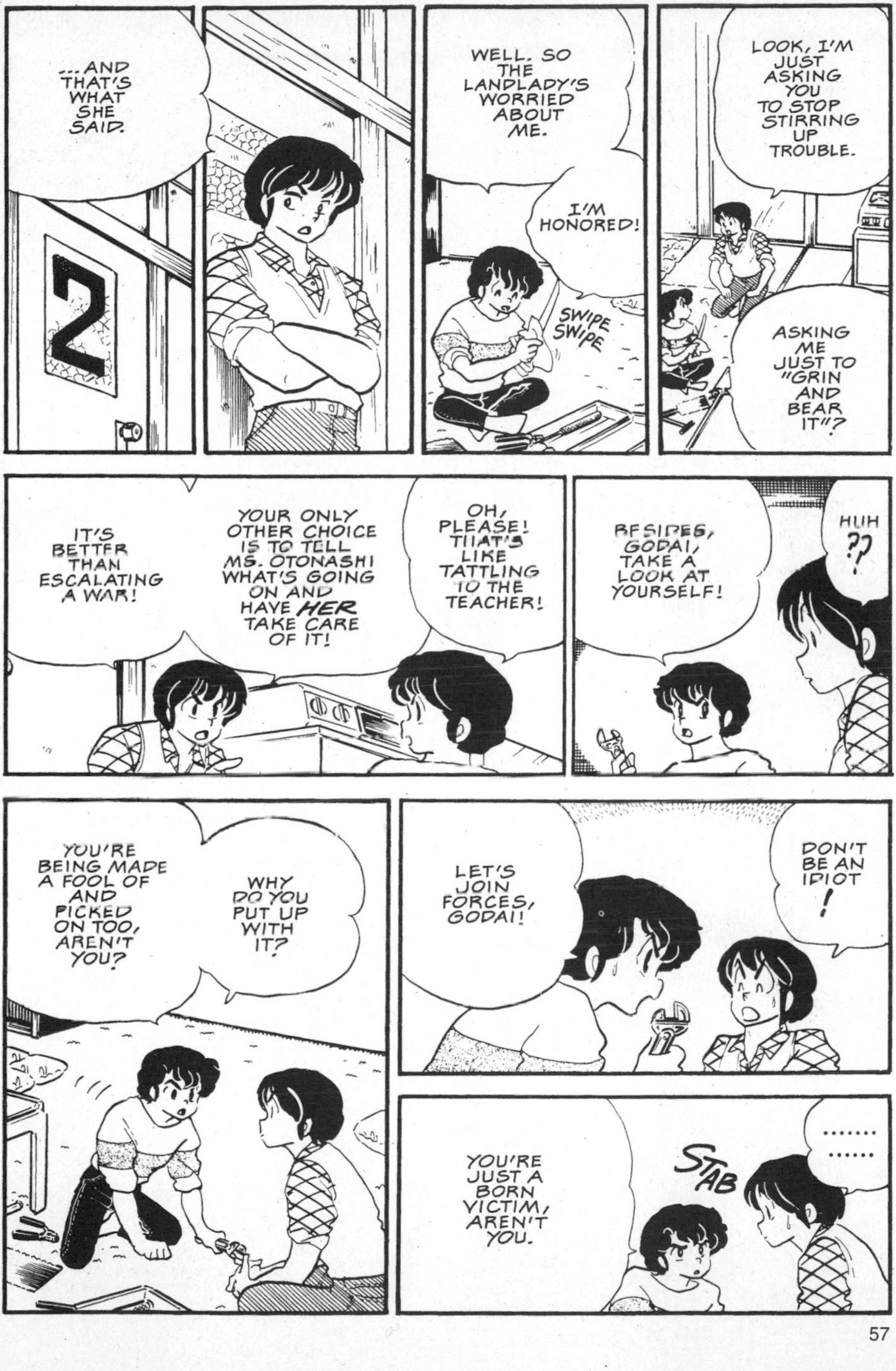
...AND THAT'S WHAT SHE SAID.
WELL. SO THE LANDLADY'S WORRIED ABOUT ME.
I'M HONORED!
SWIPE SWIPE
LOOK, I'M JUST ASKING YOU TO STOP STIRRING UP TROUBLE.
ASKING ME JUST TO "GRIN AND BEAR IT"?
IT'S BETTER THAN ESCALATING A WAR!
YOUR ONLY OTHER CHOICE IS TO TELL MS. OTONASHI WHAT'S GOING ON AND HAVE HER TAKE CARE OF IT!
OH, PLEASE! THAT'S LIKE TATTLING TO THE TEACHER!
BESIDES, GODAI, TAKE A LOOK AT YOURSELF!
HUH ??
YOU'RE BEING MADE A FOOL OF AND PICKED ON TOO, AREN'T YOU?
WHY DO YOU PUT UP WITH IT?
LET'S JOIN FORCES, GODAI!
DON'T BE AN IDIOT !
YOU'RE JUST A BORN VICTIM, AREN'T YOU.
STAB
....
....

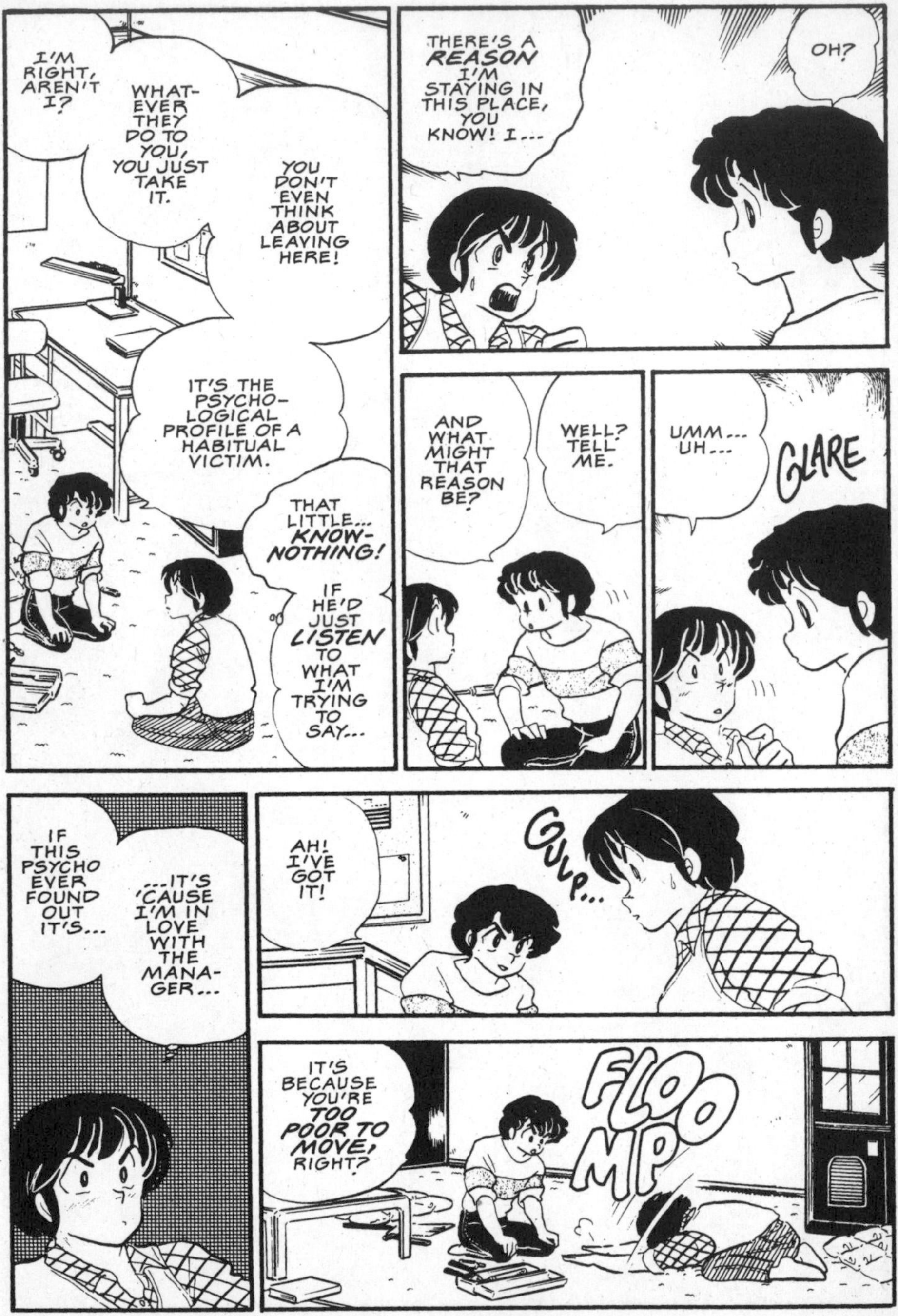
I'M RIGHT, AREN'T I?
WHAT-EVER THEY DO TO YOU, YOU JUST TAKE IT.
YOU DON'T EVEN THINK ABOUT LEAVING HERE!
IT'S THE PSYCHO-LOGICAL PROFILE OF A HABITUAL VICTIM.
THAT LITTLE... *KNOW-NOTHING!*
IF HE'D JUST *LISTEN* TO WHAT I'M TRYING TO SAY...
THERE'S A *REASON* I'M STAYING IN THIS PLACE, YOU KNOW! I...
OH?
AND WHAT MIGHT THAT REASON BE?
WELL? TELL ME.
UMM... UH...
GLARE
IF THIS PSYCHO EVER FOUND OUT IT'S...
...IT'S 'CAUSE I'M IN LOVE WITH THE MANA-GER...
AH! I'VE GOT IT!
GULP...
IT'S BECAUSE YOU'RE *TOO POOR TO MOVE,* RIGHT?
FLOOMP

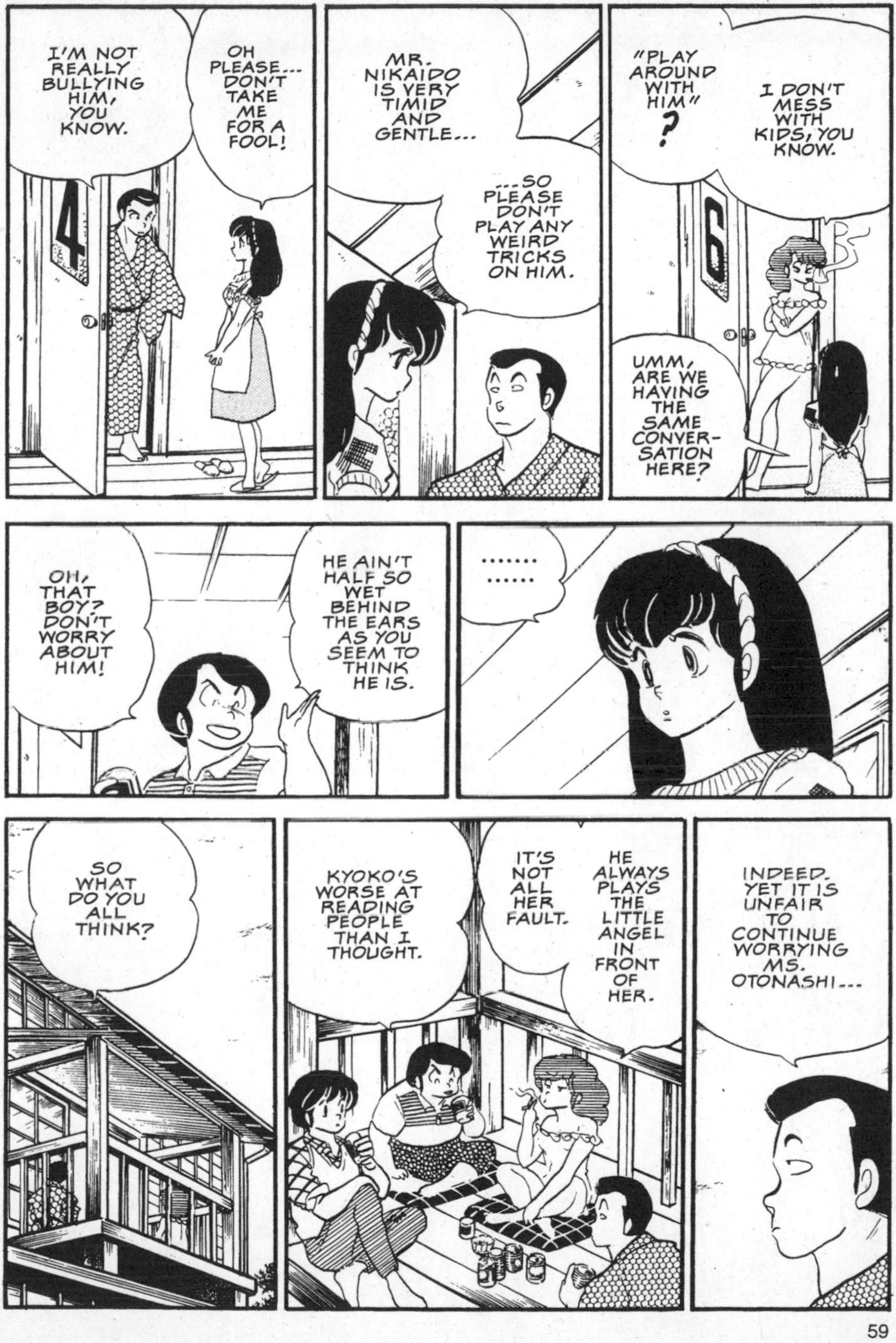
I'M NOT REALLY BULLYING HIM, YOU KNOW.
OH PLEASE... DON'T TAKE ME FOR A FOOL!
MR. NIKAIDO IS VERY TIMID AND GENTLE...
...SO PLEASE DON'T PLAY ANY WEIRD TRICKS ON HIM.
"PLAY AROUND WITH HIM"?
I DON'T MESS WITH KIDS, YOU KNOW.
UMM, ARE WE HAVING THE SAME CONVER-SATION HERE?
OH, THAT BOY? DON'T WORRY ABOUT HIM!
HE AIN'T HALF SO WET BEHIND THE EARS AS YOU SEEM TO THINK HE IS.
....
......
SO WHAT DO YOU ALL THINK?
KYOKO'S WORSE AT READING PEOPLE THAN I THOUGHT.
IT'S NOT ALL HER FAULT.
HE ALWAYS PLAYS THE LITTLE ANGEL IN FRONT OF HER.
INDEED. YET IT IS UNFAIR TO CONTINUE WORRYING MS. OTONASHI...

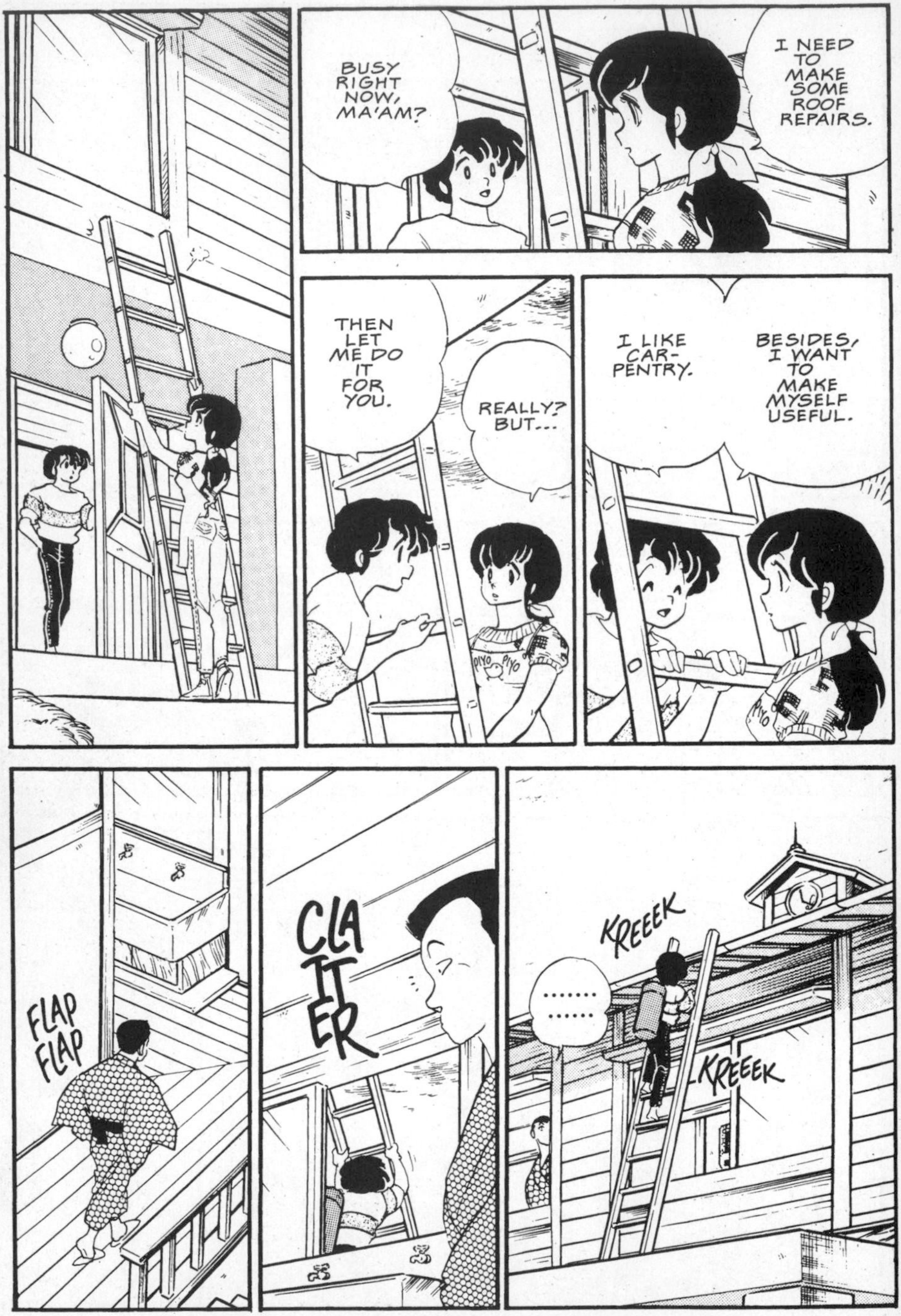
BUSY RIGHT NOW, MA'AM?
I NEED TO MAKE SOME ROOF REPAIRS.
THEN LET ME DO IT FOR YOU.
REALLY? BUT...
I LIKE CAR-PENTRY.
BESIDES, I WANT TO MAKE MYSELF USEFUL.
FLAP FLAP
CLATTER
KREEEK
....
....
KREEEK
PIYO PIYO

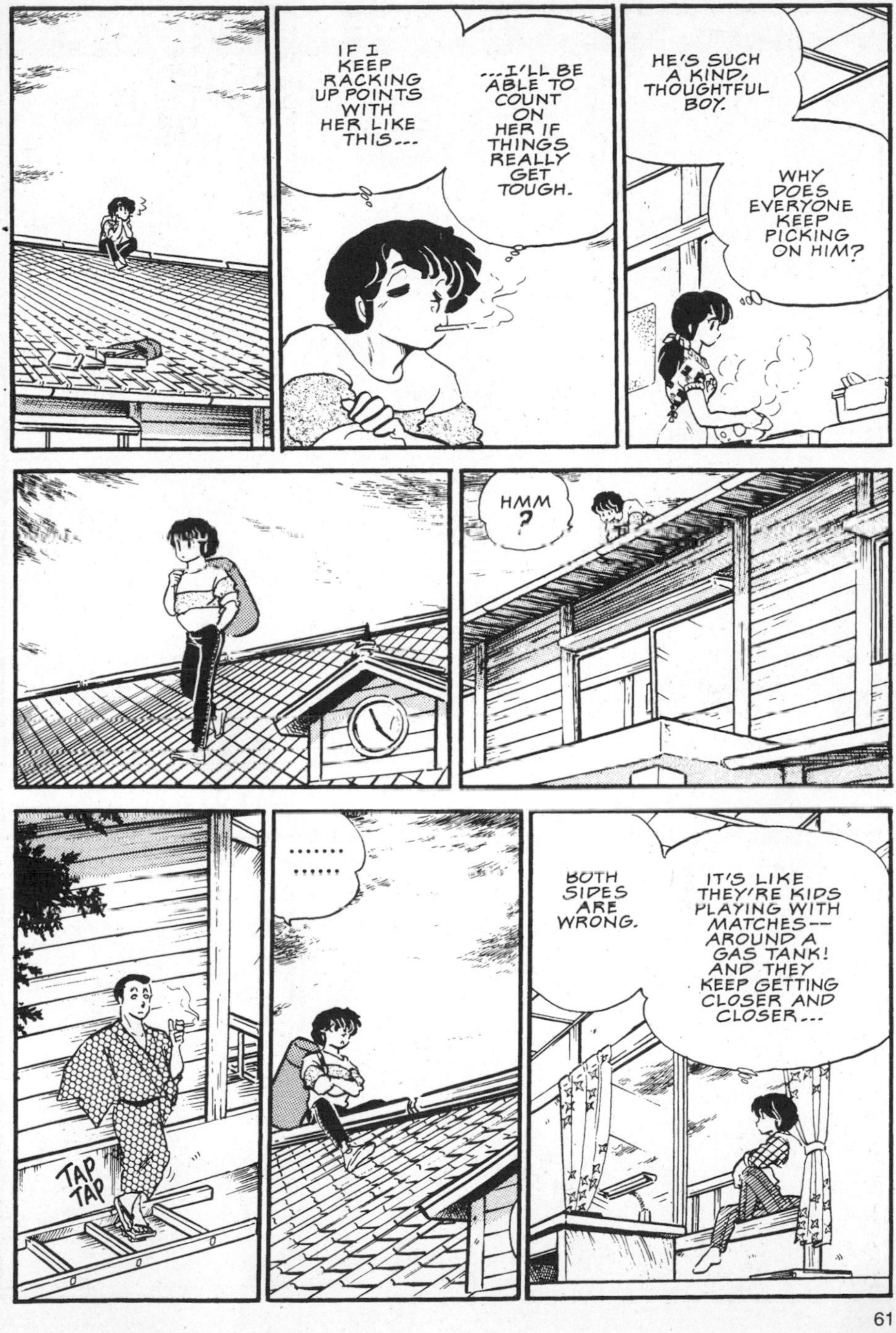
IF I KEEP RACKING UP POINTS WITH HER LIKE THIS...
...I'LL BE ABLE TO COUNT ON HER IF THINGS REALLY GET TOUGH.
HE'S SUCH A KIND, THOUGHTFUL BOY.
WHY DOES EVERYONE KEEP PICKING ON HIM?
HMM ?
TAP TAP
....
......
BOTH SIDES ARE WRONG.
IT'S LIKE THEY'RE KIDS PLAYING WITH MATCHES-- AROUND A GAS TANK! AND THEY KEEP GETTING CLOSER AND CLOSER...

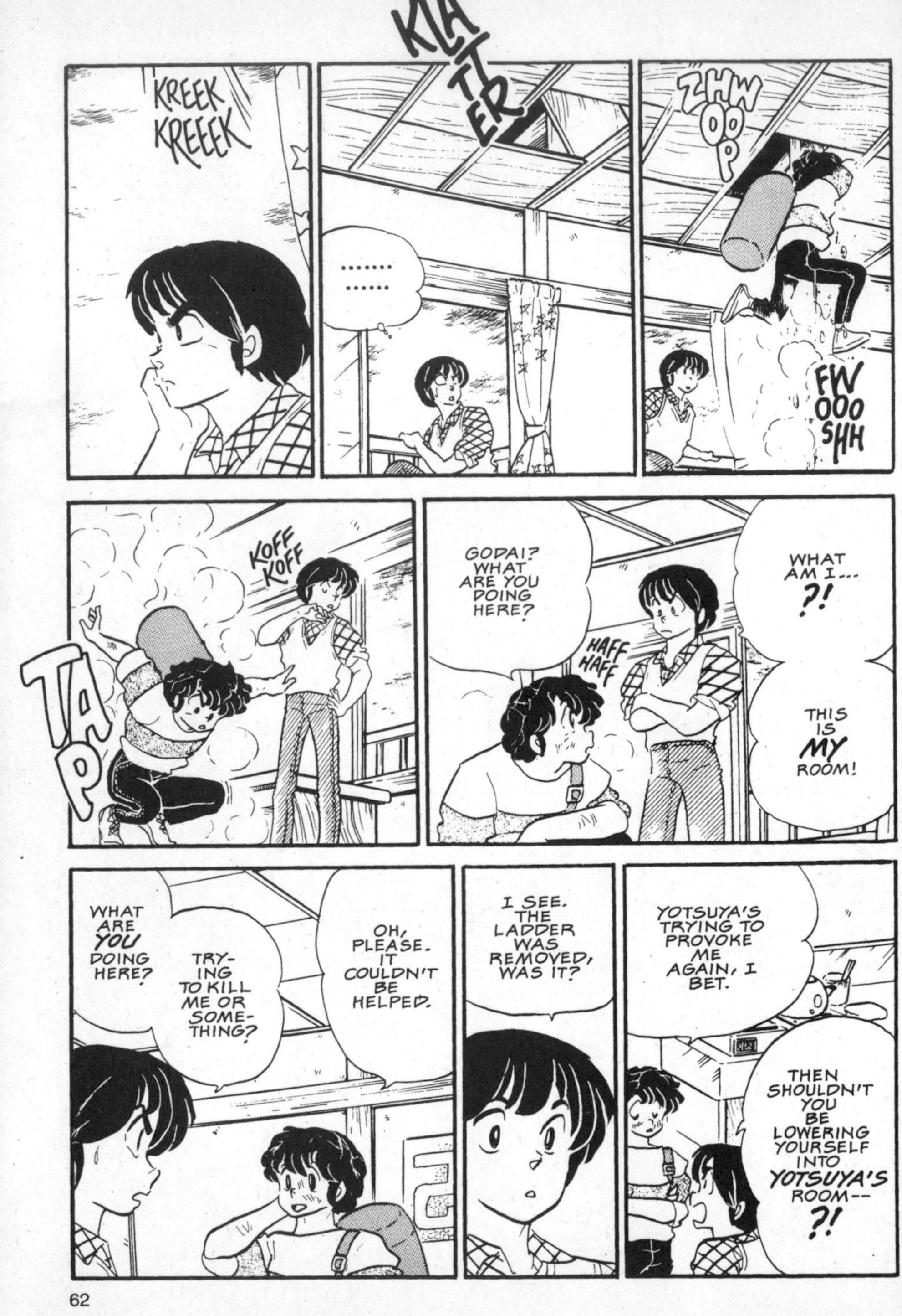

KLATTER
KREEK KREEEK
....
......
ZHWOOP
FWOOOSHH
TAP
KOFF KOFF
GODAI? WHAT ARE YOU DOING HERE?
HAFF HAFF
WHAT AM I... ?!
THIS IS MY ROOM!
WHAT ARE YOU DOING HERE?
TRYING TO KILL ME OR SOMETHING?
OH, PLEASE. IT COULDN'T BE HELPED.
I SEE. THE LADDER WAS REMOVED, WAS IT?
YOTSUYA'S TRYING TO PROVOKE ME AGAIN, I BET.
THEN SHOULDN'T YOU BE LOWERING YOURSELF INTO YOTSUYA'S ROOM-- ?!

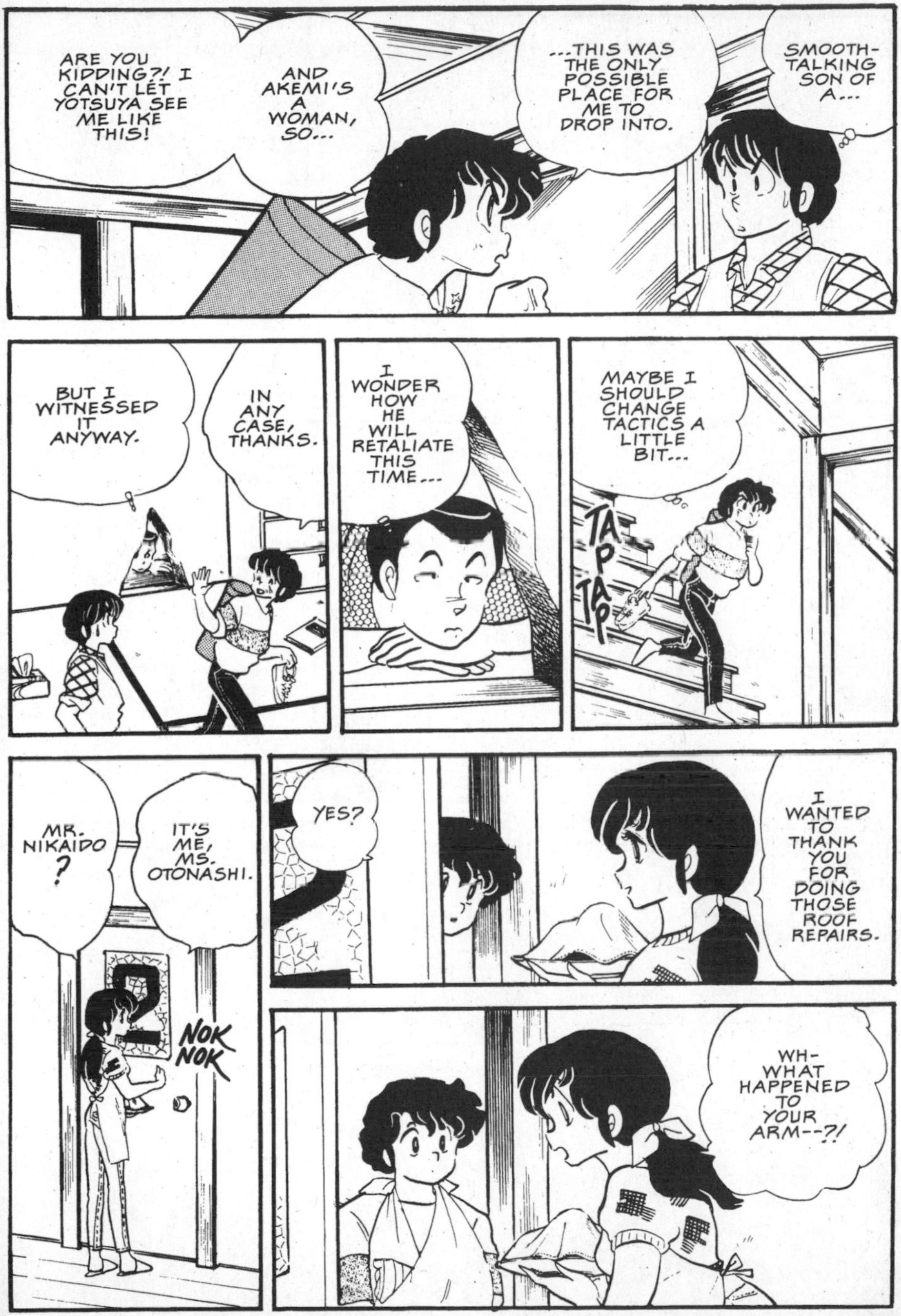
ARE YOU KIDDING?! I CAN'T LET YOTSUYA SEE ME LIKE THIS!
AND AKEMI'S A WOMAN, SO...
...THIS WAS THE ONLY POSSIBLE PLACE FOR ME TO DROP INTO.
SMOOTH-TALKING SON OF A...
BUT I WITNESSED IT ANYWAY.
IN ANY CASE, THANKS.
I WONDER HOW HE WILL RETALIATE THIS TIME...
MAYBE I SHOULD CHANGE TACTICS A LITTLE BIT...
TAP TAP TAP
MR. NIKAIDO?
IT'S ME, MS. OTONASHI.
NOK NOK
YES?
I WANTED TO THANK YOU FOR DOING THOSE ROOF REPAIRS.
WH-WHAT HAPPENED TO YOUR ARM--?!

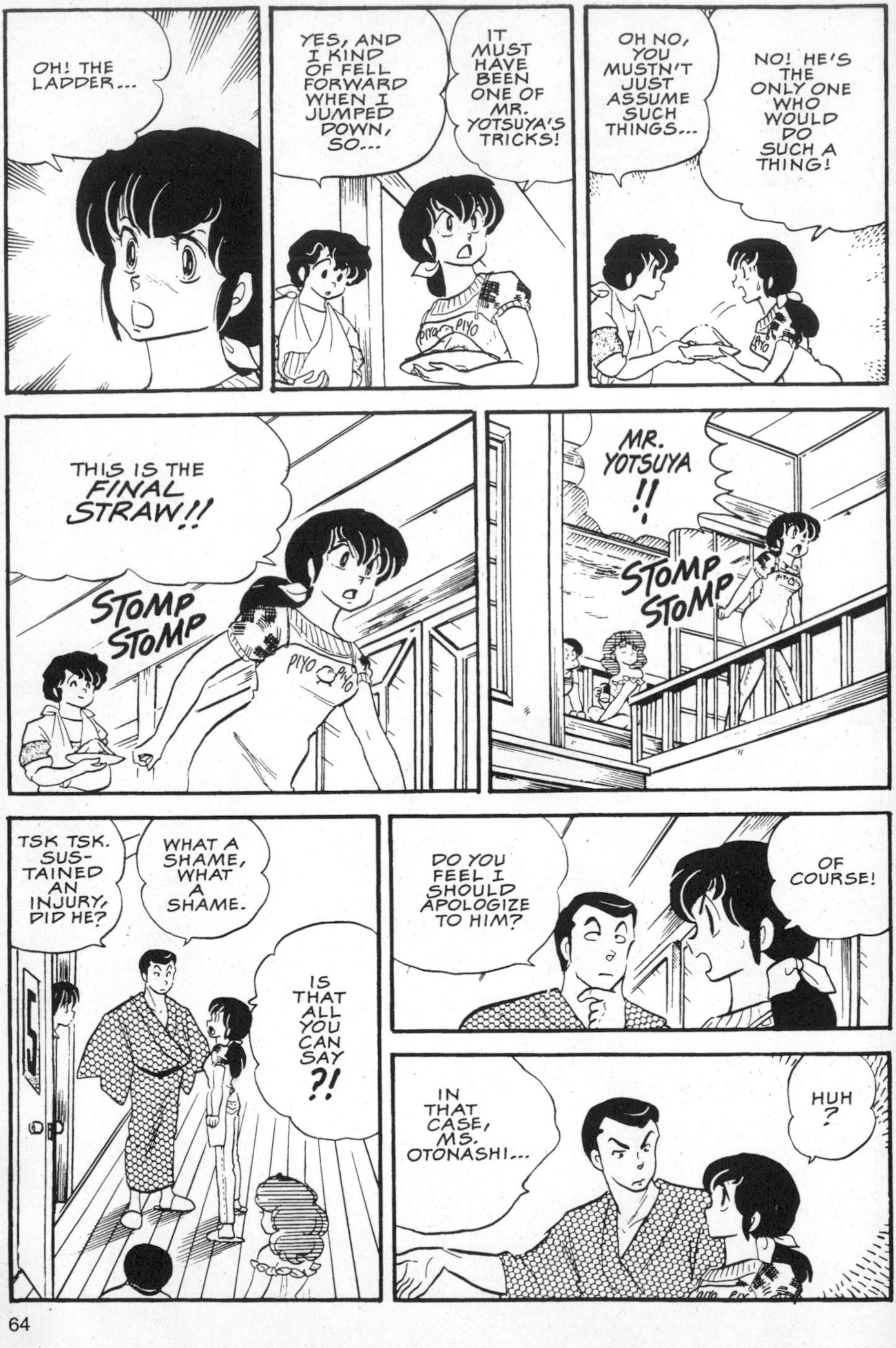
OH! THE LADDER...
YES, AND I KIND OF FELL FORWARD WHEN I JUMPED DOWN, SO...
IT MUST HAVE BEEN ONE OF MR. YOTSUYA'S TRICKS!
OH NO, YOU MUSTN'T JUST ASSUME SUCH THINGS...
NO! HE'S THE ONLY ONE WHO WOULD DO SUCH A THING!
THIS IS THE FINAL STRAW!!
STOMP STOMP
MR. YOTSUYA!!
STOMP STOMP
TSK TSK. SUS-TAINED AN INJURY, DID HE?
WHAT A SHAME, WHAT A SHAME.
IS THAT ALL YOU CAN SAY?!
DO YOU FEEL I SHOULD APOLOGIZE TO HIM?
OF COURSE!
IN THAT CASE, MS. OTONASHI...
HUH?

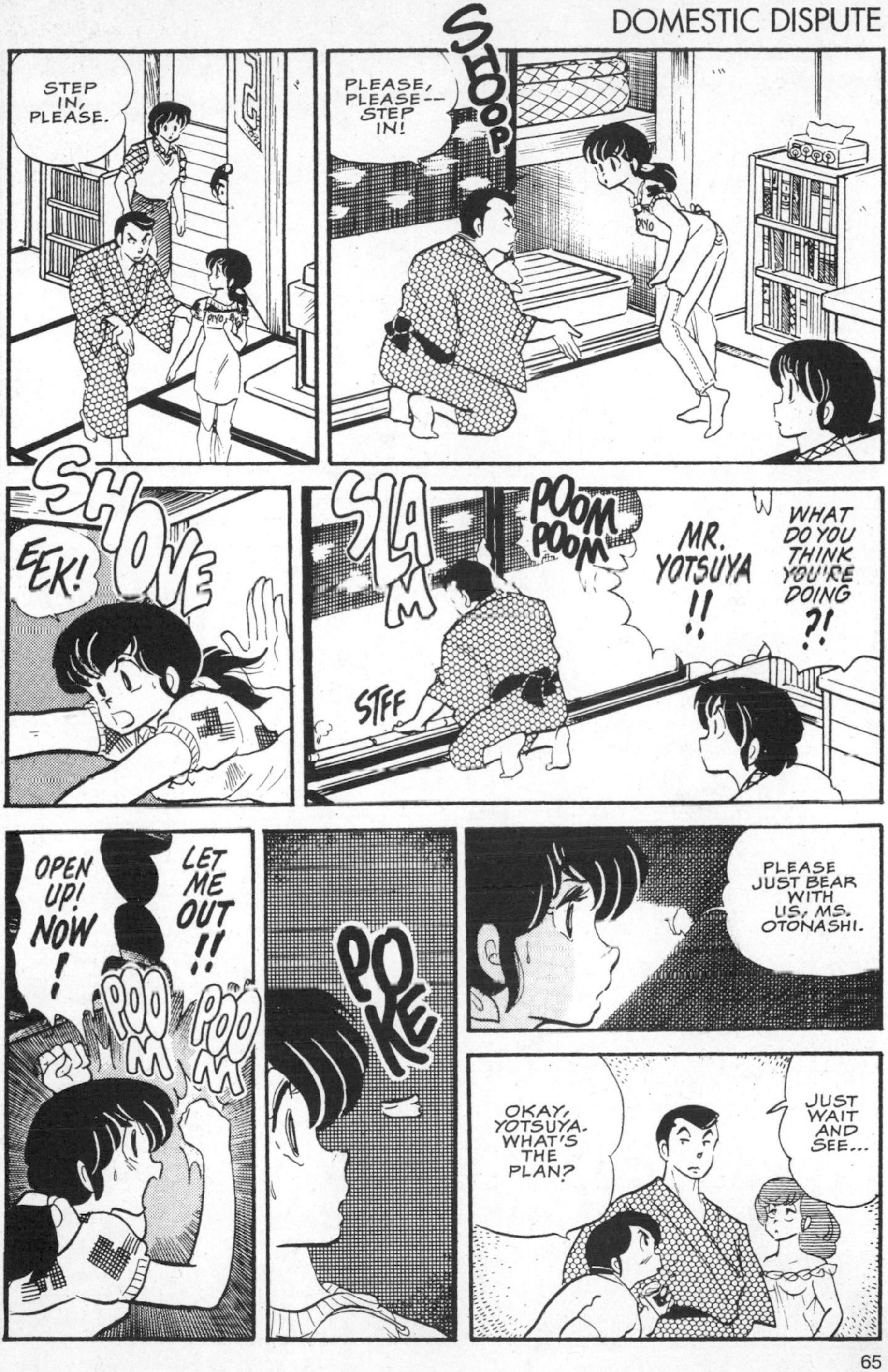
STEP IN, PLEASE.
PLEASE, PLEASE-- STEP IN!
SHOOP
SHOVE
EEK!
SLAM
POOM POOM
MR. YOTSUYA!!
WHAT DO YOU THINK YOU'RE DOING?!
STFF
OPEN UP! NOW!
LET ME OUT!!
POOM
POOM
POKE
PLEASE JUST BEAR WITH US, MS. OTONASHI.
OKAY, YOTSUYA. WHAT'S THE PLAN?
JUST WAIT AND SEE...

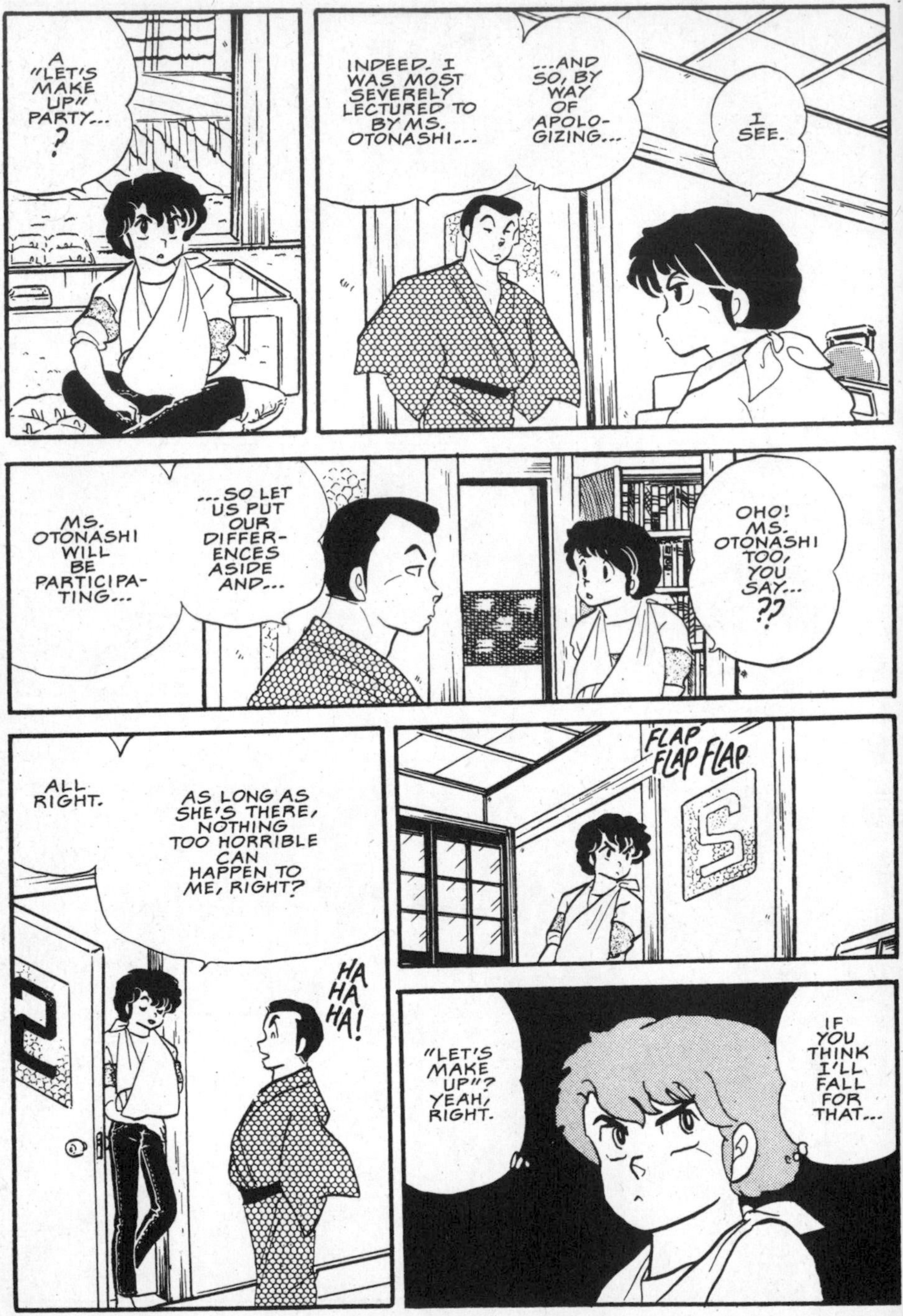
A "LET'S MAKE UP" PARTY...?
INDEED. I WAS MOST SEVERELY LECTURED TO BY MS. OTONASHI...
...AND SO, BY WAY OF APOLOGIZING...
I SEE.
MS. OTONASHI WILL BE PARTICIPATING...
...SO LET US PUT OUR DIFFERENCES ASIDE AND...
OHO! MS. OTONASHI TOO, YOU SAY...??
ALL RIGHT.
AS LONG AS SHE'S THERE, NOTHING TOO HORRIBLE CAN HAPPEN TO ME, RIGHT?
HA HA HA!
FLAP FLAP FLAP
"LET'S MAKE UP"? YEAH, RIGHT.
IF YOU THINK I'LL FALL FOR THAT...

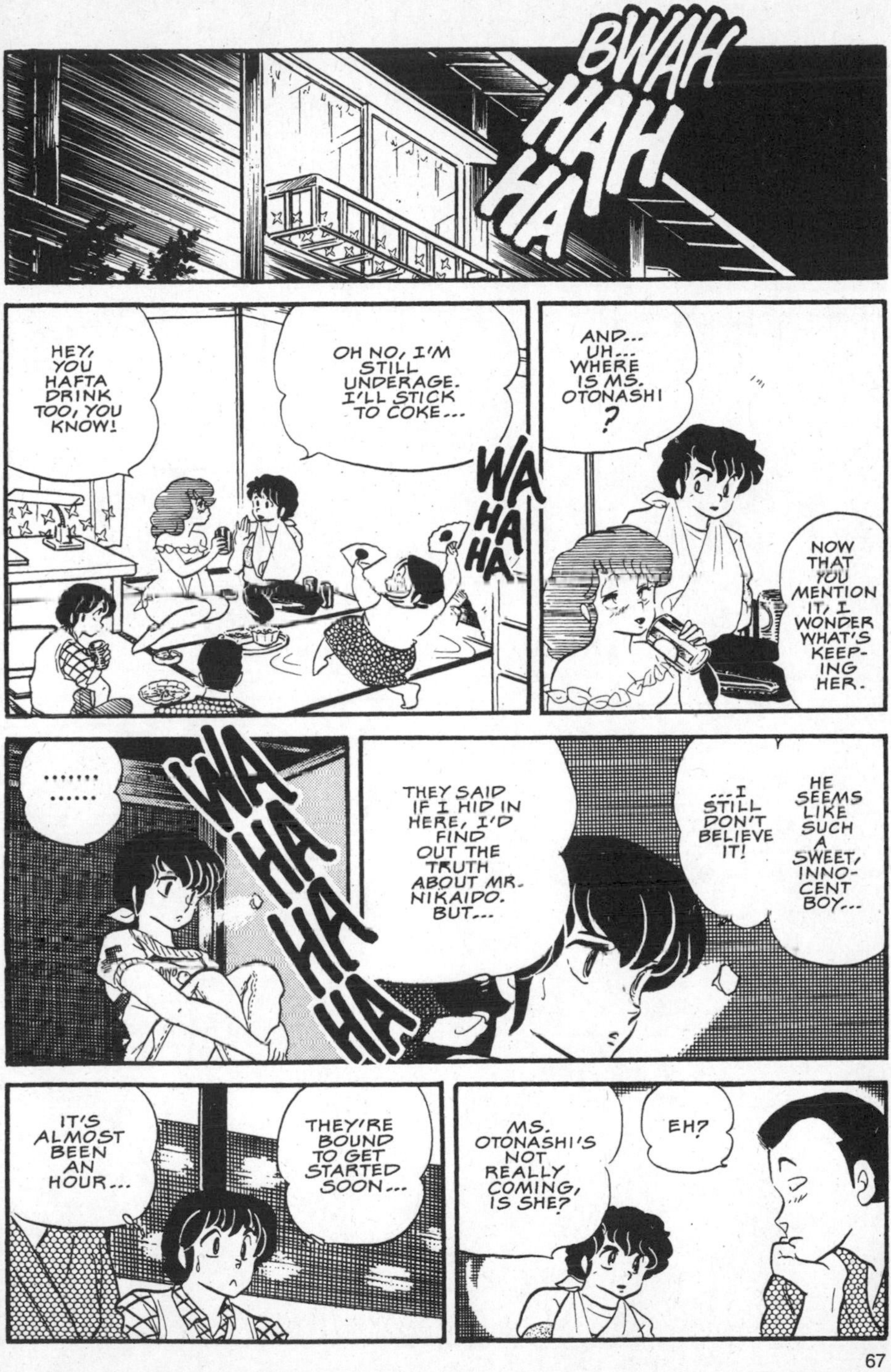
BWAH HAH HAH HA
HEY, YOU HAFTA DRINK TOO, YOU KNOW!
OH NO, I'M STILL UNDERAGE. I'LL STICK TO COKE...
WA HA HA HA
AND... UH... WHERE IS MS. OTONASHI ?
NOW THAT YOU MENTION IT, I WONDER WHAT'S KEEPING HER.
....
WA HA HA HA HA
THEY SAID IF I HID IN HERE, I'D FIND OUT THE TRUTH ABOUT MR. NIKAIDO. BUT...
...I STILL DON'T BELIEVE IT!
HE SEEMS LIKE SUCH A SWEET, INNOCENT BOY...
IT'S ALMOST BEEN AN HOUR...
THEY'RE BOUND TO GET STARTED SOON...
MS. OTONASHI'S NOT REALLY COMING, IS SHE?
EH?

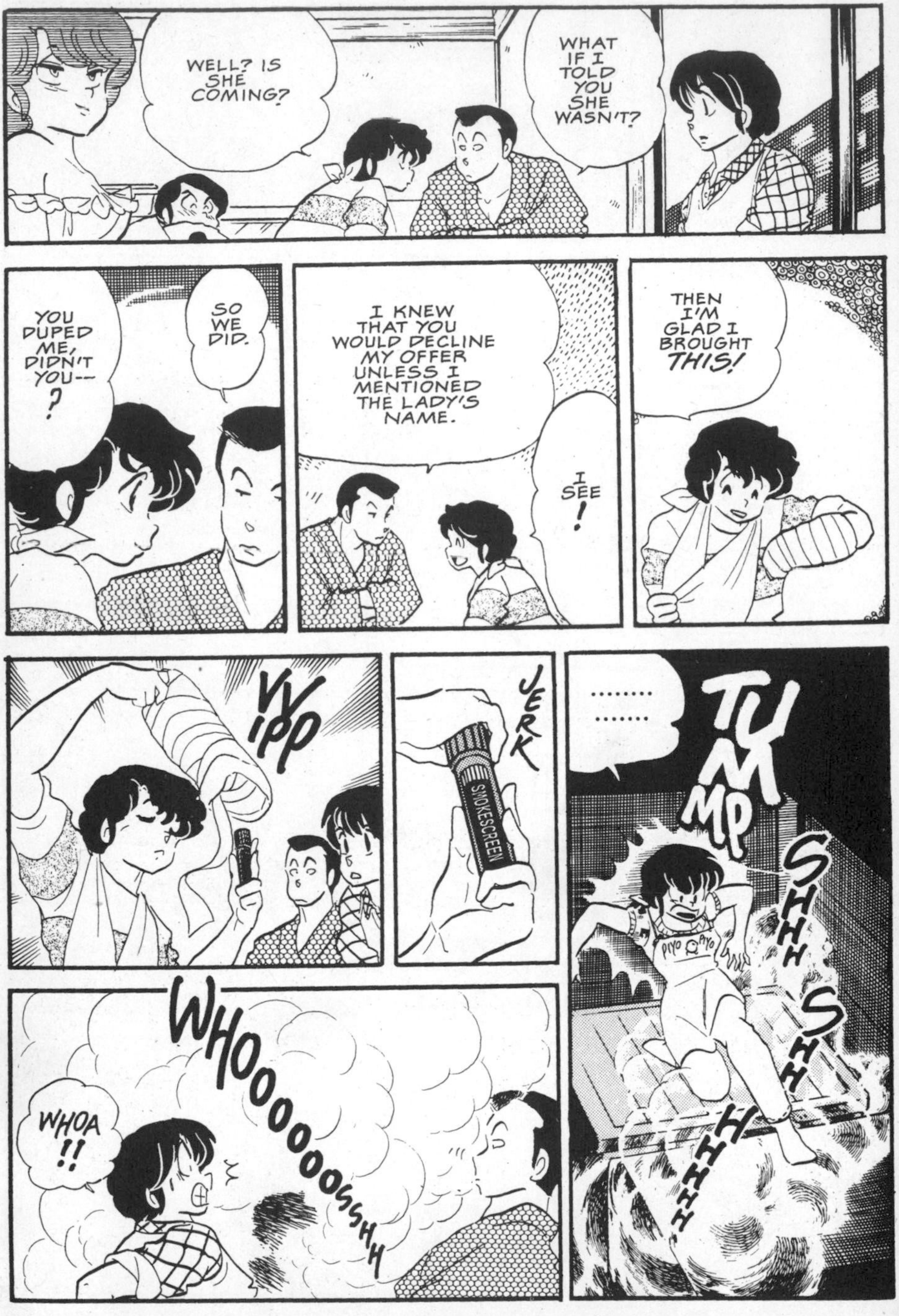

WELL? IS SHE COMING?
WHAT IF I TOLD YOU SHE WASN'T?
YOU DUPED ME, DIDN'T YOU--?
SO WE DID.
I KNEW THAT YOU WOULD DECLINE MY OFFER UNLESS I MENTIONED THE LADY'S NAME.
I SEE!
THEN I'M GLAD I BROUGHT THIS!
VVIPP
JERK
SMOKESCREEN
....
....
TUMMP
PIYO PIYO
SHHHSSHHHHHHHH
WHOOOOOOOSSHHH
WHOA!!

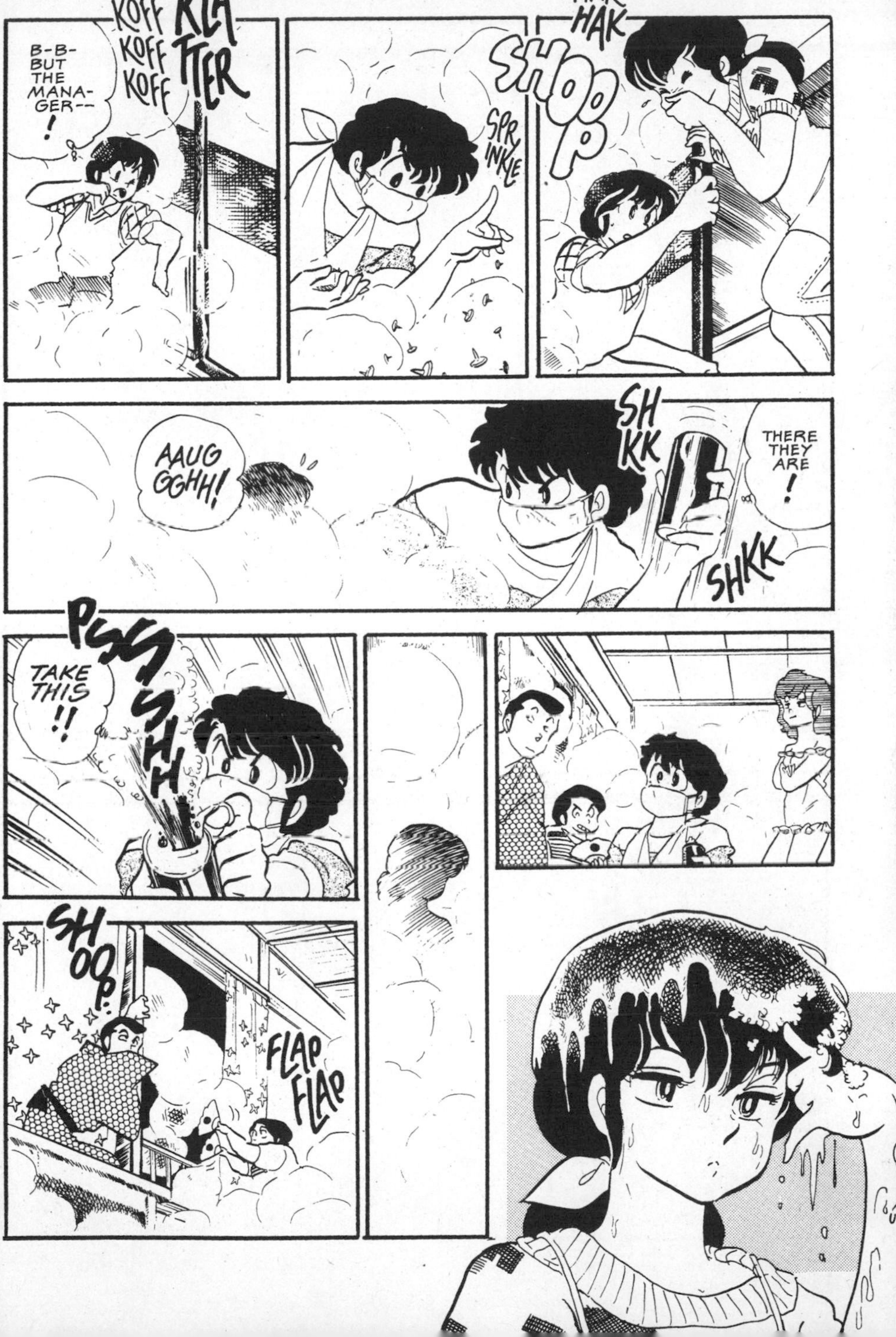
B-B-BUT THE MANAGER--!
KOFF KOFF KOFF
KLATTER
SPRINKLE
HAK HAK
SHOOOP
AAUGGHH!
SHKK
THERE THEY ARE!
SHKK
PUSSHHH
TAKE THIS!!
SHOOP...
FLAP FLAP

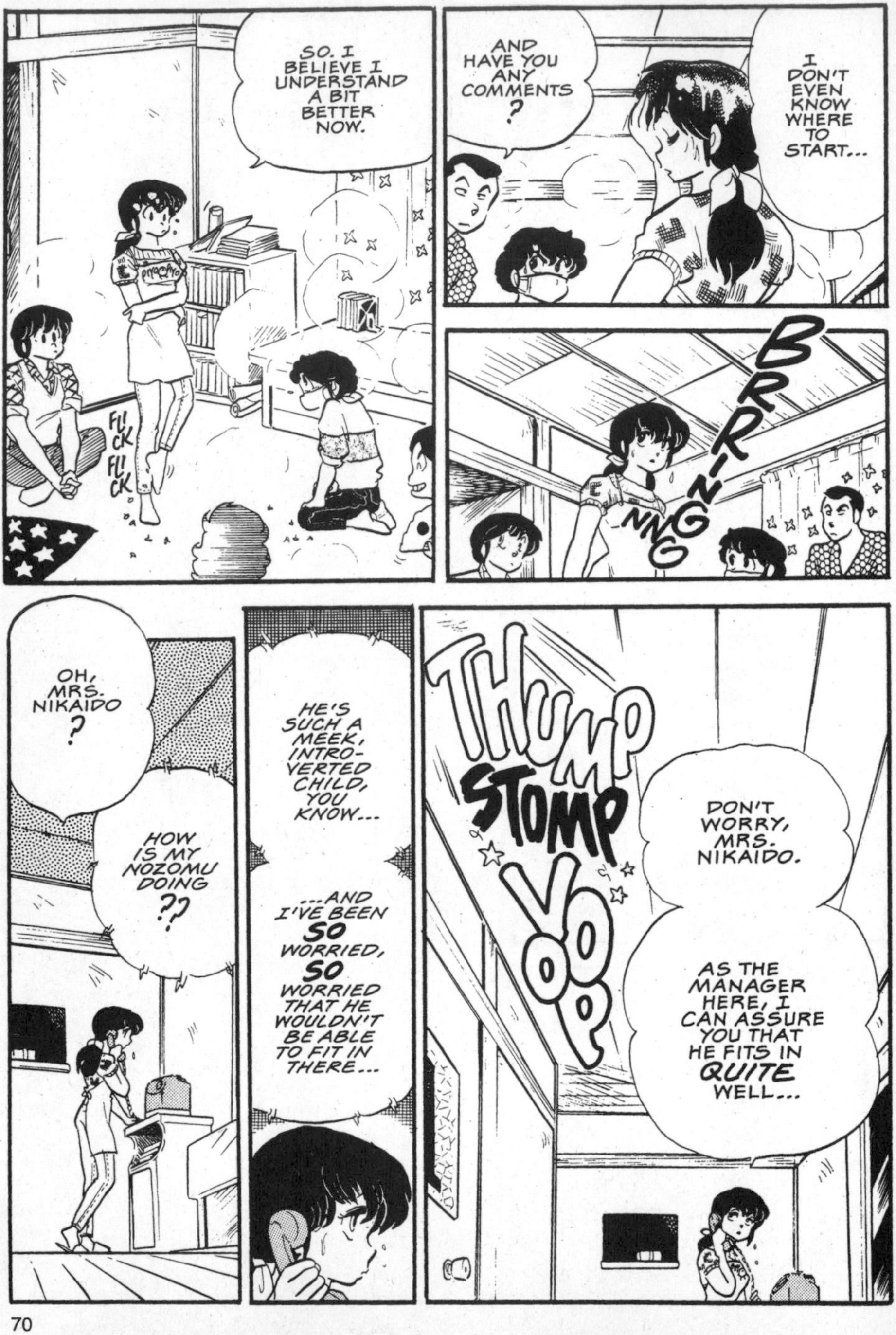
SO. I BELIEVE I UNDERSTAND A BIT BETTER NOW.
FLICK FLICK
AND HAVE YOU ANY COMMENTS?
I DON'T EVEN KNOW WHERE TO START...
BRRRINNNG
OH, MRS. NIKAIDO?
HOW IS MY NOZOMU DOING??
HE'S SUCH A MEEK, INTRO-VERTED CHILD, YOU KNOW...
...AND I'VE BEEN SO WORRIED, SO WORRIED THAT HE WOULDN'T BE ABLE TO FIT IN THERE...
THUMP STOMP VOOOP
DON'T WORRY, MRS. NIKAIDO.
AS THE MANAGER HERE, I CAN ASSURE YOU THAT HE FITS IN QUITE WELL...

PART 4
EVEN IF WE'RE CAUGHT IN THE RAIN...

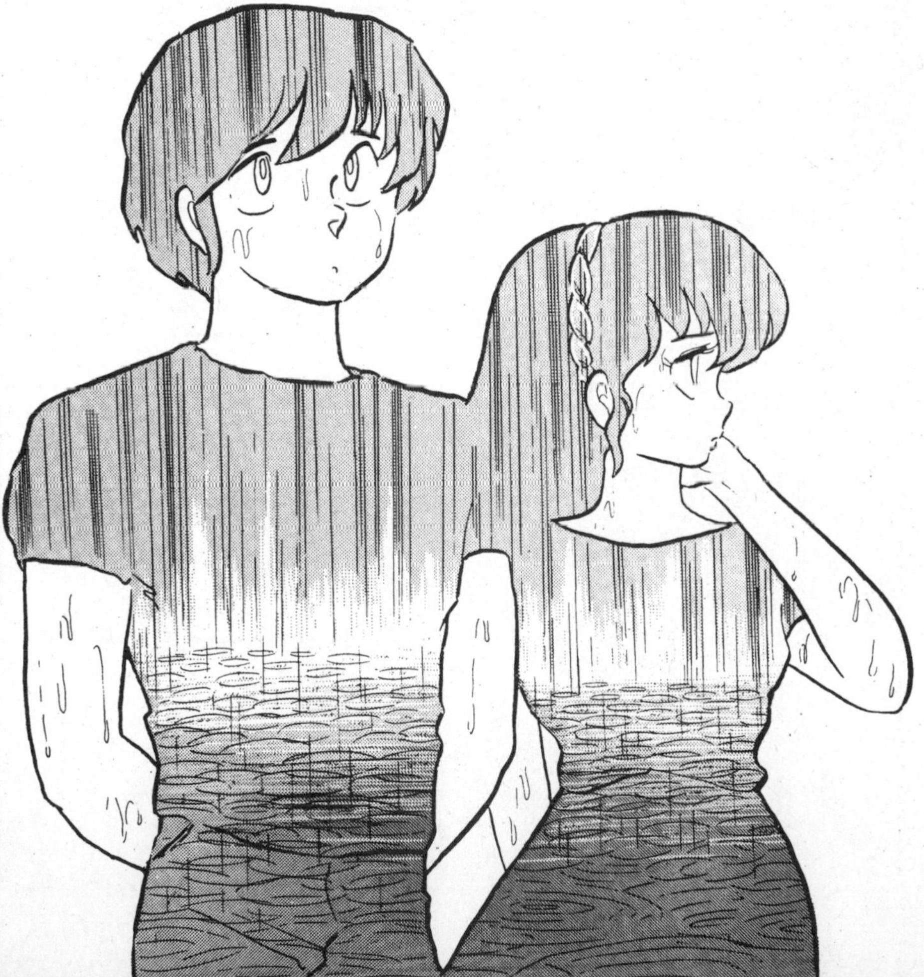

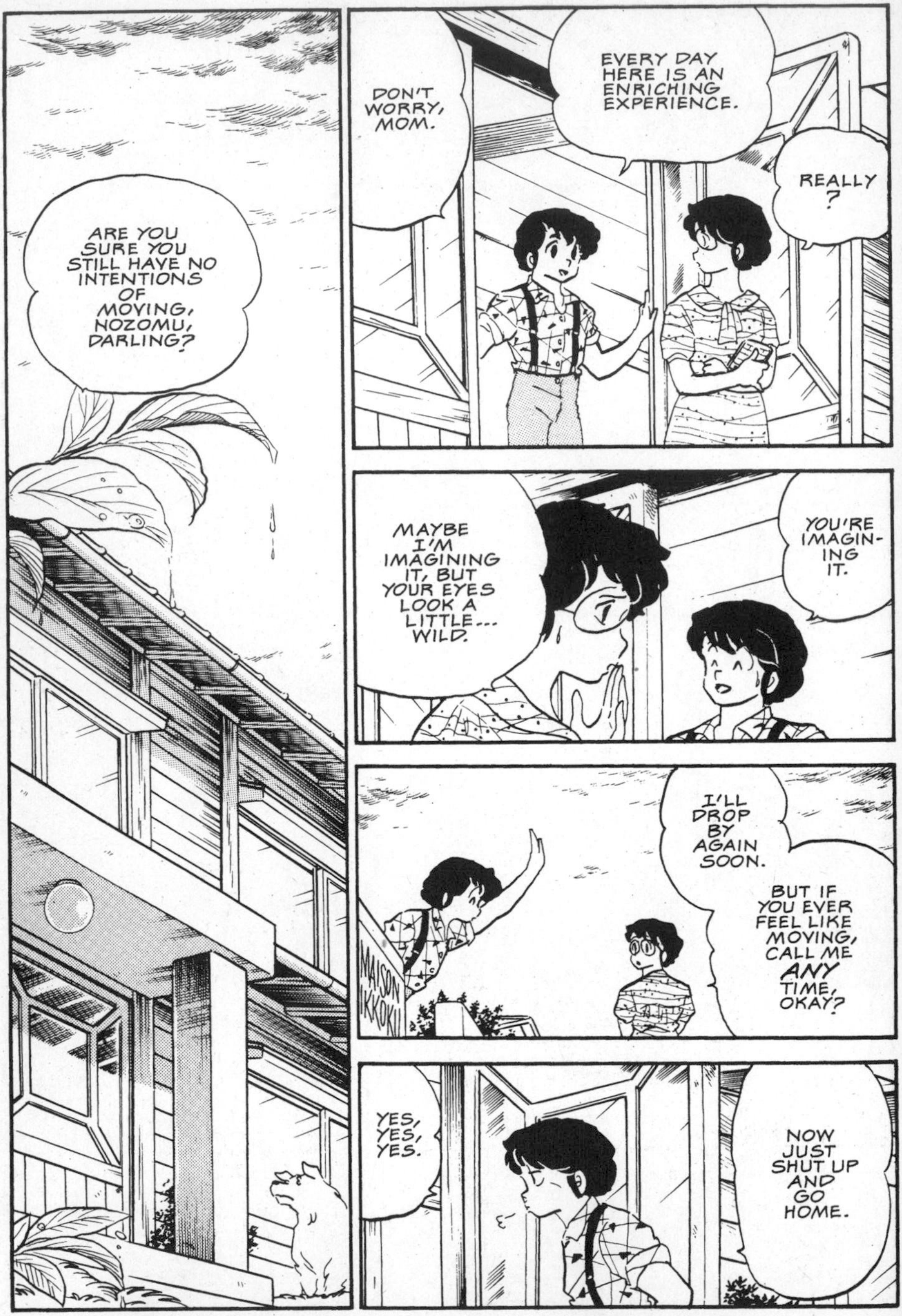
ARE YOU SURE YOU STILL HAVE NO INTENTIONS OF MOVING, NOZOMU, DARLING?
DON'T WORRY, MOM.
EVERY DAY HERE IS AN ENRICHING EXPERIENCE.
REALLY?
MAYBE I'M IMAGINING IT, BUT YOUR EYES LOOK A LITTLE... WILD.
YOU'RE IMAGINING IT.
MAISON IKKOKU
I'LL DROP BY AGAIN SOON.
BUT IF YOU EVER FEEL LIKE MOVING, CALL ME ANY TIME, OKAY?
YES, YES, YES.
NOW JUST SHUT UP AND GO HOME.

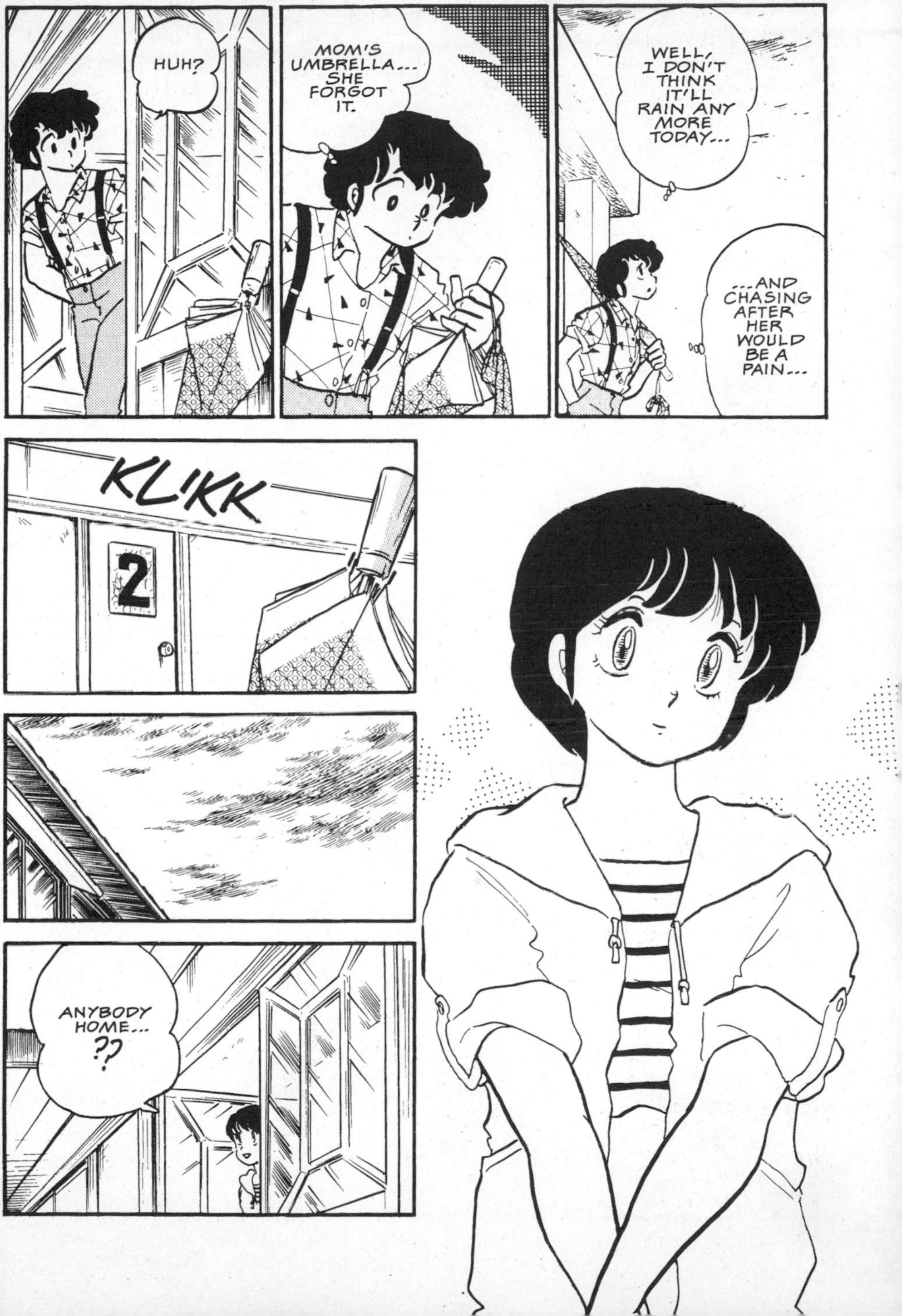
HUH?
MOM'S UMBRELLA... SHE FORGOT IT.
WELL, I DON'T THINK IT'LL RAIN ANY MORE TODAY...
...AND CHASING AFTER HER WOULD BE A PAIN...
KLIKK
2
ANYBODY HOME... ??

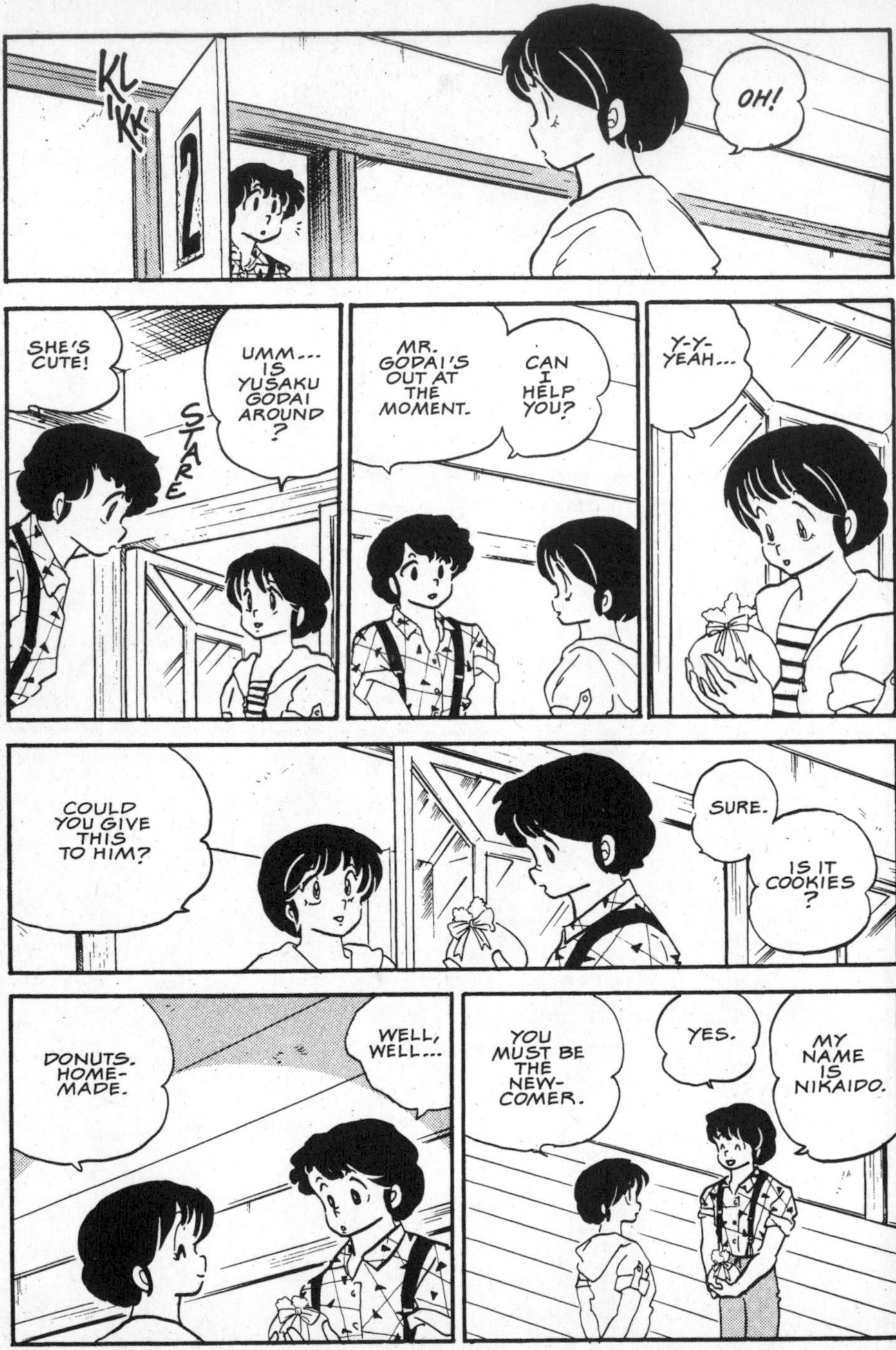

KLIKK
OH!
SHE'S CUTE!
UMM... IS YUSAKU GODAI AROUND?
STARE
MR. GODAI'S OUT AT THE MOMENT.
CAN I HELP YOU?
Y-Y-YEAH...
COULD YOU GIVE THIS TO HIM?
SURE.
IS IT COOKIES?
DONUTS. HOME-MADE.
WELL, WELL...
YOU MUST BE THE NEW-COMER.
YES.
MY NAME IS NIKAIDO.

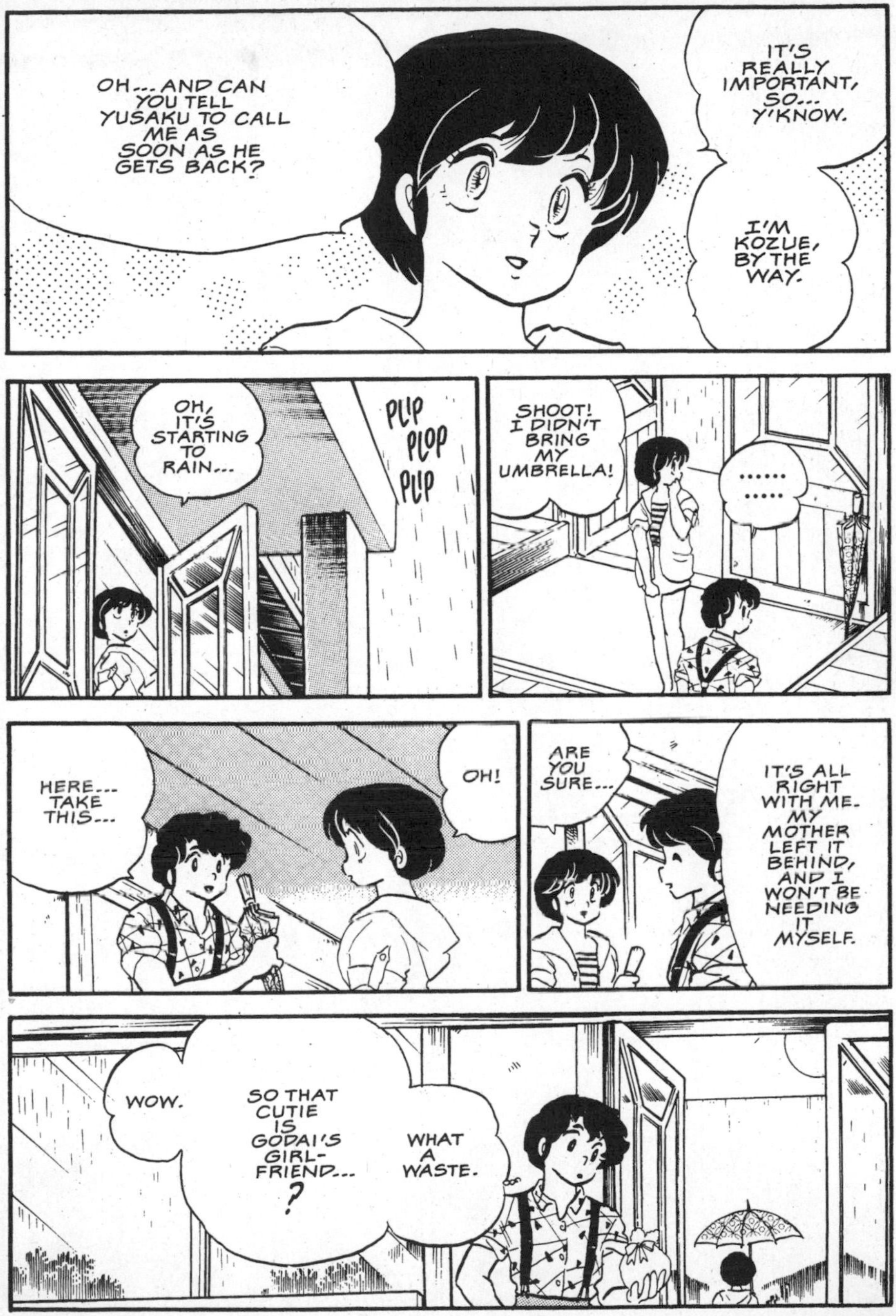
OH... AND CAN YOU TELL YUSAKU TO CALL ME AS SOON AS HE GETS BACK?
IT'S REALLY IMPORTANT, SO... Y'KNOW.
I'M KOZUE, BY THE WAY.
OH, IT'S STARTING TO RAIN...
PLIP PLOP PLIP
SHOOT! I DIDN'T BRING MY UMBRELLA!
......
......
HERE... TAKE THIS...
OH!
ARE YOU SURE...
IT'S ALL RIGHT WITH ME. MY MOTHER LEFT IT BEHIND, AND I WON'T BE NEEDING IT MYSELF.
WOW.
SO THAT CUTIE IS GODAI'S GIRL-FRIEND...?
WHAT A WASTE.

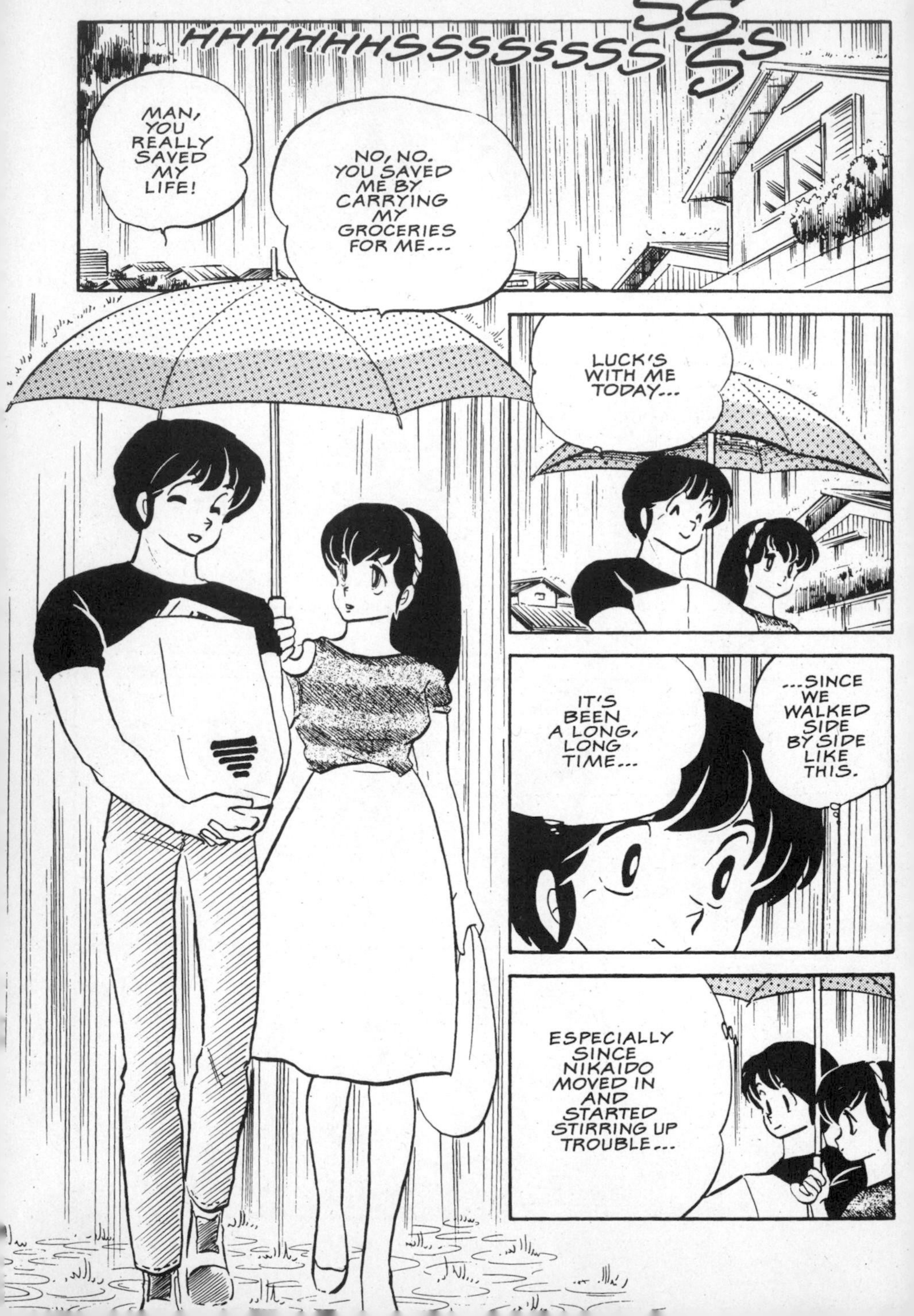
HHHHHHSSSSSSSSSSSS
MAN, YOU REALLY SAVED MY LIFE!
NO, NO. YOU SAVED ME BY CARRYING MY GROCERIES FOR ME...
LUCK'S WITH ME TODAY...
IT'S BEEN A LONG, LONG TIME...
...SINCE WE WALKED SIDE BY SIDE LIKE THIS.
ESPECIALLY SINCE NIKAIDO MOVED IN AND STARTED STIRRING UP TROUBLE...

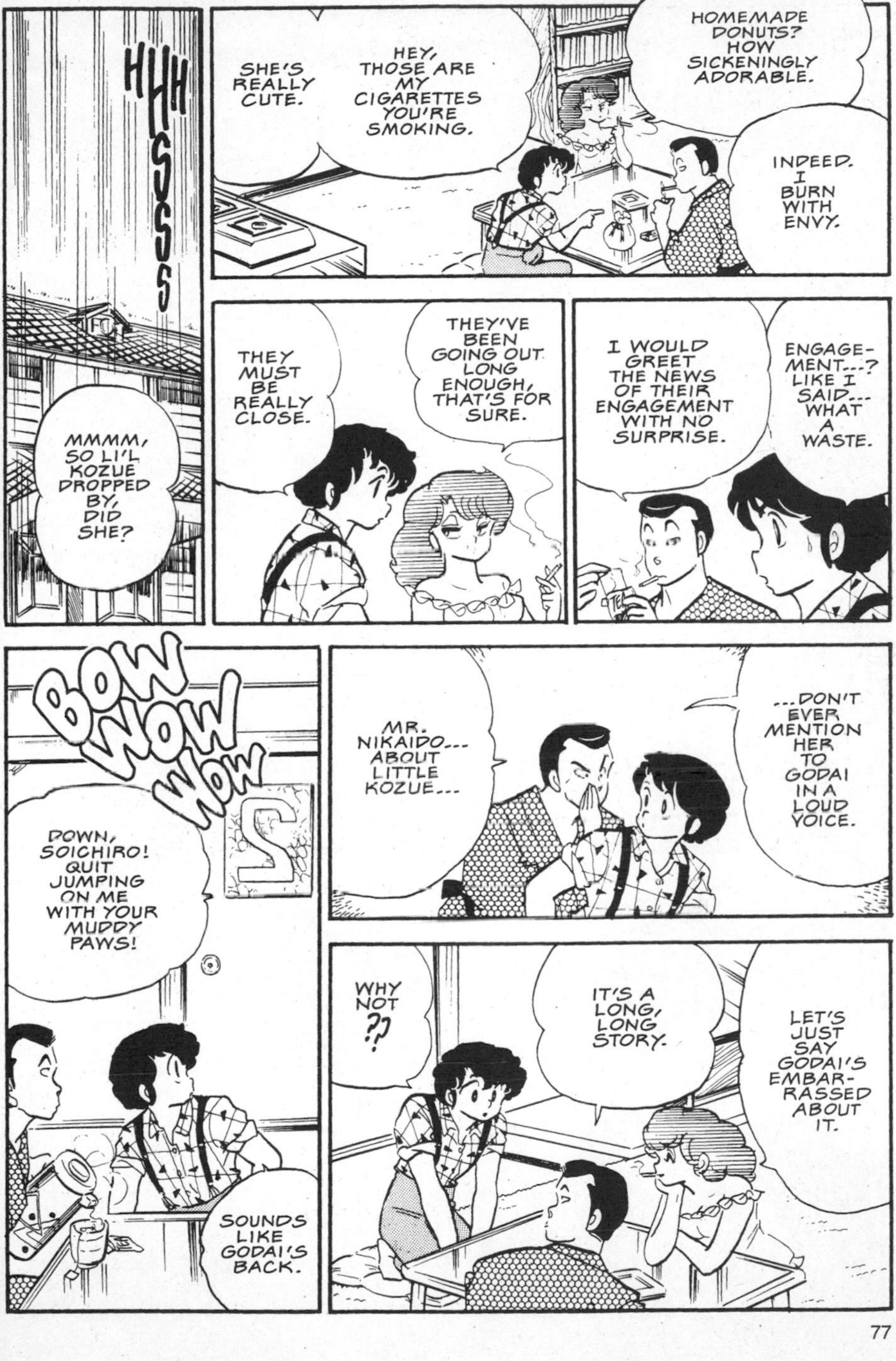
HHHISSSS
MMMM, SO LI'L KOZUE DROPPED BY, DID SHE?
SHE'S REALLY CUTE.
HEY, THOSE ARE MY CIGARETTES YOU'RE SMOKING.
HOMEMADE DONUTS? HOW SICKENINGLY ADORABLE.
INDEED. I BURN WITH ENVY.
THEY MUST BE REALLY CLOSE.
THEY'VE BEEN GOING OUT LONG ENOUGH, THAT'S FOR SURE.
I WOULD GREET THE NEWS OF THEIR ENGAGEMENT WITH NO SURPRISE.
ENGAGE-MENT...? LIKE I SAID... WHAT A WASTE.
BOW WOW WOW
DOWN, SOICHIRO! QUIT JUMPING ON ME WITH YOUR MUDDY PAWS!
SOUNDS LIKE GODAI'S BACK.
MR. NIKAIDO... ABOUT LITTLE KOZUE...
...DON'T EVER MENTION HER TO GODAI IN A LOUD VOICE.
WHY NOT ??
IT'S A LONG, LONG STORY.
LET'S JUST SAY GODAI'S EMBAR-RASSED ABOUT IT.

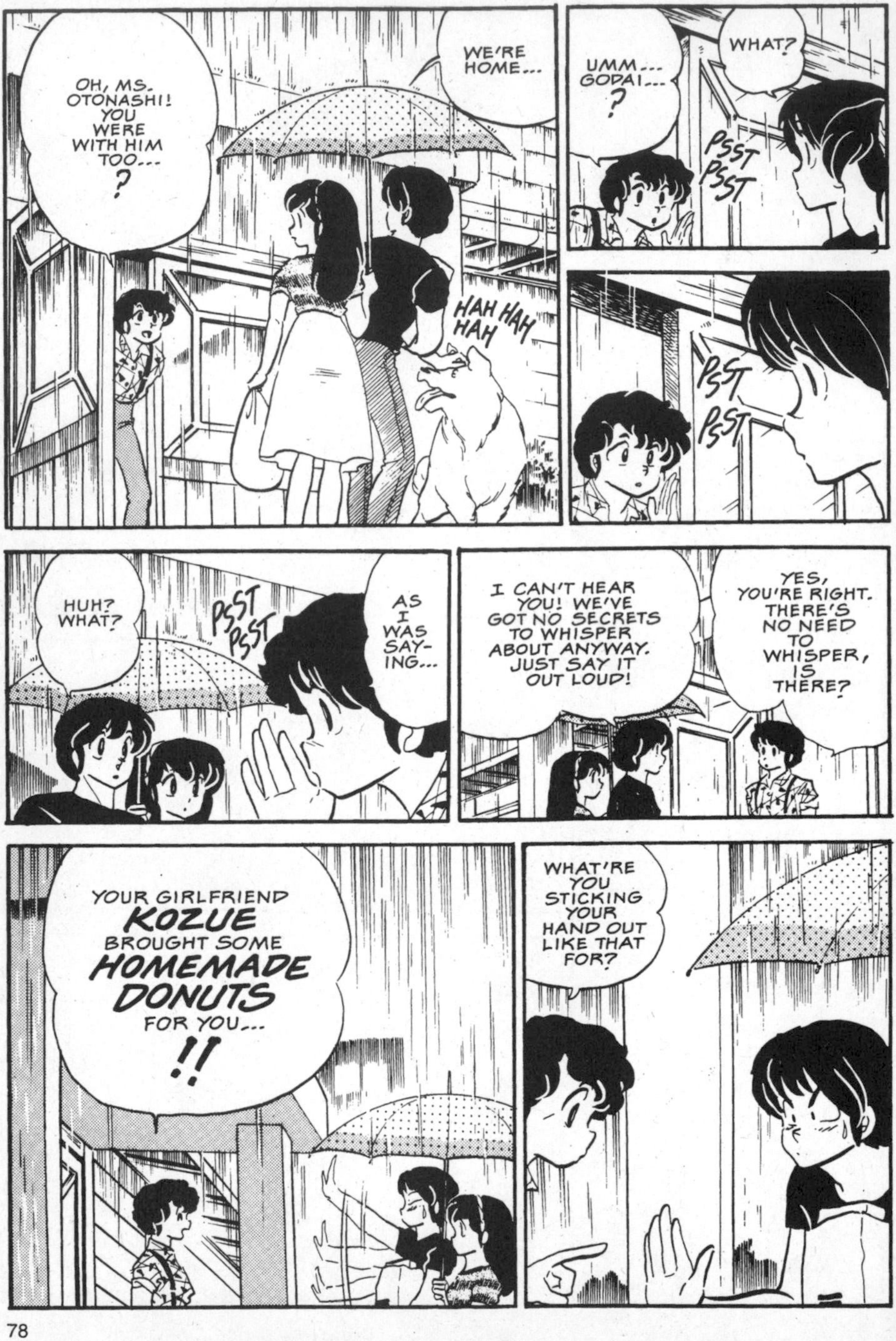
OH, MS. OTONASHI! YOU WERE WITH HIM TOO...?
WE'RE HOME...
HAH HAH HAH
UMM... GODAI...?
WHAT?
PSST PSST
PSST PSST
HUH? WHAT?
AS I WAS SAYING...
PSST PSST
I CAN'T HEAR YOU! WE'VE GOT NO SECRETS TO WHISPER ABOUT ANYWAY. JUST SAY IT OUT LOUD!
YES, YOU'RE RIGHT. THERE'S NO NEED TO WHISPER, IS THERE?
YOUR GIRLFRIEND KOZUE BROUGHT SOME HOMEMADE DONUTS FOR YOU... !!
WHAT'RE YOU STICKING YOUR HAND OUT LIKE THAT FOR?

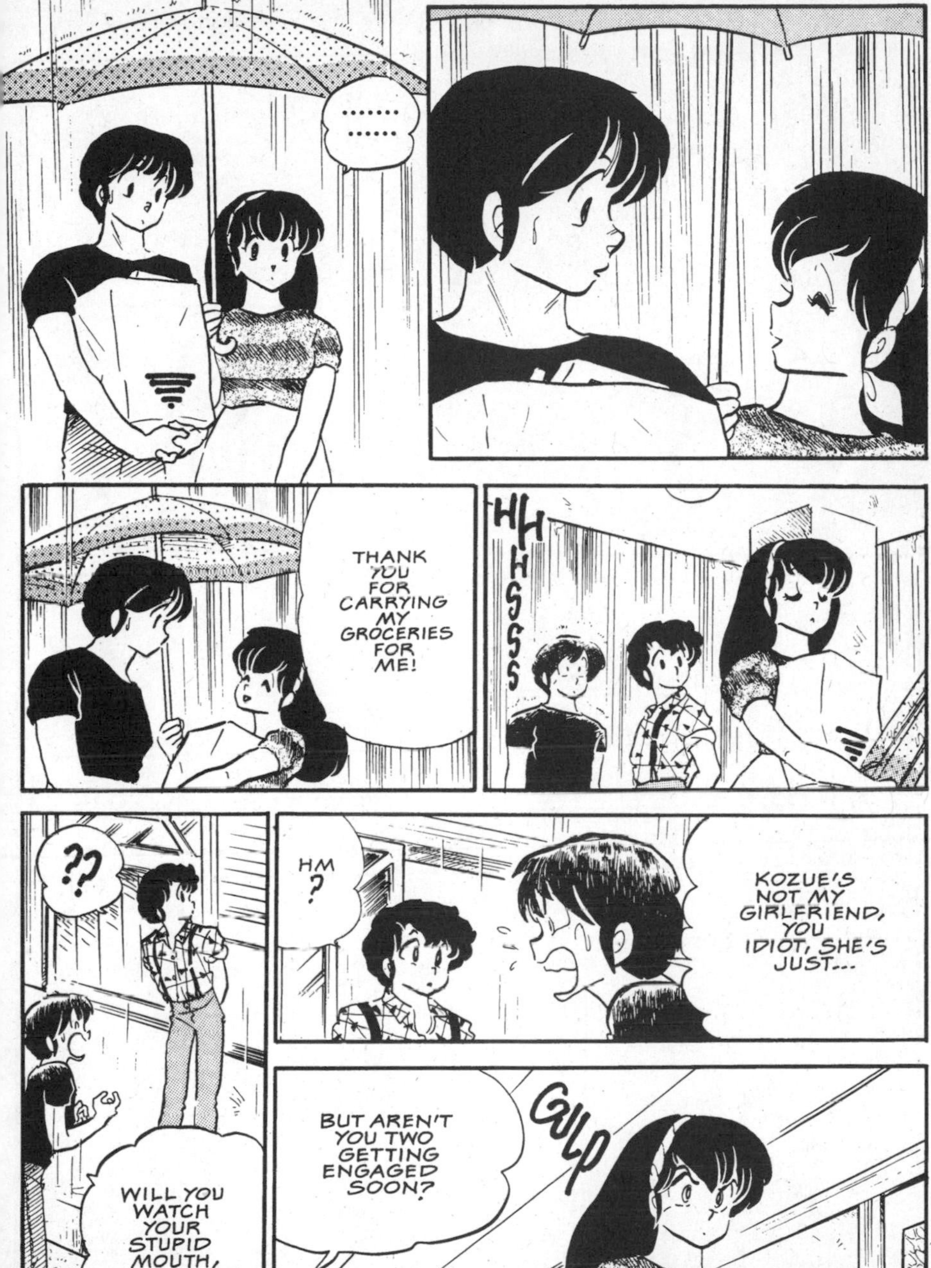
……
……
THANK YOU FOR CARRYING MY GROCERIES FOR ME!
HHHSSS
??
WILL YOU WATCH YOUR STUPID MOUTH, PLEASE?!
HM ?
KOZUE'S NOT MY GIRLFRIEND, YOU IDIOT, SHE'S JUST...
BUT AREN'T YOU TWO GETTING ENGAGED SOON?
GULP

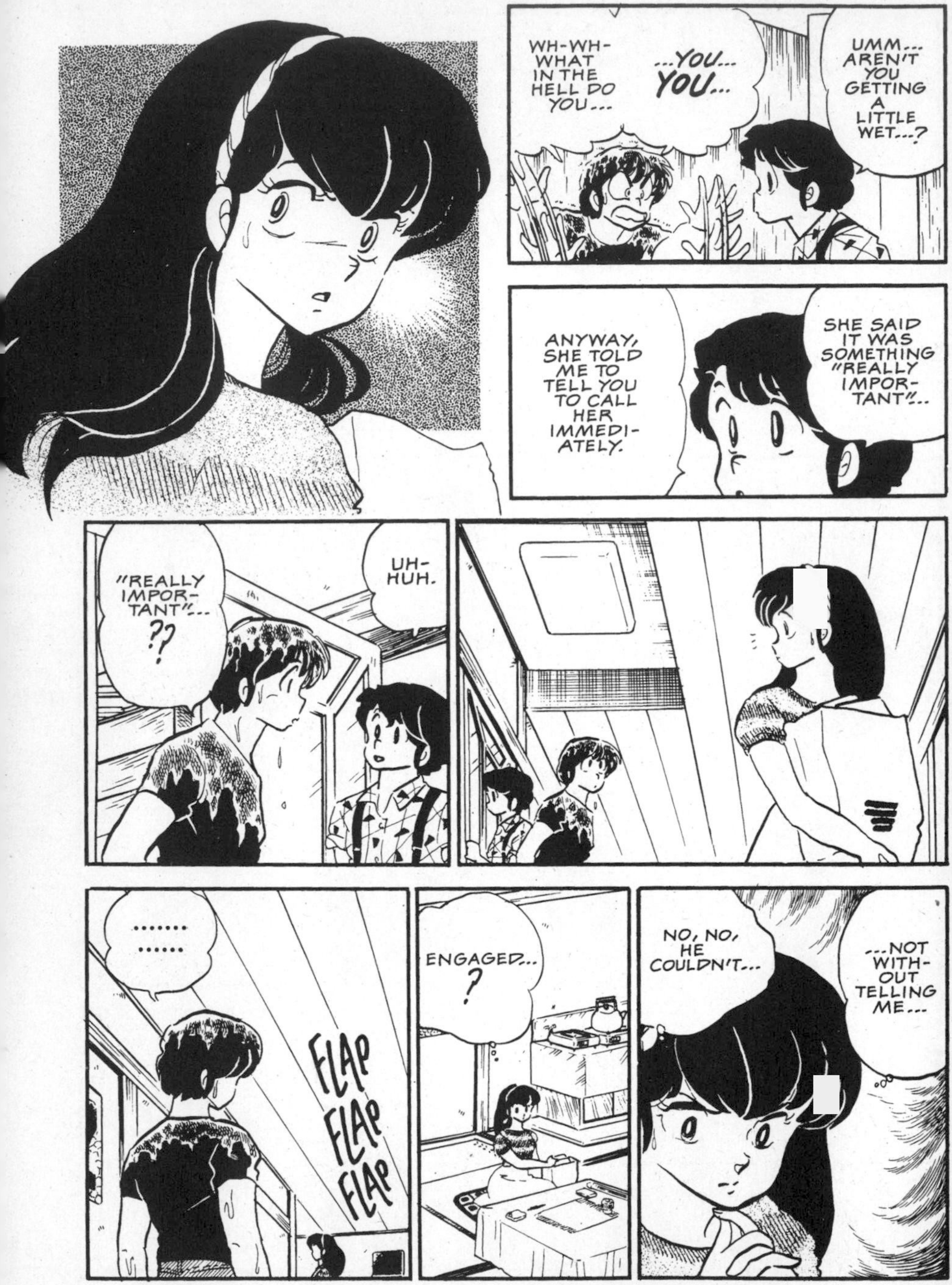
WH-WH- WHAT IN THE HELL DO YOU...
...YOU... YOU...
UMM... AREN'T YOU GETTING A LITTLE WET...?
SHE SAID IT WAS SOMETHING "REALLY IMPORTANT"...
ANYWAY, SHE TOLD ME TO TELL YOU TO CALL HER IMMEDIATELY.
"REALLY IMPORTANT"... ??
UH-HUH.
....
FLAP FLAP FLAP
ENGAGED... ?
NO, NO, HE COULDN'T...
...NOT WITHOUT TELLING ME...

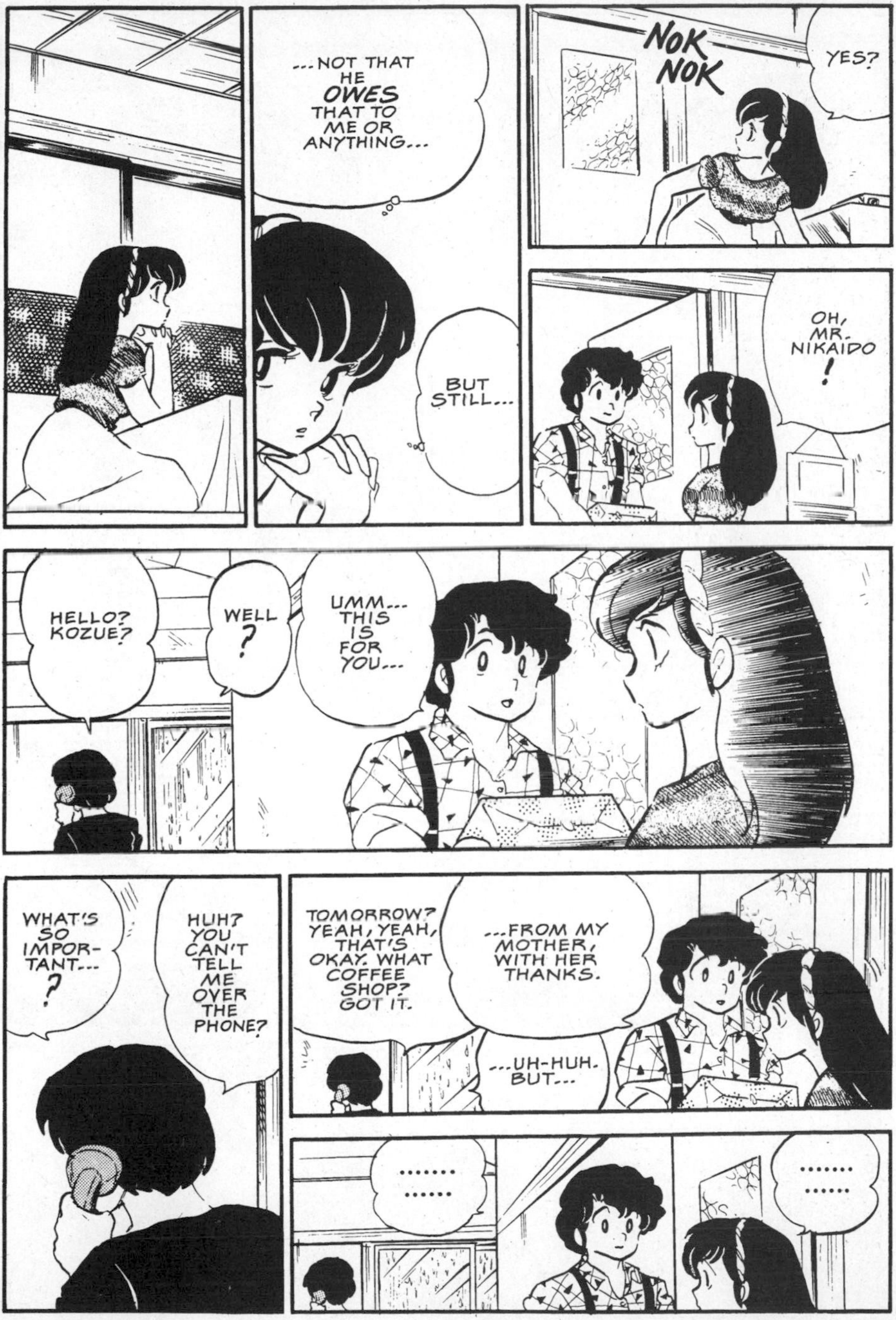
...NOT THAT HE OWES THAT TO ME OR ANYTHING...
BUT STILL...
NOK NOK
YES?
OH, MR. NIKAIDO!
HELLO? KOZUE?
WELL?
UMM... THIS IS FOR YOU...
WHAT'S SO IMPORTANT...?
HUH? YOU CAN'T TELL ME OVER THE PHONE?
TOMORROW? YEAH, YEAH, THAT'S OKAY. WHAT COFFEE SHOP? GOT IT.
...FROM MY MOTHER, WITH HER THANKS.
...UH-HUH. BUT...
....
......
....
......

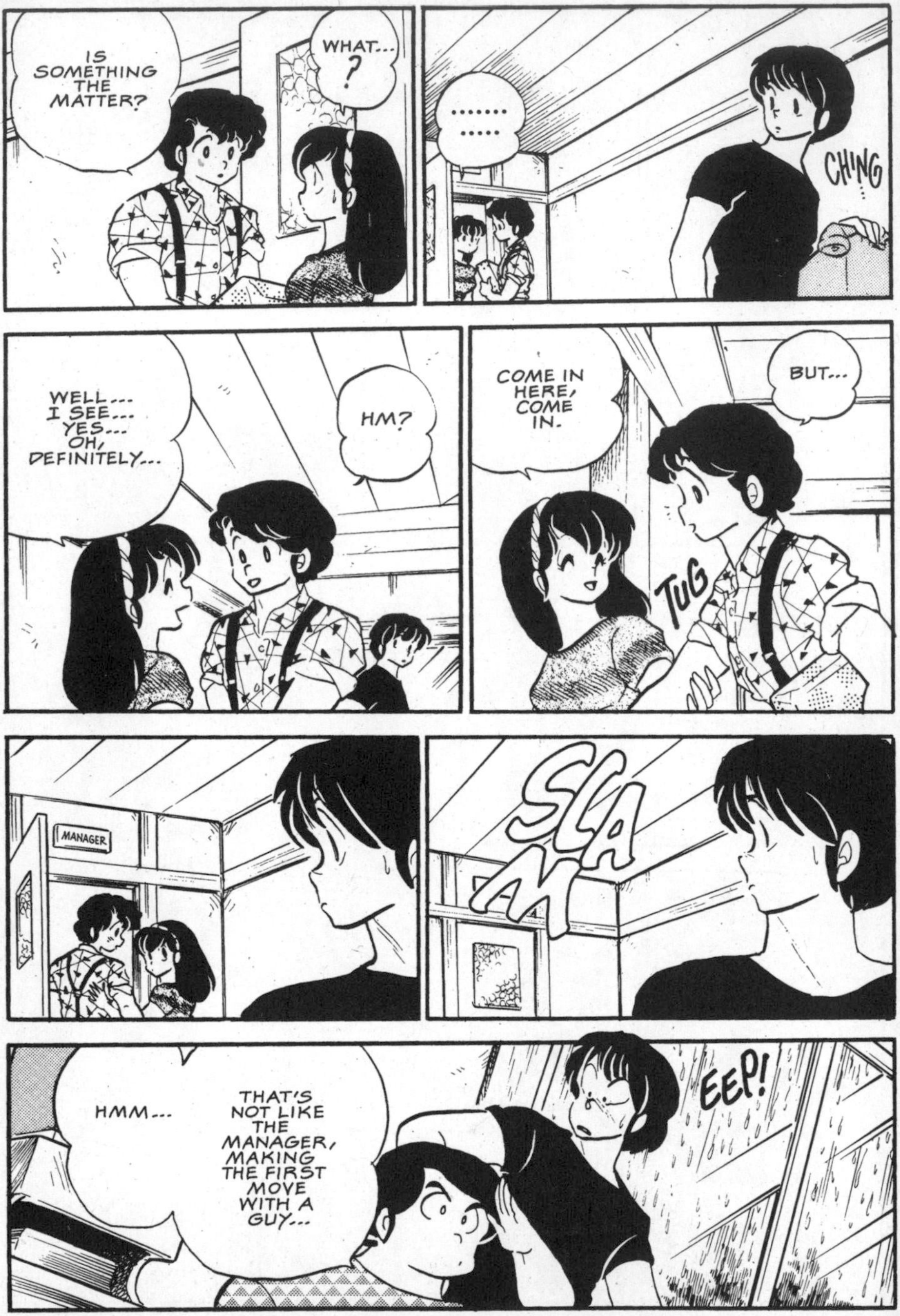
IS SOMETHING THE MATTER?
WHAT...?
......
......
CHING
WELL... I SEE... YES... OH, DEFINITELY...
HM?
COME IN HERE, COME IN.
BUT...
TUG
MANAGER
SLAM
HMM...
THAT'S NOT LIKE THE MANAGER, MAKING THE FIRST MOVE WITH A GUY...
EEP!

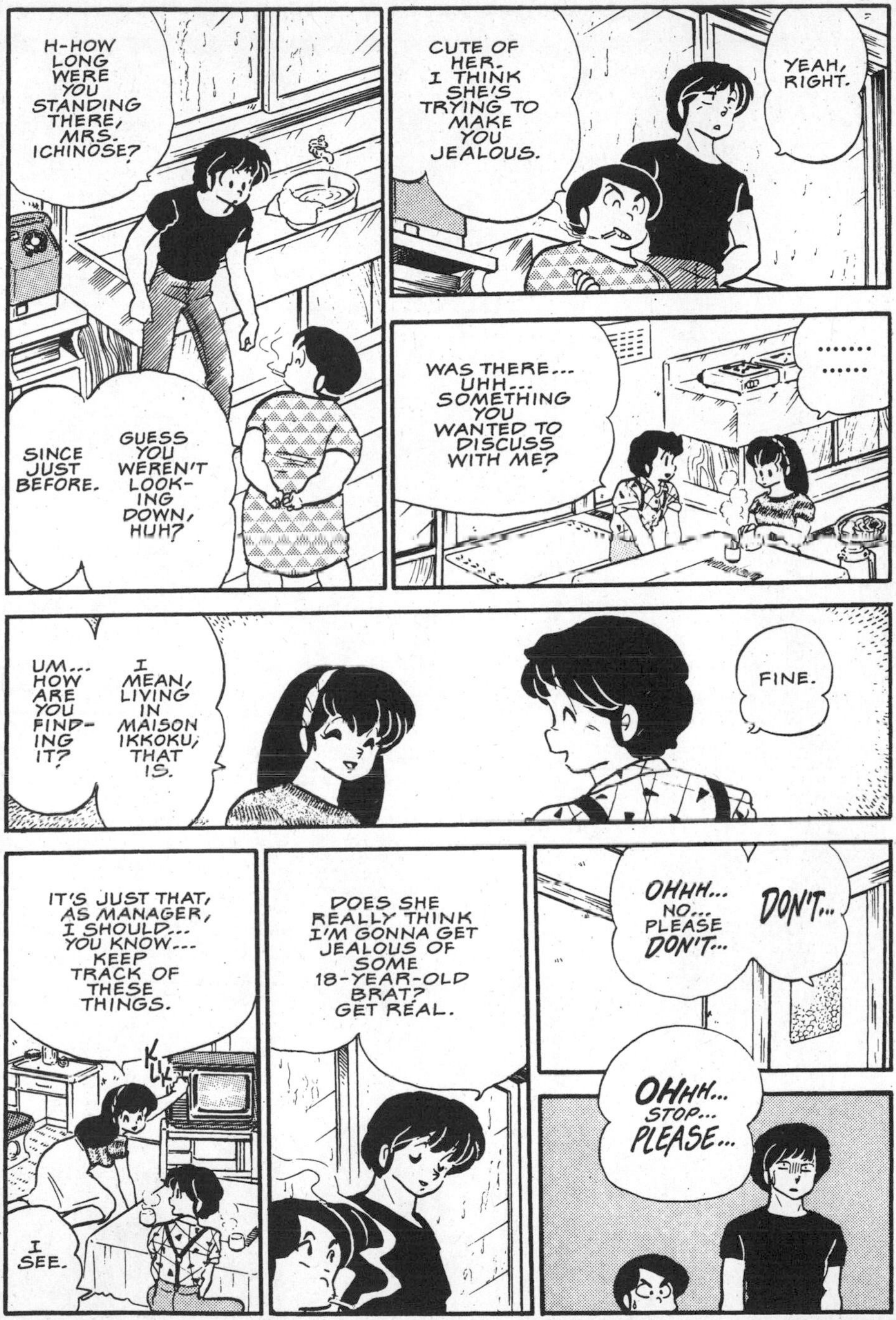
H-HOW LONG WERE YOU STANDING THERE, MRS. ICHINOSE?
SINCE JUST BEFORE.
GUESS YOU WEREN'T LOOKING DOWN, HUH?
CUTE OF HER. I THINK SHE'S TRYING TO MAKE YOU JEALOUS.
YEAH, RIGHT.
WAS THERE... UHH... SOMETHING YOU WANTED TO DISCUSS WITH ME?
....
UM... HOW ARE YOU FINDING IT?
I MEAN, LIVING IN MAISON IKKOKU, THAT IS.
FINE.
IT'S JUST THAT, AS MANAGER, I SHOULD... YOU KNOW... KEEP TRACK OF THESE THINGS.
KLIK
I SEE.
DOES SHE REALLY THINK I'M GONNA GET JEALOUS OF SOME 18-YEAR-OLD BRAT? GET REAL.
OHHH... NO... PLEASE DON'T...
DON'T...
OHHH... STOP... PLEASE...

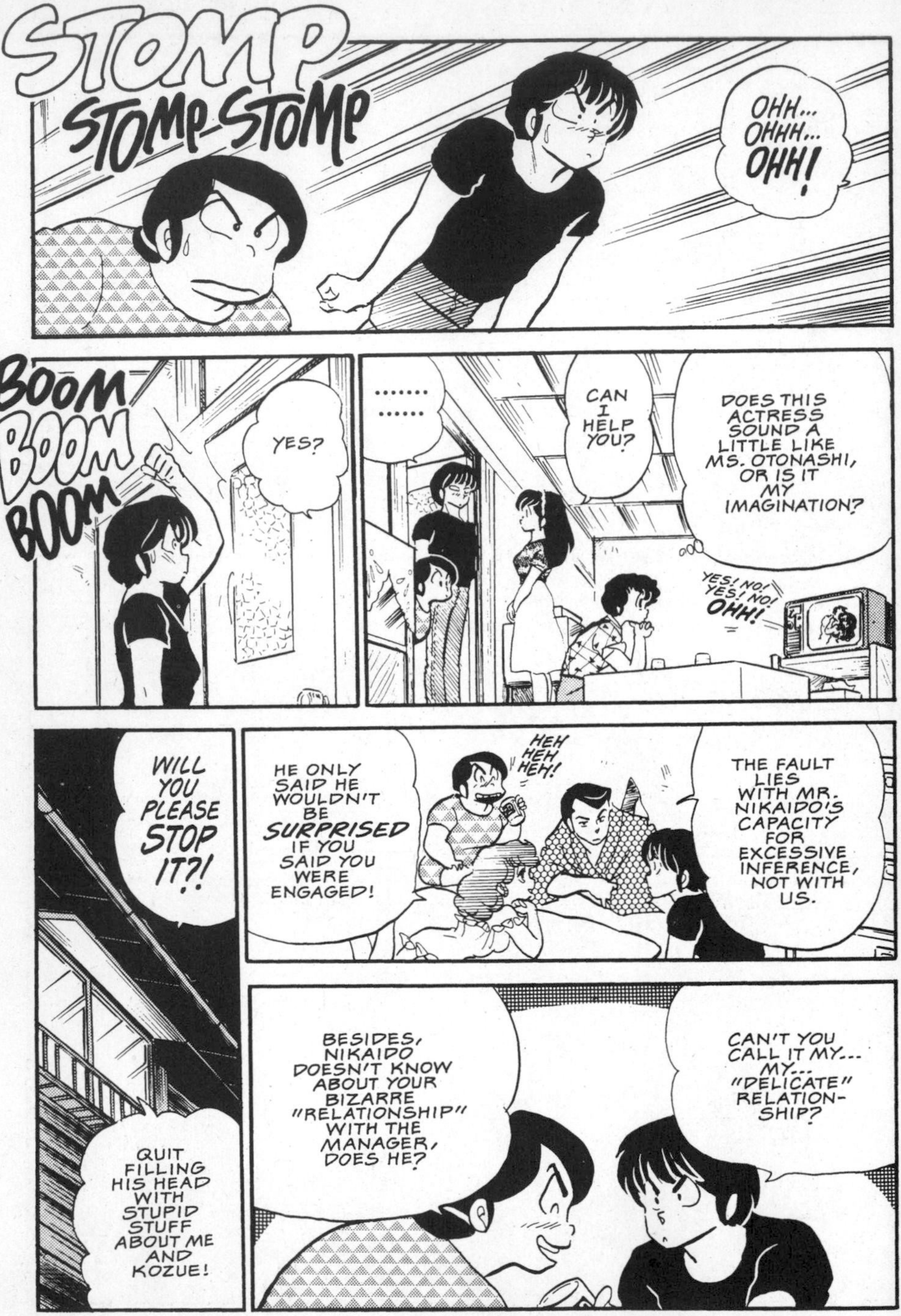
STOMP
STOMP-STOMP
OHH... OHHH... OHH!
BOOM BOOM BOOM
YES?
....
....
CAN I HELP YOU?
DOES THIS ACTRESS SOUND A LITTLE LIKE MS. OTONASHI, OR IS IT MY IMAGINATION?
YES! NO! YES! NO! OHH!
WILL YOU PLEASE STOP IT?!
QUIT FILLING HIS HEAD WITH STUPID STUFF ABOUT ME AND KOZUE!
HE ONLY SAID HE WOULDN'T BE SURPRISED IF YOU SAID YOU WERE ENGAGED!
HEH HEH HEH!
THE FAULT LIES WITH MR. NIKAIDO'S CAPACITY FOR EXCESSIVE INFERENCE, NOT WITH US.
BESIDES, NIKAIDO DOESN'T KNOW ABOUT YOUR BIZARRE "RELATIONSHIP" WITH THE MANAGER, DOES HE?
CAN'T YOU CALL IT MY... MY... "DELICATE" RELATION-SHIP?

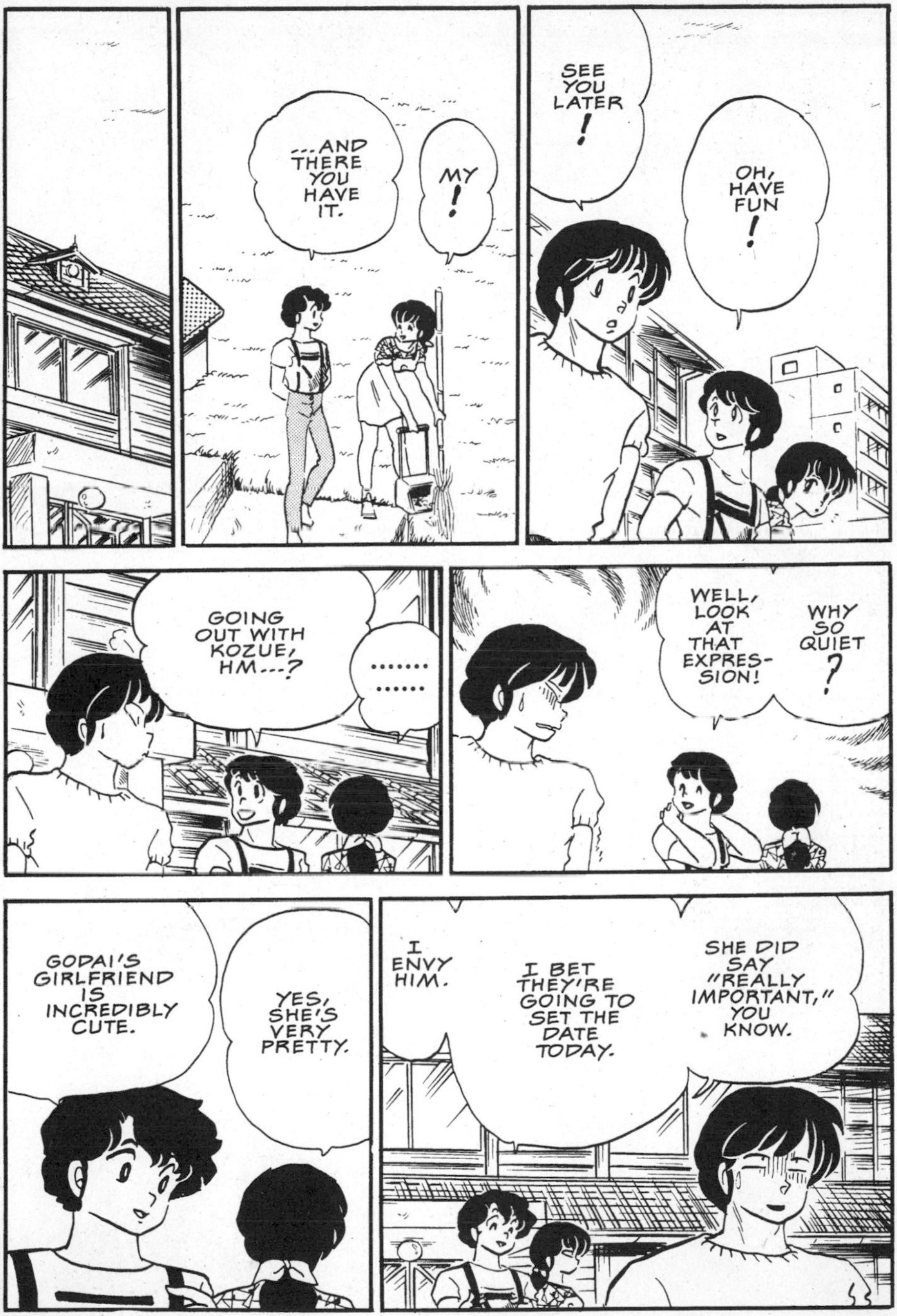
...AND THERE YOU HAVE IT.
MY!
SEE YOU LATER!
OH, HAVE FUN!
GOING OUT WITH KOZUE, HM...?
....
WELL, LOOK AT THAT EXPRESSION!
WHY SO QUIET?
GODAI'S GIRLFRIEND IS INCREDIBLY CUTE.
YES, SHE'S VERY PRETTY.
I ENVY HIM.
I BET THEY'RE GOING TO SET THE DATE TODAY.
SHE DID SAY "REALLY IMPORTANT," YOU KNOW.

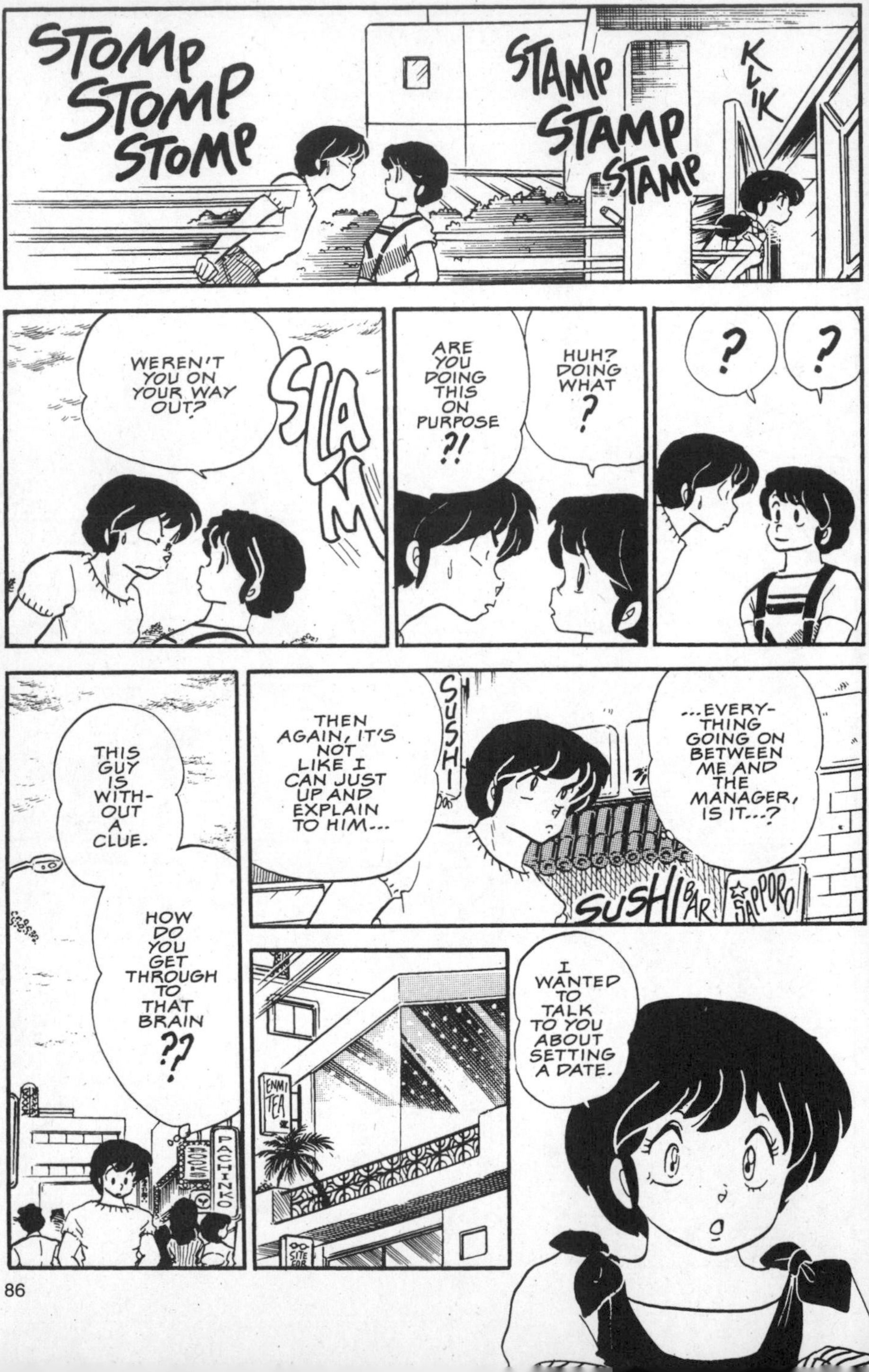
STOMP STOMP STOMP
STAMP STAMP STAMP
KLIK
WEREN'T YOU ON YOUR WAY OUT?
SLAM
ARE YOU DOING THIS ON PURPOSE?!
HUH? DOING WHAT?
?
?
THIS GUY IS WITHOUT A CLUE.
HOW DO YOU GET THROUGH TO THAT BRAIN??
PACHINKO
SUSHI
THEN AGAIN, IT'S NOT LIKE I CAN JUST UP AND EXPLAIN TO HIM...
...EVERYTHING GOING ON BETWEEN ME AND THE MANAGER, IS IT...?
SUSHI BAR
SAPPORO
ENMI TEA
I WANTED TO TALK TO YOU ABOUT SETTING A DATE.

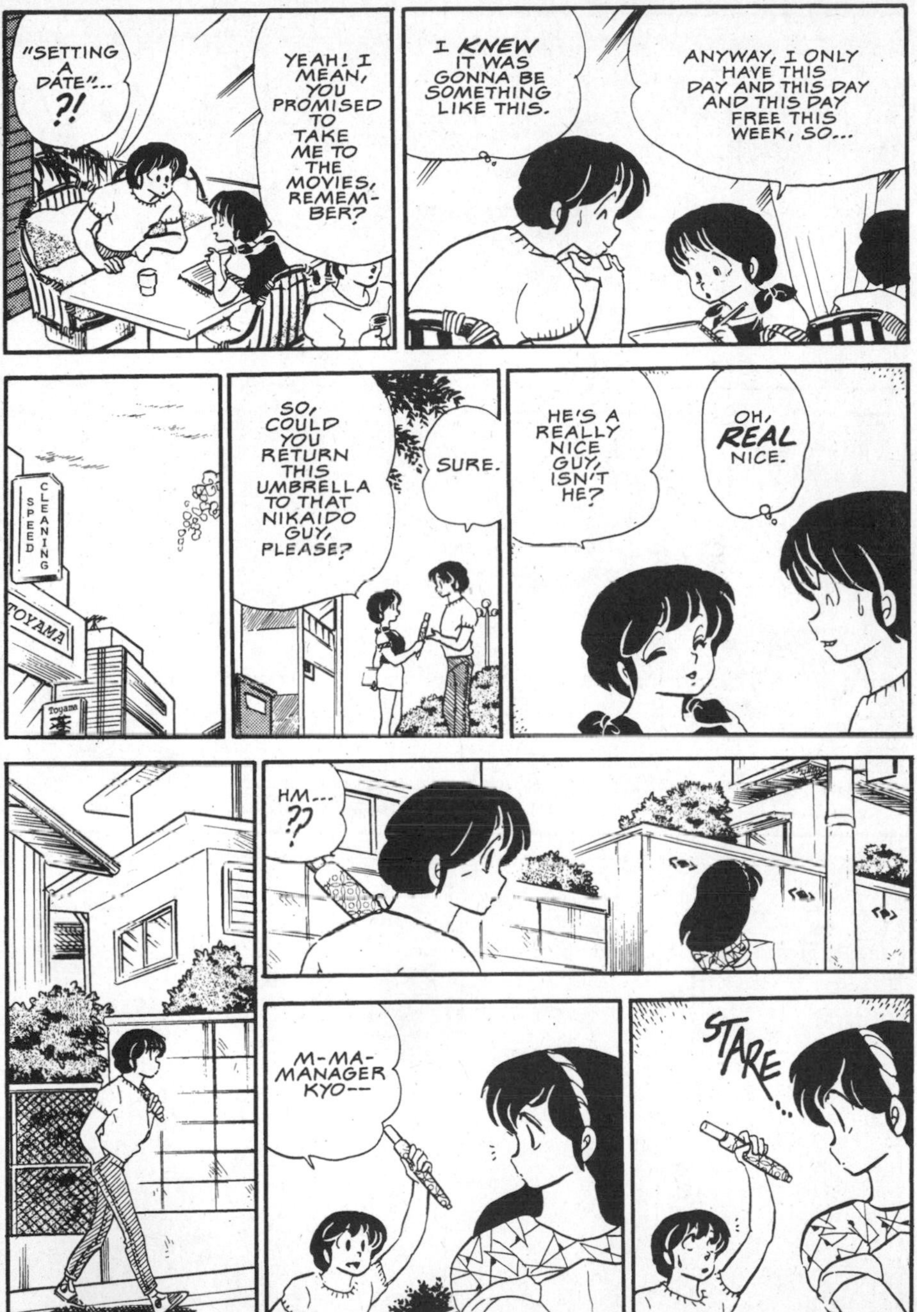
"SETTING A DATE"...?!
YEAH! I MEAN, YOU PROMISED TO TAKE ME TO THE MOVIES, REMEMBER?
I KNEW IT WAS GONNA BE SOMETHING LIKE THIS.
ANYWAY, I ONLY HAVE THIS DAY AND THIS DAY AND THIS DAY FREE THIS WEEK, SO...
SPEED CLEANING
TOYAMA
Toyama
SO, COULD YOU RETURN THIS UMBRELLA TO THAT NIKAIDO GUY, PLEASE?
SURE.
HE'S A REALLY NICE GUY, ISN'T HE?
OH, REAL NICE.
HM... ??
M-MA-MANAGER KYO--
STARE...

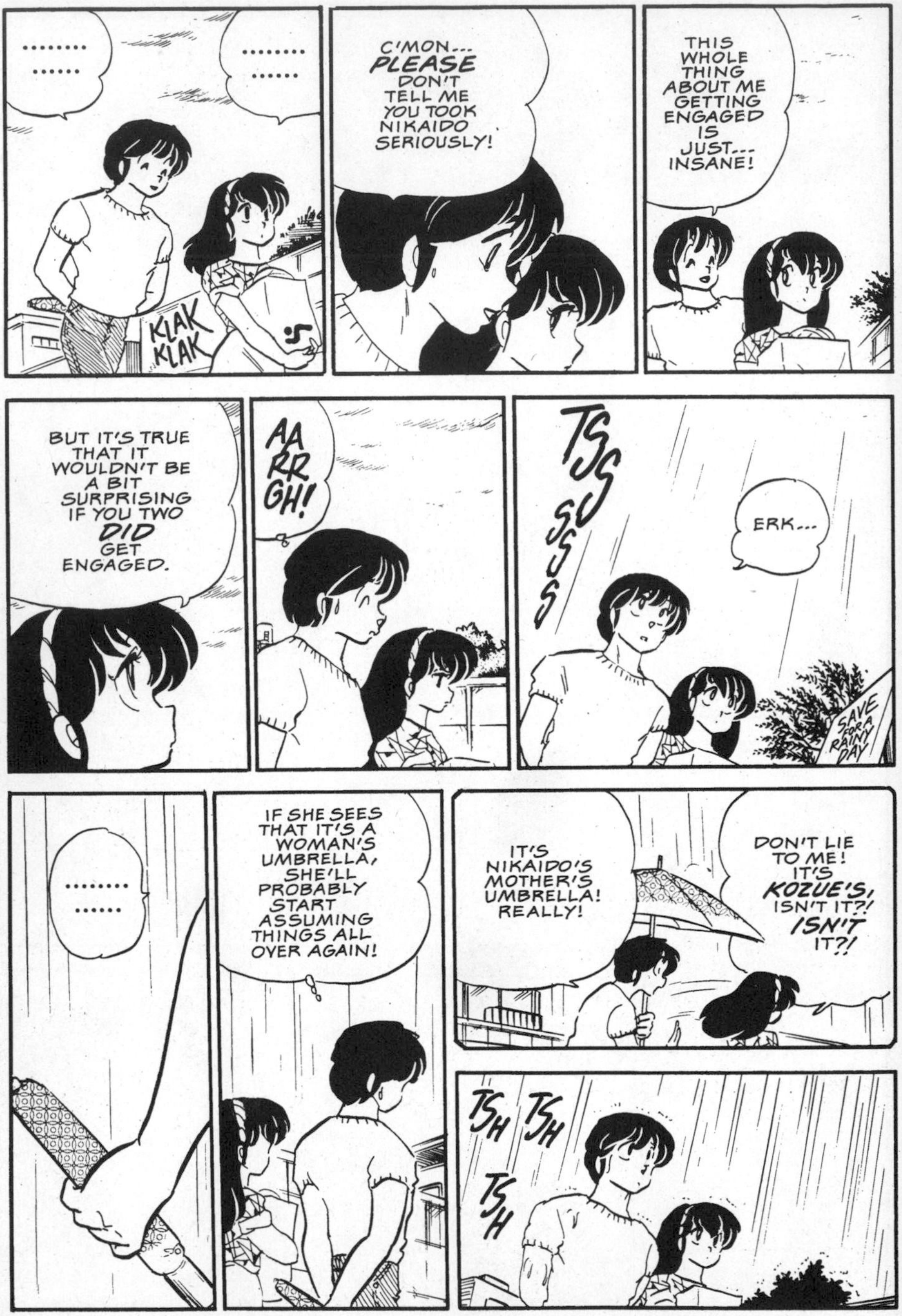

....
....
KLAK KLAK
C'MON... PLEASE DON'T TELL ME YOU TOOK NIKAIDO SERIOUSLY!
THIS WHOLE THING ABOUT ME GETTING ENGAGED IS JUST... INSANE!
BUT IT'S TRUE THAT IT WOULDN'T BE A BIT SURPRISING IF YOU TWO DID GET ENGAGED.
AARRGH!
TSSSSSSS
ERK...
SAVE FOR A RAINY DAY
....
IF SHE SEES THAT IT'S A WOMAN'S UMBRELLA, SHE'LL PROBABLY START ASSUMING THINGS ALL OVER AGAIN!
IT'S NIKAIDO'S MOTHER'S UMBRELLA! REALLY!
DON'T LIE TO ME! IT'S KOZUE'S, ISN'T IT?! ISN'T IT?!
TSH TSH
TSH

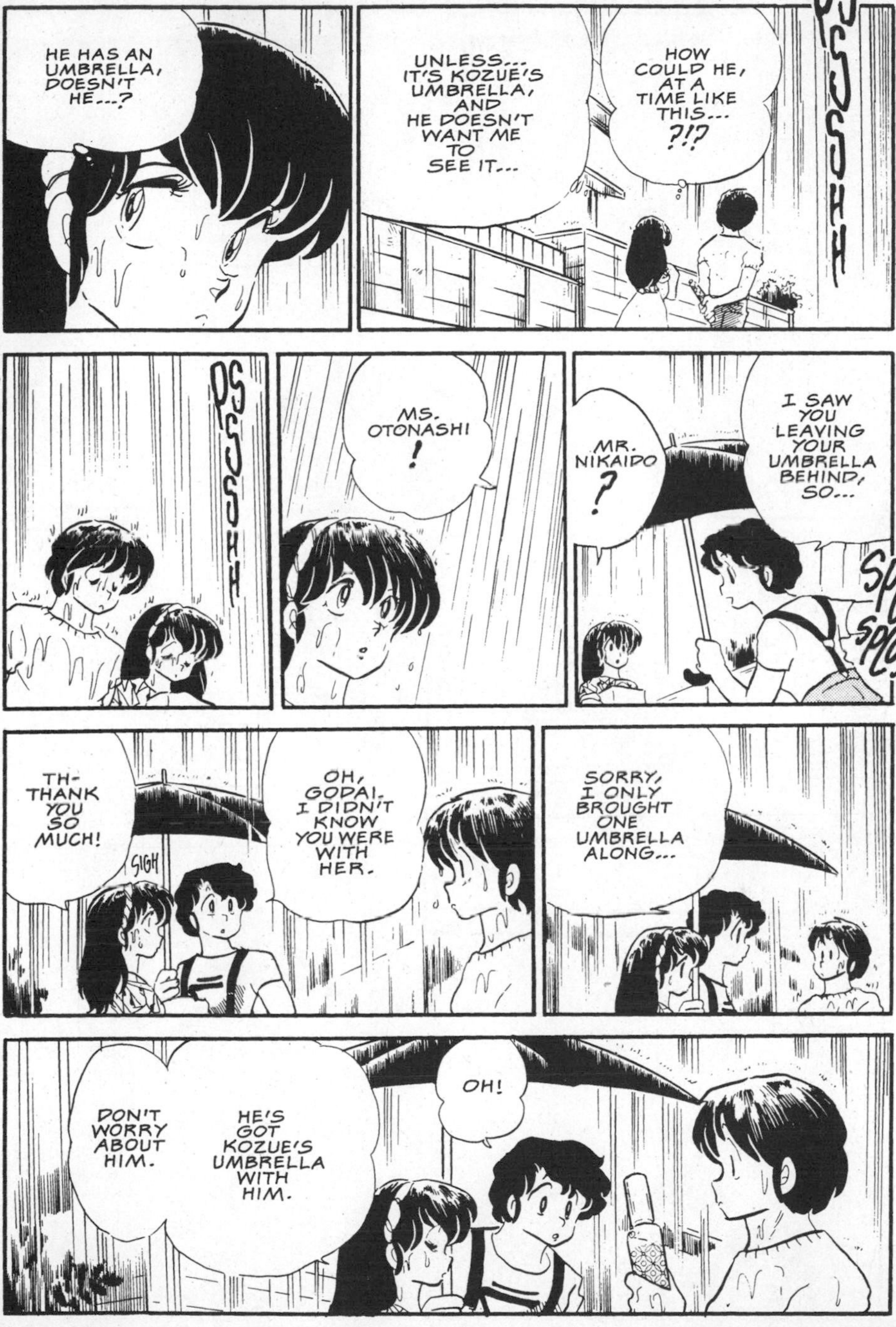
HE HAS AN UMBRELLA, DOESN'T HE...?
UNLESS... IT'S KOZUE'S UMBRELLA, AND HE DOESN'T WANT ME TO SEE IT...
HOW COULD HE, AT A TIME LIKE THIS... ?!?
PSSSSHH
PSSSSHH
MS. OTONASHI !
MR. NIKAIDO ?
I SAW YOU LEAVING YOUR UMBRELLA BEHIND, SO...
SPLOSH SPLOSH
TH-THANK YOU SO MUCH!
SIGH
OH, GODAI. I DIDN'T KNOW YOU WERE WITH HER.
SORRY, I ONLY BROUGHT ONE UMBRELLA ALONG...
DON'T WORRY ABOUT HIM.
HE'S GOT KOZUE'S UMBRELLA WITH HIM.
OH!

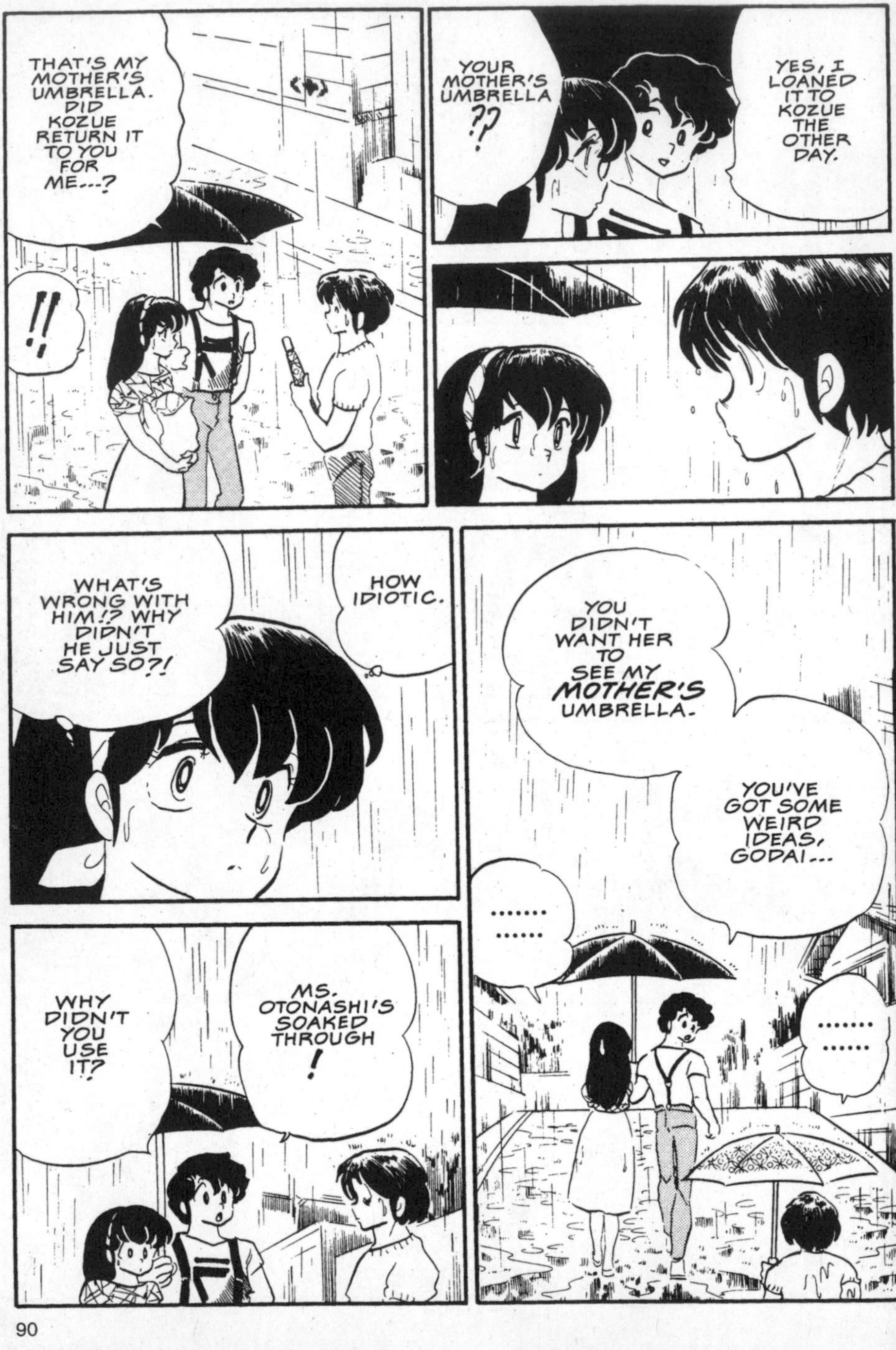

THAT'S MY MOTHER'S UMBRELLA. DID KOZUE RETURN IT TO YOU FOR ME...?
!!
YOUR MOTHER'S UMBRELLA ??
YES, I LOANED IT TO KOZUE THE OTHER DAY.
WHAT'S WRONG WITH HIM!? WHY DIDN'T HE JUST SAY SO?!
HOW IDIOTIC.
YOU DIDN'T WANT HER TO SEE MY MOTHER'S UMBRELLA.
YOU'VE GOT SOME WEIRD IDEAS, GODAI...
......
......
......
......
WHY DIDN'T YOU USE IT?
MS. OTONASHI'S SOAKED THROUGH !

PART 5
TOTAL INSENSITIVITY

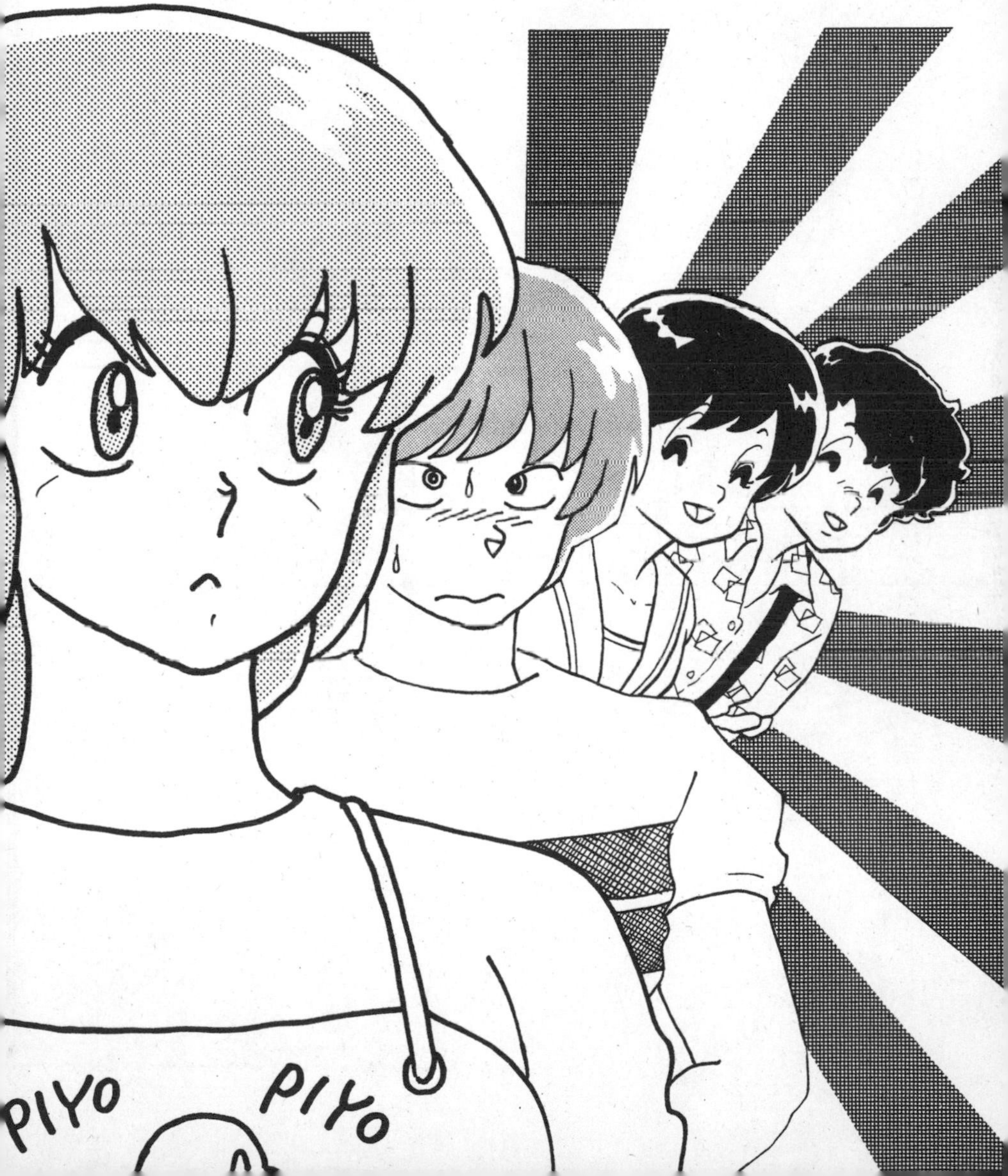
PIYO PIYO

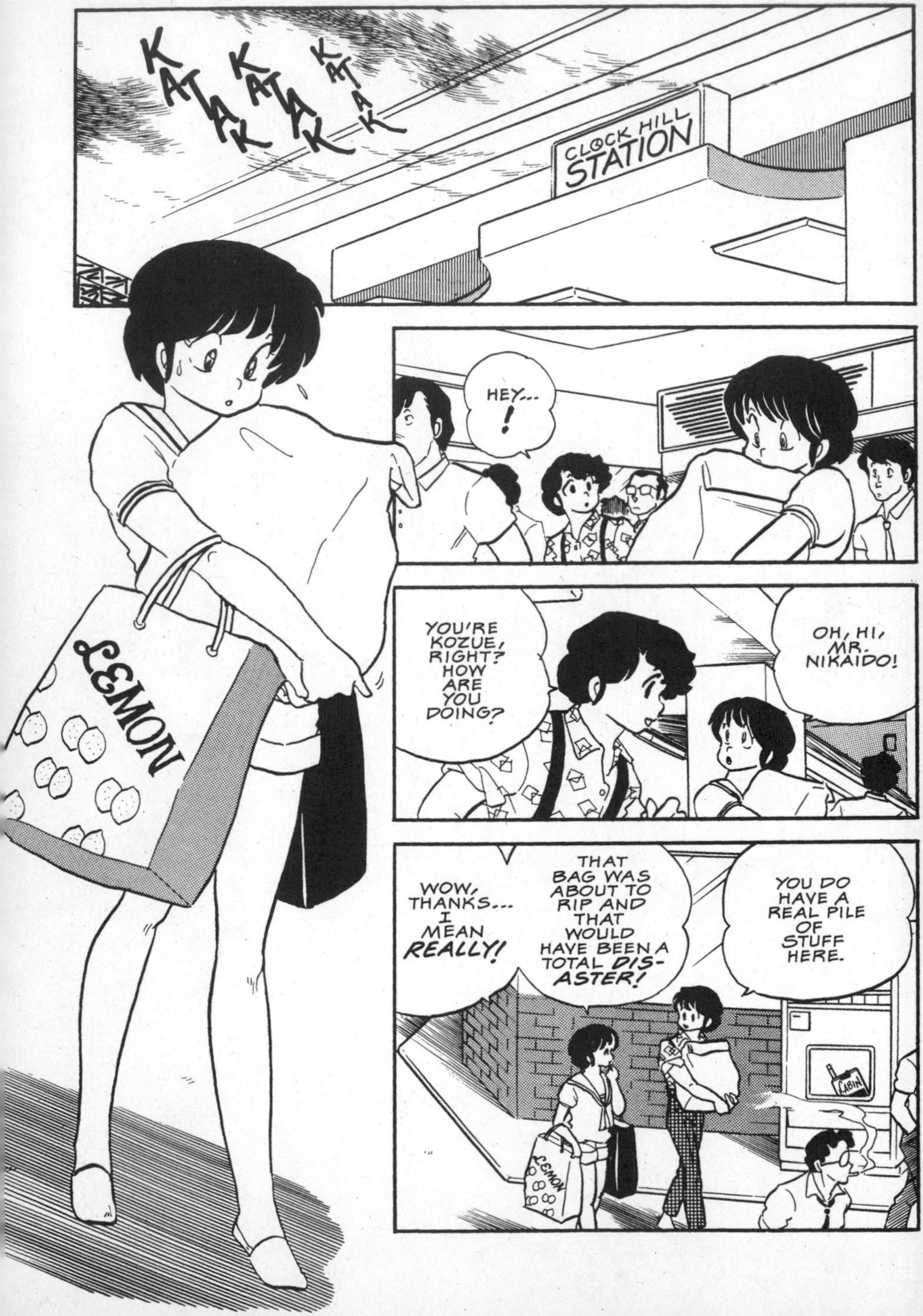
KATAK KATAK KATAK
CLOCK HILL STATION
LEMON
HEY... !
YOU'RE KOZUE, RIGHT? HOW ARE YOU DOING?
OH, HI, MR. NIKAIDO!
WOW, THANKS... I MEAN *REALLY!*
THAT BAG WAS ABOUT TO RIP AND THAT WOULD HAVE BEEN A TOTAL *DIS-ASTER!*
YOU DO HAVE A REAL PILE OF STUFF HERE.
LEMON
CABIN

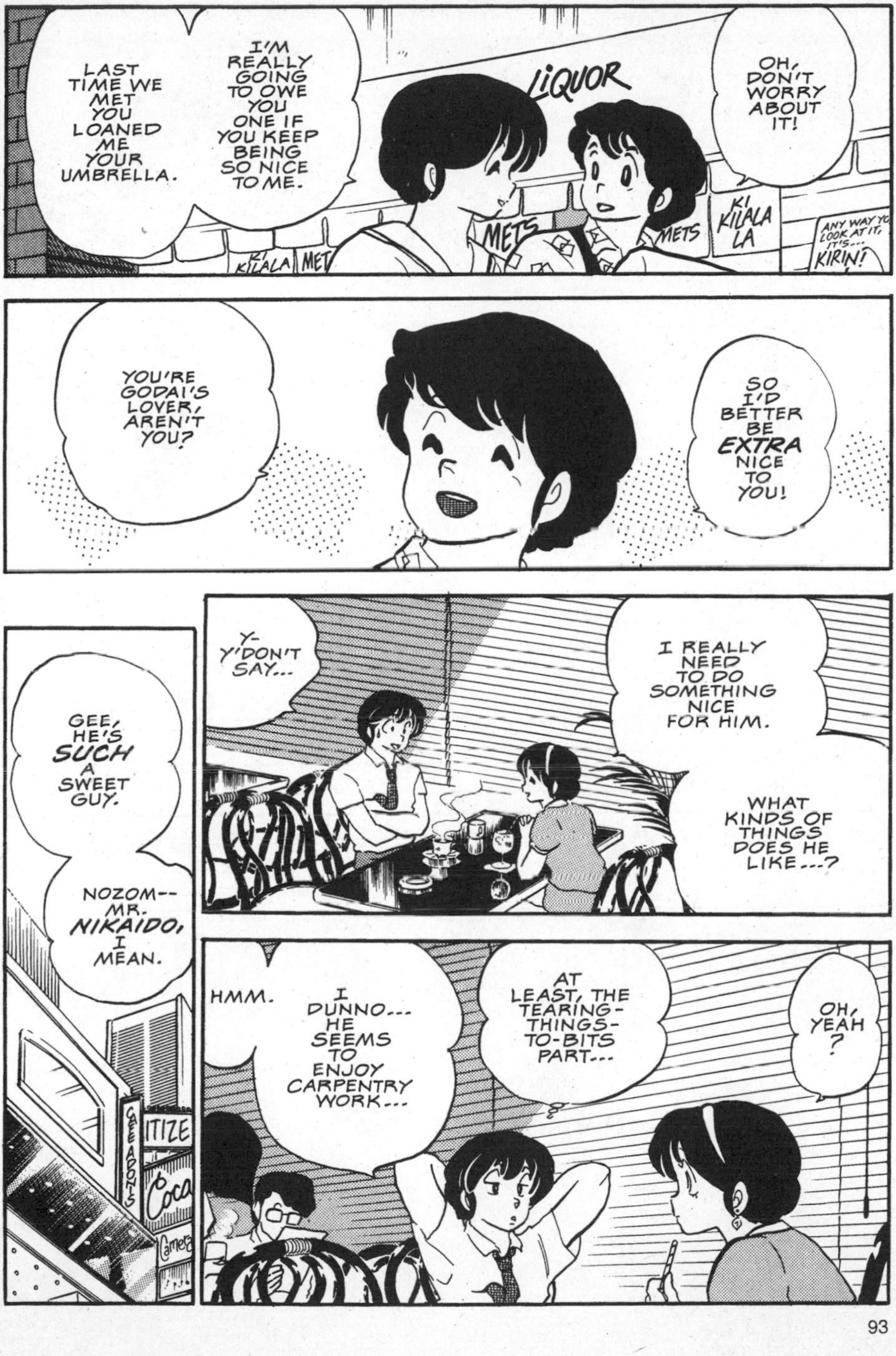
LAST TIME WE MET YOU LOANED ME YOUR UMBRELLA.
I'M REALLY GOING TO OWE YOU ONE IF YOU KEEP BEING SO NICE TO ME.
LIQUOR
OH, DON'T WORRY ABOUT IT!
YOU'RE GODAI'S LOVER, AREN'T YOU?
SO I'D BETTER BE EXTRA NICE TO YOU!
GEE, HE'S SUCH A SWEET GUY.
NOZOM-- MR. NIKAIDO, I MEAN.
Y-Y'DON'T SAY...
I REALLY NEED TO DO SOMETHING NICE FOR HIM.
WHAT KINDS OF THINGS DOES HE LIKE...?
HMM.
I DUNNO... HE SEEMS TO ENJOY CARPENTRY WORK...
AT LEAST, THE TEARING-THINGS-TO-BITS PART...
OH, YEAH?

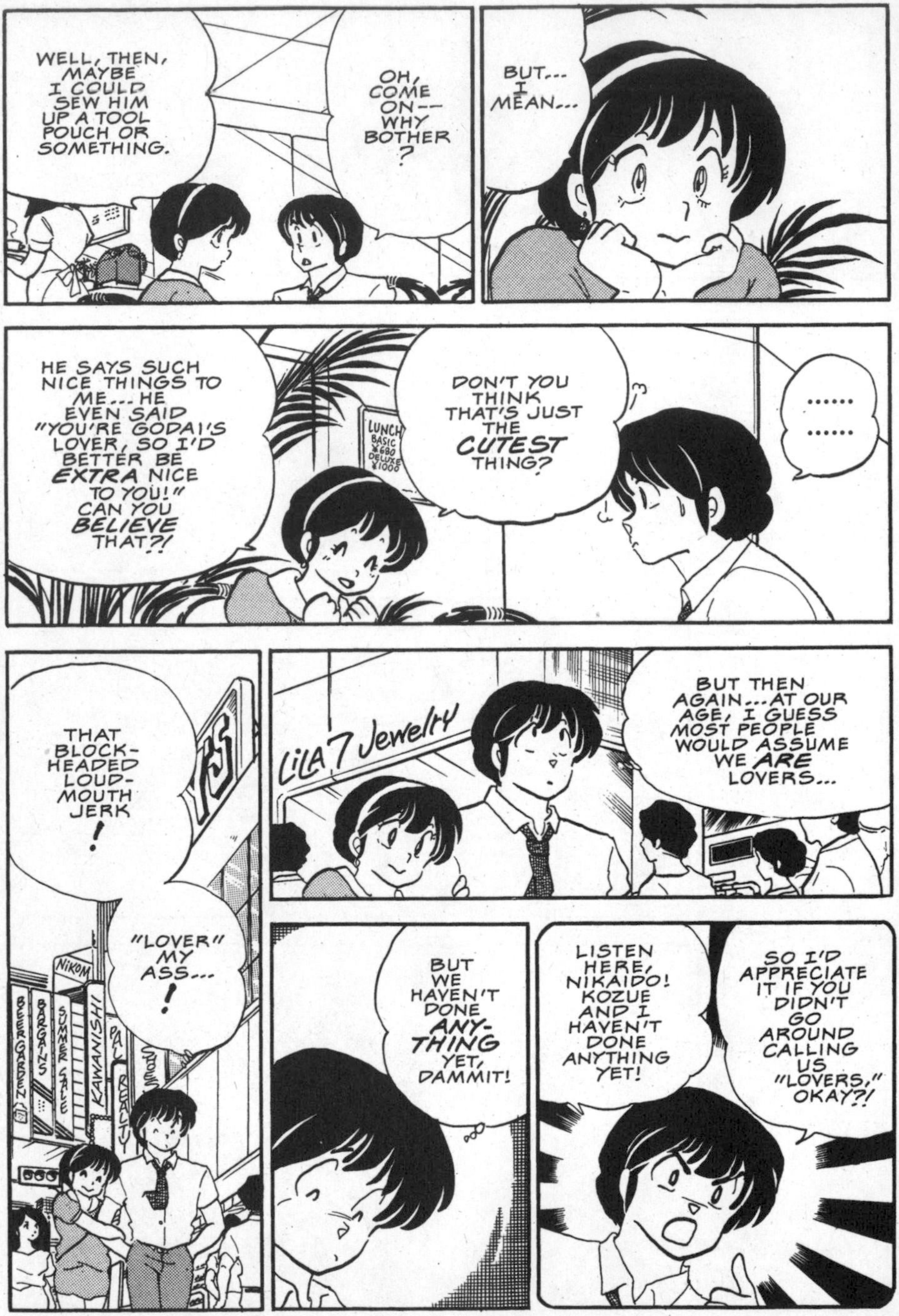
WELL, THEN, MAYBE I COULD SEW HIM UP A TOOL POUCH OR SOMETHING.
OH, COME ON-- WHY BOTHER?
BUT... I MEAN...
HE SAYS SUCH NICE THINGS TO ME... HE EVEN SAID "YOU'RE GODAI'S LOVER, SO I'D BETTER BE EXTRA NICE TO YOU!" CAN YOU BELIEVE THAT?!
LUNCH BASIC ¥680 DELUXE ¥1000
DON'T YOU THINK THAT'S JUST THE CUTEST THING?
......
......
THAT BLOCK-HEADED LOUD-MOUTH JERK!
"LOVER" MY ASS...!
NIKOM
BEER GARDEN
BARGAINS
SUMMER SALE
KAWANISHI
PAK REALTY
LILA 7 Jewelry
BUT THEN AGAIN... AT OUR AGE, I GUESS MOST PEOPLE WOULD ASSUME WE ARE LOVERS...
BUT WE HAVEN'T DONE ANY-THING YET, DAMMIT!
LISTEN HERE, NIKAIDO! KOZUE AND I HAVEN'T DONE ANYTHING YET!
SO I'D APPRECIATE IT IF YOU DIDN'T GO AROUND CALLING US "LOVERS," OKAY?!

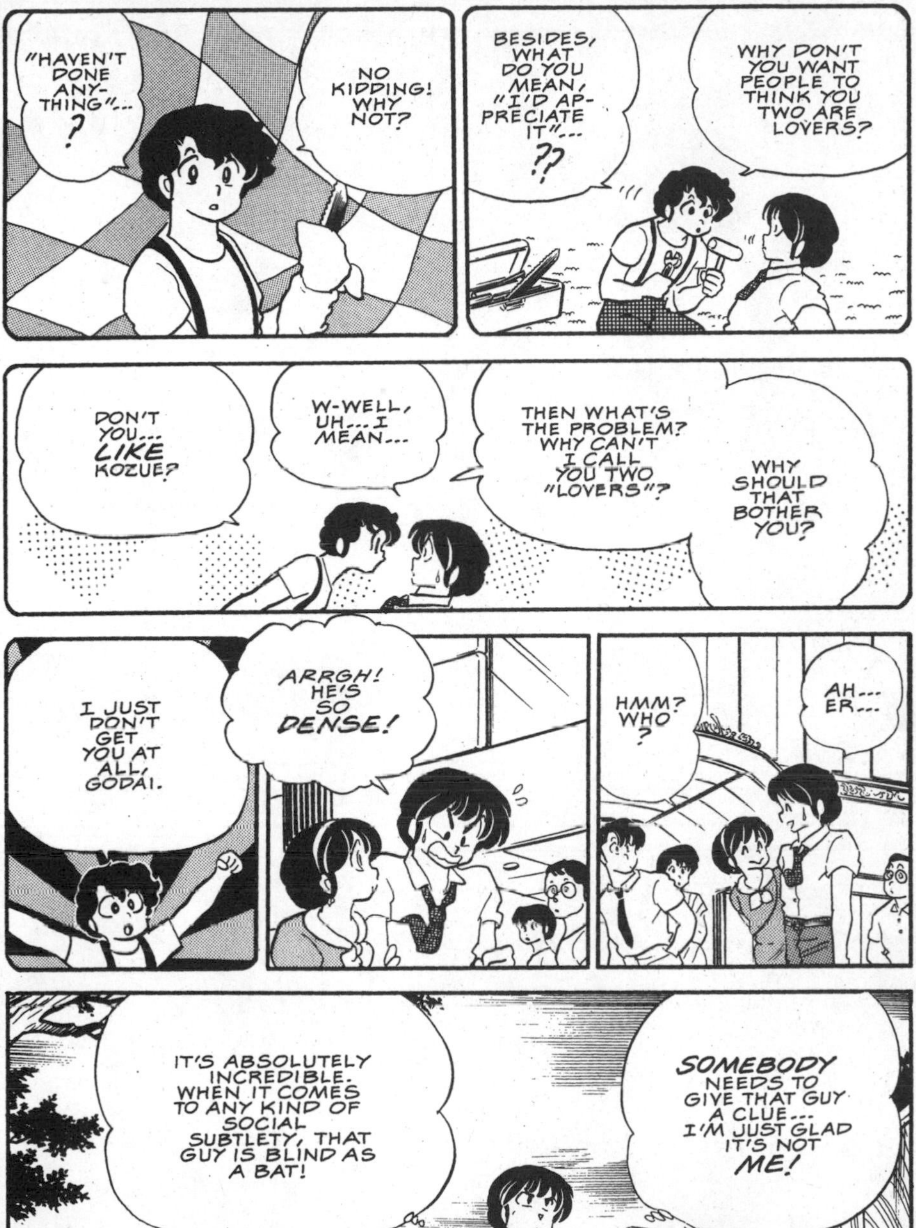
"HAVEN'T DONE ANYTHING"... ?
NO KIDDING! WHY NOT?
BESIDES, WHAT DO YOU MEAN, "I'D APPRECIATE IT"... ??
WHY DON'T YOU WANT PEOPLE TO THINK YOU TWO ARE LOVERS?
DON'T YOU... LIKE KOZUE?
W-WELL, UH... I MEAN...
THEN WHAT'S THE PROBLEM? WHY CAN'T I CALL YOU TWO "LOVERS"?
WHY SHOULD THAT BOTHER YOU?
I JUST DON'T GET YOU AT ALL, GODAI.
ARRGH! HE'S SO DENSE!
HMM? WHO?
AH... ER...
IT'S ABSOLUTELY INCREDIBLE. WHEN IT COMES TO ANY KIND OF SOCIAL SUBTLETY, THAT GUY IS BLIND AS A BAT!
SOMEBODY NEEDS TO GIVE THAT GUY A CLUE... I'M JUST GLAD IT'S NOT ME!

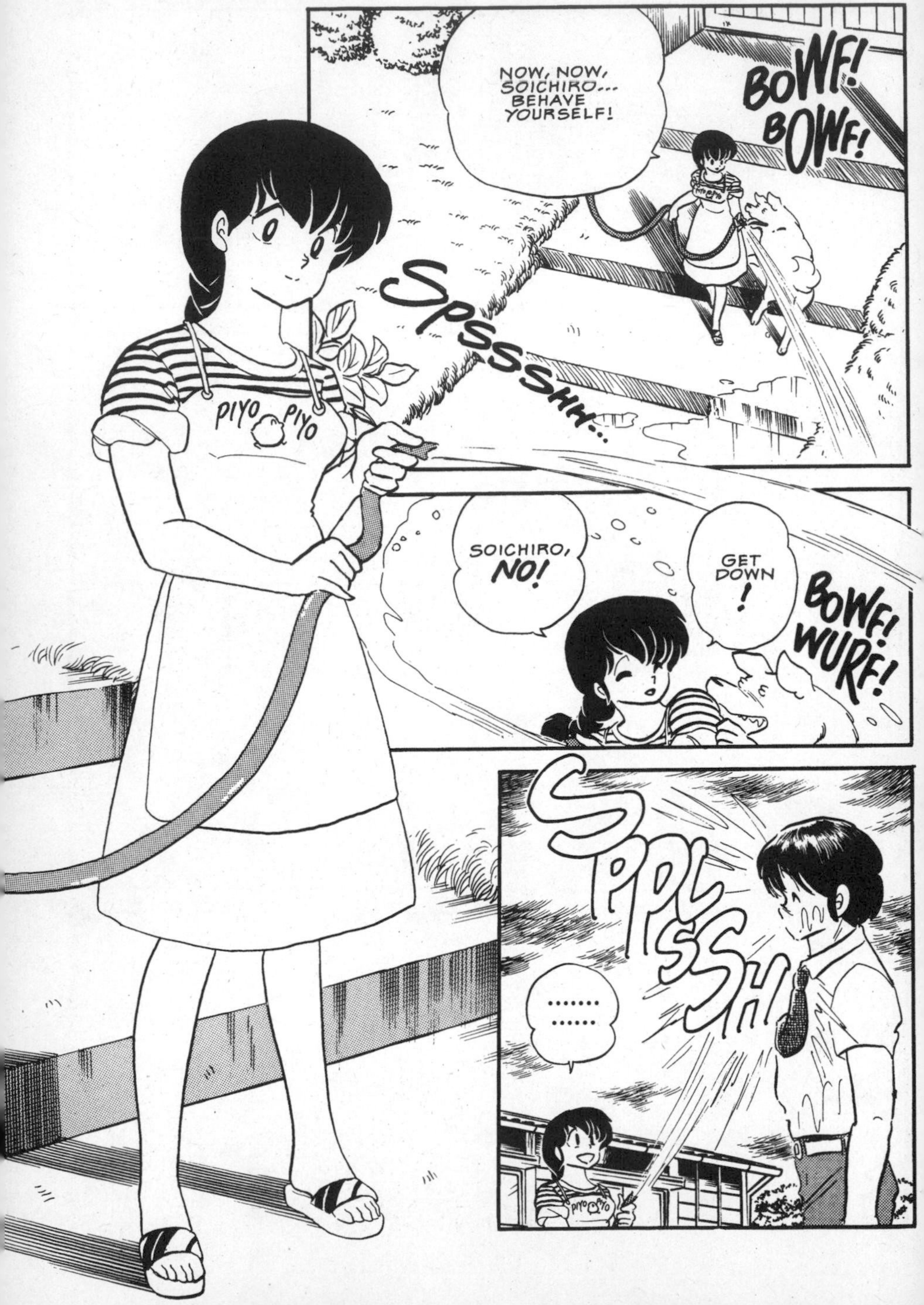
PIYO PIYO
Spsssshh...
NOW, NOW, SOICHIRO... BEHAVE YOURSELF!
BOWF! BOWF!
SOICHIRO, NO!
GET DOWN!
BOWF! WURF!
SPPLSSH!
....
....
PIYO PIYO

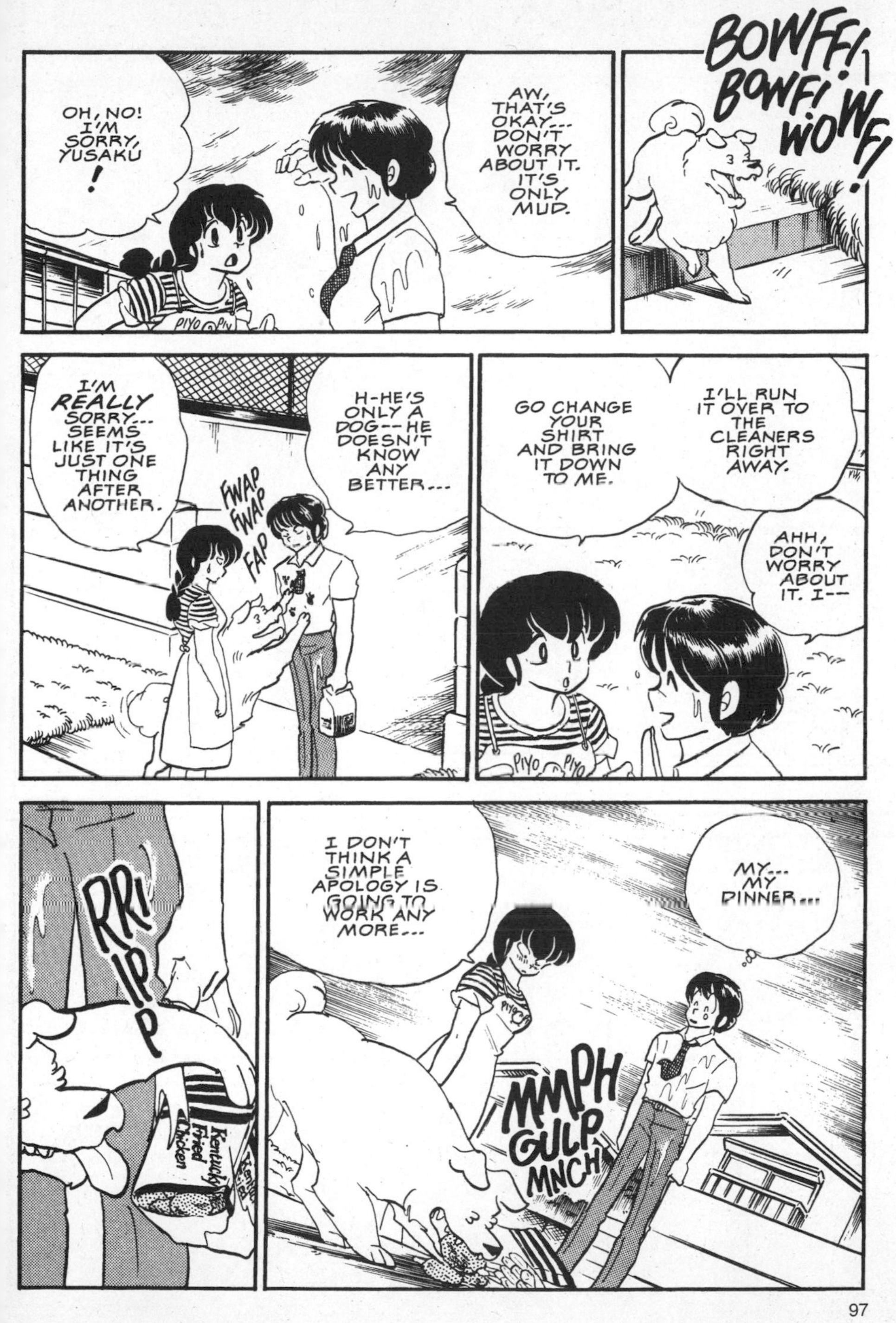
OH, NO! I'M SORRY, YUSAKU!
AW, THAT'S OKAY... DON'T WORRY ABOUT IT. IT'S ONLY MUD.
BOWFF! BOWF! WOWF!
I'M REALLY SORRY... SEEMS LIKE IT'S JUST ONE THING AFTER ANOTHER.
H-HE'S ONLY A DOG--HE DOESN'T KNOW ANY BETTER...
FWAP FWAP FAP
GO CHANGE YOUR SHIRT AND BRING IT DOWN TO ME.
I'LL RUN IT OVER TO THE CLEANERS RIGHT AWAY.
AHH, DON'T WORRY ABOUT IT. I--
RRIPPP
Kentucky Fried Chicken
I DON'T THINK A SIMPLE APOLOGY IS GOING TO WORK ANY MORE...
MY... MY DINNER...
MMPH GULP MNCH

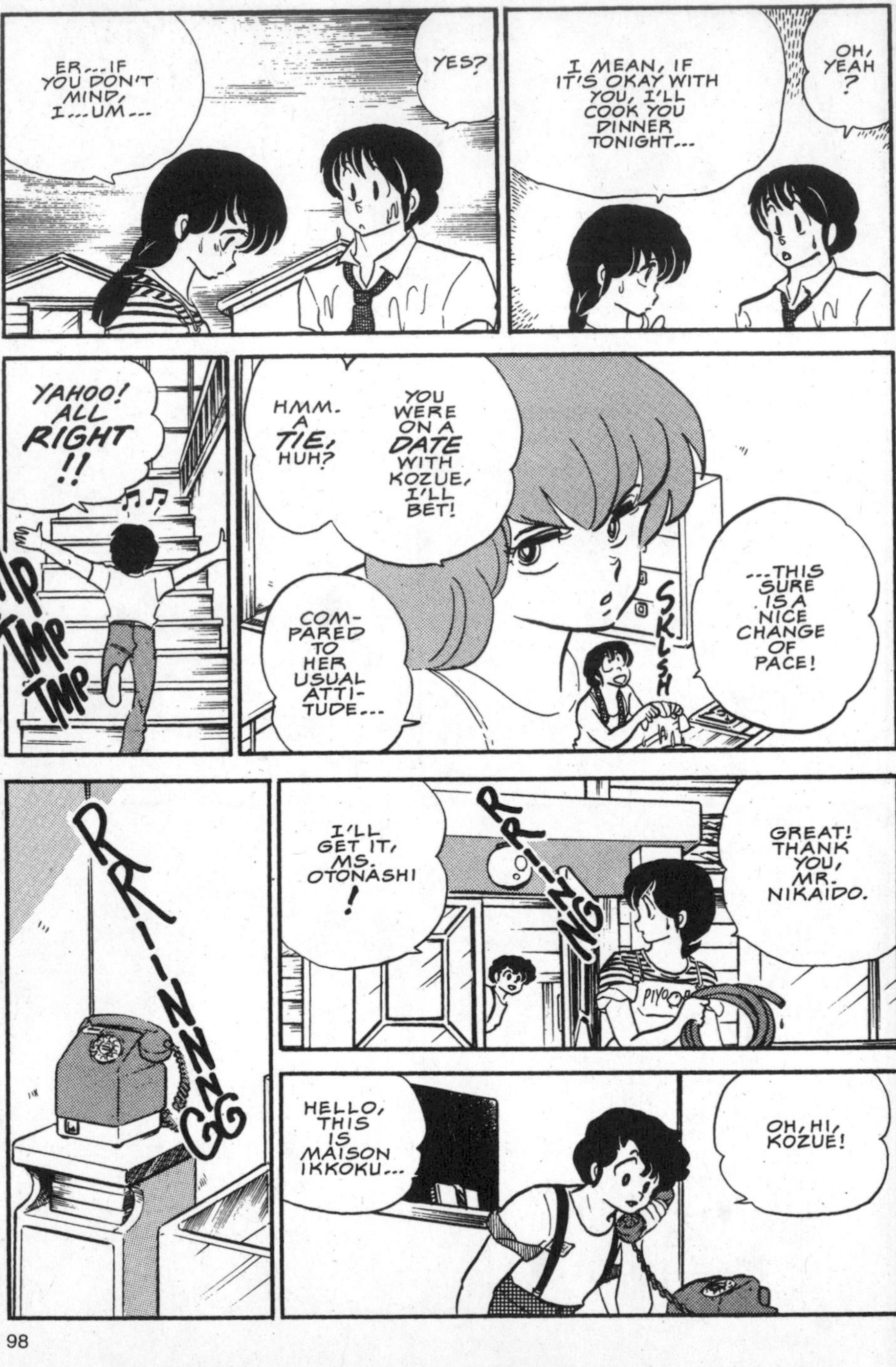
ER... IF YOU DON'T MIND, I... UM...
YES?
I MEAN, IF IT'S OKAY WITH YOU, I'LL COOK YOU DINNER TONIGHT...
OH, YEAH?
YAHOO! ALL RIGHT!!
TMP TMP TMP
HMM. A TIE, HUH?
YOU WERE ON A DATE WITH KOZUE, I'LL BET!
COMPARED TO HER USUAL ATTITUDE...
SKLSH
...THIS SURE IS A NICE CHANGE OF PACE!
RRI-NNNGG
I'LL GET IT, MS. OTONASHI!
RRI-NNG
GREAT! THANK YOU, MR. NIKAIDO.
PIYO
HELLO, THIS IS MAISON IKKOKU...
OH, HI, KOZUE!

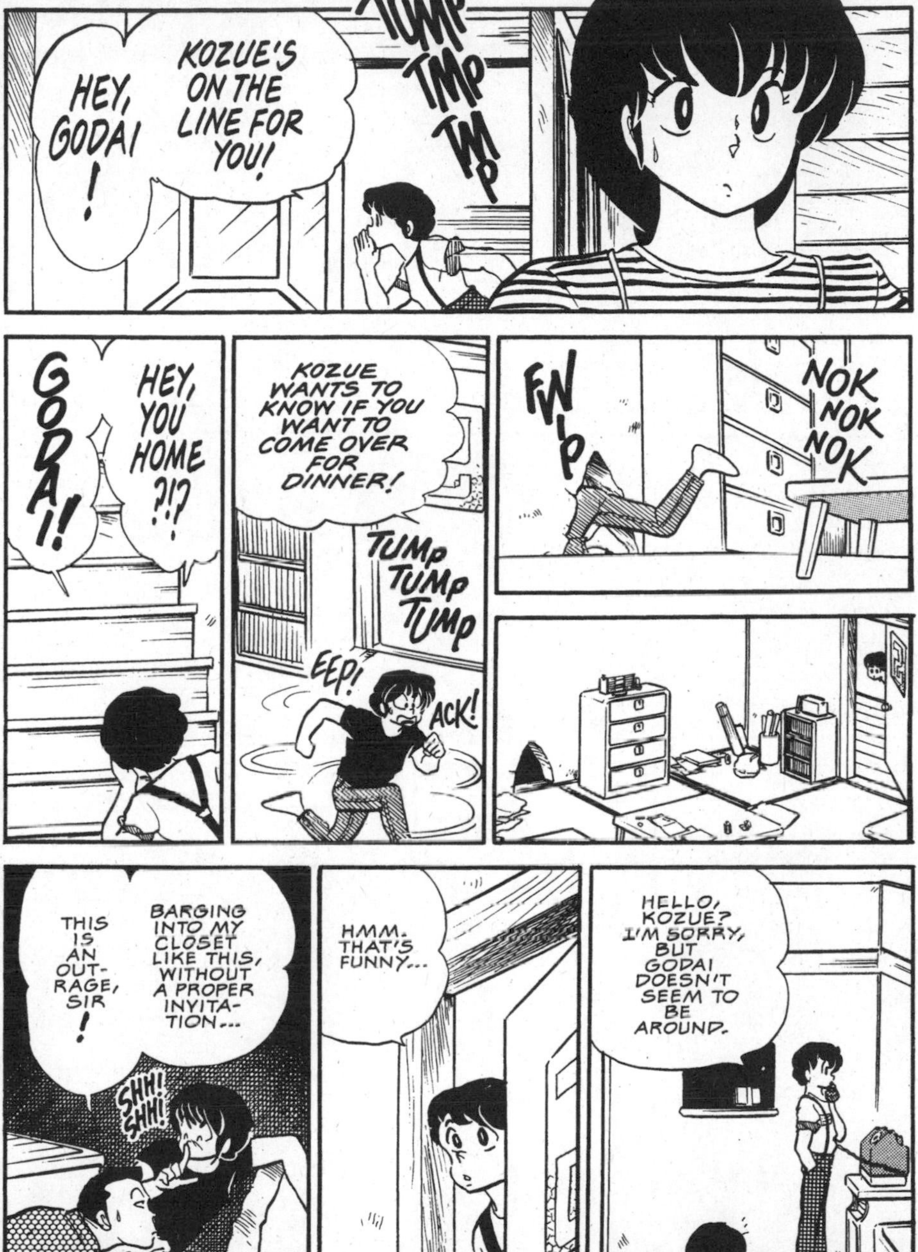
HEY, GODAI!
KOZUE'S ON THE LINE FOR YOU!
TUMP TMP TMP
GODAI!
HEY, YOU HOME ?!?
KOZUE WANTS TO KNOW IF YOU WANT TO COME OVER FOR DINNER!
TUMP TUMP TUMP
EEP!
ACK!
FWIP
NOK NOK NOK
THIS IS AN OUTRAGE, SIR!
BARGING INTO MY CLOSET LIKE THIS, WITHOUT A PROPER INVITATION...
SHH! SHH!
HMM. THAT'S FUNNY...
HELLO, KOZUE? I'M SORRY, BUT GODAI DOESN'T SEEM TO BE AROUND.

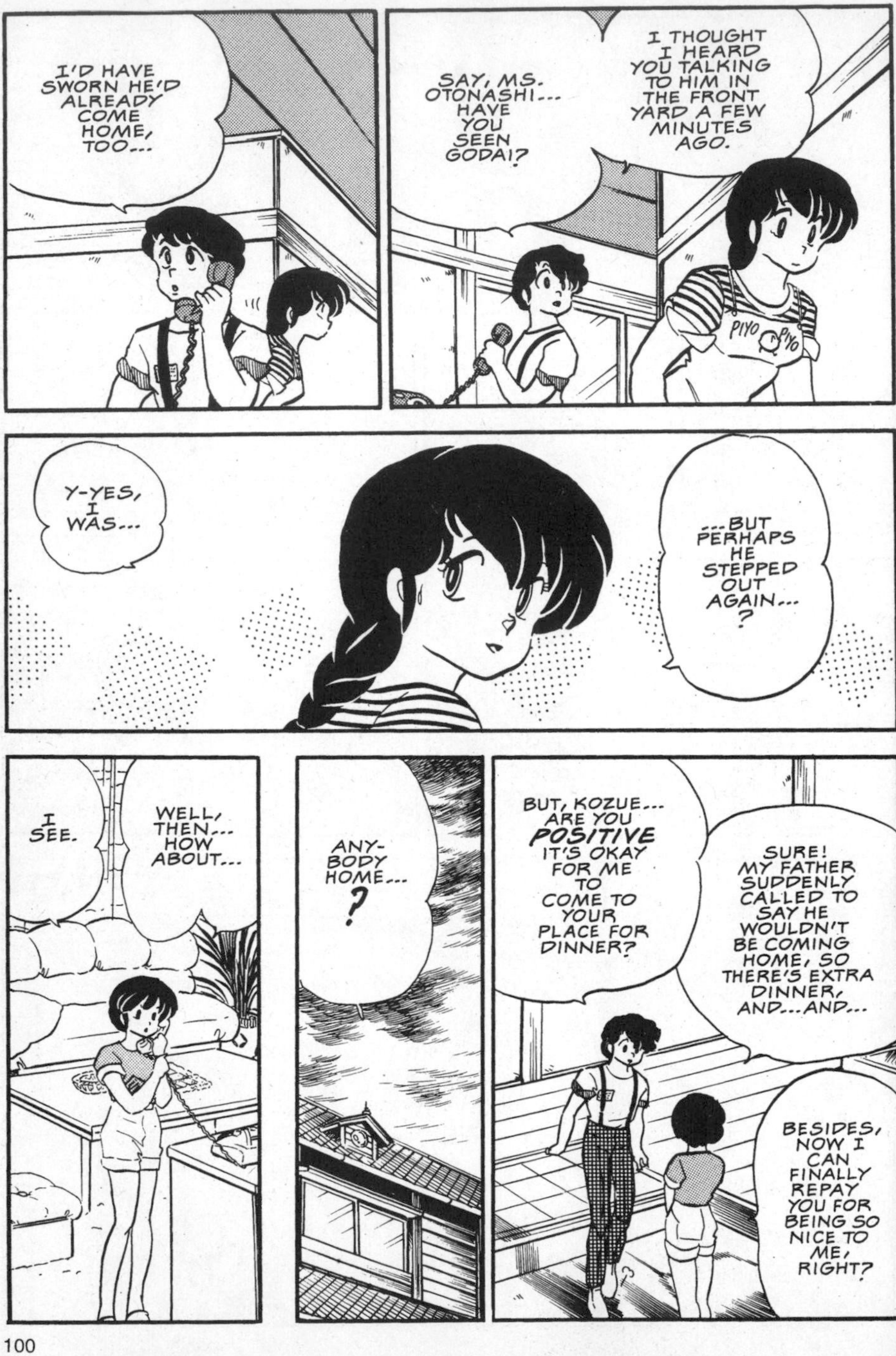
I'D HAVE SWORN HE'D ALREADY COME HOME, TOO...
SAY, MS. OTONASHI... HAVE YOU SEEN GODAI?
I THOUGHT I HEARD YOU TALKING TO HIM IN THE FRONT YARD A FEW MINUTES AGO.
PIYO PIYO
Y-YES, I WAS...
...BUT PERHAPS HE STEPPED OUT AGAIN...?
I SEE.
WELL, THEN... HOW ABOUT...
ANY-BODY HOME...?
BUT, KOZUE... ARE YOU *POSITIVE* IT'S OKAY FOR ME TO COME TO YOUR PLACE FOR DINNER?
SURE! MY FATHER SUDDENLY CALLED TO SAY HE WOULDN'T BE COMING HOME, SO THERE'S EXTRA DINNER, AND...AND...
BESIDES, NOW I CAN FINALLY REPAY YOU FOR BEING SO NICE TO ME, RIGHT?

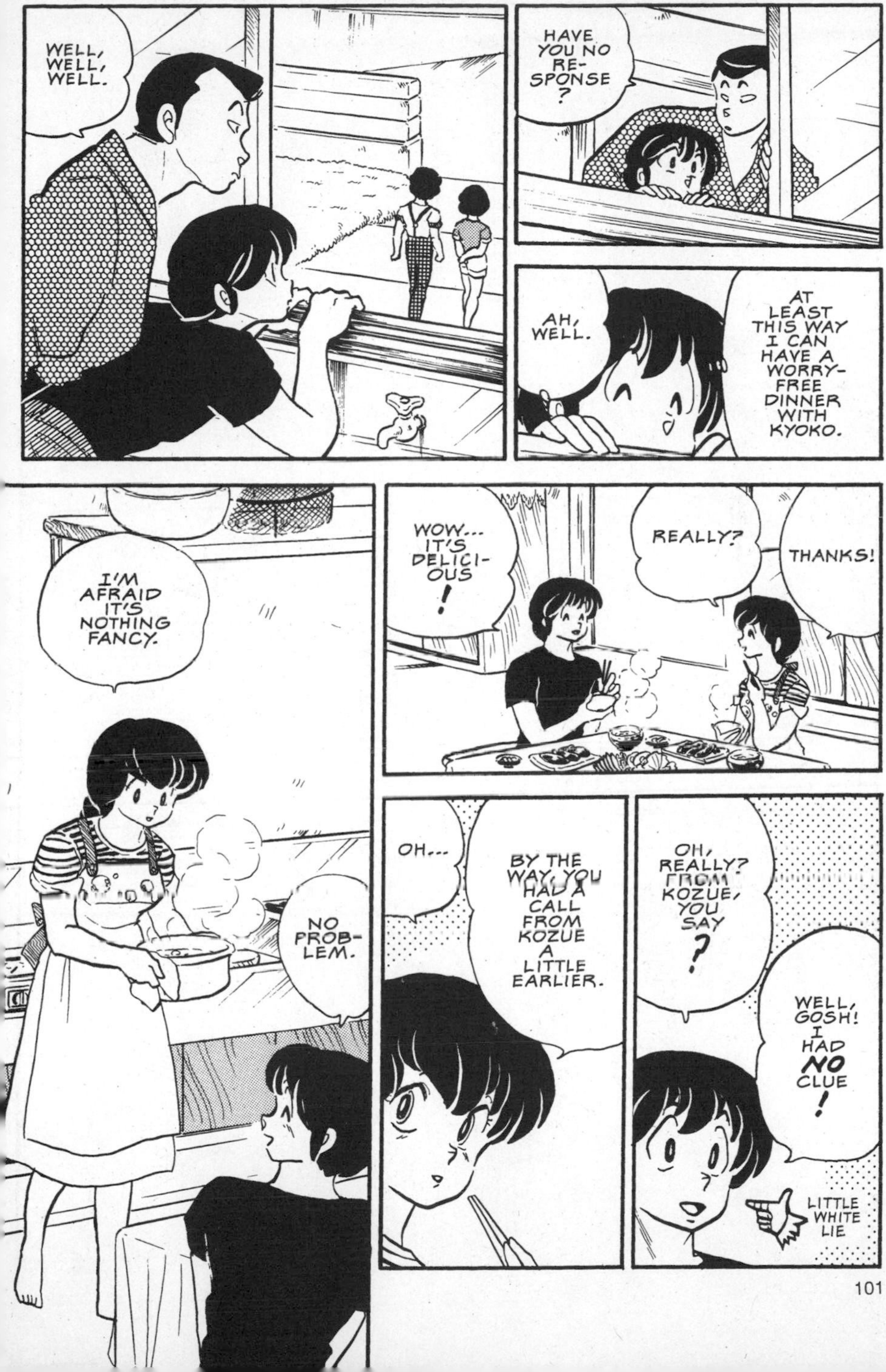
WELL, WELL, WELL.
HAVE YOU NO RE-SPONSE ?
AH, WELL.
AT LEAST THIS WAY I CAN HAVE A WORRY-FREE DINNER WITH KYOKO.
I'M AFRAID IT'S NOTHING FANCY.
NO PROB-LEM.
WOW... IT'S DELICI-OUS !
REALLY?
THANKS!
OH...
BY THE WAY, YOU HAD A CALL FROM KOZUE A LITTLE EARLIER.
OH, REALLY? FROM KOZUE, YOU SAY ?
WELL, GOSH! I HAD NO CLUE !
LITTLE WHITE LIE

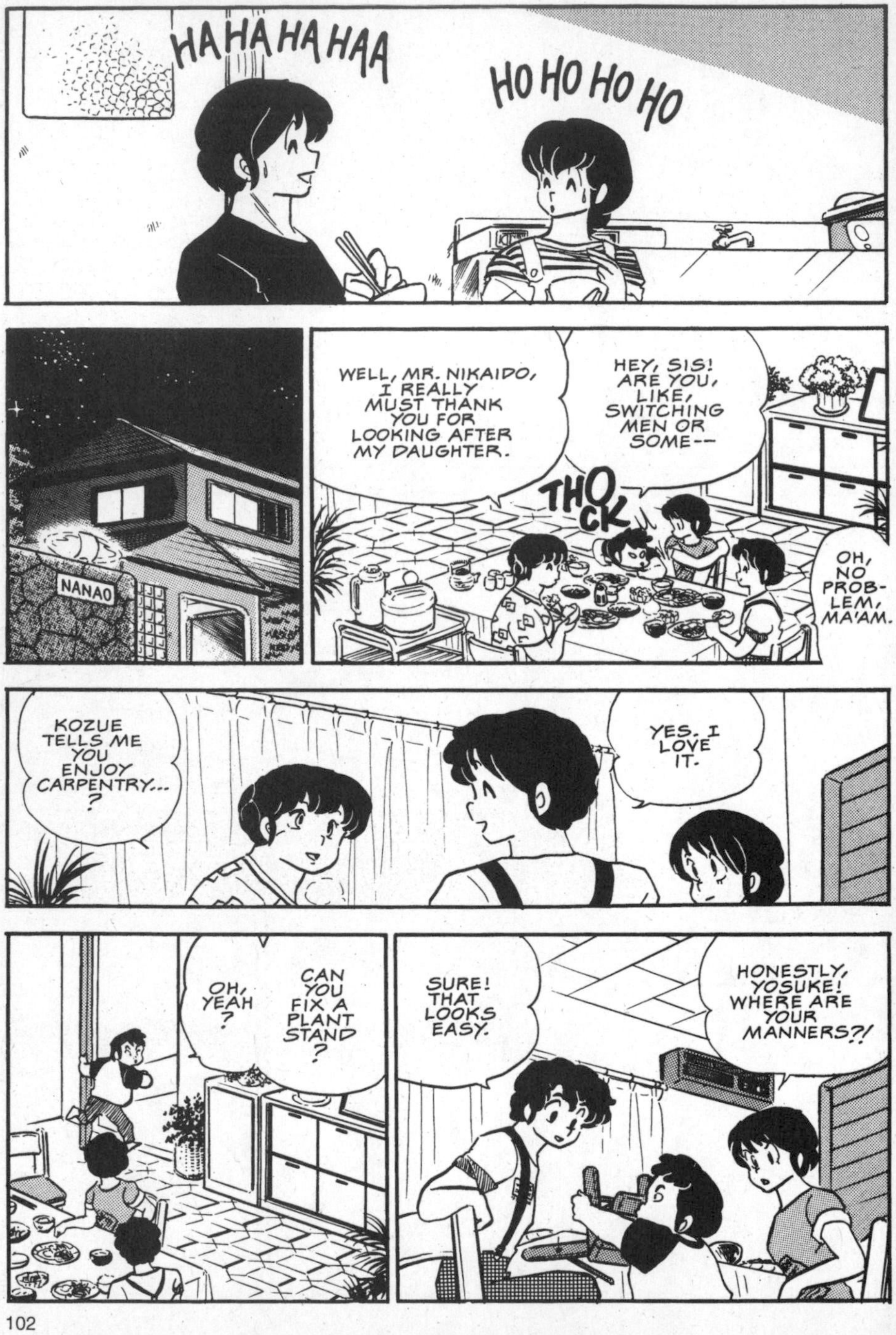
HAHAHAHAA
HO HO HO HO
WELL, MR. NIKAIDO, I REALLY MUST THANK YOU FOR LOOKING AFTER MY DAUGHTER.
HEY, SIS! ARE YOU, LIKE, SWITCHING MEN OR SOME--
THOCK
OH, NO PROBLEM, MA'AM.
NANAO
KOZUE TELLS ME YOU ENJOY CARPENTRY...?
YES. I LOVE IT.
OH, YEAH?
CAN YOU FIX A PLANT STAND?
SURE! THAT LOOKS EASY.
HONESTLY, YOSUKE! WHERE ARE YOUR MANNERS?!

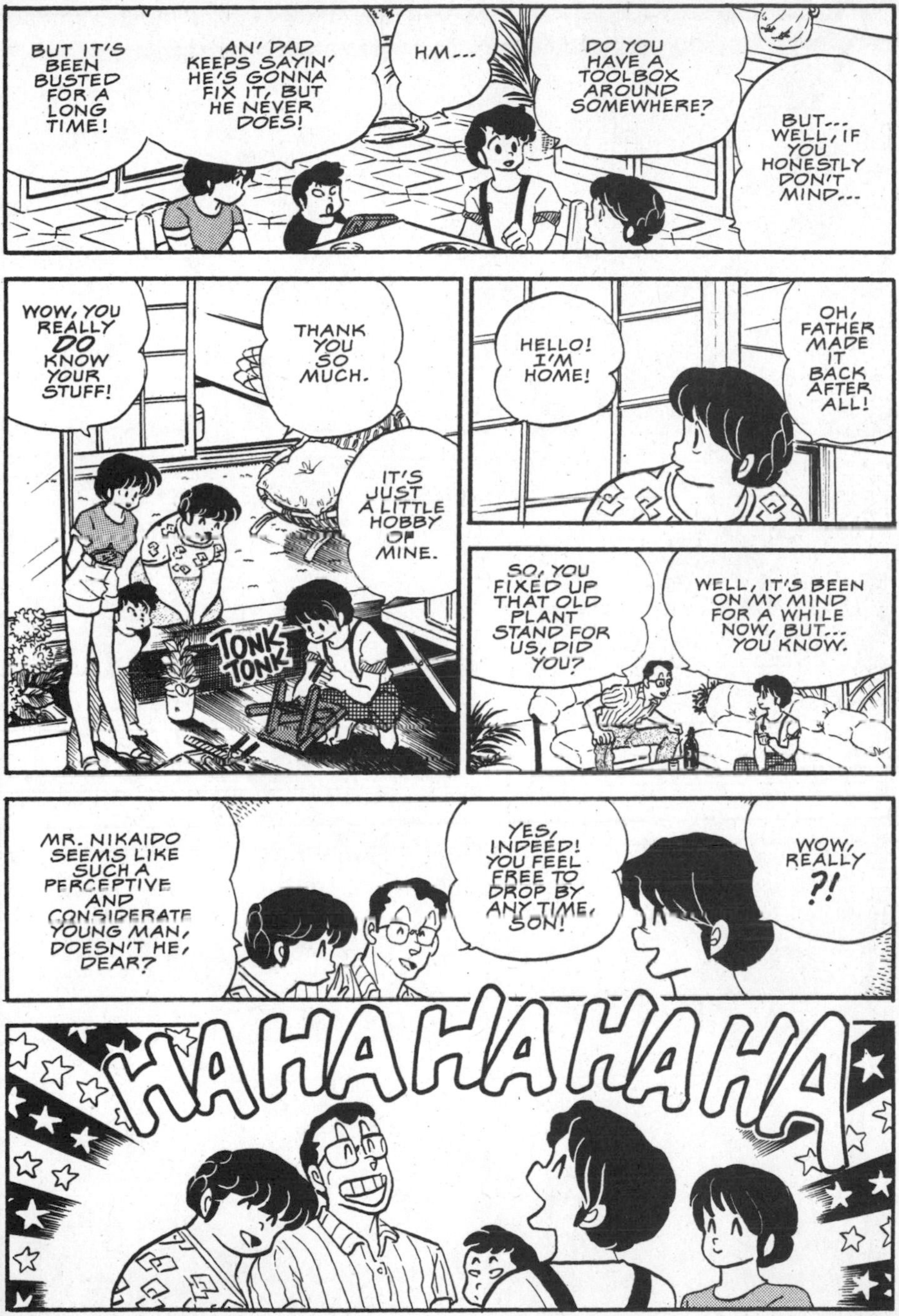
BUT IT'S BEEN BUSTED FOR A LONG TIME!
AN' DAD KEEPS SAYIN' HE'S GONNA FIX IT, BUT HE NEVER DOES!
HM...
DO YOU HAVE A TOOLBOX AROUND SOMEWHERE?
BUT... WELL, IF YOU HONESTLY DON'T MIND...
WOW, YOU REALLY DO KNOW YOUR STUFF!
THANK YOU SO MUCH.
IT'S JUST A LITTLE HOBBY OF MINE.
TONK TONK
HELLO! I'M HOME!
OH, FATHER MADE IT BACK AFTER ALL!
SO, YOU FIXED UP THAT OLD PLANT STAND FOR US, DID YOU?
WELL, IT'S BEEN ON MY MIND FOR A WHILE NOW, BUT... YOU KNOW.
MR. NIKAIDO SEEMS LIKE SUCH A PERCEPTIVE AND CONSIDERATE YOUNG MAN, DOESN'T HE, DEAR?
YES, INDEED! YOU FEEL FREE TO DROP BY ANY TIME, SON!
WOW, REALLY ?!
HAHAHAHAHAHA

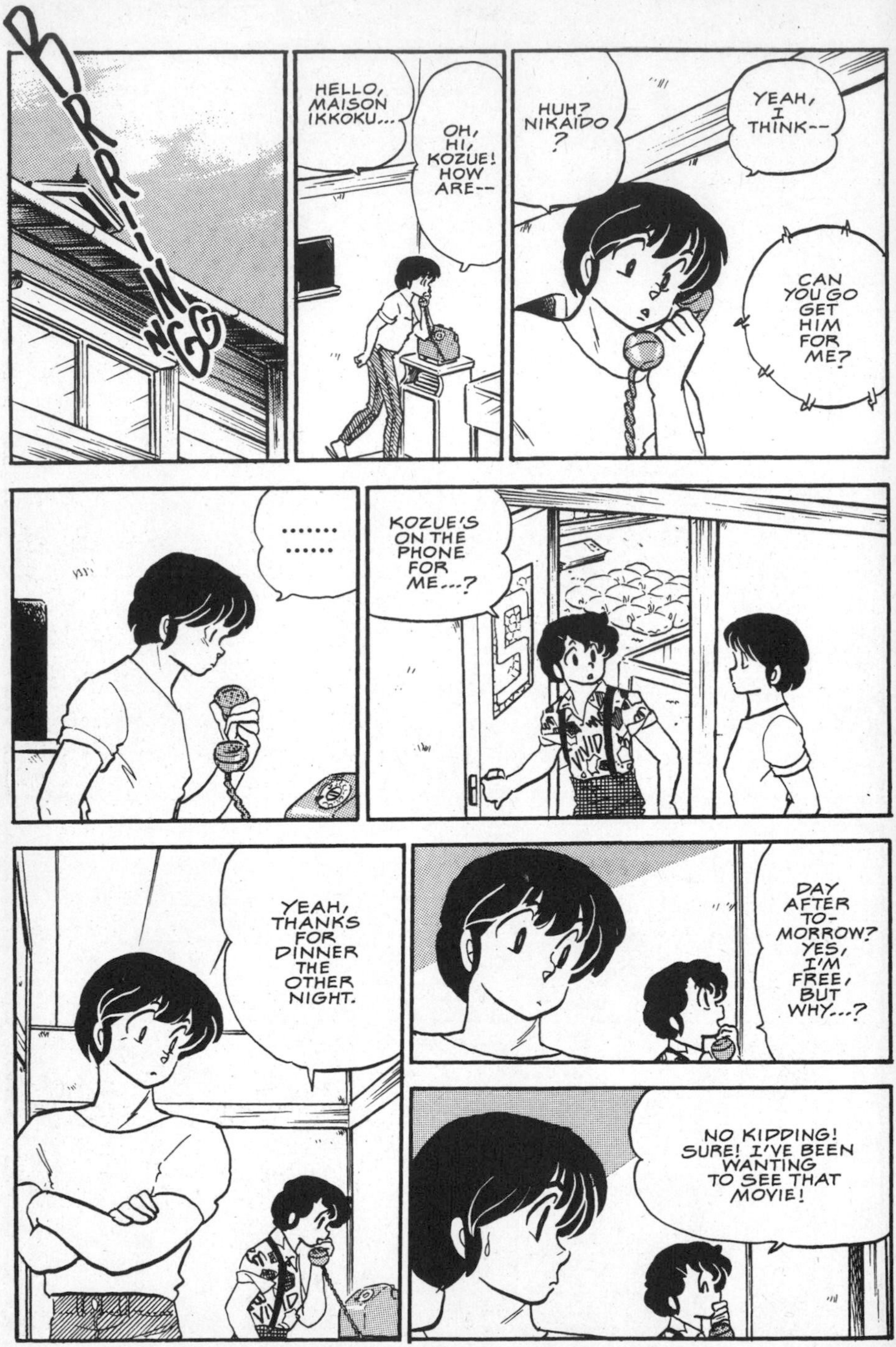
BRRRIIINNGG
HELLO, MAISON IKKOKU...
OH, HI, KOZUE! HOW ARE--
HUH? NIKAIDO?
YEAH, I THINK--
CAN YOU GO GET HIM FOR ME?
....
....
KOZUE'S ON THE PHONE FOR ME...?
YEAH, THANKS FOR DINNER THE OTHER NIGHT.
DAY AFTER TO-MORROW? YES, I'M FREE, BUT WHY...?
NO KIDDING! SURE! I'VE BEEN WANTING TO SEE THAT MOVIE!

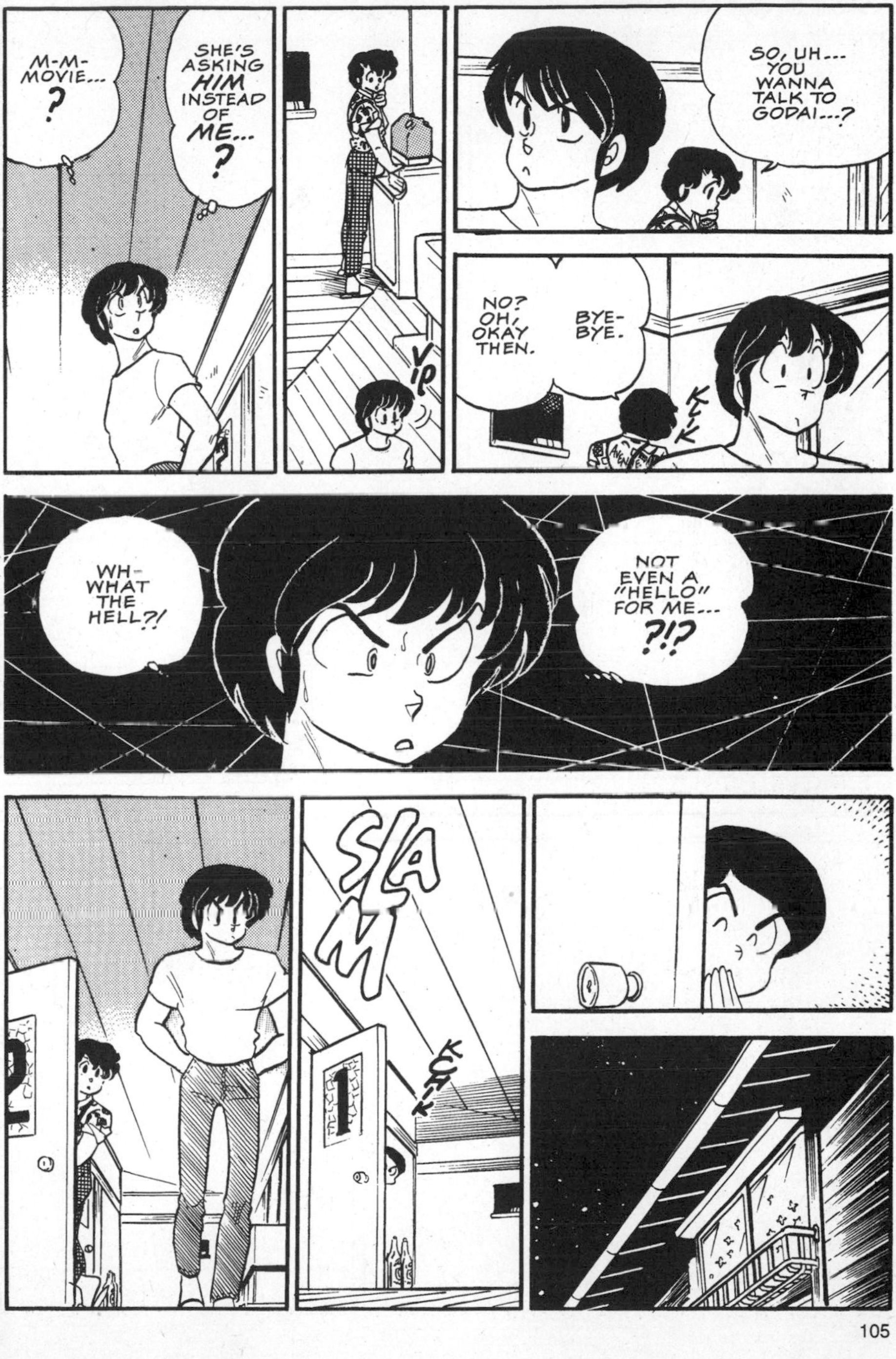
M-M-MOVIE...?
SHE'S ASKING HIM INSTEAD OF ME...?
VIP
SO, UH... YOU WANNA TALK TO GODAI...?
NO? OH, OKAY THEN.
BYE-BYE.
WH-WHAT THE HELL?!
NOT EVEN A "HELLO" FOR ME...?!?
SLAM

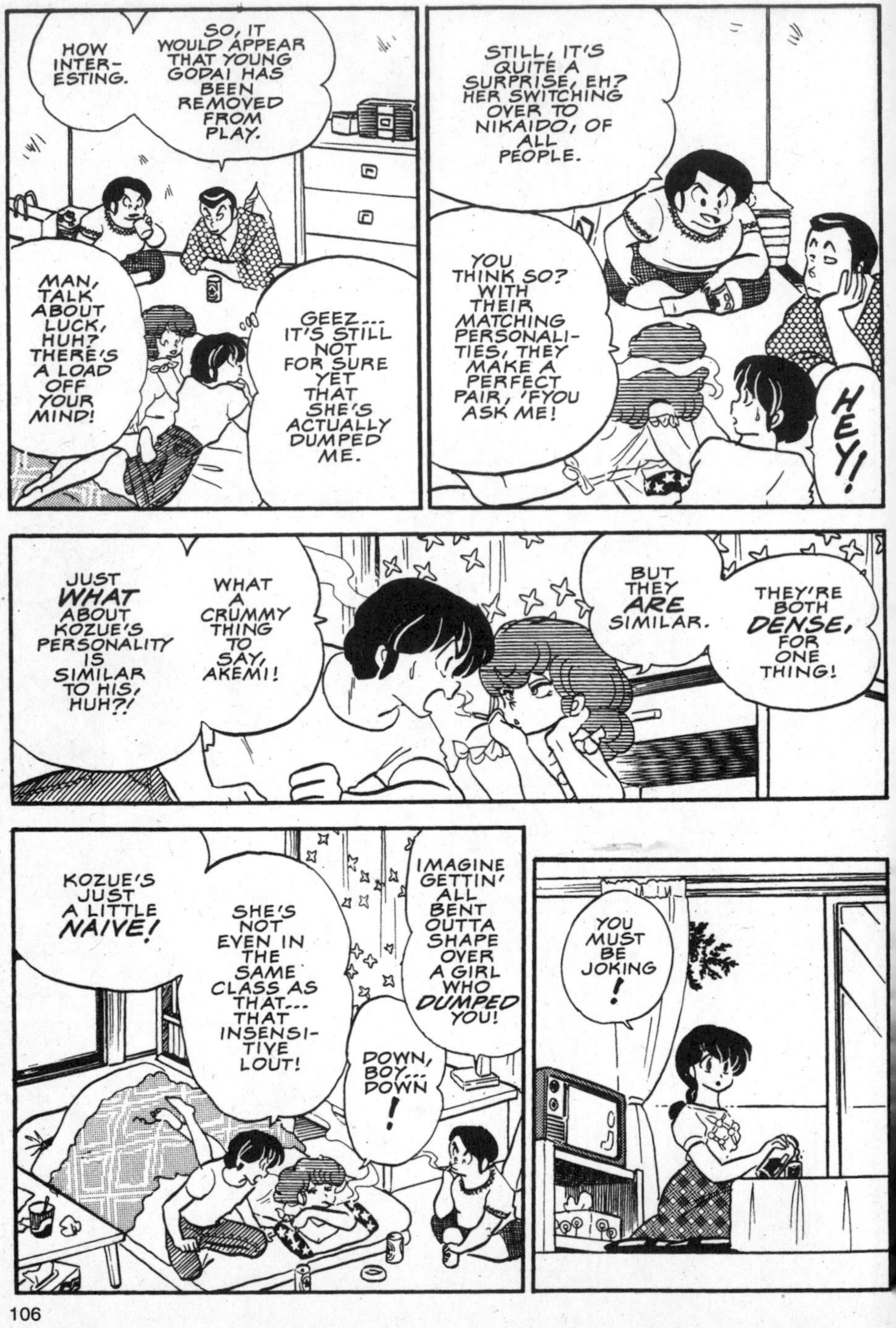
HOW INTER-ESTING.
SO, IT WOULD APPEAR THAT YOUNG GODAI HAS BEEN REMOVED FROM PLAY.
MAN, TALK ABOUT LUCK, HUH? THERE'S A LOAD OFF YOUR MIND!
GEEZ... IT'S STILL NOT FOR SURE YET THAT SHE'S ACTUALLY DUMPED ME.
STILL, IT'S QUITE A SURPRISE, EH? HER SWITCHING OVER TO NIKAIDO, OF ALL PEOPLE.
YOU THINK SO? WITH THEIR MATCHING PERSONALI-TIES, THEY MAKE A PERFECT PAIR, 'FYOU ASK ME!
HEY!
JUST WHAT ABOUT KOZUE'S PERSONALITY IS SIMILAR TO HIS, HUH?!
WHAT A CRUMMY THING TO SAY, AKEMI!
BUT THEY ARE SIMILAR.
THEY'RE BOTH DENSE, FOR ONE THING!
KOZUE'S JUST A LITTLE NAIVE!
SHE'S NOT EVEN IN THE SAME CLASS AS THAT... THAT INSENSI-TIVE LOUT!
IMAGINE GETTIN' ALL BENT OUTTA SHAPE OVER A GIRL WHO DUMPED YOU!
DOWN, BOY... DOWN!
YOU MUST BE JOKING!

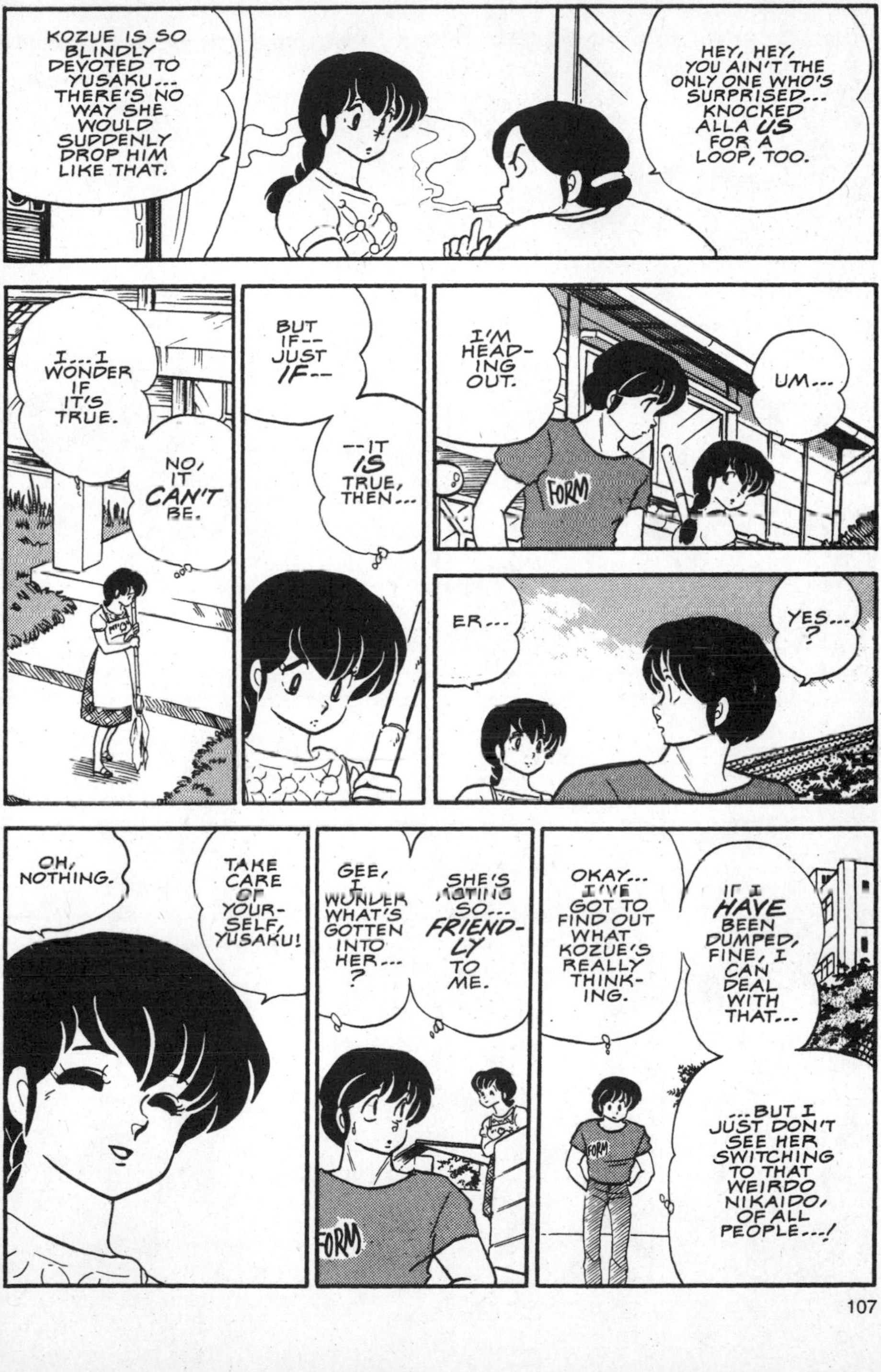
KOZUE IS SO BLINDLY DEVOTED TO YUSAKU... THERE'S NO WAY SHE WOULD SUDDENLY DROP HIM LIKE THAT.
HEY, HEY, YOU AIN'T THE ONLY ONE WHO'S SURPRISED... KNOCKED ALLA *US* FOR A LOOP, TOO.
I... I WONDER IF IT'S TRUE.
NO, IT *CAN'T* BE.
BUT IF-- JUST *IF*--
--IT *IS* TRUE, THEN...
I'M HEADING OUT.
UM...
ER...
YES...?
OH, NOTHING.
TAKE CARE OF YOURSELF, YUSAKU!
GEE, I WONDER WHAT'S GOTTEN INTO HER...?
SHE'S ACTING SO... *FRIENDLY* TO ME.
OKAY... I'VE GOT TO FIND OUT WHAT KOZUE'S REALLY THINKING.
IF I *HAVE* BEEN DUMPED, FINE, I CAN DEAL WITH THAT...
...BUT I JUST DON'T SEE HER SWITCHING TO THAT WEIRDO NIKAIDO, OF ALL PEOPLE...!

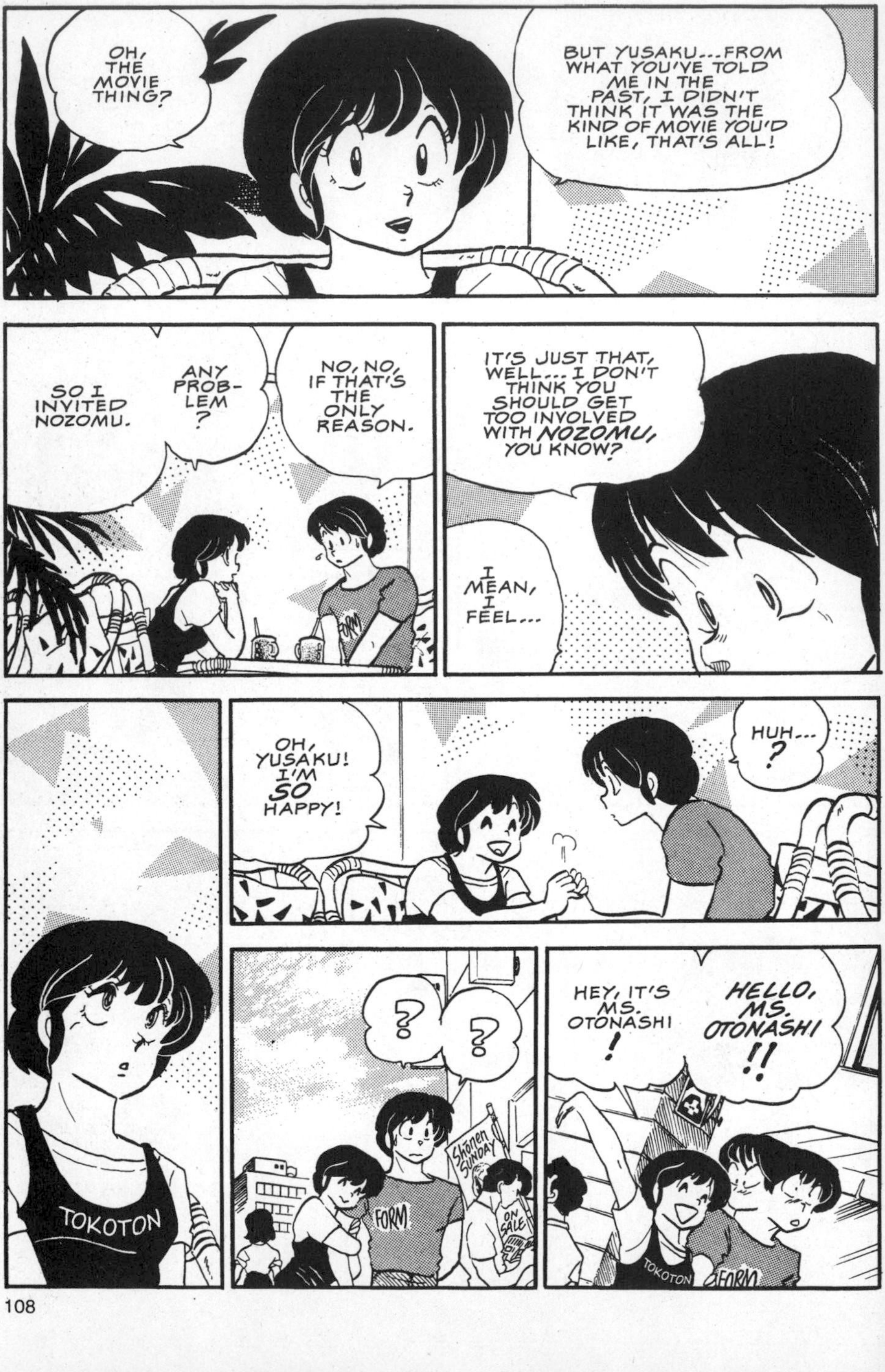
OH, THE MOVIE THING?
BUT YUSAKU...FROM WHAT YOU'VE TOLD ME IN THE PAST, I DIDN'T THINK IT WAS THE KIND OF MOVIE YOU'D LIKE, THAT'S ALL!
SO I INVITED NOZOMU.
ANY PROB-LEM?
NO, NO, IF THAT'S THE ONLY REASON.
FORM
IT'S JUST THAT, WELL... I DON'T THINK YOU SHOULD GET TOO INVOLVED WITH NOZOMU, YOU KNOW?
I MEAN, I FEEL...
TOKOTON
OH, YUSAKU! I'M SO HAPPY!
HUH...?
?
?
FORM
Shōnen SUNDAY
ON SALE
HEY, IT'S MS. OTONASHI!
HELLO, MS. OTONASHI!!
TOKOTON
FORM

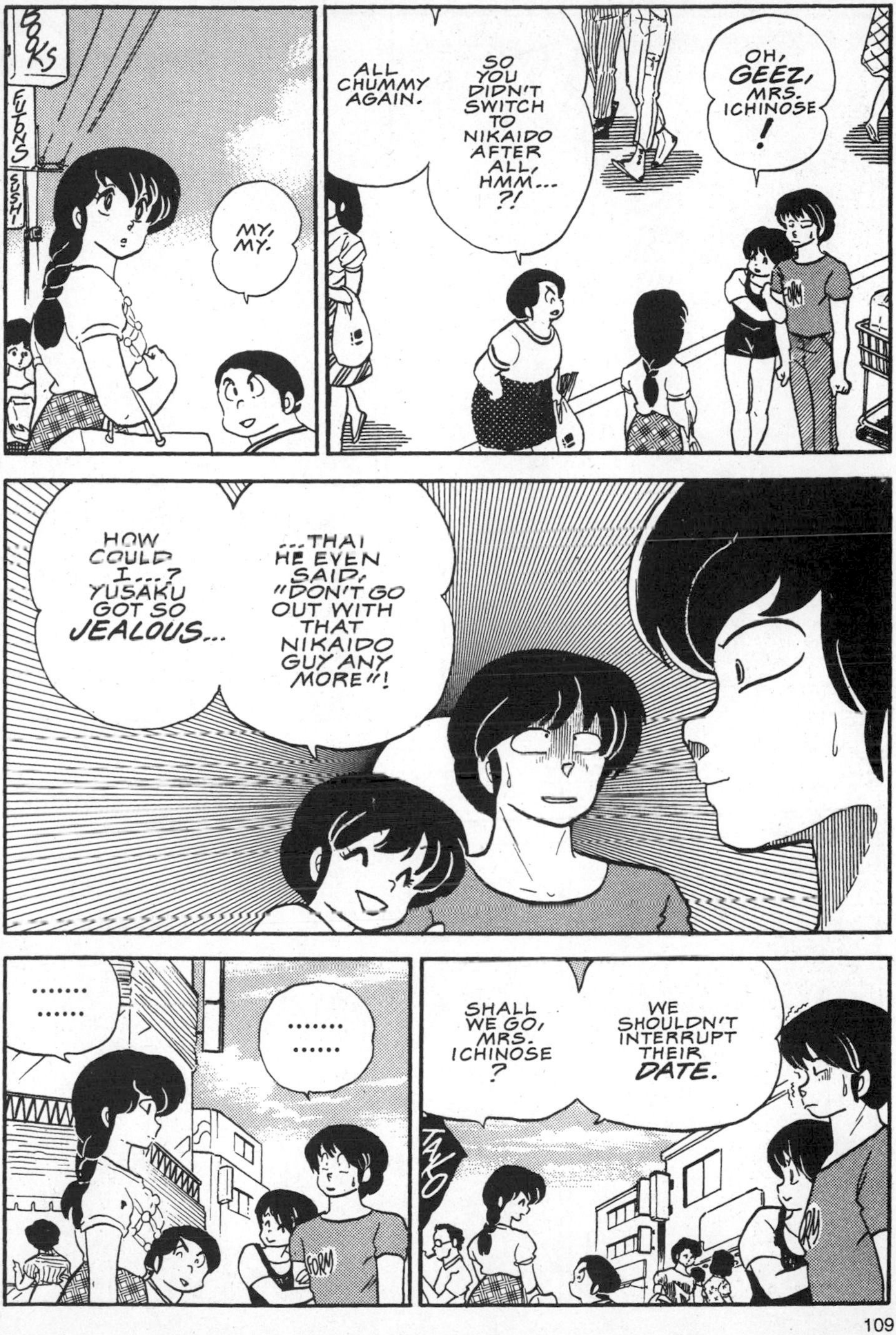
BOOKS
FUTONS
SUSHI
MY, MY.
ALL CHUMMY AGAIN.
SO YOU DIDN'T SWITCH TO NIKAIDO AFTER ALL, HMM...?!
OH, GEEZ, MRS. ICHINOSE!
FORM
HOW COULD I...? YUSAKU GOT SO JEALOUS...
...THAT HE EVEN SAID, "DON'T GO OUT WITH THAT NIKAIDO GUY ANY MORE"!
....
....
FORM
SHALL WE GO, MRS. ICHINOSE?
WE SHOULDN'T INTERRUPT THEIR DATE.

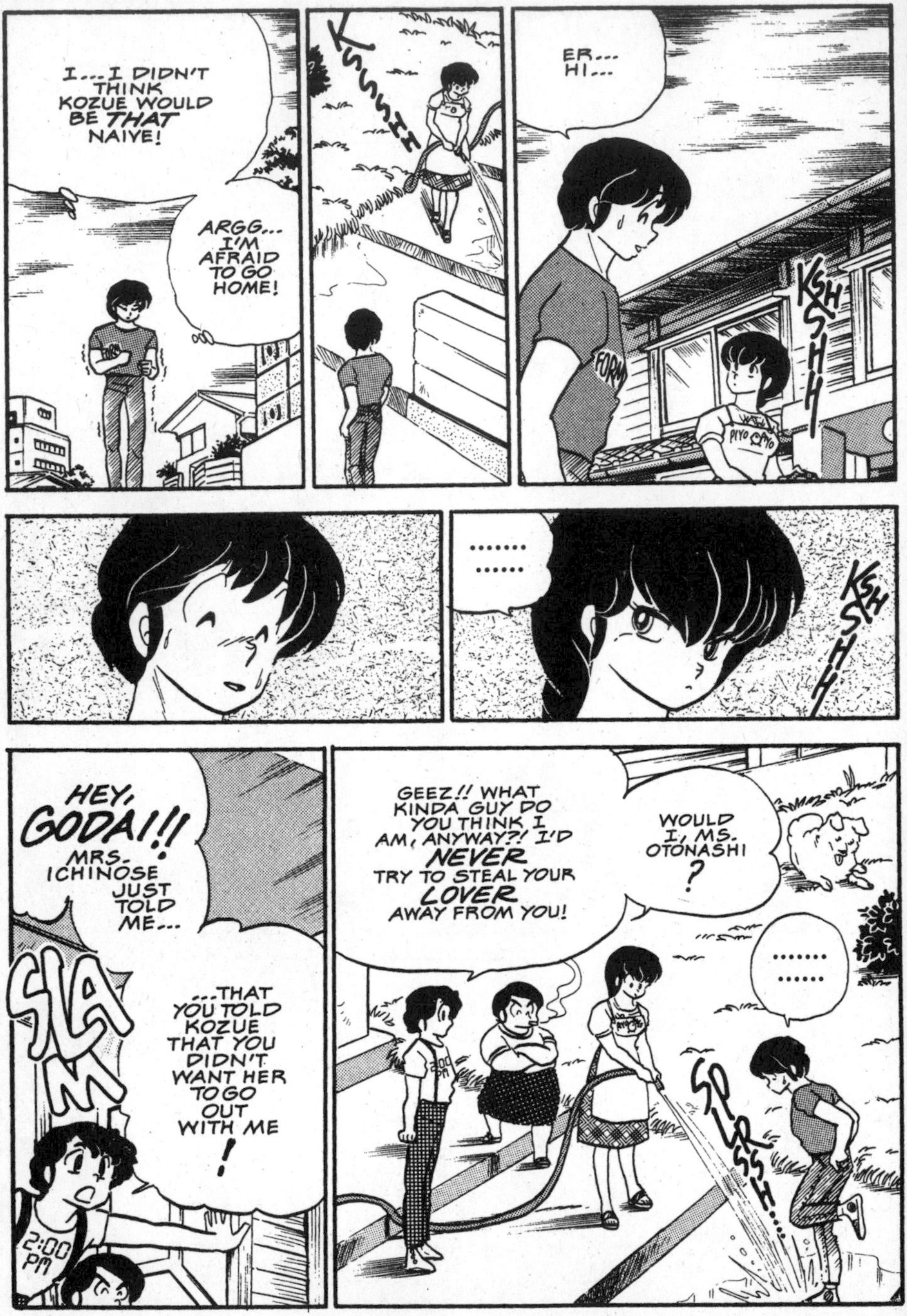
I...I DIDN'T THINK KOZUE WOULD BE THAT NAIYE!
ARGG... I'M AFRAID TO GO HOME!
KSSSSHH
ER... HI...
KSHSHHH
....
......
KSHSHHH
HEY, GODAI!!! MRS. ICHINOSE JUST TOLD ME...
...THAT YOU TOLD KOZUE THAT YOU DIDN'T WANT HER TO GO OUT WITH ME!
SLAM
GEEZ!! WHAT KINDA GUY DO YOU THINK I AM, ANYWAY?! I'D NEVER TRY TO STEAL YOUR LOVER AWAY FROM YOU!
WOULD I, MS. OTONASHI?
....
......
SPLRSSH....

PART 6
NOTHING...NOTHING AT ALL!

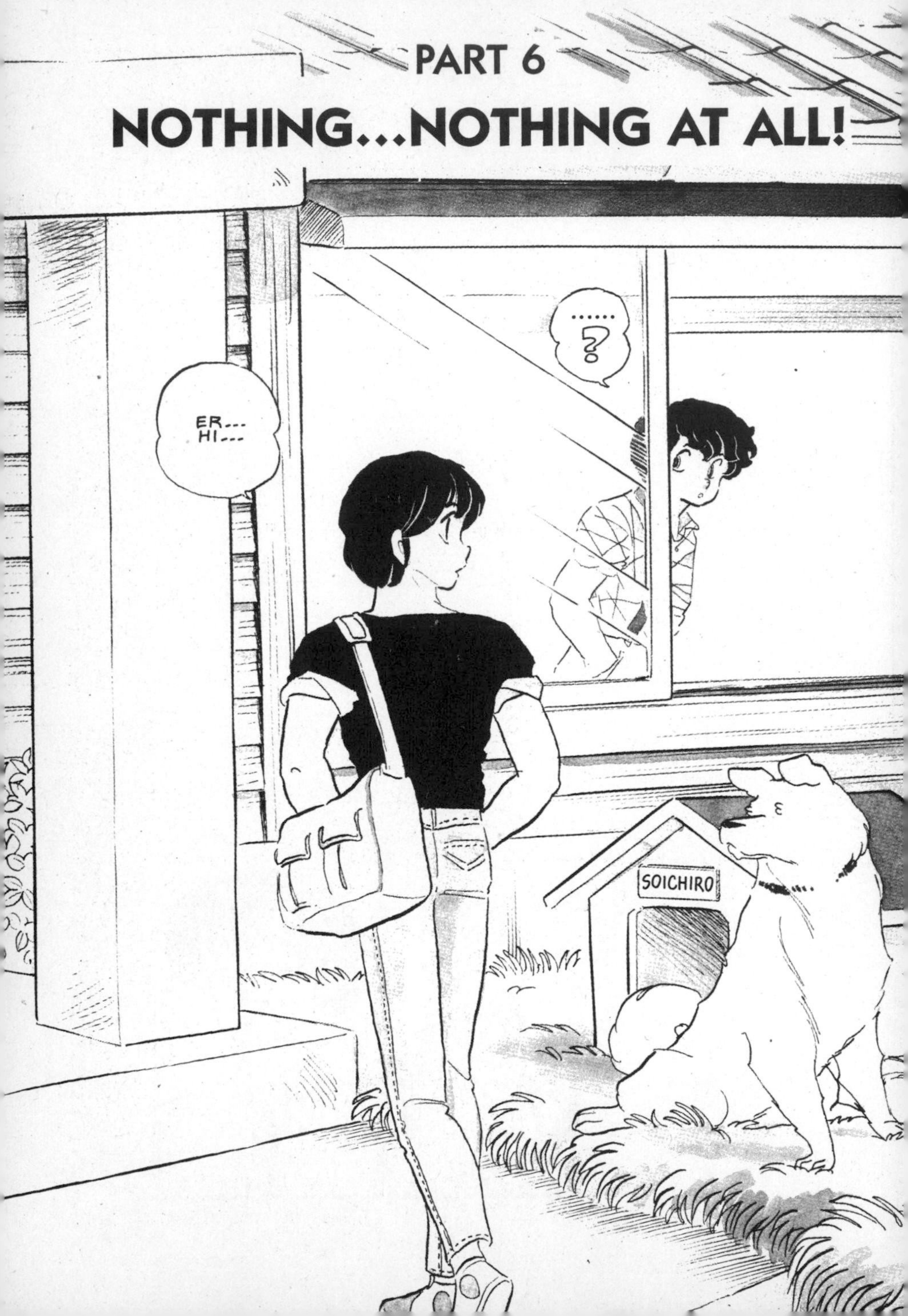
ER...
HI...
......
?
SOICHIRO

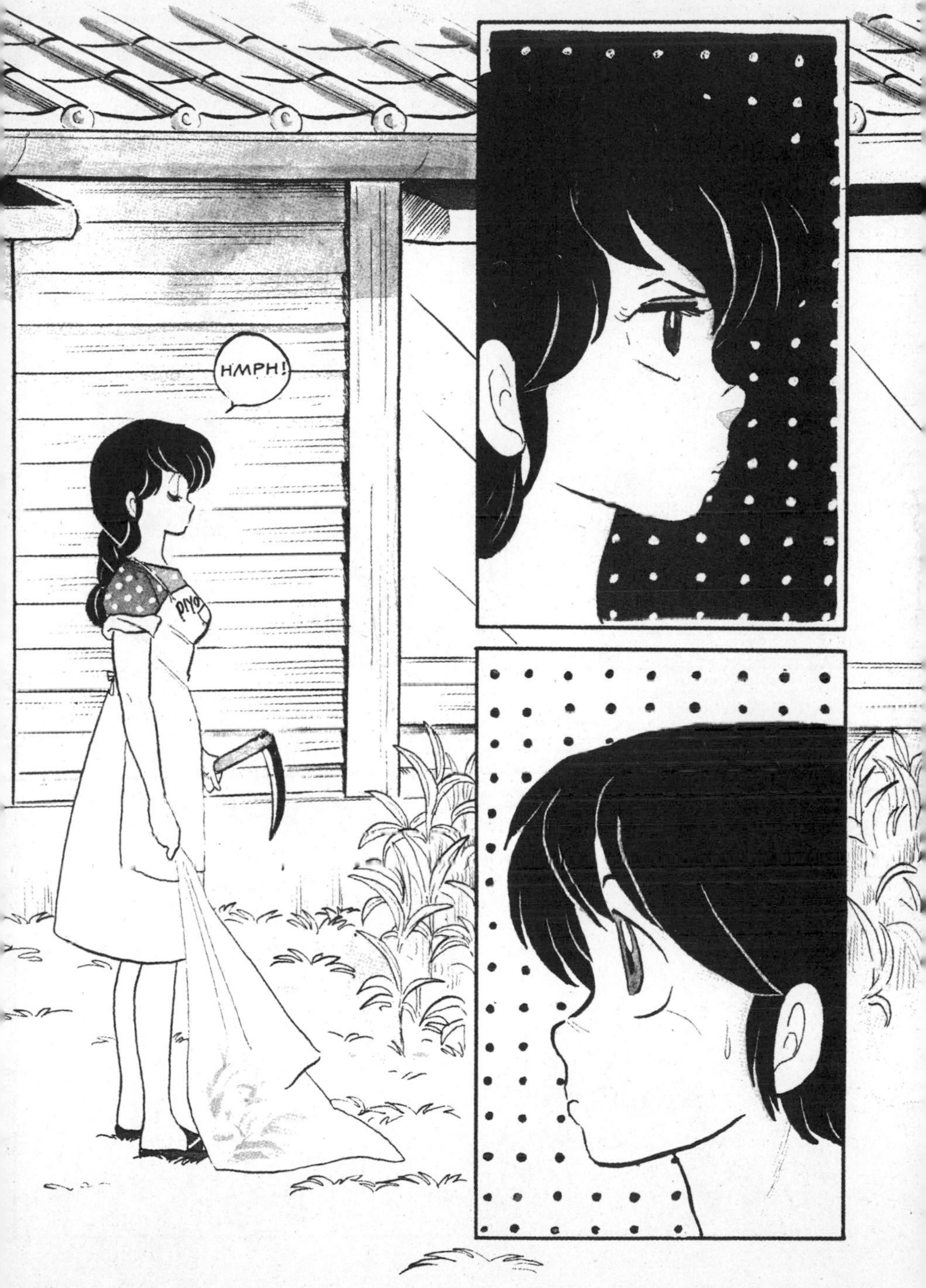
HMPH!
PIYO

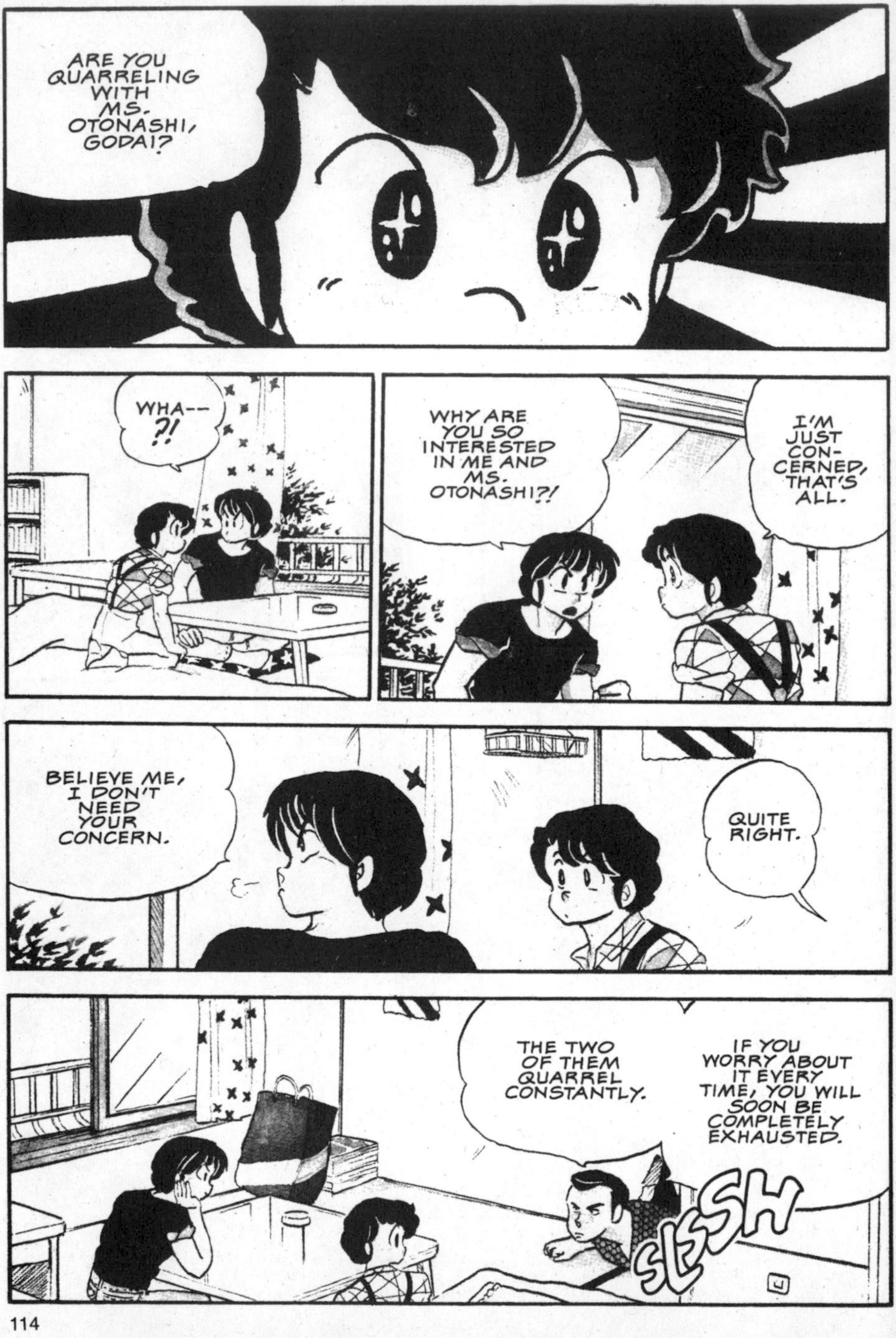
ARE YOU QUARRELING WITH MS. OTONASHI, GODAI!?
WHA-- ?!
WHY ARE YOU SO INTERESTED IN ME AND MS. OTONASHI!?!
I'M JUST CON-CERNED, THAT'S ALL.
BELIEVE ME, I DON'T NEED YOUR CONCERN.
QUITE RIGHT.
THE TWO OF THEM QUARREL CONSTANTLY.
IF YOU WORRY ABOUT IT EVERY TIME, YOU WILL SOON BE COMPLETELY EXHAUSTED.
SLSSH

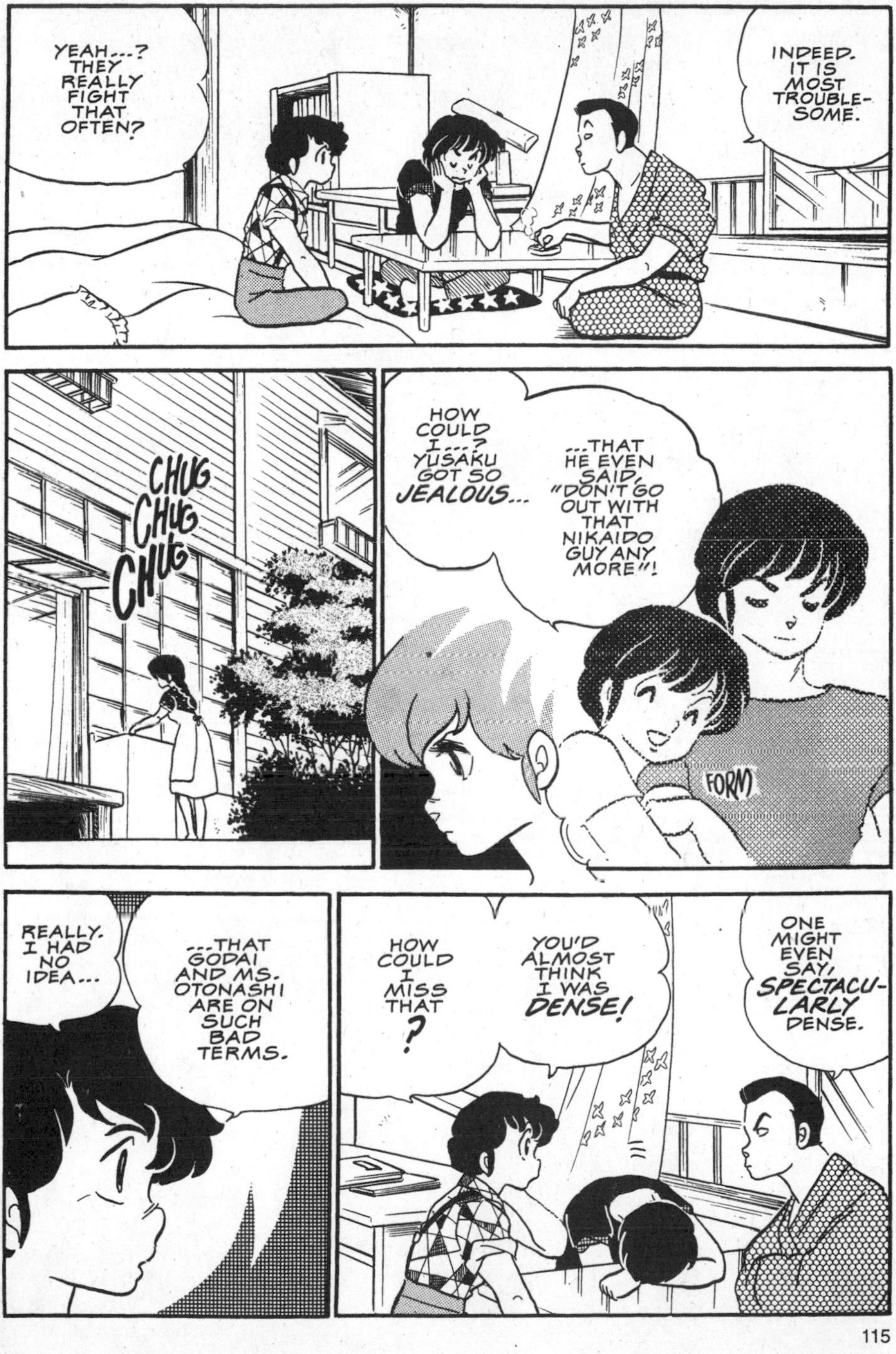
YEAH...? THEY REALLY FIGHT THAT OFTEN?
INDEED. IT IS MOST TROUBLE-SOME.
CHUG CHUG CHUG
HOW COULD I...? YUSAKU GOT SO JEALOUS...
...THAT HE EVEN SAID, "DON'T GO OUT WITH THAT NIKAIDO GUY ANY MORE"!
FORM
REALLY. I HAD NO IDEA...
...THAT GODAI AND MS. OTONASHI ARE ON SUCH BAD TERMS.
HOW COULD I MISS THAT ?
YOU'D ALMOST THINK I WAS DENSE!
ONE MIGHT EVEN SAY, SPECTACU-LARLY DENSE.

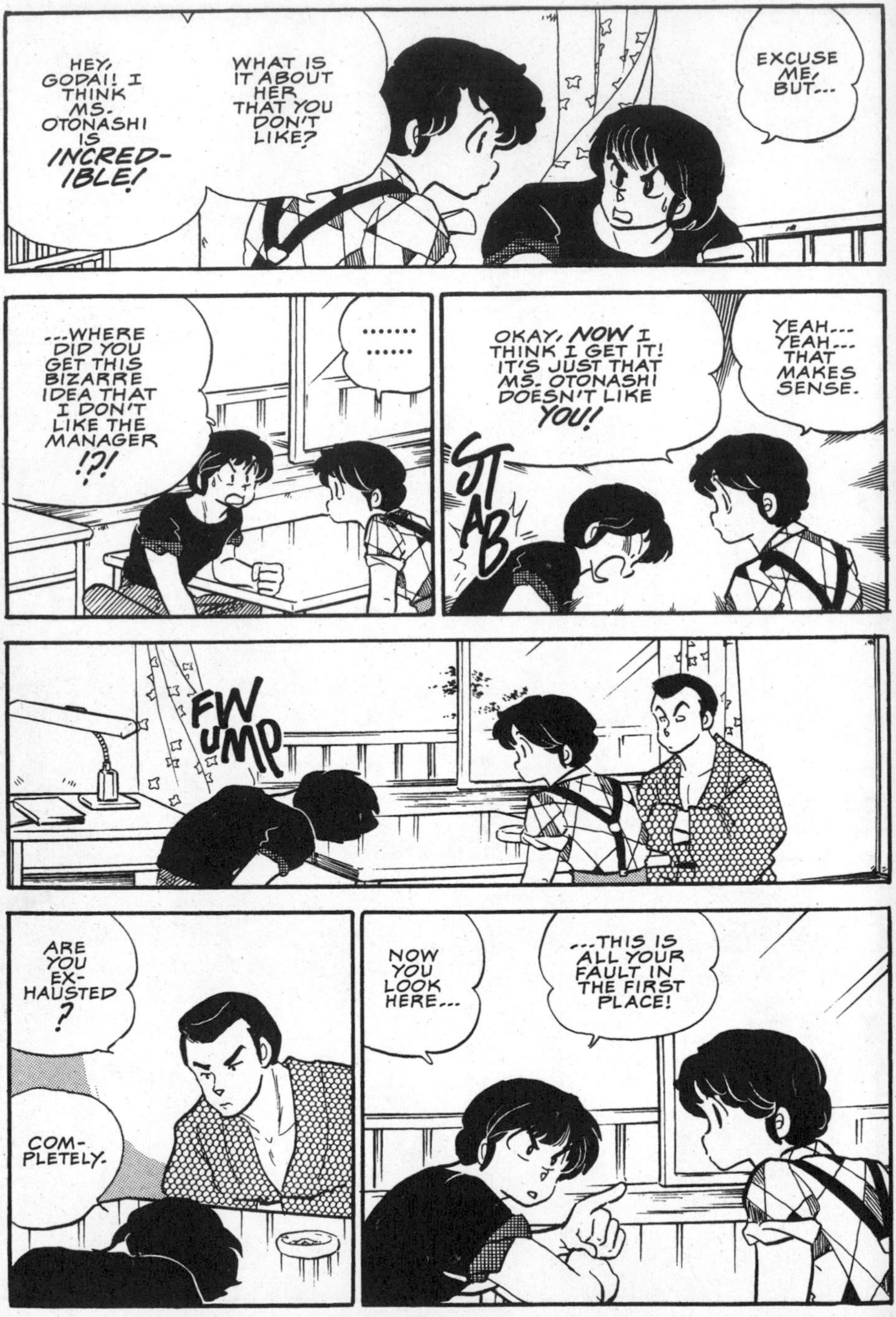
HEY, GODAI! I THINK MS. OTONASHI IS INCREDIBLE!
WHAT IS IT ABOUT HER THAT YOU DON'T LIKE?
EXCUSE ME, BUT...
...WHERE DID YOU GET THIS BIZARRE IDEA THAT I DON'T LIKE THE MANAGER !?!
....
......
STAB
OKAY, NOW I THINK I GET IT! IT'S JUST THAT MS. OTONASHI DOESN'T LIKE YOU!
YEAH... YEAH... THAT MAKES SENSE.
FWUMP
ARE YOU EX-HAUSTED ?
COM-PLETELY.
NOW YOU LOOK HERE...
...THIS IS ALL YOUR FAULT IN THE FIRST PLACE!

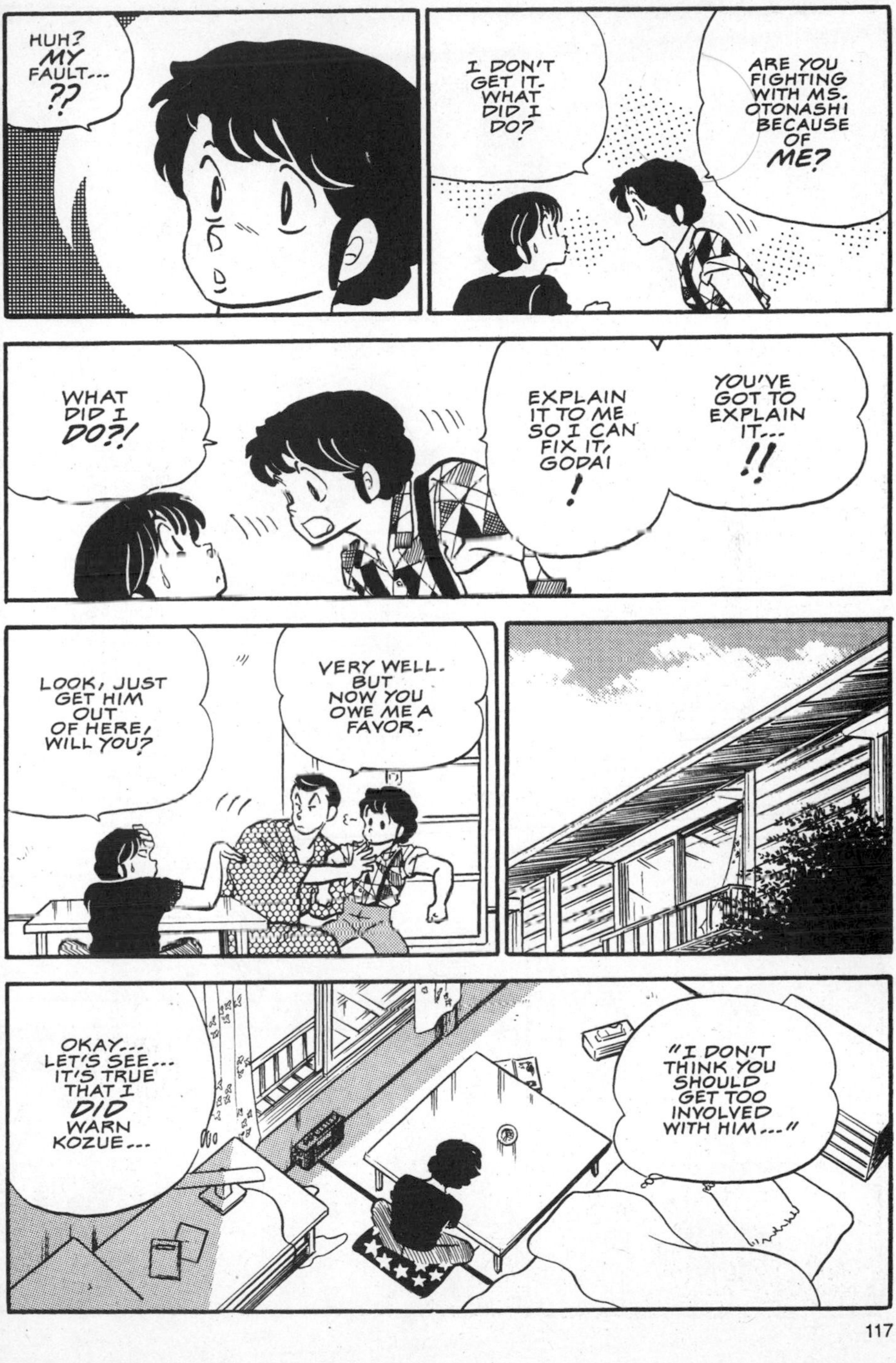
HUH? MY FAULT... ??
I DON'T GET IT. WHAT DID I DO?
ARE YOU FIGHTING WITH MS. OTONASHI BECAUSE OF ME?
WHAT DID I DO?!
EXPLAIN IT TO ME SO I CAN FIX IT, GODAI!
YOU'VE GOT TO EXPLAIN IT...!!
LOOK, JUST GET HIM OUT OF HERE, WILL YOU?
VERY WELL. BUT NOW YOU OWE ME A FAVOR.
OKAY... LET'S SEE... IT'S TRUE THAT I DID WARN KOZUE...
"I DON'T THINK YOU SHOULD GET TOO INVOLVED WITH HIM..."

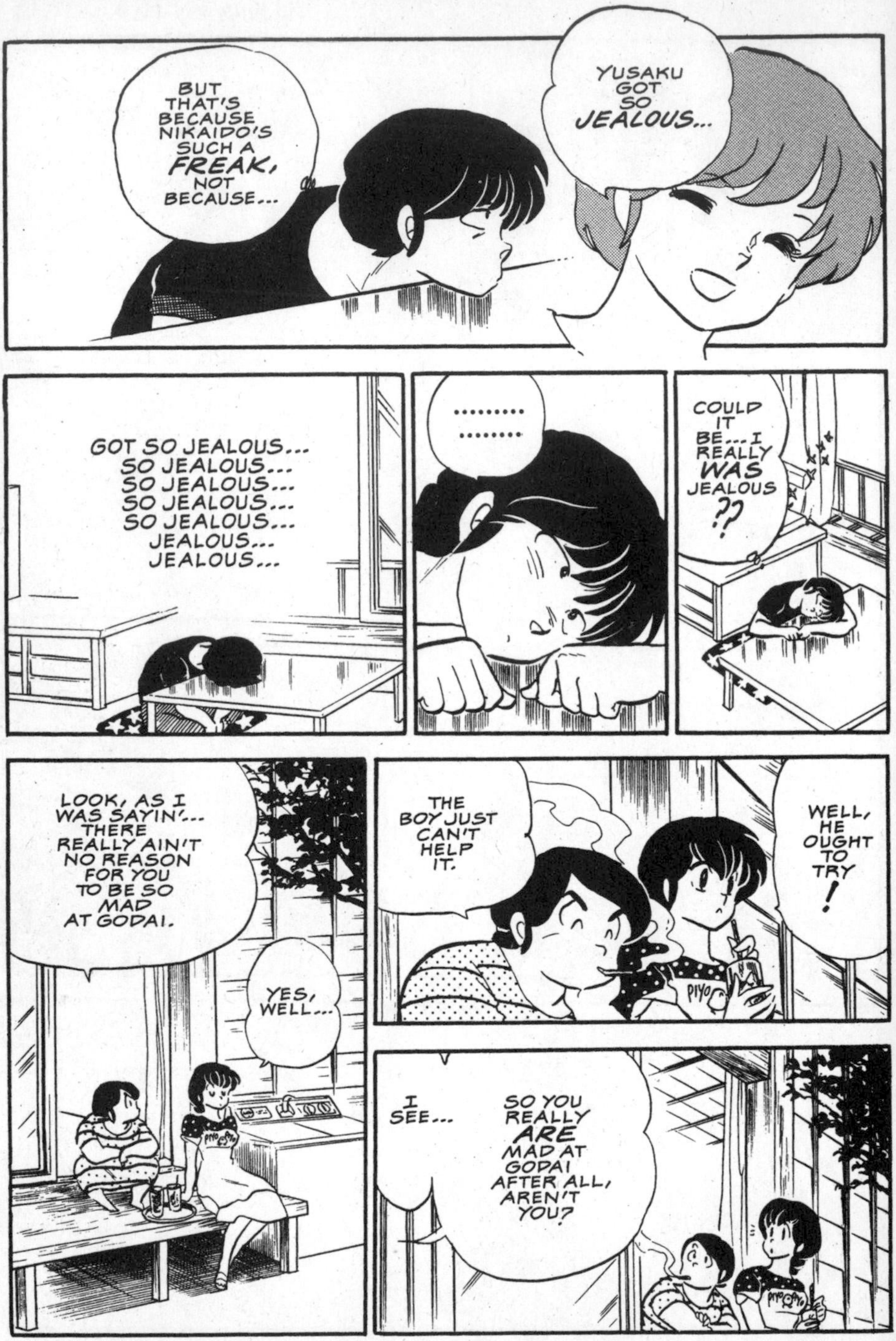
BUT THAT'S BECAUSE NIKAIDO'S SUCH A FREAK, NOT BECAUSE...
YUSAKU GOT SO JEALOUS...
GOT SO JEALOUS... SO JEALOUS... SO JEALOUS... SO JEALOUS... SO JEALOUS... JEALOUS... JEALOUS...
....
COULD IT BE... I REALLY WAS JEALOUS ??
LOOK, AS I WAS SAYIN'... THERE REALLY AIN'T NO REASON FOR YOU TO BE SO MAD AT GODAI.
YES, WELL...
THE BOY JUST CAN'T HELP IT.
WELL, HE OUGHT TO TRY!
PIYO
I SEE...
SO YOU REALLY ARE MAD AT GODAI AFTER ALL, AREN'T YOU?

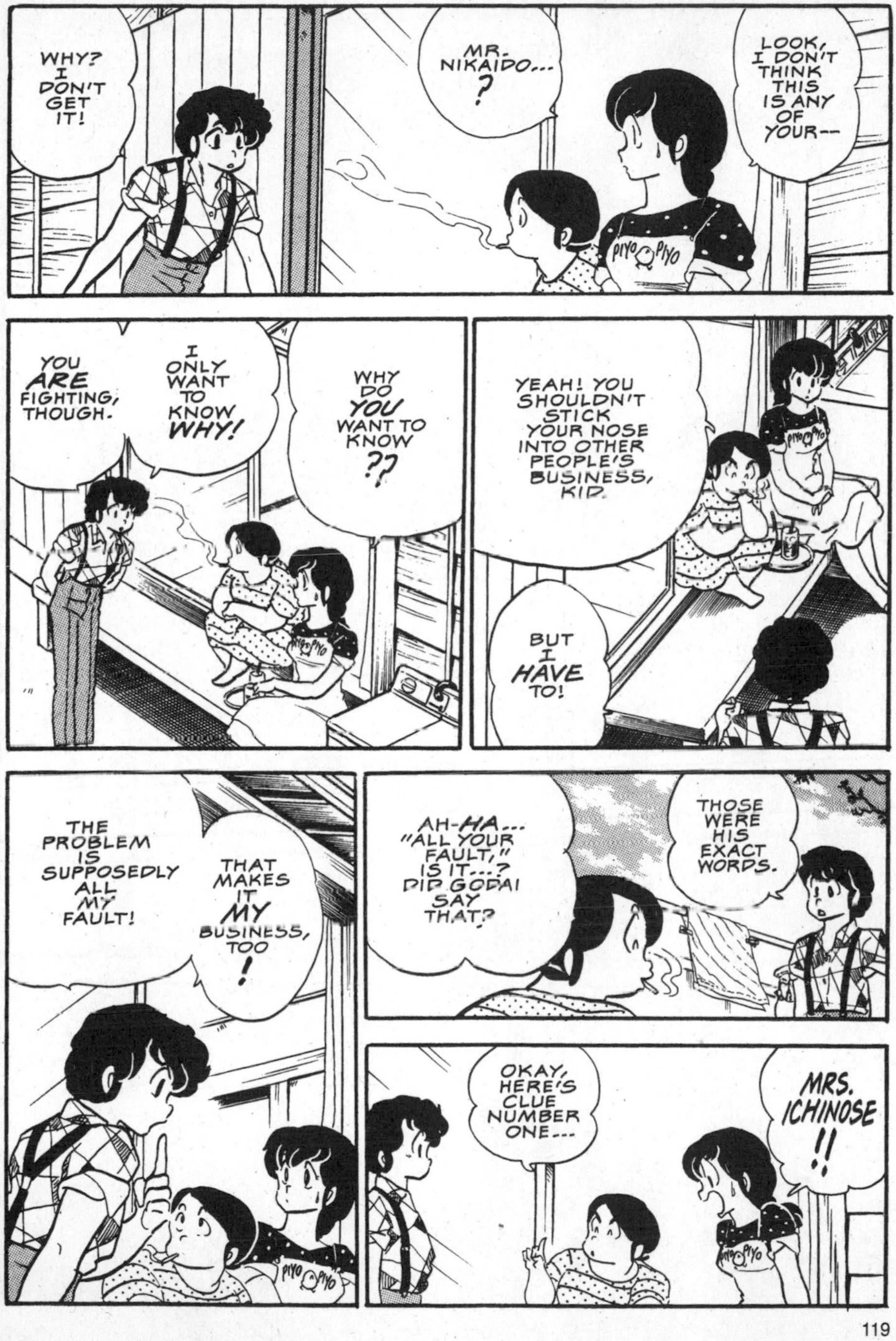
WHY? I DON'T GET IT!
MR. NIKAIDO...?
LOOK, I DON'T THINK THIS IS ANY OF YOUR--
YOU ARE FIGHTING, THOUGH.
I ONLY WANT TO KNOW WHY!
WHY DO YOU WANT TO KNOW??
YEAH! YOU SHOULDN'T STICK YOUR NOSE INTO OTHER PEOPLE'S BUSINESS, KID.
BUT I HAVE TO!
THE PROBLEM IS SUPPOSEDLY ALL MY FAULT!
THAT MAKES IT MY BUSINESS, TOO!
AH-HA... "ALL YOUR FAULT," IS IT...? DID GODAI SAY THAT?
THOSE WERE HIS EXACT WORDS.
OKAY, HERE'S CLUE NUMBER ONE...
MRS. ICHINOSE!!

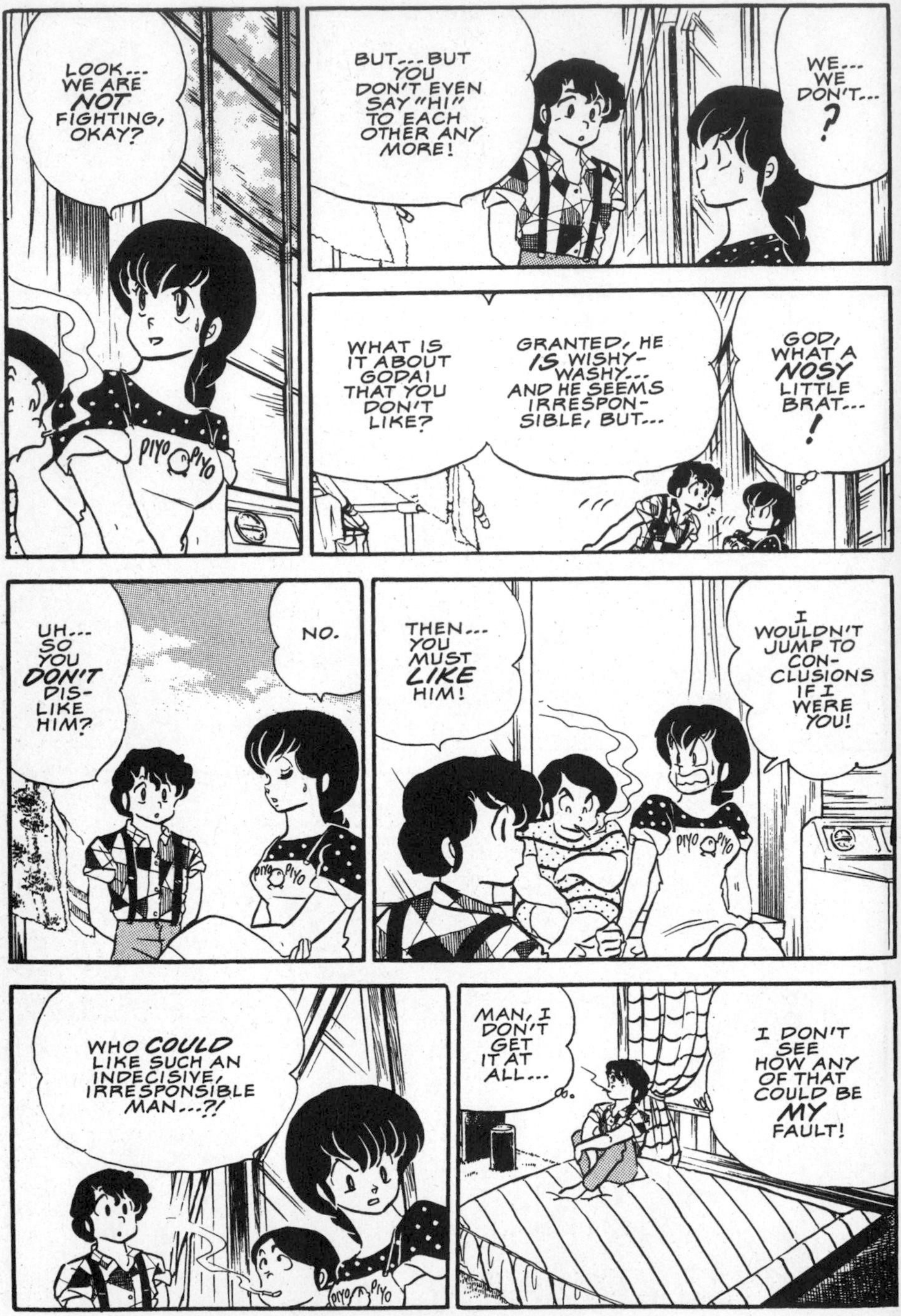
LOOK... WE ARE NOT FIGHTING, OKAY?
BUT... BUT YOU DON'T EVEN SAY "HI" TO EACH OTHER ANY MORE!
WE... WE DON'T...?
WHAT IS IT ABOUT GODAI THAT YOU DON'T LIKE?
GRANTED, HE IS WISHY-WASHY... AND HE SEEMS IRRESPON-SIBLE, BUT...
GOD, WHAT A NOSY LITTLE BRAT...!
UH... SO YOU DON'T DIS-LIKE HIM?
NO.
THEN... YOU MUST LIKE HIM!
I WOULDN'T JUMP TO CON-CLUSIONS IF I WERE YOU!
WHO COULD LIKE SUCH AN INDECISIVE, IRRESPONSIBLE MAN...?!
MAN, I DON'T GET IT AT ALL...
I DON'T SEE HOW ANY OF THAT COULD BE MY FAULT!

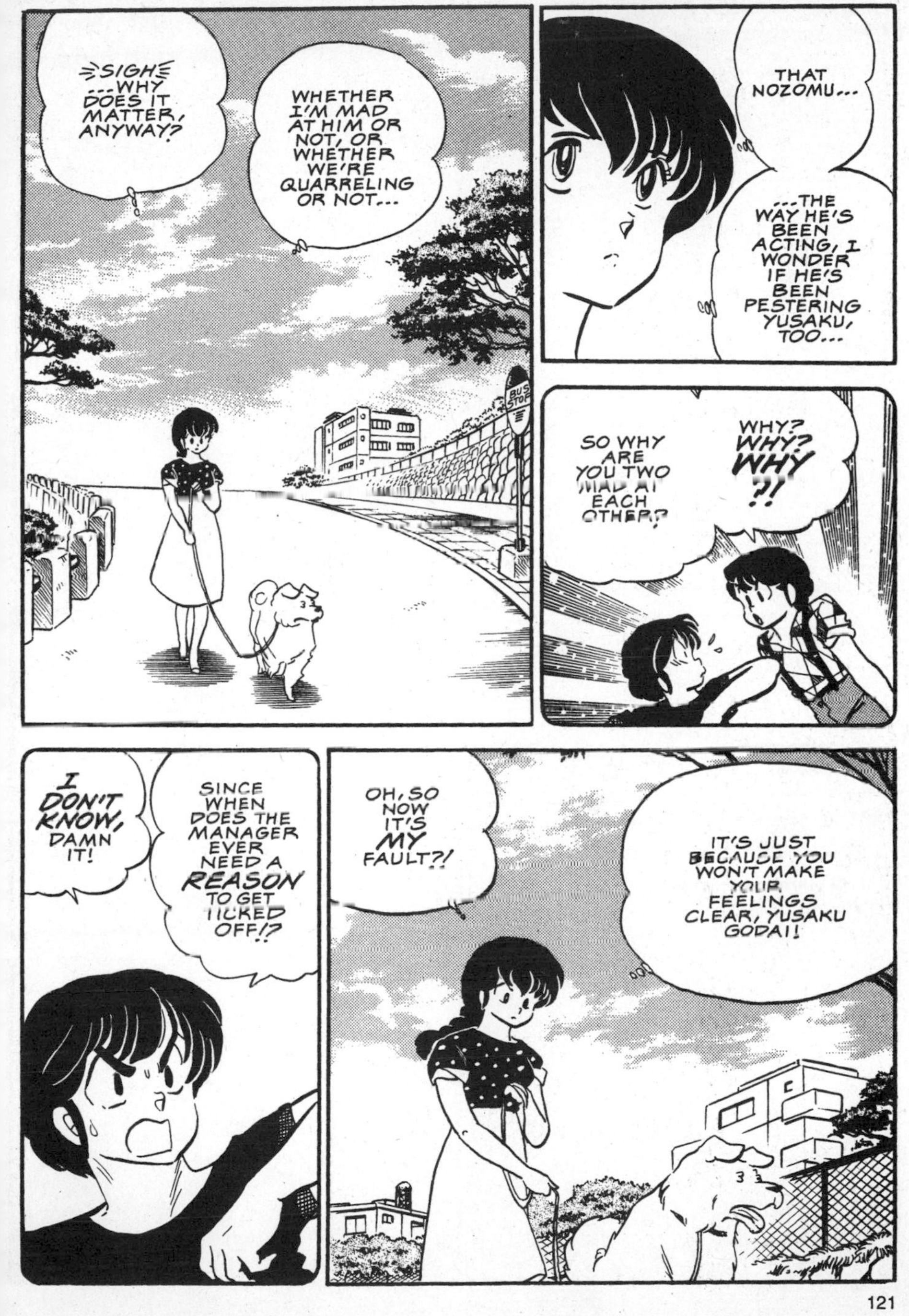
SIGH ...WHY DOES IT MATTER, ANYWAY?
WHETHER I'M MAD AT HIM OR NOT, OR WHETHER WE'RE QUARRELING OR NOT...
BUS STOP
THAT NOZOMU...
...THE WAY HE'S BEEN ACTING, I WONDER IF HE'S BEEN PESTERING YUSAKU, TOO...
SO WHY ARE YOU TWO MAD AT EACH OTHER?
WHY? WHY? WHY ?!
I DON'T KNOW, DAMN IT!
SINCE WHEN DOES THE MANAGER EVER NEED A REASON TO GET TICKED OFF!?
OH, SO NOW IT'S MY FAULT?!
IT'S JUST BECAUSE YOU WON'T MAKE YOUR FEELINGS CLEAR, YUSAKU GODAI!

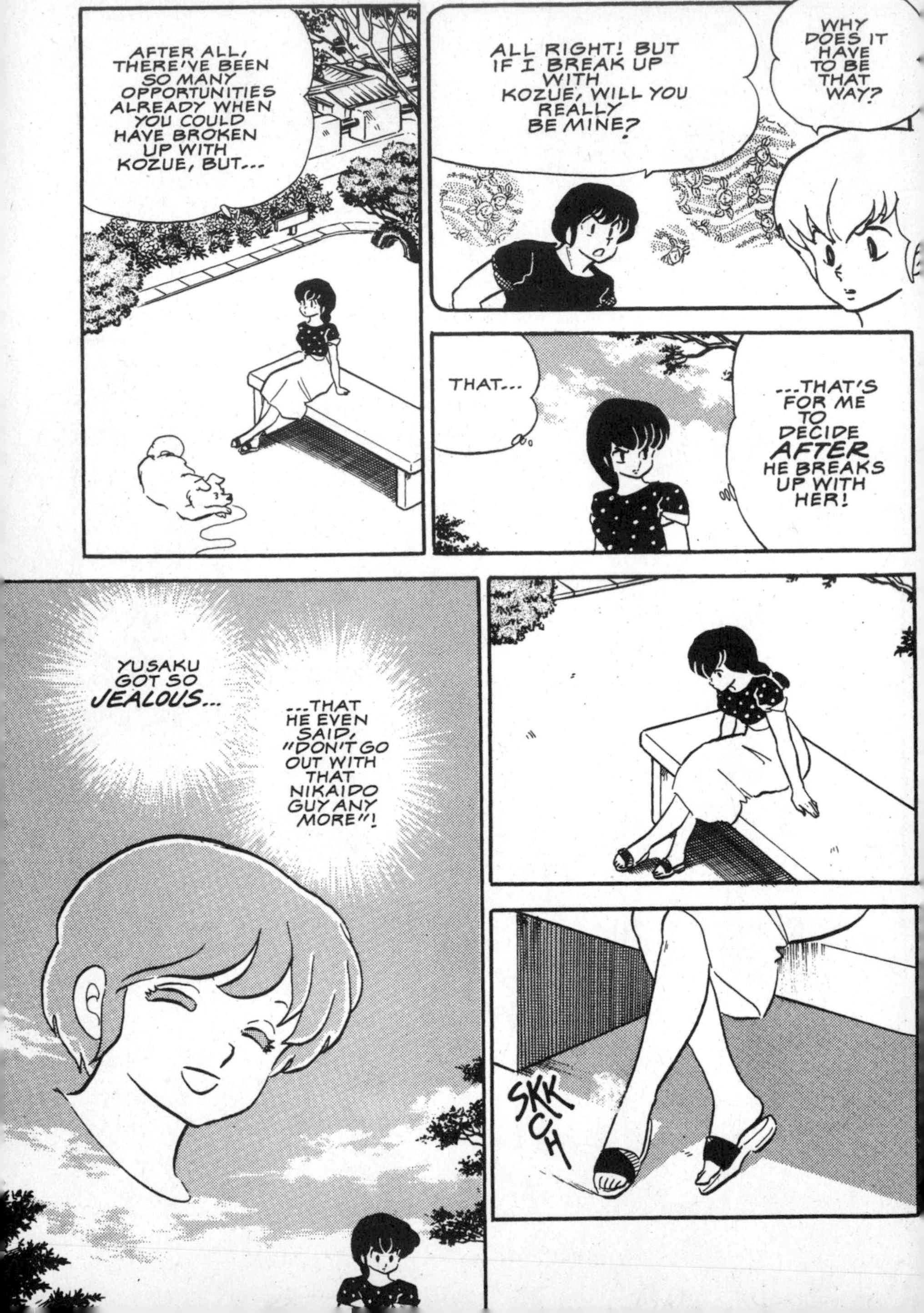
AFTER ALL, THERE'VE BEEN SO MANY OPPORTUNITIES ALREADY WHEN YOU COULD HAVE BROKEN UP WITH KOZUE, BUT...
ALL RIGHT! BUT IF I BREAK UP WITH KOZUE, WILL YOU REALLY BE MINE?
WHY DOES IT HAVE TO BE THAT WAY?
THAT...
...THAT'S FOR ME TO DECIDE AFTER HE BREAKS UP WITH HER!
YUSAKU GOT SO JEALOUS...
...THAT HE EVEN SAID, "DON'T GO OUT WITH THAT NIKAIDO GUY ANY MORE"!
SKK CH

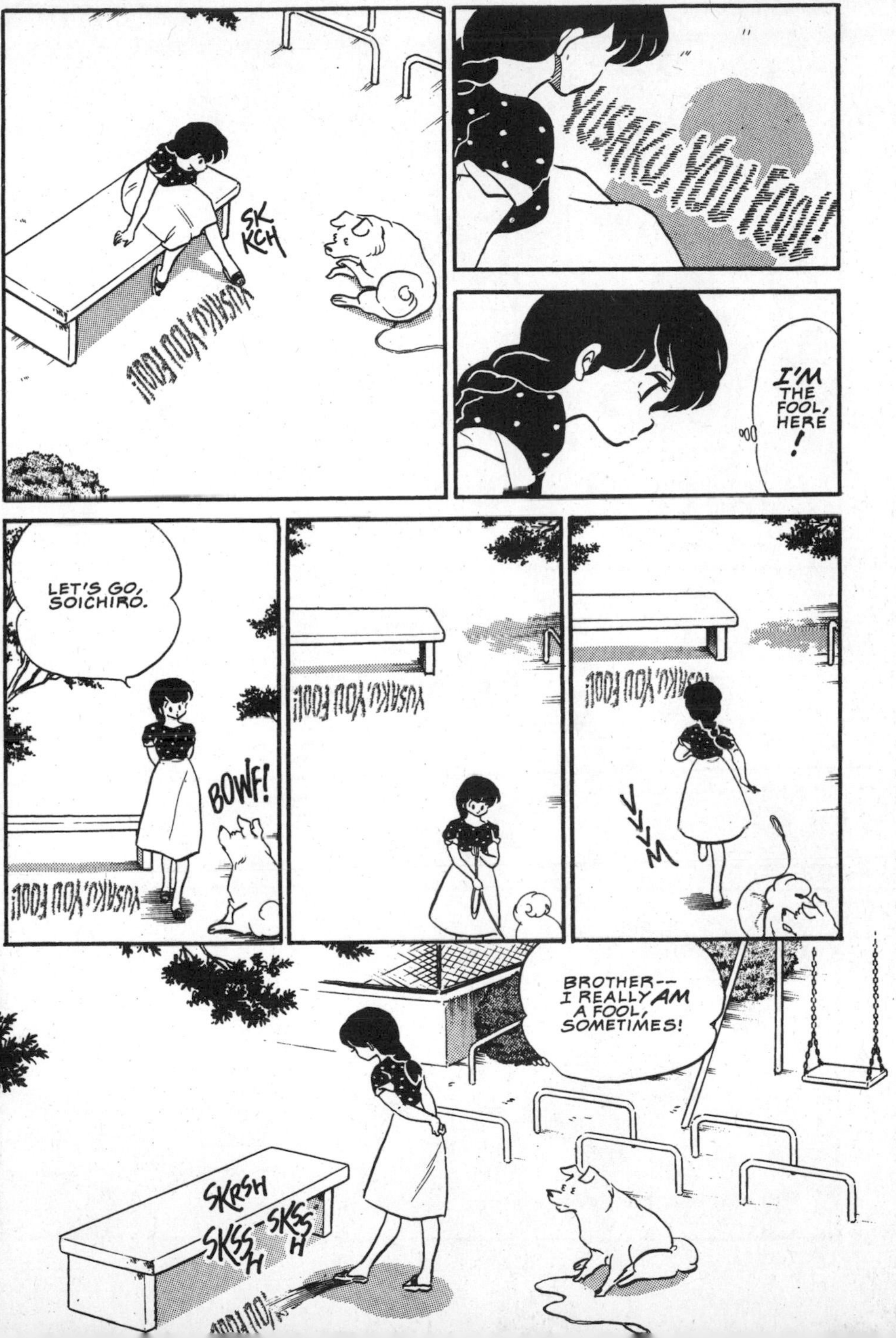
SK KCH
YUSAKU, YOU FOOL!
YUSAKU, YOU FOOL!
I'M THE FOOL, HERE!
LET'S GO, SOICHIRO.
BOWF!
YUSAKU, YOU FOOL!
YUSAKU, YOU FOOL!
YUSAKU, YOU FOOL!
BROTHER-- I REALLY AM A FOOL, SOMETIMES!
SKRSH
SKSSH SKSSH

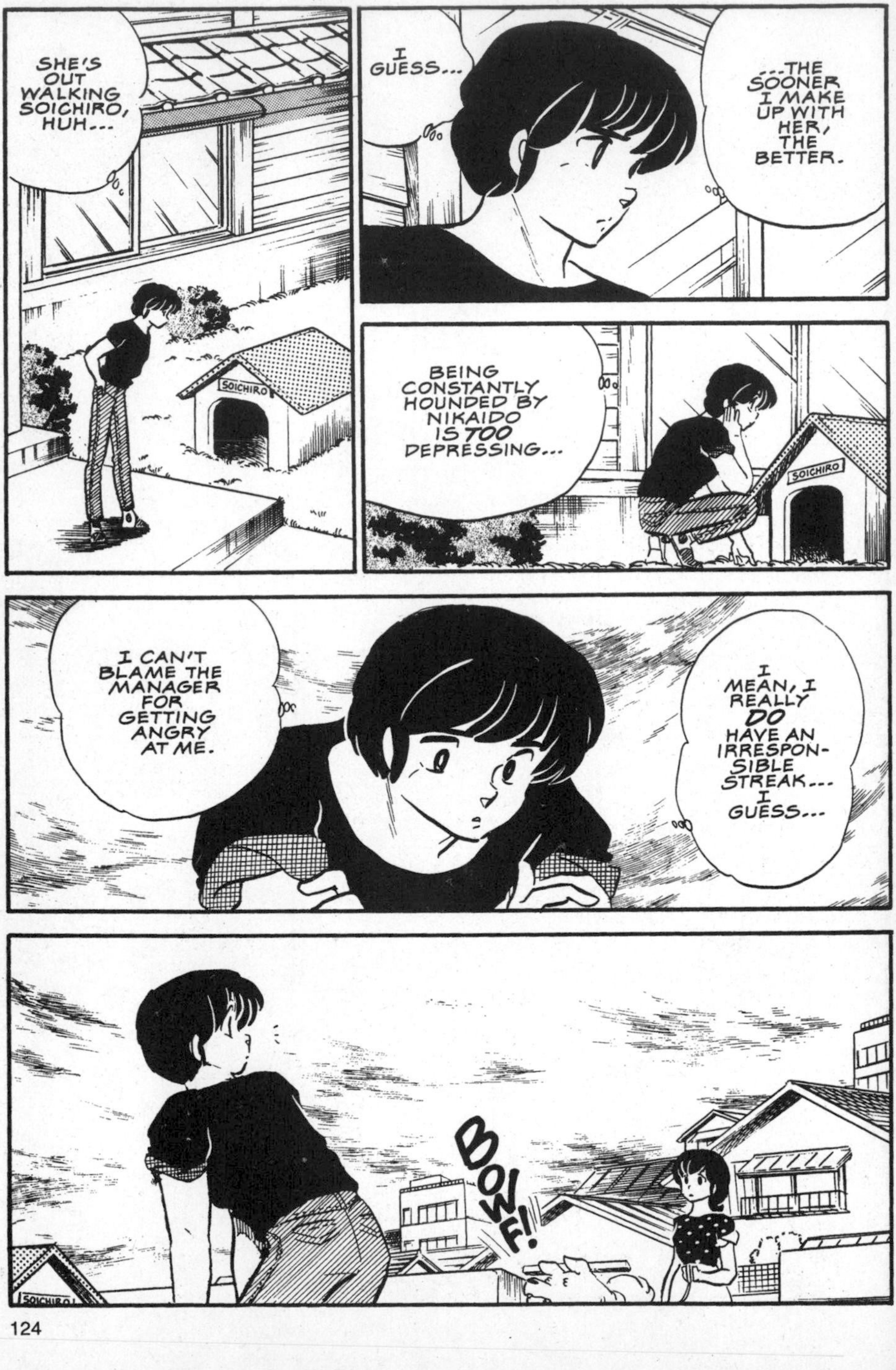
SHE'S OUT WALKING SOICHIRO, HUH...
SOICHIRO
I GUESS...
...THE SOONER I MAKE UP WITH HER, THE BETTER.
BEING CONSTANTLY HOUNDED BY NIKAIDO IS TOO DEPRESSING...
SOICHIRO
I CAN'T BLAME THE MANAGER FOR GETTING ANGRY AT ME.
I MEAN, I REALLY DO HAVE AN IRRESPON-SIBLE STREAK... I GUESS...
BOWF!
SOICHIRO

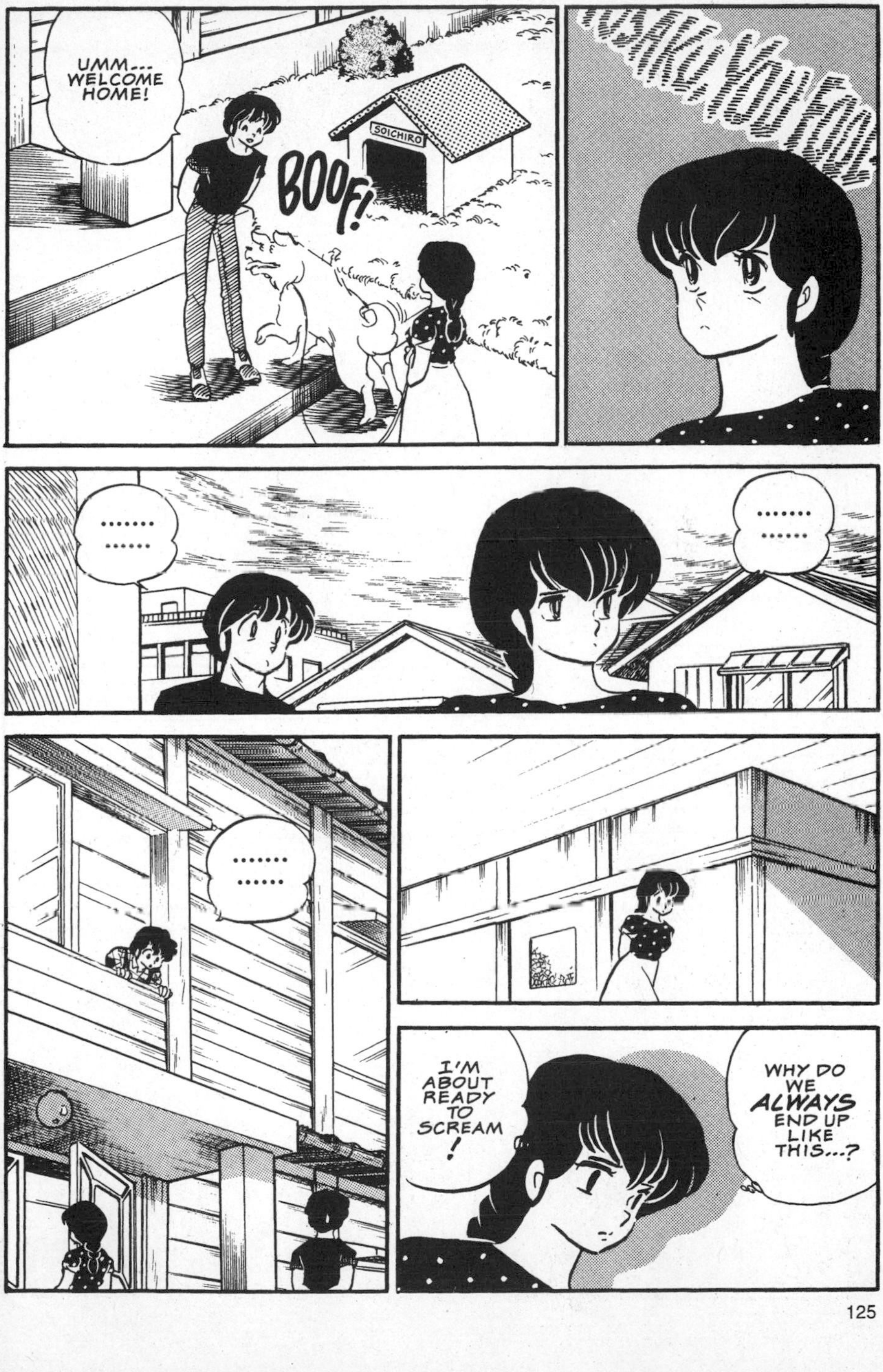
UMM... WELCOME HOME!
SOICHIRO
BOOF!
SAKU, YOU FOOL!
....
......
....
......
....
......
I'M ABOUT READY TO SCREAM!
WHY DO WE ALWAYS END UP LIKE THIS...?

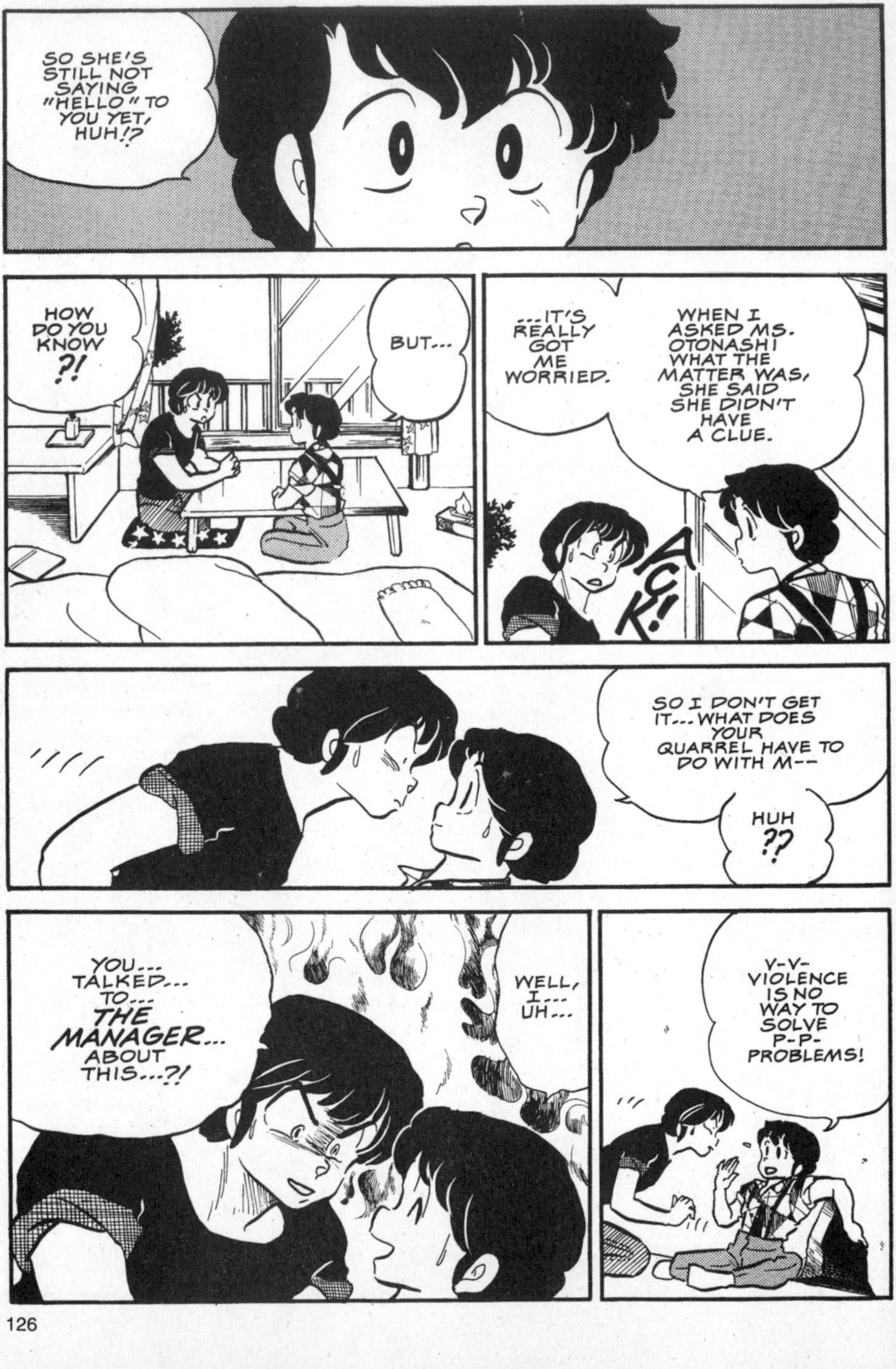
SO SHE'S STILL NOT SAYING "HELLO" TO YOU YET, HUH!?
HOW DO YOU KNOW ?!
BUT...
...IT'S REALLY GOT ME WORRIED.
WHEN I ASKED MS. OTONASHI WHAT THE MATTER WAS, SHE SAID SHE DIDN'T HAVE A CLUE.
ACK!
SO I DON'T GET IT... WHAT DOES YOUR QUARREL HAVE TO DO WITH M--
HUH ??
YOU... TALKED... TO... THE MANAGER... ABOUT THIS...?!
WELL, I... UH...
V-V-VIOLENCE IS NO WAY TO SOLVE P-P-PROBLEMS!

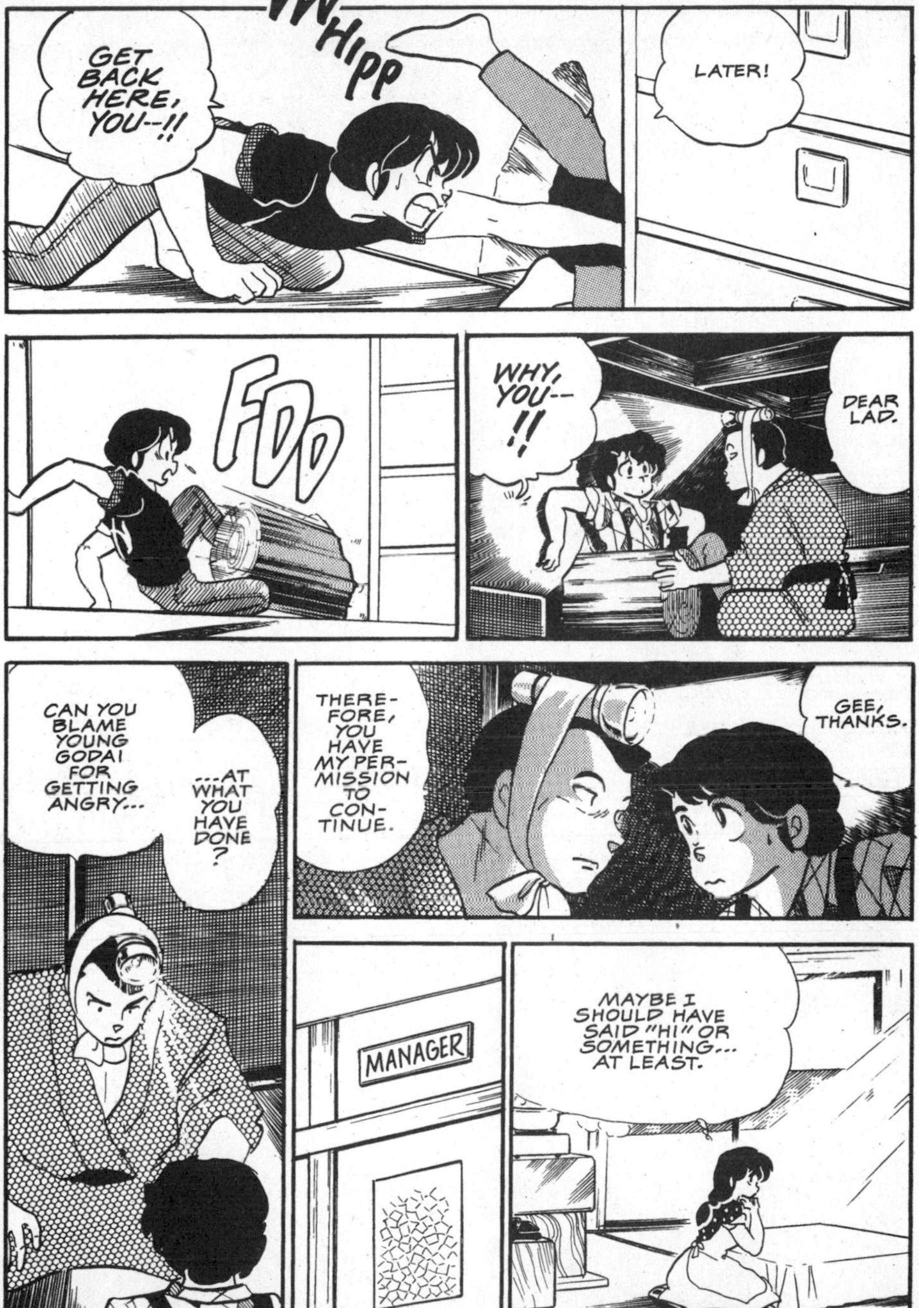
VWHIPP
GET BACK HERE, YOU--!!
LATER!
FDD
WHY, YOU--!!
DEAR LAD.
CAN YOU BLAME YOUNG GODAI FOR GETTING ANGRY...
...AT WHAT YOU HAVE DONE?
THEREFORE, YOU HAVE MY PERMISSION TO CONTINUE.
GEE, THANKS.
MANAGER
MAYBE I SHOULD HAVE SAID "HI" OR SOMETHING... AT LEAST.

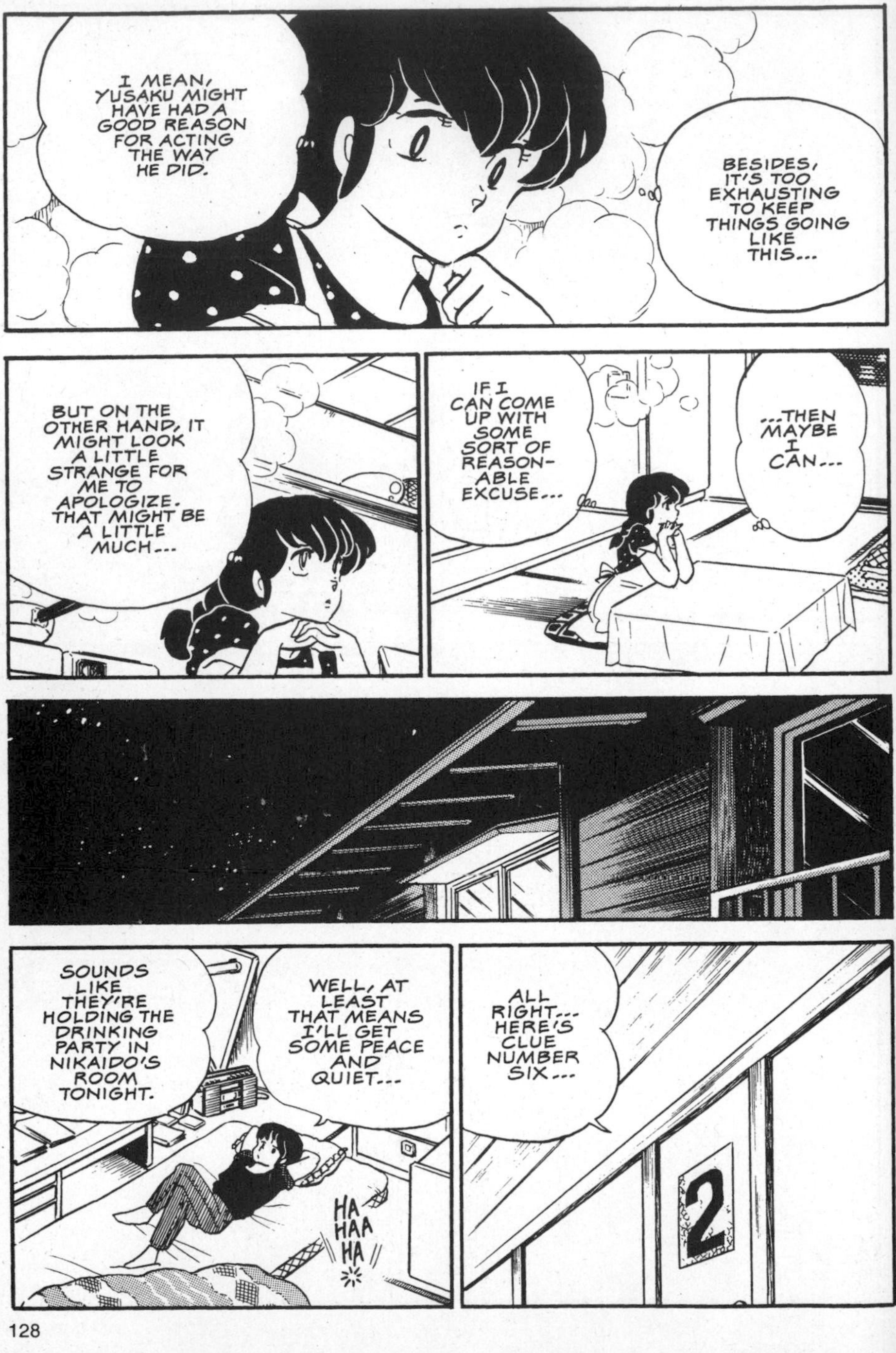
I MEAN, YUSAKU MIGHT HAVE HAD A GOOD REASON FOR ACTING THE WAY HE DID.
BESIDES, IT'S TOO EXHAUSTING TO KEEP THINGS GOING LIKE THIS...
BUT ON THE OTHER HAND, IT MIGHT LOOK A LITTLE STRANGE FOR ME TO APOLOGIZE. THAT MIGHT BE A LITTLE MUCH...
IF I CAN COME UP WITH SOME SORT OF REASON-ABLE EXCUSE...
...THEN MAYBE I CAN...
SOUNDS LIKE THEY'RE HOLDING THE DRINKING PARTY IN NIKAIDO'S ROOM TONIGHT.
WELL, AT LEAST THAT MEANS I'LL GET SOME PEACE AND QUIET...
HA HAA HA
ALL RIGHT... HERE'S CLUE NUMBER SIX...
2

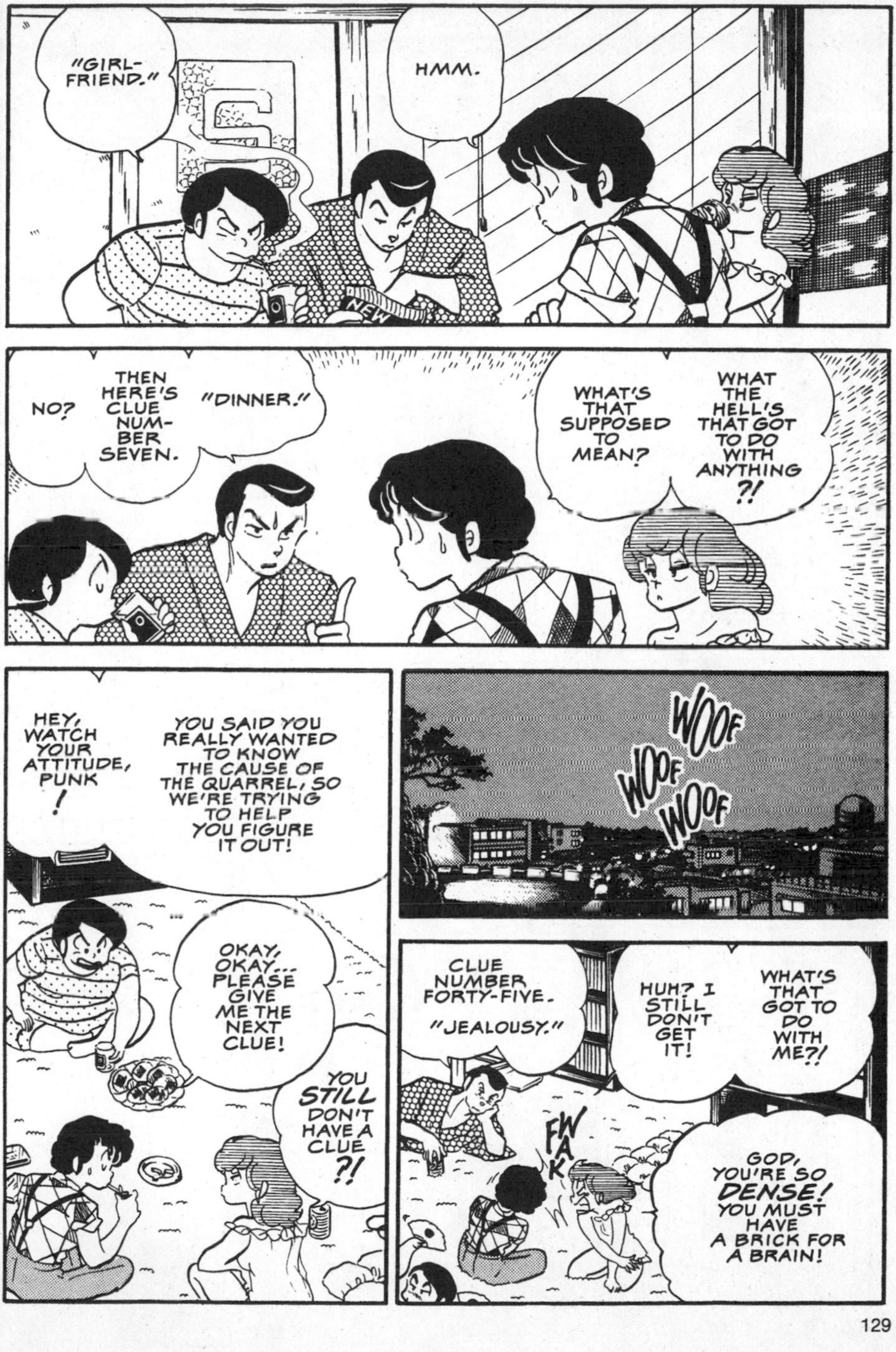
"GIRL-FRIEND."
HMM.
NO?
THEN HERE'S CLUE NUMBER SEVEN.
"DINNER."
WHAT'S THAT SUPPOSED TO MEAN?
WHAT THE HELL'S THAT GOT TO DO WITH ANYTHING ?!
HEY, WATCH YOUR ATTITUDE, PUNK !
YOU SAID YOU REALLY WANTED TO KNOW THE CAUSE OF THE QUARREL, SO WE'RE TRYING TO HELP YOU FIGURE IT OUT!
OKAY, OKAY... PLEASE GIVE ME THE NEXT CLUE!
YOU STILL DON'T HAVE A CLUE ?!
WOOF
WOOF
WOOF
CLUE NUMBER FORTY-FIVE.
"JEALOUSY."
HUH? I STILL DON'T GET IT!
WHAT'S THAT GOT TO DO WITH ME?!
FWAK
GOD, YOU'RE SO DENSE! YOU MUST HAVE A BRICK FOR A BRAIN!

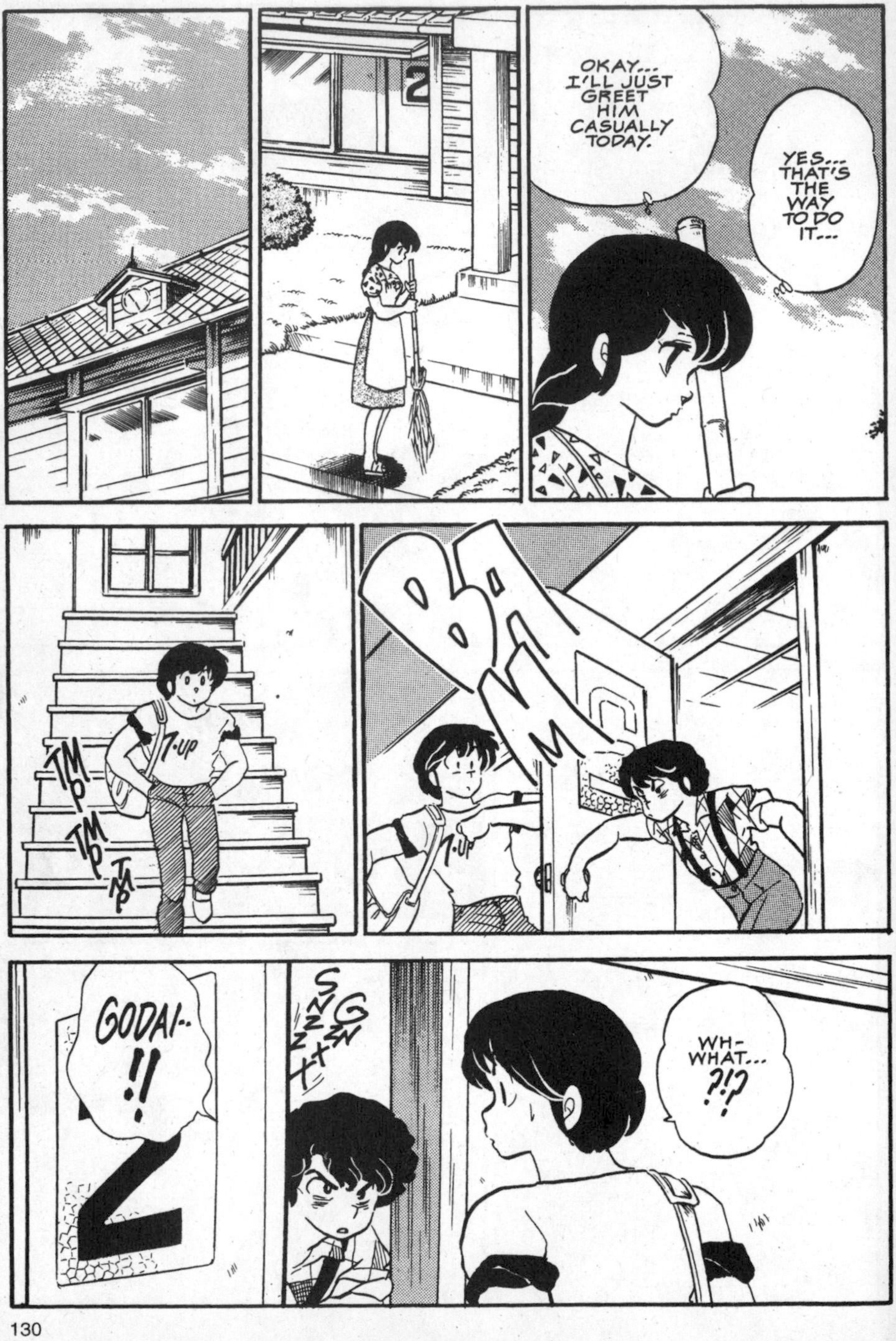
OKAY... I'LL JUST GREET HIM CASUALLY TODAY.
YES... THAT'S THE WAY TO DO IT...
TMP TMP TMP
BAM
GODAI..!!
WH-WHAT...?!?

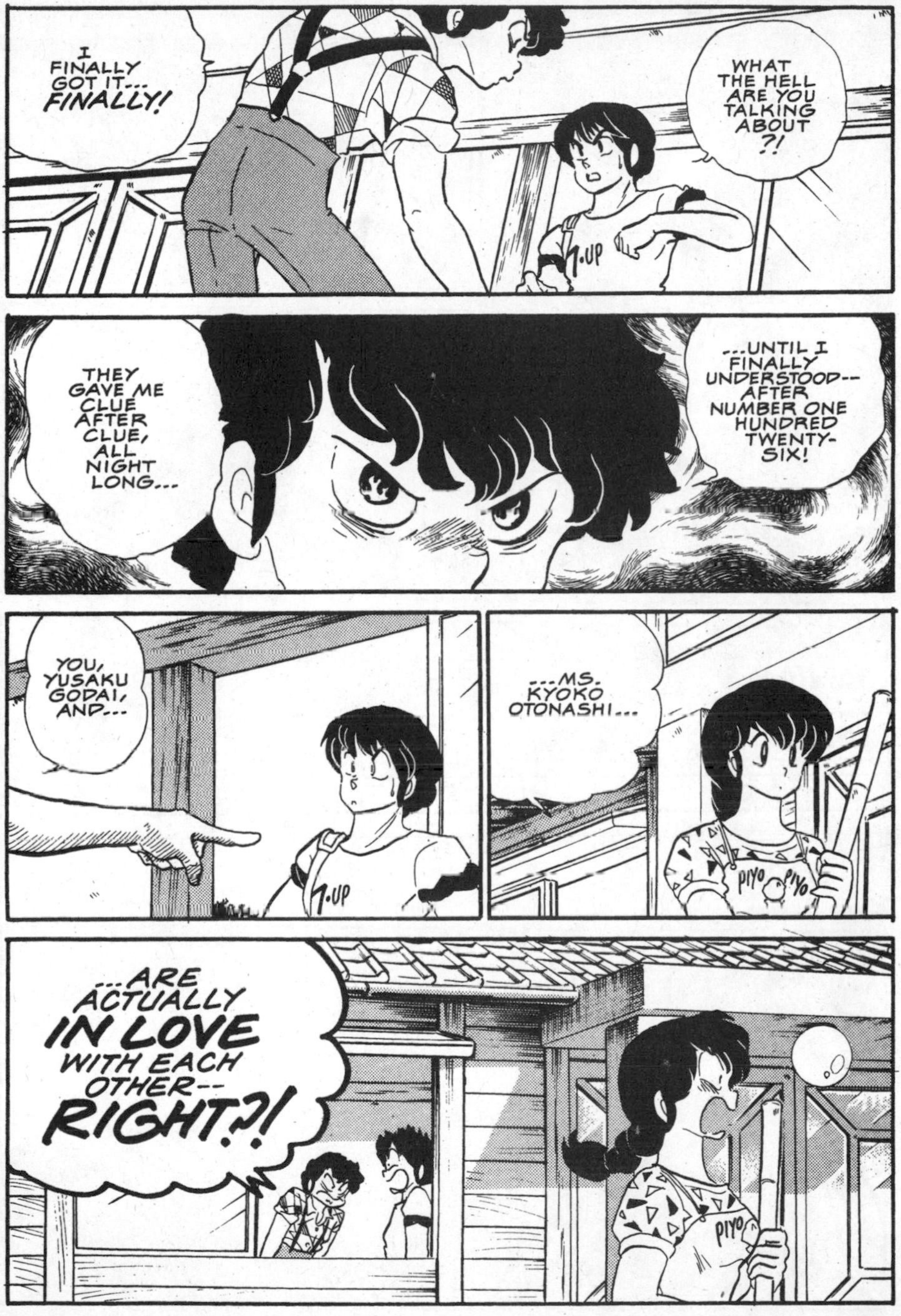
I FINALLY GOT IT... FINALLY!
WHAT THE HELL ARE YOU TALKING ABOUT ?!
THEY GAVE ME CLUE AFTER CLUE, ALL NIGHT LONG...
...UNTIL I FINALLY UNDERSTOOD-- AFTER NUMBER ONE HUNDRED TWENTY-SIX!
YOU, YUSAKU GODAI, AND...
...MS. KYOKO OTONASHI...
PIYO PIYO
...ARE ACTUALLY IN LOVE WITH EACH OTHER-- RIGHT?!
PIYO

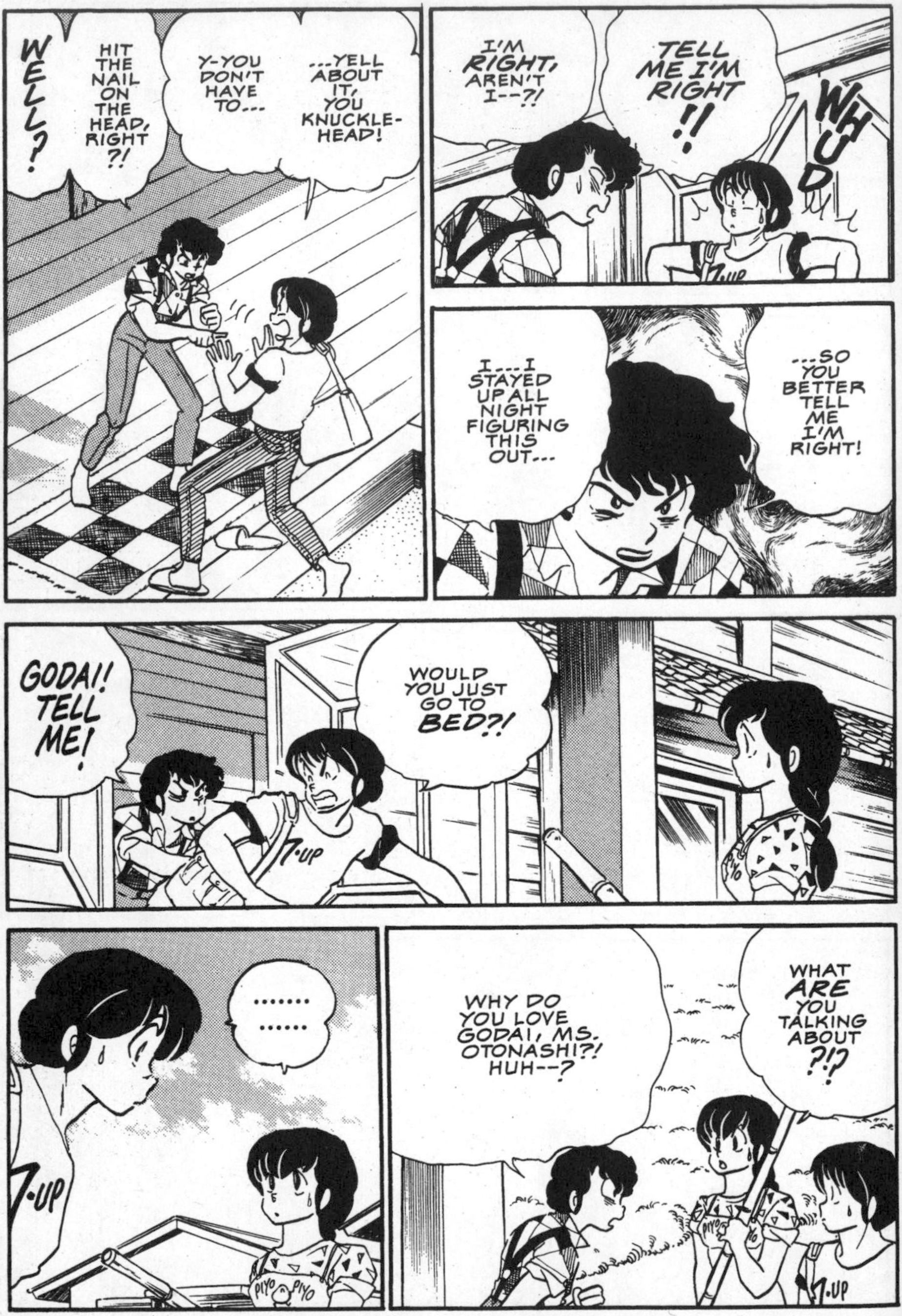
WELL?
HIT THE NAIL ON THE HEAD, RIGHT ?!
Y-YOU DON'T HAVE TO...
...YELL ABOUT IT, YOU KNUCKLE-HEAD!
I'M RIGHT, AREN'T I--?!
TELL ME I'M RIGHT !!
WHUD
I...I STAYED UP ALL NIGHT FIGURING THIS OUT...
...SO YOU BETTER TELL ME I'M RIGHT!
GODAI!! TELL ME!
WOULD YOU JUST GO TO BED?!
7-UP
....
....
WHY DO YOU LOVE GODAI, MS. OTONASHI?! HUH--?
WHAT ARE YOU TALKING ABOUT ?!?

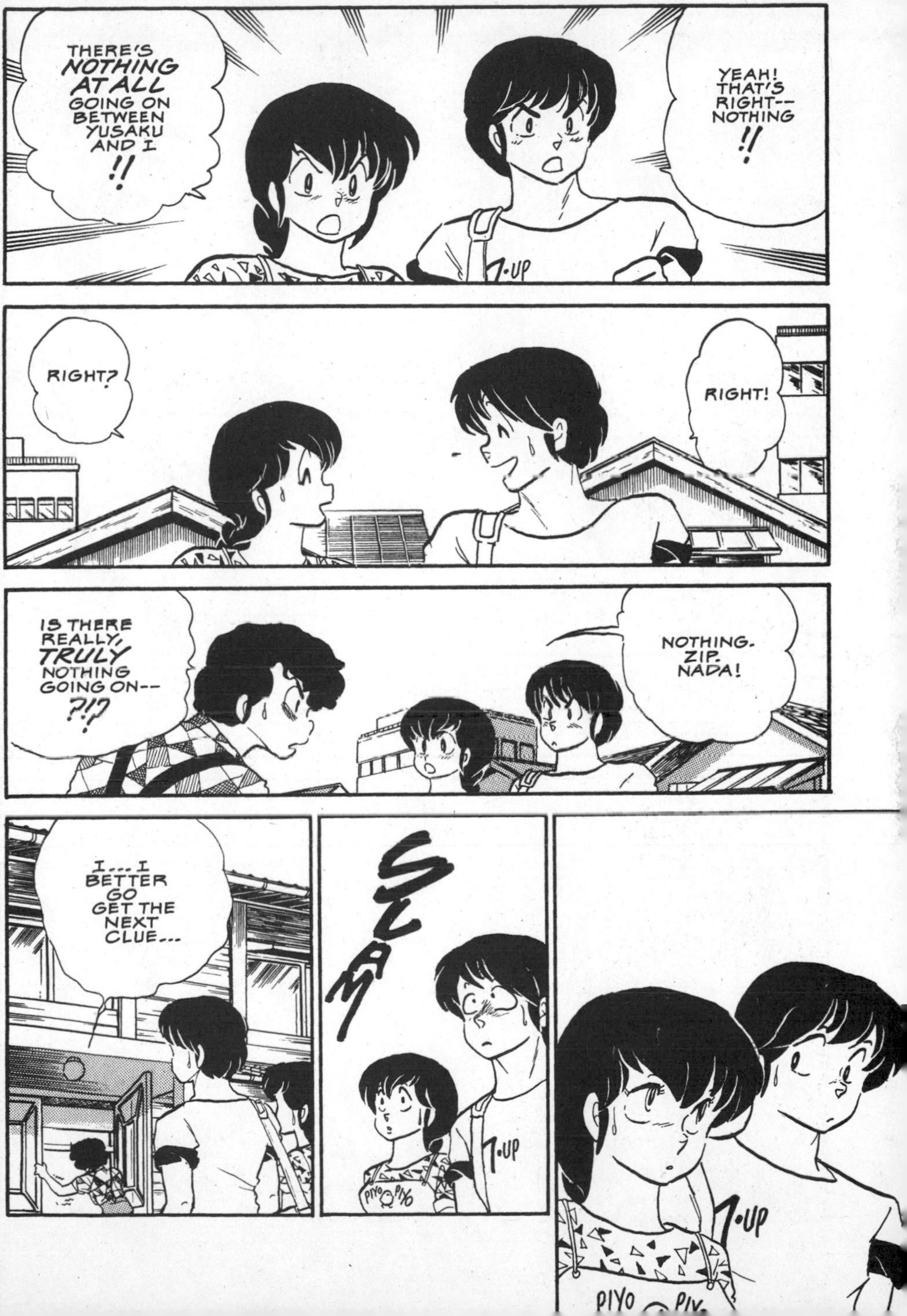
THERE'S *NOTHING AT ALL* GOING ON BETWEEN YUSAKU AND I !!
YEAH! THAT'S RIGHT-- NOTHING !!
7-UP
RIGHT?
RIGHT!
IS THERE REALLY, *TRULY* NOTHING GOING ON-- ?!?
NOTHING. ZIP. NADA!
I... I BETTER GO GET THE NEXT CLUE...
SLAM
7-UP
PIYO PIYO
7-UP
PIYO

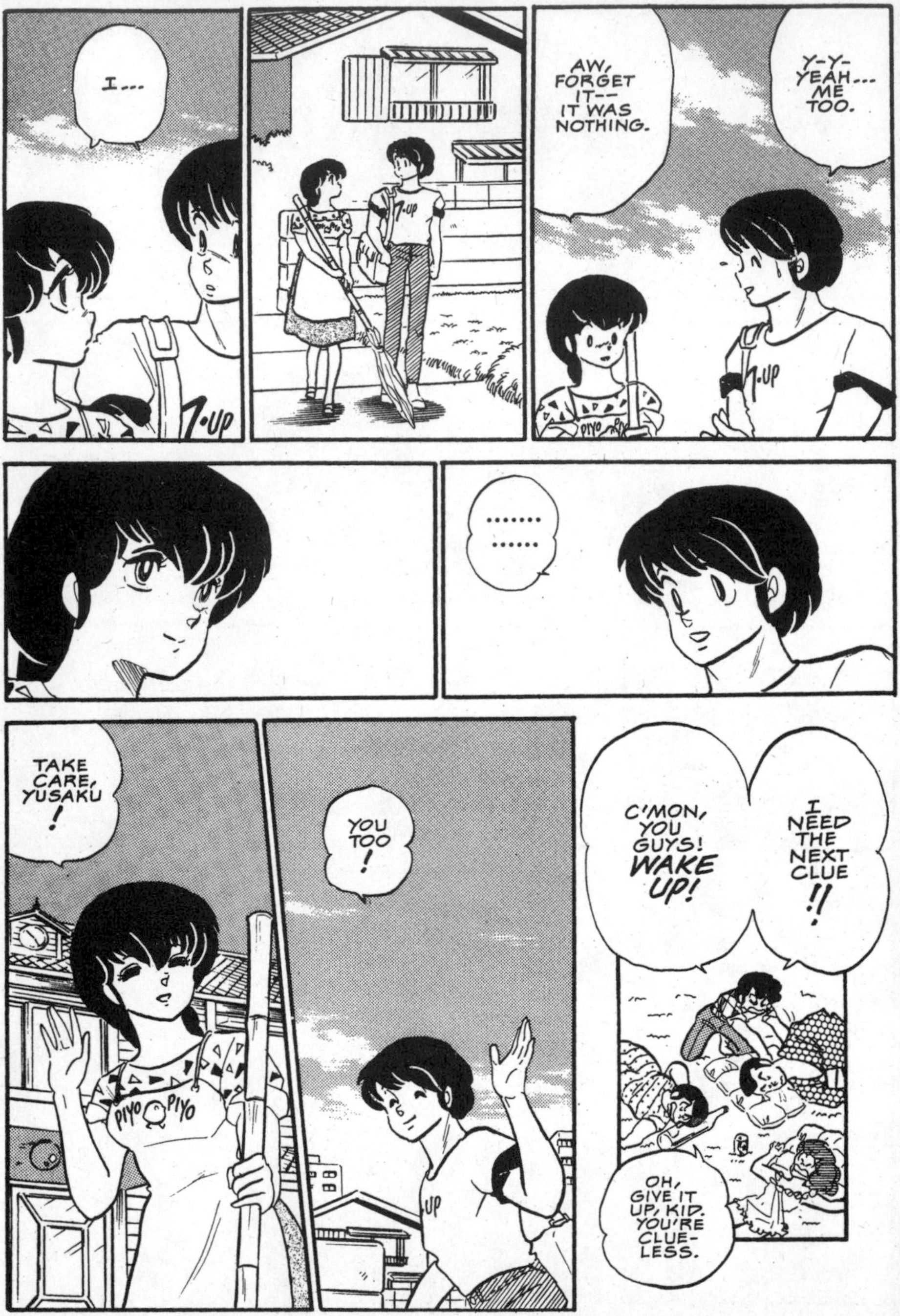

I...
AW, FORGET IT-- IT WAS NOTHING.
Y-Y-YEAH... ME TOO.
....
TAKE CARE, YUSAKU!
YOU TOO!
C'MON, YOU GUYS! WAKE UP!
I NEED THE NEXT CLUE!!
OH, GIVE IT UP, KID. YOU'RE CLUE-LESS.

PART 7

THE SCRAMBLE KID

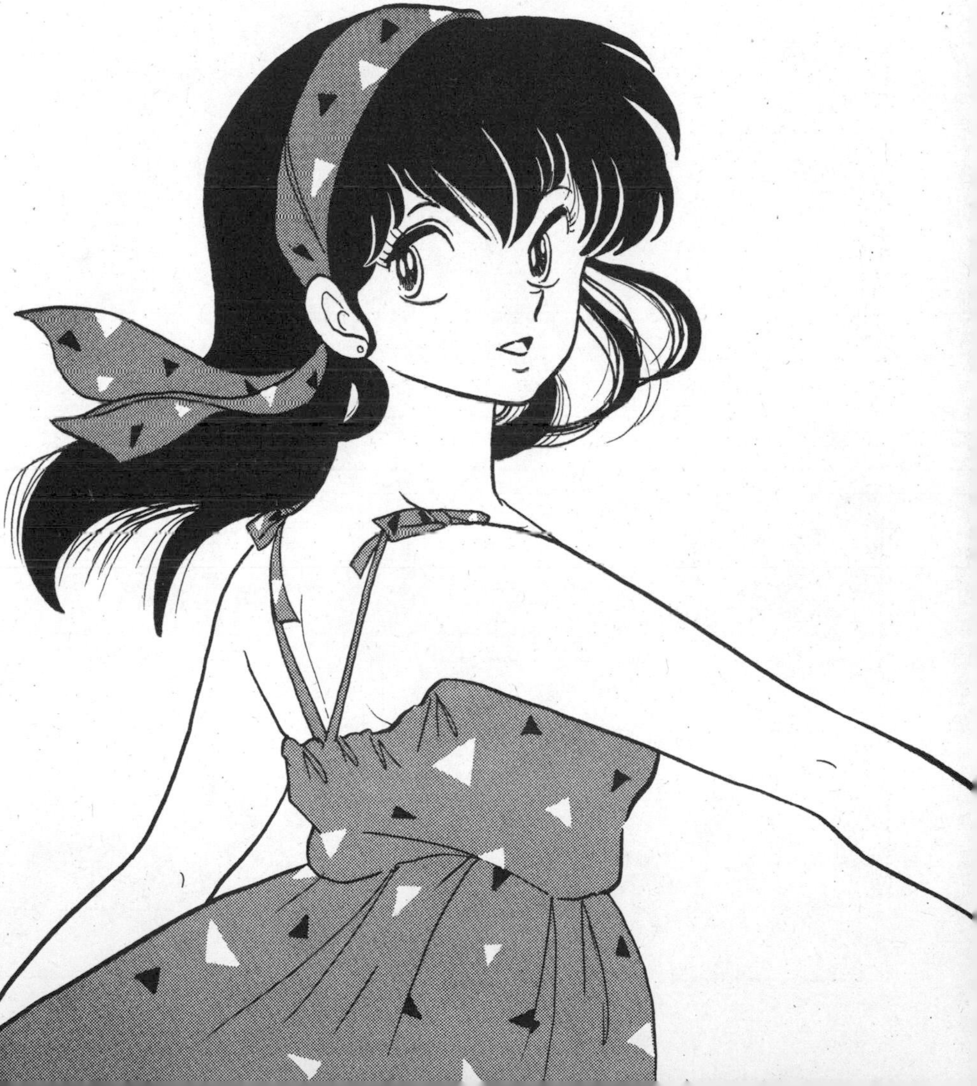

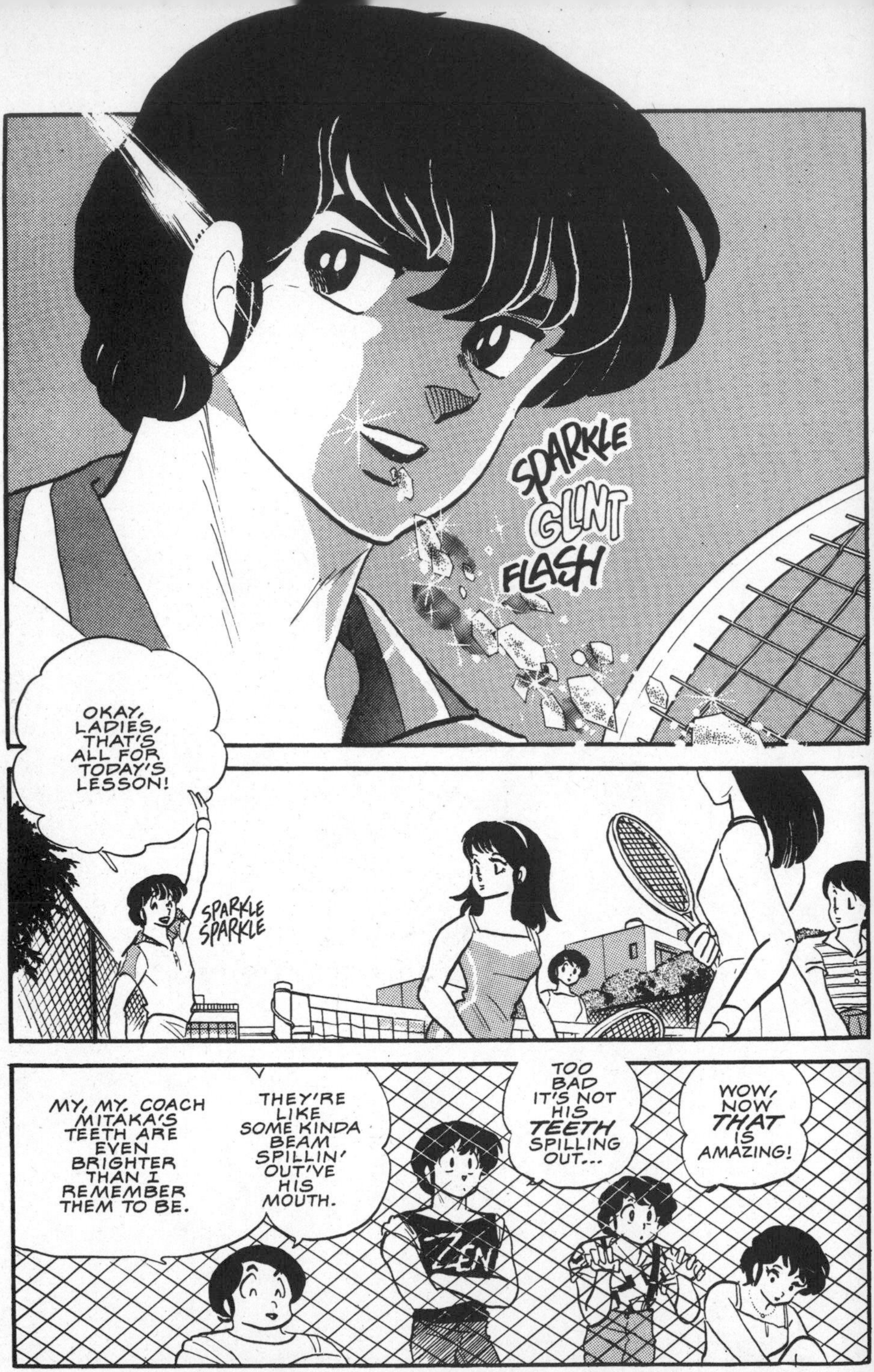
SPARKLE
GLINT
FLASH
OKAY, LADIES, THAT'S ALL FOR TODAY'S LESSON!
SPARKLE SPARKLE
MY, MY. COACH MITAKA'S TEETH ARE EVEN BRIGHTER THAN I REMEMBER THEM TO BE.
THEY'RE LIKE SOME KINDA BEAM SPILLIN' OUT'VE HIS MOUTH.
TOO BAD IT'S NOT HIS *TEETH* SPILLING OUT...
WOW, NOW *THAT* IS AMAZING!

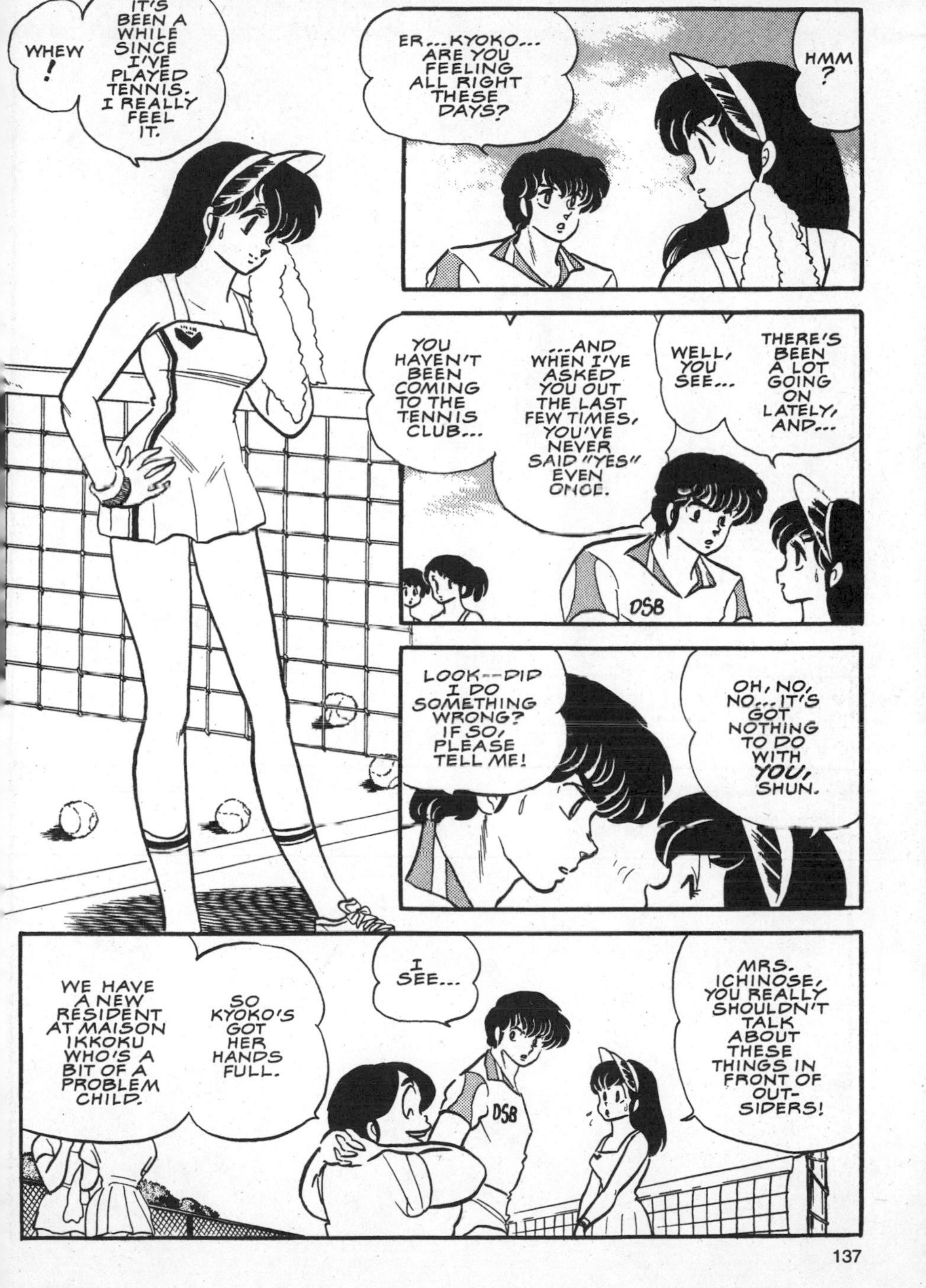
WHEW!
IT'S BEEN A WHILE SINCE I'VE PLAYED TENNIS. I REALLY FEEL IT.
ER...KYOKO... ARE YOU FEELING ALL RIGHT THESE DAYS?
HMM?
YOU HAVEN'T BEEN COMING TO THE TENNIS CLUB...
...AND WHEN I'VE ASKED YOU OUT THE LAST FEW TIMES, YOU'VE NEVER SAID "YES" EVEN ONCE.
WELL, YOU SEE...
THERE'S BEEN A LOT GOING ON LATELY, AND...
LOOK--DID I DO SOMETHING WRONG? IF SO, PLEASE TELL ME!
OH, NO, NO... IT'S GOT NOTHING TO DO WITH YOU, SHUN.
WE HAVE A NEW RESIDENT AT MAISON IKKOKU WHO'S A BIT OF A PROBLEM CHILD.
SO KYOKO'S GOT HER HANDS FULL.
I SEE...
MRS. ICHINOSE, YOU REALLY SHOULDN'T TALK ABOUT THESE THINGS IN FRONT OF OUT-SIDERS!

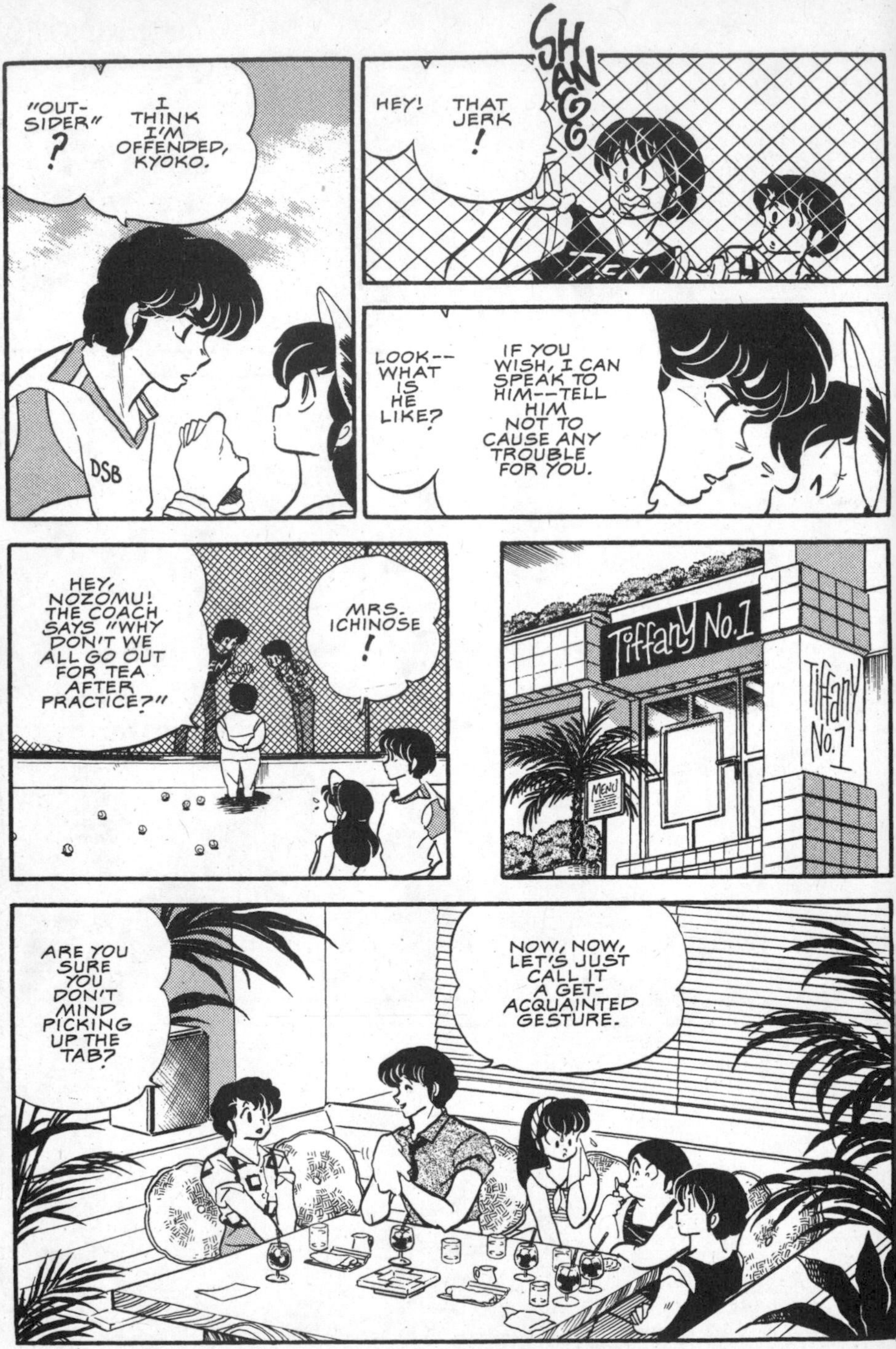
"OUT-SIDER" ?
I THINK I'M OFFENDED, KYOKO.
SHANGG
HEY! THAT JERK !
LOOK-- WHAT IS HE LIKE?
IF YOU WISH, I CAN SPEAK TO HIM--TELL HIM NOT TO CAUSE ANY TROUBLE FOR YOU.
HEY, NOZOMU! THE COACH SAYS "WHY DON'T WE ALL GO OUT FOR TEA AFTER PRACTICE?"
MRS. ICHINOSE !
Tiffany No.1
Tiffany No.1
MENU
ARE YOU SURE YOU DON'T MIND PICKING UP THE TAB?
NOW, NOW, LET'S JUST CALL IT A GET-ACQUAINTED GESTURE.

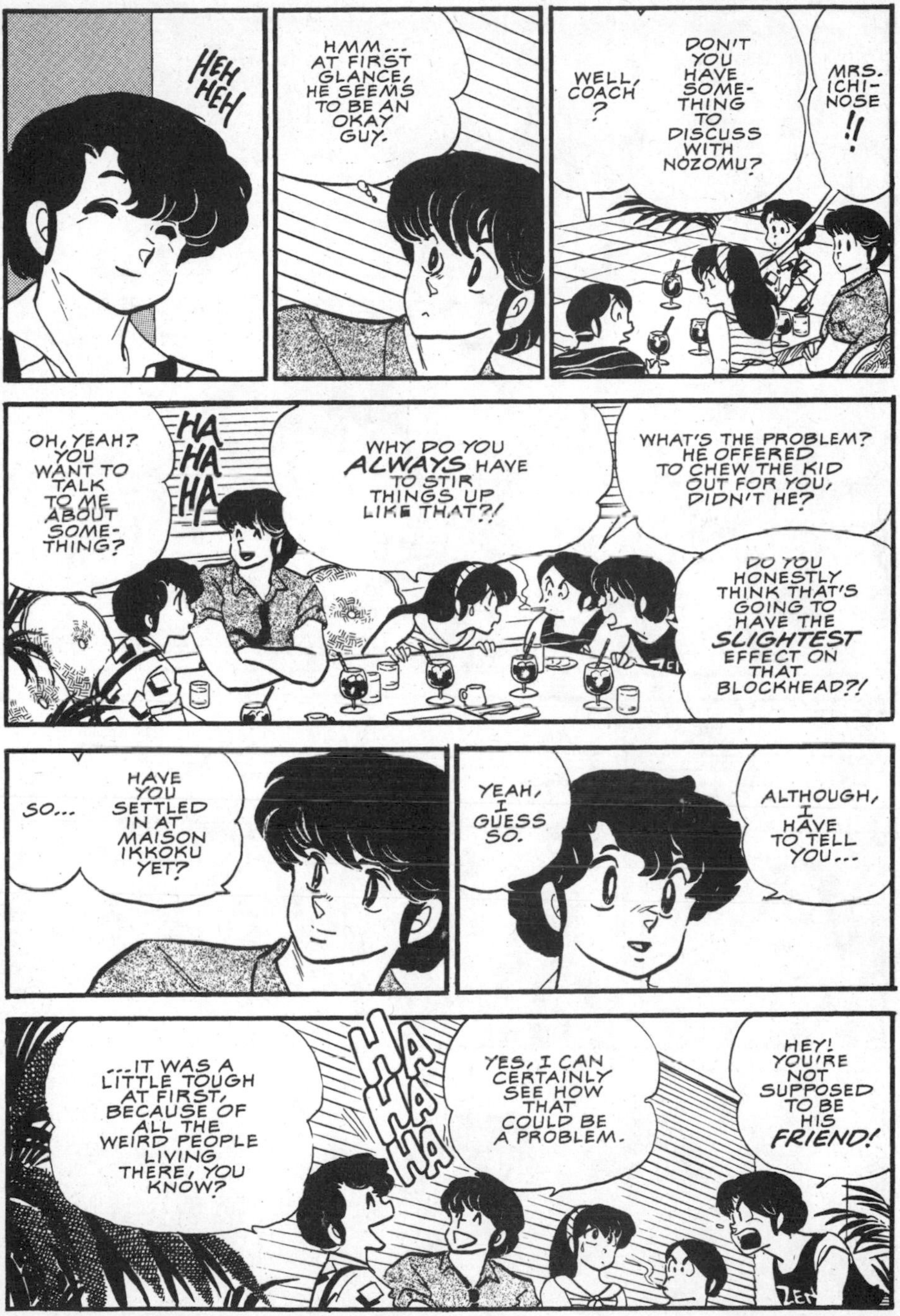
HEH HEH
HMM... AT FIRST GLANCE, HE SEEMS TO BE AN OKAY GUY.
WELL, COACH?
DON'T YOU HAVE SOMETHING TO DISCUSS WITH NOZOMU?
MRS. ICHINOSE!!
OH, YEAH? YOU WANT TO TALK TO ME ABOUT SOMETHING?
HA HA HA
WHY DO YOU ALWAYS HAVE TO STIR THINGS UP LIKE THAT?!
WHAT'S THE PROBLEM? HE OFFERED TO CHEW THE KID OUT FOR YOU, DIDN'T HE?
DO YOU HONESTLY THINK THAT'S GOING TO HAVE THE SLIGHTEST EFFECT ON THAT BLOCKHEAD?!
SO...
HAVE YOU SETTLED IN AT MAISON IKKOKU YET?
YEAH, I GUESS SO.
ALTHOUGH, I HAVE TO TELL YOU...
...IT WAS A LITTLE TOUGH AT FIRST, BECAUSE OF ALL THE WEIRD PEOPLE LIVING THERE, YOU KNOW?
HA HA HA HA
YES, I CAN CERTAINLY SEE HOW THAT COULD BE A PROBLEM.
HEY! YOU'RE NOT SUPPOSED TO BE HIS FRIEND!

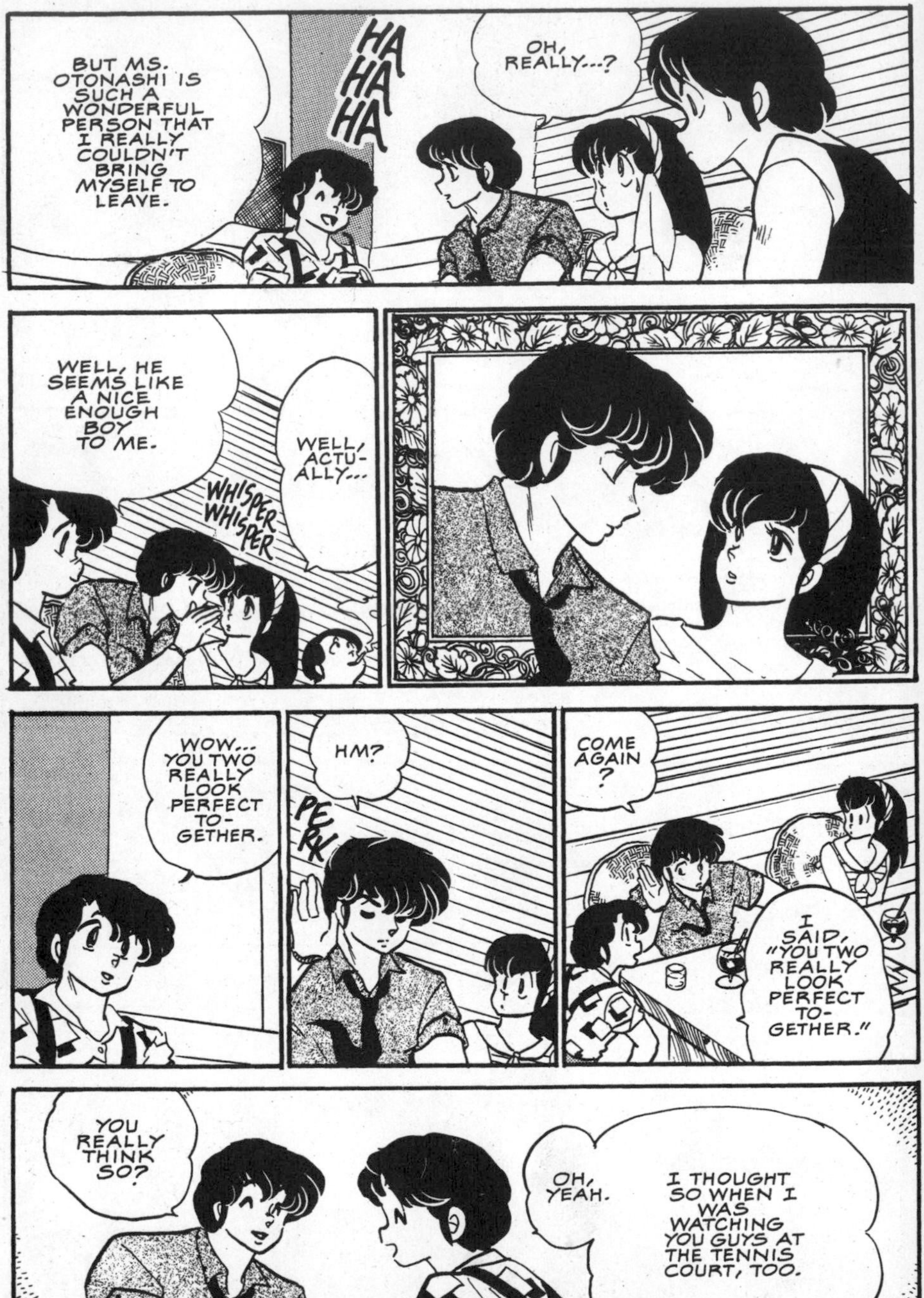
BUT MS. OTONASHI IS SUCH A WONDERFUL PERSON THAT I REALLY COULDN'T BRING MYSELF TO LEAVE.
HA HA HA HA
OH, REALLY...?
WELL, HE SEEMS LIKE A NICE ENOUGH BOY TO ME.
WHISPER WHISPER
WELL, ACTU-ALLY...
WOW... YOU TWO REALLY LOOK PERFECT TO-GETHER.
HM?
PERK
COME AGAIN ?
I SAID, "YOU TWO REALLY LOOK PERFECT TO-GETHER."
YOU REALLY THINK SO?
OH, YEAH.
I THOUGHT SO WHEN I WAS WATCHING YOU GUYS AT THE TENNIS COURT, TOO.

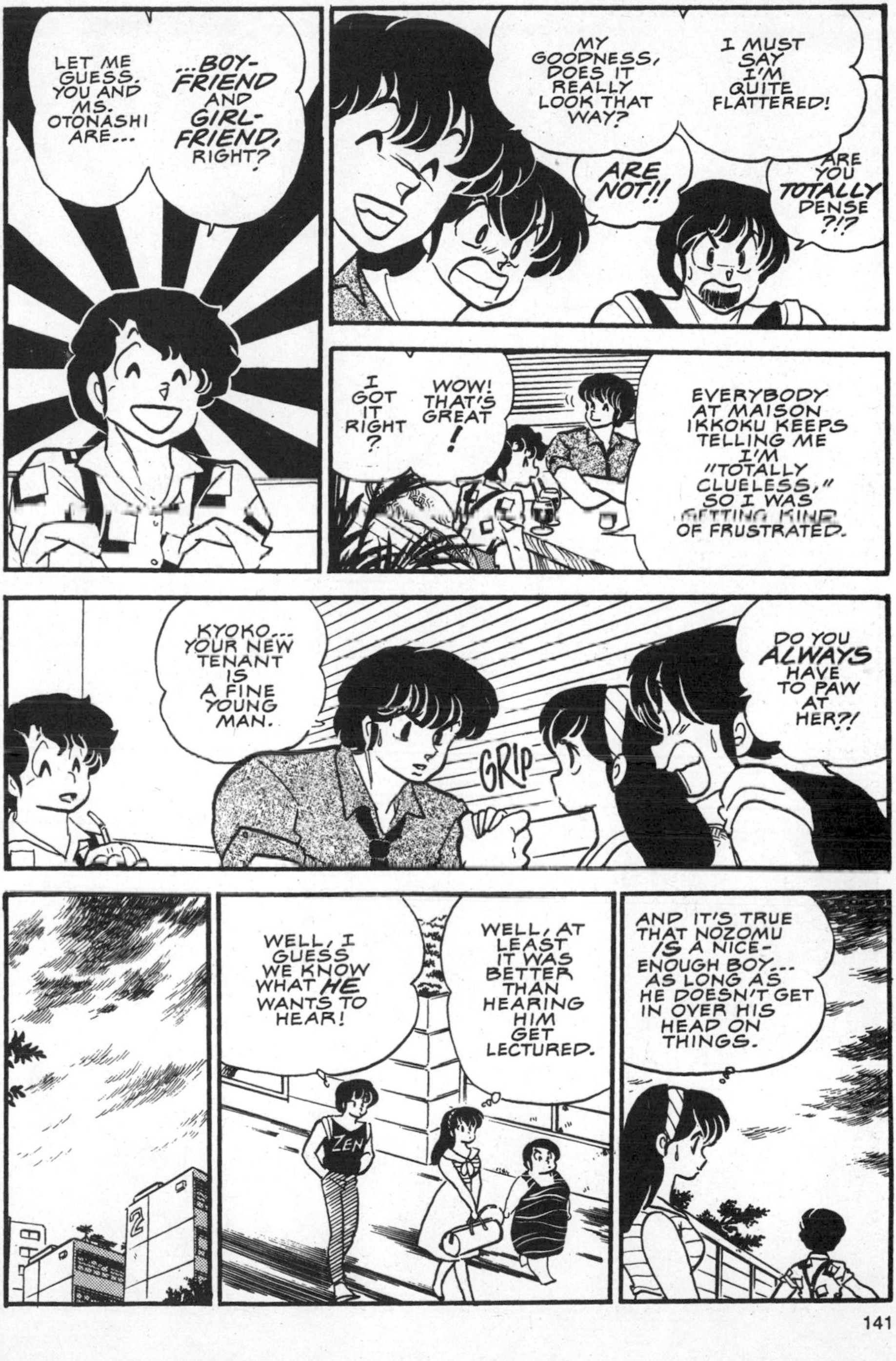
LET ME GUESS. YOU AND MS. OTONASHI ARE...
...BOY-FRIEND AND GIRL-FRIEND, RIGHT?
MY GOODNESS, DOES IT REALLY LOOK THAT WAY?
I MUST SAY I'M QUITE FLATTERED!
ARE NOT!!
ARE YOU TOTALLY DENSE ?!?
I GOT IT RIGHT ?
WOW! THAT'S GREAT !
EVERYBODY AT MAISON IKKOKU KEEPS TELLING ME I'M "TOTALLY CLUELESS," SO I WAS GETTING KIND OF FRUSTRATED.
KYOKO... YOUR NEW TENANT IS A FINE YOUNG MAN.
GRIP
DO YOU ALWAYS HAVE TO PAW AT HER?!
WELL, I GUESS WE KNOW WHAT HE WANTS TO HEAR!
WELL, AT LEAST IT WAS BETTER THAN HEARING HIM GET LECTURED.
AND IT'S TRUE THAT NOZOMU IS A NICE-ENOUGH BOY... AS LONG AS HE DOESN'T GET IN OVER HIS HEAD ON THINGS.
ZEN
2

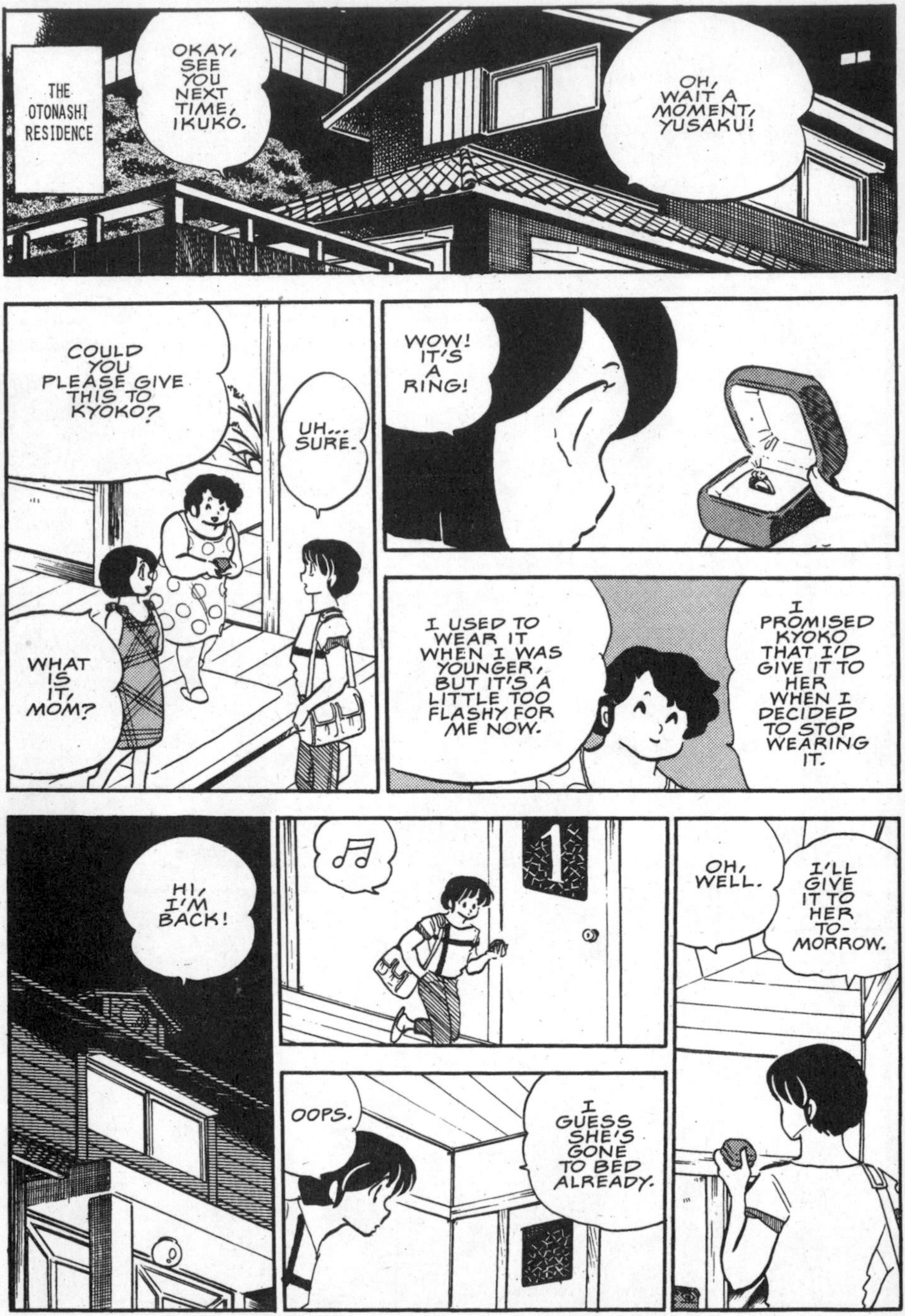

THE OTONASHI RESIDENCE
OKAY, SEE YOU NEXT TIME, IKUKO.
OH, WAIT A MOMENT, YUSAKU!
COULD YOU PLEASE GIVE THIS TO KYOKO?
UH... SURE.
WHAT IS IT, MOM?
WOW! IT'S A RING!
I USED TO WEAR IT WHEN I WAS YOUNGER, BUT IT'S A LITTLE TOO FLASHY FOR ME NOW.
I PROMISED KYOKO THAT I'D GIVE IT TO HER WHEN I DECIDED TO STOP WEARING IT.
HI, I'M BACK!
1
OOPS.
I GUESS SHE'S GONE TO BED ALREADY.
OH, WELL.
I'LL GIVE IT TO HER TO-MORROW.

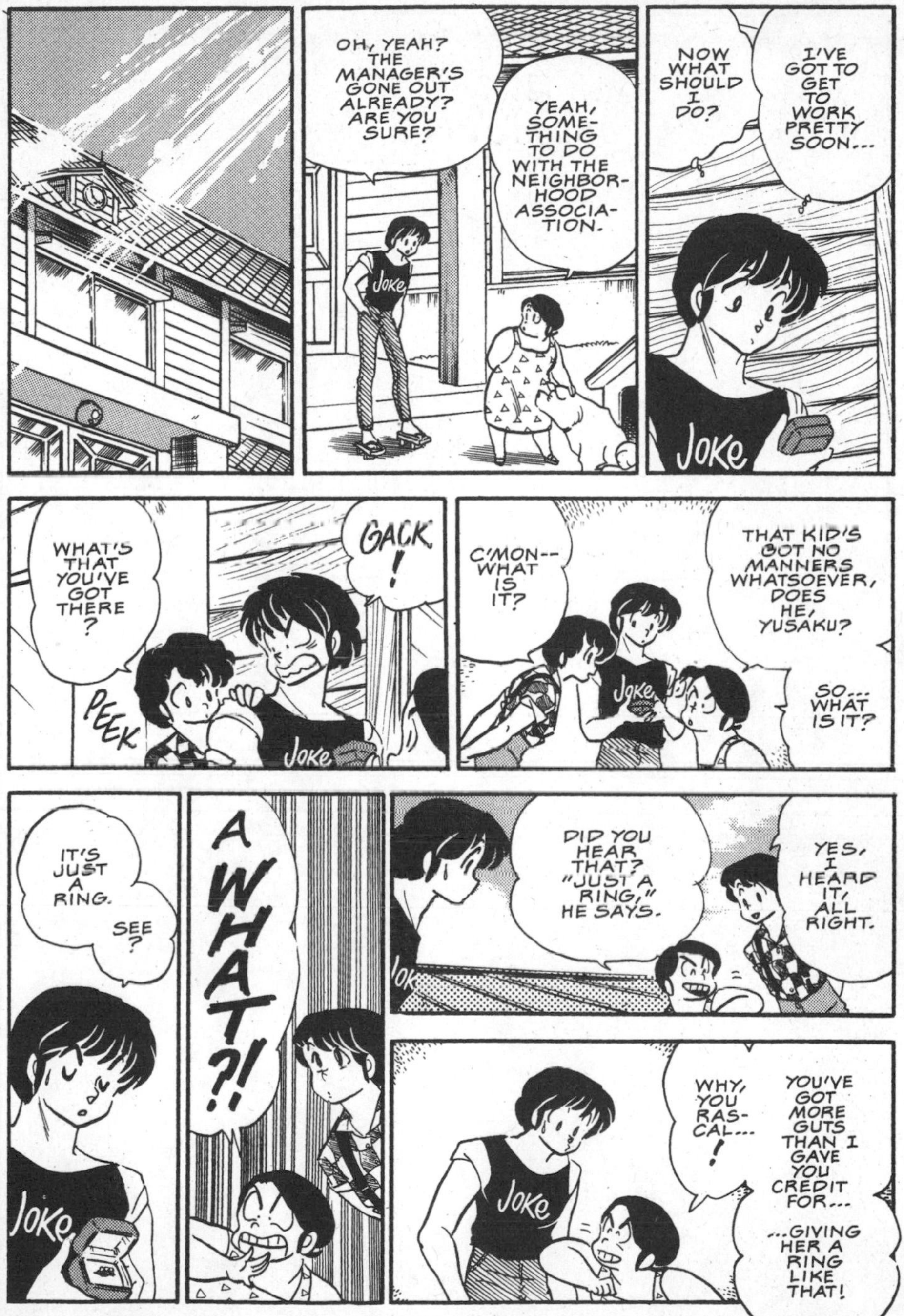
OH, YEAH? THE MANAGER'S GONE OUT ALREADY? ARE YOU SURE?
YEAH, SOMETHING TO DO WITH THE NEIGHBORHOOD ASSOCIATION.
NOW WHAT SHOULD I DO?
I'VE GOT TO GET TO WORK PRETTY SOON...
WHAT'S THAT YOU'VE GOT THERE?
GACK!
PEEK
C'MON-- WHAT IS IT?
THAT KID'S GOT NO MANNERS WHATSOEVER, DOES HE, YUSAKU?
SO... WHAT IS IT?
IT'S JUST A RING.
SEE?
A WHAT?!
DID YOU HEAR THAT? "JUST A RING," HE SAYS.
YES, I HEARD IT, ALL RIGHT.
WHY, YOU RASCAL...!
YOU'VE GOT MORE GUTS THAN I GAVE YOU CREDIT FOR...
...GIVING HER A RING LIKE THAT!

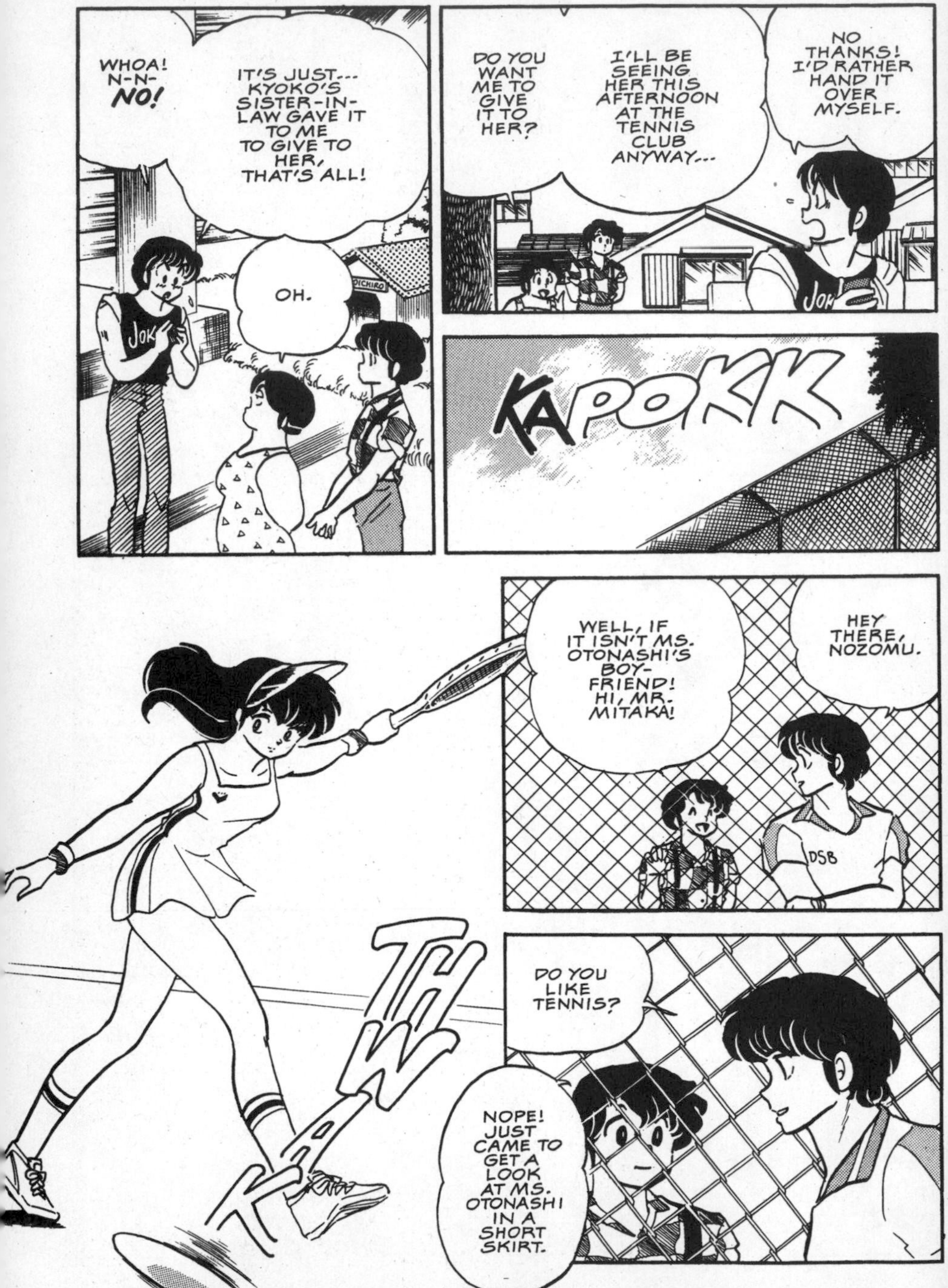
WHOA! N-N-NO!
IT'S JUST... KYOKO'S SISTER-IN-LAW GAVE IT TO ME TO GIVE TO HER, THAT'S ALL!
OH.
DO YOU WANT ME TO GIVE IT TO HER?
I'LL BE SEEING HER THIS AFTERNOON AT THE TENNIS CLUB ANYWAY...
NO THANKS! I'D RATHER HAND IT OVER MYSELF.
KAPOKK
THWAK
WELL, IF IT ISN'T MS. OTONASHI'S BOY-FRIEND! HI, MR. MITAKA!
HEY THERE, NOZOMU.
DO YOU LIKE TENNIS?
NOPE! JUST CAME TO GET A LOOK AT MS. OTONASHI IN A SHORT SKIRT.

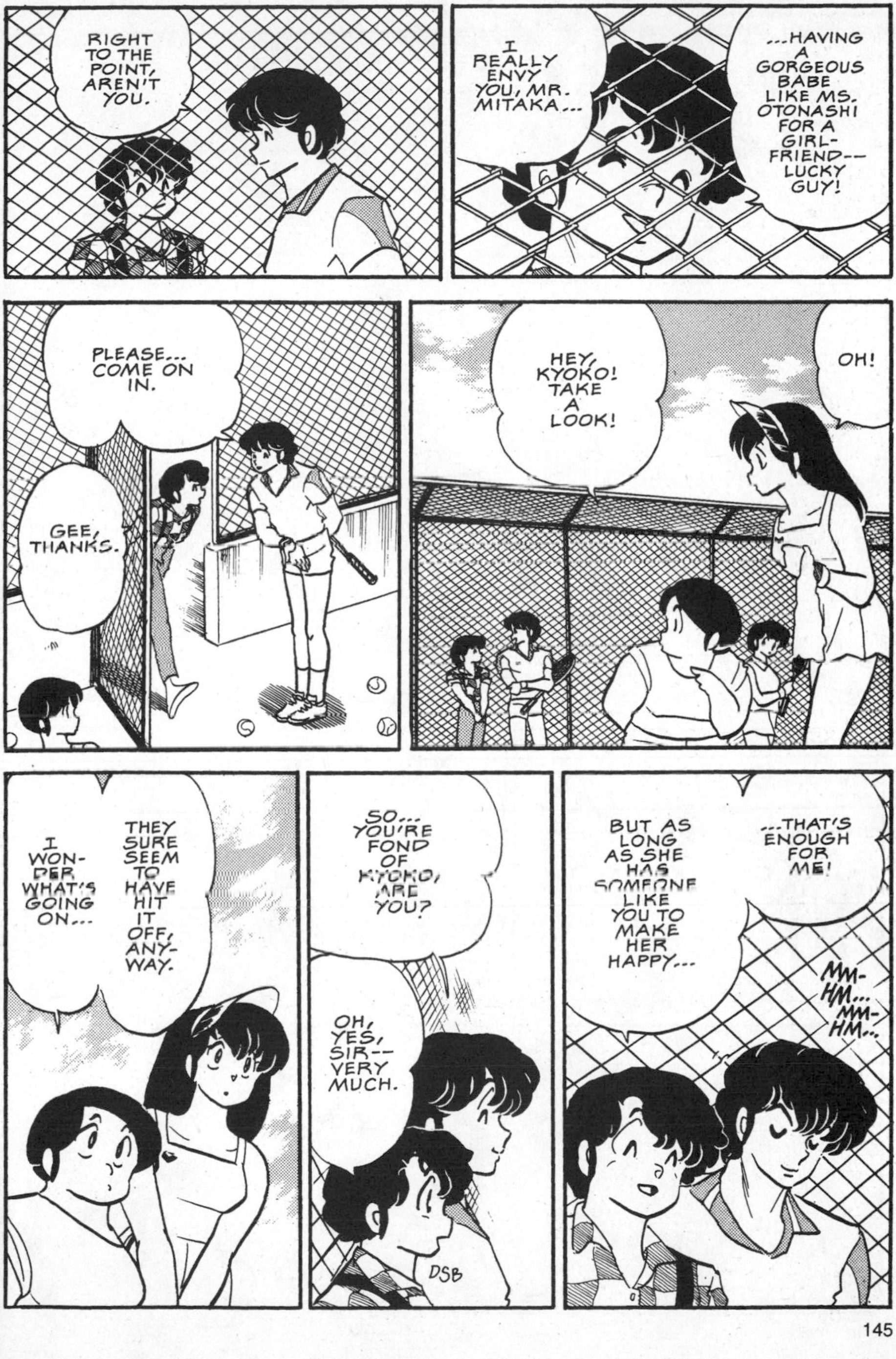
RIGHT TO THE POINT, AREN'T YOU.
I REALLY ENVY YOU, MR. MITAKA...
...HAVING A GORGEOUS BABE LIKE MS. OTONASHI FOR A GIRLFRIEND--LUCKY GUY!
PLEASE... COME ON IN.
GEE, THANKS.
HEY, KYOKO! TAKE A LOOK!
OH!
I WONDER WHAT'S GOING ON...
THEY SURE SEEM TO HAVE HIT IT OFF, ANYWAY.
SO... YOU'RE FOND OF KYOKO, ARE YOU?
OH, YES, SIR--VERY MUCH.
DSB
BUT AS LONG AS SHE HAS SOMEONE LIKE YOU TO MAKE HER HAPPY...
...THAT'S ENOUGH FOR ME!
MM-HM... MM-HM...

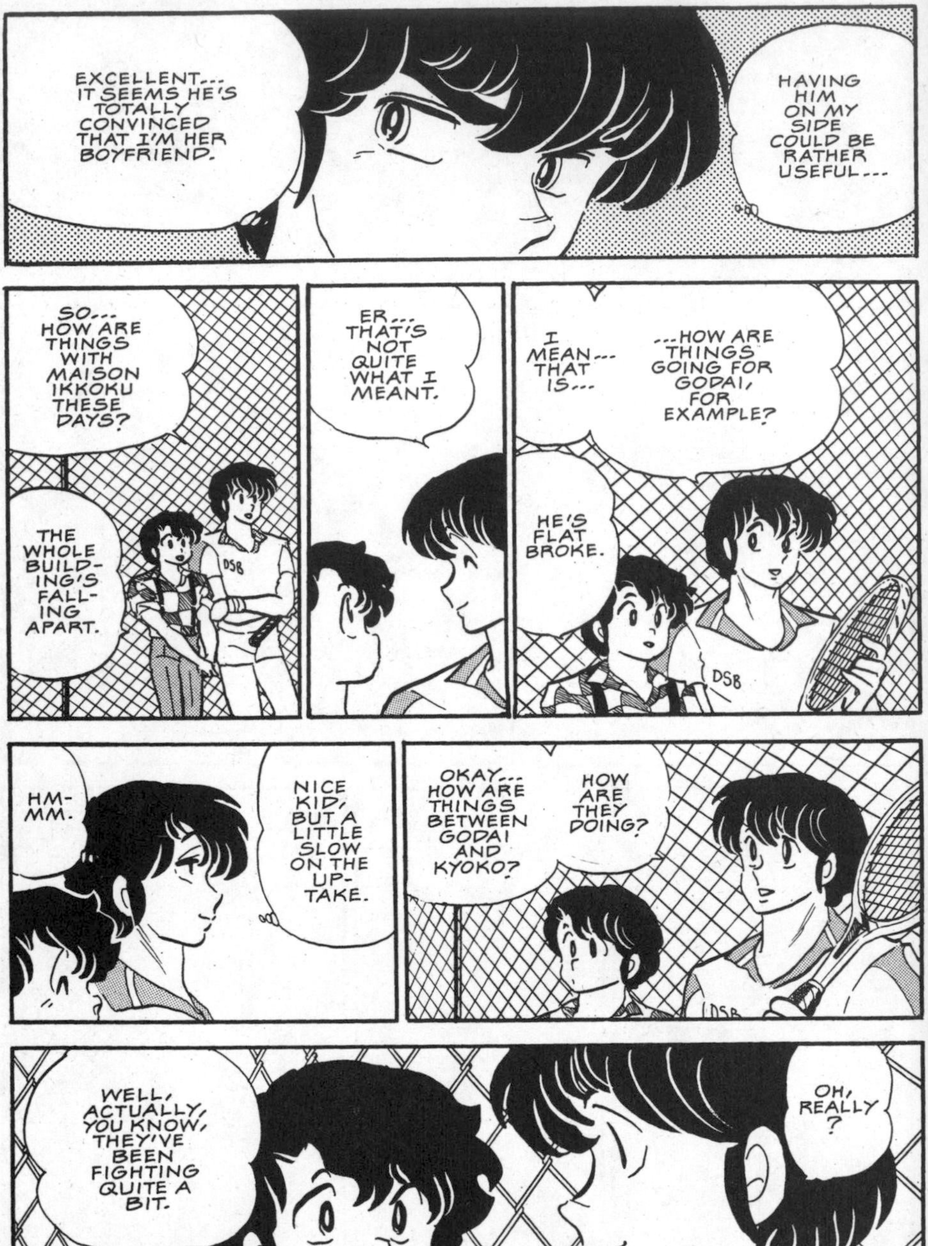
EXCELLENT... IT SEEMS HE'S TOTALLY CONVINCED THAT I'M HER BOYFRIEND.
HAVING HIM ON MY SIDE COULD BE RATHER USEFUL...
SO... HOW ARE THINGS WITH MAISON IKKOKU THESE DAYS?
THE WHOLE BUILDING'S FALLING APART.
ER... THAT'S NOT QUITE WHAT I MEANT.
I MEAN... THAT IS...
...HOW ARE THINGS GOING FOR GODAI, FOR EXAMPLE?
HE'S FLAT BROKE.
HMM.
NICE KID, BUT A LITTLE SLOW ON THE UPTAKE.
OKAY... HOW ARE THINGS BETWEEN GODAI AND KYOKO?
HOW ARE THEY DOING?
WELL, ACTUALLY, YOU KNOW, THEY'VE BEEN FIGHTING QUITE A BIT.
OH, REALLY?

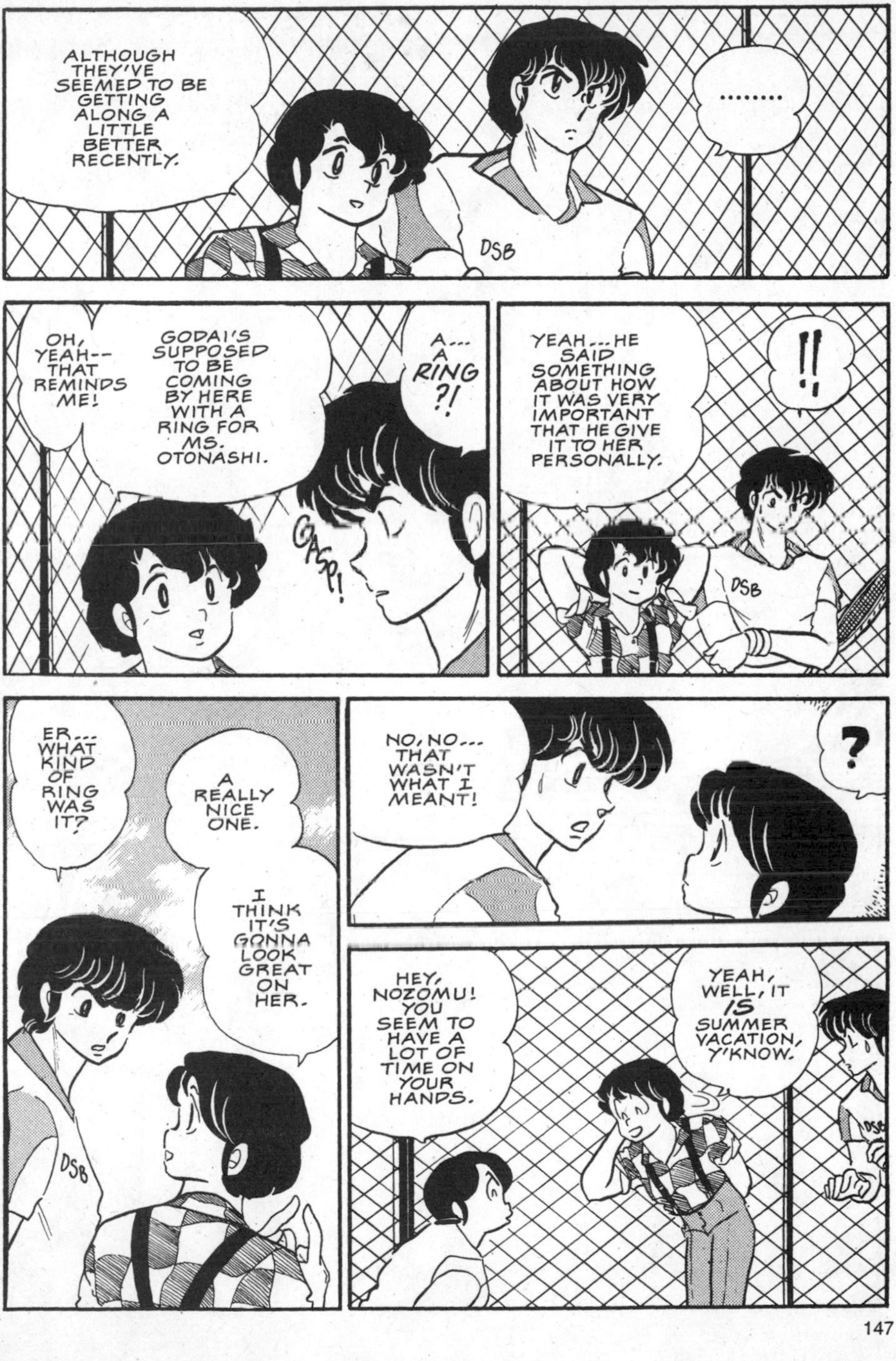
ALTHOUGH THEY'VE SEEMED TO BE GETTING ALONG A LITTLE BETTER RECENTLY.
....
OH, YEAH-- THAT REMINDS ME!
GODAI'S SUPPOSED TO BE COMING BY HERE WITH A RING FOR MS. OTONASHI.
A... A RING ?!
GASP!
YEAH... HE SAID SOMETHING ABOUT HOW IT WAS VERY IMPORTANT THAT HE GIVE IT TO HER PERSONALLY.
!!
ER... WHAT KIND OF RING WAS IT?
A REALLY NICE ONE.
I THINK IT'S GONNA LOOK GREAT ON HER.
NO, NO... THAT WASN'T WHAT I MEANT!
?
HEY, NOZOMU! YOU SEEM TO HAVE A LOT OF TIME ON YOUR HANDS.
YEAH, WELL, IT *IS* SUMMER VACATION, Y'KNOW.

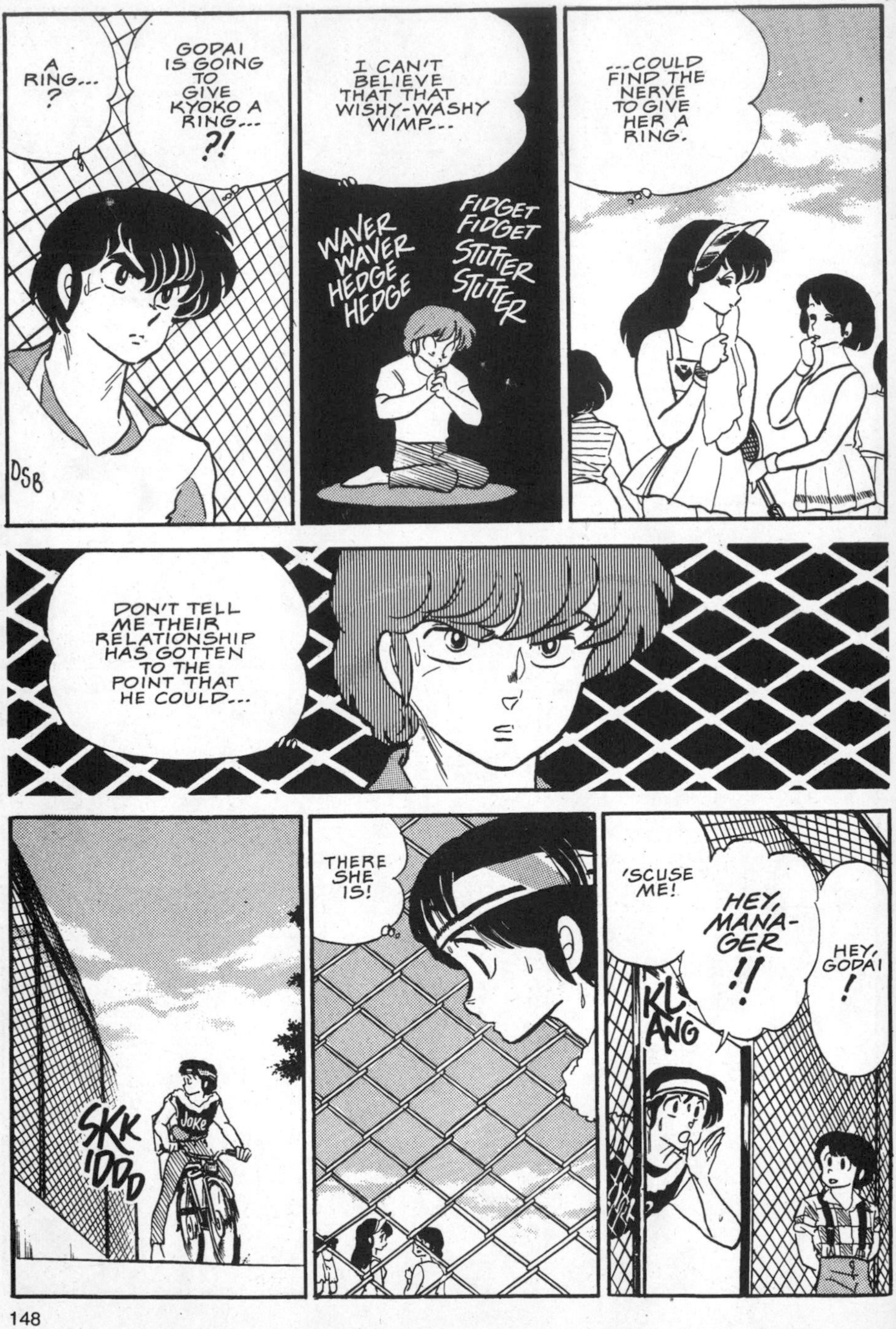
A RING... ?
GODAI IS GOING TO GIVE KYOKO A RING... ?!
I CAN'T BELIEVE THAT THAT WISHY-WASHY WIMP...
WAVER WAVER HEDGE HEDGE
FIDGET FIDGET STUTTER STUTTER
...COULD FIND THE NERVE TO GIVE HER A RING.
DON'T TELL ME THEIR RELATIONSHIP HAS GOTTEN TO THE POINT THAT HE COULD...
SKK !DDD
THERE SHE IS!
'SCUSE ME!
HEY, MANAGER !!
KLANG
HEY, GODAI !

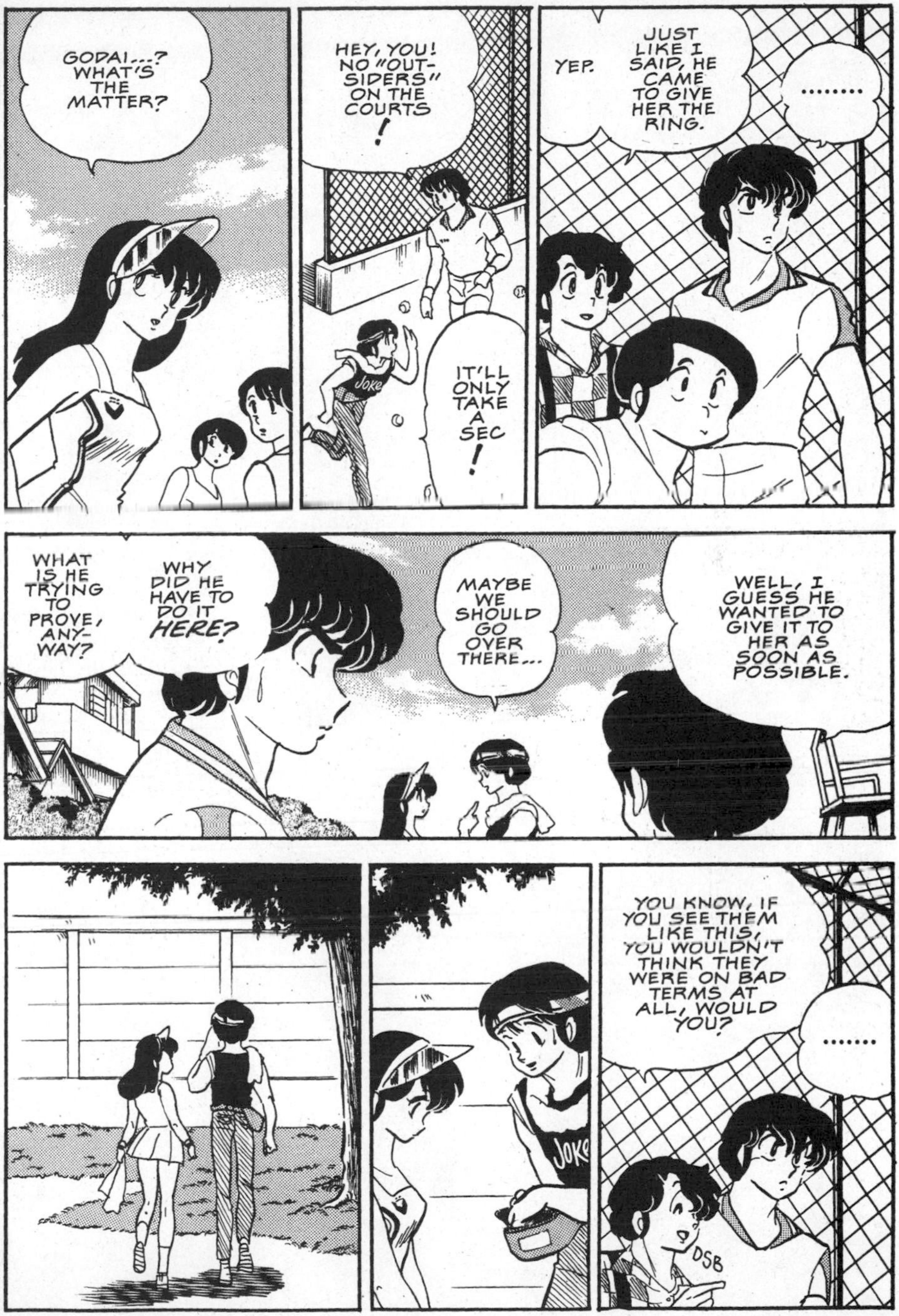
GODAI...? WHAT'S THE MATTER?
HEY, YOU! NO "OUT-SIDERS" ON THE COURTS!
IT'LL ONLY TAKE A SEC!
YEP.
JUST LIKE I SAID, HE CAME TO GIVE HER THE RING.
....
WHAT IS HE TRYING TO PROVE, ANYWAY?
WHY DID HE HAVE TO DO IT HERE?
MAYBE WE SHOULD GO OVER THERE...
WELL, I GUESS HE WANTED TO GIVE IT TO HER AS SOON AS POSSIBLE.
YOU KNOW, IF YOU SEE THEM LIKE THIS, YOU WOULDN'T THINK THEY WERE ON BAD TERMS AT ALL, WOULD YOU?
....
DSB

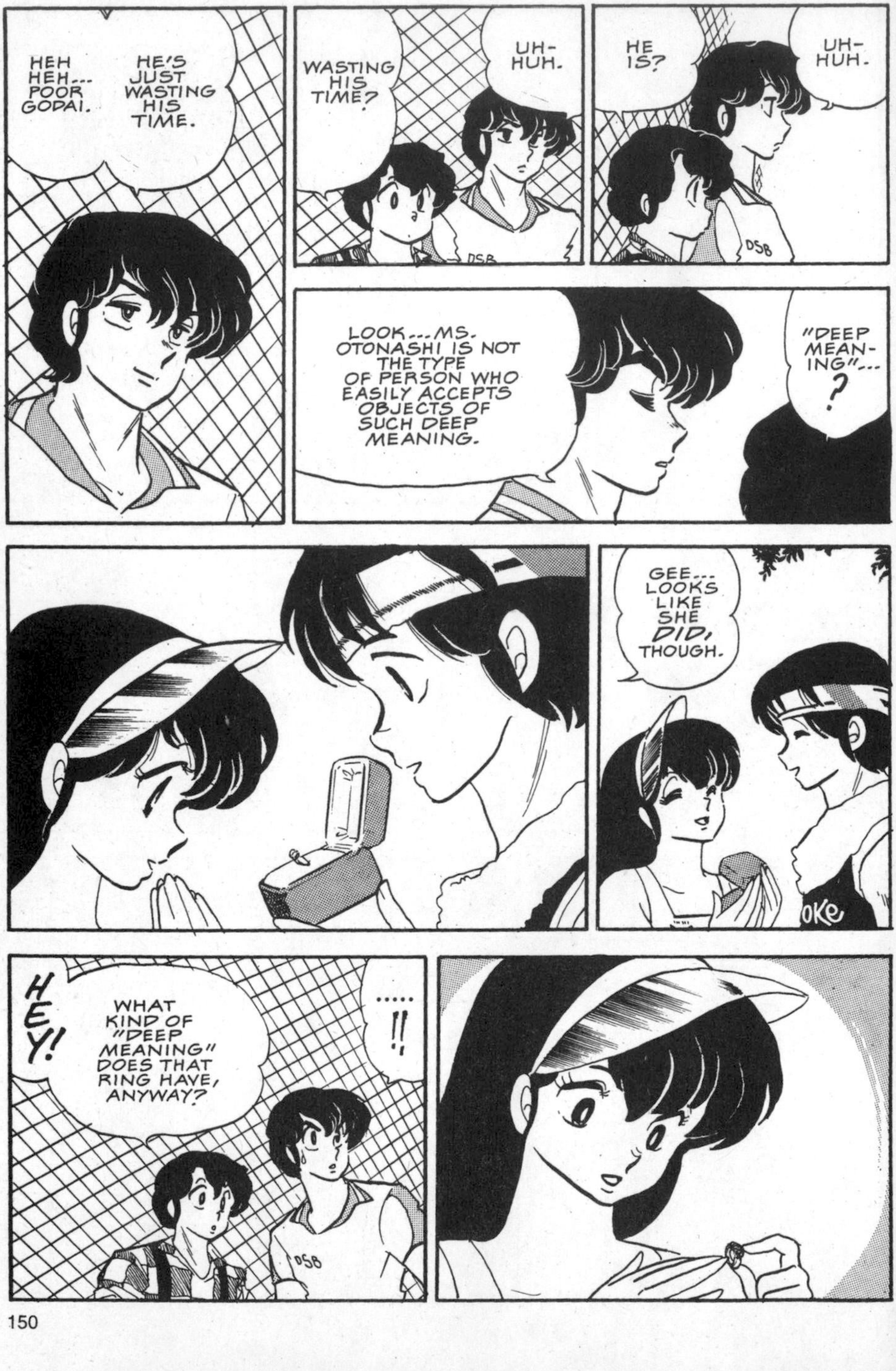
HEH HEH... POOR GODAI.
HE'S JUST WASTING HIS TIME.
WASTING HIS TIME?
UH-HUH.
HE IS?
UH-HUH.
LOOK...MS. OTONASHI IS NOT THE TYPE OF PERSON WHO EASILY ACCEPTS OBJECTS OF SUCH DEEP MEANING.
"DEEP MEANING"... ?
GEE... LOOKS LIKE SHE DID, THOUGH.
HEY!
WHAT KIND OF "DEEP MEANING" DOES THAT RING HAVE, ANYWAY?
.....!!

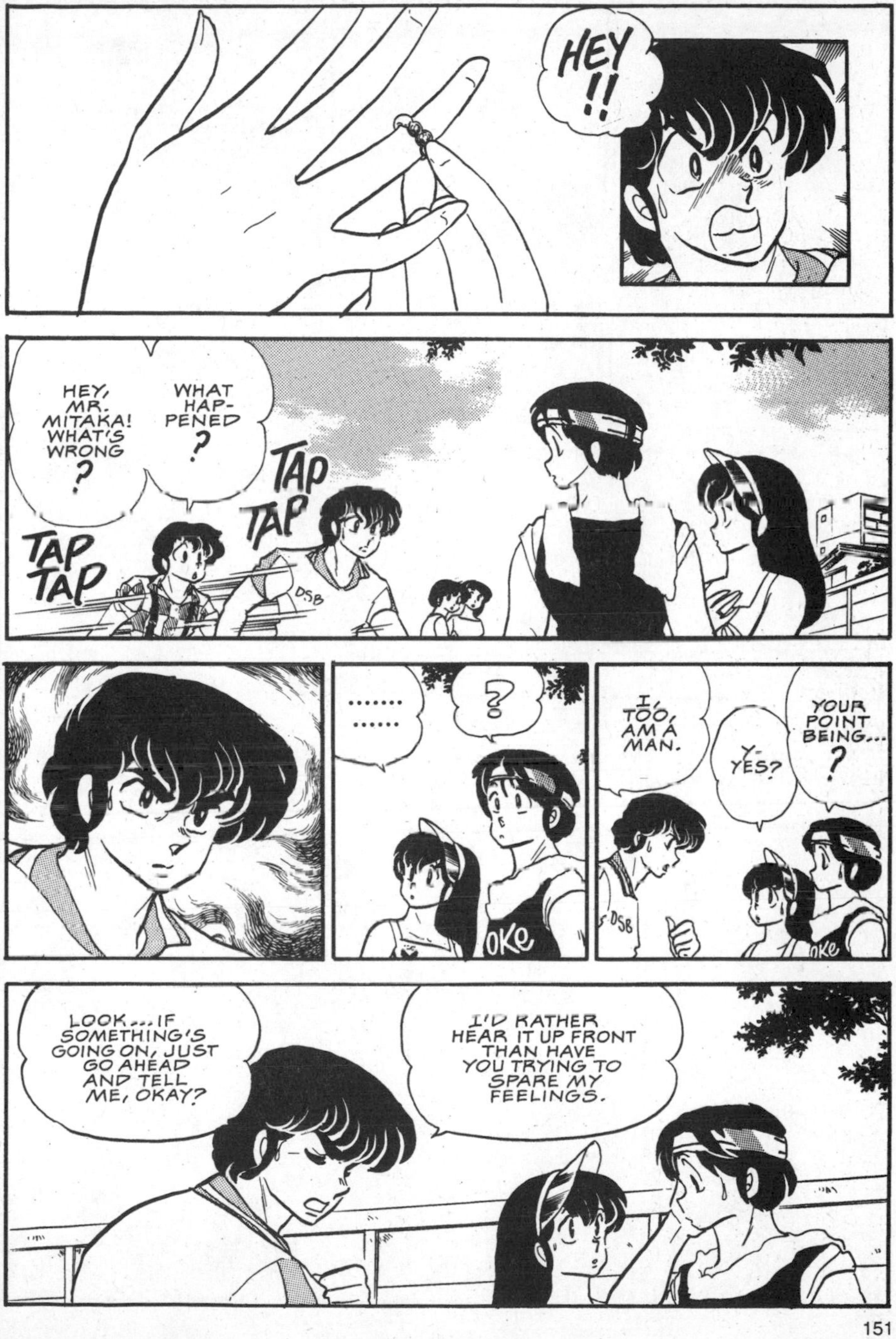
HEY !!
HEY, MR. MITAKA! WHAT'S WRONG ?
WHAT HAP-PENED ?
TAP TAP
TAP TAP
....
?
I, TOO, AM A MAN.
Y-YES?
YOUR POINT BEING... ?
LOOK... IF SOMETHING'S GOING ON, JUST GO AHEAD AND TELL ME, OKAY?
I'D RATHER HEAR IT UP FRONT THAN HAVE YOU TRYING TO SPARE MY FEELINGS.

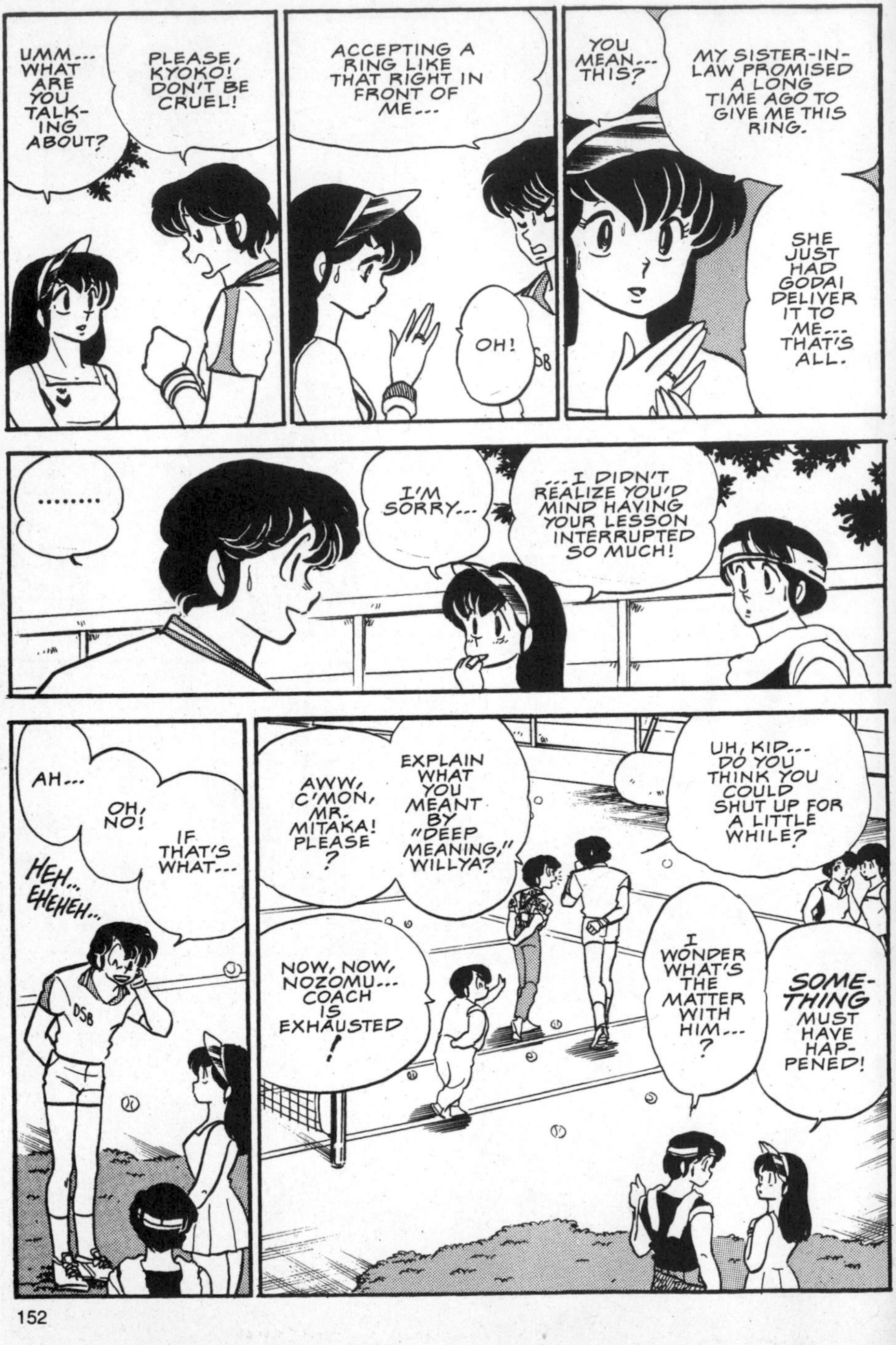

UMM... WHAT ARE YOU TALKING ABOUT?
PLEASE, KYOKO! DON'T BE CRUEL!
ACCEPTING A RING LIKE THAT RIGHT IN FRONT OF ME...
OH!
YOU MEAN... THIS?
MY SISTER-IN-LAW PROMISED A LONG TIME AGO TO GIVE ME THIS RING.
SHE JUST HAD GODAI DELIVER IT TO ME... THAT'S ALL.
....
I'M SORRY...
...I DIDN'T REALIZE YOU'D MIND HAVING YOUR LESSON INTERRUPTED SO MUCH!
AH...
OH, NO!
IF THAT'S WHAT...
HEH... EHEHEH...
AWW, C'MON, MR. MITAKA! PLEASE?
EXPLAIN WHAT YOU MEANT BY "DEEP MEANING," WILLYA?
UH, KID... DO YOU THINK YOU COULD SHUT UP FOR A LITTLE WHILE?
NOW, NOW, NOZOMU... COACH IS EXHAUSTED!
I WONDER WHAT'S THE MATTER WITH HIM...?
SOMETHING MUST HAVE HAPPENED!

PART 8

QUÉ SERÁ, SERÁ...

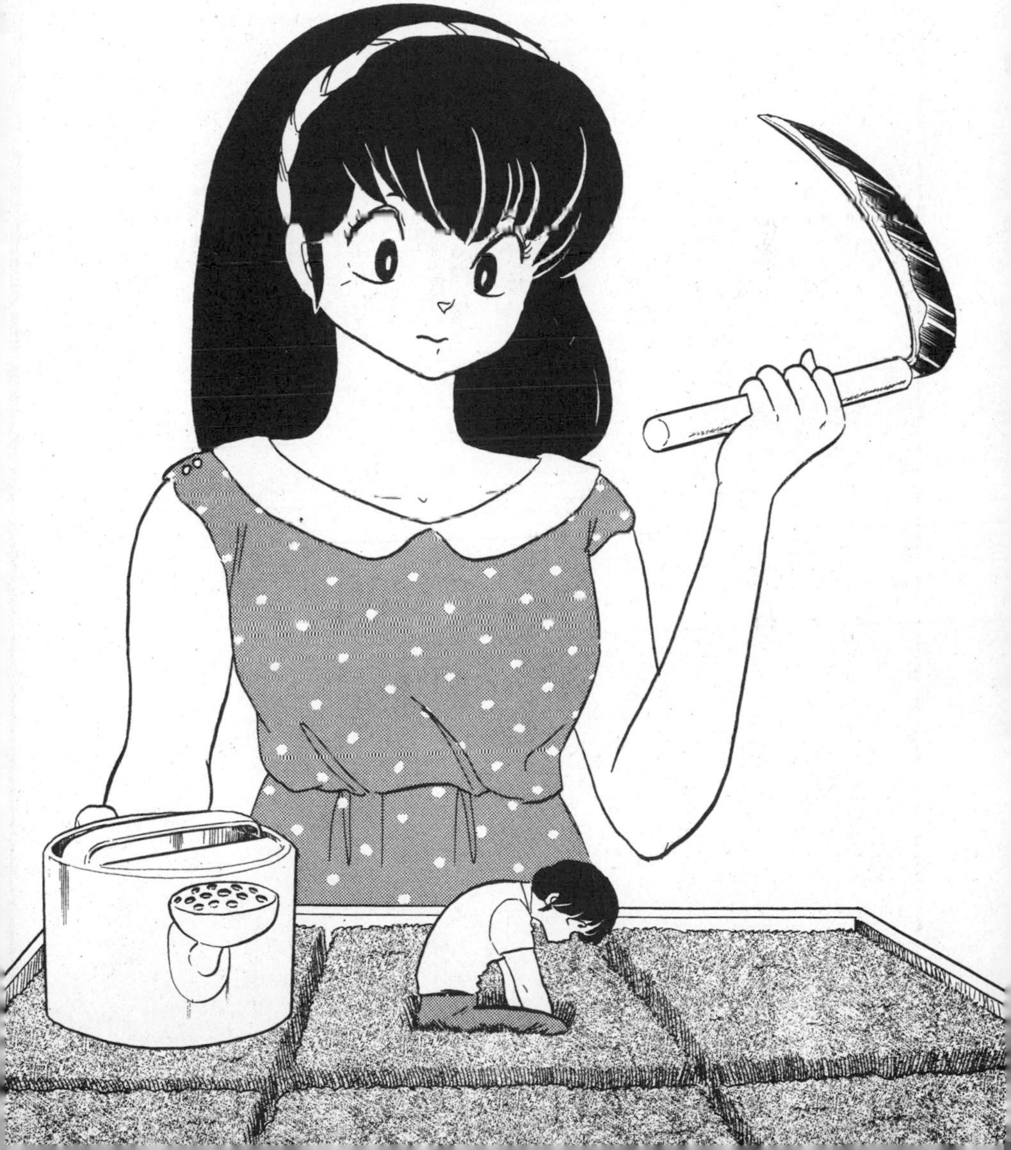

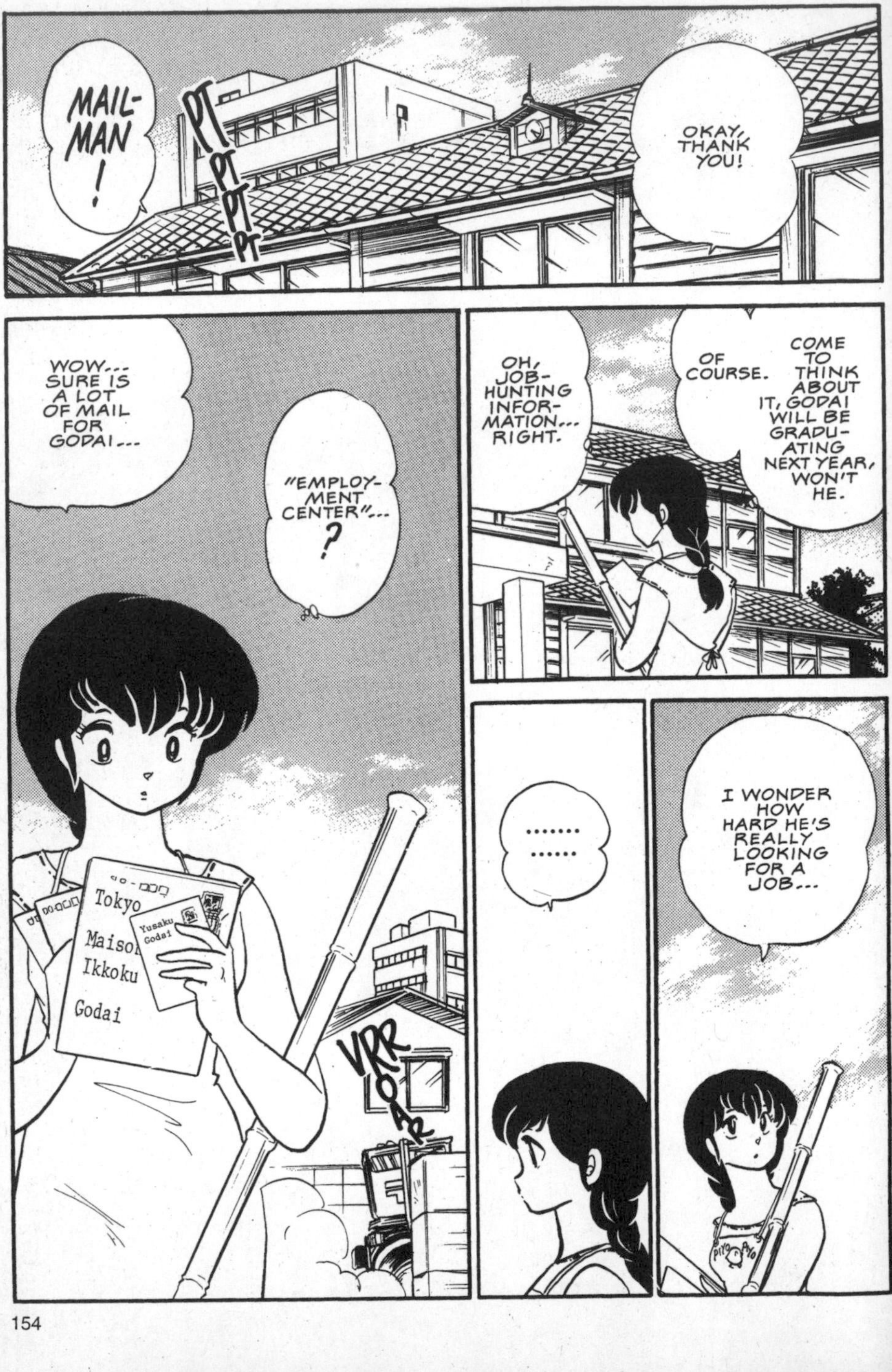
MAIL-MAN!
PT PT PT PT PT
OKAY, THANK YOU!
WOW... SURE IS A LOT OF MAIL FOR GODAI...
"EMPLOYMENT CENTER"...?
Tokyo
Maison Ikkoku
Godai
Yusaku Godai
VRR ROAR
OH, JOB-HUNTING INFORMATION... RIGHT.
OF COURSE.
COME TO THINK ABOUT IT, GODAI WILL BE GRADUATING NEXT YEAR, WON'T HE.
....
I WONDER HOW HARD HE'S REALLY LOOKING FOR A JOB...

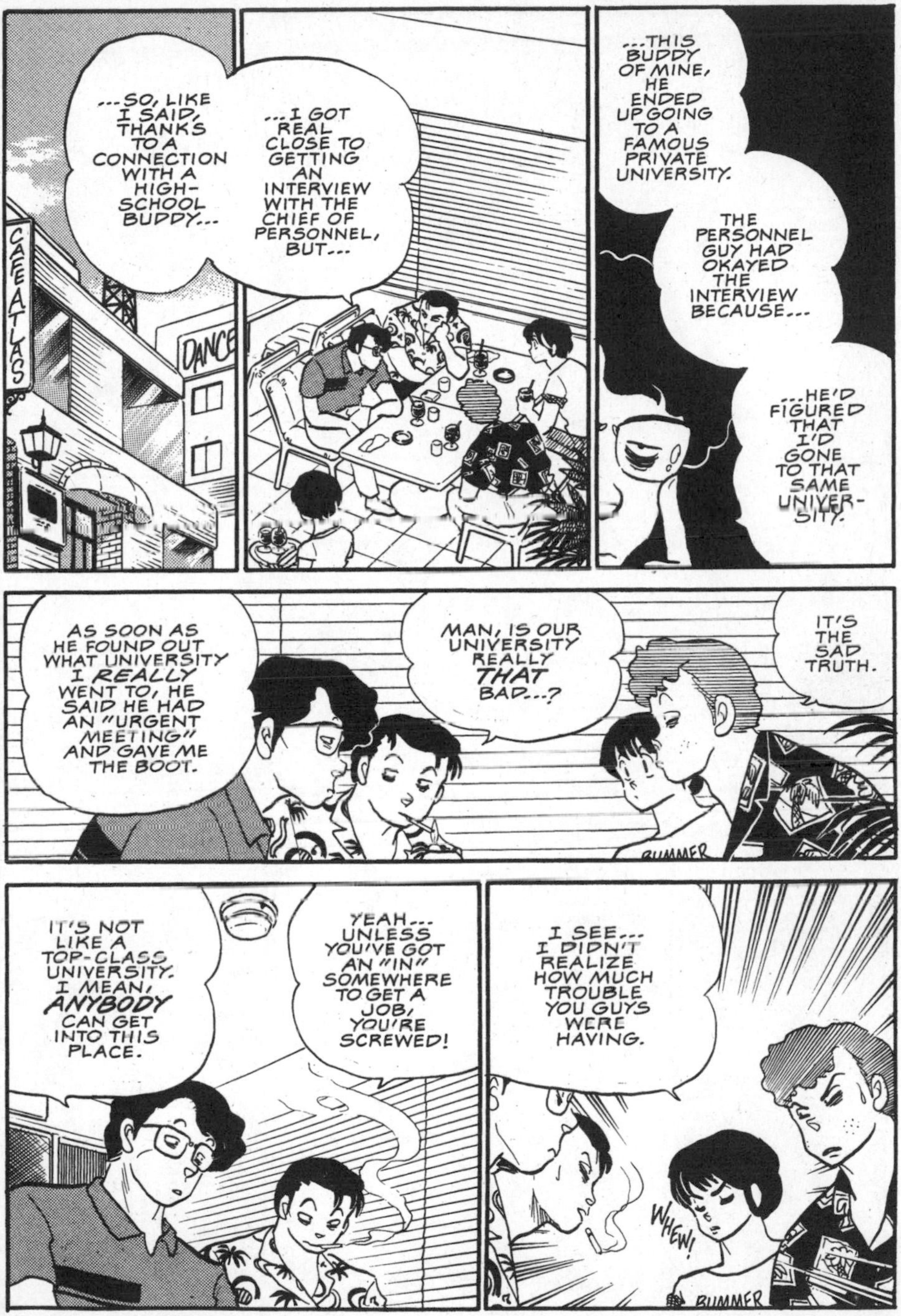
...SO, LIKE I SAID, THANKS TO A CONNECTION WITH A HIGH-SCHOOL BUDDY...
CAFE ATLAS
DANCE
...I GOT REAL CLOSE TO GETTING AN INTERVIEW WITH THE CHIEF OF PERSONNEL, BUT...
...THIS BUDDY OF MINE, HE ENDED UP GOING TO A FAMOUS PRIVATE UNIVERSITY.
THE PERSONNEL GUY HAD OKAYED THE INTERVIEW BECAUSE...
...HE'D FIGURED THAT I'D GONE TO THAT SAME UNIVER-SITY.
AS SOON AS HE FOUND OUT WHAT UNIVERSITY I *REALLY* WENT TO, HE SAID HE HAD AN "URGENT MEETING" AND GAVE ME THE BOOT.
MAN, IS OUR UNIVERSITY REALLY *THAT* BAD...?
IT'S THE SAD TRUTH.
BUMMER
IT'S NOT LIKE A TOP-CLASS UNIVERSITY. I MEAN, *ANYBODY* CAN GET INTO THIS PLACE.
YEAH... UNLESS YOU'VE GOT AN "IN" SOMEWHERE TO GET A JOB, YOU'RE SCREWED!
I SEE... I DIDN'T REALIZE HOW MUCH TROUBLE YOU GUYS WERE HAVING.
WHEW!
BUMMER

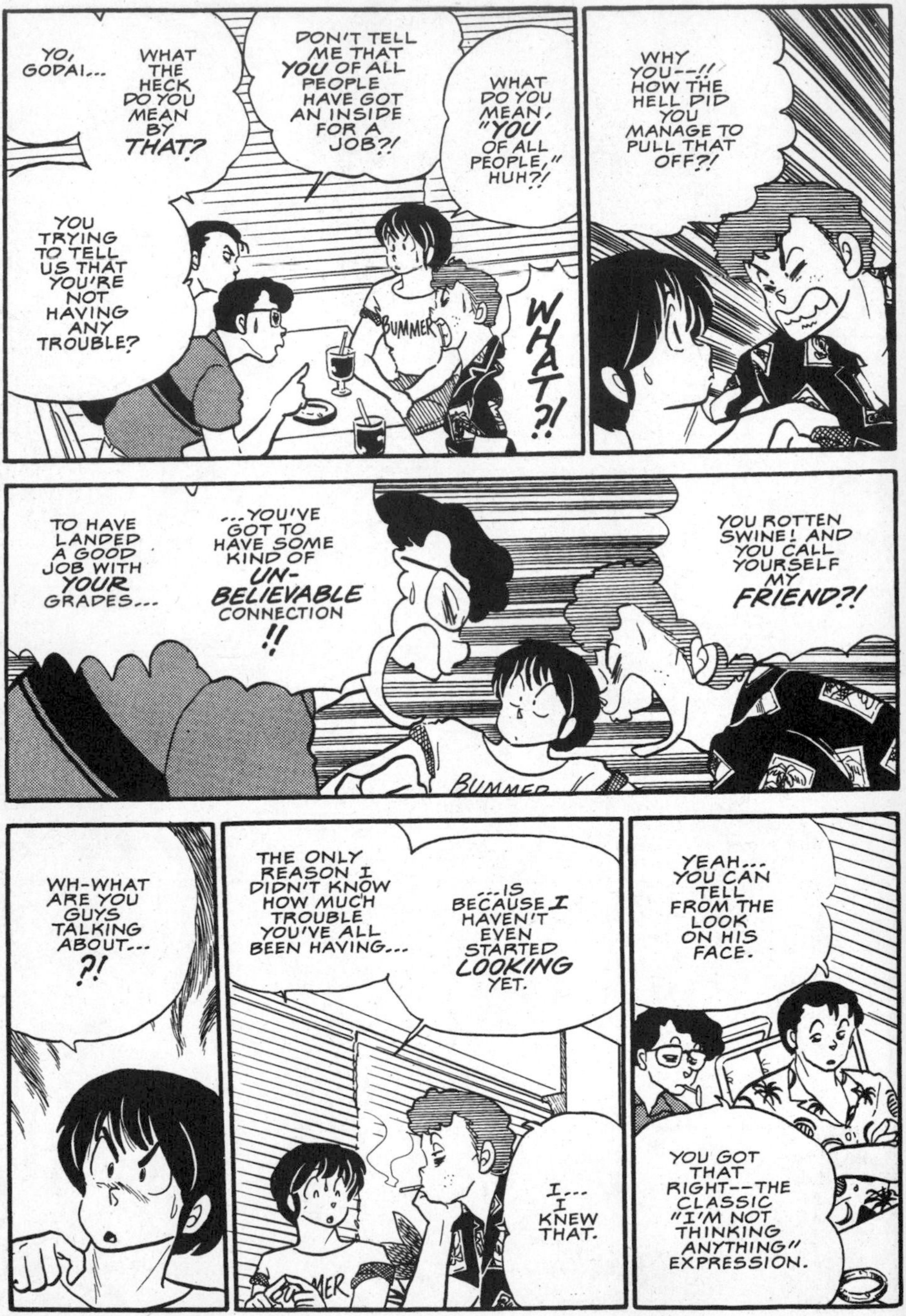
YO, GODAI...
WHAT THE HECK DO YOU MEAN BY THAT?
DON'T TELL ME THAT YOU OF ALL PEOPLE HAVE GOT AN INSIDE FOR A JOB?!
WHAT DO YOU MEAN, "YOU OF ALL PEOPLE," HUH?!
YOU TRYING TO TELL US THAT YOU'RE NOT HAVING ANY TROUBLE?
BUMMER
WHAT?!
WHY YOU--!! HOW THE HELL DID YOU MANAGE TO PULL THAT OFF?!
TO HAVE LANDED A GOOD JOB WITH YOUR GRADES...
...YOU'VE GOT TO HAVE SOME KIND OF UN-BELIEVABLE CONNECTION!!
YOU ROTTEN SWINE! AND YOU CALL YOURSELF MY FRIEND?!
WH-WHAT ARE YOU GUYS TALKING ABOUT...?!
THE ONLY REASON I DIDN'T KNOW HOW MUCH TROUBLE YOU'VE ALL BEEN HAVING...
...IS BECAUSE I HAVEN'T EVEN STARTED LOOKING YET.
I... I KNEW THAT.
YEAH... YOU CAN TELL FROM THE LOOK ON HIS FACE.
YOU GOT THAT RIGHT--THE CLASSIC "I'M NOT THINKING ANYTHING" EXPRESSION.

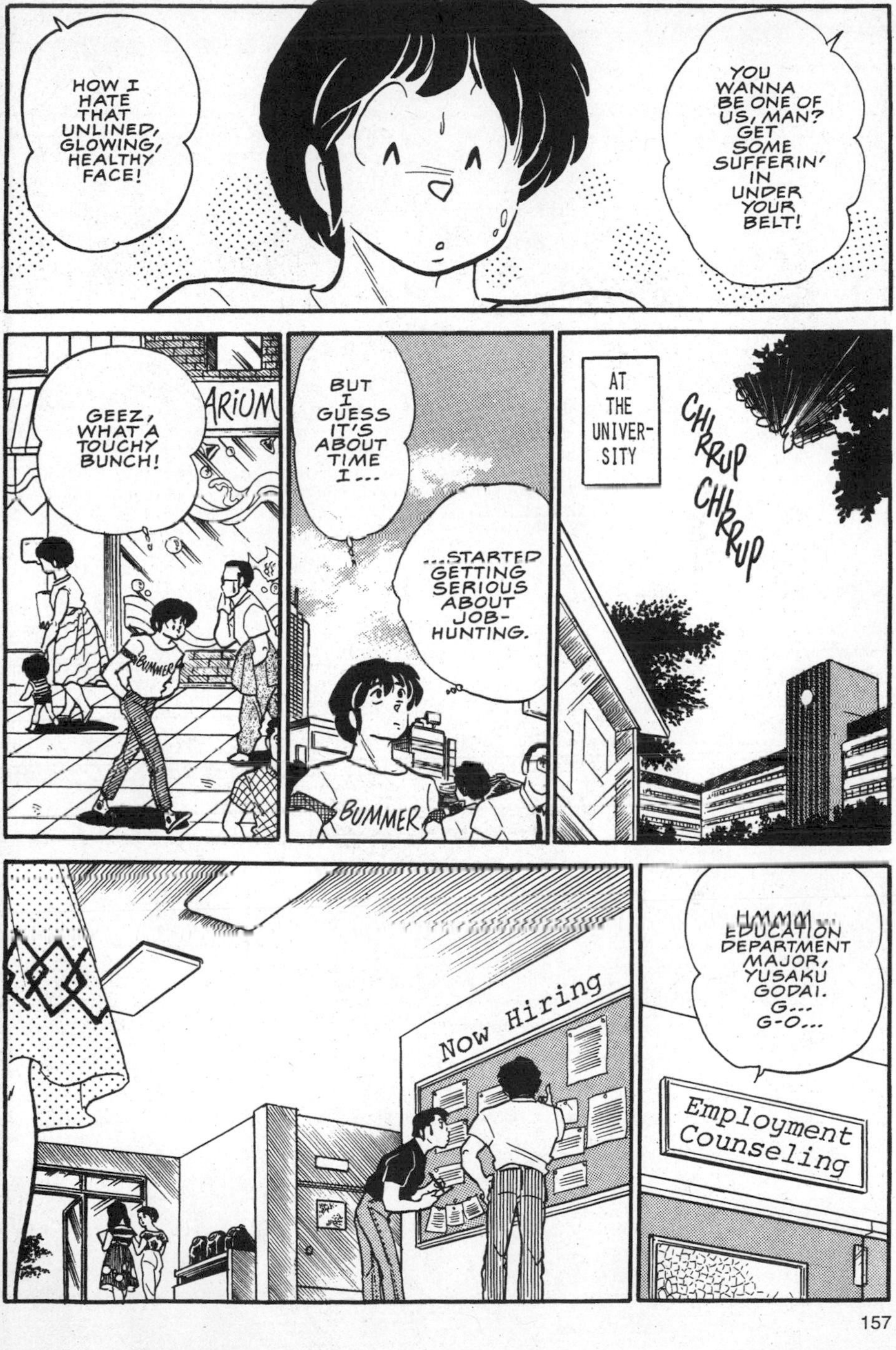
HOW I HATE THAT UNLINED, GLOWING, HEALTHY FACE!
YOU WANNA BE ONE OF US, MAN? GET SOME SUFFERIN' IN UNDER YOUR BELT!
ARIUM
GEEZ, WHAT A TOUCHY BUNCH!
BUMMER
BUT I GUESS IT'S ABOUT TIME I...
...STARTED GETTING SERIOUS ABOUT JOB-HUNTING.
BUMMER
AT THE UNIVERSITY
CHIRRUP
CHIRRUP
Now Hiring
HMMM EDUCATION DEPARTMENT MAJOR, YUSAKU GODAI. G... G-O...
Employment Counseling

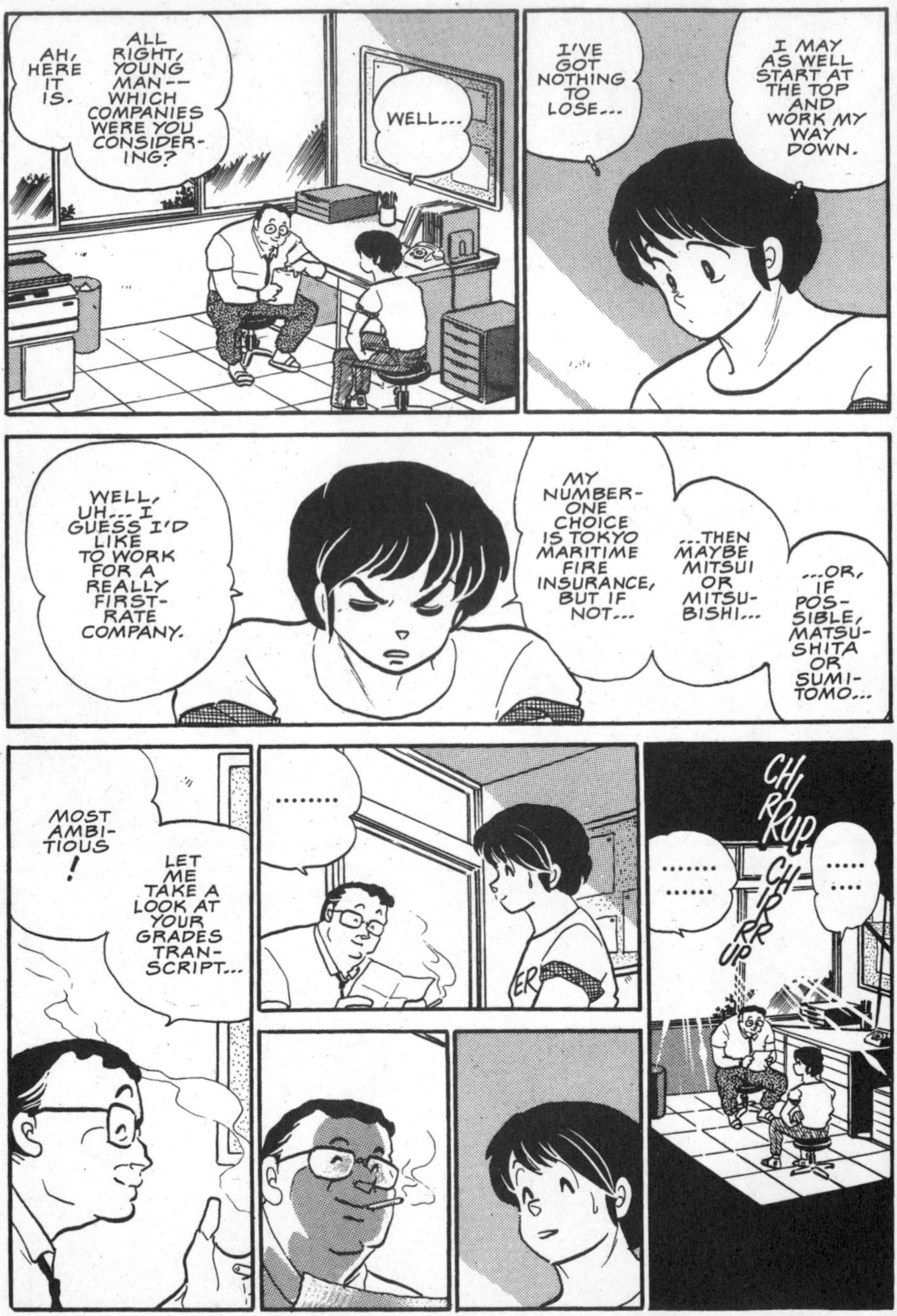
AH, HERE IT IS.
ALL RIGHT, YOUNG MAN-- WHICH COMPANIES WERE YOU CONSIDERING?
WELL...
I'VE GOT NOTHING TO LOSE...
I MAY AS WELL START AT THE TOP AND WORK MY WAY DOWN.
WELL, UH... I GUESS I'D LIKE TO WORK FOR A REALLY FIRST-RATE COMPANY.
MY NUMBER-ONE CHOICE IS TOKYO MARITIME FIRE INSURANCE, BUT IF NOT...
...THEN MAYBE MITSUI OR MITSUBISHI...
...OR, IF POSSIBLE, MATSUSHITA OR SUMITOMO...
MOST AMBITIOUS!
LET ME TAKE A LOOK AT YOUR GRADES TRANSCRIPT...
....
CHIRRUP
CHIRRRUP
....
....
.....
.....

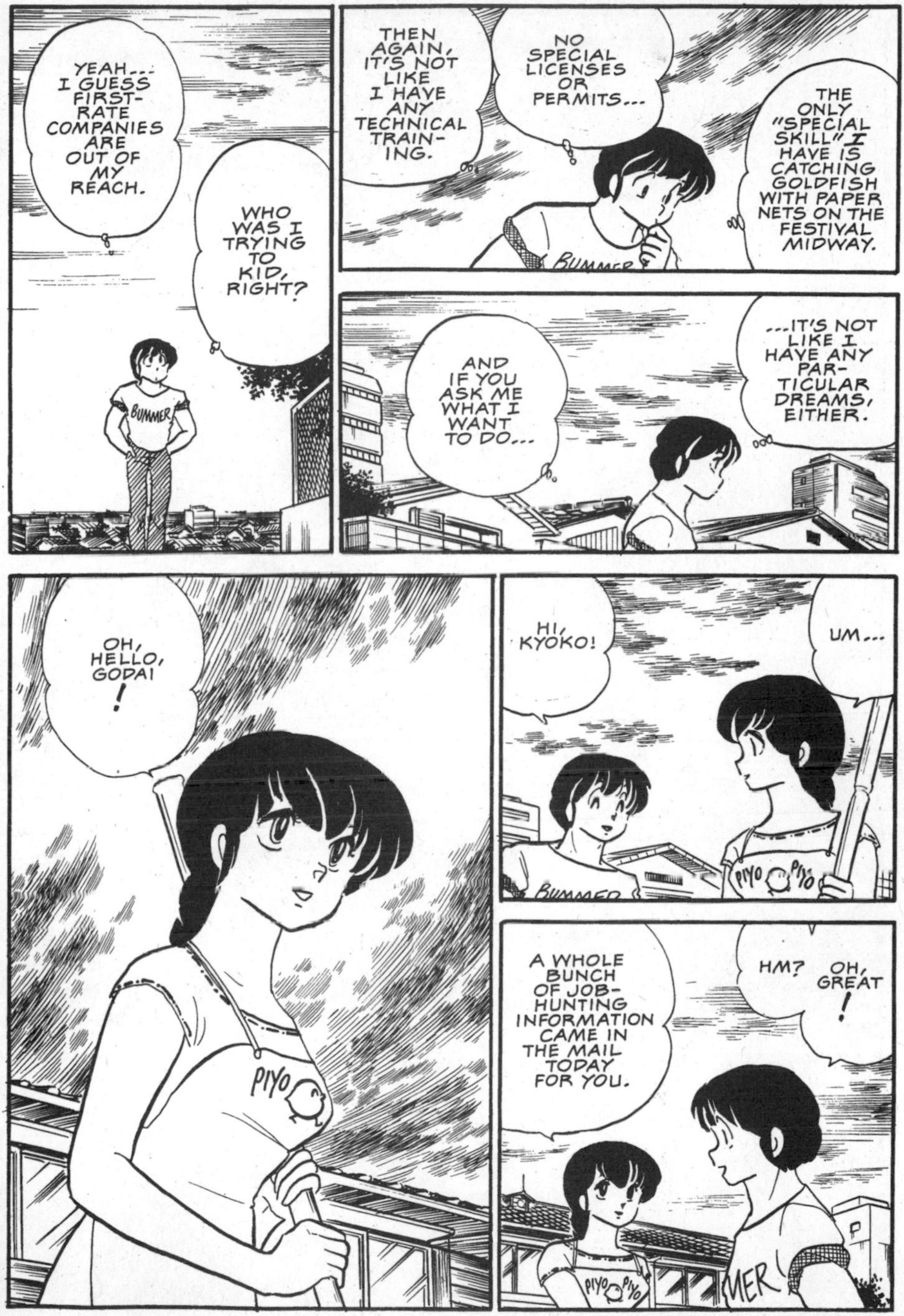
YEAH... I GUESS FIRST-RATE COMPANIES ARE OUT OF MY REACH.
WHO WAS I TRYING TO KID, RIGHT?
BUMMER
THEN AGAIN, IT'S NOT LIKE I HAVE ANY TECHNICAL TRAIN-ING.
NO SPECIAL LICENSES OR PERMITS...
THE ONLY "SPECIAL SKILL" I HAVE IS CATCHING GOLDFISH WITH PAPER NETS ON THE FESTIVAL MIDWAY.
AND IF YOU ASK ME WHAT I WANT TO DO...
...IT'S NOT LIKE I HAVE ANY PAR-TICULAR DREAMS, EITHER.
OH, HELLO, GODAI!
PIYO
HI, KYOKO!
UM...
A WHOLE BUNCH OF JOB-HUNTING INFORMATION CAME IN THE MAIL TODAY FOR YOU.
HM? OH, GREAT!

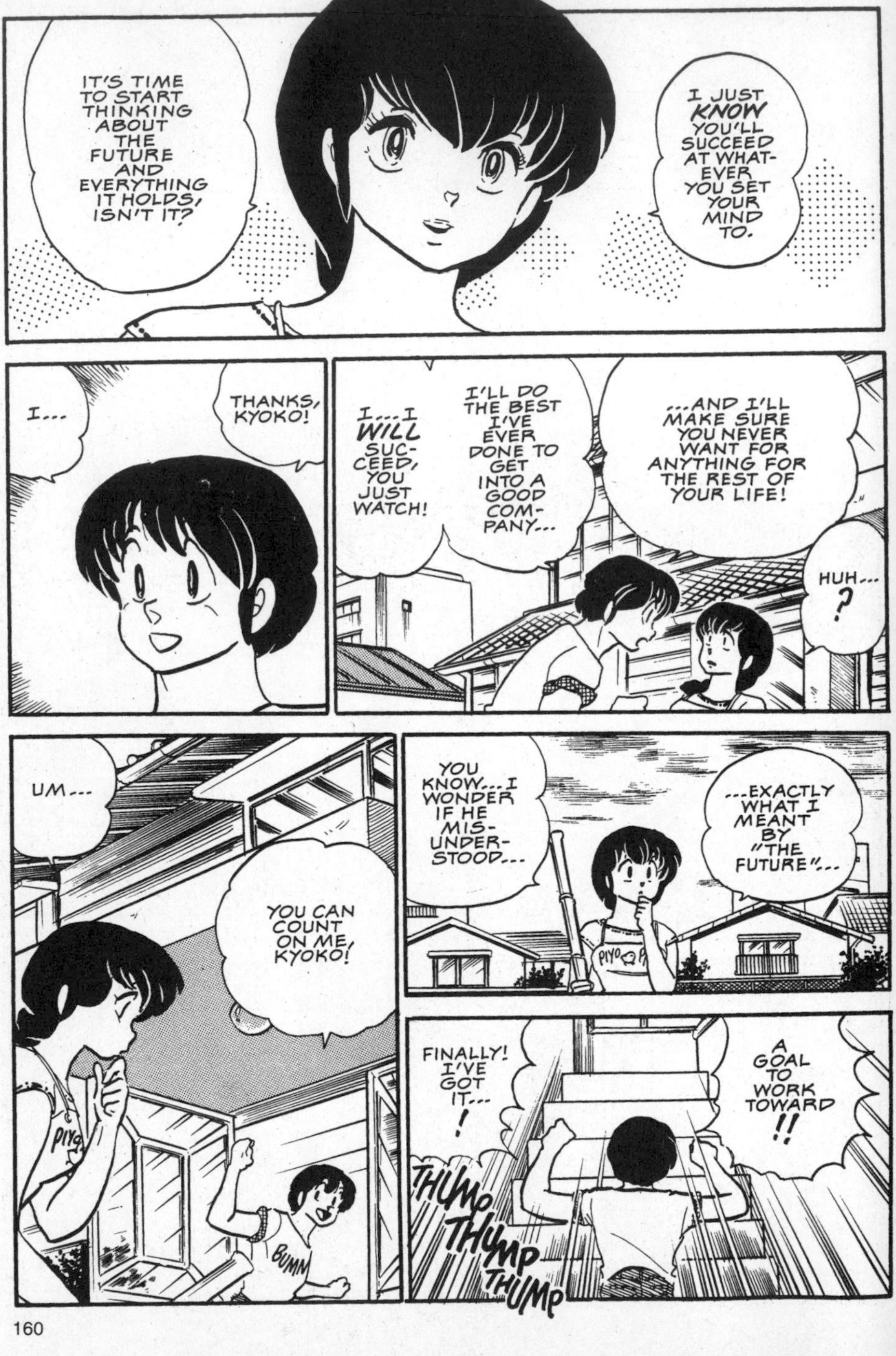
IT'S TIME TO START THINKING ABOUT THE FUTURE AND EVERYTHING IT HOLDS, ISN'T IT?
I JUST KNOW YOU'LL SUCCEED AT WHAT-EVER YOU SET YOUR MIND TO.
I...
THANKS, KYOKO!
I...I WILL SUC-CEED, YOU JUST WATCH!
I'LL DO THE BEST I'VE EVER DONE TO GET INTO A GOOD COM-PANY...
...AND I'LL MAKE SURE YOU NEVER WANT FOR ANYTHING FOR THE REST OF YOUR LIFE!
HUH...?
UM...
YOU CAN COUNT ON ME, KYOKO!
PIYO
BUMM
YOU KNOW...I WONDER IF HE MIS-UNDER-STOOD...
...EXACTLY WHAT I MEANT BY "THE FUTURE"...
PIYO
FINALLY! I'VE GOT IT...!
A GOAL TO WORK TOWARD!!
THUMP THUMP THUMP THUMP

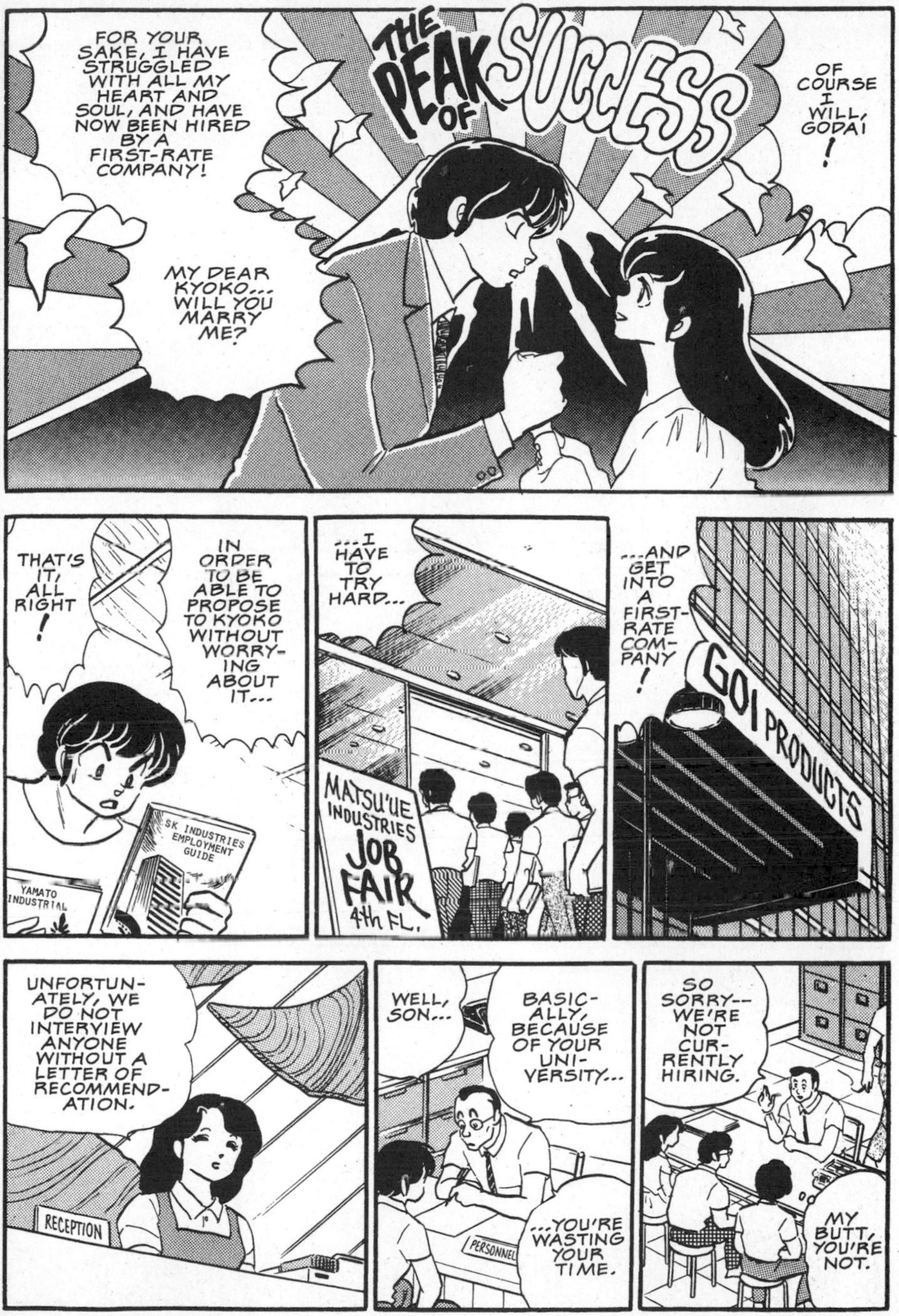
FOR YOUR SAKE, I HAVE STRUGGLED WITH ALL MY HEART AND SOUL, AND HAVE NOW BEEN HIRED BY A FIRST-RATE COMPANY!
THE PEAK OF SUCCESS
MY DEAR KYOKO... WILL YOU MARRY ME?
OF COURSE I WILL, GODAI!
THAT'S IT, ALL RIGHT!
IN ORDER TO BE ABLE TO PROPOSE TO KYOKO WITHOUT WORRYING ABOUT IT...
SK INDUSTRIES EMPLOYMENT GUIDE
YAMATO INDUSTRIAL
...I HAVE TO TRY HARD...
MATSU'UE INDUSTRIES JOB FAIR 4th FL.
...AND GET INTO A FIRST-RATE COMPANY!
GOI PRODUCTS
UNFORTUNATELY, WE DO NOT INTERVIEW ANYONE WITHOUT A LETTER OF RECOMMENDATION.
RECEPTION
WELL, SON...
BASICALLY, BECAUSE OF YOUR UNIVERSITY...
...YOU'RE WASTING YOUR TIME.
PERSONNEL
SO SORRY--WE'RE NOT CURRENTLY HIRING.
MY BUTT, YOU'RE NOT.

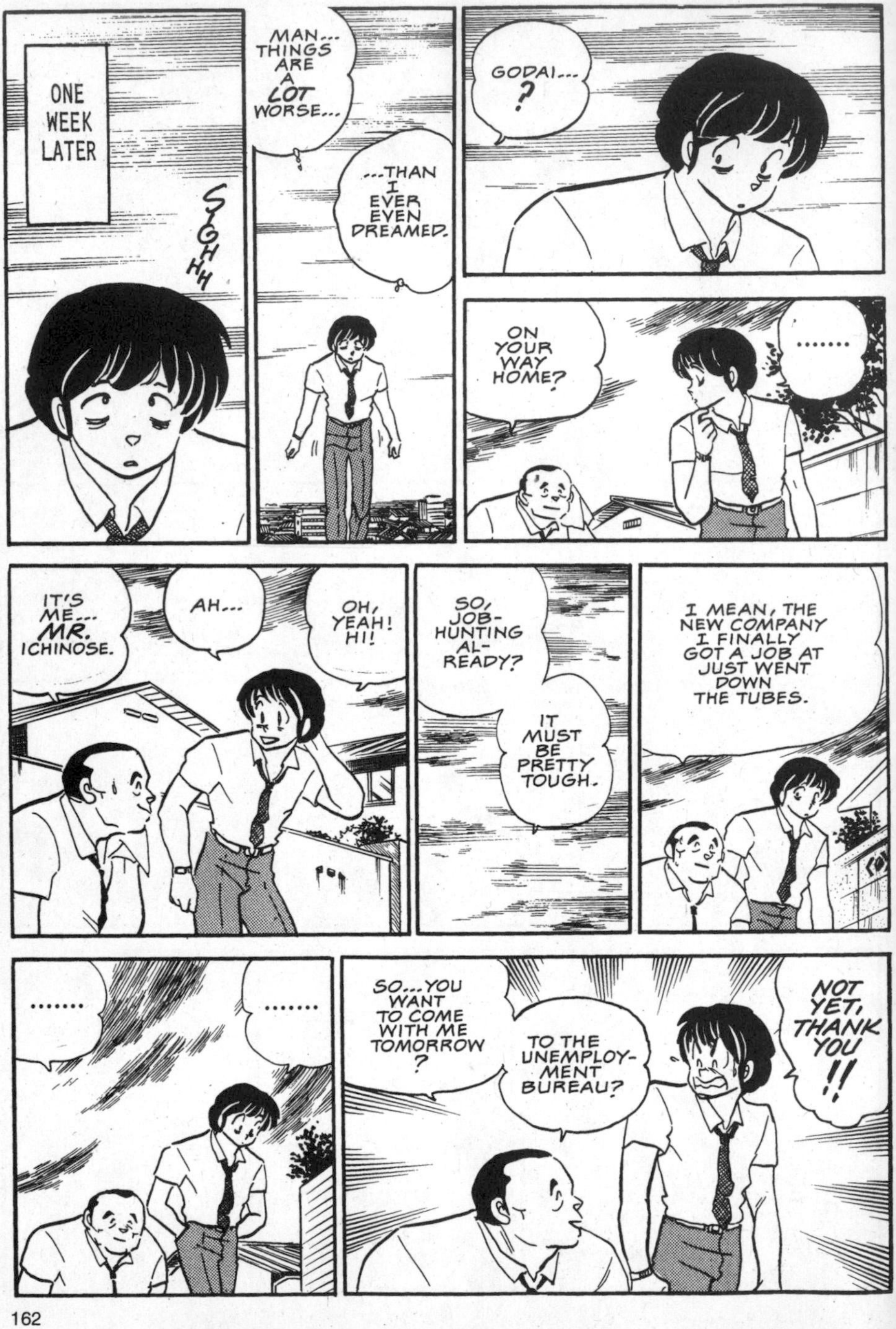

ONE WEEK LATER
SIGHHH
MAN... THINGS ARE A LOT WORSE...
...THAN I EVER EVEN DREAMED.
GODAI... ?
ON YOUR WAY HOME?
....
IT'S ME... MR. ICHINOSE.
AH...
OH, YEAH! HI!
SO, JOB-HUNTING AL-READY?
IT MUST BE PRETTY TOUGH.
I MEAN, THE NEW COMPANY I FINALLY GOT A JOB AT JUST WENT DOWN THE TUBES.
....
....
SO...YOU WANT TO COME WITH ME TOMORROW ?
TO THE UNEMPLOY-MENT BUREAU?
NOT YET, THANK YOU !!

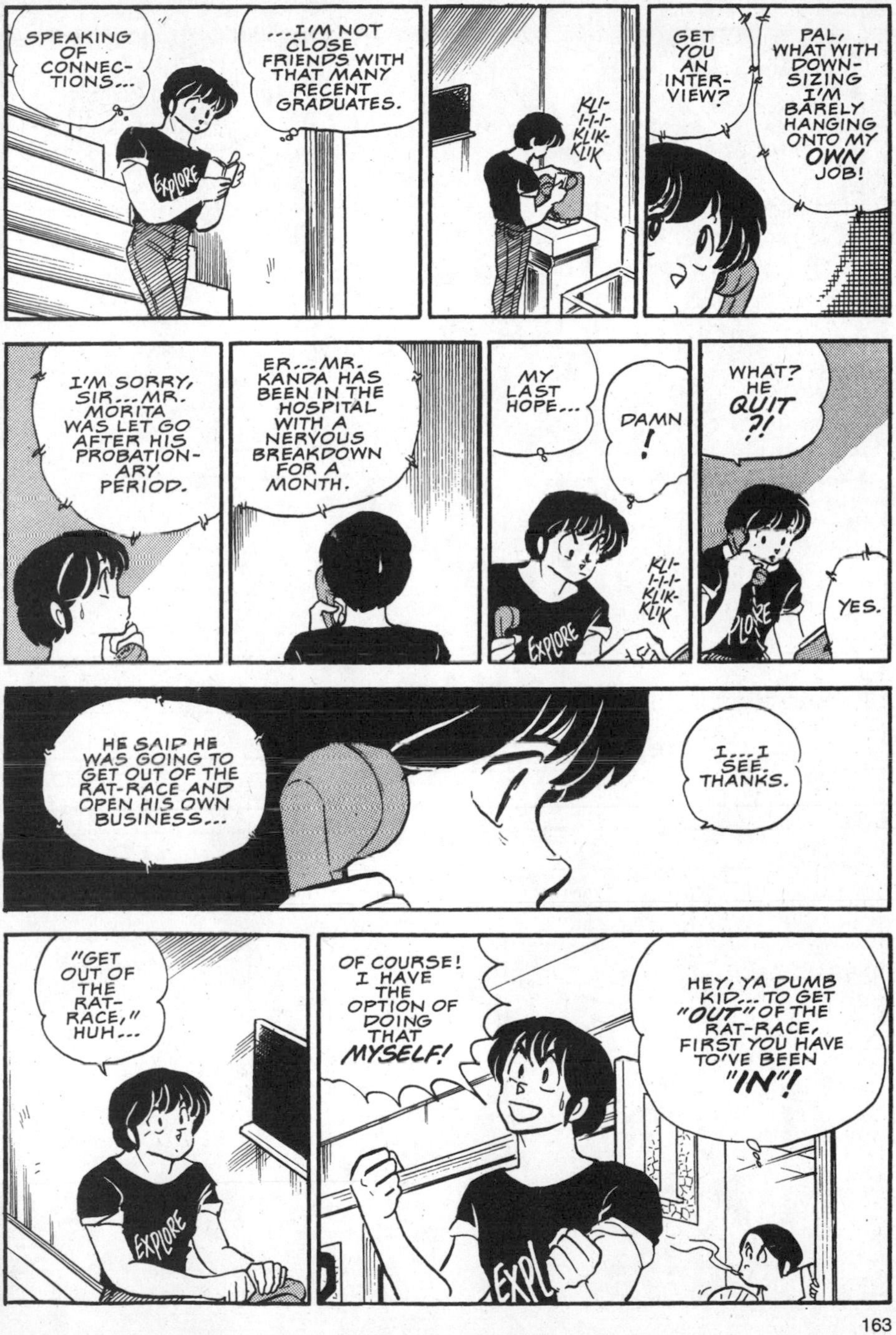
SPEAKING OF CONNECTIONS...
...I'M NOT CLOSE FRIENDS WITH THAT MANY RECENT GRADUATES.
KLI-I-I-I-KLIK-KLIK
GET YOU AN INTERVIEW?
PAL, WHAT WITH DOWN-SIZING I'M BARELY HANGING ONTO MY OWN JOB!
I'M SORRY, SIR... MR. MORITA WAS LET GO AFTER HIS PROBATIONARY PERIOD.
ER... MR. KANDA HAS BEEN IN THE HOSPITAL WITH A NERVOUS BREAKDOWN FOR A MONTH.
MY LAST HOPE...
DAMN!
KLI-I-I-I-KLIK-KLIK
WHAT? HE QUIT?!
YES.
HE SAID HE WAS GOING TO GET OUT OF THE RAT-RACE AND OPEN HIS OWN BUSINESS...
I... I SEE. THANKS.
"GET OUT OF THE RAT-RACE," HUH...
OF COURSE! I HAVE THE OPTION OF DOING THAT MYSELF!
HEY, YA DUMB KID... TO GET "OUT" OF THE RAT-RACE, FIRST YOU HAVE TO'VE BEEN "IN"!

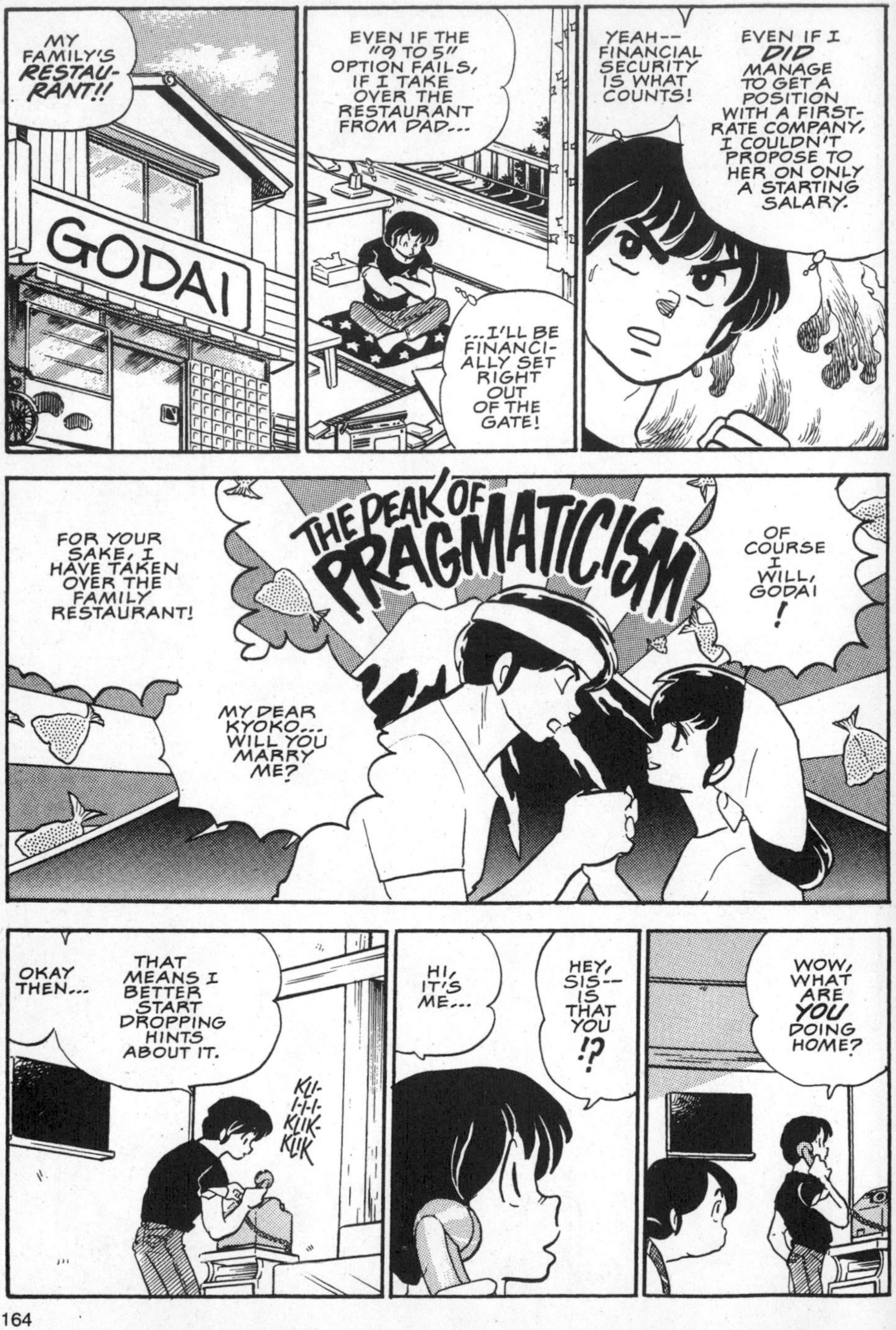
MY FAMILY'S RESTAURANT!!
GODAI
EVEN IF THE "9 TO 5" OPTION FAILS, IF I TAKE OVER THE RESTAURANT FROM DAD...
...I'LL BE FINANCIALLY SET RIGHT OUT OF THE GATE!
YEAH-- FINANCIAL SECURITY IS WHAT COUNTS!
EVEN IF I DID MANAGE TO GET A POSITION WITH A FIRST-RATE COMPANY, I COULDN'T PROPOSE TO HER ON ONLY A STARTING SALARY.
THE PEAK OF PRAGMATICISM
FOR YOUR SAKE, I HAVE TAKEN OVER THE FAMILY RESTAURANT!
MY DEAR KYOKO... WILL YOU MARRY ME?
OF COURSE I WILL, GODAI!
OKAY THEN...
THAT MEANS I BETTER START DROPPING HINTS ABOUT IT.
KLI-I-I-I-KLIK-KLIK
HI, IT'S ME...
HEY, SIS-- IS THAT YOU!?
WOW, WHAT ARE YOU DOING HOME?

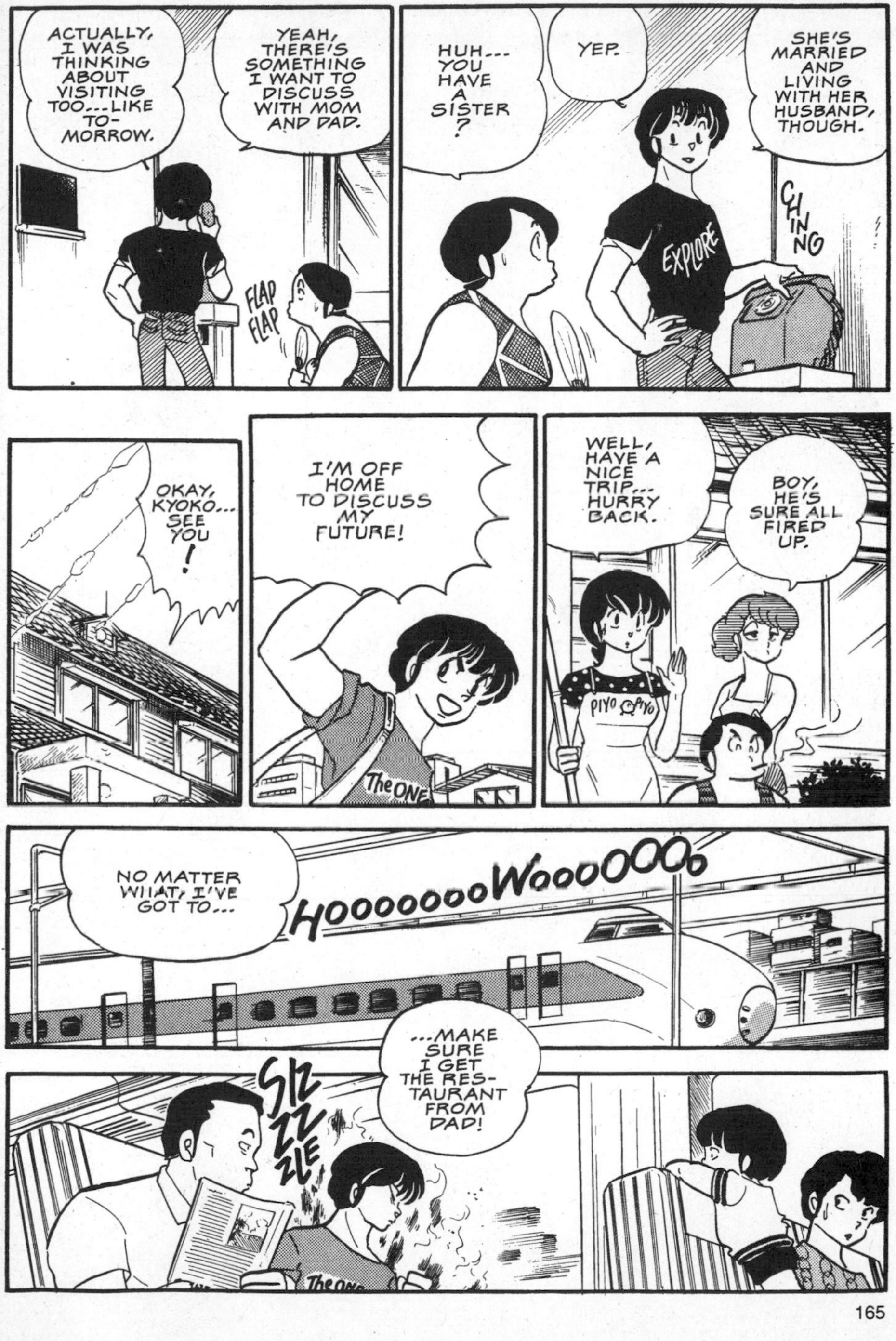
ACTUALLY, I WAS THINKING ABOUT VISITING TOO...LIKE TO-MORROW.
YEAH, THERE'S SOMETHING I WANT TO DISCUSS WITH MOM AND DAD.
FLAP FLAP
HUH... YOU HAVE A SISTER?
YEP.
SHE'S MARRIED AND LIVING WITH HER HUSBAND, THOUGH.
EXPLORE
CHING
OKAY, KYOKO... SEE YOU!
I'M OFF HOME TO DISCUSS MY FUTURE!
The ONE
WELL, HAVE A NICE TRIP... HURRY BACK.
BOY, HE'S SURE ALL FIRED UP.
PIYO PIYO
NO MATTER WHAT, I'VE GOT TO...
HOOOOOOOWOOOOOOO
...MAKE SURE I GET THE RES-TAURANT FROM DAD!
SIZZZZLE

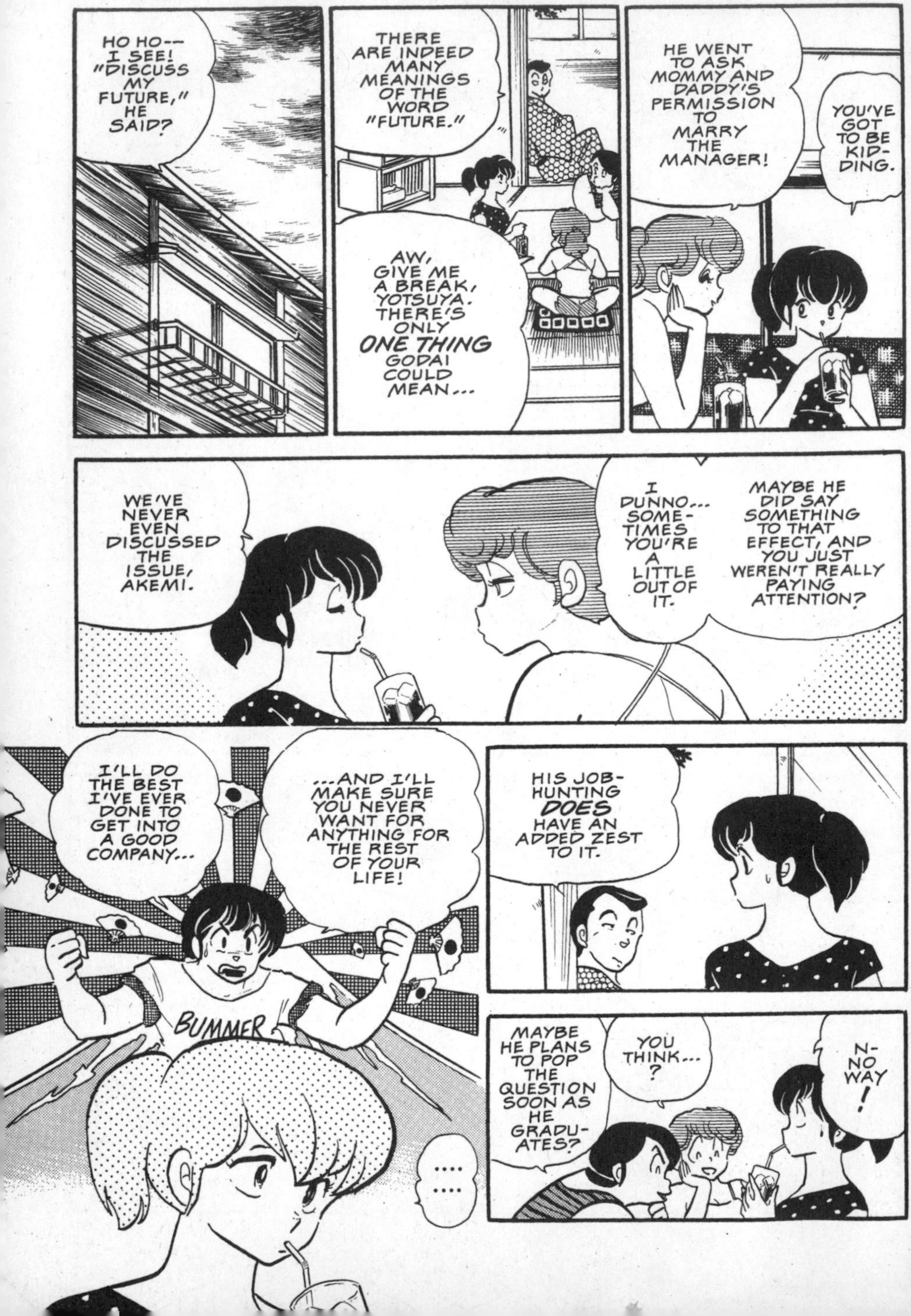
HO HO-- I SEE! "DISCUSS MY FUTURE," HE SAID?
THERE ARE INDEED MANY MEANINGS OF THE WORD "FUTURE."
AW, GIVE ME A BREAK, YOTSUYA. THERE'S ONLY ONE THING GODAI COULD MEAN...
HE WENT TO ASK MOMMY AND DADDY'S PERMISSION TO MARRY THE MANAGER!
YOU'VE GOT TO BE KID-DING.
WE'VE NEVER EVEN DISCUSSED THE ISSUE, AKEMI.
I DUNNO... SOME-TIMES YOU'RE A LITTLE OUT OF IT.
MAYBE HE DID SAY SOMETHING TO THAT EFFECT, AND YOU JUST WEREN'T REALLY PAYING ATTENTION?
I'LL DO THE BEST I'VE EVER DONE TO GET INTO A GOOD COMPANY...
...AND I'LL MAKE SURE YOU NEVER WANT FOR ANYTHING FOR THE REST OF YOUR LIFE!
BUMMER
....
....
HIS JOB-HUNTING DOES HAVE AN ADDED ZEST TO IT.
MAYBE HE PLANS TO POP THE QUESTION SOON AS HE GRADU-ATES?
YOU THINK... ?
N-NO WAY!

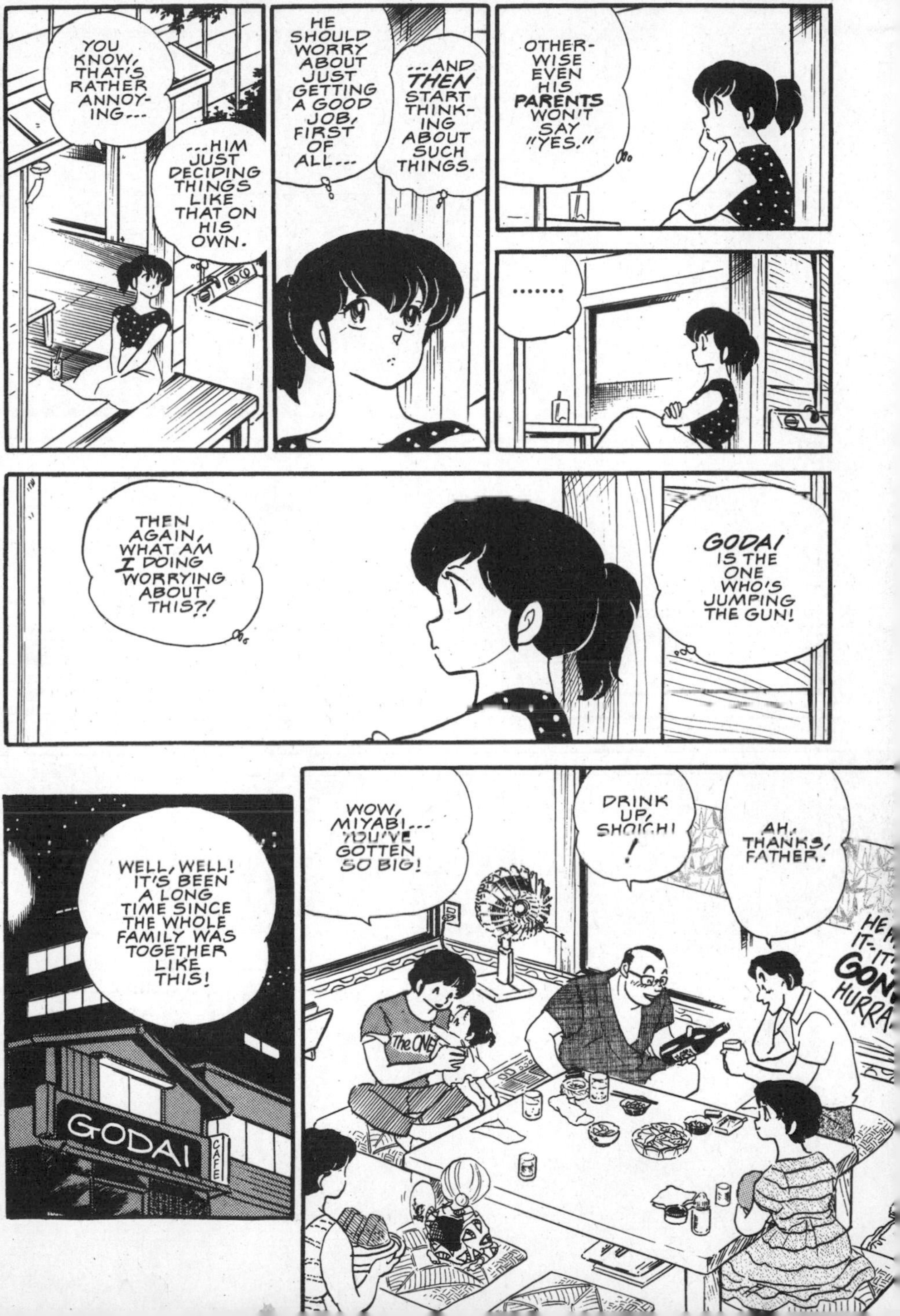
YOU KNOW, THAT'S RATHER ANNOY-ING...
...HIM JUST DECIDING THINGS LIKE THAT ON HIS OWN.
HE SHOULD WORRY ABOUT JUST GETTING A GOOD JOB, FIRST OF ALL...
...AND THEN START THINK-ING ABOUT SUCH THINGS.
OTHER-WISE EVEN HIS PARENTS WON'T SAY "YES."
....
THEN AGAIN, WHAT AM I DOING WORRYING ABOUT THIS?!
GODAI IS THE ONE WHO'S JUMPING THE GUN!
WELL, WELL! IT'S BEEN A LONG TIME SINCE THE WHOLE FAMILY WAS TOGETHER LIKE THIS!
GODAI
CAFE
WOW, MIYABI... YOU'VE GOTTEN SO BIG!
DRINK UP, SHOICHI!
AH, THANKS, FATHER.
The ONE

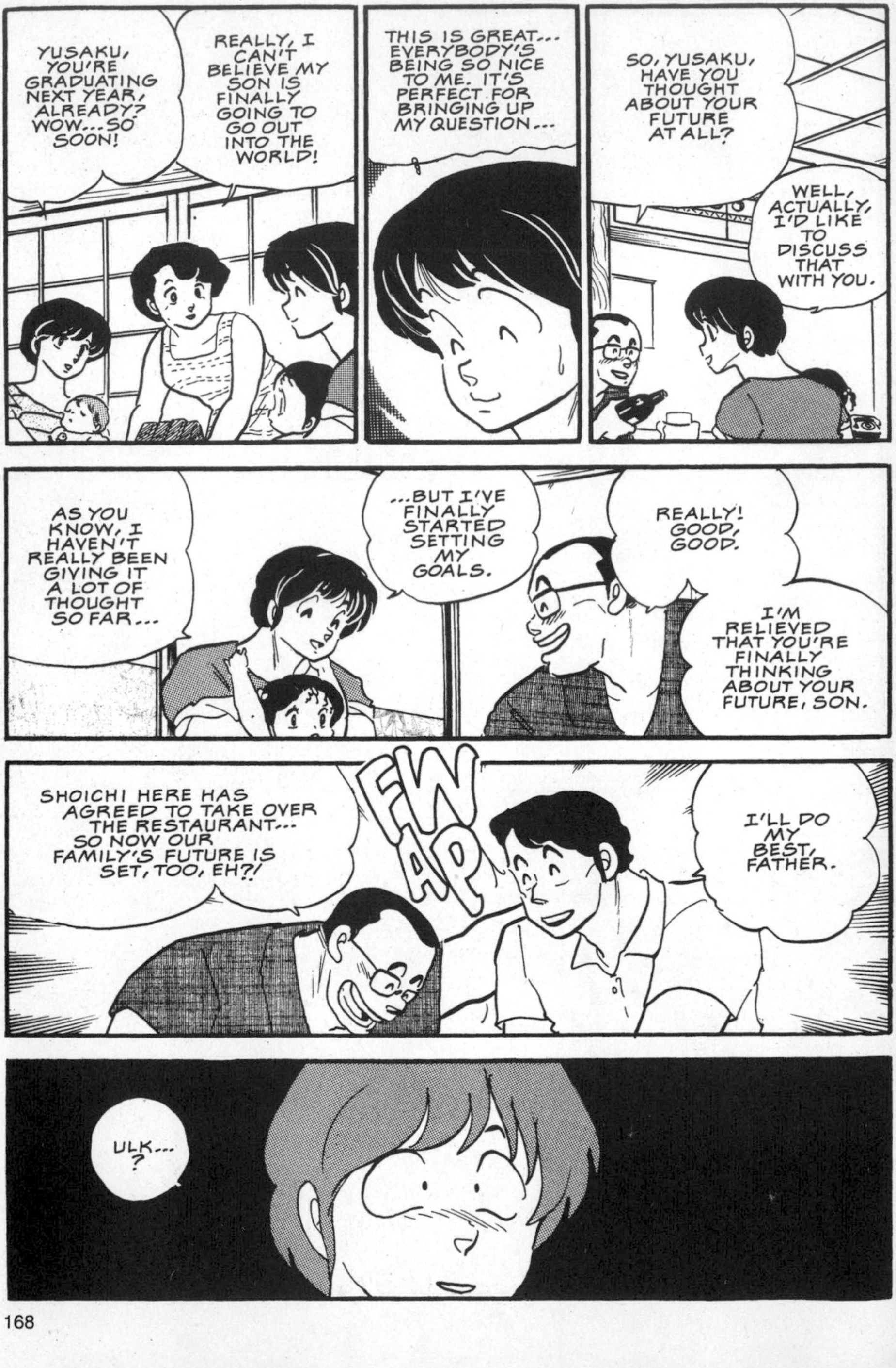
YUSAKU, YOU'RE GRADUATING NEXT YEAR, ALREADY? WOW... SO SOON!
REALLY, I CAN'T BELIEVE MY SON IS FINALLY GOING TO GO OUT INTO THE WORLD!
THIS IS GREAT... EVERYBODY'S BEING SO NICE TO ME. IT'S PERFECT FOR BRINGING UP MY QUESTION...
SO, YUSAKU, HAVE YOU THOUGHT ABOUT YOUR FUTURE AT ALL?
WELL, ACTUALLY, I'D LIKE TO DISCUSS THAT WITH YOU.
AS YOU KNOW, I HAVEN'T REALLY BEEN GIVING IT A LOT OF THOUGHT SO FAR...
...BUT I'VE FINALLY STARTED SETTING MY GOALS.
REALLY! GOOD, GOOD.
I'M RELIEVED THAT YOU'RE FINALLY THINKING ABOUT YOUR FUTURE, SON.
SHOICHI HERE HAS AGREED TO TAKE OVER THE RESTAURANT... SO NOW OUR FAMILY'S FUTURE IS SET, TOO, EH?!
FWAP
I'LL DO MY BEST, FATHER.
ULK... ?

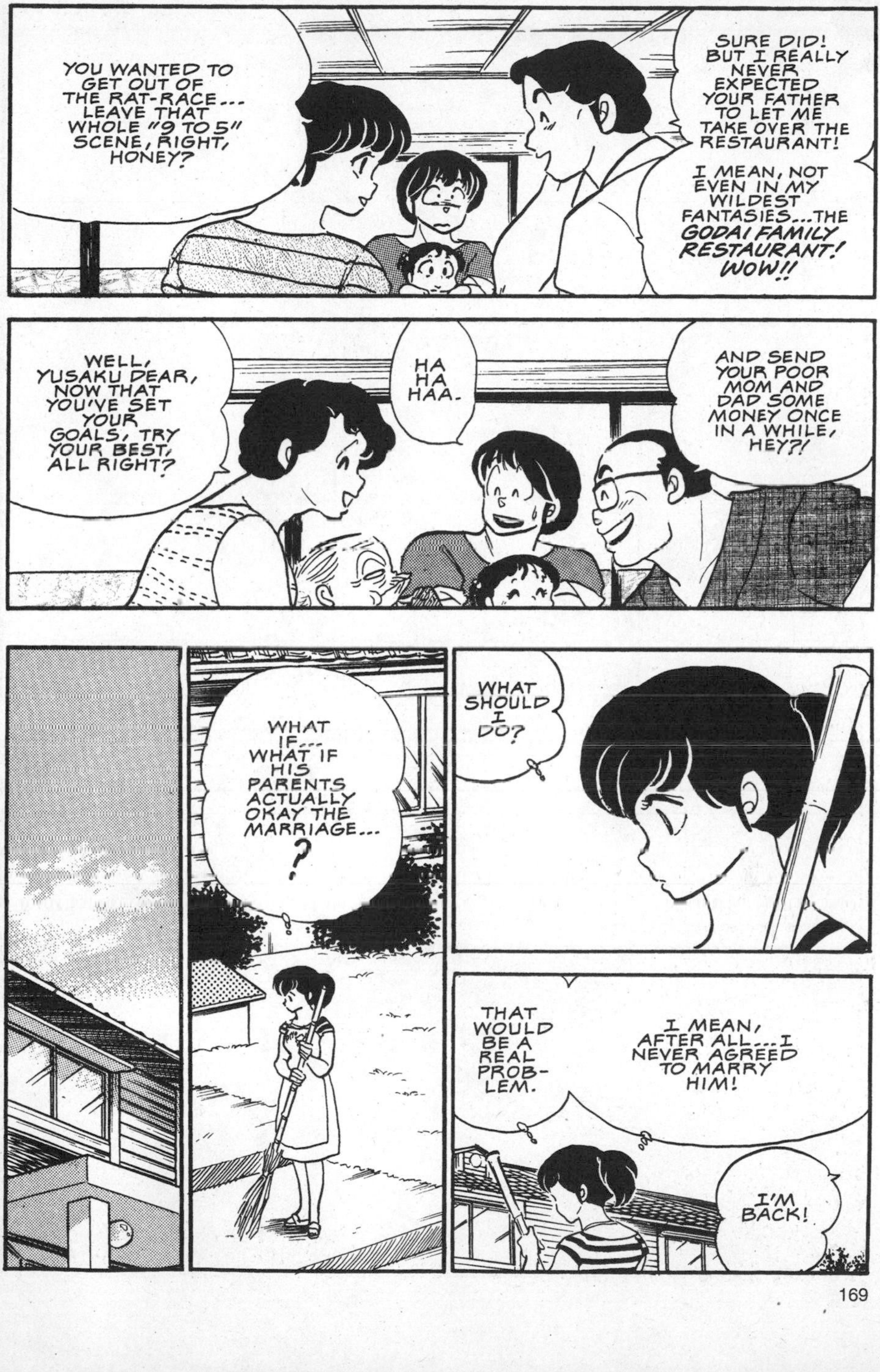
YOU WANTED TO GET OUT OF THE RAT-RACE... LEAVE THAT WHOLE "9 TO 5" SCENE, RIGHT, HONEY?
SURE DID! BUT I REALLY NEVER EXPECTED YOUR FATHER TO LET ME TAKE OVER THE RESTAURANT!
I MEAN, NOT EVEN IN MY WILDEST FANTASIES...THE *GODAI FAMILY RESTAURANT! WOW!!*
WELL, YUSAKU DEAR, NOW THAT YOU'VE SET YOUR GOALS, TRY YOUR BEST, ALL RIGHT?
HA HA HAA.
AND SEND YOUR POOR MOM AND DAD SOME MONEY ONCE IN A WHILE, HEY?!
WHAT IF... WHAT IF HIS PARENTS ACTUALLY OKAY THE MARRIAGE...?
WHAT SHOULD I DO?
THAT WOULD BE A REAL PROB-LEM.
I MEAN, AFTER ALL...I NEVER AGREED TO MARRY HIM!
I'M BACK!

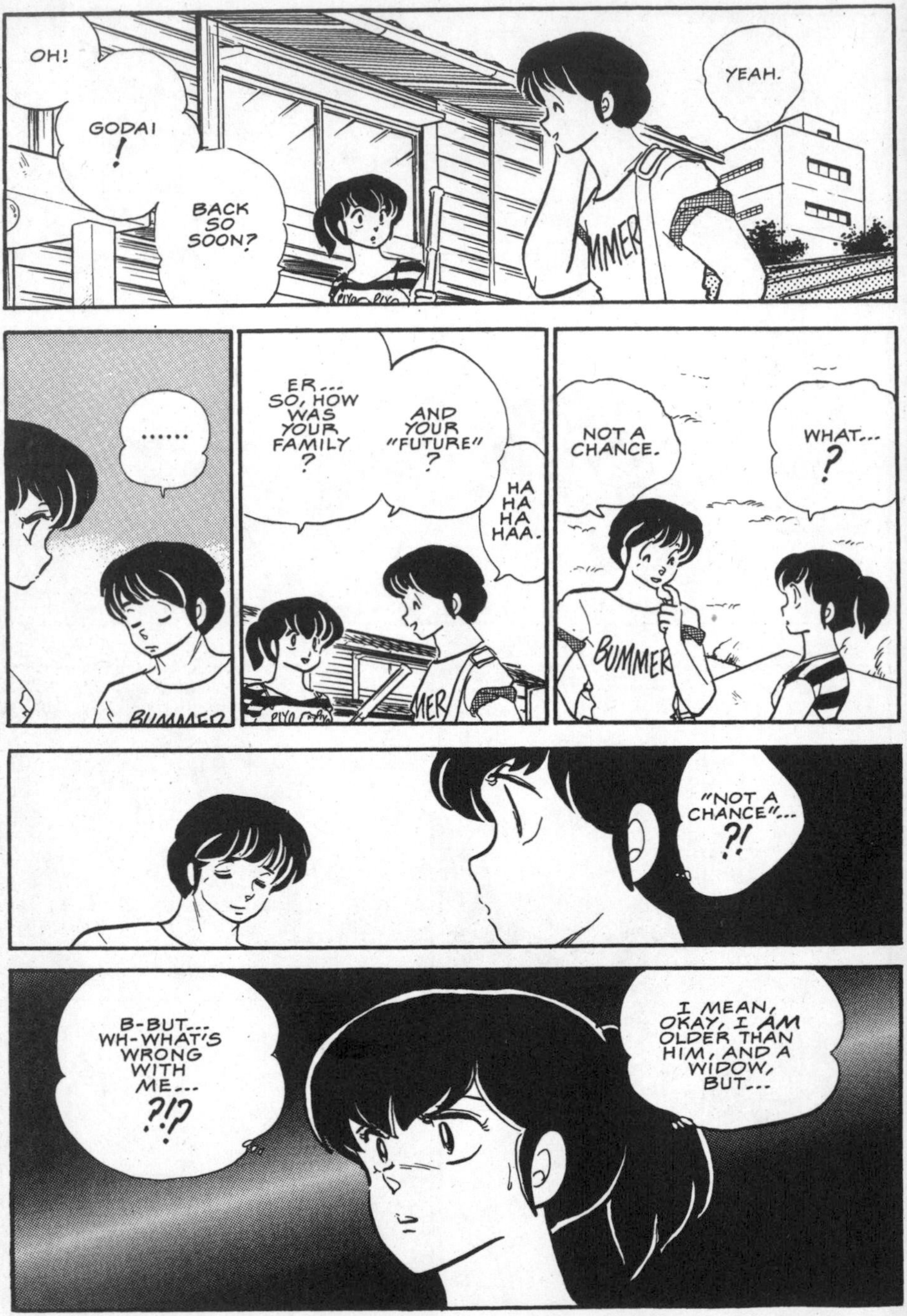
OH!
GODAI !
BACK SO SOON?
YEAH.
PIYO PIYO
BUMMER
......
BUMMER
ER... SO, HOW WAS YOUR FAMILY ?
AND YOUR "FUTURE" ?
HA HA HA HAA.
NOT A CHANCE.
WHAT... ?
BUMMER
"NOT A CHANCE"... ?!
B-BUT... WH-WHAT'S WRONG WITH ME... ?!?
I MEAN, OKAY, I AM OLDER THAN HIM, AND A WIDOW, BUT...

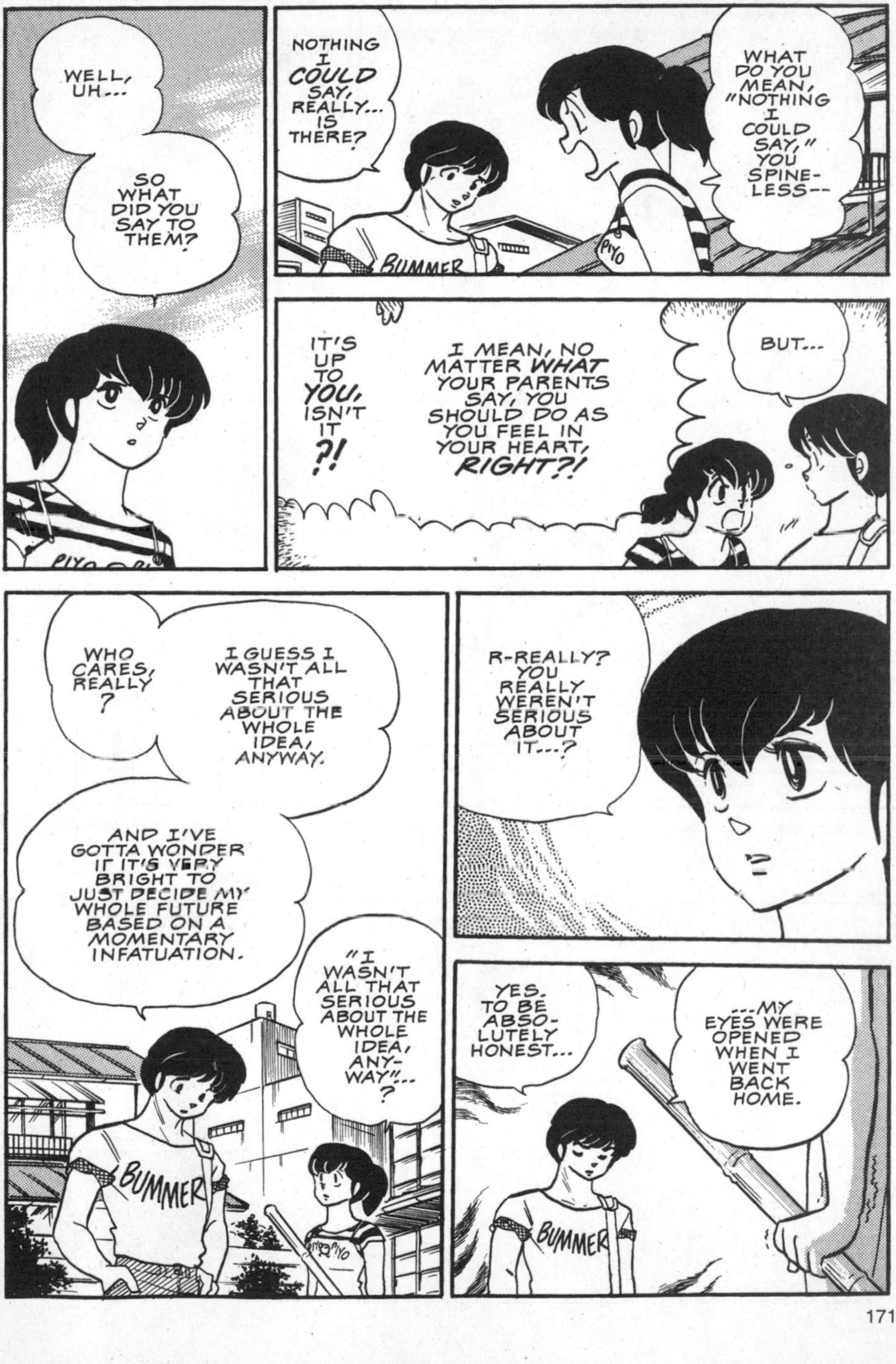
WELL, UH...
SO WHAT DID YOU SAY TO THEM?
NOTHING I COULD SAY, REALLY... IS THERE?
WHAT DO YOU MEAN, "NOTHING I COULD SAY," YOU SPINE-LESS--
IT'S UP TO YOU, ISN'T IT ?!
I MEAN, NO MATTER WHAT YOUR PARENTS SAY, YOU SHOULD DO AS YOU FEEL IN YOUR HEART, RIGHT?!
BUT...
WHO CARES, REALLY ?
I GUESS I WASN'T ALL THAT SERIOUS ABOUT THE WHOLE IDEA, ANYWAY.
AND I'VE GOTTA WONDER IF IT'S VERY BRIGHT TO JUST DECIDE MY WHOLE FUTURE BASED ON A MOMENTARY INFATUATION.
"I WASN'T ALL THAT SERIOUS ABOUT THE WHOLE IDEA, ANY-WAY"!...?
R-REALLY? YOU REALLY WEREN'T SERIOUS ABOUT IT...?
YES. TO BE ABSO-LUTELY HONEST...
...MY EYES WERE OPENED WHEN I WENT BACK HOME.

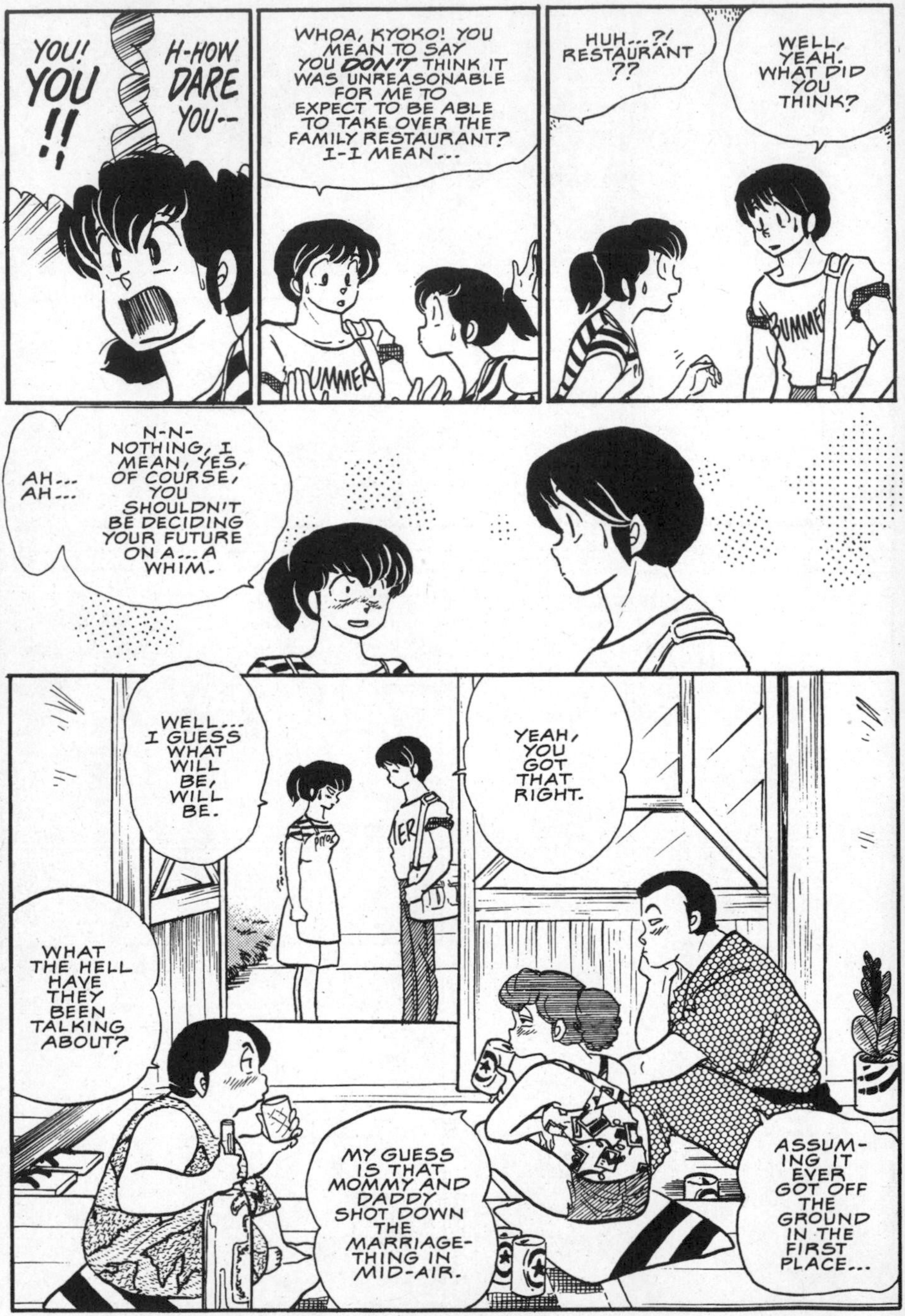
YOU! YOU!!
H-HOW DARE YOU--
WHOA, KYOKO! YOU MEAN TO SAY YOU ***DON'T*** THINK IT WAS UNREASONABLE FOR ME TO EXPECT TO BE ABLE TO TAKE OVER THE FAMILY RESTAURANT? I-I MEAN...
HUH...?! RESTAURANT??
WELL, YEAH. WHAT DID YOU THINK?
AH... AH...
N-N-NOTHING, I MEAN, YES, OF COURSE, YOU SHOULDN'T BE DECIDING YOUR FUTURE ON A...A WHIM.
WELL... I GUESS WHAT WILL BE, WILL BE.
YEAH, YOU GOT THAT RIGHT.
WHAT THE HELL HAVE THEY BEEN TALKING ABOUT?
MY GUESS IS THAT MOMMY AND DADDY SHOT DOWN THE MARRIAGE-THING IN MID-AIR.
ASSUMING IT EVER GOT OFF THE GROUND IN THE FIRST PLACE...

PART 9
VANITY RECRUIT

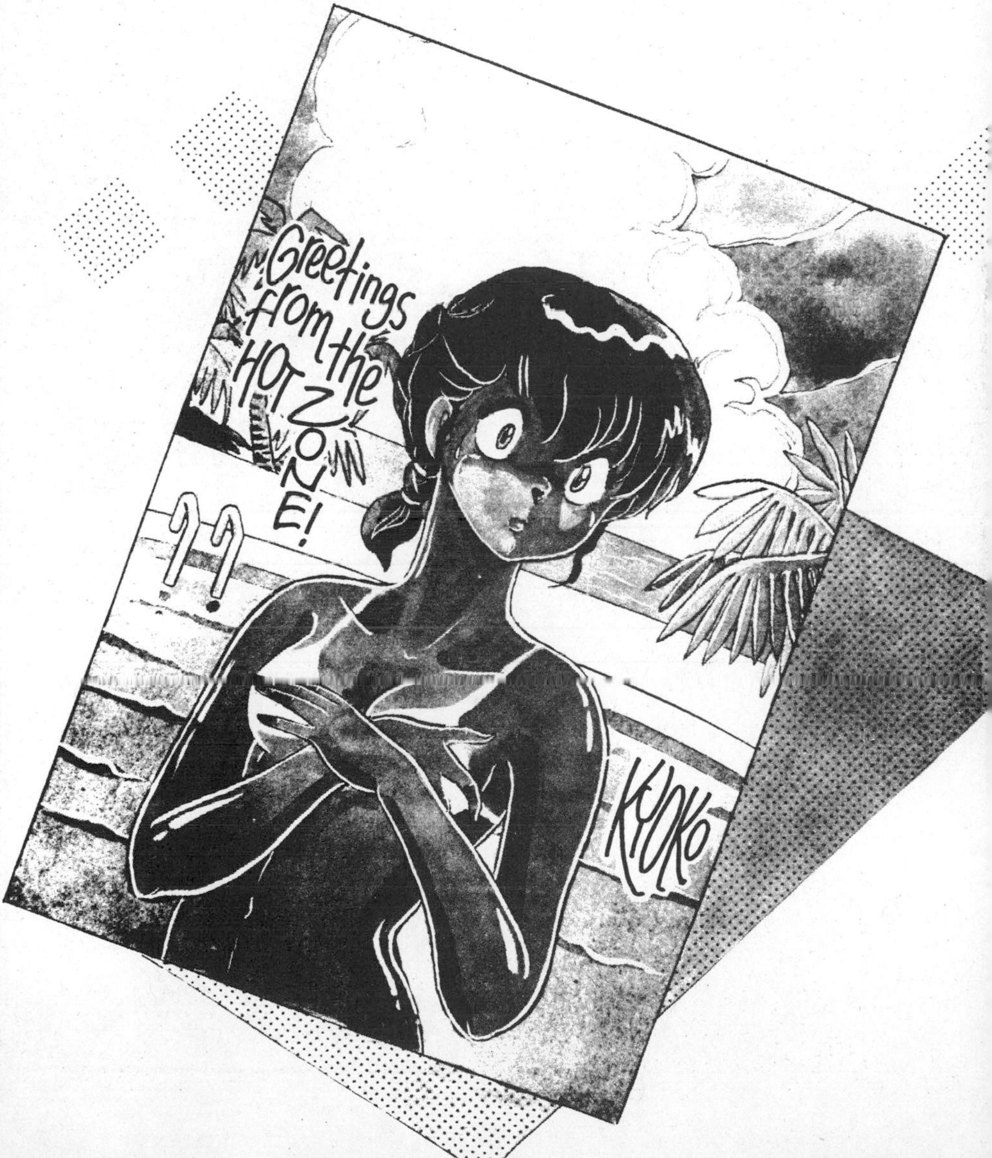

Greetings from the HOT ZONE!
!?
KYUKO

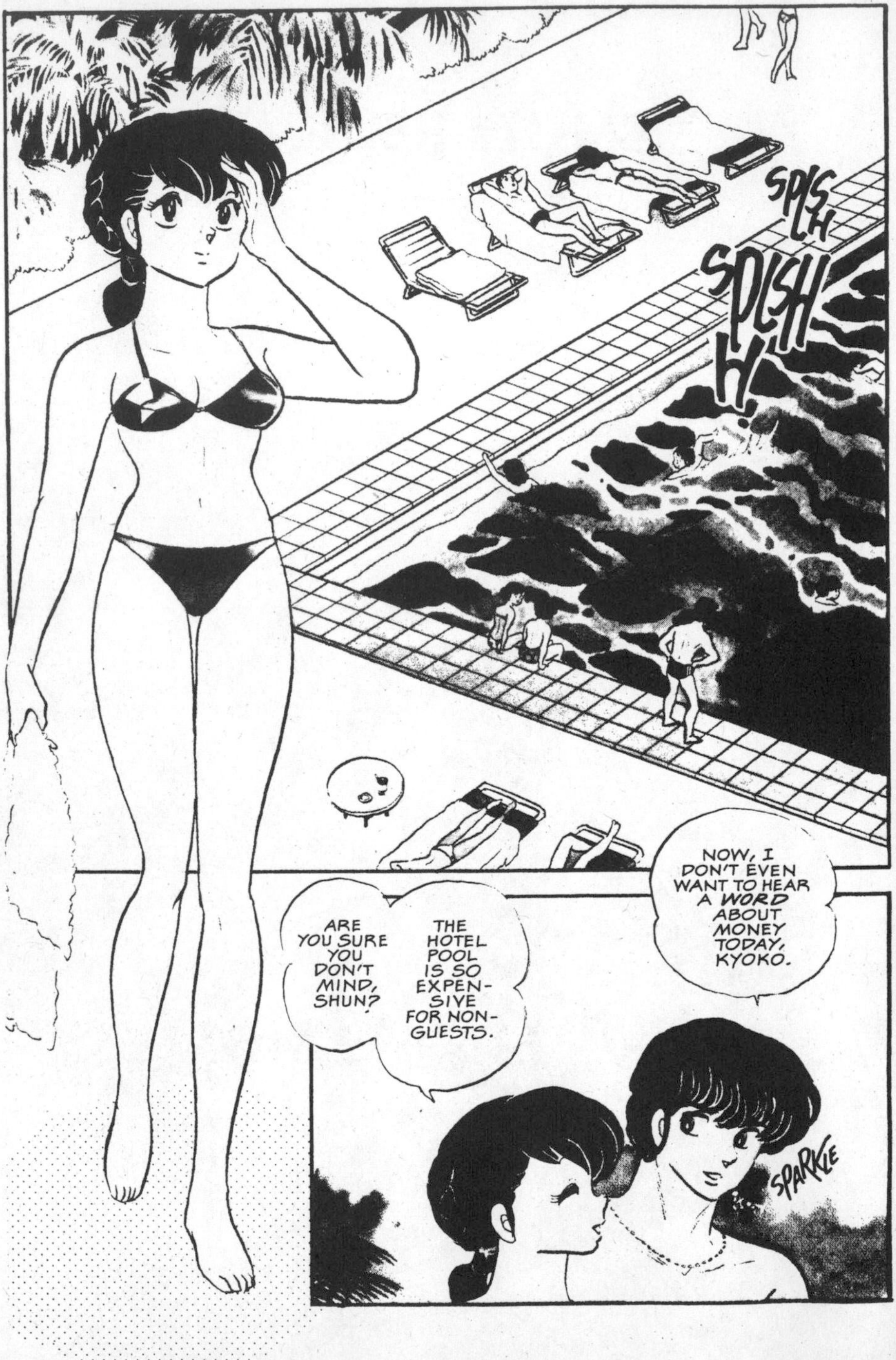
SPLSH
SPLSH
SPLSHH!
ARE YOU SURE YOU DON'T MIND, SHUN?
THE HOTEL POOL IS SO EXPENSIVE FOR NONGUESTS.
NOW, I DON'T EVEN WANT TO HEAR A WORD ABOUT MONEY TODAY, KYOKO.
SPARKLE

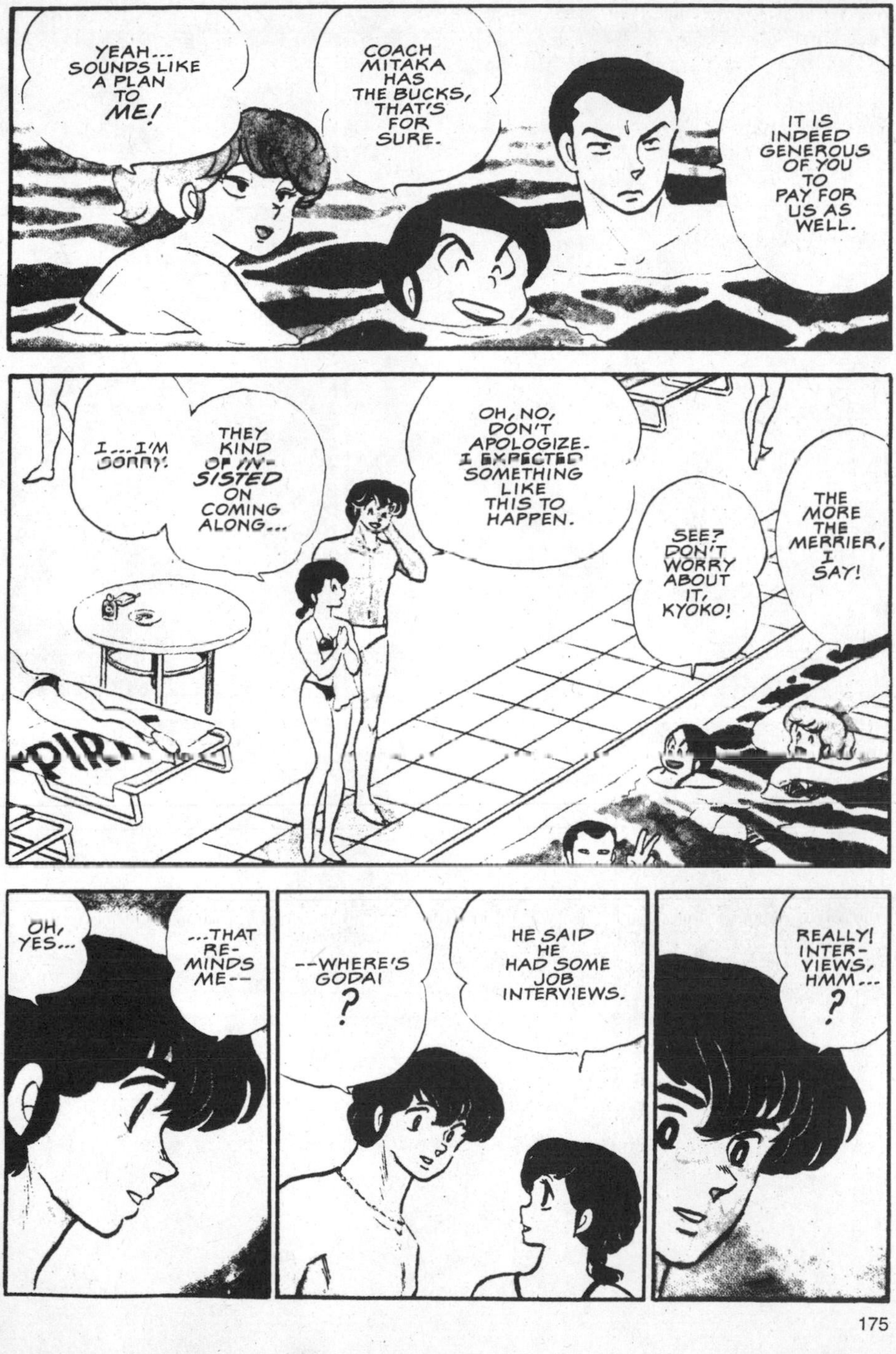
YEAH... SOUNDS LIKE A PLAN TO ME!
COACH MITAKA HAS THE BUCKS, THAT'S FOR SURE.
IT IS INDEED GENEROUS OF YOU TO PAY FOR US AS WELL.
I...I'M SORRY!
THEY KIND OF IN-SISTED ON COMING ALONG...
OH, NO, DON'T APOLOGIZE. I EXPECTED SOMETHING LIKE THIS TO HAPPEN.
SEE? DON'T WORRY ABOUT IT, KYOKO!
THE MORE THE MERRIER, I SAY!
OH, YES...
...THAT RE-MINDS ME--
--WHERE'S GODAI ?
HE SAID HE HAD SOME JOB INTERVIEWS.
REALLY! INTER-VIEWS, HMM... ?

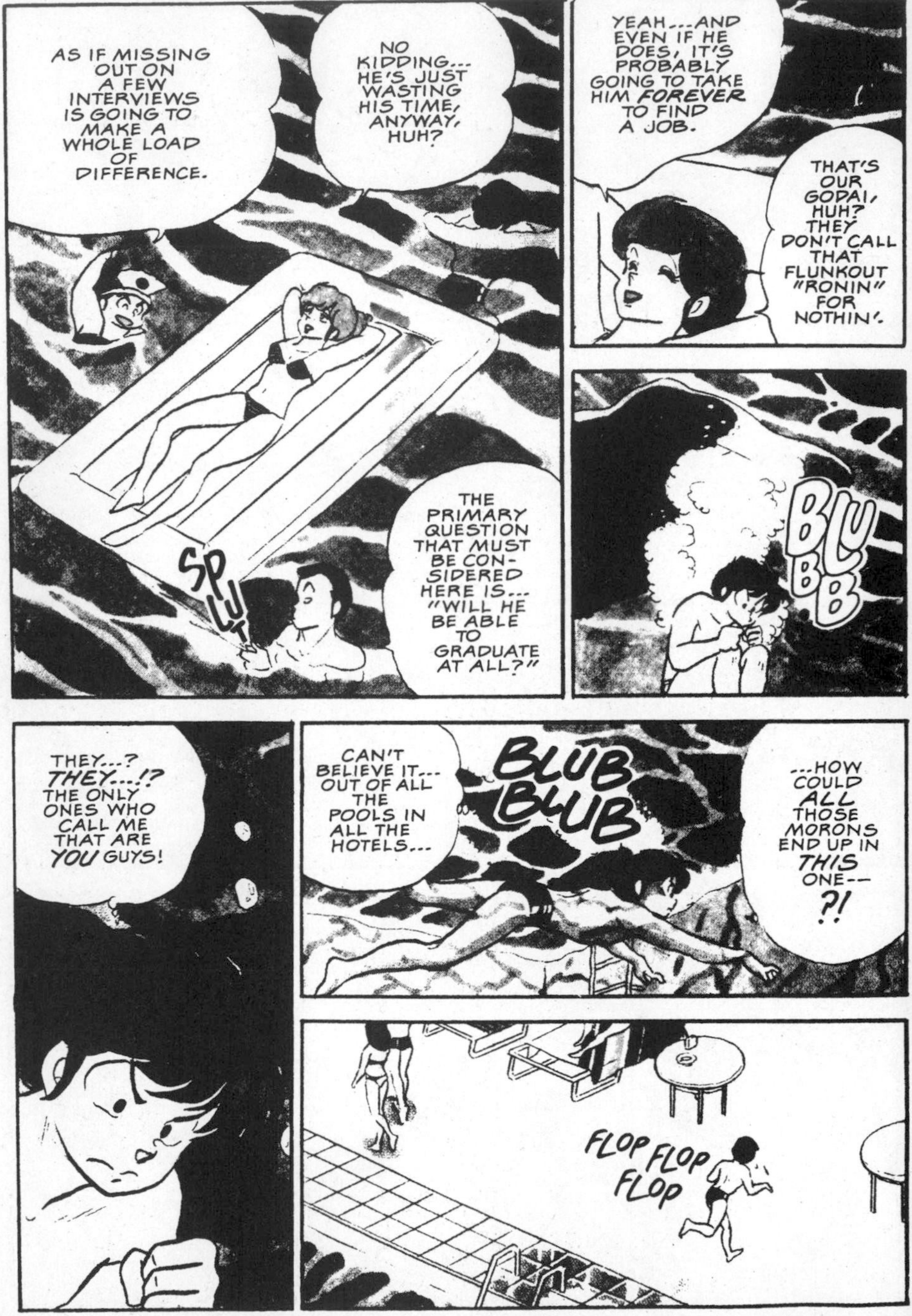
AS IF MISSING OUT ON A FEW INTERVIEWS IS GOING TO MAKE A WHOLE LOAD OF DIFFERENCE.
NO KIDDING... HE'S JUST WASTING HIS TIME, ANYWAY, HUH?
THE PRIMARY QUESTION THAT MUST BE CON-SIDERED HERE IS... "WILL HE BE ABLE TO GRADUATE AT ALL?"
SPLUT
YEAH...AND EVEN IF HE DOES, IT'S PROBABLY GOING TO TAKE HIM FOREVER TO FIND A JOB.
THAT'S OUR GODAI, HUH? THEY DON'T CALL THAT FLUNKOUT "RONIN" FOR NOTHIN'.
BLUBB
THEY...? THEY...!? THE ONLY ONES WHO CALL ME THAT ARE YOU GUYS!
CAN'T BELIEVE IT... OUT OF ALL THE POOLS IN ALL THE HOTELS...
BLUB BLUB
...HOW COULD ALL THOSE MORONS END UP IN THIS ONE--?!
FLOP FLOP FLOP

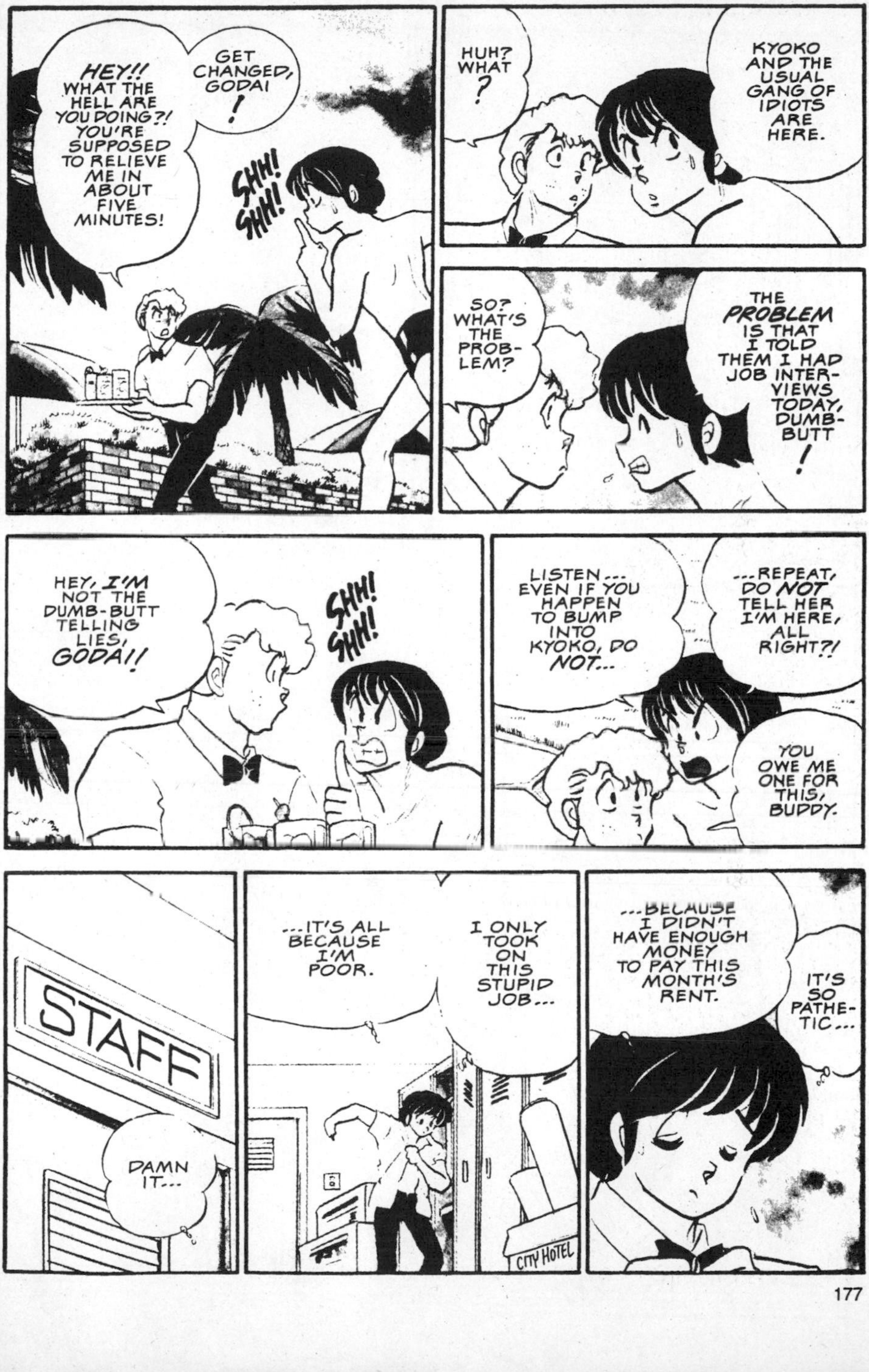
HEY!! WHAT THE HELL ARE YOU DOING?! YOU'RE SUPPOSED TO RELIEVE ME IN ABOUT FIVE MINUTES!
GET CHANGED, GODAI!
SHH! SHH!
HUH? WHAT?
KYOKO AND THE USUAL GANG OF IDIOTS ARE HERE.
SO? WHAT'S THE PROB-LEM?
THE PROBLEM IS THAT I TOLD THEM I HAD JOB INTER-VIEWS TODAY, DUMB-BUTT!
HEY, I'M NOT THE DUMB-BUTT TELLING LIES, GODAI!!
SHH! SHH!
LISTEN... EVEN IF YOU HAPPEN TO BUMP INTO KYOKO, DO NOT...
...REPEAT, DO NOT TELL HER I'M HERE, ALL RIGHT?!
YOU OWE ME ONE FOR THIS, BUDDY.
STAFF
DAMN IT...
...IT'S ALL BECAUSE I'M POOR.
I ONLY TOOK ON THIS STUPID JOB...
CITY HOTEL
...BECAUSE I DIDN'T HAVE ENOUGH MONEY TO PAY THIS MONTH'S RENT.
IT'S SO PATHE-TIC...

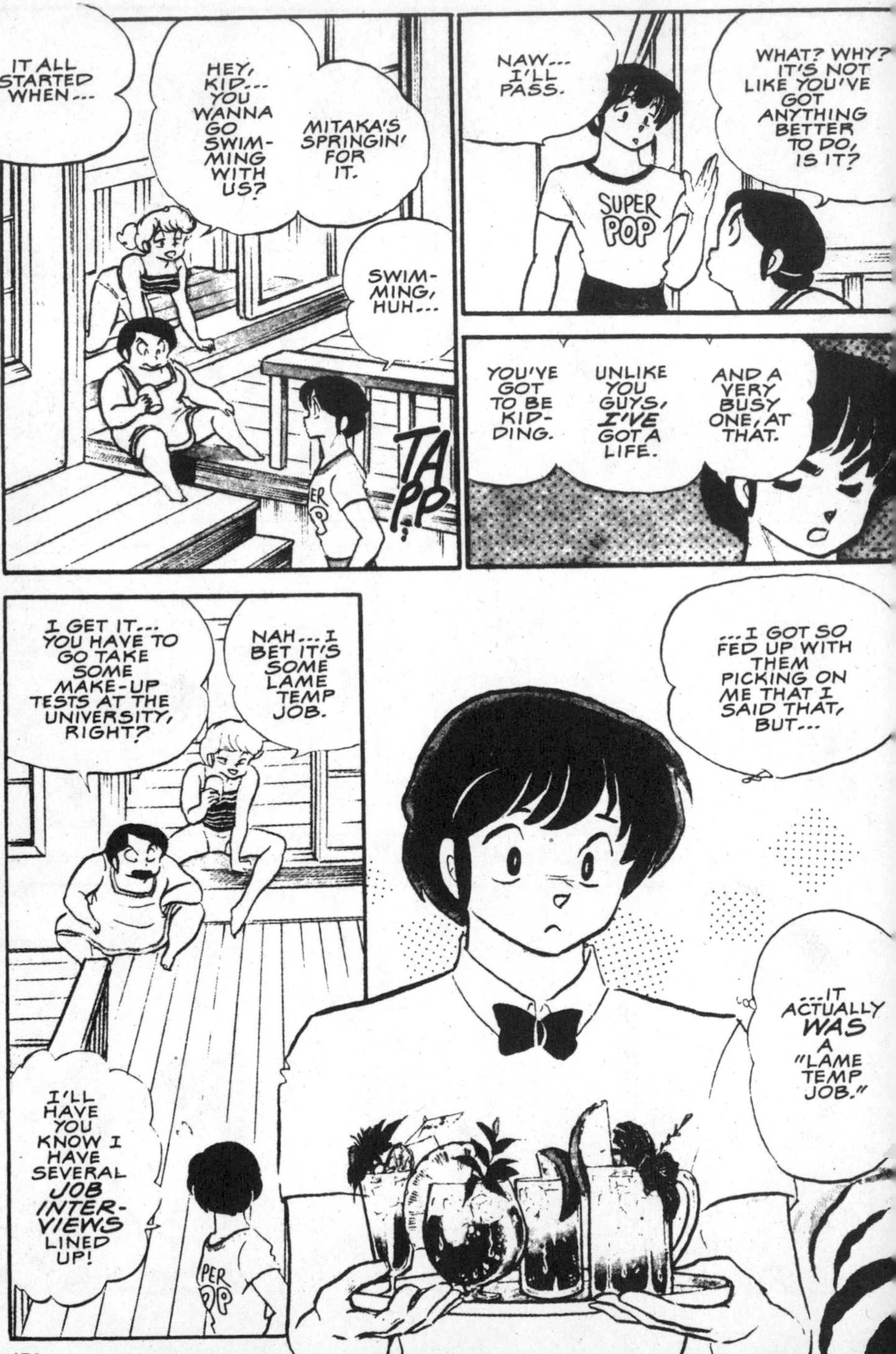
IT ALL STARTED WHEN...
HEY, KID... YOU WANNA GO SWIMMING WITH US?
MITAKA'S SPRINGIN' FOR IT.
SWIMMING, HUH...
TAPP
NAW... I'LL PASS.
SUPER POP
WHAT? WHY? IT'S NOT LIKE YOU'VE GOT ANYTHING BETTER TO DO, IS IT?
YOU'VE GOT TO BE KIDDING.
UNLIKE YOU GUYS, *I'VE* GOT A LIFE.
AND A VERY BUSY ONE, AT THAT.
I GET IT... YOU HAVE TO GO TAKE SOME MAKE-UP TESTS AT THE UNIVERSITY, RIGHT?
NAH... I BET IT'S SOME LAME TEMP JOB.
I'LL HAVE YOU KNOW I HAVE SEVERAL *JOB INTERVIEWS* LINED UP!
...I GOT SO FED UP WITH THEM PICKING ON ME THAT I SAID THAT, BUT...
...IT ACTUALLY *WAS* A "LAME TEMP JOB."

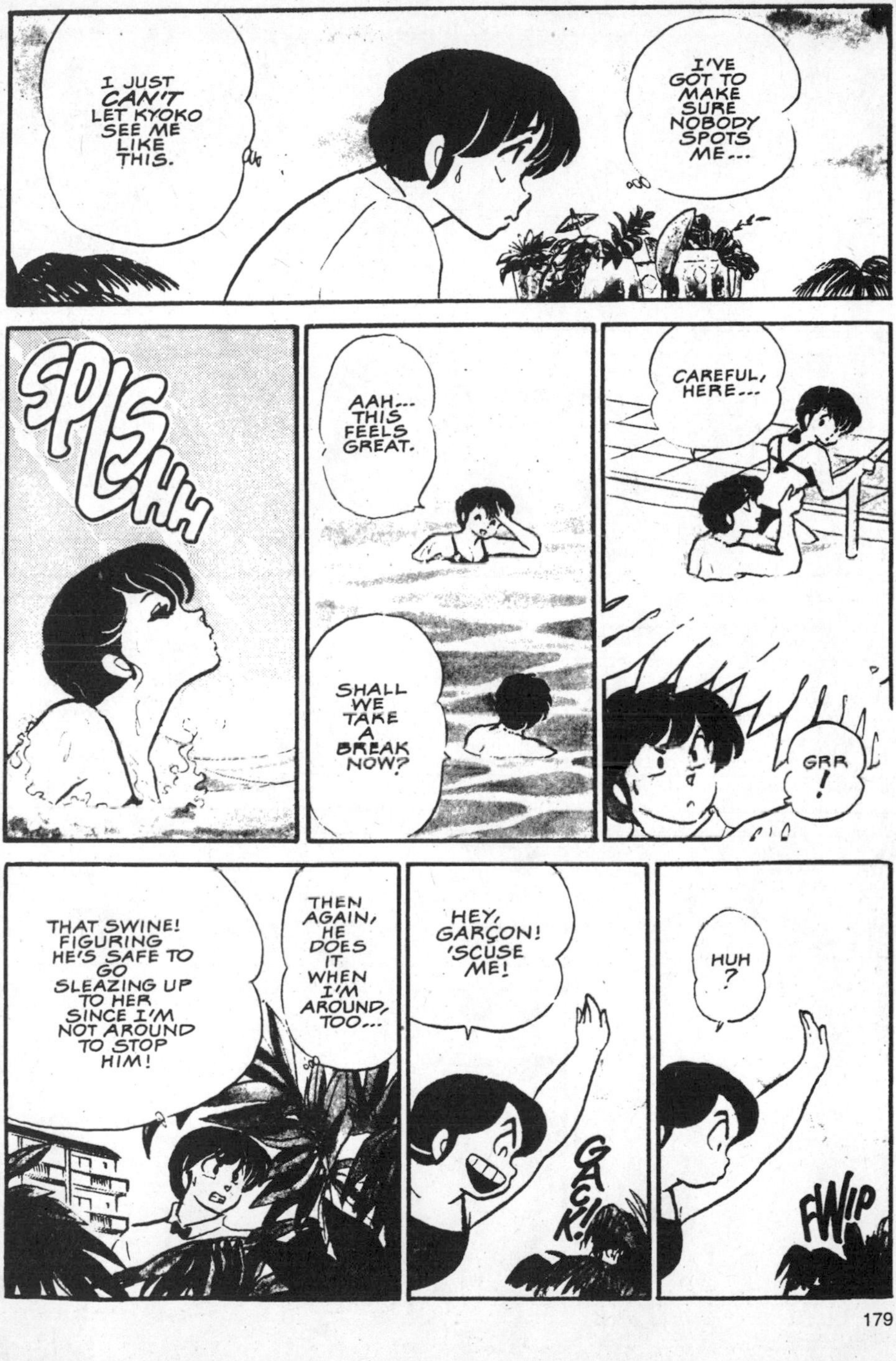
I JUST CAN'T LET KYOKO SEE ME LIKE THIS.
I'VE GOT TO MAKE SURE NOBODY SPOTS ME...
SPLISHH
AAH... THIS FEELS GREAT.
SHALL WE TAKE A BREAK NOW?
CAREFUL, HERE...
GRR!
THAT SWINE! FIGURING HE'S SAFE TO GO SLEAZING UP TO HER SINCE I'M NOT AROUND TO STOP HIM!
THEN AGAIN, HE DOES IT WHEN I'M AROUND, TOO...
HEY, GARÇON! 'SCUSE ME!
GACK!
HUH?
FWIP

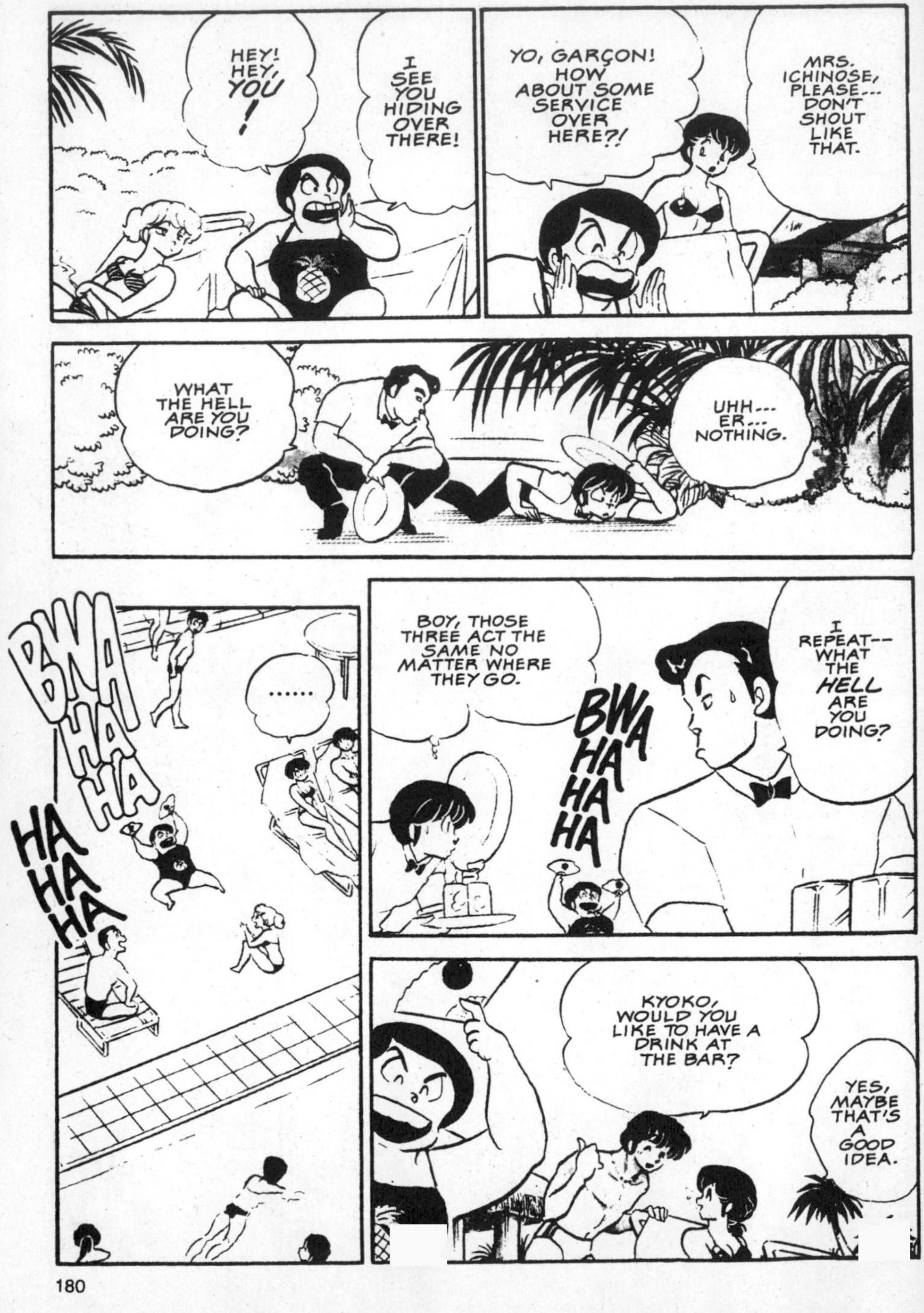
HEY! HEY, YOU!
I SEE YOU HIDING OVER THERE!
YO, GARÇON! HOW ABOUT SOME SERVICE OVER HERE?!
MRS. ICHINOSE, PLEASE--- DON'T SHOUT LIKE THAT.
WHAT THE HELL ARE YOU DOING?
UHH--- ER--- NOTHING.
BWA HA HA HA
HA HA HA
....
BOY, THOSE THREE ACT THE SAME NO MATTER WHERE THEY GO.
BWA HA HA HA HA
I REPEAT-- WHAT THE HELL ARE YOU DOING?
KYOKO, WOULD YOU LIKE TO HAVE A DRINK AT THE BAR?
YES, MAYBE THAT'S A GOOD IDEA.

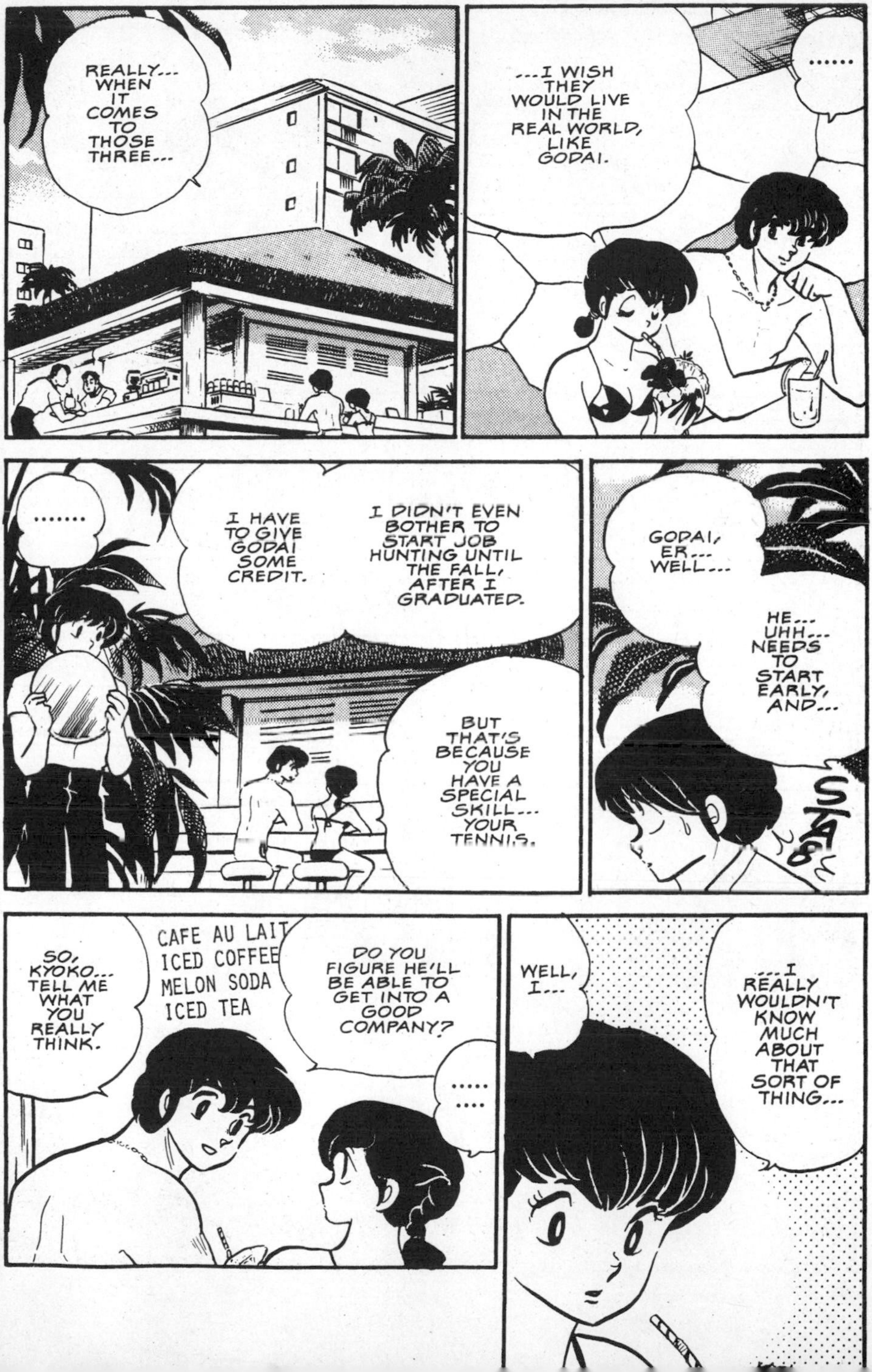
REALLY... WHEN IT COMES TO THOSE THREE...
...I WISH THEY WOULD LIVE IN THE REAL WORLD, LIKE GODAI.
......
....
I HAVE TO GIVE GODAI SOME CREDIT.
I DIDN'T EVEN BOTHER TO START JOB HUNTING UNTIL THE FALL, AFTER I GRADUATED.
BUT THAT'S BECAUSE YOU HAVE A SPECIAL SKILL... YOUR TENNIS.
GODAI, ER... WELL...
HE... UHH... NEEDS TO START EARLY, AND...
STAB
SO, KYOKO... TELL ME WHAT YOU REALLY THINK.
CAFE AU LAIT
ICED COFFEE
MELON SODA
ICED TEA
DO YOU FIGURE HE'LL BE ABLE TO GET INTO A GOOD COMPANY?
....
WELL, I...
...I REALLY WOULDN'T KNOW MUCH ABOUT THAT SORT OF THING...

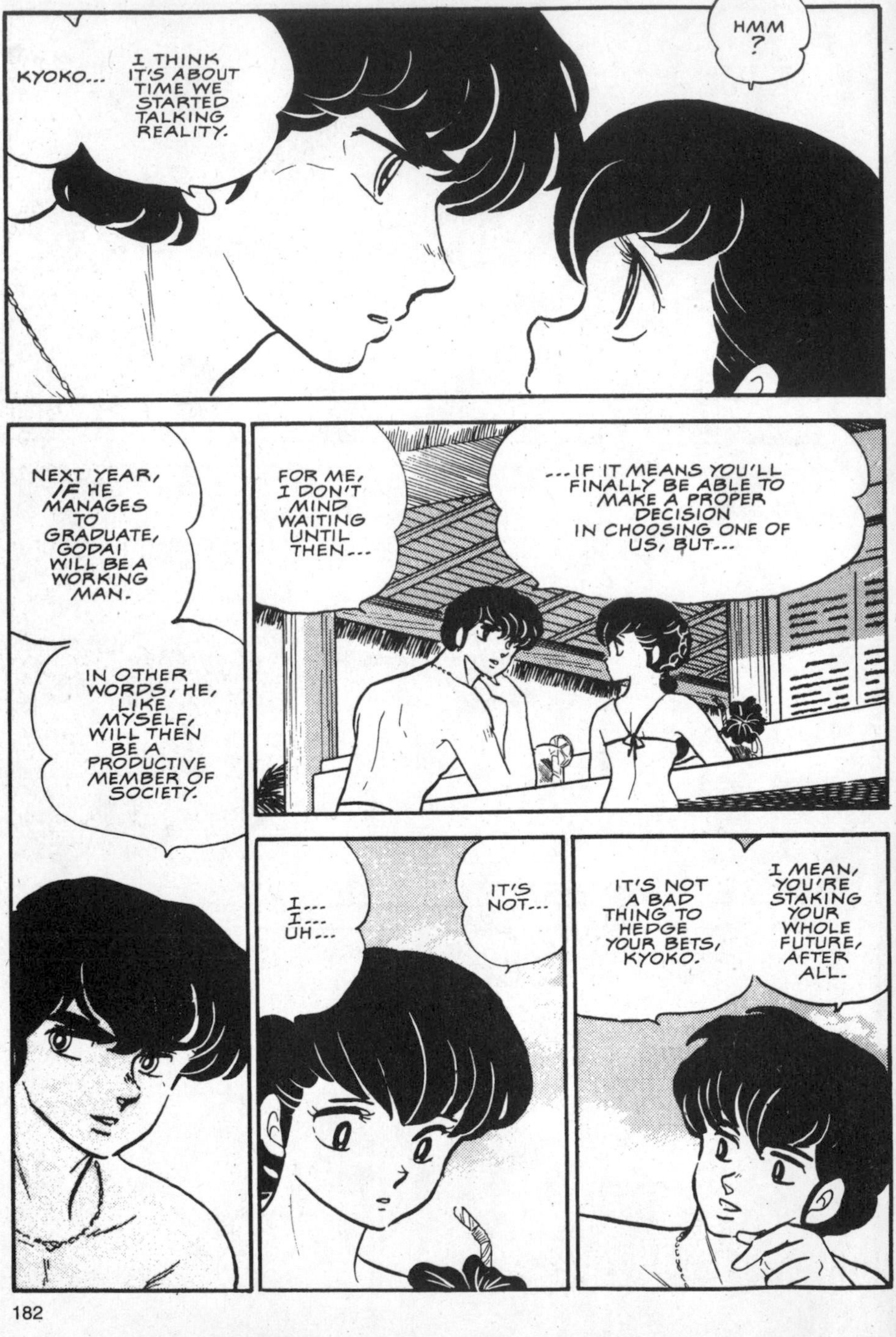
KYOKO...
I THINK IT'S ABOUT TIME WE STARTED TALKING REALITY.
HMM ?
NEXT YEAR, *IF* HE MANAGES TO GRADUATE, GODAI WILL BE A WORKING MAN.
IN OTHER WORDS, HE, LIKE MYSELF, WILL THEN BE A PRODUCTIVE MEMBER OF SOCIETY.
FOR ME, I DON'T MIND WAITING UNTIL THEN...
...IF IT MEANS YOU'LL FINALLY BE ABLE TO MAKE A PROPER DECISION IN CHOOSING ONE OF US, BUT...
I... I... UH...
IT'S NOT...
IT'S NOT A BAD THING TO HEDGE YOUR BETS, KYOKO.
I MEAN, YOU'RE STAKING YOUR WHOLE FUTURE, AFTER ALL.

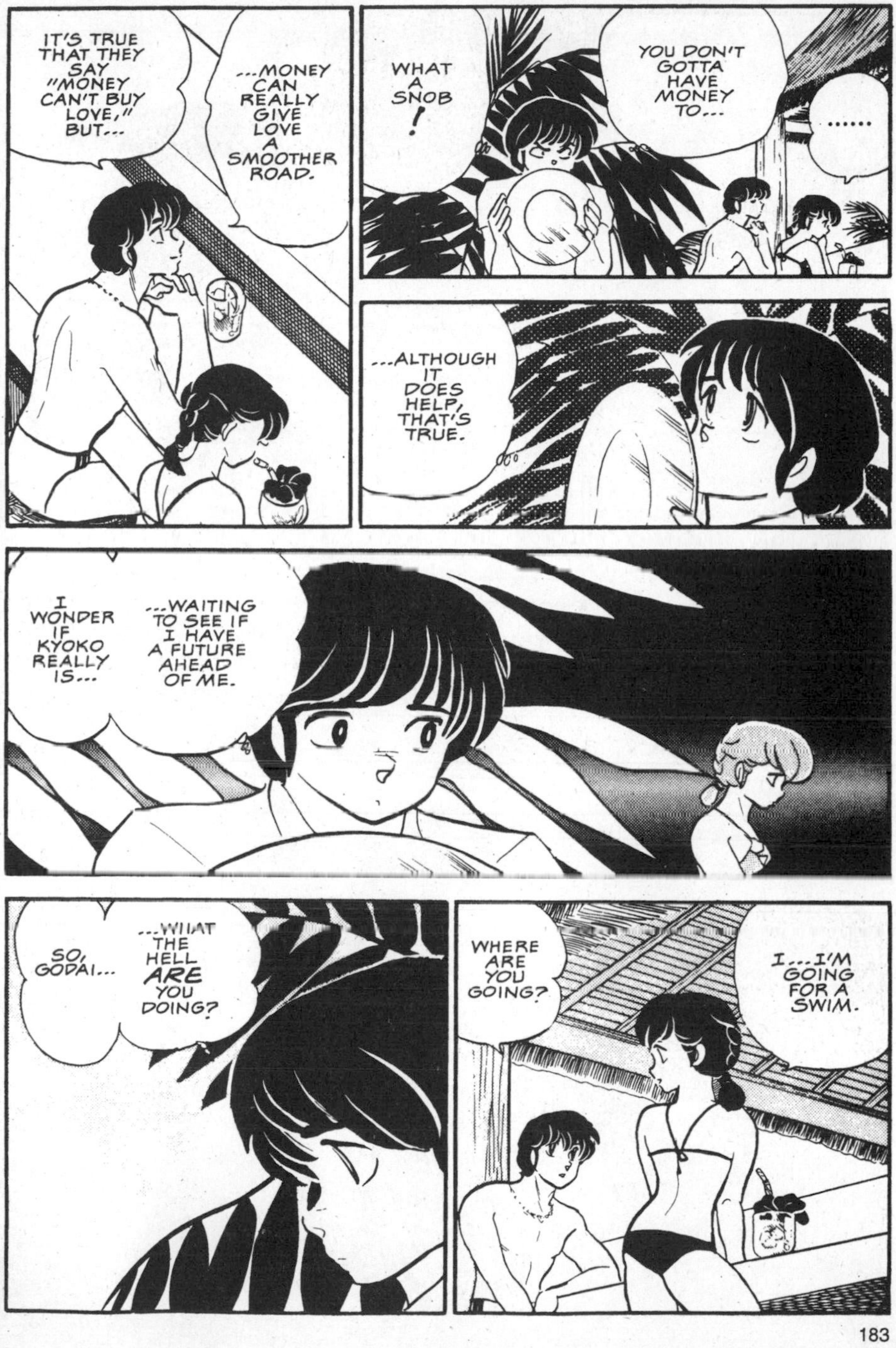
IT'S TRUE THAT THEY SAY "MONEY CAN'T BUY LOVE," BUT...
...MONEY CAN REALLY GIVE LOVE A SMOOTHER ROAD.
WHAT A SNOB!
YOU DON'T GOTTA HAVE MONEY TO...
......
...ALTHOUGH IT DOES HELP, THAT'S TRUE.
I WONDER IF KYOKO REALLY IS...
...WAITING TO SEE IF I HAVE A FUTURE AHEAD OF ME.
SO, GODAI...
...WHAT THE HELL ARE YOU DOING?
WHERE ARE YOU GOING?
I...I'M GOING FOR A SWIM.

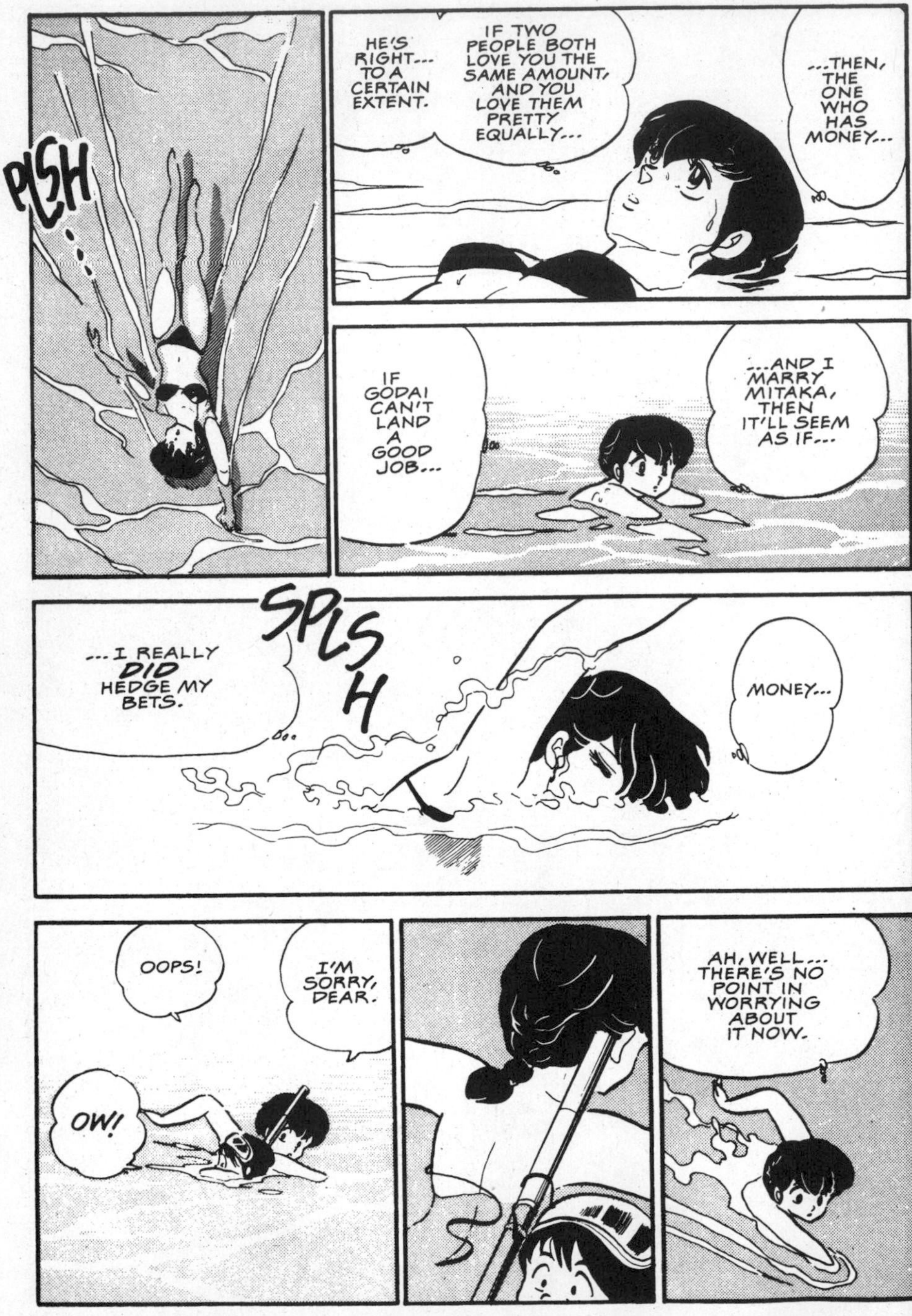
PLSH
HE'S RIGHT... TO A CERTAIN EXTENT.
IF TWO PEOPLE BOTH LOVE YOU THE SAME AMOUNT, AND YOU LOVE THEM PRETTY EQUALLY...
...THEN, THE ONE WHO HAS MONEY...
IF GODAI CAN'T LAND A GOOD JOB...
...AND I MARRY MITAKA, THEN IT'LL SEEM AS IF...
SPLSH
...I REALLY *DID* HEDGE MY BETS.
MONEY...
OOPS!
I'M SORRY, DEAR.
OW!
AH, WELL... THERE'S NO POINT IN WORRYING ABOUT IT NOW.

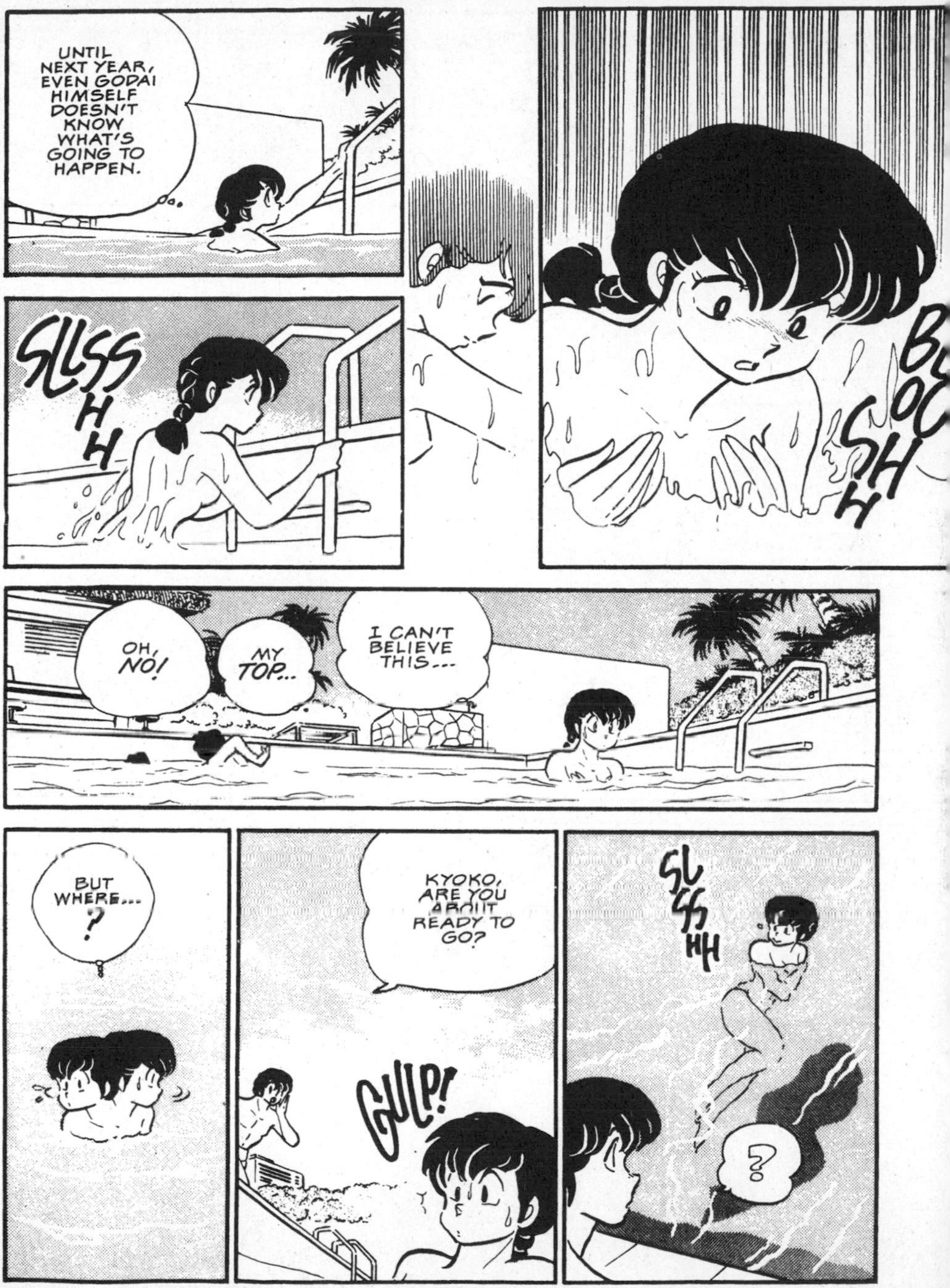
UNTIL NEXT YEAR, EVEN GODAI HIMSELF DOESN'T KNOW WHAT'S GOING TO HAPPEN.
SLLSSHH
OH, NO!
MY TOP...
I CAN'T BELIEVE THIS...
BUT WHERE...?
KYOKO, ARE YOU ABOUT READY TO GO?
GULP!
SLSSHH
?

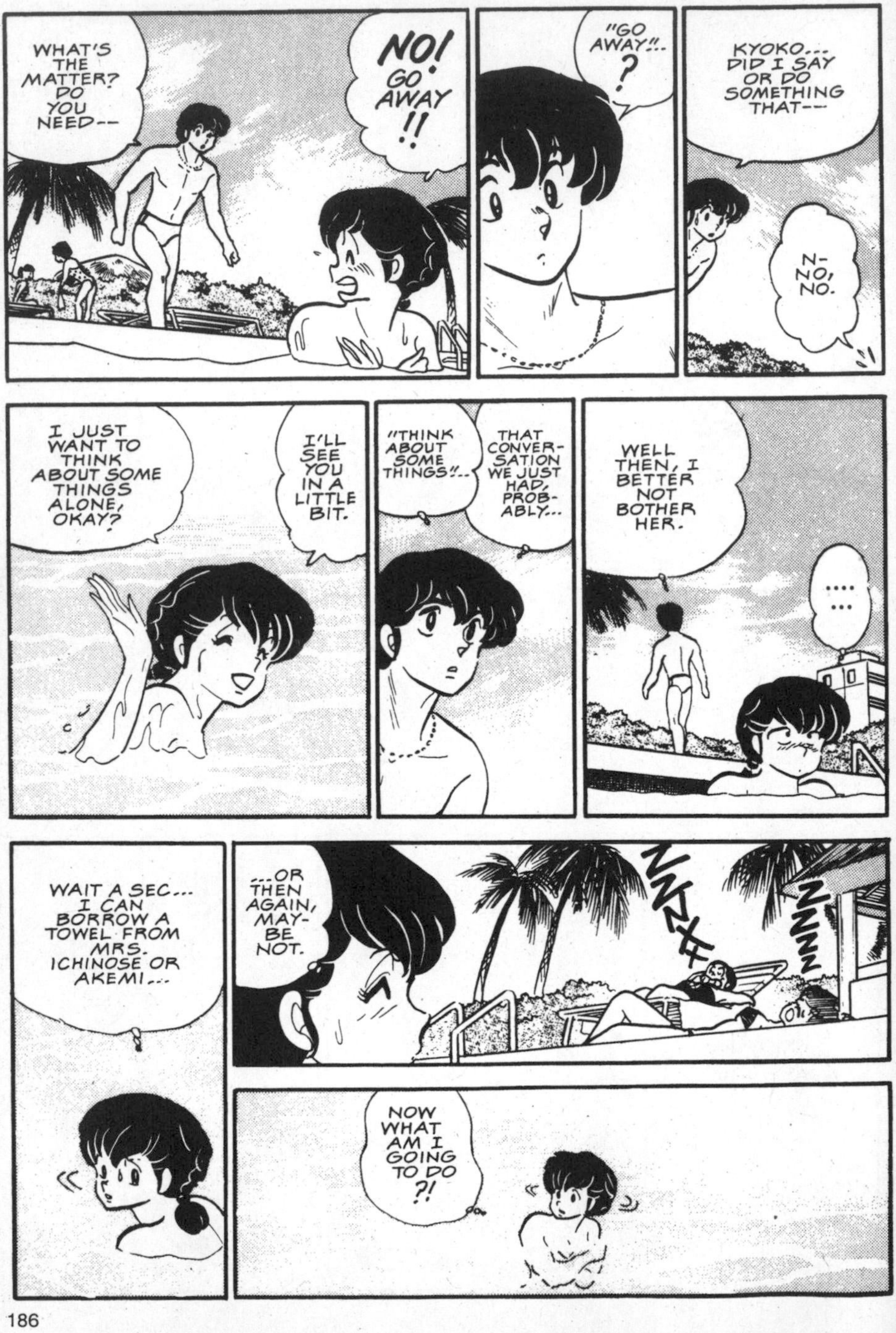
WHAT'S THE MATTER? DO YOU NEED--
NO! GO AWAY!!
"GO AWAY!"..?
KYOKO... DID I SAY OR DO SOMETHING THAT--
N-NO, NO.
I JUST WANT TO THINK ABOUT SOME THINGS ALONE, OKAY?
I'LL SEE YOU IN A LITTLE BIT.
"THINK ABOUT SOME THINGS"..
THAT CONVERSATION WE JUST HAD, PROBABLY...
WELL THEN, I BETTER NOT BOTHER HER.
....
WAIT A SEC... I CAN BORROW A TOWEL FROM MRS. ICHINOSE OR AKEMI...
...OR THEN AGAIN, MAYBE NOT.
NOW WHAT AM I GOING TO DO?!

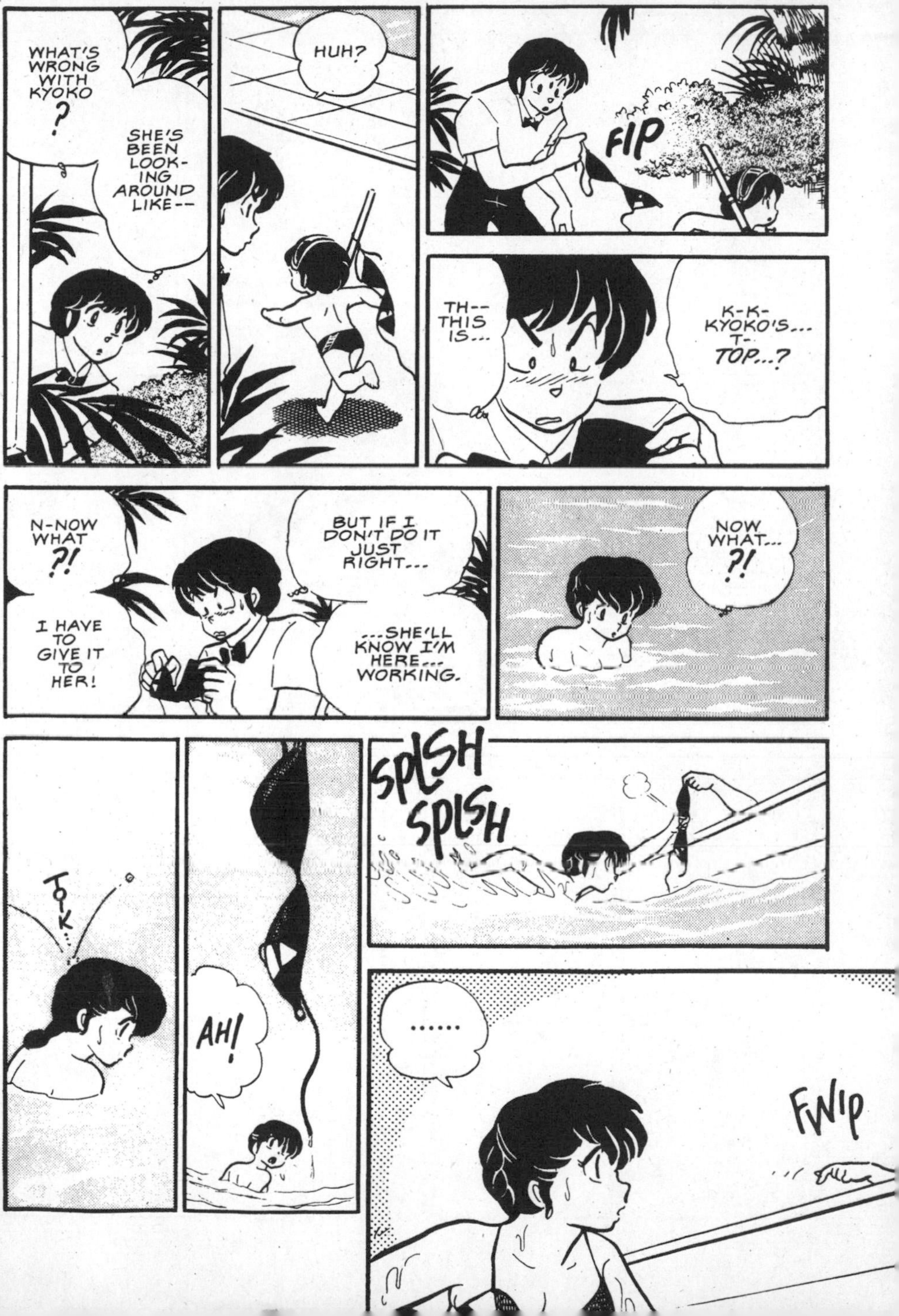
WHAT'S WRONG WITH KYOKO?
SHE'S BEEN LOOKING AROUND LIKE--
HUH?
FIP
TH-- THIS IS...
K-K-KYOKO'S... T-TOP...?
N-NOW WHAT?!
I HAVE TO GIVE IT TO HER!
BUT IF I DON'T DO IT JUST RIGHT...
...SHE'LL KNOW I'M HERE... WORKING.
NOW WHAT...?!
TOK...
AH!
SPLSH SPLSH
......
FWIP

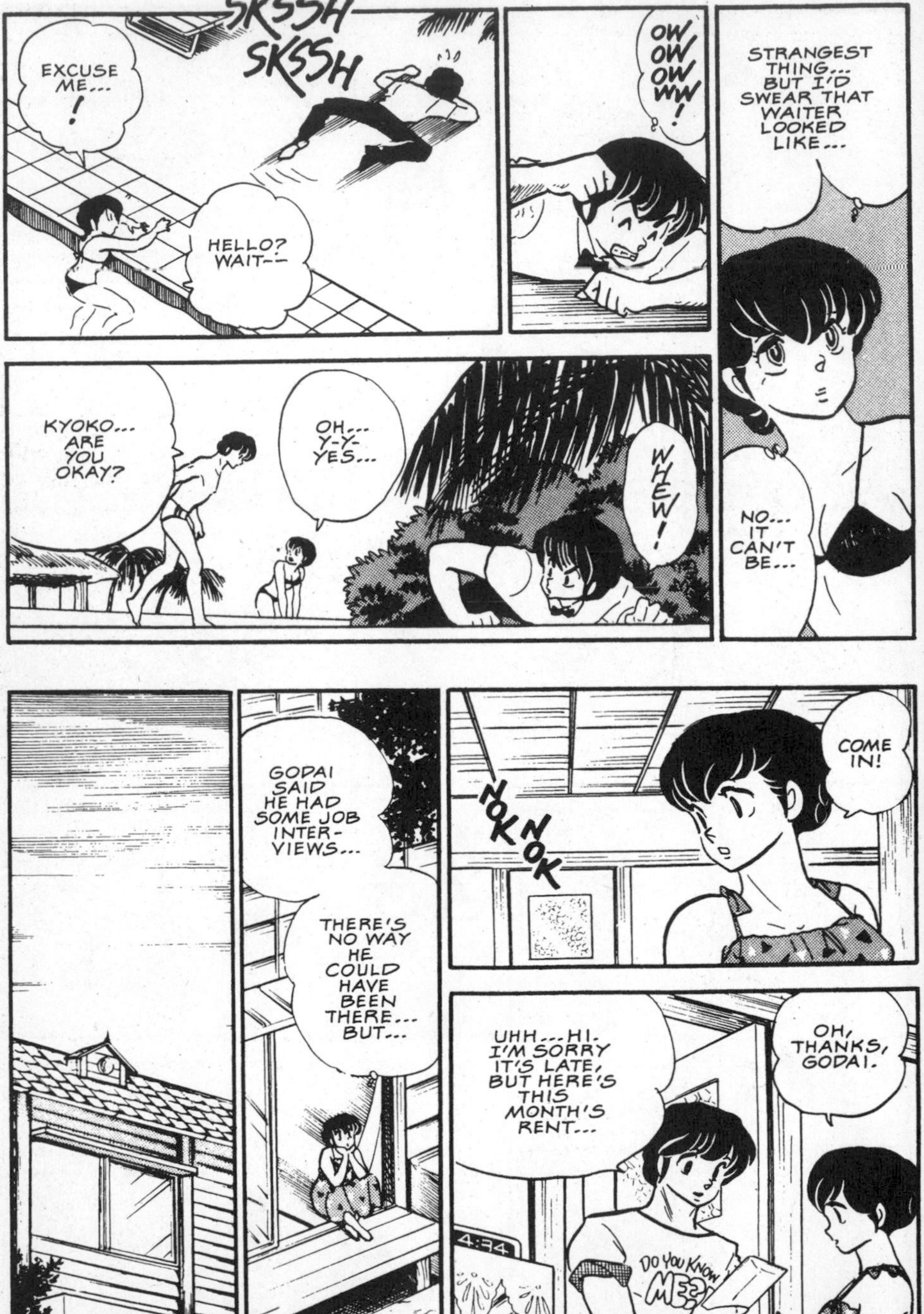
SKSSH SKSSH
EXCUSE ME... !
HELLO? WAIT--
OW OW OW WW!
KYOKO... ARE YOU OKAY?
OH... Y-Y-YES...
WHEW!
STRANGEST THING... BUT I'D SWEAR THAT WAITER LOOKED LIKE...
NO... IT CAN'T BE...
GODAI SAID HE HAD SOME JOB INTER-VIEWS...
THERE'S NO WAY HE COULD HAVE BEEN THERE... BUT...
NOK NOK
COME IN!
UHH...HI. I'M SORRY IT'S LATE, BUT HERE'S THIS MONTH'S RENT...
OH, THANKS, GODAI.
DO YOU KNOW ME?

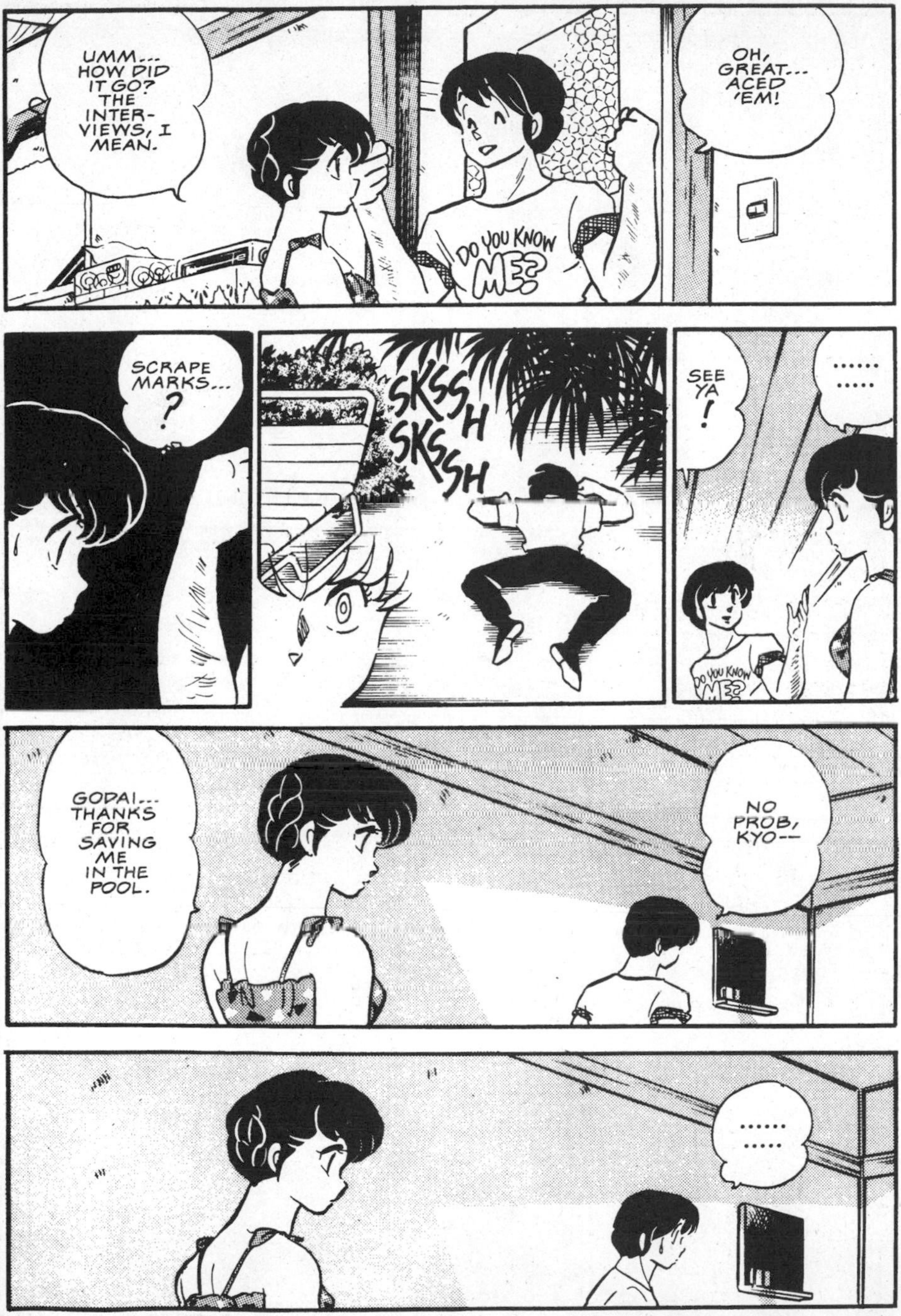
UMM... HOW DID IT GO? THE INTER-VIEWS, I MEAN.
OH, GREAT... ACED 'EM!
DO YOU KNOW ME?
SCRAPE MARKS...?
SKSSH SKSSSH
SEE YA!
......
......
DO YOU KNOW ME?
GODAI... THANKS FOR SAVING ME IN THE POOL.
NO PROB, KYO--
......
......

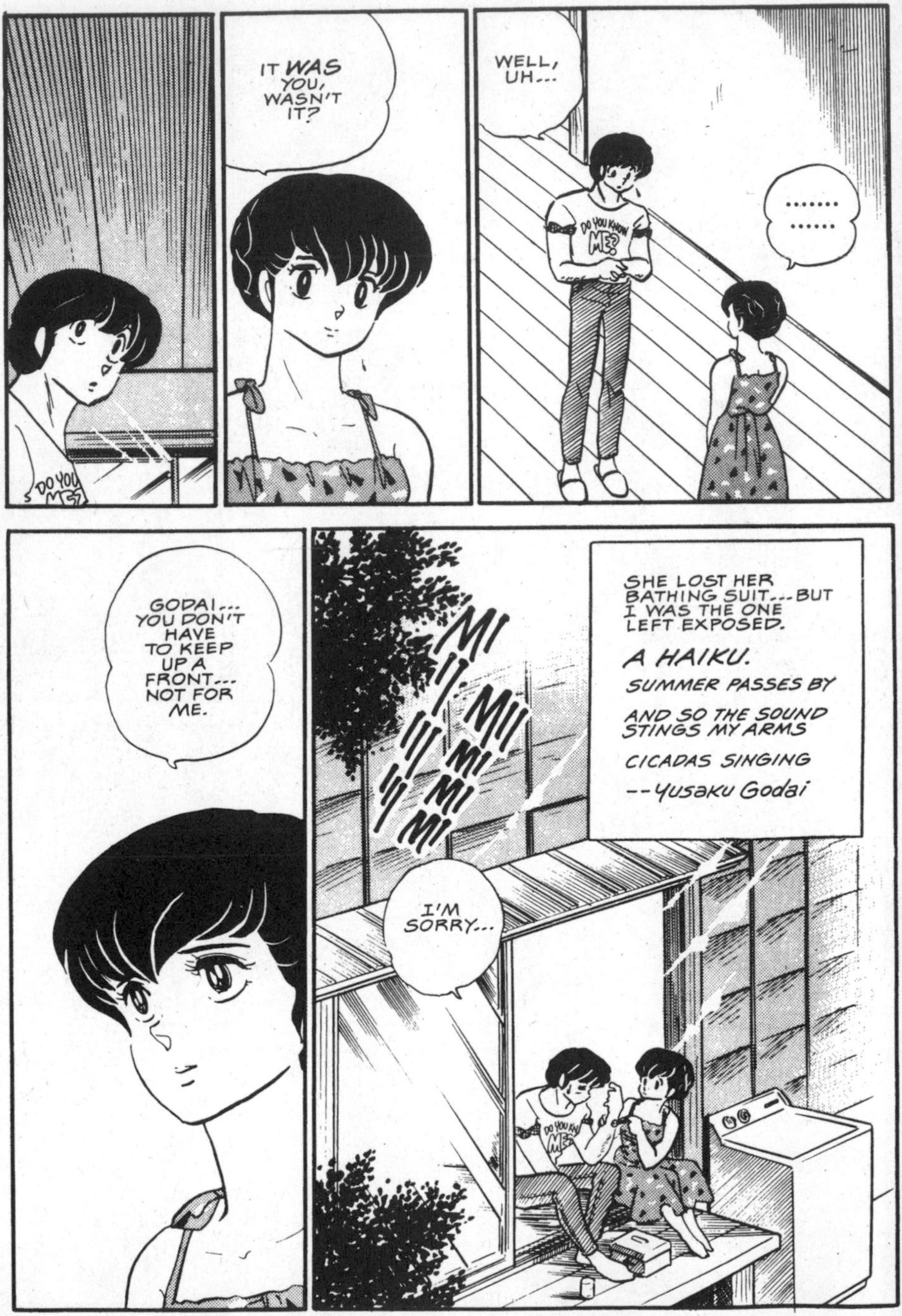

IT WAS YOU, WASN'T IT?
WELL, UH...
DO YOU KNOW ME?
....
......
GODAI... YOU DON'T HAVE TO KEEP UP A FRONT... NOT FOR ME.
SHE LOST HER BATHING SUIT... BUT I WAS THE ONE LEFT EXPOSED.
A HAIKU.
SUMMER PASSES BY
AND SO THE SOUND STINGS MY ARMS
CICADAS SINGING
--Yusaku Godai
MI MI MI MI MI MI
I'M SORRY...

PART 10

MAN VS. MAIDEN

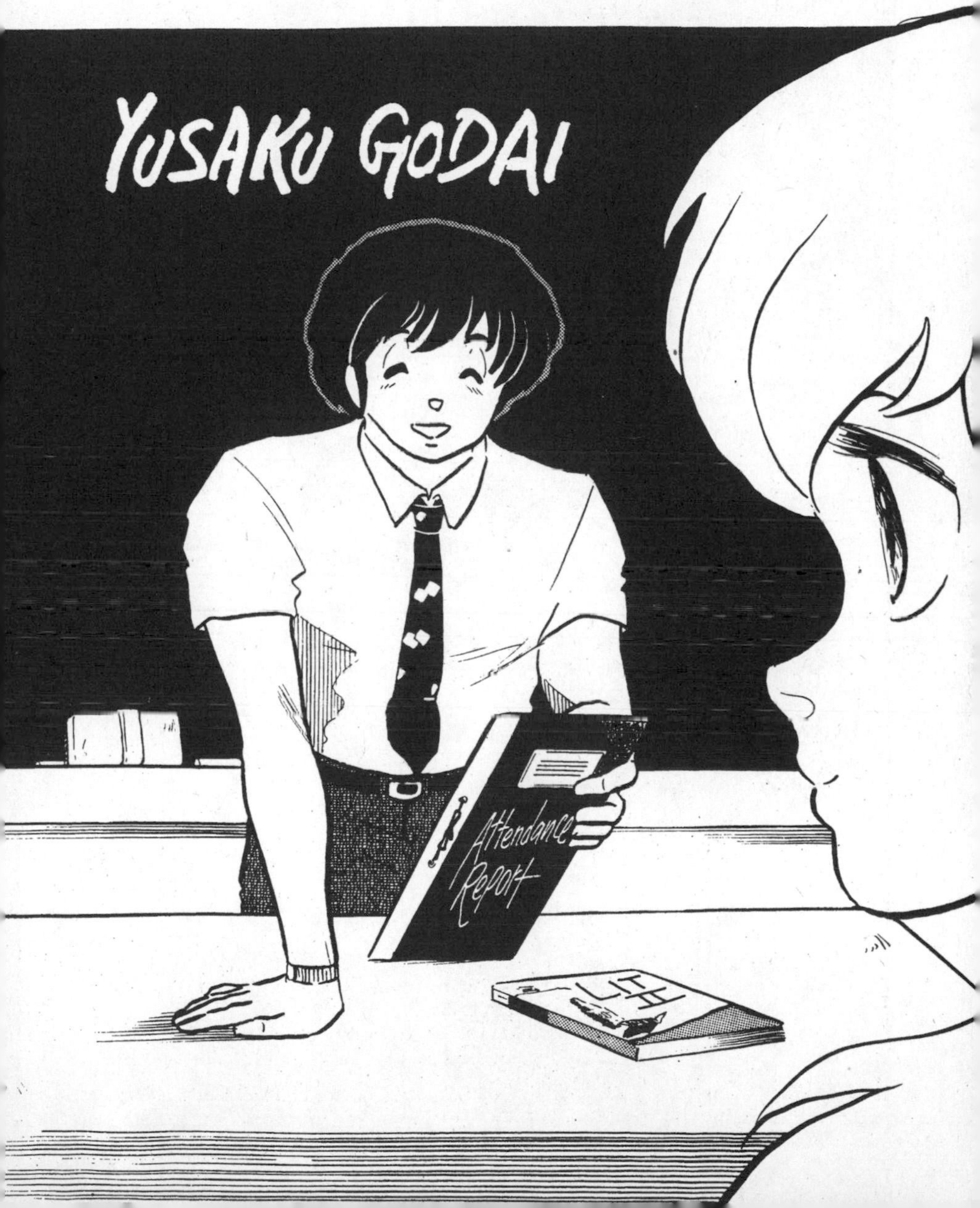
YUSAKU GODAI
Attendance Report
LIT II

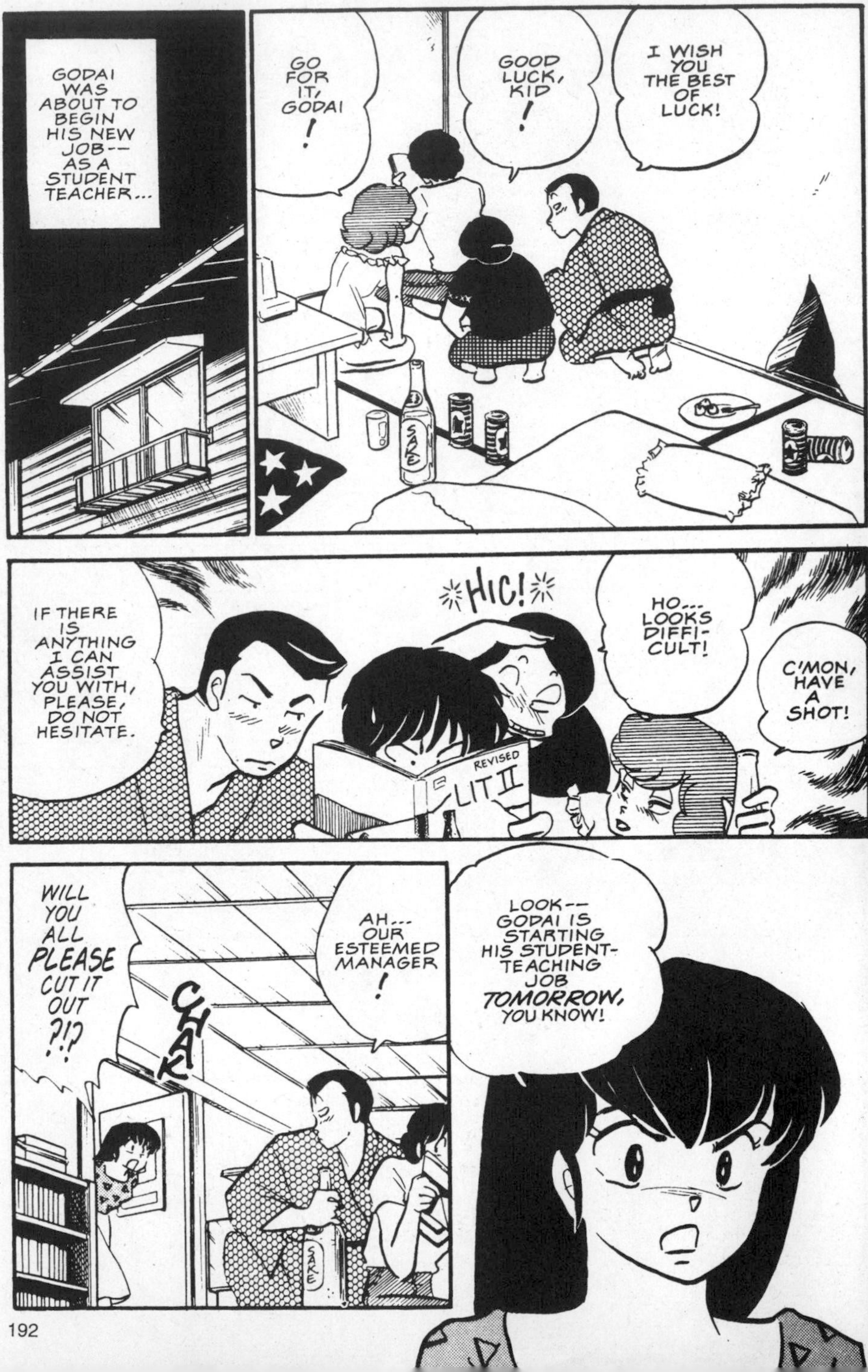

GODAI WAS ABOUT TO BEGIN HIS NEW JOB-- AS A STUDENT TEACHER...
GO FOR IT, GODAI!
GOOD LUCK, KID!
I WISH YOU THE BEST OF LUCK!
SAKE
IF THERE IS ANYTHING I CAN ASSIST YOU WITH, PLEASE, DO NOT HESITATE.
HIC!
HO... LOOKS DIFFI-CULT!
C'MON, HAVE A SHOT!
REVISED LIT II
WILL YOU ALL PLEASE CUT IT OUT?!?
CHAK
AH... OUR ESTEEMED MANAGER!
LOOK-- GODAI IS STARTING HIS STUDENT-TEACHING JOB TOMORROW, YOU KNOW!
SAKE

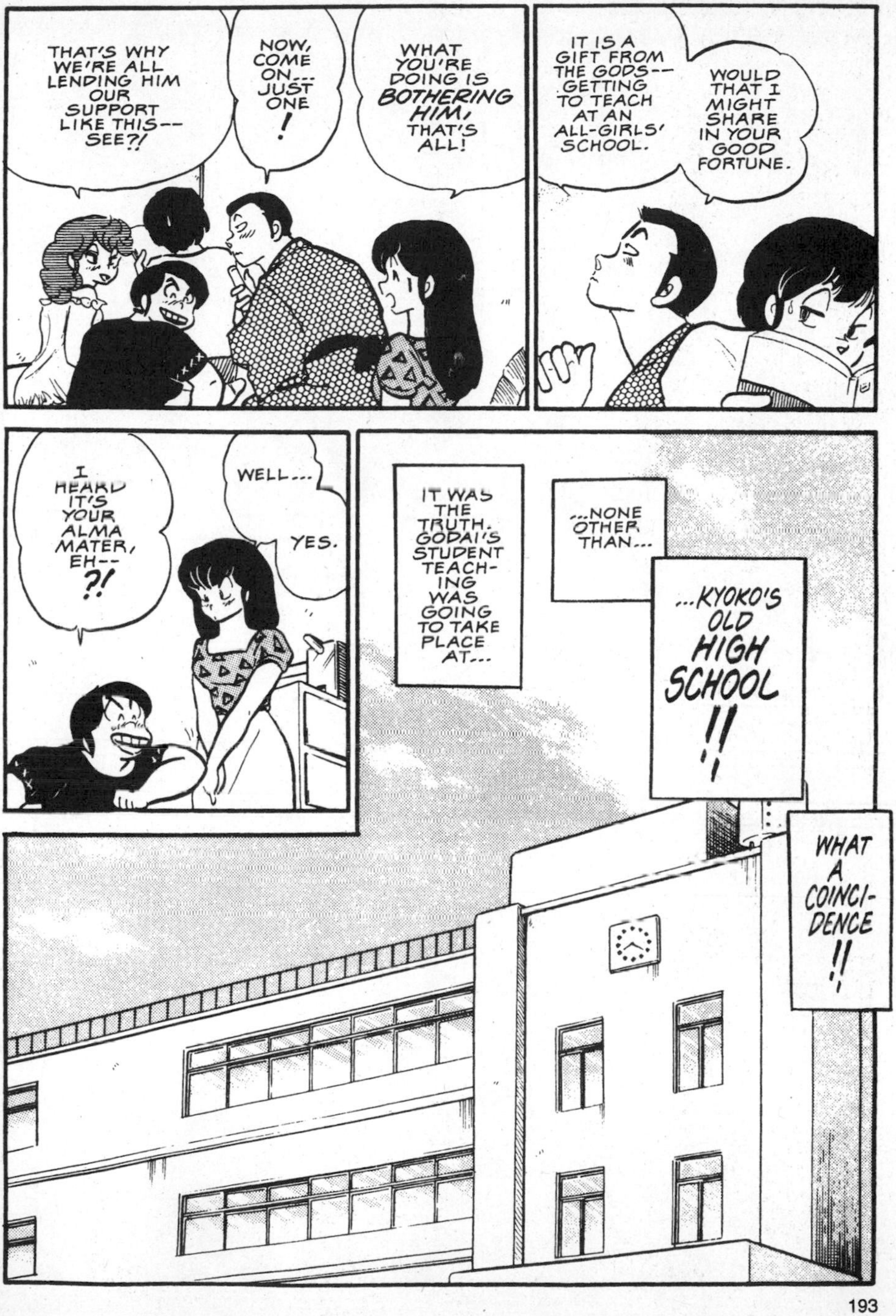
THAT'S WHY WE'RE ALL LENDING HIM OUR SUPPORT LIKE THIS-- SEE?!
NOW, COME ON... JUST ONE !
WHAT YOU'RE DOING IS BOTHERING HIM, THAT'S ALL!
IT IS A GIFT FROM THE GODS-- GETTING TO TEACH AT AN ALL-GIRLS' SCHOOL.
WOULD THAT I MIGHT SHARE IN YOUR GOOD FORTUNE.
I HEARD IT'S YOUR ALMA MATER, EH--?!
WELL... YES.
IT WAS THE TRUTH. GODAI'S STUDENT TEACHING WAS GOING TO TAKE PLACE AT...
...NONE OTHER THAN...
...KYOKO'S OLD HIGH SCHOOL!!
WHAT A COINCIDENCE!!

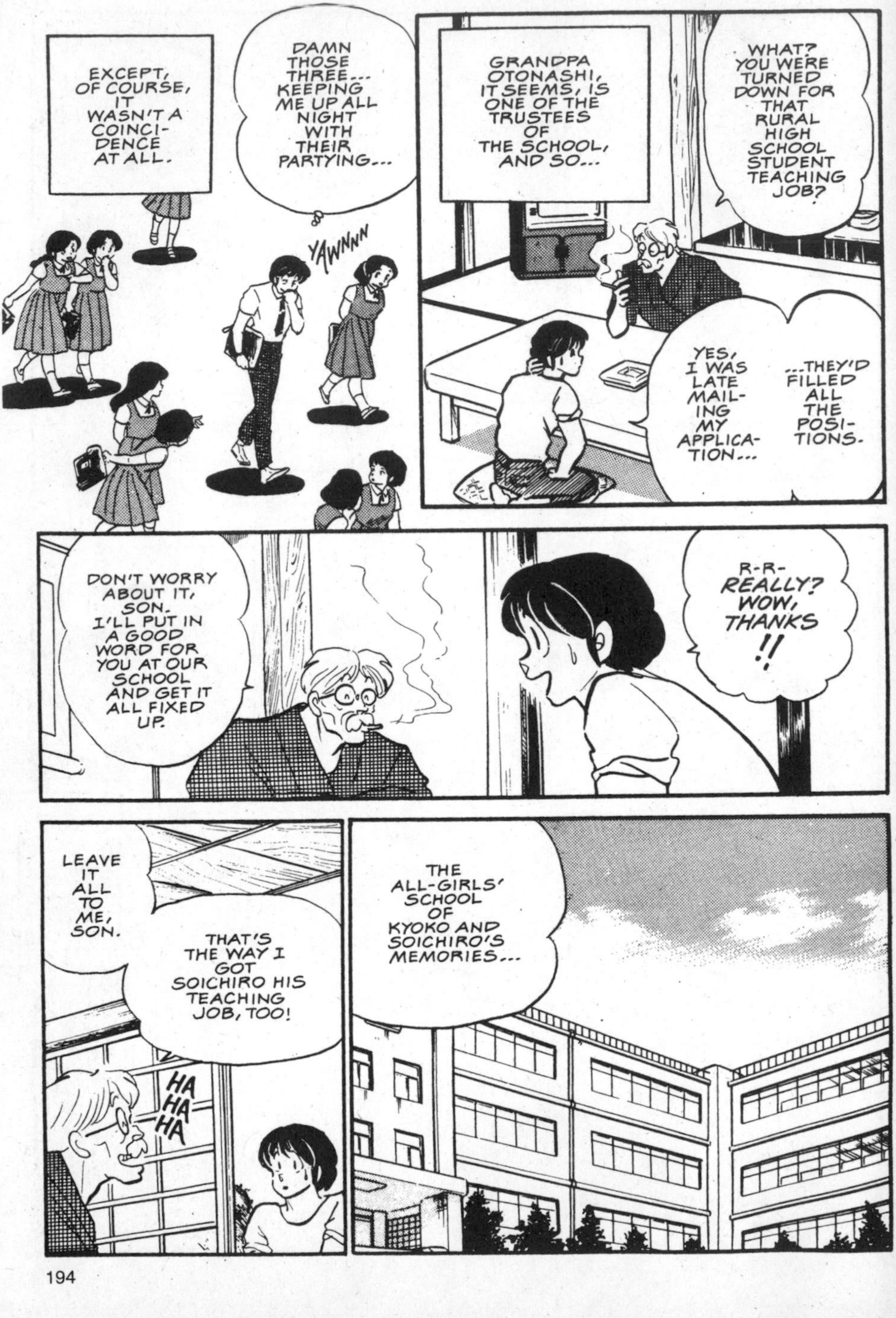
EXCEPT, OF COURSE, IT WASN'T A COINCIDENCE AT ALL.
DAMN THOSE THREE... KEEPING ME UP ALL NIGHT WITH THEIR PARTYING...
YAWNNN
GRANDPA OTONASHI, IT SEEMS, IS ONE OF THE TRUSTEES OF THE SCHOOL, AND SO...
WHAT? YOU WERE TURNED DOWN FOR THAT RURAL HIGH SCHOOL STUDENT TEACHING JOB?
YES, I WAS LATE MAILING MY APPLICATION...
...THEY'D FILLED ALL THE POSITIONS.
DON'T WORRY ABOUT IT, SON. I'LL PUT IN A GOOD WORD FOR YOU AT OUR SCHOOL AND GET IT ALL FIXED UP.
R-R-REALLY? WOW, THANKS!!
LEAVE IT ALL TO ME, SON.
THAT'S THE WAY I GOT SOICHIRO HIS TEACHING JOB, TOO!
HA HA HA
THE ALL-GIRLS' SCHOOL OF KYOKO AND SOICHIRO'S MEMORIES...

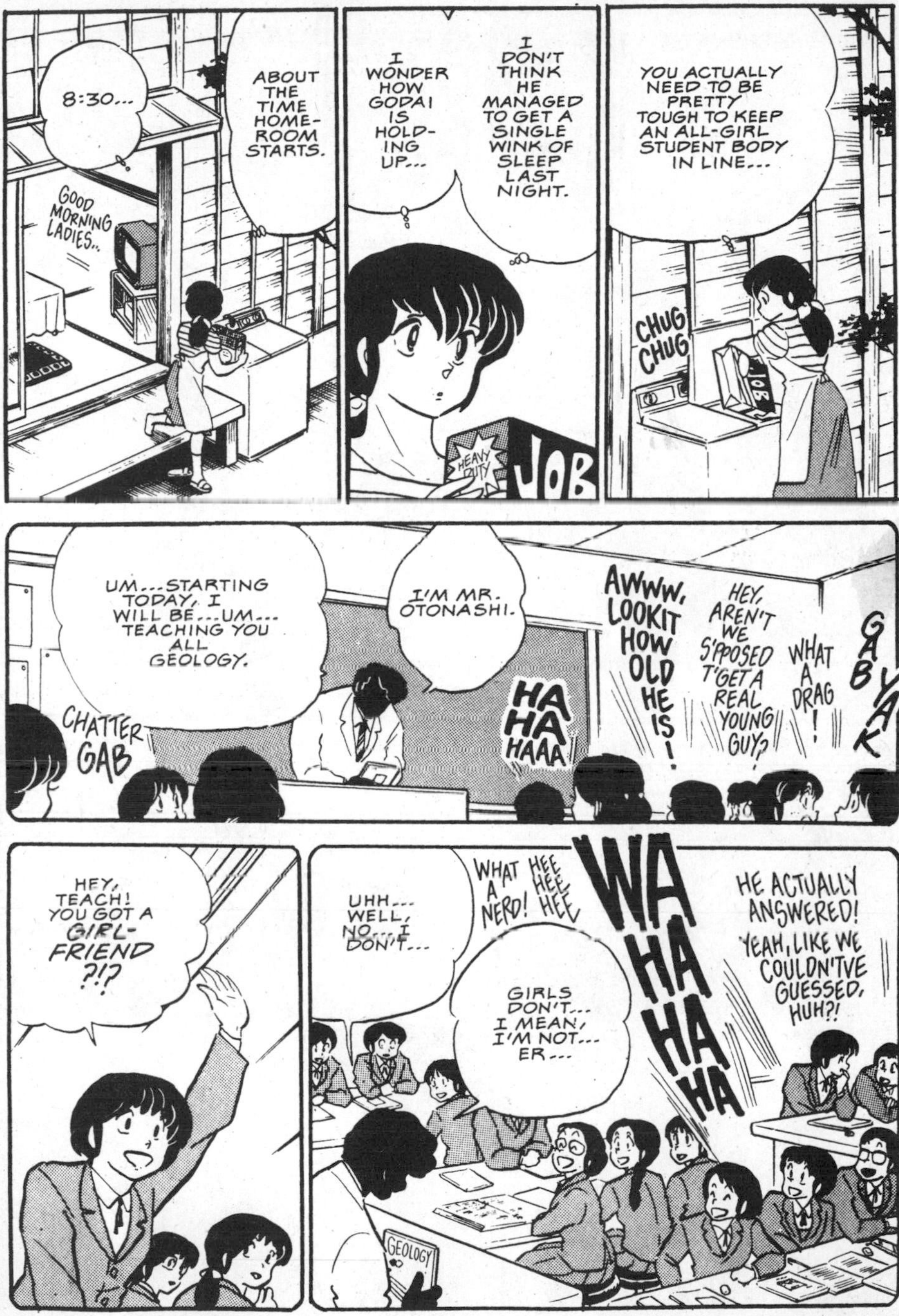
8:30...
GOOD MORNING LADIES...
ABOUT THE TIME HOME-ROOM STARTS.
I WONDER HOW GODAI IS HOLD-ING UP...
I DON'T THINK HE MANAGED TO GET A SINGLE WINK OF SLEEP LAST NIGHT.
HEAVY DUTY
JOB
YOU ACTUALLY NEED TO BE PRETTY TOUGH TO KEEP AN ALL-GIRL STUDENT BODY IN LINE...
CHUG CHUG
JOB
UM...STARTING TODAY, I WILL BE...UM... TEACHING YOU ALL GEOLOGY.
CHATTER GAB
I'M MR. OTONASHI.
HA HA HAAA
AWWW, LOOKIT HOW OLD HE IS!
HEY, AREN'T WE S'PPOSED T'GET A REAL YOUNG GUY?
WHAT A DRAG!
GAB YAK
HEY, TEACH! YOU GOT A GIRL-FRIEND ?!?
UHH... WELL, NO...I DON'T...
WHAT A NERD!
HEE, HEE, HEE
GIRLS DON'T... I MEAN, I'M NOT... ER...
GEOLOGY
WA HA HA HA HA HA
HE ACTUALLY ANSWERED!
YEAH, LIKE WE COULDN'T'VE GUESSED, HUH?!

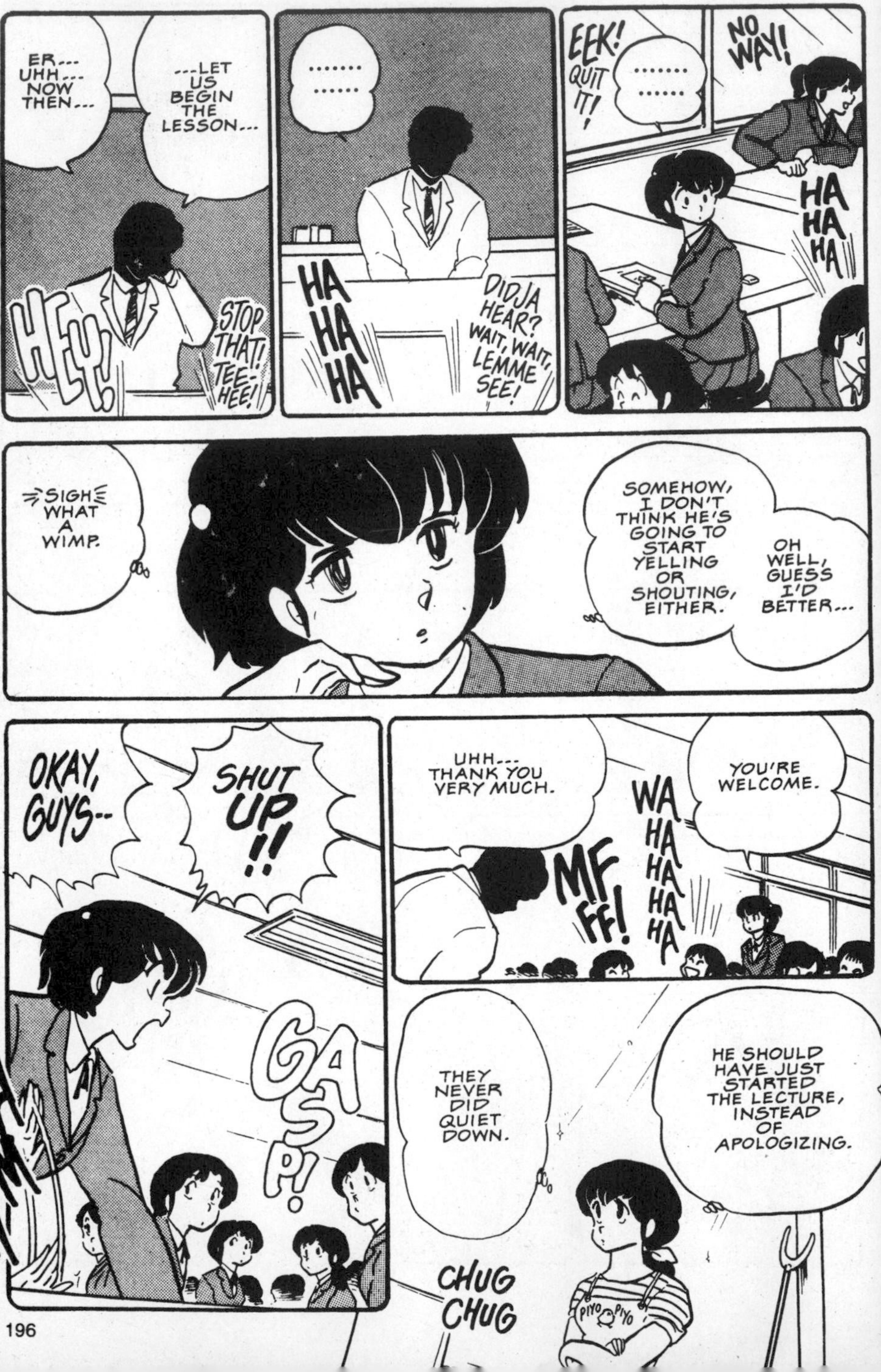
ER--- UHH--- NOW THEN---
---LET US BEGIN THE LESSON---
HEY!
STOP THAT! TEE-HEE!
....
HA HA HA
DIDJA HEAR? WAIT, WAIT, LEMME SEE!
EEK! QUIT IT!
....
NO WAY!
HA HA HA
SIGH WHAT A WIMP.
SOMEHOW, I DON'T THINK HE'S GOING TO START YELLING OR SHOUTING, EITHER.
OH WELL, GUESS I'D BETTER...
OKAY, GUYS--
SHUT UP!!
GASP!
UHH--- THANK YOU VERY MUCH.
YOU'RE WELCOME.
MF FF!
WA HA HA HA HA HA
THEY NEVER DID QUIET DOWN.
HE SHOULD HAVE JUST STARTED THE LECTURE, INSTEAD OF APOLOGIZING.
CHUG CHUG
PIYO PIYO

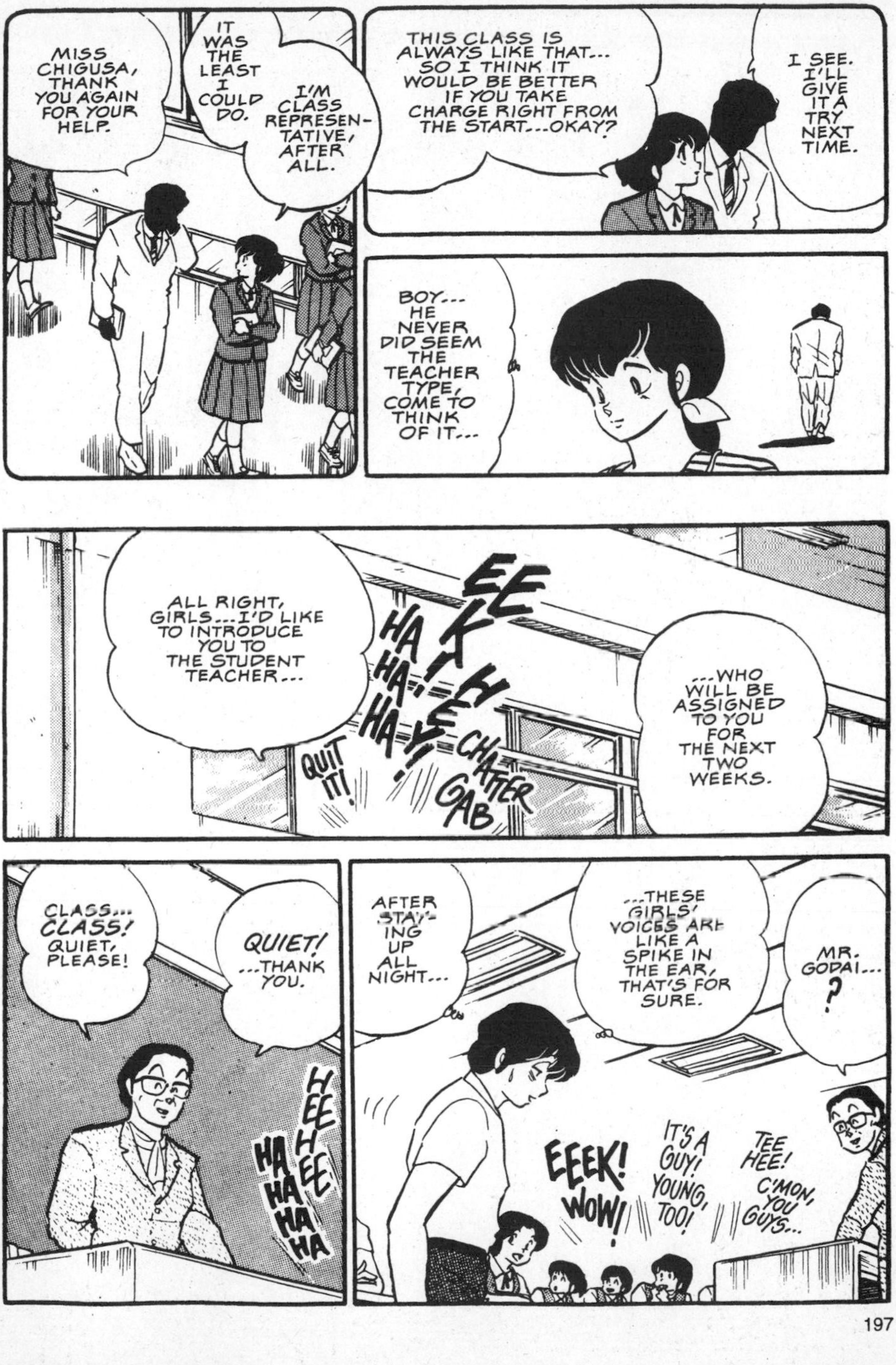
MISS CHIGUSA, THANK YOU AGAIN FOR YOUR HELP.
IT WAS THE LEAST I COULD DO.
I'M CLASS REPRESENTATIVE, AFTER ALL.
THIS CLASS IS ALWAYS LIKE THAT... SO I THINK IT WOULD BE BETTER IF YOU TAKE CHARGE RIGHT FROM THE START...OKAY?
I SEE. I'LL GIVE IT A TRY NEXT TIME.
BOY... HE NEVER DID SEEM THE TEACHER TYPE, COME TO THINK OF IT...
ALL RIGHT, GIRLS...I'D LIKE TO INTRODUCE YOU TO THE STUDENT TEACHER...
EEK
HA HA HA!
HEE HEE!
QUIT IT!
CHATTER
GAB
...WHO WILL BE ASSIGNED TO YOU FOR THE NEXT TWO WEEKS.
CLASS... CLASS! QUIET, PLEASE!
QUIET! ...THANK YOU.
HEE HEE
HA HA HA HA HA
AFTER STAYING UP ALL NIGHT...
...THESE GIRLS' VOICES ARE LIKE A SPIKE IN THE EAR, THAT'S FOR SURE.
MR. GODAI... ?
EEEK! WOW!
IT'S A GUY! YOUNG, TOO!
TEE HEE!
C'MON, YOU GUYS...

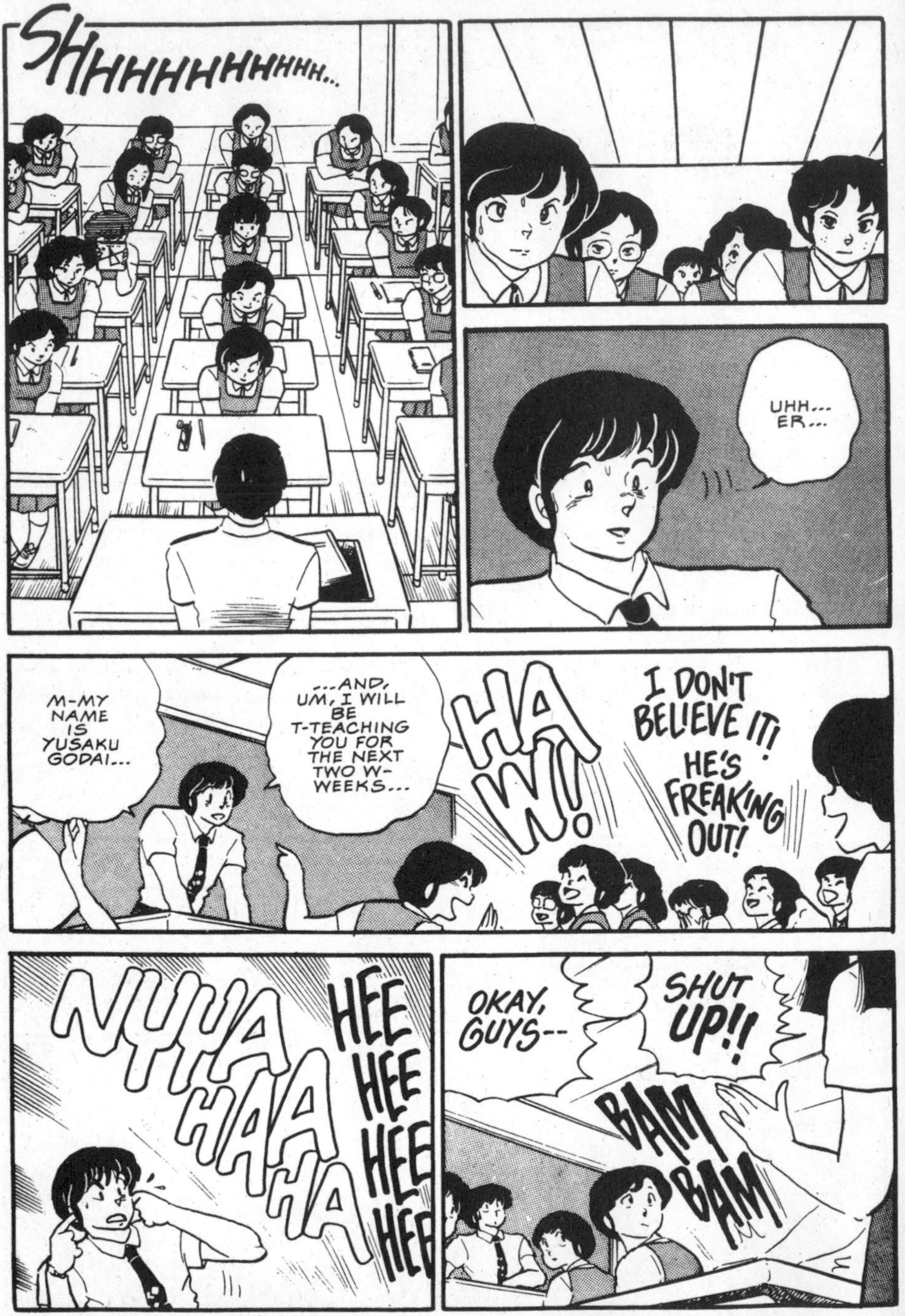
SHHHHHHHHHHH...
UHH... ER...
M-MY NAME IS YUSAKU GODAI...
...AND, UM, I WILL BE T-TEACHING YOU FOR THE NEXT TWO W-WEEKS...
HAW!
I DON'T BELIEVE IT!
HE'S FREAKING OUT!
NYUA HAA HA
HEE HEE HEE HEE
OKAY, GUYS--
SHUT UP!!
BAM BAM

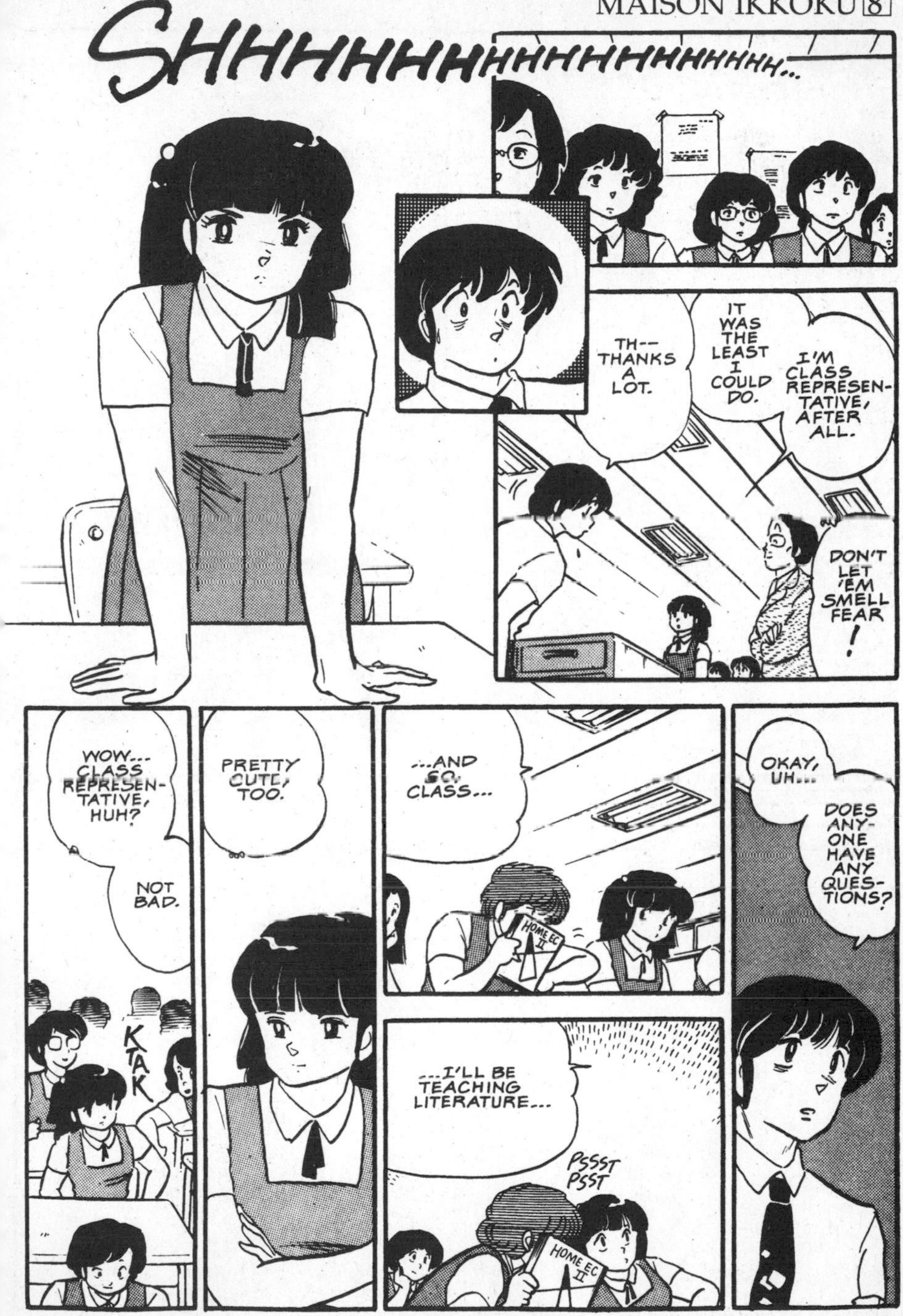
SHHHHHHHHHHHHHHHHHH...
TH-- THANKS A LOT.
IT WAS THE LEAST I COULD DO.
I'M CLASS REPRESENTATIVE, AFTER ALL.
DON'T LET 'EM SMELL FEAR!
WOW... CLASS REPRESENTATIVE, HUH?
NOT BAD.
KTAK
PRETTY CUTE, TOO.
...AND SO, CLASS...
HOME EC II
...I'LL BE TEACHING LITERATURE...
PSSST PSST
HOME EC II
OKAY, UH...
DOES ANYONE HAVE ANY QUESTIONS?

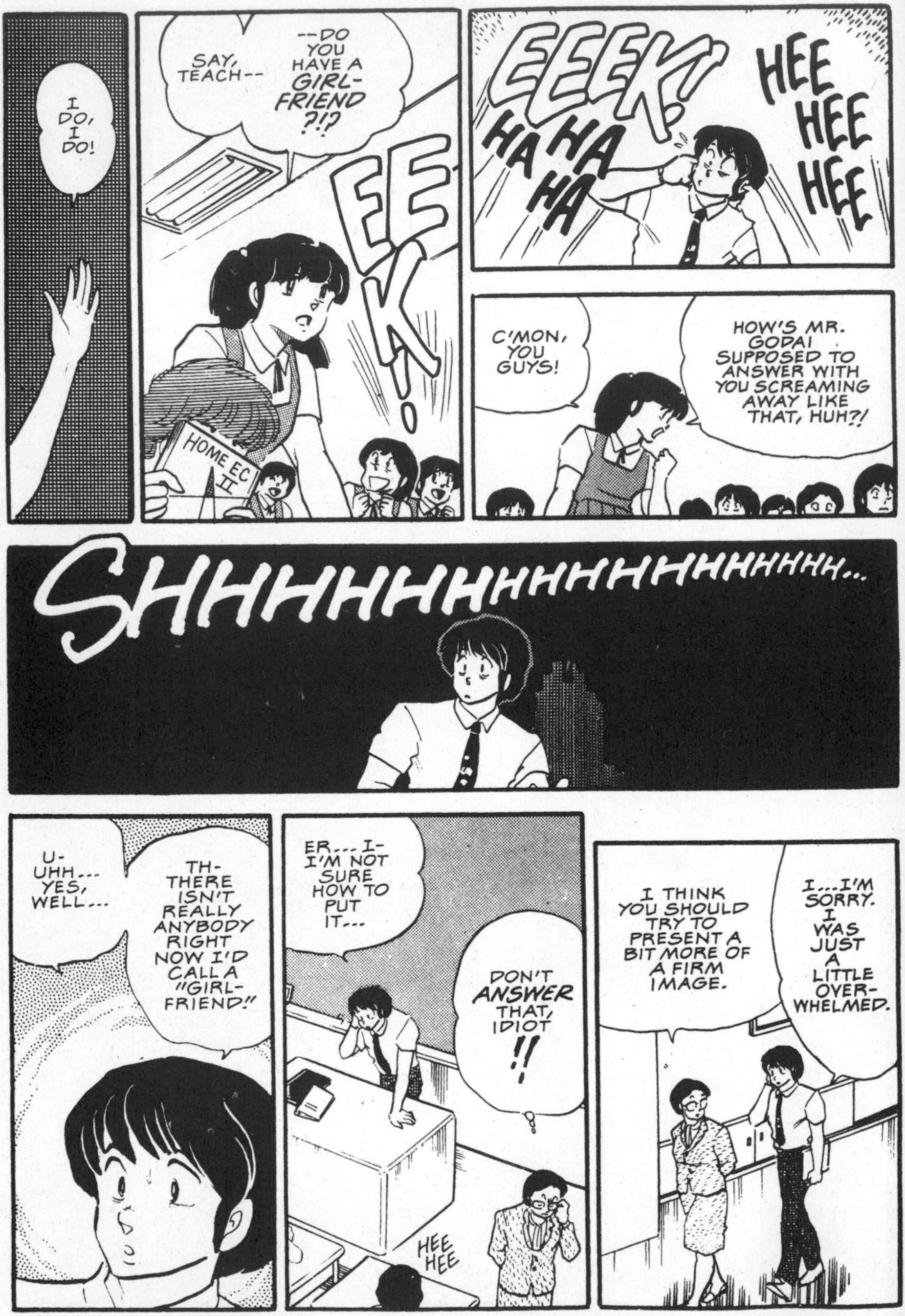
I DO, I DO!
SAY, TEACH--
--DO YOU HAVE A GIRL-FRIEND ?!?
EEEK!
HOME EC II
EEEK!
HA HA HA HA HA
HEE HEE HEE
C'MON, YOU GUYS!
HOW'S MR. GODAI SUPPOSED TO ANSWER WITH YOU SCREAMING AWAY LIKE THAT, HUH?!
SHHHHHHHHHHHHHHHH...
U-UHH... YES, WELL...
TH-THERE ISN'T REALLY ANYBODY RIGHT NOW I'D CALL A "GIRL-FRIEND."
ER... I-I'M NOT SURE HOW TO PUT IT...
DON'T ANSWER THAT, IDIOT !!
HEE HEE
I THINK YOU SHOULD TRY TO PRESENT A BIT MORE OF A FIRM IMAGE.
I... I'M SORRY. I WAS JUST A LITTLE OVER-WHELMED.

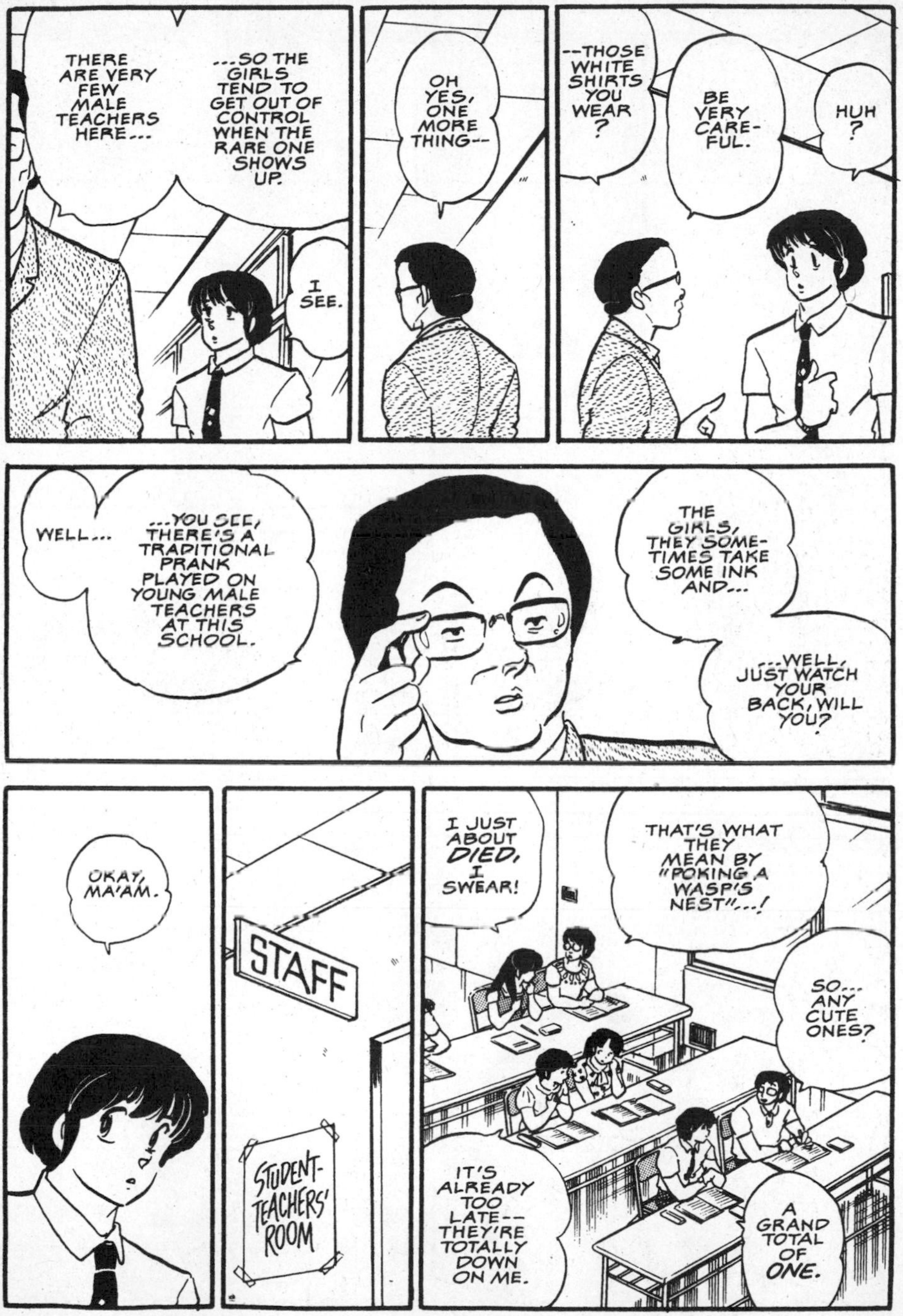
THERE ARE VERY FEW MALE TEACHERS HERE...
...SO THE GIRLS TEND TO GET OUT OF CONTROL WHEN THE RARE ONE SHOWS UP.
I SEE.
OH YES, ONE MORE THING--
--THOSE WHITE SHIRTS YOU WEAR?
BE VERY CARE-FUL.
HUH?
WELL...
...YOU SEE, THERE'S A TRADITIONAL PRANK PLAYED ON YOUNG MALE TEACHERS AT THIS SCHOOL.
THE GIRLS, THEY SOMETIMES TAKE SOME INK AND...
...WELL, JUST WATCH YOUR BACK, WILL YOU?
OKAY, MA'AM.
STAFF
STUDENT-TEACHERS' ROOM
I JUST ABOUT DIED, I SWEAR!
THAT'S WHAT THEY MEAN BY "POKING A WASP'S NEST"...!
SO... ANY CUTE ONES?
IT'S ALREADY TOO LATE--THEY'RE TOTALLY DOWN ON ME.
A GRAND TOTAL OF ONE.

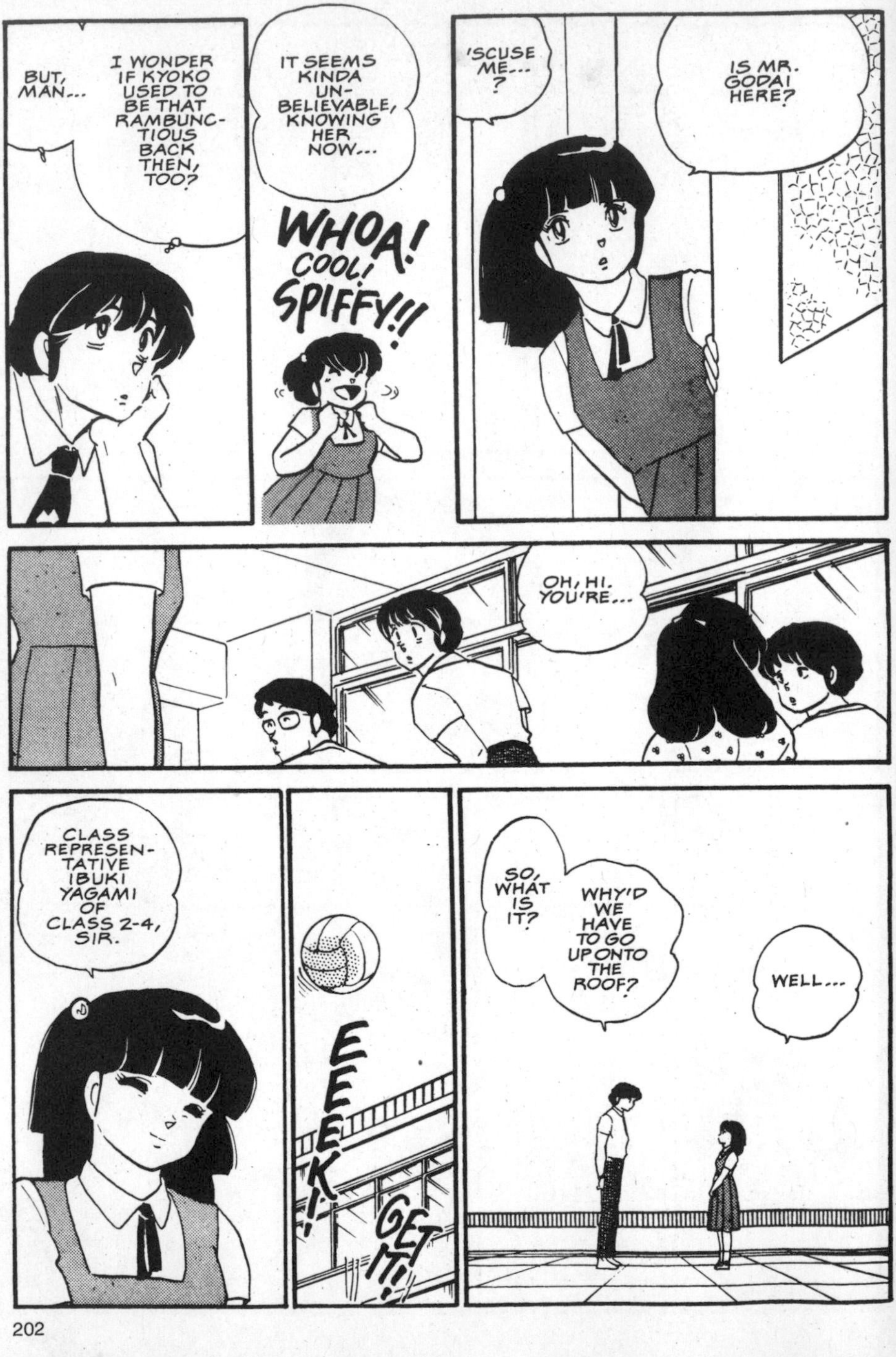
BUT, MAN...
I WONDER IF KYOKO USED TO BE THAT RAMBUNCTIOUS BACK THEN, TOO?
IT SEEMS KINDA UNBELIEVABLE, KNOWING HER NOW...
WHOA! COOL! SPIFFY!!
'SCUSE ME...?
IS MR. GODAI HERE?
OH, HI. YOU'RE...
CLASS REPRESENTATIVE IBUKI YAGAMI OF CLASS 2-4, SIR.
EEEEK!!
GET IT!!
SO, WHAT IS IT?
WHY'D WE HAVE TO GO UP ONTO THE ROOF?
WELL...

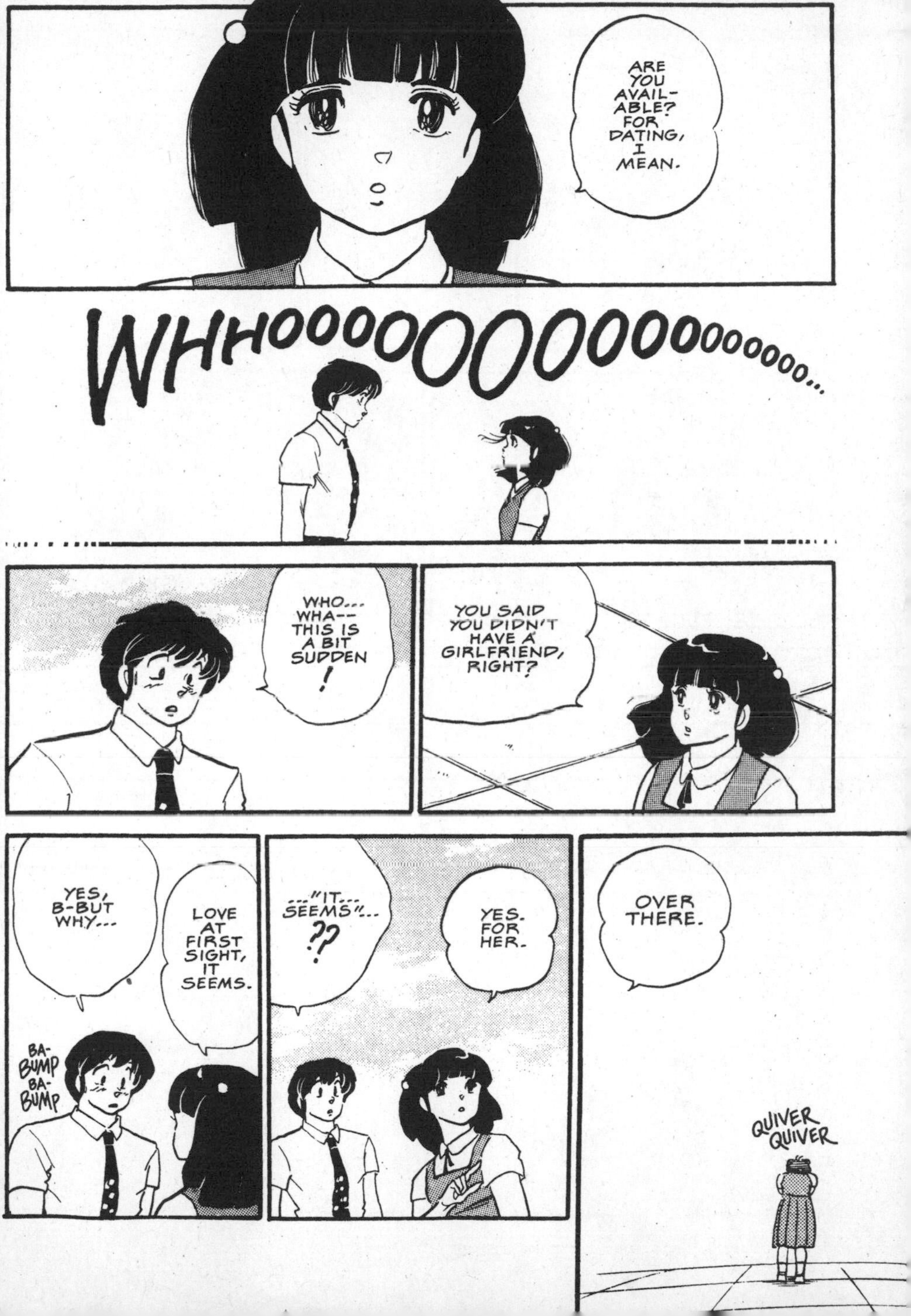
ARE YOU AVAILABLE? FOR DATING, I MEAN.
WHHOOOOOOOOOOOOOOOOOOO...
WHO... WHA-- THIS IS A BIT SUDDEN!
YOU SAID YOU DIDN'T HAVE A GIRLFRIEND, RIGHT?
YES, B-BUT WHY...
LOVE AT FIRST SIGHT, IT SEEMS.
BA-BUMP BA-BUMP
..."IT... SEEMS"...
??
YES. FOR HER.
OVER THERE.
QUIVER QUIVER

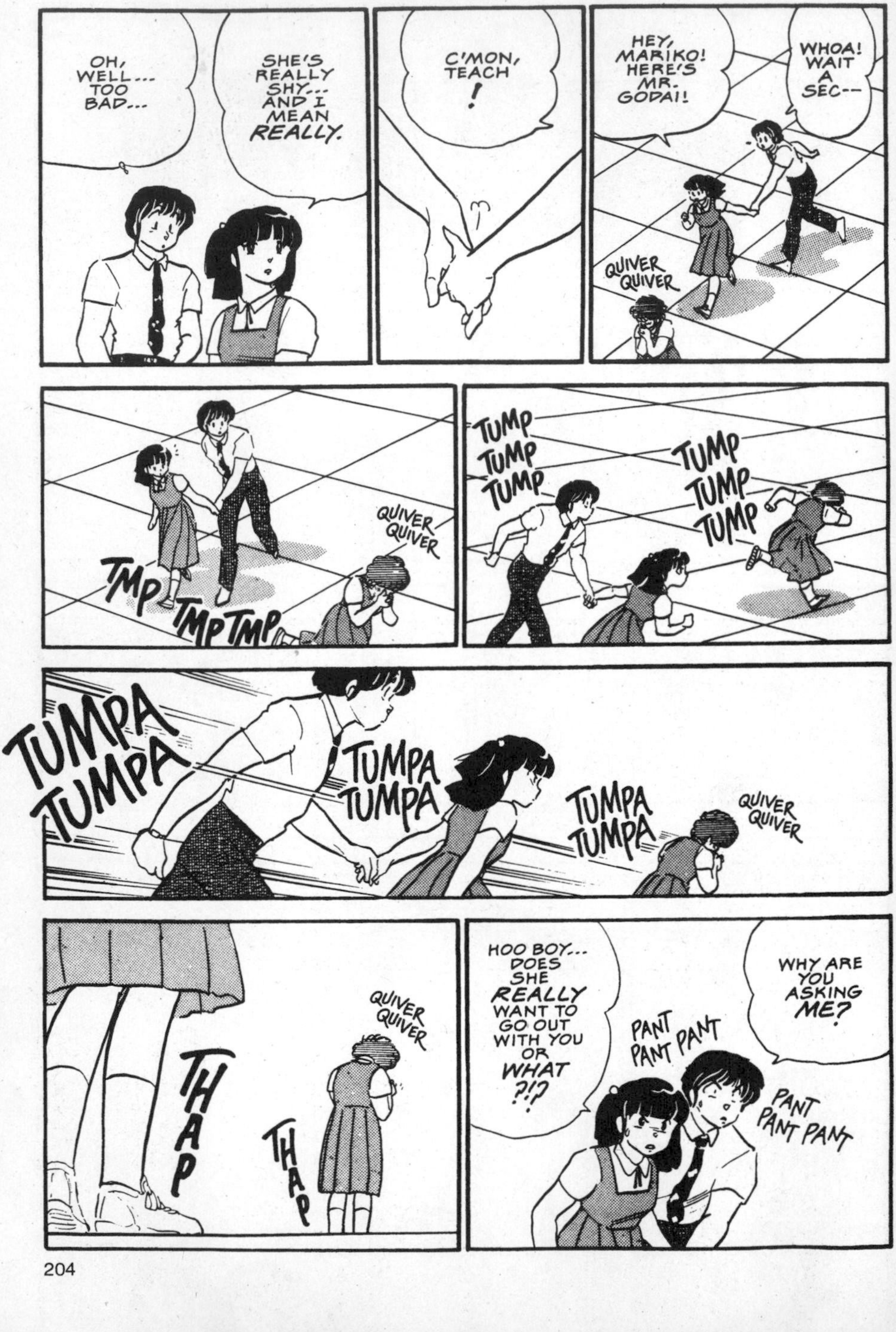

OH, WELL... TOO BAD...
SHE'S REALLY SHY... AND I MEAN REALLY.
C'MON, TEACH!
HEY, MARIKO! HERE'S MR. GODAI!
WHOA! WAIT A SEC--
QUIVER QUIVER
QUIVER QUIVER
TMP TMP TMP
TUMP TUMP TUMP
TUMP TUMP TUMP
TUMPA TUMPA
TUMPA TUMPA
TUMPA TUMPA
QUIVER QUIVER
QUIVER QUIVER
THAP
THAP
HOO BOY... DOES SHE REALLY WANT TO GO OUT WITH YOU OR WHAT ?!?
WHY ARE YOU ASKING ME?
PANT PANT PANT
PANT PANT PANT

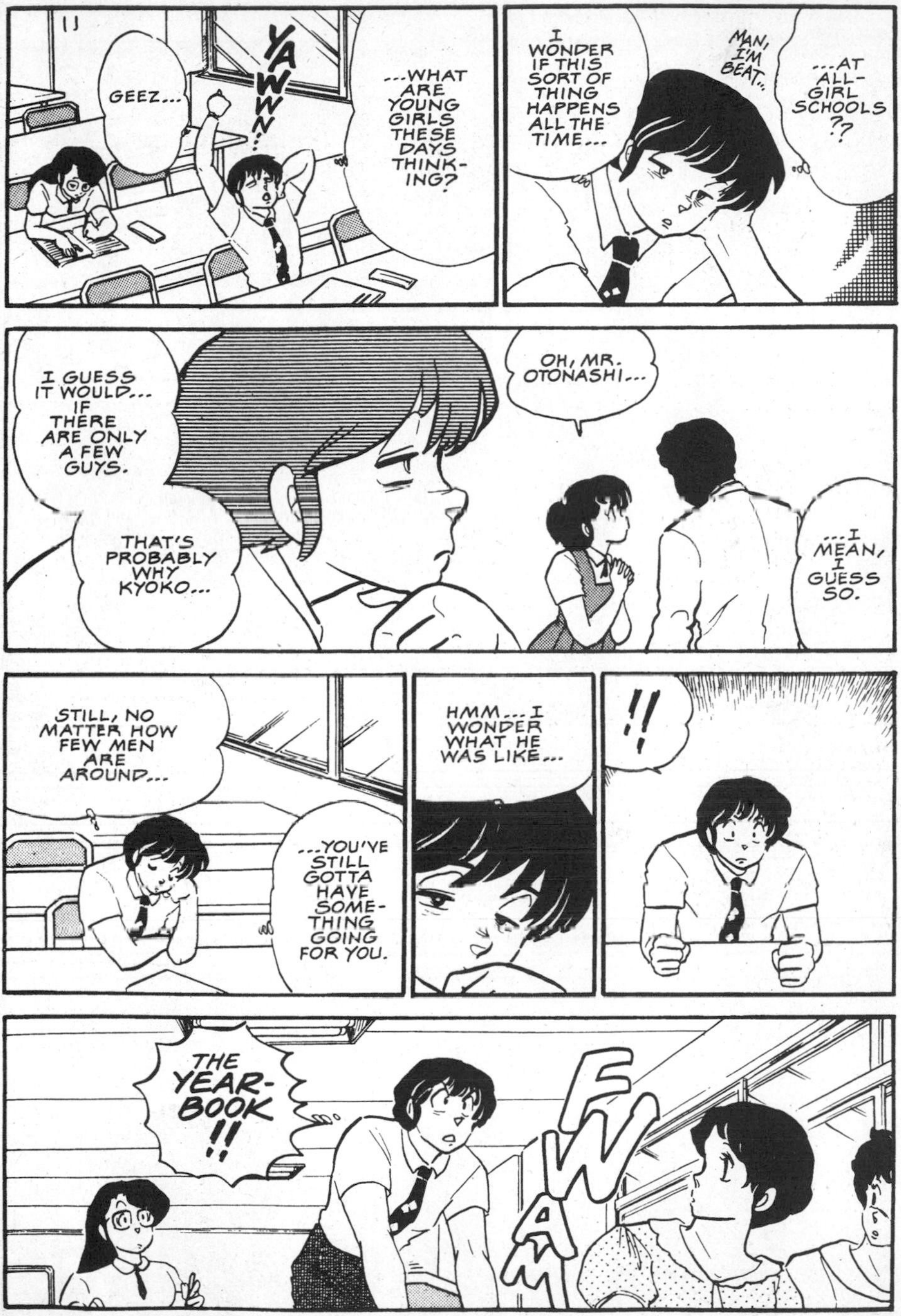
GEEZ...
YAWWN!
...WHAT ARE YOUNG GIRLS THESE DAYS THINKING?
I WONDER IF THIS SORT OF THING HAPPENS ALL THE TIME...
MAN, I'M BEAT..
...AT ALL-GIRL SCHOOLS ??
I GUESS IT WOULD... IF THERE ARE ONLY A FEW GUYS.
THAT'S PROBABLY WHY KYOKO...
OH, MR. OTONASHI...
...I MEAN, I GUESS SO.
STILL, NO MATTER HOW FEW MEN ARE AROUND...
...YOU'VE STILL GOTTA HAVE SOMETHING GOING FOR YOU.
HMM... I WONDER WHAT HE WAS LIKE...
!!
THE YEAR-BOOK !!
FWAM

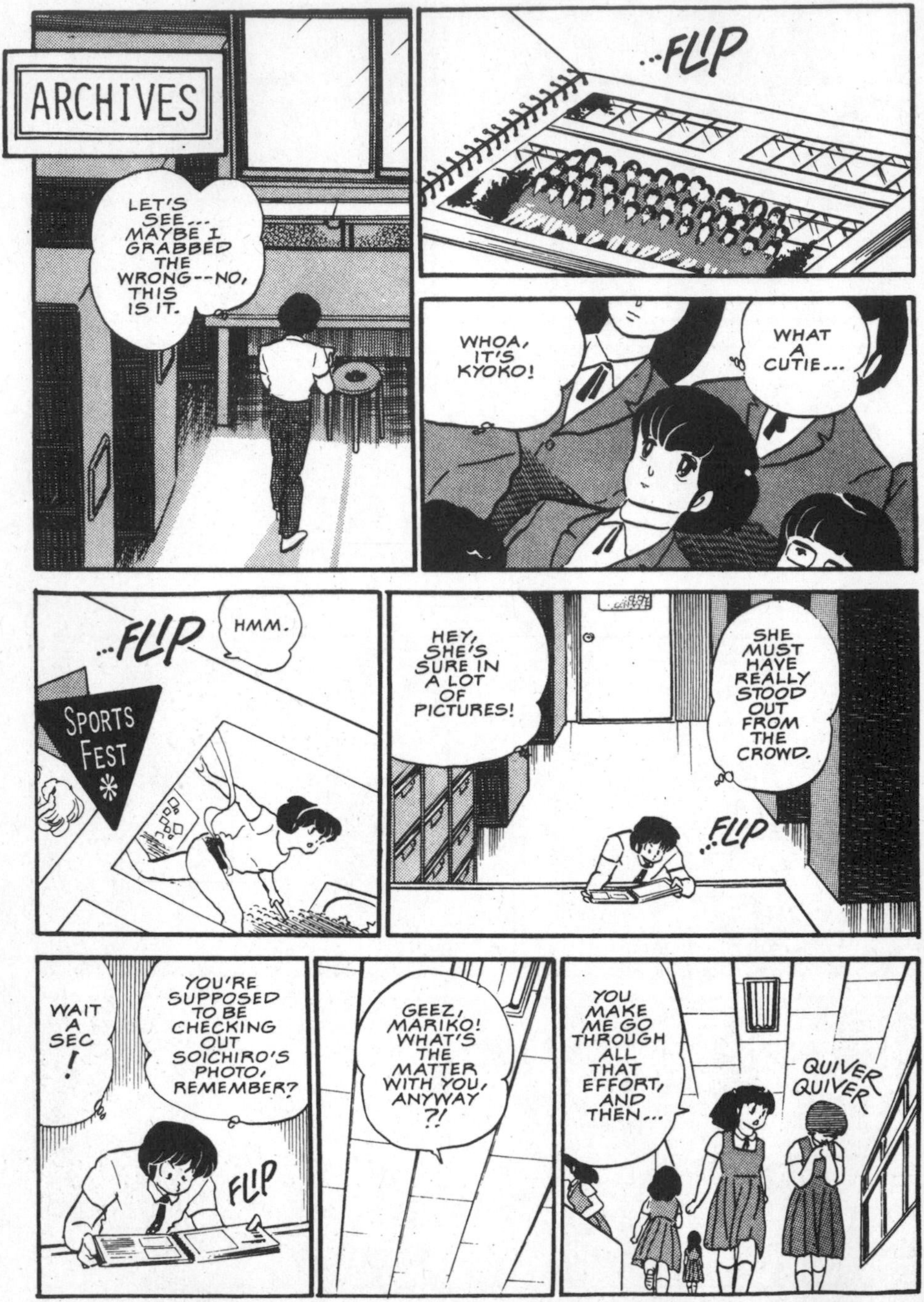
ARCHIVES
LET'S SEE... MAYBE I GRABBED THE WRONG--NO, THIS IS IT.
...FLIP
WHOA, IT'S KYOKO!
WHAT A CUTIE...
...FLIP
HMM.
SPORTS FEST
HEY, SHE'S SURE IN A LOT OF PICTURES!
SHE MUST HAVE REALLY STOOD OUT FROM THE CROWD.
...FLIP
WAIT A SEC!
YOU'RE SUPPOSED TO BE CHECKING OUT SOICHIRO'S PHOTO, REMEMBER?
FLIP
GEEZ, MARIKO! WHAT'S THE MATTER WITH YOU, ANYWAY?!
YOU MAKE ME GO THROUGH ALL THAT EFFORT, AND THEN...
QUIVER QUIVER

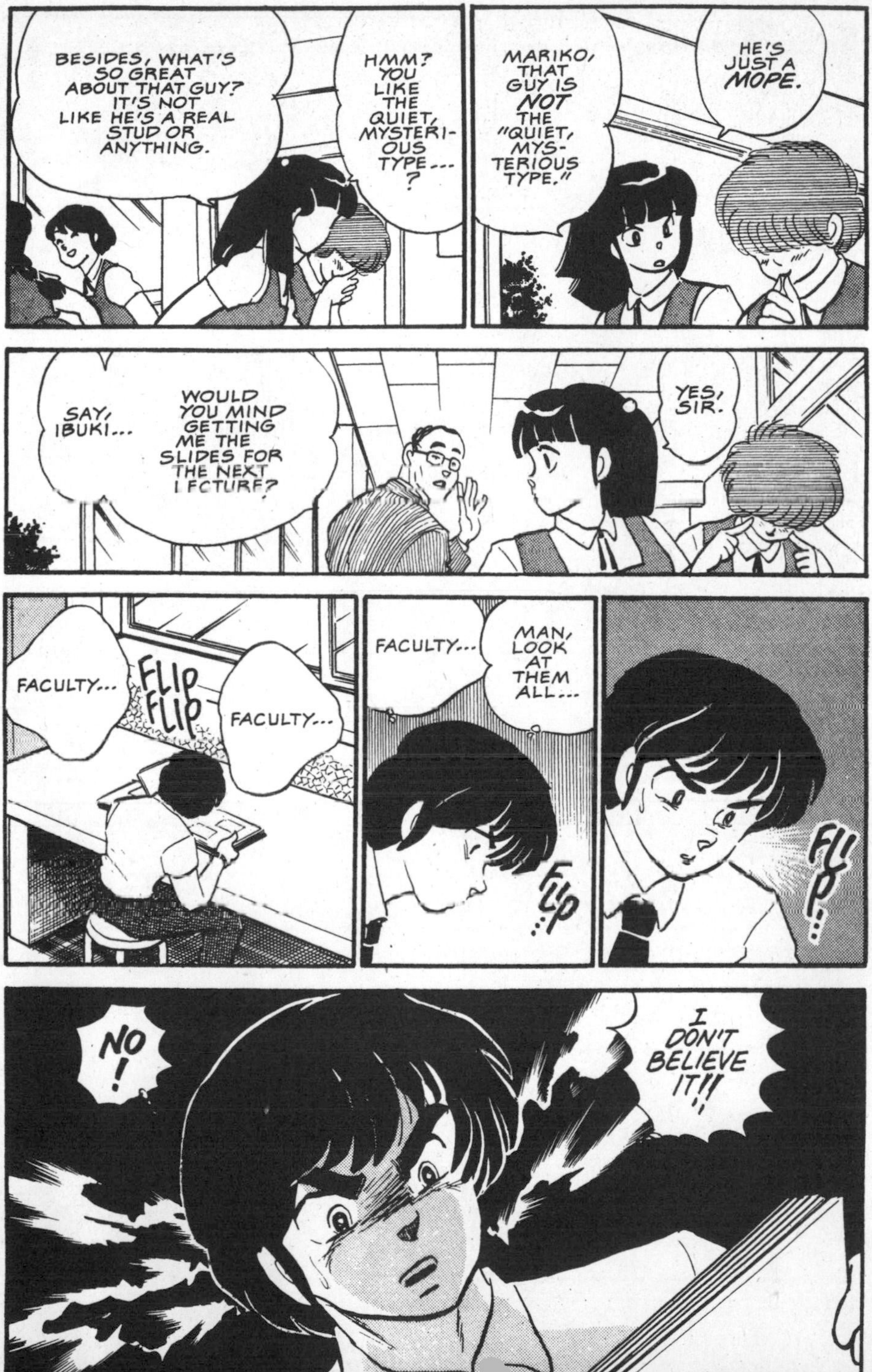
BESIDES, WHAT'S SO GREAT ABOUT THAT GUY? IT'S NOT LIKE HE'S A REAL STUD OR ANYTHING.
HMM? YOU LIKE THE QUIET, MYSTERIOUS TYPE...?
MARIKO, THAT GUY IS NOT THE "QUIET, MYSTERIOUS TYPE."
HE'S JUST A MOPE.
SAY, IBUKI...
WOULD YOU MIND GETTING ME THE SLIDES FOR THE NEXT LECTURE?
YES, SIR.
FACULTY...
FLIP FLIP
FACULTY...
FACULTY...
MAN, LOOK AT THEM ALL...
FLIP...
FLIP...
NO!
I DON'T BELIEVE IT!!

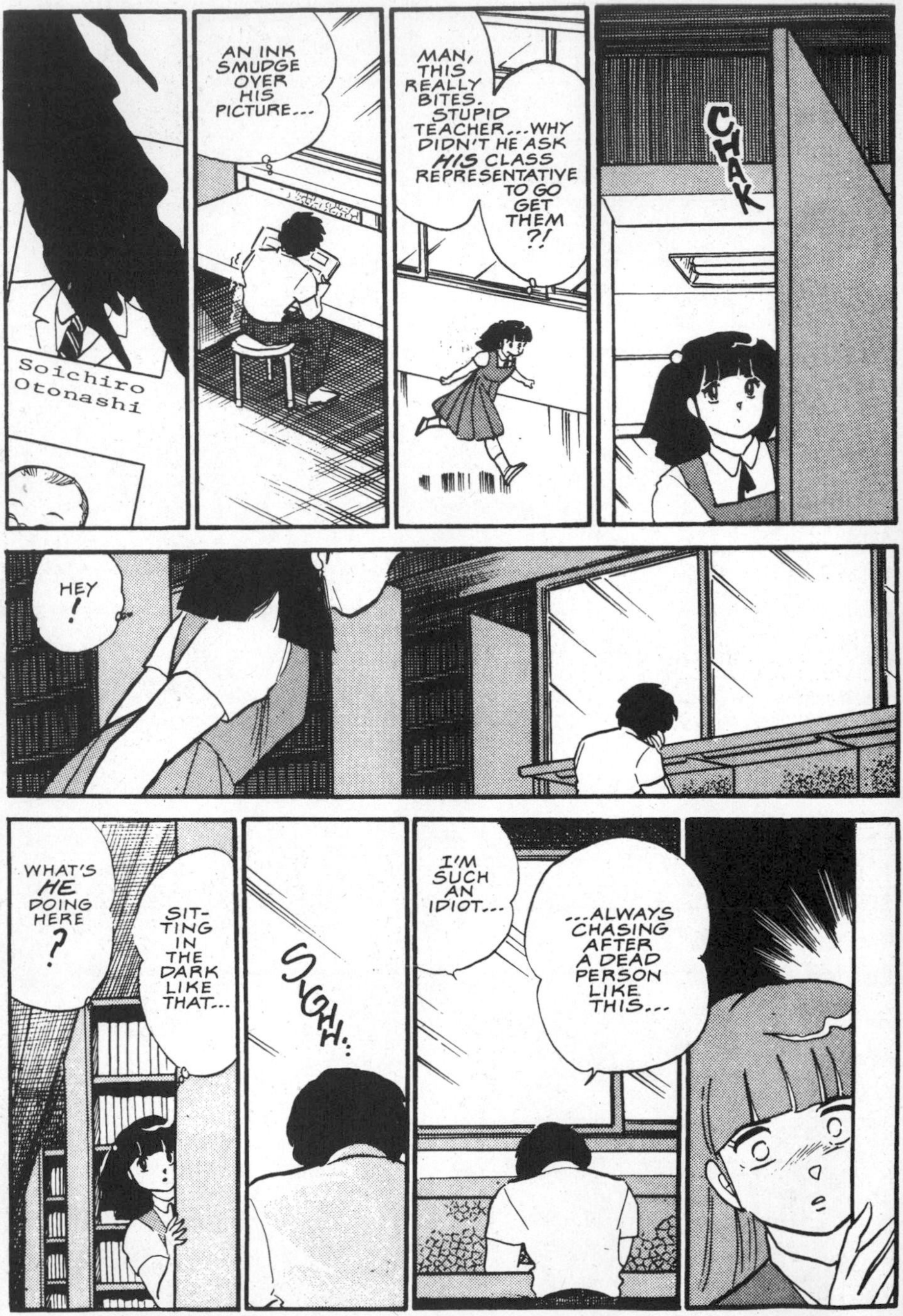
Soichiro Otonashi
AN INK SMUDGE OVER HIS PICTURE...
MAN, THIS REALLY BITES. STUPID TEACHER...WHY DIDN'T HE ASK HIS CLASS REPRESENTATIVE TO GO GET THEM?!
CHAK
HEY!
WHAT'S HE DOING HERE?
SIT-TING IN THE DARK LIKE THAT...
SIGHH...
I'M SUCH AN IDIOT...
...ALWAYS CHASING AFTER A DEAD PERSON LIKE THIS...

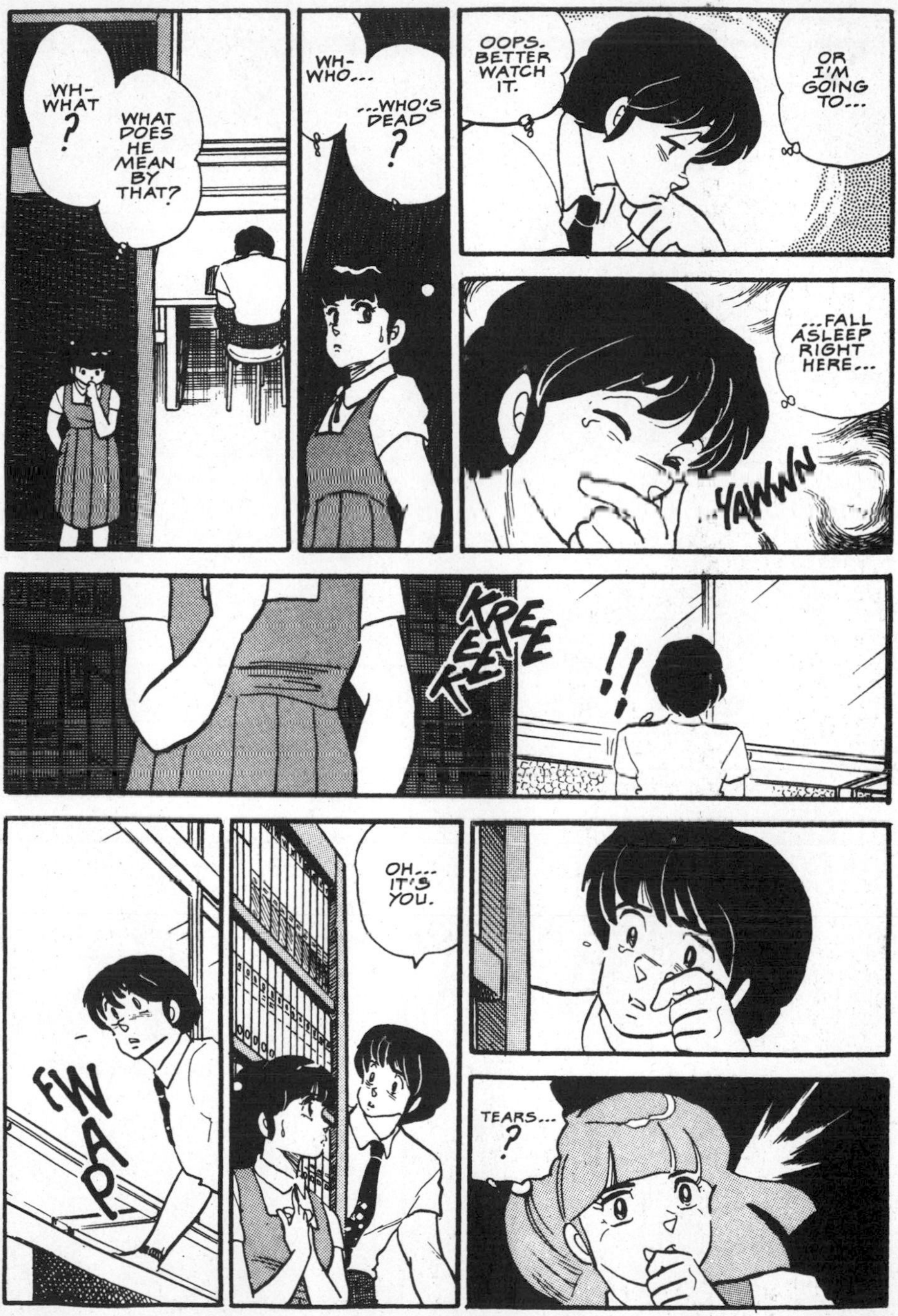
WH- WHAT?
WHAT DOES HE MEAN BY THAT?
WH- WHO...
...WHO'S DEAD?
OOPS. BETTER WATCH IT.
OR I'M GOING TO...
...FALL ASLEEP RIGHT HERE...
YAWWN
KREEEE
!!
FWAP
OH... IT'S YOU.
TEARS...?

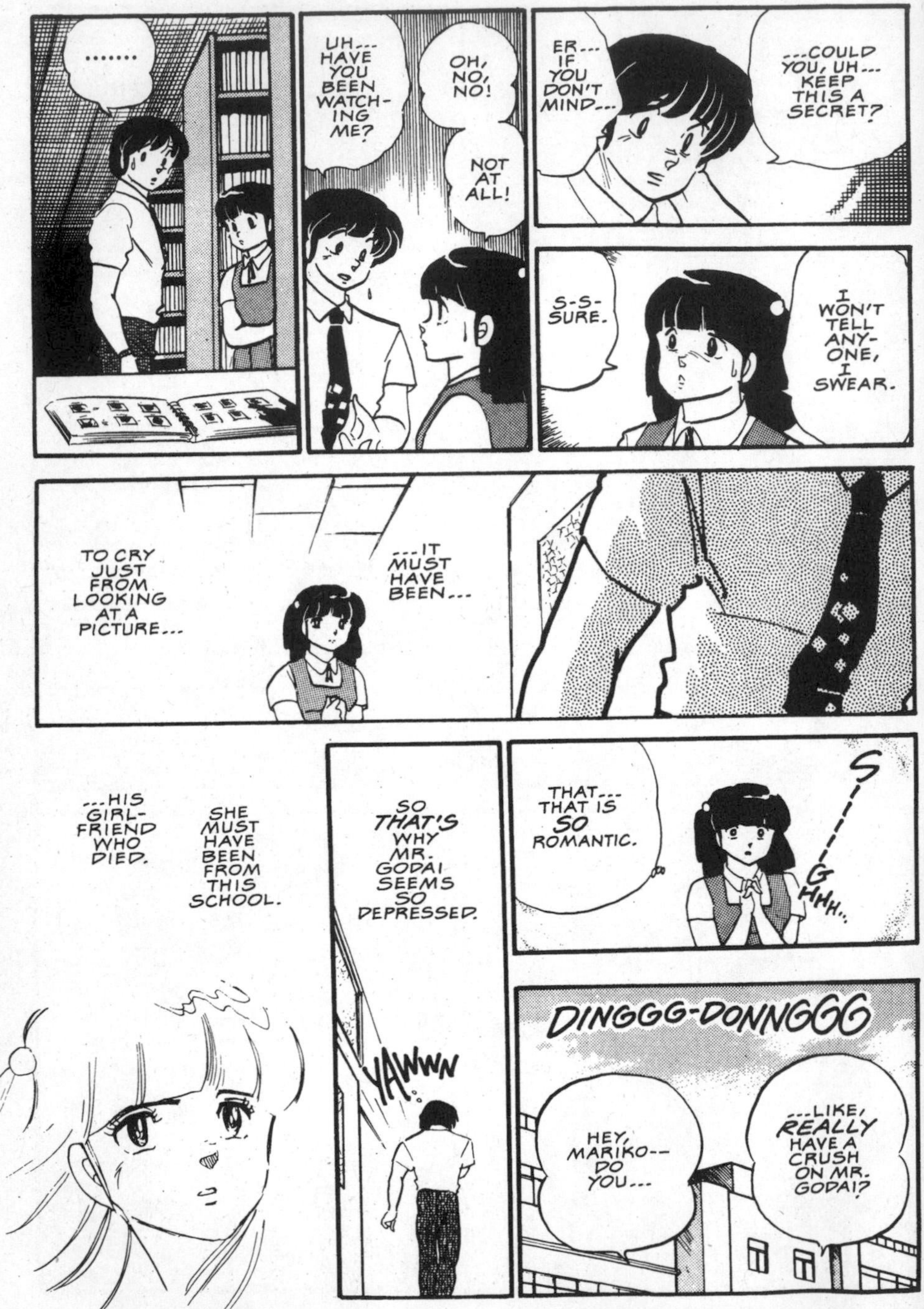
....
UH... HAVE YOU BEEN WATCHING ME?
OH, NO, NO!
NOT AT ALL!
ER... IF YOU DON'T MIND...
...COULD YOU, UH... KEEP THIS A SECRET?
S-S-SURE.
I WON'T TELL ANYONE, I SWEAR.
TO CRY JUST FROM LOOKING AT A PICTURE...
...IT MUST HAVE BEEN...
...HIS GIRLFRIEND WHO DIED.
SHE MUST HAVE BEEN FROM THIS SCHOOL.
SO *THAT'S* WHY MR. GODAI SEEMS SO DEPRESSED.
YAWWN
THAT... THAT IS *SO* ROMANTIC.
SIIIGHHH..
DINGGG-DONNGGG
HEY, MARIKO-- DO YOU...
...LIKE, *REALLY* HAVE A CRUSH ON MR. GODAI?

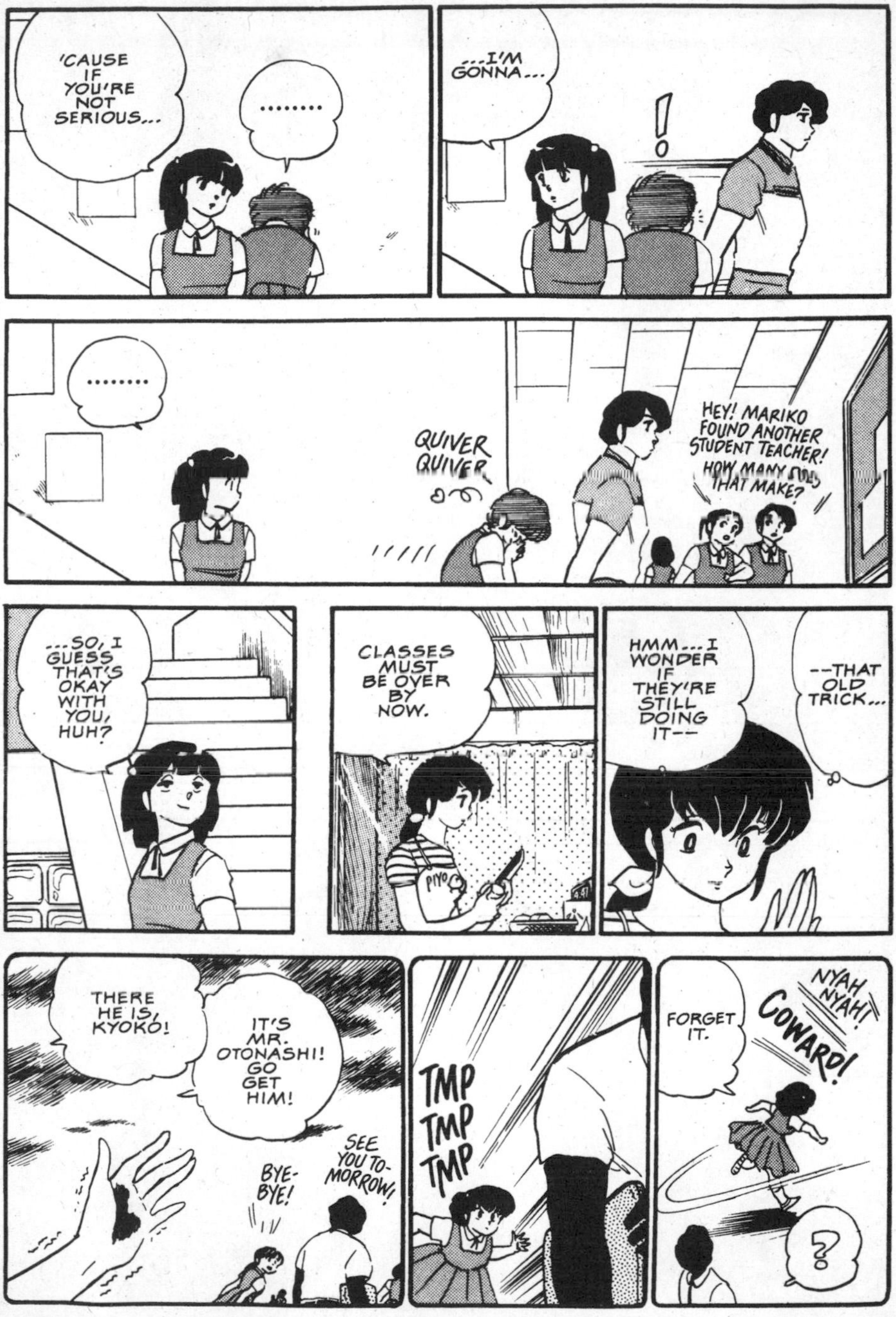
'CAUSE IF YOU'RE NOT SERIOUS...
....
...I'M GONNA...
!
....
QUIVER QUIVER
HEY! MARIKO FOUND ANOTHER STUDENT TEACHER!
HOW MANY THAT MAKE?
...SO, I GUESS THAT'S OKAY WITH YOU, HUH?
CLASSES MUST BE OVER BY NOW.
PIYO
HMM... I WONDER IF THEY'RE STILL DOING IT--
--THAT OLD TRICK...
THERE HE IS, KYOKO!
IT'S MR. OTONASHI! GO GET HIM!
BYE-BYE!
SEE YOU TO-MORROW!
TMP TMP TMP
FORGET IT.
NYAH NYAH!
COWARD!
?

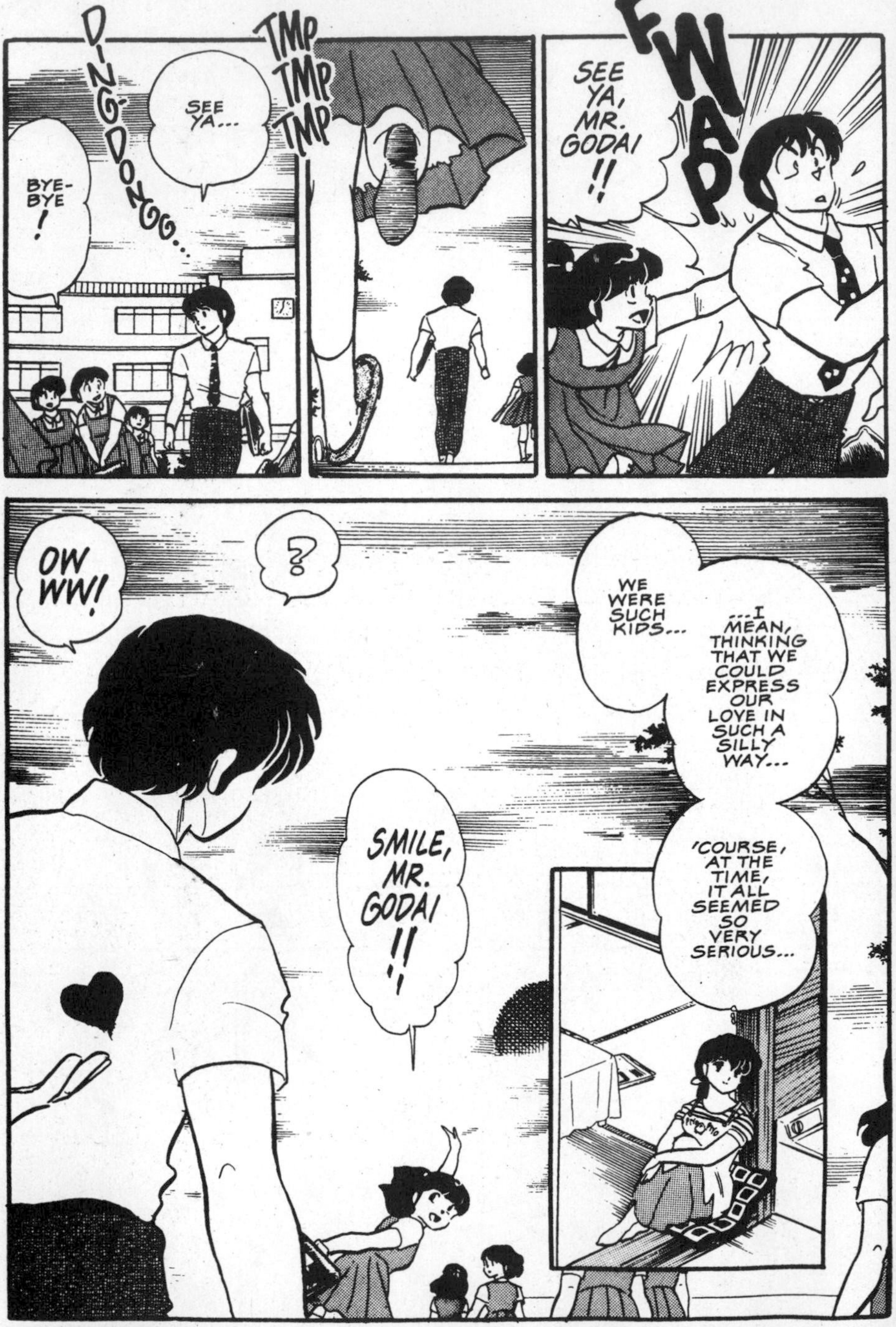
DING-DONGGG...
BYE-BYE!
SEE YA...
TMP TMP TMP
SEE YA, MR. GODAI!!
FWAP
OWWW!
?
SMILE, MR. GODAI!!
WE WERE SUCH KIDS...
...I MEAN, THINKING THAT WE COULD EXPRESS OUR LOVE IN SUCH A SILLY WAY...
'COURSE, AT THE TIME, IT ALL SEEMED SO VERY SERIOUS...

PART 11

"KOKORO"

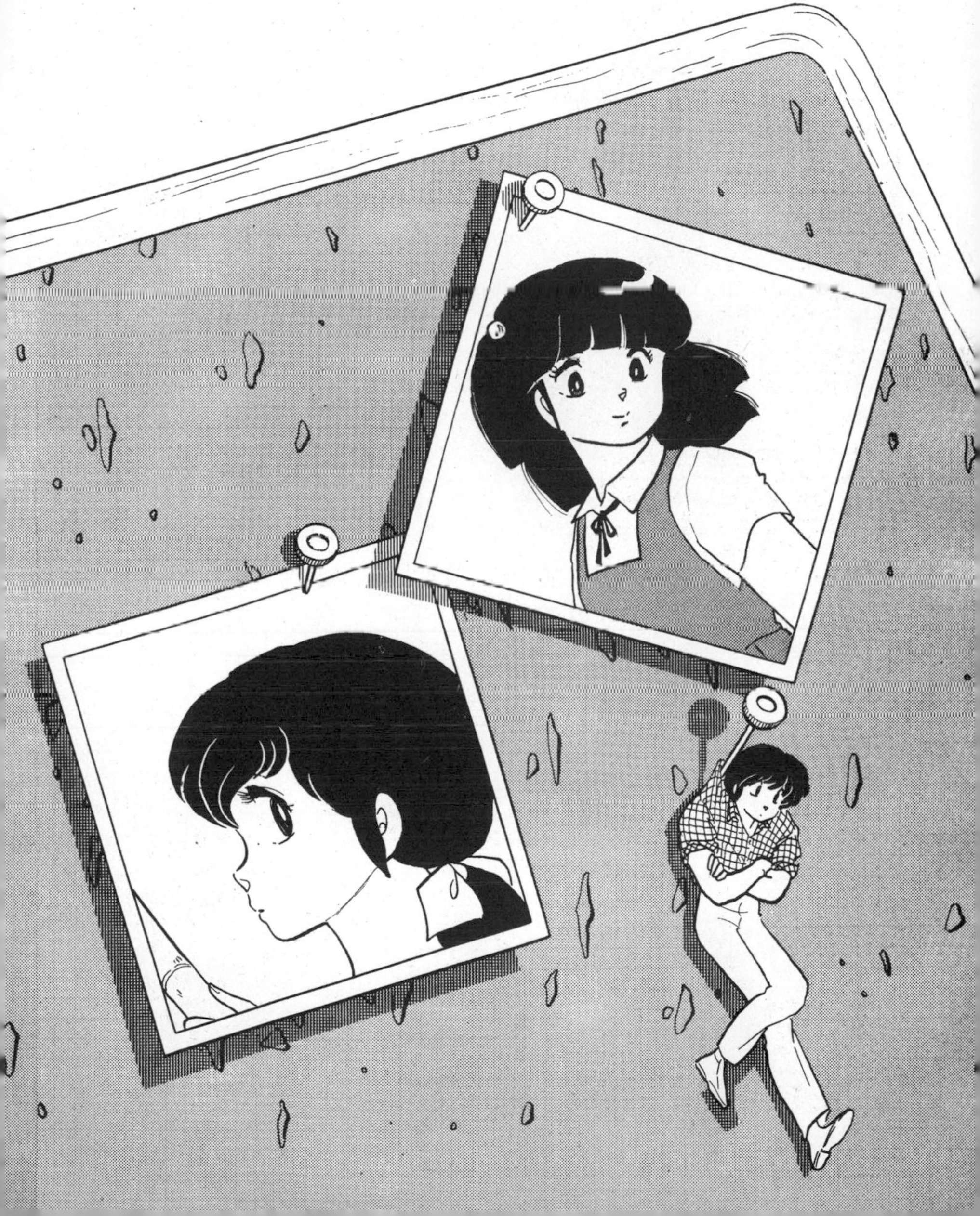

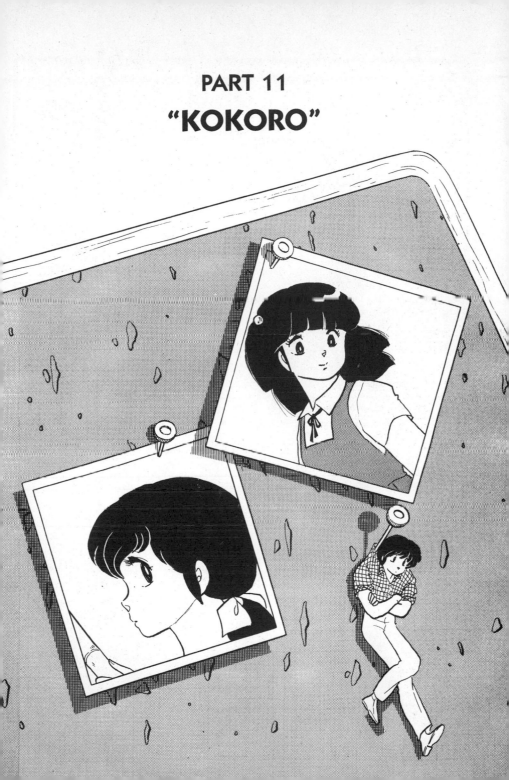

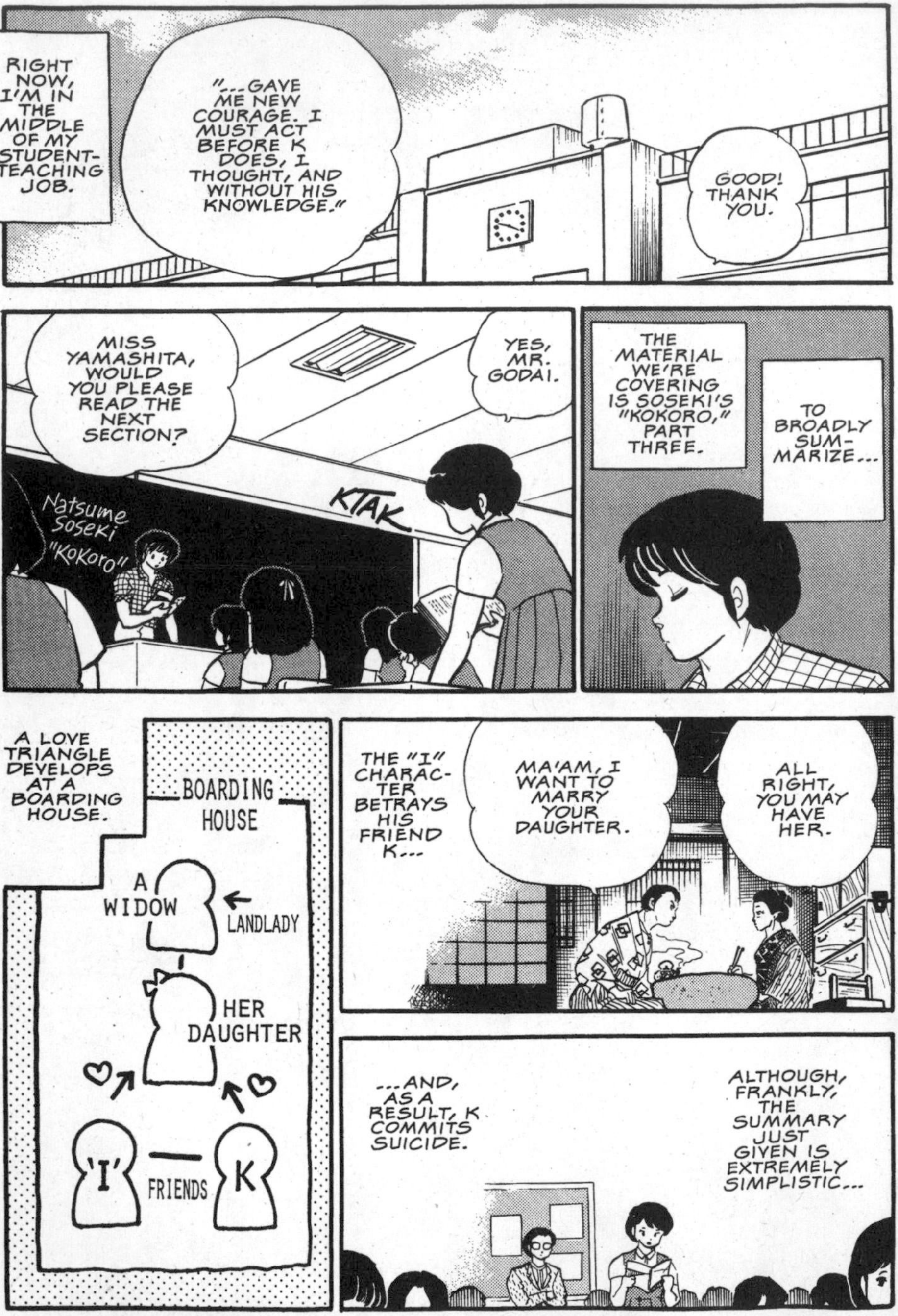
RIGHT NOW, I'M IN THE MIDDLE OF MY STUDENT-TEACHING JOB.
"...GAVE ME NEW COURAGE. I MUST ACT BEFORE K DOES, I THOUGHT, AND WITHOUT HIS KNOWLEDGE."
GOOD! THANK YOU.
MISS YAMASHITA, WOULD YOU PLEASE READ THE NEXT SECTION?
YES, MR. GODAI.
Natsume Soseki "Kokoro"
KTAK
THE MATERIAL WE'RE COVERING IS SOSEKI'S "KOKORO," PART THREE.
TO BROADLY SUMMARIZE...
A LOVE TRIANGLE DEVELOPS AT A BOARDING HOUSE.
BOARDING HOUSE
A WIDOW
LANDLADY
HER DAUGHTER
'I'
FRIENDS
K
THE "I" CHARACTER BETRAYS HIS FRIEND K...
MA'AM, I WANT TO MARRY YOUR DAUGHTER.
ALL RIGHT, YOU MAY HAVE HER.
...AND, AS A RESULT, K COMMITS SUICIDE.
ALTHOUGH, FRANKLY, THE SUMMARY JUST GIVEN IS EXTREMELY SIMPLISTIC...

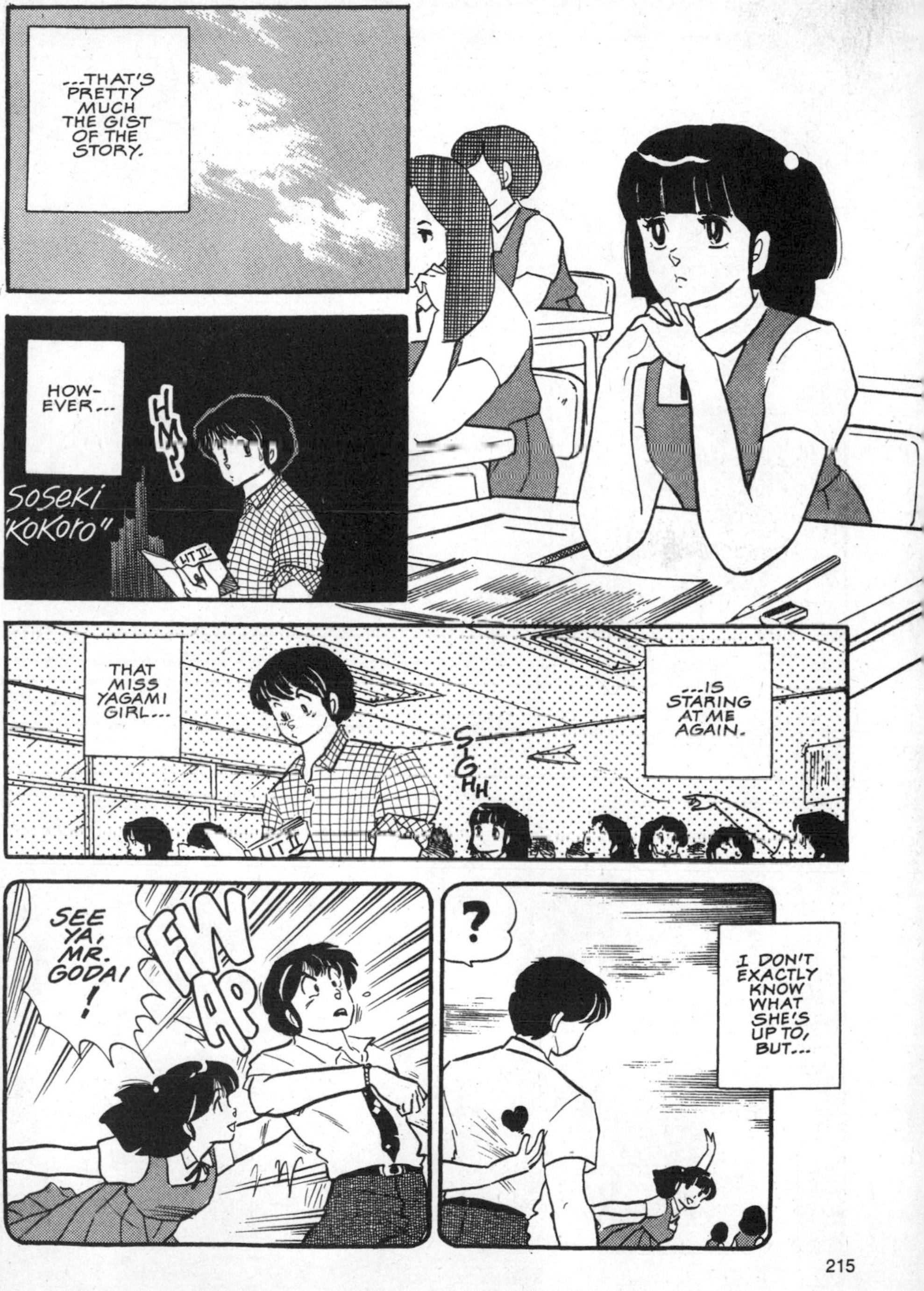
...THAT'S PRETTY MUCH THE GIST OF THE STORY.
HOW-EVER...
HM?
Soseki "Kokoro"
LIT II
THAT MISS YAGAMI GIRL...
SIGHH
...IS STARING AT ME AGAIN.
LIT II
SEE YA, MR. GODAI!
FWAP
?
I DON'T EXACTLY KNOW WHAT SHE'S UP TO, BUT...

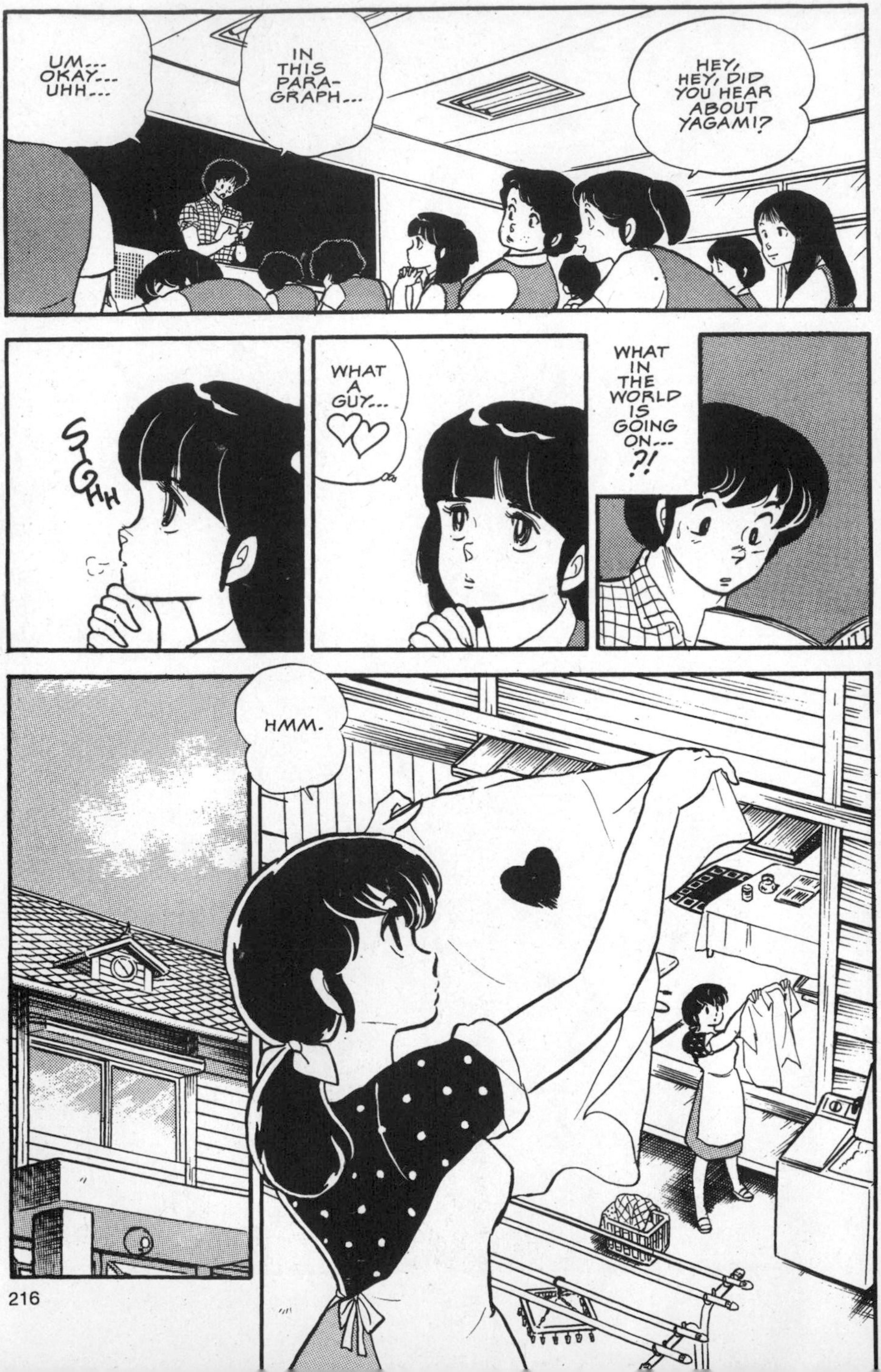
UM... OKAY... UHH...
IN THIS PARA-GRAPH...
HEY, HEY, DID YOU HEAR ABOUT YAGAMI!?
SIGHH
WHAT A GUY...
WHAT IN THE WORLD IS GOING ON...?!
HMM.

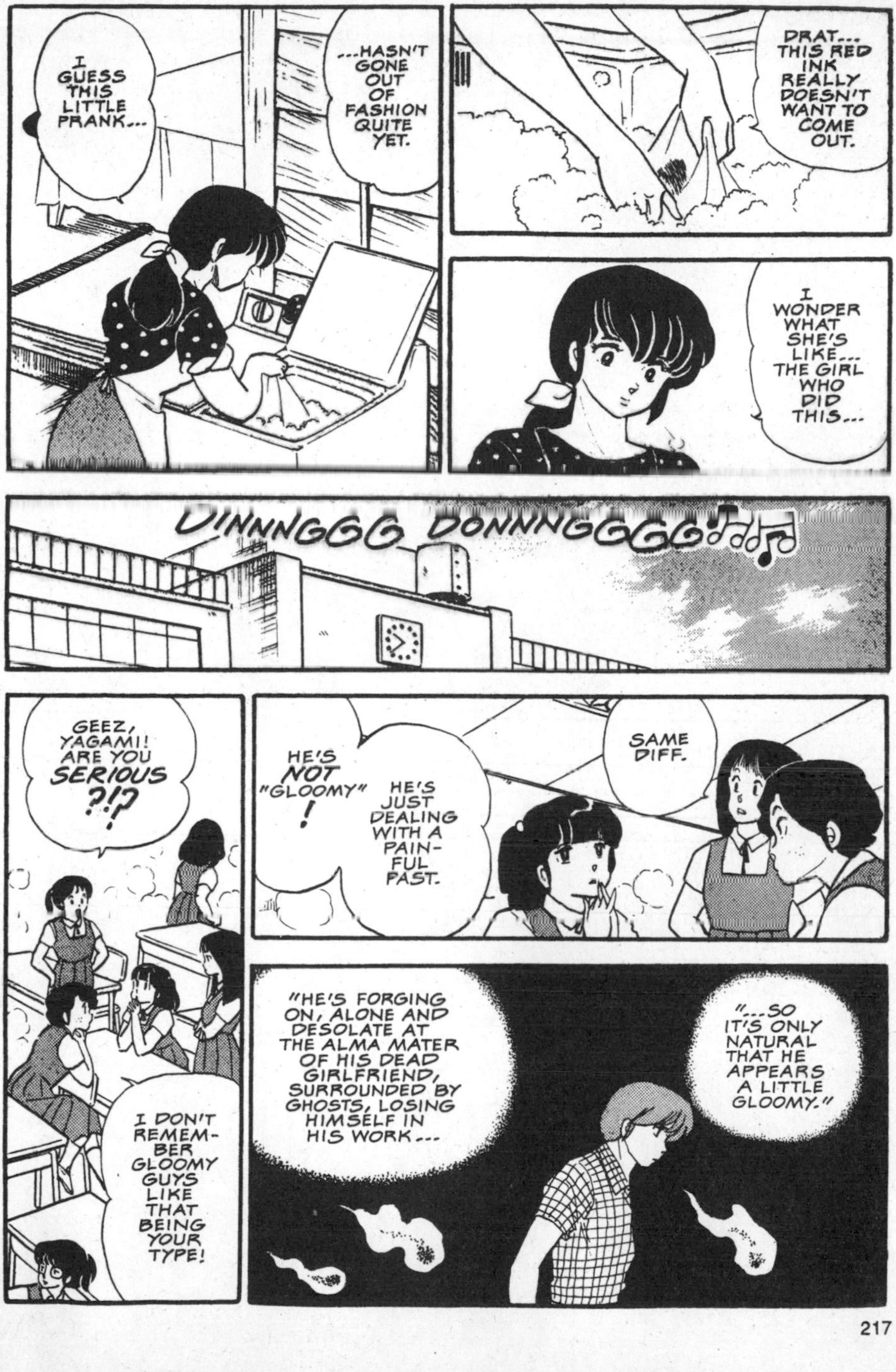
I GUESS THIS LITTLE PRANK...
...HASN'T GONE OUT OF FASHION QUITE YET.
DRAT... THIS RED INK REALLY DOESN'T WANT TO COME OUT.
I WONDER WHAT SHE'S LIKE... THE GIRL WHO DID THIS...
DINNNGGG DONNNGGGG
GEEZ, YAGAMI! ARE YOU SERIOUS ?!?
I DON'T REMEMBER GLOOMY GUYS LIKE THAT BEING YOUR TYPE!
HE'S NOT "GLOOMY"!
HE'S JUST DEALING WITH A PAINFUL PAST.
SAME DIFF.
"HE'S FORGING ON, ALONE AND DESOLATE AT THE ALMA MATER OF HIS DEAD GIRLFRIEND, SURROUNDED BY GHOSTS, LOSING HIMSELF IN HIS WORK...
"...SO IT'S ONLY NATURAL THAT HE APPEARS A LITTLE GLOOMY."

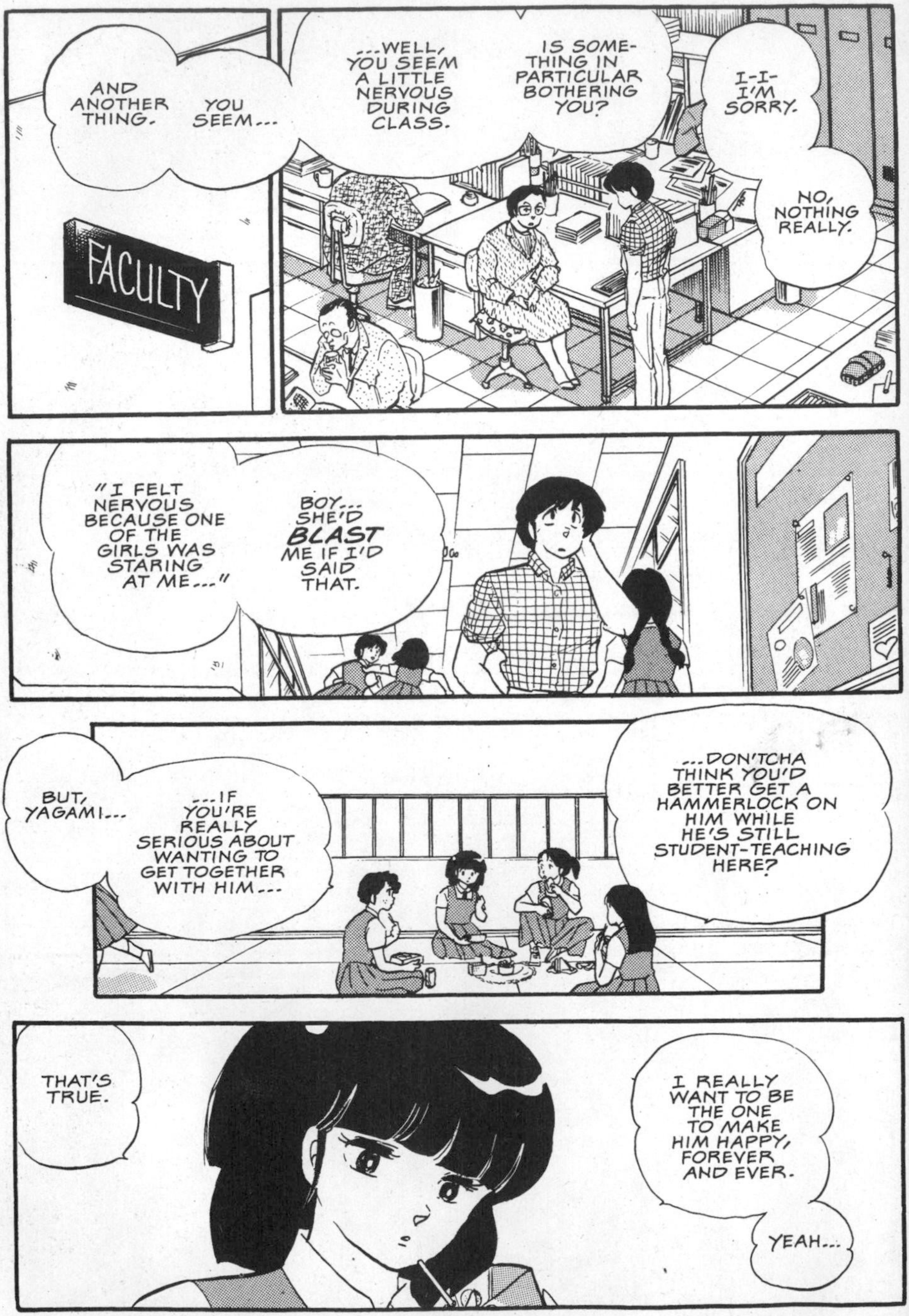
AND ANOTHER THING. YOU SEEM...
FACULTY
...WELL, YOU SEEM A LITTLE NERVOUS DURING CLASS.
IS SOMETHING IN PARTICULAR BOTHERING YOU?
I-I-I'M SORRY.
NO, NOTHING REALLY.
"I FELT NERVOUS BECAUSE ONE OF THE GIRLS WAS STARING AT ME..."
BOY... SHE'D BLAST ME IF I'D SAID THAT.
BUT, YAGAMI...
...IF YOU'RE REALLY SERIOUS ABOUT WANTING TO GET TOGETHER WITH HIM...
...DON'TCHA THINK YOU'D BETTER GET A HAMMERLOCK ON HIM WHILE HE'S STILL STUDENT-TEACHING HERE?
THAT'S TRUE.
I REALLY WANT TO BE THE ONE TO MAKE HIM HAPPY, FOREVER AND EVER.
YEAH...

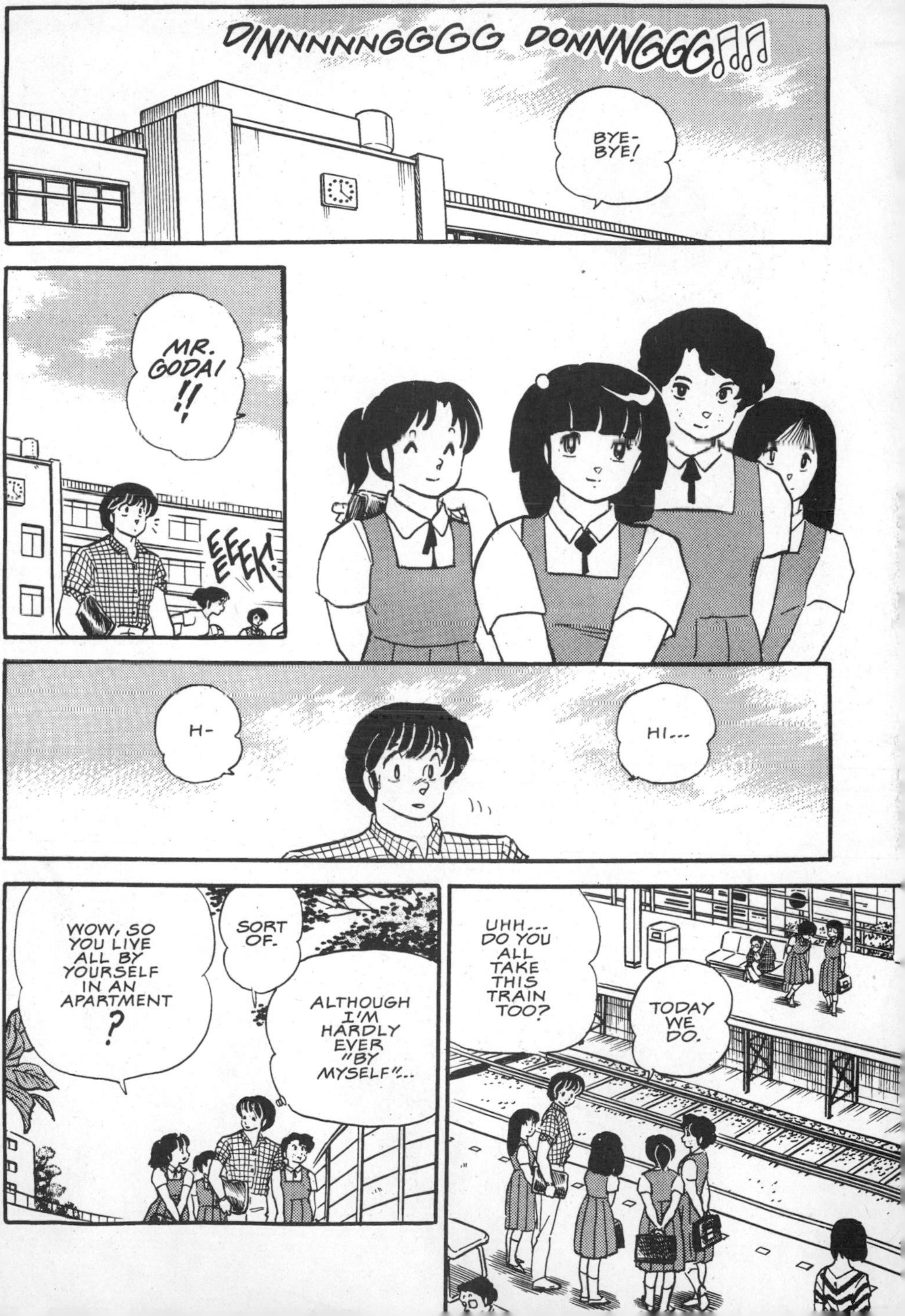
DINNNNNGGGG DONNNGGG
BYE-BYE!
MR. GODAI!!
EEEEK!
H-
HI...
WOW, SO YOU LIVE ALL BY YOURSELF IN AN APARTMENT?
SORT OF.
ALTHOUGH I'M HARDLY EVER "BY MYSELF"...
UHH... DO YOU ALL TAKE THIS TRAIN TOO?
TODAY WE DO.

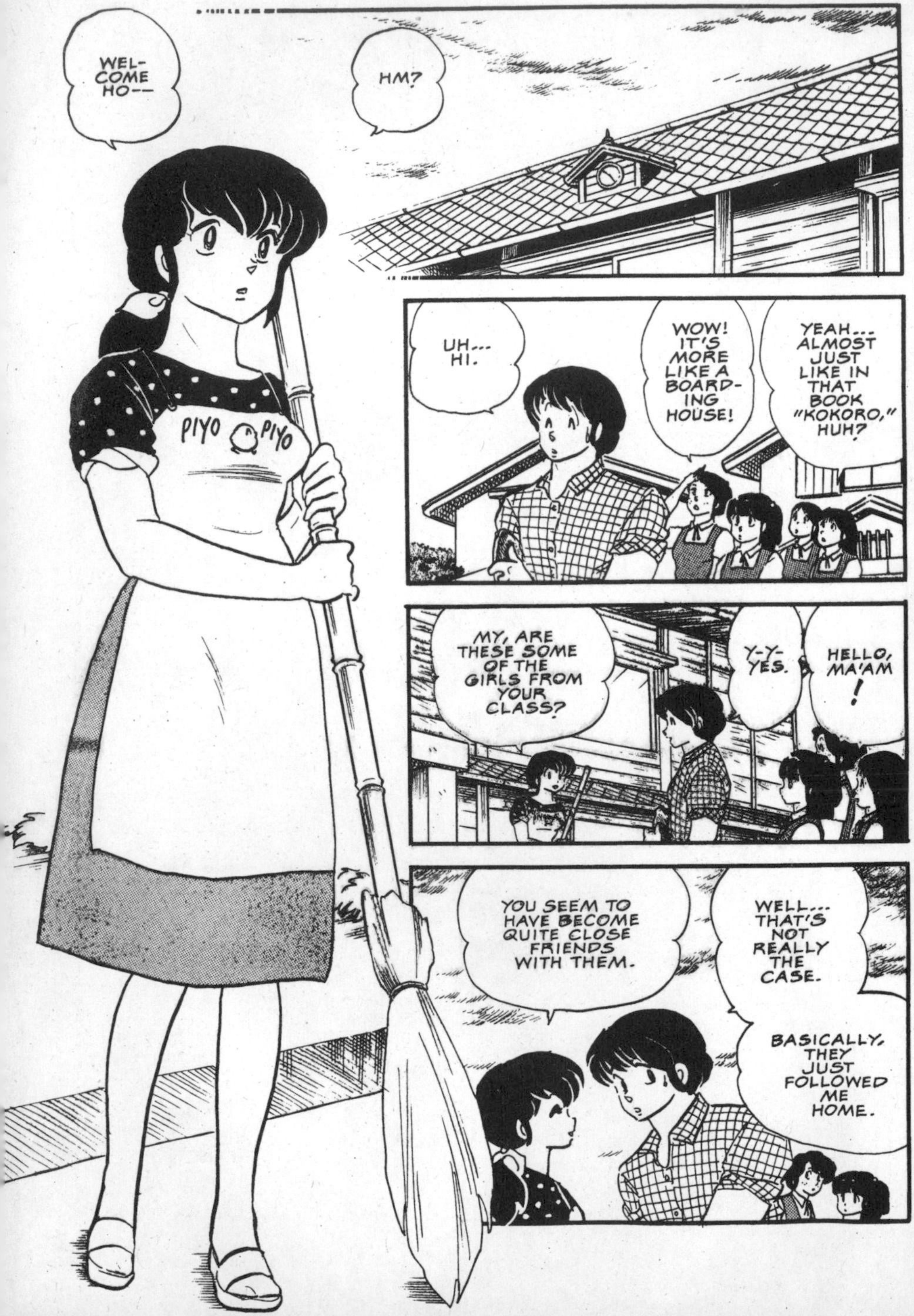
WEL-COME HO--
PIYO PIYO
HM?
UH... HI.
WOW! IT'S MORE LIKE A BOARDING HOUSE!
YEAH... ALMOST JUST LIKE IN THAT BOOK "KOKORO," HUH?
MY, ARE THESE SOME OF THE GIRLS FROM YOUR CLASS?
Y-Y-YES.
HELLO, MA'AM!
YOU SEEM TO HAVE BECOME QUITE CLOSE FRIENDS WITH THEM.
WELL... THAT'S NOT REALLY THE CASE.
BASICALLY, THEY JUST FOLLOWED ME HOME.

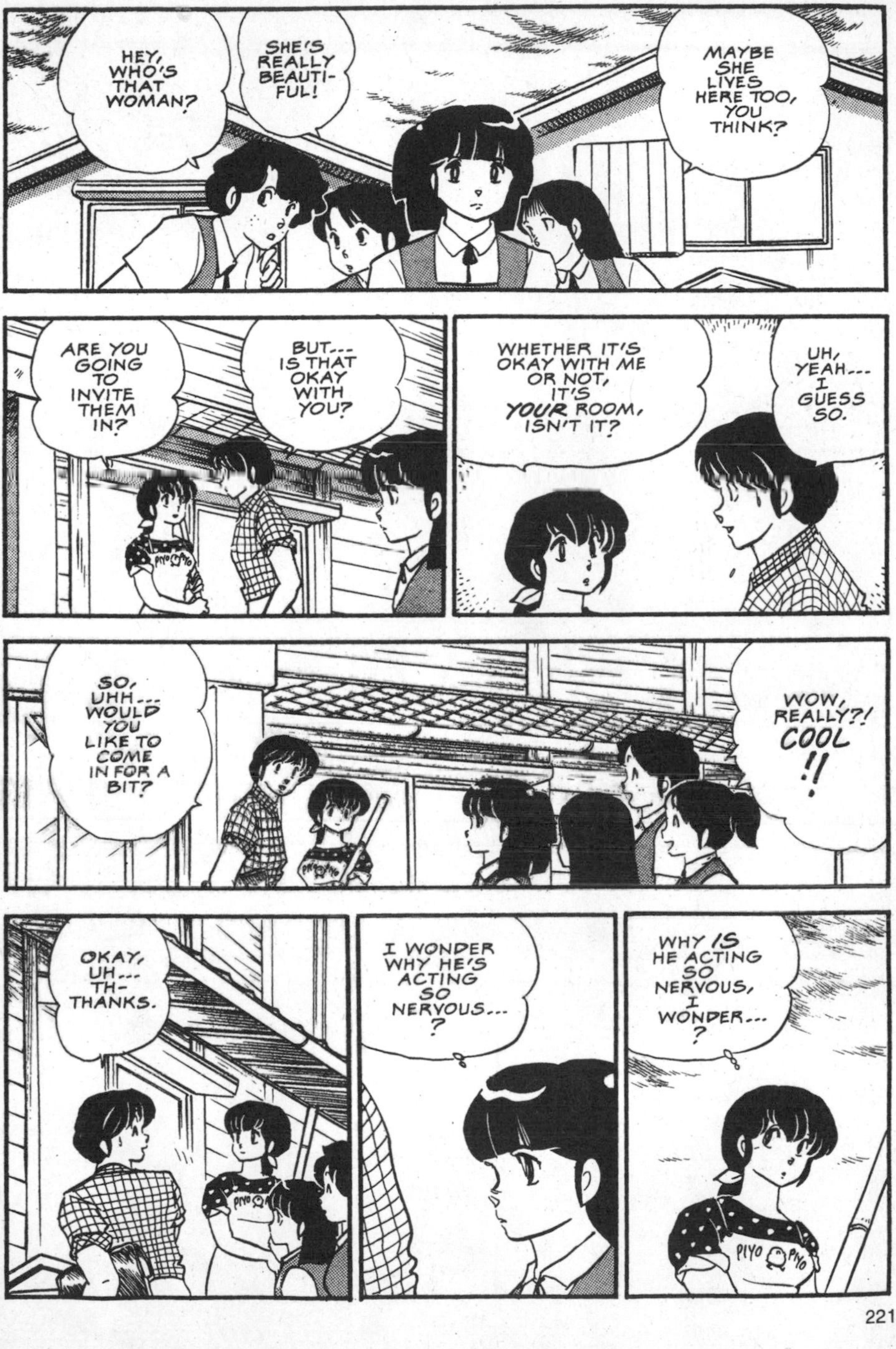
HEY, WHO'S THAT WOMAN?
SHE'S REALLY BEAUTI-FUL!
MAYBE SHE LIVES HERE TOO, YOU THINK?
ARE YOU GOING TO INVITE THEM IN?
BUT... IS THAT OKAY WITH YOU?
WHETHER IT'S OKAY WITH ME OR NOT, IT'S YOUR ROOM, ISN'T IT?
UH, YEAH... I GUESS SO.
SO, UHH... WOULD YOU LIKE TO COME IN FOR A BIT?
WOW, REALLY?! COOL!!
OKAY, UH... TH-THANKS.
I WONDER WHY HE'S ACTING SO NERVOUS...?
WHY IS HE ACTING SO NERVOUS, I WONDER...?

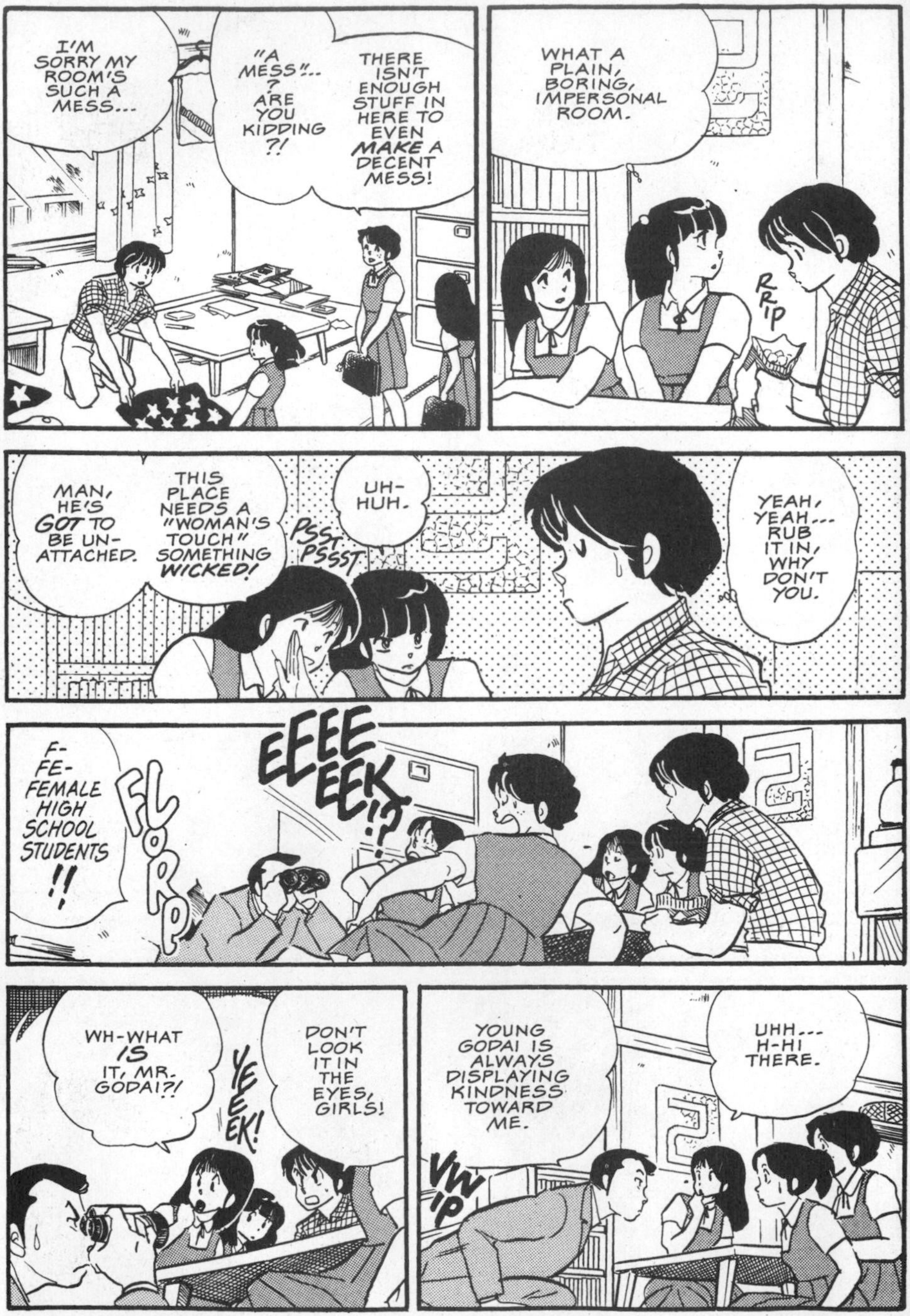
I'M SORRY MY ROOM'S SUCH A MESS...
"A MESS"...? ARE YOU KIDDING?!
THERE ISN'T ENOUGH STUFF IN HERE TO EVEN MAKE A DECENT MESS!
WHAT A PLAIN, BORING, IMPERSONAL ROOM.
RRIP
MAN, HE'S GOT TO BE UN-ATTACHED.
THIS PLACE NEEDS A "WOMAN'S TOUCH" SOMETHING WICKED!
PSST PSSST
UH-HUH.
YEAH, YEAH... RUB IT IN, WHY DON'T YOU.
F-FE-FEMALE HIGH SCHOOL STUDENTS!!
FLORP
EEEEEEK!?
WH-WHAT IS IT, MR. GODAI?!
YEEEK!
DON'T LOOK IT IN THE EYES, GIRLS!
YOUNG GODAI IS ALWAYS DISPLAYING KINDNESS TOWARD ME.
VWIP
UHH... H-HI THERE.

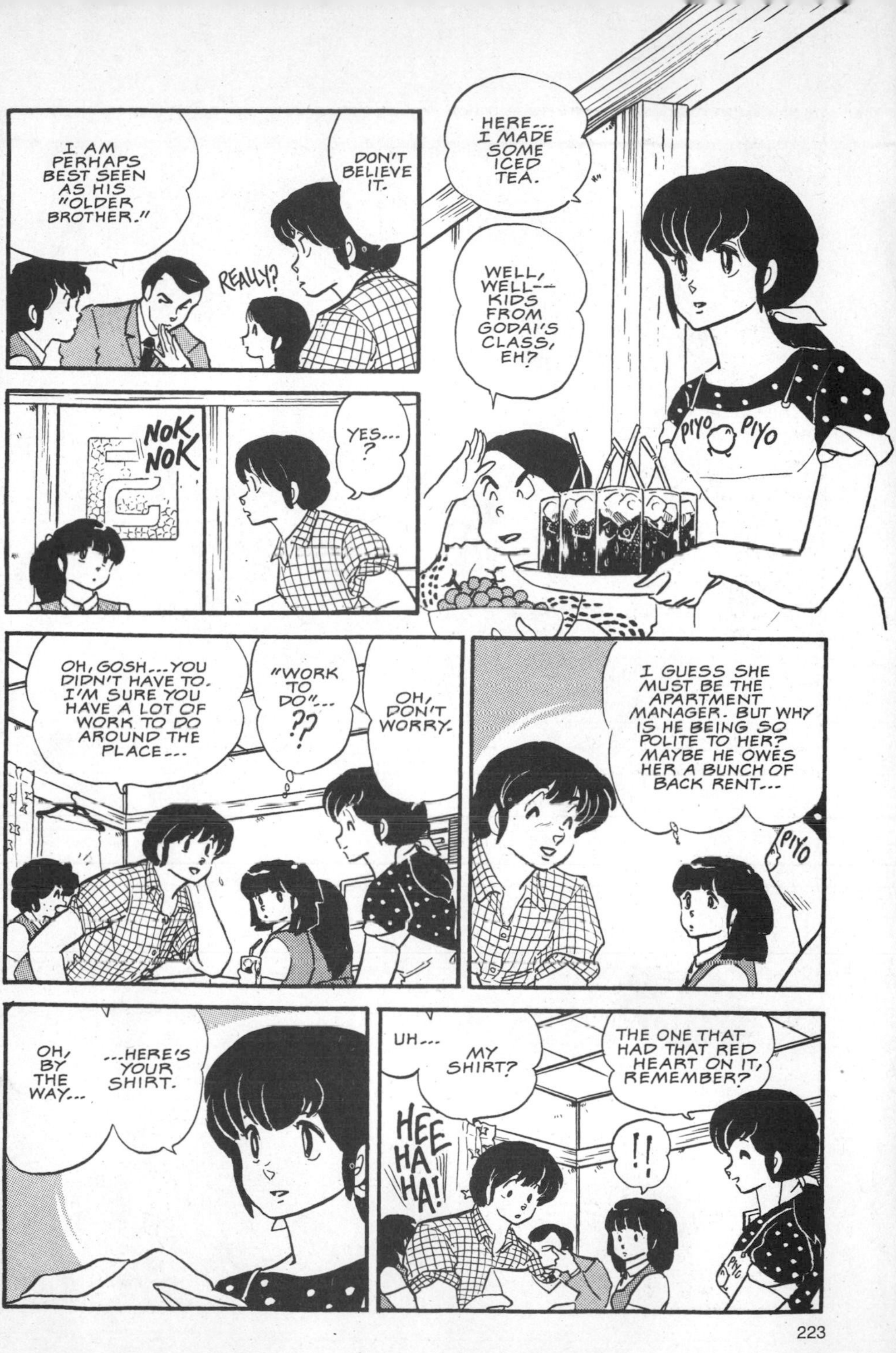
I AM PERHAPS BEST SEEN AS HIS "OLDER BROTHER."
DON'T BELIEVE IT.
REALLY?
HERE... I MADE SOME ICED TEA.
WELL, WELL-- KIDS FROM GODAI'S CLASS, EH?
NOK NOK
YES... ?
PIYO PIYO
OH, GOSH... YOU DIDN'T HAVE TO. I'M SURE YOU HAVE A LOT OF WORK TO DO AROUND THE PLACE...
"WORK TO DO"... ??
OH, DON'T WORRY.
I GUESS SHE MUST BE THE APARTMENT MANAGER. BUT WHY IS HE BEING SO POLITE TO HER? MAYBE HE OWES HER A BUNCH OF BACK RENT...
PIYO
OH, BY THE WAY...
...HERE'S YOUR SHIRT.
UH...
MY SHIRT?
THE ONE THAT HAD THAT RED HEART ON IT, REMEMBER?
HEE HA HA!
!!

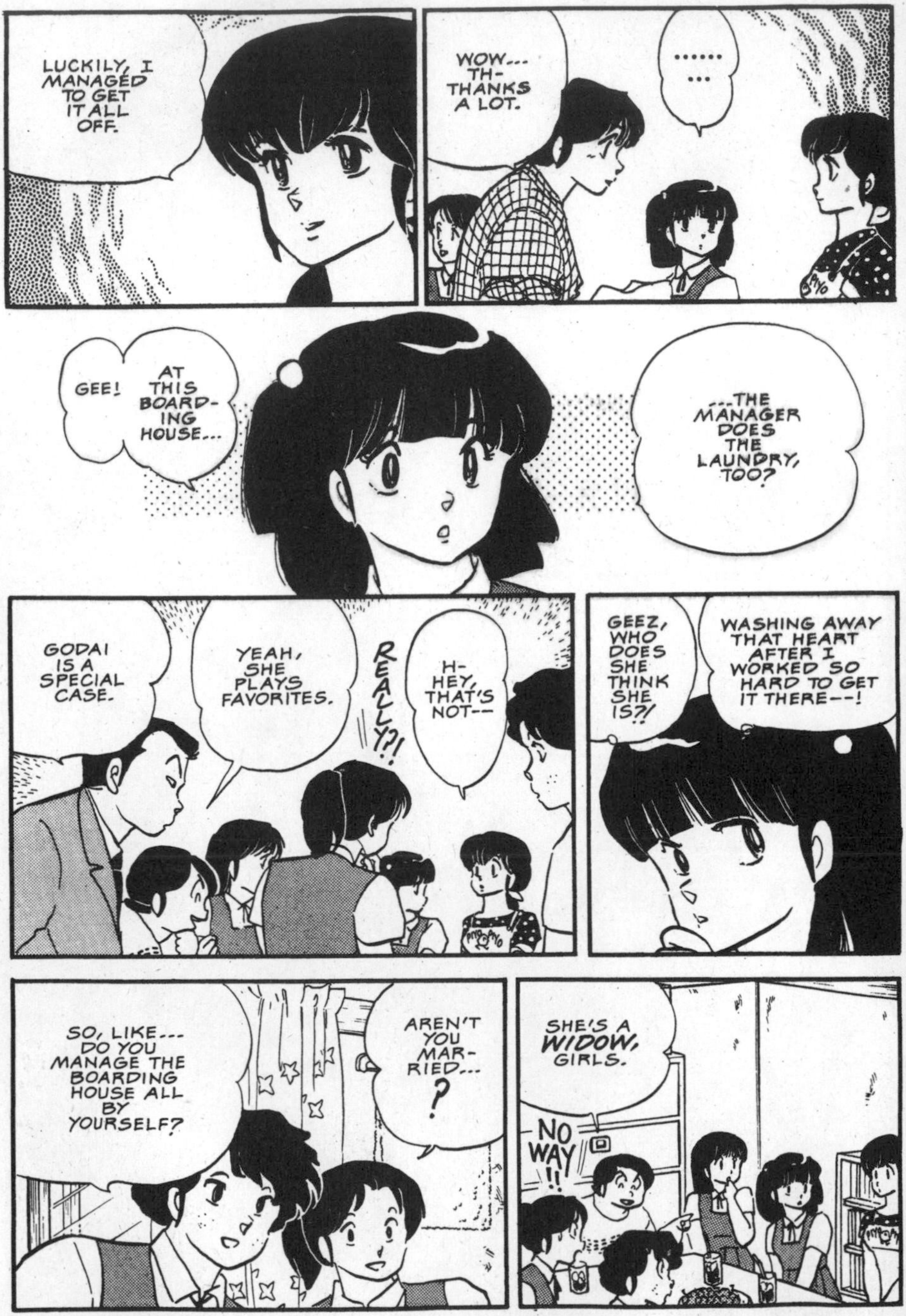
LUCKILY, I MANAGED TO GET IT ALL OFF.
WOW... TH-THANKS A LOT.
....
GEE!
AT THIS BOARDING-HOUSE...
...THE MANAGER DOES THE LAUNDRY, TOO?
GODAI IS A SPECIAL CASE.
YEAH, SHE PLAYS FAVORITES.
REALLY?!
H-HEY, THAT'S NOT--
GEEZ, WHO DOES SHE THINK SHE IS?!
WASHING AWAY THAT HEART AFTER I WORKED SO HARD TO GET IT THERE--!
SO, LIKE... DO YOU MANAGE THE BOARDING HOUSE ALL BY YOURSELF?
AREN'T YOU MAR-RIED...?
SHE'S A WIDOW, GIRLS.
NO WAY!!

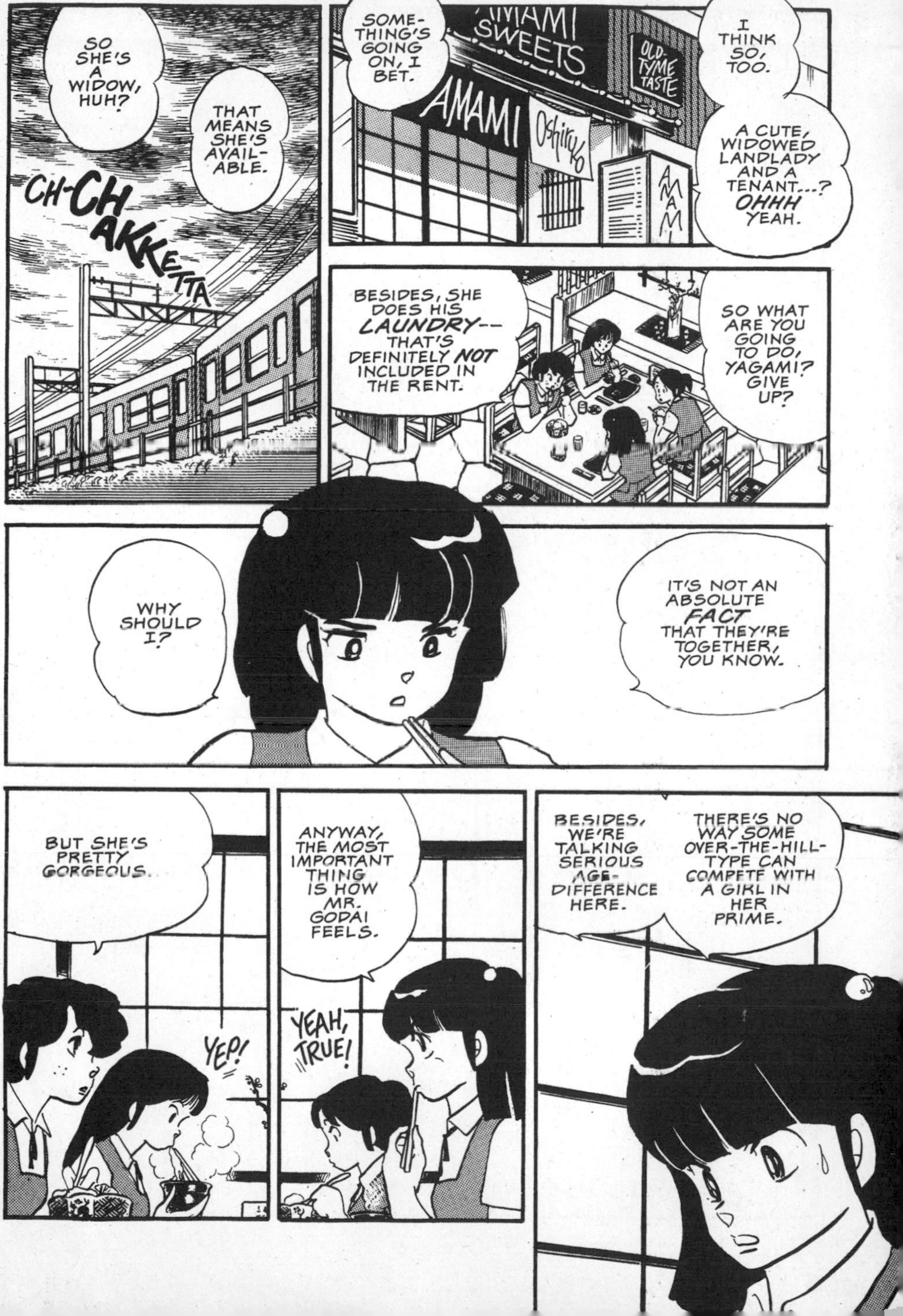
SO SHE'S A WIDOW, HUH?
THAT MEANS SHE'S AVAIL-ABLE.
CH-CHAKKETTA
SOME-THING'S GOING ON, I BET.
AMAMI SWEETS
OLD-TYME TASTE
AMAMI
Oshiruko
AMAMI
I THINK SO, TOO.
A CUTE, WIDOWED LANDLADY AND A TENANT...? OHHH YEAH.
BESIDES, SHE DOES HIS LAUNDRY-- THAT'S DEFINITELY NOT INCLUDED IN THE RENT.
SO WHAT ARE YOU GOING TO DO, YAGAMI? GIVE UP?
WHY SHOULD I?
IT'S NOT AN ABSOLUTE FACT THAT THEY'RE TOGETHER, YOU KNOW.
BUT SHE'S PRETTY GORGEOUS...
YEP!
ANYWAY, THE MOST IMPORTANT THING IS HOW MR. GODAI FEELS.
YEAH, TRUE!
BESIDES, WE'RE TALKING SERIOUS AGE-DIFFERENCE HERE.
THERE'S NO WAY SOME OVER-THE-HILL-TYPE CAN COMPETE WITH A GIRL IN HER PRIME.

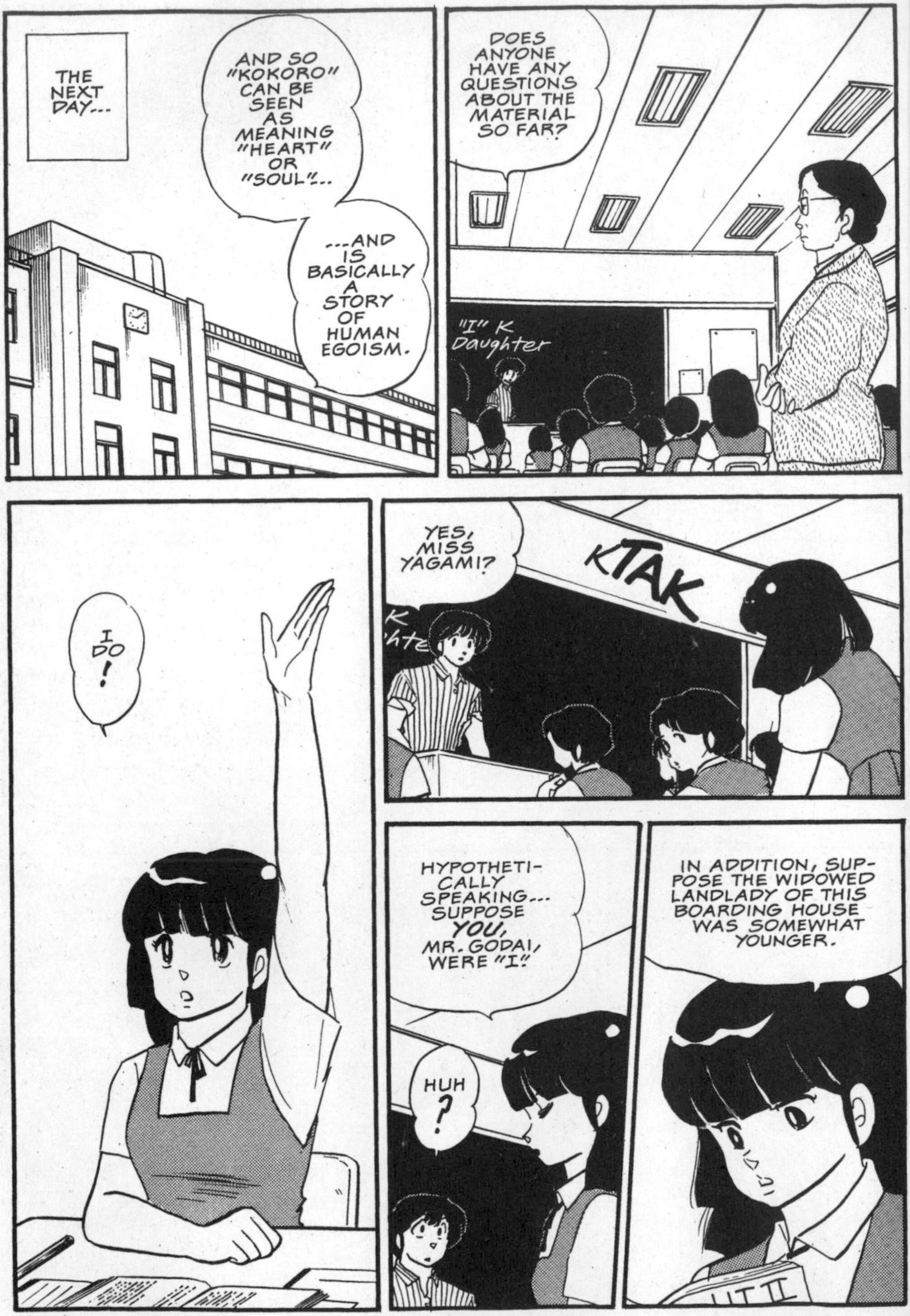
THE NEXT DAY...
AND SO "KOKORO" CAN BE SEEN AS MEANING "HEART" OR "SOUL"...
...AND IS BASICALLY A STORY OF HUMAN EGOISM.
DOES ANYONE HAVE ANY QUESTIONS ABOUT THE MATERIAL SO FAR?
"I" K
Daughter
I DO!
YES, MISS YAGAMI?
KTAK
HYPOTHETICALLY SPEAKING... SUPPOSE YOU, MR. GODAI, WERE "I."
HUH?
IN ADDITION, SUPPOSE THE WIDOWED LANDLADY OF THIS BOARDING HOUSE WAS SOMEWHAT YOUNGER.

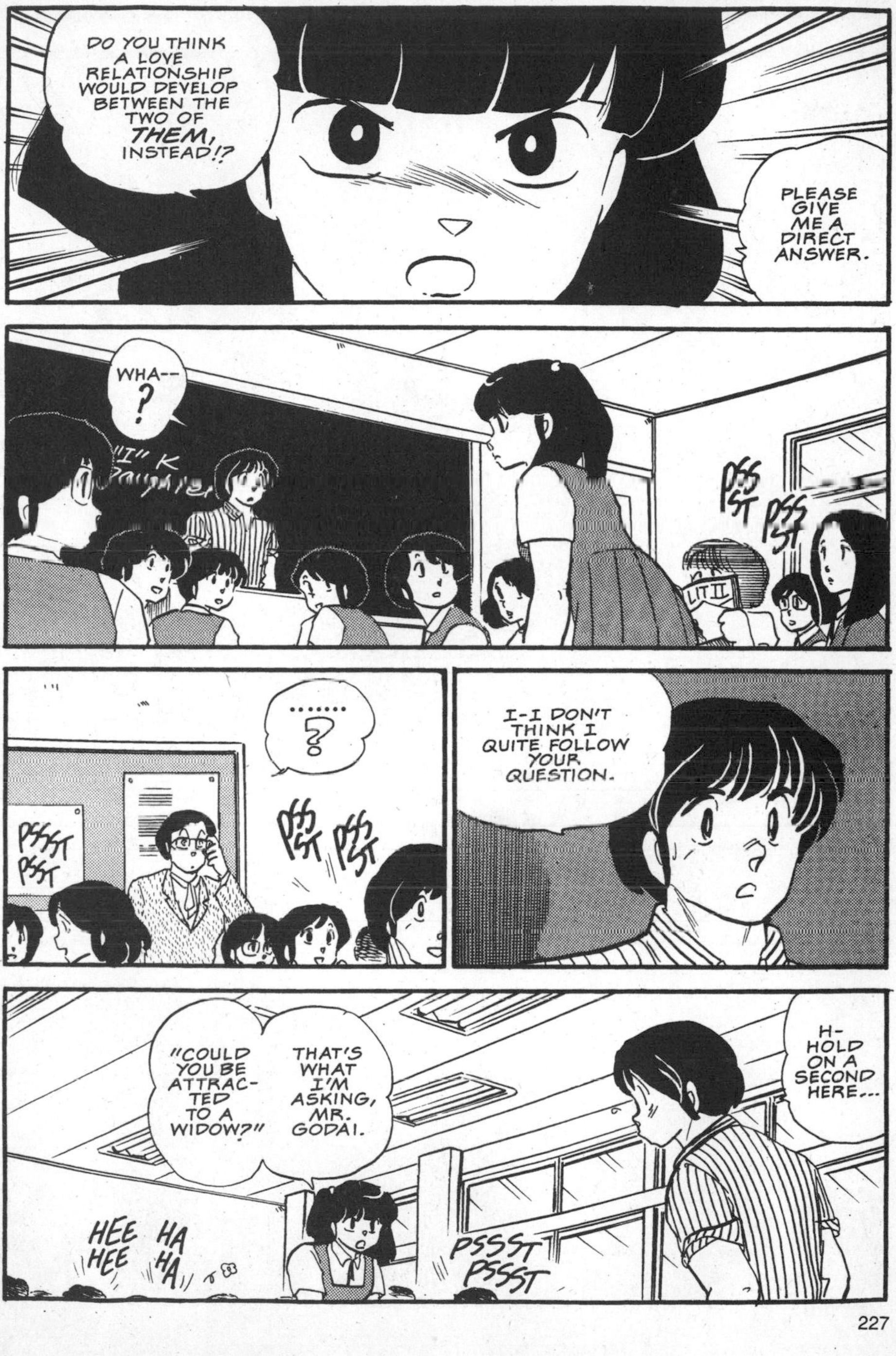
DO YOU THINK A LOVE RELATIONSHIP WOULD DEVELOP BETWEEN THE TWO OF *THEM,* INSTEAD!?
PLEASE GIVE ME A DIRECT ANSWER.
WHA-- ?
PSS ST
PSS ST
LIT II
.... ?
PSSST PSST
際 際
I-I DON'T THINK I QUITE FOLLOW YOUR QUESTION.
"COULD YOU BE ATTRACTED TO A WIDOW?"
THAT'S WHAT I'M ASKING, MR. GODAI.
H-HOLD ON A SECOND HERE...
HEE HEE
HA HA
PSSST PSSST

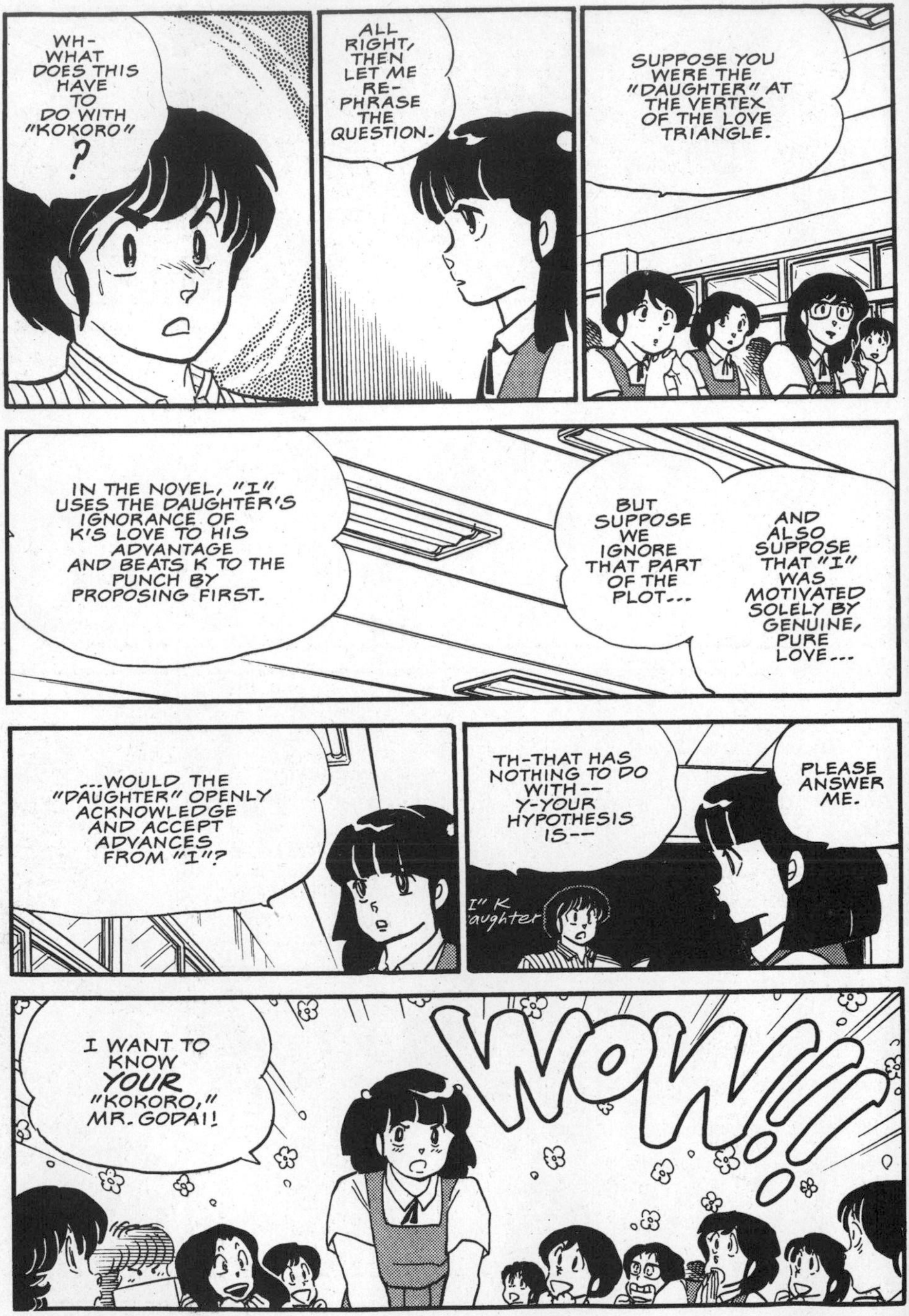

WH-WHAT DOES THIS HAVE TO DO WITH "KOKORO"?
ALL RIGHT, THEN LET ME RE-PHRASE THE QUESTION.
SUPPOSE YOU WERE THE "DAUGHTER" AT THE VERTEX OF THE LOVE TRIANGLE.
IN THE NOVEL, "I" USES THE DAUGHTER'S IGNORANCE OF K'S LOVE TO HIS ADVANTAGE AND BEATS K TO THE PUNCH BY PROPOSING FIRST.
BUT SUPPOSE WE IGNORE THAT PART OF THE PLOT...
AND ALSO SUPPOSE THAT "I" WAS MOTIVATED SOLELY BY GENUINE, PURE LOVE...
...WOULD THE "DAUGHTER" OPENLY ACKNOWLEDGE AND ACCEPT ADVANCES FROM "I"?
TH-THAT HAS NOTHING TO DO WITH-- Y-YOUR HYPOTHESIS IS--
PLEASE ANSWER ME.
I WANT TO KNOW YOUR "KOKORO," MR. GODAI!
WOW!!!

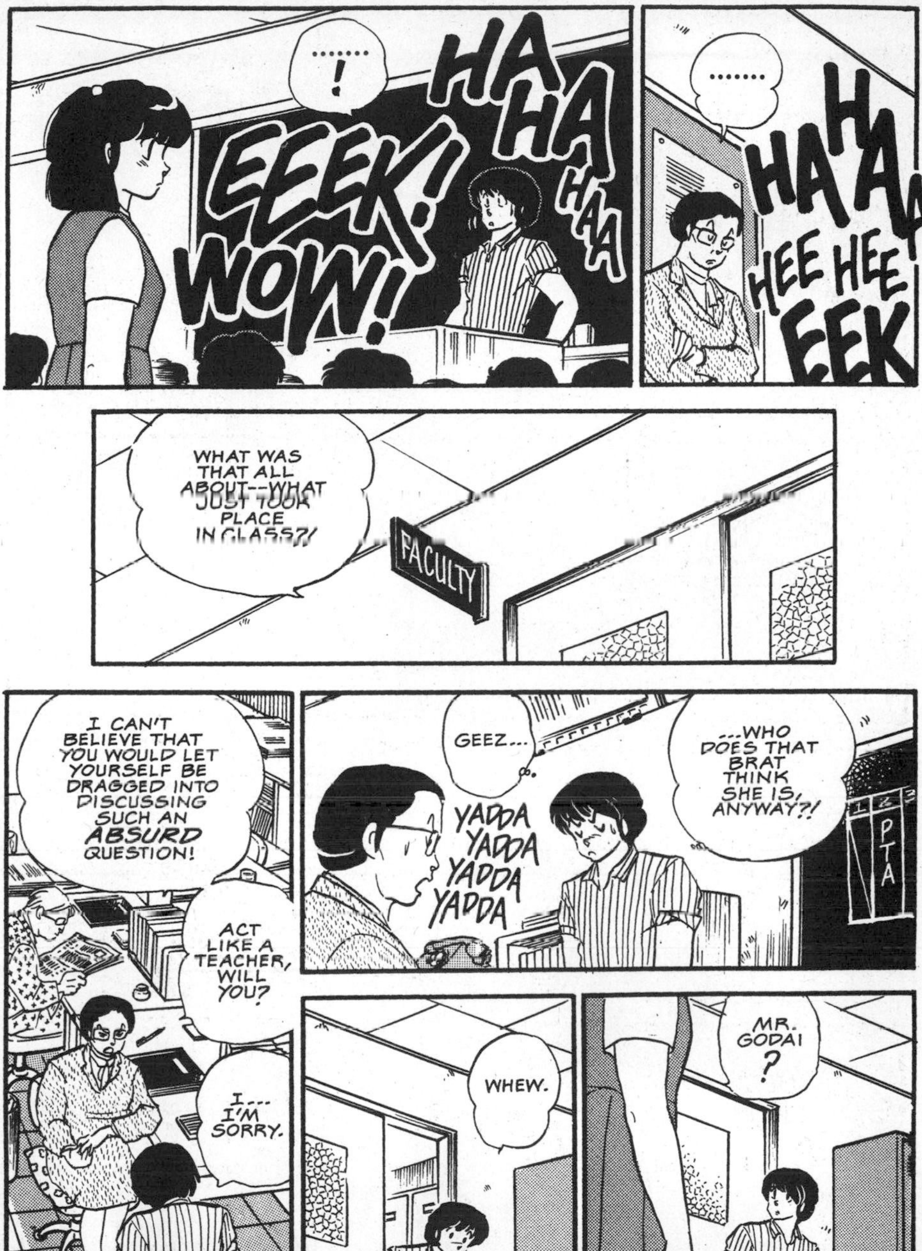
.... !
HA HA HAAA
EEEK! WOW!
....
HA HA AAA
HEE HEE EEK
WHAT WAS THAT ALL ABOUT--WHAT JUST TOOK PLACE IN CLASS?!
FACULTY
I CAN'T BELIEVE THAT YOU WOULD LET YOURSELF BE DRAGGED INTO DISCUSSING SUCH AN ABSURD QUESTION!
ACT LIKE A TEACHER, WILL YOU?
I... I'M SORRY.
GEEZ...
YADDA YADDA YADDA YADDA
...WHO DOES THAT BRAT THINK SHE IS, ANYWAY?!
PTA
WHEW.
MR. GODAI ?

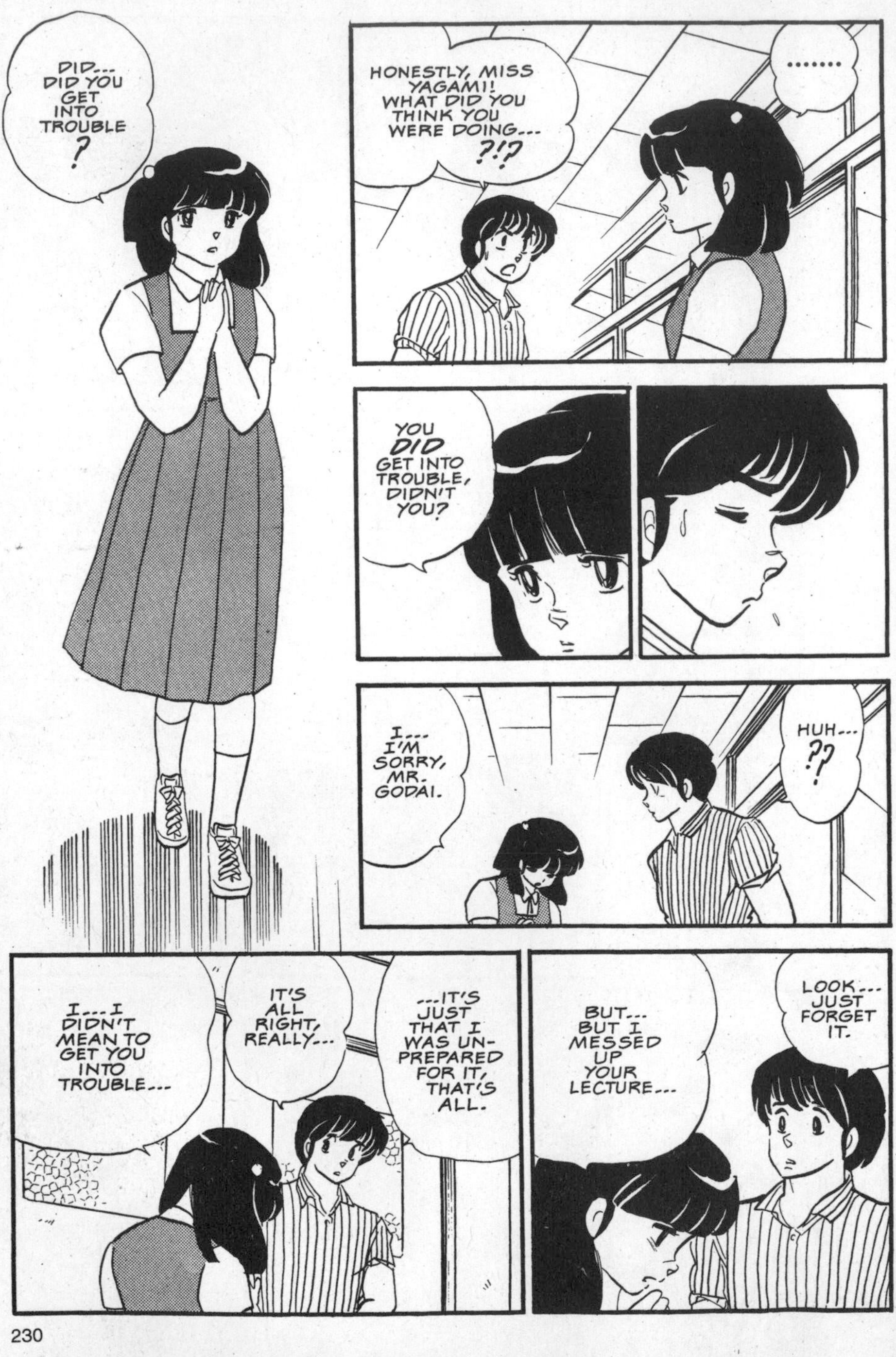
DID... DID YOU GET INTO TROUBLE ?
HONESTLY, MISS YAGAMI! WHAT DID YOU THINK YOU WERE DOING... ?!?
....
YOU DID GET INTO TROUBLE, DIDN'T YOU?
I... I'M SORRY, MR. GODAI.
HUH... ??
I... I DIDN'T MEAN TO GET YOU INTO TROUBLE...
IT'S ALL RIGHT, REALLY...
...IT'S JUST THAT I WAS UN-PREPARED FOR IT, THAT'S ALL.
BUT... BUT I MESSED UP YOUR LECTURE...
LOOK... JUST FORGET IT.

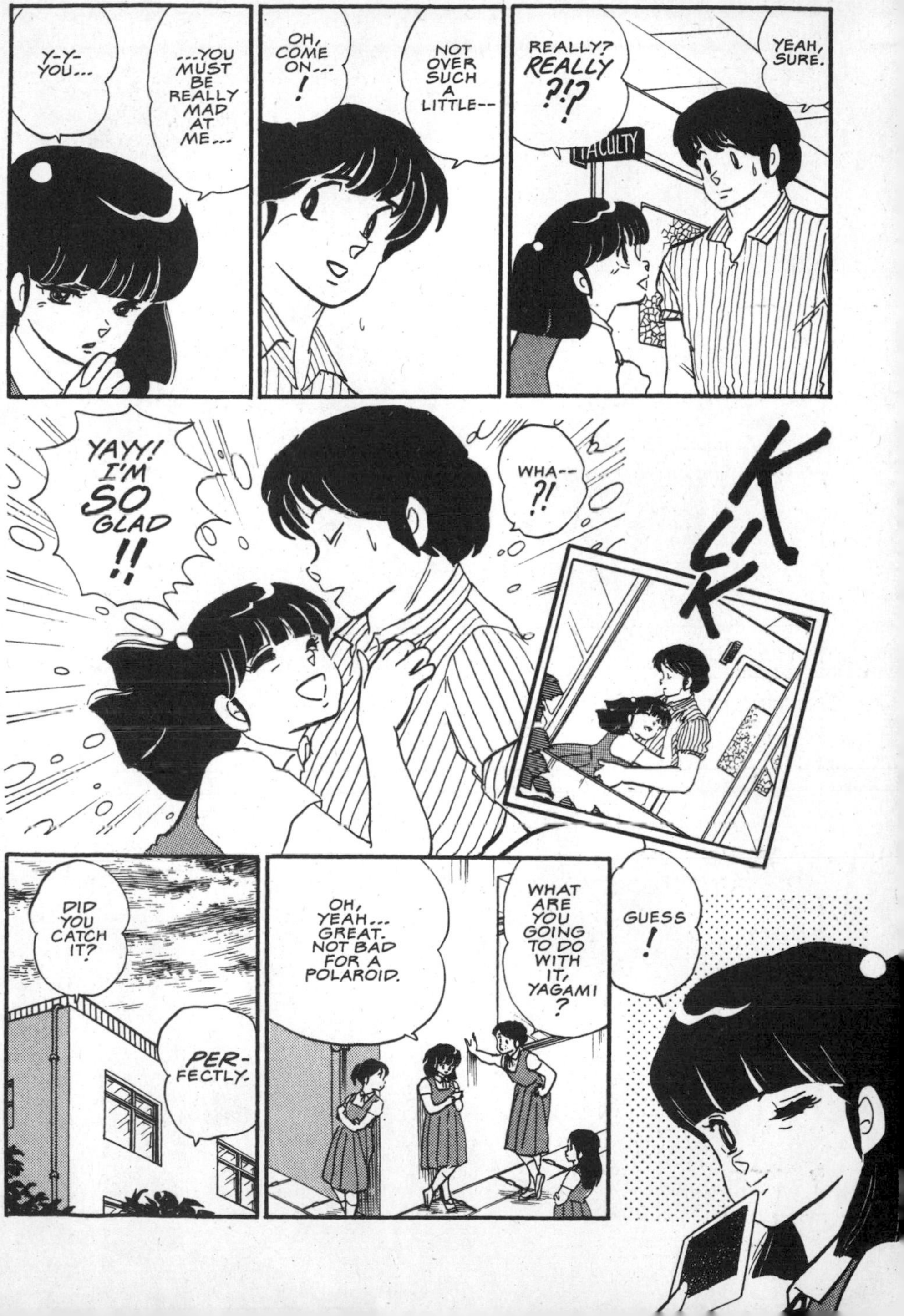
Y-Y-YOU...
...YOU MUST BE REALLY MAD AT ME...
OH, COME ON...!
NOT OVER SUCH A LITTLE--
REALLY? REALLY ?!?
YEAH, SURE.
YAYY! I'M SO GLAD !!
WHA-- ?!
KLIK
DID YOU CATCH IT?
PER-FECTLY.
OH, YEAH... GREAT. NOT BAD FOR A POLAROID.
WHAT ARE YOU GOING TO DO WITH IT, YAGAMI ?
GUESS !

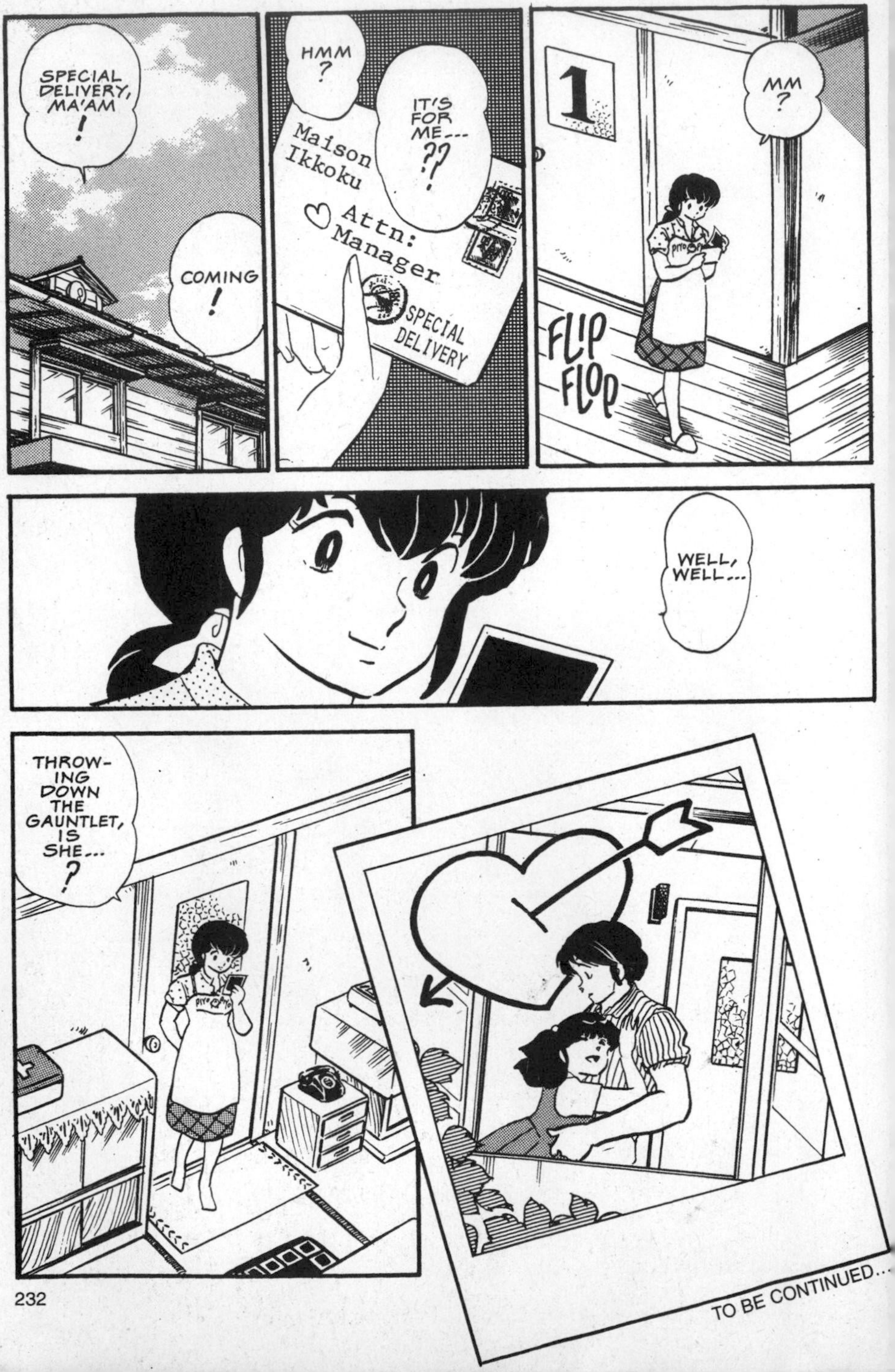
SPECIAL DELIVERY, MA'AM!
COMING!
HMM?
IT'S FOR ME...??
Maison Ikkoku
Attn: Manager
SPECIAL DELIVERY
MM?
FLIP FLOP
WELL, WELL...
THROWING-ING DOWN THE GAUNTLET, IS SHE...?
TO BE CONTINUED...